Contingent Countryside

*Settlement, Economy, and Land Use in
the Southern Argolid Since 1700*

Contributors

KEITH W. ADAMS

CLAUDIA CHANG

MARI H. CLARKE

HAMISH A. FORBES

MICHAEL H. JAMESON

P. NICK KARDULIAS

HAROLD A. KOSTER

JOAN BOUZA KOSTER

PRISCILLA M. MURRAY

MARINA PETRONOTI

SUSAN BUCK SUTTON

PETER W. TOPPING

Contingent Countryside

Settlement, Economy, and Land Use in
the Southern Argolid Since 1700

Edited by Susan Buck Sutton

A Publication of the Argolid Exploration Project

STANFORD UNIVERSITY PRESS
STANFORD, CALIFORNIA

Stanford University Press

Stanford, California

© 2000 by the Board of Trustees of the

Leland Stanford Junior University

Printed in the United States of America

CIP data appear at the end of the book

NOTE: Except as otherwise noted, all photographs,
illustrations, and maps were produced
by the authors.

In Memory of Robert McCorkle Netting

This volume is dedicated to the memory of Robert McCorkle Netting, a remarkable scholar of great integrity, wisdom, warmth, and generosity—qualities that won him international recognition and a circle of dedicated students and friends who were shocked by his sudden death in 1995. He played a vital role in designing and bringing to fruition an essential aspect of the Argolid Exploration Project (AEP).

Netting's pursuit of greater understanding of the interactions between population growth, social stratification, agricultural intensification, and the long term stability of human ecosystems placed him at the center of ecological anthropology. These interests also made him a logical and important contributor to the AEP. Thus it was that in the late 1960s Michael Jameson, then in the Department of Classics at the University of Pennsylvania, contacted Netting when he sought to expand the ethnographic component of the AEP, a component that had been an essential element of the project since its original conception.

More specifically, it was after a conference at the University of Pennsylvania on the intensification of agriculture and population growth that Jameson asked Netting to collaborate in the AEP. The conference was a general examination of the implications of Ester Boserup's hypotheses about the relationship between population growth and agricultural intensification (1965). It produced the volume *Population Growth: Anthropological Implications* (Spooner 1972). At this time Netting had completed a pioneering ecological monograph on intensive farming and household organization on the Jos Plateau in Nigeria (*Hill Farmers of Nigeria*, 1968) and had begun work on a general introduction to the subject reflected in the title of his book *Cultural Ecology* (first published in 1977 and issued in a second edition in 1986).

In response to Jameson's invitation, Netting explained that he had already made plans for research in Switzerland—an innovative study combining ethnography with historical demography that ultimately resulted in *Balancing on an Alp: Ecological Change and Continuity in a Swiss Mountain Community* (1981). He observed, however, with characteristic practicality and humor, "you can have several students for the price of me." He subsequently announced the opportunity for research in Greece in his cultural ecology class, and four careers took an unexpected turn to the Aegean—those of Harold Koster, who began work in Dhidhima with Joan Bouza Koster, and of Hamish Forbes and Mari Clarke, who initiated their research on Methana.

During his research in Switzerland, and after his move from the University of Pennsylvania to the University of Arizona, Bob Netting supervised these students and continued to give them valuable advice. He also paid a visit to the Argolid in 1974 and offered his insights on key issues and approaches during a tour of the region in a Volkswagen bug.

Harold Koster's student, Claudia Chang, continued this legacy when she conducted ethnoarchaeological research on pastoralists in Dhidhima, while Clarke, Forbes (accompanied by Lin Foxhall), and Hal and Joan Koster carried on their work in the area, continuing to the present. Others, such as Nicolas Gavrielides, Susan Sutton, Priscilla Murray, and Nick Kardulias joined with the AEP during the late 1970s and early 1980s. All were influenced by Netting's interest in the region and his evolving work on smallholders and the household economy, as presented over the last two decades with *Households: Comparative and Historical Studies*, edited by Netting, Richard Wilk, and Eric Arnould (1984), Netting's paper "Smallholders, Householders, Freeholders: Why the Family Farm Works Well Worldwide" (1989), and his most recent and important book, *Smallholders, Householders: Farm Families and the Ecology of Intensive, Sustainable Agriculture* (1993).

The AEP has expanded in various directions since its early days, and other anthropological approaches are certainly represented in this volume. It is fair to say, however, that without Netting's writings and his powerful influence, this work would be missing one of its most critical elements.

Mari H. Clarke and Michael H. Jameson

Acknowledgments

There are four sets of people without whom the work presented in this volume would not have occurred. First among these are the contemporary residents of the southern Argolid themselves. The many people in various communities who took us into their homes, told us of their lives, and let us walk their fields, as well as the public officials who shared local records and archives, created an atmosphere of generosity and openness that made the process of research a genuine pleasure. Many are thanked in the chapters that follow. At the outset, however, I would like to express particular gratitude to the two families in Koiladha who served as gracious hosts for the Argolid Exploration Project throughout its duration. Angelos and Stamatina Iatrou and Yeorghos and Litsa Lafiotis provided all of those associated with the AEP with much appreciated food, shelter, comfort, and wisdom during the many years of the project.

This volume also reflects the vision and support of several remarkable scholars, who, while they did not carry out research on the modern southern Argolid themselves, strongly encouraged those of us who did. Indeed, it was the commitment of archaeologists Michael H. Jameson and Thomas W. Jacobsen to the development of a comprehensive, multiperiod understanding of the region that brought many of us to the southern Argolid in the first place. Their belief that studies of the Greek past and present had something to say to each other served as invitation and support for much of the work reported in this volume. In this conviction they were ultimately joined by three others who contributed greatly to the interdisciplinary discussions that have guided our research: archaeologist Curtis N. Runnels, geologist Tjeerd H. Van Andel, and cultural ecologist Robert McC. Netting.

Thanks, too, must go to those who assisted in the production of this volume. The staff at Stanford University Press, especially Director Norris Pope and Associate Editor Nathan Mac-Brien, gave considerable guidance and encouragement in turning our rough manuscripts into smooth copy. Copy Editor Charles Spencer went far beyond the call of duty, approaching our contributions with equal measures of insight, patience, and thoroughness. The constructive comments of the reviewers to whom this volume was sent were uniformly helpful. In this regard, we are particularly grateful to Vance Watrous for his many insights and suggestions. Aristea Vareldzis-Pappas, Evelyn Oliver, Nicole Wright, Lauren Cronin, George Mitsas, Will O'Daix, Cathie Corrigan, and Janine Beckley played key roles in readying the text of this volume at IUPUI, while Samuel Mattes, Joy Kramer, Wayne Husted, Nathaniel Husted, Jeffrey Wilson, and Melody Johnson lent their computer expertise to the preparation of tables and figures.

Finally, each of the contributors to this volume operated with the significant help of various research assistants and personal support networks. My own work was greatly advanced by the able assistance of Bitten Skartvedt and Susan Langdon in data analysis. Above all, I am eternally grateful to my husband, Robert F. Sutton, Jr., who took a break in his interpretation of ancient vase painting to help me better understand the contemporary countryside, and my son, Peter Buck Sutton, who grew to be taller than his mother as the idea of this collaborative volume moved slowly toward its conclusion.

Susan Buck Sutton

Contents

Foreword

The studies collected in *Contingent Countryside* constitute the third unit in the publication program of the Argolid Exploration Project. In 1994 a comprehensive presentation of the results of the archaeological, historical, and environmental research in the southern Argolid of Greece was offered in *A Greek Countryside: The Southern Argolid from Prehistory to the Present Day* (Jameson, Runnels, and van Andel 1994); it had been preceded by a more popular introduction to the problems and the proposed conclusions in *Beyond the Acropolis: A Rural Greek Past* (van Andel and Runnels 1987). The second unit in the publication program, *Artifact and Assemblage*, presented the finds from the field survey on which the dating and interpretation of sites are based (for vol. I, see Runnels, Pullen, and Langdon 1995; vol. II, edited by M. H. Munn and M. L. Z. Munn, is forthcoming).

The ethnographic and historical studies in the present volume illustrate a dimension integral to the project from its beginning (cf. Jameson 1954, 1976a, and 1976b). Both *A Greek Countryside* and *Beyond the Acropolis* acknowledged their debt to the ongoing ethnographic studies and to Peter Topping's unlocking of the treasure house of Venetian cadastres. Both must now be supplemented and corrected by the more detailed and up-to-date contributions to the present volume. (The first publications of ethnographers associated with the project appeared in Dimen and Friedl 1976, as did a valuable article by Peter Topping, 1976a, and in "A Greek Countryside: Reports from the Argolid Exploration Project," *Expedition* 19 [1976b]). The subject of our research has comprised all periods of human settlement, including the contemporary, in a particular regional environment. We have asked how the region was settled and its resources exploited over a period of some 50,000 years, what were the processes of change, and what was the interaction between those who lived here and their environment.

Fieldwork and study by this volume's contributors sometimes led in unexpected directions, resulting in conclusions and hypotheses important for the archaeologists and scientists involved in the project. Two points made explicit in Chapter 5, "Liquid Landscapes," may be selected as examples: (1) The fluidity and flexibility of the nature of settlement over time, a perception that can help free the archaeologist and the anthropologist from what is in effect the tyranny of the nuclear settlement—taking the major settlement or archaeological site as the lens through which all the historical processes of the area are viewed. (2) The importance of the relationship of the subject area to neighboring regions, in the case of the southern Argolid usually with larger populations and more complex economic and social structures. For the historian this middle range view of influence and exchange offers an alternate to the extremes of hypothetically self-sufficient social entities, in which the great majority of the inhabitants were sustained by subsistence agriculture, and the modernist model of widespread trade and a reliance on market mechanisms.

A final, perhaps paradoxical observation on the utility of these studies: Susan Sutton in her Introduction notes that attention has shifted from the so-called Golden Age of Classical Greece and that other periods of Greece's long history are now receiving more attention. This is certainly true of research. Neglected periods, regions, and topics may well be more commonly the subject of monographs and articles than, say, Periclean Athens. But for the wider public and not least the university student, the texts, history, art, and monuments of a few centuries in the first millennium before the Common Era continue to fascinate. While respecting fully the independent significance of other eras and the issues attached to them, I freely confess, as one who remains in thrall to that fascination, that it was in part to see the Classical world in a broad social, economic, historical, and natural context that this large project was set in motion. We went "beyond the Acropolis" in part because some of us expected to return to it, better able to understand it.

Michael H. Jameson

Contingent Countryside

*Settlement, Economy, and Land Use in
the Southern Argolid Since 1700*

CHAPTER ONE

Introduction: Past and Present in Rural Greece

Susan Buck Sutton

The essays that follow are united by attention to the many ways in which residents of the coastal regions of the southern Argolid peninsula of Greece have attempted to shelter, feed, and advance the situations of their families during the last three centuries. The separate parts of this volume are linked not only by geography and history but also by a common interest in the complexities of settlement, economy, and land use in rural Greece. While this is a regionally organized volume, it is the kind that asks us to think carefully about what we mean by "region," as well as many other terms commonly employed in discussions of the Greek countryside. Its papers explore processes by which the material essentials of rural Greek life have formed and reformed, combined and recombined over the last three hundred years. They present the positioning of fields and settlements, the relationship of farmers to shepherds, and the inwardness or expansiveness of market systems as historically shifting and intricately intertwined. In so doing, they conceive the southern Argolid as a contingent countryside whose boundaries and characteristics have been reconfigured time and again. Such notions strengthen general reformulations that have been occurring within Greek ethnography and, as part of the Argolid Exploration Project publication series, speak directly to archaeological attempts to connect the Greek past and present.

Over the last twenty-five years, the series of largely independent research projects presented in this volume have collectively built this understanding of the southern Argolid, through work on land use and settlement practices in several communities in the southeastern section of the peninsula. Some of these investigations were undertaken by cultural anthropologists, some by archaeologists who turned their gaze toward the modern landscape, one by an historian, and one by a geographer. Taken together, these studies have made the southern Argolid the focus of more ethnographic and ethnohistorical attention than any other comparable region of Greece.

While the scholars whose work is presented here focused on the recent history and current state of the southern Argolid, almost all were influenced by contact with the archaeologists studying the region's ancient past. Indeed, the intensity of research on modern life in the southern Argolid has been a direct result of the interests and vision of the archaeologists also working there.[1] In the 1950s, epigraphic finds drew archaeologist Michael Jameson to this region, which lay some distance from the major cities and sanctuaries of the classical world. Increasingly intrigued by the notion that such ancient hinterlands had their own story to tell, Jameson soon brought other archaeologists to the area. In the 1960s, excavations were begun at the ancient town of Halieis and the prehistoric Franchthi Cave.[2] By 1970, Jameson and fellow archaeologist Thomas Jacobsen had developed an interest in looking beyond specific sites to the area as a whole, and thus began the initial stages of what became the multiphase, multi-institutional Argolid Exploration Project (AEP).[3]

From its inception, the archaeologists involved in the AEP encouraged historians, geographers, and cultural anthropologists to join in their examination of the region, believing connections could be made between the contemporary and ancient Greek countrysides. Following discussions with Jameson and Jacobsen, anthropologist Robert Netting, to whom this volume is dedicated, encouraged several contributors to this volume to conduct ecological studies in the area in the early 1970s. Other scholars of modern Greek life were drawn to the Argolid in connection with later stages of the AEP, particularly the phase of work directed by Jameson, archaeologist Curtis Runnels, and geologist Tjeerd van Andel in conjunction with Stanford University between 1979 and 1983. Such early work on modern life in the Argolid inspired all who followed. Even researchers operating independently of the AEP inevitably found themselves articulating with its studies of the region's economy, settlement, and agriculture.

By conjoining these various investigations of the contemporary Argolid peninsula in a single volume, we aim at insights of connection and contrast reflecting an evolving understanding of how to approach the modern Greek countryside and link it to its past. The two decades over which this work has been conducted have witnessed a sustained process of growth and reflection. They have provided time to rethink our relationship to the people whose lives we attempt to represent. They have enabled us to weave our understandings together and to fit them to the ideas of two other anthropologists who have worked in the region, Nicolas Gavrielides (1976a, 1976b) and Maria Vellioti (1987). We have been influenced by revelations of settlement complexity from archaeological surveys of the region, as well as by recent disciplinary challenges within cultural anthropology. We have also been transformed by the southern Argolid itself. None of these studies is quite what we intended when we began. As we came to look outward as well as inward, to explore how boundaries were created as well as what happened within them, and to place the ethnographic present in the sweep of history, we increasingly saw the value of bringing our various projects into closer juxtaposition.

This volume is the result of that resolve. It brings the regional history presented in the archaeological volumes of the AEP publication series forward to the present. It sets forth an understanding of the material conditions of rural Greek life as mutable and negotiated in ways that complement both archaeological interest in the settlement fluctuations of the Greek past and recent shifts in anthropological conceptions of modern Greek kinship, religion, gender, and identity. The same processes that have led individuals to create, contest, maintain, or reformulate the nature of family ties and religious belief have also given Greek houses, settlements, land tenure rules, and production methods a variability not well recognized when this work began. Behaviors once seen in terms of normative rules and enduring cycles are now perceived as having been repeatedly reshaped by strategy and by circumstance. In this contextualized notion of settlement, land use, and rural economy, boundaries blur, old and new mix, and the connections to antiquity become more complex. By the same token, statements of honor, family, and identity are given deeper meaning.

The questions before us have thus become more complex since this research began. Assumptions of village longevity have been replaced by investigations into what has caused villages to form, grow, or decline at various points in Greek history. Idealized inheritance patterns have been placed alongside records of actual land transactions. The categorical boundaries between shepherds, farmers, and sailors have blurred as personal occupational histories emerged. Production methods of supposed great antiquity are now recognized as operating within and reflecting contemporary political and economic conditions. It has not only become clear that the local cannot be understood outside the national but also that the way individuals negotiate their relationship to long-distance forces reveals an agency that goes beyond mere acceptance and imitation. Such conclusions concerning the mutability of rural Greek economic and settlement strategies contribute a materialist perspective to the rethinking of Greek life that has been occurring in other modes of ethnography.

The essays that follow thus also carry meaning for ethnoarchaeological efforts to interpret the material evidence of the rural Greek past. While the dynamism of the modern countryside at first appeared to rend it completely from previous periods of Greek history, we now see this dynamism as providing parallels for understanding the frequent shifts revealed by archaeological investigations of ancient landscapes. In our efforts to move beyond static, categorical understandings of the Greek present, we have also found a powerful way of relating that present to the Greek past.

This introduction contains, of course, my own particular understanding of the ideas that have grown from this multiyear dialogue. My thinking has been extensively and constructively shaped by my interaction with the other contributors. Each chapter, however, should be read for its own definition and interpretation of the issues. What follows are certain themes I see as integrating the volume. These are presented in four steps: identification of the geographical and chronological parameters that frame the volume, a brief account of how the modern Greek countryside has historically been represented, consideration of what these essays contribute to such discussions, and an assessment of the ethnoarchaeological implications of this work.

The Southern Argolid Since 1700

The papers in this volume concern the eastern and southern sections of the Argolid peninsula, the eastern finger of the Peloponnesos that separates the Saronic Gulf from the Argolic Gulf (Figure 1.1). The Adheres and Dhidhima mountains divide this area from the uplands of Epidavros and the plains of Argos and Nafplio.[4] The district contains a series of narrow coastal plains and valleys, and the mountains and rolling hills that frame and punctuate them (Jameson, Runnels, and van Andel 1994: 13–56). Many of the settlements discussed in this volume are found in the southernmost part of this region, currently designated as the *eparkhia* (administrative district) of the Ermionidha, a 421 km² section of the *nomos* (state or province) of the Argolid (Argolidha). Others are located on the small, mountainous peninsula of Methana, which juts off the mainland roughly 15 km north of the Ermionidha. Methana was placed under the

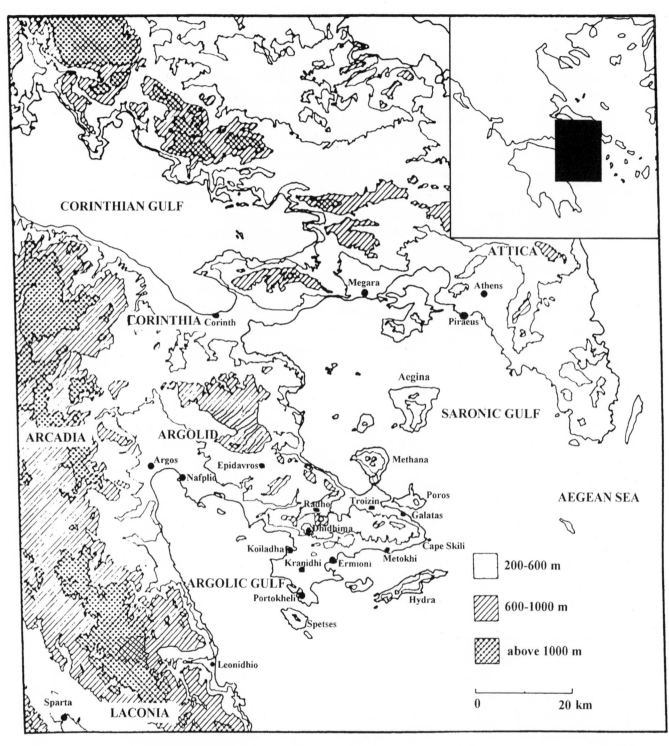

Figure 1.1. The Southern Argolid: Regional topography and major settlements. Based on Jameson, Runnels, and van Andel (1994: 14).

Figure 1.2.   Panorama of the eastern Ermionidha, taken from Iliokastro, facing toward Ermioni and Hydra, 1983.

nomos of Attica (Attiki) in 1925, but until that time, these two sections of the southern Argolid were connected administratively as well as geographically.

There are few places within this area that are very far from either sea or mountains, an environmental mix capable of supporting the variety of economic strategies discussed in this volume.[5] The twin peaks of Dhidhima stand at 1,124 m and 1,133 m respectively. Gathered around their base are the small mountain villages of Radho and Pelei, as well as the larger, interconnected settlements of Dhidhima, Loukaiti, and Iliokastro. Only 16 km south of Dhidhima, in an area of small valleys and hills 300–400 m in elevation, lies Kranidhi, the largest settlement in the area. Kranidhi is closely tied to the ports of Koiladha and Portokheli on the west and south. The coastal town of Ermioni, some 8 km to the east, is a second major commercial center and port. From this point, Thermisi and a string of small communities spread eastward for 18 km along the coast to Metokhi, the farming estate of a monastery on the nearby island of Hydra. The present-day road then rounds rugged Cape Skili and continues to the village of Galatas, the coastal plains of Troizinia, and the mountainous Methana peninsula. Immediately offshore and clearly visible from this section of the mainland are the Saronic Islands of Spetses, Hydra, Poros, and Aegina.[6]

Passes, pathways, and now hard-surfaced roads have long connected this area to the mountainous interior of the Peloponnesos, while the surrounding sea has provided transport to other ports, both near and distant. The harbor of Portokheli lies roughly 100 km from Piraeus, 45 km from Nafplio, and 35 km from Leonidhio. In the past, ships traveling between the western

Mediterranean and Constantinople held to and sometimes stopped along this coast, as do those plying the tourist trade between Athens and Nafplio today.

The places discussed in this volume thus share a common general location. Our goal in assembling these studies is not so much to characterize the region as a whole, however, as it is to describe the flux and variation within it. The extent to which the southern Argolid is a unified, recognized, and bounded system is an interesting and open question that would require a different type of analysis than undertaken here. Our interest is in the varied responses that neighboring communities have had to relatively similar circumstances, as well as in the ways the actions of these communities have shaped and altered each other. We wish to dissect the region rather than wrap it up, to show the fluidity of its components and the malleability of its borders. We also want to reveal something of the dynamism and heterogeneity of the Greek countryside, as well as the complex interaction of local, regional, national, and even international forces. The juxtaposition of studies on several settlements in the same area enables us to move beyond the false sense of closure that sometimes arises from studies of single villages. It also allows us to explore the give-and-take that has long characterized rural Greek life. The regional history that emerges from this volume is not one of an orderly, self-repeating system with each place playing its assigned role. It is rather the story of people who have moved from place to place and occupation to occupation. It is a tale in which the array, nature, and positioning of settlements have changed time and again. This volume is not so much a comprehensive study of a particular region as it is an assessment of how various communities and groups have participated in that region. It operates on a level that connects village and region with the aim of seeing each of these units in new ways.

Temporally, the essays in this volume examine such local and regional changes in the southern Argolid from the time of the Second Venetian Occupation of the Peloponnesos (1685–1715) to the present.[7] Primarily agricultural during the first period of Turkish control,[8] as well as under the brief Venetian reoccupation at the start of the period covered by this volume, the region embarked on a very different path after the Ottoman Empire regained control in 1715. The entry of Hydra and Spetses into international shipping in the 18th century had a ripple effect on the southern Argolid, which furnished sailors and provisions for this trade and sent out small fleets of its own. While both islands and mainland were active participants in the successful Greek Revolution against the Ottomans in the 1820s, their economic fortunes soon diverged. As first Syros and then Athens rose to dominate shipping in the new Greek nation, Hydra and Spetses went into demographic and economic decline. Many parts of the southern Argolid were more successful in holding their own, however, by combining various cash producing strategies, including sponging, fishing, tourism, and commercial agriculture. Indeed, the region's population has grown to several times its eighteenth-century levels.

The recent history of the southern Argolid thus stands in some contrast to the depopulation and economic decline which have characterized so much of the Greek countryside. This trend was not immediately obvious, however, to those of us who began research in the region in the early 1970s (e.g., Bintliff 1977: 221). At that time, the Ermionidha ranked among the lowest areas in the Peloponnesos on indexes of such amenities as automobiles, telephones, running water, indoor toilets, electricity, hard-surfaced roads, and radios (Baxevanis 1972: 56). These consumption patterns figured greatly into our experience of daily life in the region, making it seem remote and not yet greatly changed by modern times. That the same statistical study also showed the area to be among the highest in per capita income and most stable in population, however, was a clue, only dimly perceived at first, that more complex analytic frames were required. As we moved in this direction we joined in an evolving discourse on the nature of rural Greece in general.

Representing Rural Greece

Anthropologists began their first village studies in Greece, and archaeologists moved toward the contemporary form of surface survey there within a decade of each other. The initial ethnographic fieldwork of Friedl and Campbell was undertaken in the late 1950s, while the archaeological survey known as the Minnesota Messenia Expedition (MME) commenced in the 1960s (Friedl 1962; Campbell 1964; McDonald and Rapp 1972). Each initiative brought questions new to its field. Friedl and Campbell were among the first to turn from cultural anthropology's preoccupation with horticultural and foraging societies. Similarly, the MME broadened the archaeological field of vision to include more than cities and sanctuaries and was explicitly interested in parallels between contemporary and ancient rural life.

Even if archaeologists and anthropologists had not seriously considered it before, however, the modern Greek countryside had already been the object of considerable discussion by others. The nature and impact of village ethnography and survey archaeology in Greece can only be fully understood by considering the broader conceptual climate in which they operated. These new approaches resonated, in ways both intended and accidental, with a much longer discursive history on rural Greece that involved both foreign travels to a Greece of the imagination and nationalist efforts to defend the modern Greek state.

In this discourse, Greek villagers were often consigned to mythic time, rather than contemporary history, except for a brief philhellenic glorification of their dynamism and valor around the time of the Revolution (Angelomatis-Tsougarakis 1990; Augustinos 1994: 228–64; Eisner 1991; Spencer 1954; Sutton 1997; Tsigakou 1981: 50–68). Many scholars, travelers, urbanites, and politicians—both Greek and foreign—portrayed these ruralites as a folk who, until quite recently, lived outside the events shaping modern times. Various processes of exoticism, Orientalism, and even nationalism operated to underscore how these villagers were different from those who wrote about them.[9] Whether these differences were seen as good or bad depended on other dimensions in the viewpoints of particular observers.

While there have been many variations, three overlapping ways of conceiving this timelessness have been common. Perhaps the best-known and most widely discussed way has been what is sometimes termed survivalism.[10] In the search for ancient and modern parallels, survivalists have claimed that various forms of antiquity continue or survive in much of rural Greek life. While transformations in urban life have been too great to ignore, the Greek countryside has been seen as having a passive or perhaps resistant role toward the encroachments of time. The nineteenth- or twentieth-century existence of a folk song, ceramic vessel, or farming technique similar to that of antiquity has been taken as proof of unbroken continuity.

Establishing that aspects of antiquity have survived to the present has, of course, played an important political and cultural role in arguments concerning Greek national sovereignty and legitimacy. This search for connections was prompted by the nineteenth-century appropriation of classical antiquity by European political writers such as Jakob Fallmerayer, who denied any connection between modern and ancient Greeks, as well as those foreign travelers so focused on the Greek past that, as Angelomatis-Tsougarakis (1990: 1–24) has documented, they simply ignored its present. For supporters of Greek nationalism it became important to establish the Greek countryside as a place of cultural preservation only recently disrupted.

A second, closely related way in which rural Greece has been conceptually removed from history may be found in various forms of romanticism. The romantic view has emphasized the physical beauty of the Greek landscape and its points of contrast with urban and industrial settings. Only occasionally has this been connected to the ability of that landscape to evoke the glories of ancient Greece. In other formulations, antiquities have played a minor or negligible role, while sun, sea, the absence of recognizable markers of industrialism, and a peasantry perceived as both quaint and earthy have moved to the fore (Tsigakou 1981: 71). Virtually all forms of romanticism have employed this constructed form of the Greek countryside as a type of cultural critique. Travelers of the eighteenth and nineteenth centuries saw the ancient monuments and picturesque shepherds of rural Greece as contrast to corruption and repression in the capitals of Europe (Eisner 1991: 98; Morris 1994: 24). Twentieth-century tourists, whether from abroad or from Athens, have often characterized their rural visits as curing anomie and overwork (Eisner 1991: 244; Sutton 1997). In either case, the perceived contrast between rural Greece and other settings has worked to place the former somewhere outside the conditions of modernity, having resorted to a view of Greek villagers that borders on caricature.

A third way in which rural Greece has sometimes been removed from the forces of recent history is its invocation in various forms of what one might simply label as urban disdain. Such formulations have portrayed the modern Greek countryside as substandard, backward, and lagging well behind urban Greece and the industrialized world. Rural Greece has been seen as provincial, unaware of developments in the wider world, and arbitrarily resistant to change. One form of disdain emerges from travel accounts remarking on how far contemporary Greece has fallen from its grandeur and status in antiquity. In the nineteenth century, such remarks often accompanied an ideologically based questioning of the extent to which the modern Greek population was directly descended from the ancient one (Angelomatis-Tsougarakis 1990; Eisner 1991: 101; Fotiadis 1995; Jacobsen 1985). Issues of genetic continuity have died down somewhat in the twentieth century, but even guidebooks romantically extolling the seeming isolation of rural Greece can in the next paragraph derisively complain of the outdated facilities encountered when traveling outside Athens. In such views, the Greek countryside is not participating in the same world of progress and convenience as the people who visit it.

The various forms of survivalism, romanticism, and urban disdain have crosscut each other at different moments in time to create a variety of images, all of which have spoken of an eternal rural Greece.[11] Such imagery has swirled in the background of much that has been written about the Greek countryside and has continued to inform much nationalist, tourist, and popular discourse up to the present. Such representations also proved quite consonant with a certain theoretical stance that became firmly entrenched in the mainstream of social science when rural Greek life first became the subject of concentrated scholarly study in the 1950s.

In the 1950s, the approach generally known as modernization theory provided a commonly accepted explanation for increasingly apparent differences between the industrialized and developing worlds. Modernization theory, which dominated the scholarly discussion of contemporary Greek society from the 1950s through the 1970s, was used for assessing what was keeping Greece from the prosperity of the rest of Europe (Mouzelis 1996). Such studies placed much of the blame for Greece's economic position on the perceived backward nature of its peasantry (e.g., McNall 1974; Thompson 1963; Ward 1962). A rural reticence to change and inability to comprehend the larger world were held to be major factors in the nation's lagging development. Portrayed as stubbornly traditional and unable to break through into the modern world, rural Greeks thus remained another kind of people from those writing about them.

Even as the loaded dichotomies of modernization theory fell from favor[12] and as breakthrough studies of medieval and more recent periods (e.g., Kremmydhas 1972, Panayiotopoulos 1985, Mouzelis 1978, Vergopoulos 1975) revealed the extensive commercial connections and internal population shifts of rural Greek history, the linkages between these observations and contemporary Greek farmers and shepherds on the ground level were often overlooked. Couroucli (1989) has noted that studies of nineteenth-century rural Greek history have often paradoxically contained notions of village isolation and stability at their core. As Netting (1993: 10) has stated more generally, "perhaps the most stubborn and pervasive myth about smallholders is that their physical isolation in rural areas, their simple technology, and their modicum of self-sufficiency remove them from dependency on a market and the mentality of maximization."

The image of an isolated and passive Greek countryside continues to resonate every time all Greek farmers are glossed as one, the countryside is treated as uniform, the distant is seen as only recently penetrating the local, and all change is attributed to Athens. Simply employing such terms as village or region can sometimes turn a fluid process into a seemingly fixed entity. Categories whose component parts and formative processes remain unspoken take on a reified life of their own. This is only compounded when such concepts are used for symbolic purpose by local residents themselves.

Such was the arena into which both cultural anthropology and survey archaeology moved in the 1960s. One wanted to frame the rural Greek past in new ways, while the other wished to do the same for the present. Much ground has been covered, both literally and figuratively, in the ensuing decades. These two fields have developed in parallel ways, but are nevertheless not that well known to each other, despite their occasional articulation in the form of ethnoarchaeology. The following brief overview of disciplinary changes is intended to make clearer what each may have to offer the other, and hence what is to be gained by including a volume such as this one, largely written by anthropologists and focused on recent change in the Greek countryside, in an archaeological publication series.

The village studies of Friedl (1962) and Campbell (1964) were part of a postwar refiguring of the scope and concerns of anthropology to include peasant as well as primitive, and even the societies in which anthropologists themselves lived (Gamst 1974).[13] In making these shifts, anthropologists carried forward their pattern of intensive field study with small groups of people, a methodology developed to engender a personal, transformative grasp of the internal workings of a society. This approach had been central in establishing the logic of different lifeways, and supported the cultural relativism anthropologists used as their form of cultural critique. Transferring this method to peasant villages, however, eventually brought about its own transformation. An overly inward looking approach proved increasingly unsuited, even for study of the foragers or horticulturalists for whom it had originally been developed. As Wolf (1956), Barth (1959), and others began to suggest quite early, it was difficult to comprehend smallholders' lives without considering their connections to distant centers.

Such issues were not, however, immediately settled. Most village studies in peasant areas of the world up through the 1960s continued in a largely closed-system, functionalist mode (Marcus 1989; Wolf 1982). In some cases, this mode reflected insulating strategies used by particular villages to enclose and defend themselves in colonial situations (Wolf 1955). More commonly, this approach matched the desire of anthropologists such as Redfield (1956) to demonstrate an internal sense and coherence to these villages that would counter the assumptions of backwardness so prevalent in modernization theory. This counter, however, also resonated with and seemed to support the many representations of peasant villages, whether in Greece or elsewhere, that placed them in a timeless space, outside the workings of history.[14]

Combining this situation in anthropological village studies with the long-standing images of the Greek countryside already discussed, it is remarkable that Friedl and Campbell clearly aligned with those few anthropologists who, in settings outside Greece, had begun to feel uneasy with the closed-community study. Herzfeld (1987) has persuasively argued that Campbell's writings accurately reflected the Sarakatsani's marginal position in the modern Greek state. Friedl was even clearer in her deliberate choice of a cash-cropping village, as well as her use of what Marcus (1989: 13) calls categorical, rather than structural, holism (Friedl 1995). While her ethnography of Vasilika covered the standard range of topics from housing to religion, it did not portray the village as a self-contained system. These steps toward a more connected kind of community study were not yet fully theorized and articulated, however. For this reason, those not attuned to the nascent struggles over village representation in anthropology could easily have read the work of Friedl, Campbell and other early Greek ethnographers in more conventional and survivalist ways.[15]

The archaeologists drawn to survey work in Greece at this time also felt they were moving their discipline in new directions (Ammerman 1981; Cherry 1983; Keller and Rupp 1983; McDonald and Rapp 1972; Renfrew and Wagstaff 1982; Watrous 1982).[16] They envisioned an expansion beyond classical cities and sanctuaries that would give a broader view of ancient life, show the marginal and forgotten, and explore issues of political and economic dominance through study of settlement patterns and regional connections. The statements on such issues have become increasingly explicit over time (Cherry, Davis, and Mantzourani 1991; Jameson, Runnels, and van Andel 1994; Kardulias 1994; Renfrew 1984; Snodgrass 1987: 67–92; van Andel and Runnels 1987). This was as much a disciplinary refocusing, by a group sometimes viewed as pioneering, sometimes as renegade, as was the shift to peasant studies in cultural anthropology.

In attempting this broader understanding of the Greek past, virtually all archaeological surveys included some analysis, in the regions under consideration, of medieval and recent history, as well as contemporary settlement. Concern for these later periods, dismissed by many other scholars of antiquity as degenerate or irrelevant, reflected the desire of survey archaeologists to break the hold of classical Greece. The many postclassical sherds and architectural remains recovered by survey work also drew their attention in this direction. Finally, and of particular importance to this volume, survey archaeologists hoped to find parallels in contemporary Greek settlement, technology, and land use that would make the largely artifactual evidence of the ancient countryside speak more eloquently.[17] Similar efforts were under way in Americanist archaeology, where they were termed ethnoarchaeology (Kramer 1979; Gould 1980). Thus, very early on, Aschenbrenner (1972, 1986), Blitzer (1982), and many contributors to this volume were invited to work in tandem with archaeological survey projects.

The first sustained efforts to make such linkages came from the MME. Aschenbrenner's study of a modern Messenian village (1972, 1986) became a worthy prototype of Greek ethnoarchaeology. As with the early village ethnographies in Greece, this project was an exploratory venture. Assumptions and implications later seen as limiting were only dimly perceived, if at all. There has been considerable subsequent rethinking of these issues, a developmental process in which many authors included in this volume have participated. What stands out in Ashenbrenner's work, looking back some twenty-five years on this road, is its significant similarity to Friedl's in mentioning village history and commercialization. Aschenbrenner's statements on such issues were overshadowed, however, by the use some made of his work in search of direct and unchanged remnants of the past.

Fotiadis (1995) has given an incisive discussion of the initial ways in which Aschenbrenner's study was ethnoarchaeologically interpreted, ways that took Aschenbrenner's research in directions he may not have intended. Under the sway of the processual or New Archaeology, then emergent in anthropological forms of archaeology, modern Messenians were seen as universal village farmers whose agricultural cycles produced patterns that could be fitted to others far removed in space and time, including the cultivators of Bronze Age Greece. Processes of cash-cropping and urbanization were viewed as very recent, unlike anything before, and not relevant to analogies between past and present. The meshing of agricultural work with seasons of the year was read as participation in endlessly repeating, largely self-sufficient loops that were only broken in the last few decades. This, in turn, subtly fed into the many other images that removed modern Greek farmers from more linear conceptions of history and change. Much was learned about farming in Mediterranean climes, but altering one's strategies, negotiating external systems, and moving one's base of operations were not initially part of this.

This focus on seemingly repetitive and intrinsically driven agricultural cycles was reflecting, as Fotiadis (1995) has suggested, the emphasis at that time in Americanist archaeology on universal laws as the basis of archaeological inference. Compounding this were both the largely synchronic, functionalist approach that still dominated community studies in ethnography and the early, rigidly homeostatic forms of ecological anthropology. Milling around offstage were popular views that somehow peasants were different kinds of people from those who observed them. As Fotiadis has pointed out for Greece, and Stahl (1993) and Gould (1990: 24–27) have indicated more generally, ethnoarchaeology quickly slipped into selective reporting of contemporary patterns, omission of anything considered a contamination and presentations of rural life as enduringly repetitive and uniform.

The general rethinking of ethnography in the last fifteen years has been strongly felt in Greece, where it has cast ethnoarchaeological issues into sharp relief. Herzfeld's delineation and critique of various representations of contemporary Greek life have been pivotal in this regard

(1982, 1987). He and others, such as Panourgia (1994), Danforth (1989), and Dubisch (1995a), have justifiably called for greater attention to the ways in which the writer's position affects the representations being crafted. Greek ethnography has also increasingly examined the manner in which individuals interpret and contest dominant value structures and normative patterns, particularly as these actions reflect gender, ethnicity, economic class, and social marginality (Bennett 1988; Cowan 1990; Danforth 1995; Dimen and Friedl 1976; Dubisch 1986; Galani-Moutafi 1993; Herzfeld 1985; Hirschon 1989; Karakasidou 1997; Loizos and Papataxiarchis 1991; Seremetakis 1991; Stewart 1991). It has delved into the historical development of religious practices, social categories, and kinship institutions often taken for granted, as well as the workings of local memory and the various meanings of tradition (Bottomley 1992; Couroucli 1985; Hart 1992; Herzfeld 1991; Kenna 1995; Moore 1995; Sant Cassia and Bada 1992; Sutton 1986; Sutton, D. 1995).

While general debates within anthropology sometimes imply otherwise, the kinds of materialist studies represented in this volume have moved in concert with these theoretical shifts in Greek ethnography. A series of anthropological and geographical inquiries into settlement, economy, and regional relationships have explicitly worked to counter images of rural stasis and isolation (Allen 1976; Bialor 1976; Beopoulou 1981; Burgel 1981; Costa 1988; Forbes 1976a; Frangakis and Wagstaff 1987, 1992; Kayser 1976; Kolodny 1974; Petronoti 1985a, b, c; Piault 1981; Sivignon 1977; Sutton 1988; Vermeulen 1976; Wagstaff 1982). These same materialist studies have also revealed the constructed nature of such only seemingly fixed institutions as land tenure rules, village boundaries, and household composition. The issues of migration, class, and ethnicity so central to recent interpretive ethnography are greatly illuminated by materialist attention to who lives where and what economic strategies they pursue.

The ethnoarchaeological work done in connection with survey research has been much influenced by these anthropological shifts in conceiving modern Greek life, as well as the clear evidence of long-term rural change that archaeological surveys incontrovertibly revealed. By the 1990s, there were repeated admonitions against survivalist approaches to ethnoarchaeology (Chang 1994; Halstead 1990; Sutton 1988, 1990, 1994; Forbes 1993; Fotiadis 1995; Shutes 1994). Investigations of agricultural tactics are now as likely to stress historical moments of intensification as repetitive cycles (Davis 1991; Forbes 1992; Gallant 1991; Halstead and Jones 1989; Shutes 1994). The full range of structures, fields, and open spaces is examined within a landscape, not just the most typical (Alcock, Cherry, and Davis 1994; Whitelaw 1991; Chang 1992; Clarke 1995). Villages and other settlements are presumed to have life histories worth investigating (Sutton 1988, 1991, 1994, 1995; Wagstaff 1982; Wagstaff and Cherry 1982). The moment has been reached in which archaeology and ethnography are mutually able to conceive the modern countryside in a contingent way. The work reported in this volume has contributed to this development.

Settlement, Economy, and Land Use in the Southern Argolid

Our studies of the southern Argolid began with a general sense that ethnographers, historians, geographers, and classically trained as well as anthropologically trained archaeologists had something to share in examining the Greek landscape. As a minimum we had common interests in settlement, land use, and economy, even if theorized largely at the common sense level. Hamish Forbes, Harold Koster, Joan Koster, Mari Clarke, and Nicolas Gavrielides thus began a series of ecologically oriented studies in the area in the early 1970s, at the same time that Peter Topping initiated his historical demography of the region.[18] Claudia Chang and Keith Adams soon followed, pursuing issues raised by this original work. Nick Kardulias, Priscilla Murray, and I constituted a third wave, first entering the area in conjunction with the intensive phase of the AEP from 1979 to 1983, to which Forbes was also attached. Marina Petronoti's historical analysis of political and economic issues was an independent venture that began at roughly the same time. Many of us have continued working in the region up to the present, and all of us embarked on significant new analyses and rethinking of older issues in order to bring our work into articulation with each other for this volume.

The long period between initiation of some of this work and publication of this volume has been both positive and negative. Some of us would frame our fieldwork differently if we were to start over again. I would pay more attention to local conceptual frameworks for comprehending settlement shifts and patterns. Others would make their own adjustments. On the other hand, this volume records a process of growth. We have had time to reflect on our initial assumptions, to be brought up short by our observations and experiences of the southern Argolid, to shift and expand our theoretical projects. The concerns of contemporary ethnography have asked that even archaic bits of material culture be understood as shaped by present circumstance, and the concerns of contemporary survey archaeology have demanded recognition of the repeated transformations this region has historically undergone. Equally important, the multiple voices which have joined in the discussion over the years have built a comprehension of this area which goes beyond what any of us could have accomplished alone.

The longer we talked with each other and with those living in the Argolid, the more difficult it became to conceive the area's residents as rooted in a timeless soil. Finlay recognized the dynamism of the sailors of this area a century ago in a rare characterization, stemming in this case from his desire to support the new Greek state, by emphasizing how the populace had mobilized prior to the Greek Revolution (1877, 6: 30–33).[19] As we asked new questions, even of older fieldnotes, we found agency such as this among others living in the region both before and after Finlay's day. We came to perceive farming, sailing, and herding as overlapping options in a landscape where houses, fields, and settlements have repeatedly shifted over time.

In pursuing such ideas, we found ourselves venturing beyond the standard forms of ethnographic evidence. Archives and local records, historical writings and government censuses, artifacts and architecture, settlement maps and geological surveys—all combined with interviews and observations to build a dense, textured image of the shifting forms of land use in the area. Ignoring the abundance of such information for rural Greece now seems one more way of distancing these lands from the processes of history. The way in which these different sources of information support or deny each other also directly relates to the issues of representation, variation, idealization, and contestation at the heart of contemporary ethnography.

The essays that follow range between those taking a broad chronological or geographical view and those exploring how specific groups wended their way through history and landscape.

Peter Topping's contribution in Chapter 2 culminates decades of research in identifying and interpreting the often fragmentary and obscure documentary evidence about the southern Argolid during Byzantine, Venetian, and Ottoman times. Topping's investigation connects antiquity to the present and explores changes in the political, economic, and demographic structures of the southern Argolid in ways that show a clear relationship to the formative events and processes of Greek history. Agricultural production, for example, has expanded, contracted, and then expanded again, depending on the region's position within broader systems.

The first essay by Hamish Forbes in Chapter 3 gives depth and texture to one phase of this long history. He combines a close reading of census and cadastral documents from the Second Venetian Occupation with figures calculated from modern farming practices to derive some sense of settlement, land tenure, and agricultural strategies in the Ermionidha around 1700. Concurring with Topping's assessment that the area witnessed a demographic decline in the late 17th century (especially compared to previous periods when sailing and salt-production were important), Forbes suggests that agricultural activities, especially shepherding, governed the economy at this time. Neither the olive cultivation nor the shipping that later dominated the area were then much in evidence, a circumstance that underscores the repeated shifts of rural Greek history. Local monasteries and large estates controlled production levels and land use. Major centers were surrounded by smaller settlements that grew and declined with the passage of time and seasons of the year.

By examining family histories, ship records, and other local documents, Marina Petronoti reveals in Chapter 4 how dramatically the area changed once again with the rise of long-distance shipping. The essay included here recasts her previous analyses of Kranidhiote political economy in the nineteenth century to draw out even more clearly how the surrounding landscape was transformed through a mix of local agency and foreign influence. While recognizing the profound imprint of international markets and forces, she resists images of the southern Argolid as simply a peripheral reflection of the hegemony of distant centers. She also suggests ways in which the capital accumulated by Kranidhiote families during the shipping boom kindled other economic developments, including agricultural expansion.

My own examination of census counts and local demographic records in Chapter 5 investigates how population levels and settlement patterns in the Ermionidha have changed since the period discussed by Petronoti. This chapter brings the area's history forward to the present while also dissolving what has been taken as a fixed and long-standing array of settlements into its formative processes. The patterns of growth, decline, and settlement proliferation found in the records indicate a population in considerable motion and reconfigure conventional images of the Greek village. These conclusions second Forbes and Petronoti in their presentation of the active role that rural Greeks have taken in shaping their own history.

Mari H. Clarke's first chapter in this volume begins a series of essays (Chapter 6 through Chapter 9) that focus on the examination of various buildings and structures in the contemporary southern Argolid and report on interviews with those who have built or used them. Together, they give a detailed reading of the changing architectural landscape as understood through the decisions and actions of particular households. In her examination of the shifting configuration of housing in a Methana village over the last 150 years, Clarke questions ethnoarchaeological assumptions of a direct fit between house size and number of inhabitants, as well as between house form and the activities that householders pursue. By examining various phases of house building, remodeling, and abandonment, she provides a cautionary tale revealing that small houses have sometimes sheltered more residents than large ones, and that a single building can serve multiple functions and sets of occupants during its lifetime. In such manner, Clarke takes the houses of smallholding farmers from universal and hence static categories to a matter of familial strategy and circumstance. She suggests that archaeologists do the same when they examine the dwellings of the past.

The next paper, Chapter 7 by Claudia Chang, also argues against the use of universalized categories in approaching the countryside. She reflects on her own conceptual shifts after two decades of ethnoarchaeological work among pastoral groups in Greece. What emerges is her increasing discomfort with abstract analogies that reduce the specificity and variability of pastoral material culture to vague, disembodied types with strong implications of universality and immovablity. Chang's detailed study of the location, shape, and meaning of the sheep and goat folds that fan out from the village of Dhidhima makes a strong argument against using idealized site types and for recognizing the contingency and decision making that routinely alter such places over time. The present positioning of these folds reflects the ways in which families have negotiated resources, herd size, market factors, pasture availability, and household labor as they moved through historical changes and their own life cycles. For Chang, animal folds are artifacts that only have analogical validity when contextualized within particular conditions. That relatively little archaeological attention has been paid to what pastoral material culture reveals about the variability of such groups, however, has frequently produced formulaic accounts of a mythically unitary form of ancient pastoralism. Indeed, Chang feels that the search for analogies has so often led to a falsely generalized view of pastoralism that she would rather put such efforts aside and focus instead on what detailed investigation of material culture reveals about the specific history of particular areas, without comparison to others.

The joint contribution in Chapter 8 by Priscilla Murray and P. Nick Kardulias is based, like Chang's, on close inspection of sites outside village boundaries. Their study complements the full surface coverage of archaeological surveys and reveals a dense field of social activity and meaning in what is sometimes perceived as an undifferentiated countryside. Murray and Kardulias identify and examine the full range of modern structures, from chapels to kilns, scattered across the Pikrodhafni valley near Kranidhi. The chapter reworks an earlier presentation of this material to accord greater attention to the many instances of site and artifact reuse in the valley. What were once houses have sometimes become sheep folds, while large oil storage jars have been turned into terrace decorations. This demonstration of the periodic reconstitution of the nature of places supports Clarke's argument against tendencies to classify sites according to a single, sustained use. Categorical boundaries are further blurred by the identification of domestic artifacts at primarily religious sites. While Murray and Kardulias remain more sympathetic to the construction of archaeological analogies than does Chang, they nevertheless echo her sentiments about undertaking such comparisons in a careful and contextualized manner.

With Chapter 9, the second of the contributions by Clarke, the papers turn to examination of familial economic strategies and the impact such strategies have had on boundaries and population in the southern Argolid. Clarke's essay continues her analysis of life in the village on Methana, this time exploring successive transformations of local household economy that have occurred since establishment of the Greek state. By considering the household not just as a unit but also as a set of individuals with sometimes conflicting goals, Clarke reaches an understanding of change in household form and function that complements her analysis of house architecture. Of particular importance is Clarke's conclusion that the stem households so common in the village's past were born as much of economic necessity as of cultural values, while the recent decline of such households reflects new methods of income production, field placement, and family roles.

Forbes in Chapter 10 and Keith W. Adams in Chapter 11 also consider issues of household economy as they take up field fragmentation, which is often mentioned as an impediment to agricultural efficiency in contemporary Greece. In his selection, Forbes gives a strong counterargument to accusations of rural conservatism, detailing the economic advantages of scattered land holdings for families on Methana, even under the recent impact of market forces. This chapter is a critically important extension of his groundbreaking argument that in environments with great variation in climate, altitude, soils, and topographical features, households benefit from a range of fields scattered widely across available niches. Forbes here demonstrates with detailed data what had previously been argued more conceptually. Intensive examination of microenvironmental conditions, plot locations, and inheritance patterns indicates that households have purposefully sought fields in a variety of locations to guard against climatic variations and to stagger harvesting times for efficient use of limited family labor. Forbes further locates this pattern within a specific historical context that combined an emphasis on consolidated settlements with a numerical predominance of smallholders who had only household labor at their disposal.

Adams also pursues the issue of fragmentation, in this case through examination of local records on field ownership for the small village of Pelei near Dhidhima by tracking all land transfers recorded for Pelei between 1936 and 1980. His study stands as the first to call into question the generally presumed relationship between equal partible inheritance and field subdivision. Adam's data clearly show that there would have been more plots in 1980 if all parcels listed in 1936 had been equally divided among heirs. Trade and sales, particularly of poor land, served as a check on fragmentation, despite the ideal of equal division among heirs. While families still held plots scattered across a range of microenvironments, their holdings within each of these niches were more consolidated than generally assumed. The studies of Adams and Forbes thus reveal land ownership to be a conscious strategy of household economy, rather than an unfortunate side effect of maladaptive normative ideals. They also combine to depict the rural landscape as an evolving matrix where boundary lines shift with family needs and historical transitions.

In Chapter 12 Harold Koster also looks at fields, in this case pastures close to Dhidhima, that pastoralists have obtained for seasonal use through informal contract and reciprocity rather than cash rental. This analysis enables Koster to move beyond familistic understandings of village social relations to reveal the widespread use of *allilovoithia* (mutual aid) among nonkin of roughly equal social status. This system of mutual obligation through gifts and favors has enabled cash-poor shepherds to use the highly valued grazing lands near the village at below market cost. This situation has created a network of binding reciprocity that is a vital component of household economy in Dhidhima. Koster's precise documentation of such transactions counterbalances agonistic impressions of village life and gives material support for the position that social interest and family interest do sometimes merge in rural Greece.

In a closely related paper, Chapter 13, Koster and Forbes investigate how communally held pasture lands have been used in both Methana and Dhidhima. They reject the thesis that such lands have been overexploited in the pursuit of blind self-interest. Hardin's frequently cited "tragedy of the commons" does not seem to apply (Hardin 1968). Koster and Forbes show that, despite formal differences in land tenure between Dhidhima and Methana, ground-level practices have been quite similar. Public lands in both communities have been used for a combination of grazing, wild herb gathering, lime and charcoal production, and the cutting of firewood. In most cases, those using common areas have shown foresight with respect to the sustainability of key resources, a claim supported by statistics compiled on production levels and flock sizes. Cases when such foresight has been absent have reflected distant market forces rather than long-standing local social relations. As others in this volume, this study thus reveals a complexity in human use of the countryside that reaches well beyond the boundaries of village or site.

The final two essays, Chapter 14 by Kardulias and Chapter 15 by Joan Bouza Koster, examine strategies of craft production in the region, especially as affected by shifting markets and conditions at the national level. They make a strong case against timeless portrayals of either hand pottery or textile production, preferring to see these crafts as shaped by their times, even if certain aspects of technology have persisted from one period to another. Kardulias reflects on his conversations in the 1980s with a potter, Ioannis Sampson, who worked in the outskirts of Ermioni. Throughout his life Sampson made pottery by hand in a workshop attached to his house. Kardulias' study documents material aspects of a ceramic technology of great antiquity, at the same time that it explores how production levels and marketing patterns surrounding this technology have varied over time. Sampson's occupational history exposes the ways in which he balanced family needs, life cycle changes, and market shifts by adjusting levels of pottery output at various points in his career.

Joan Bouza Koster takes up the issue of why some pastoral families in Dhidhima still devote considerable time and effort to weaving textiles, while others do not. Hers is an extraordinarily rich account of historical shifts in handweaving in the region, differentiating domestic production from commodity production and identifying class distinctions involved in the continuation of this craft. Through interviews and household schedules, Koster meticulously examines the hours involved and choices made as women juggle domestic tasks, textile needs, issues of familial status, and perceived measures of modernity. Koster's analysis indicates that the selective continuation of handweaving does not reflect a distinction between isolated and market-oriented households, for all participated in external economies, but rather the wealth and resources available to each family.

The stories of these groups and places in the southern Argolid thus say much about the processes by which the material conditions of the Greek countryside have been created and recreated, conceived and reconceived over the last three hundred years. We see issues of family and village that have figured in many other accounts of rural Greece. We also see, however, themes of settlement creation and abandonment, changing land use and production patterns, boundary shifts and negotiations, occupational overlap and mobility, and many other matters that render our understanding of family and village more permeable and dynamic. The changes of postwar Greece were preceded by the changes of the Greek Revolution, which, in turn, were preceded by the changes of the Tourkokratia. The many and varied responses to such shifts described in these papers yield a contextualized view of rural life in which the landscape is diverse and the population active.

These papers develop this understanding by situating familial decision making within the changing political economy of the southern Argolid over the last three centuries. The authors thus return history and agency to those often left out of such discussions (Fox 1991; Ohnuki-Tierney 1990; O'Brien and Roseberry 1991; Wolf 1982). They also move toward some meeting between the ground-level methods of anthropology and the historical demography of scholars such as Panayiotopoulos (1985), Kolodny (1974), and Sivignon (1977, 1981). In ways both explicit and implicit, these papers follow the lead of Netting and others in focusing on household-level responses to the events of recent history (e.g., Kearney 1986; Machlachlan 1987; Netting 1993; Wilk 1991). This emphasis enables the writers to affirm the importance of regional perspectives in avoiding the enclosure of community studies (Smith 1976) without then being enclosed by a simplistic conception of the nature and boundaries of regions (Lagopoulos and Boklund-Lagopoulou 1992; Pred 1990). Wrapping up neither village nor region very tightly, these papers reveal the variations and contestations inherent in both units. They are also able to acknowledge the strength of national and international systems in shaping even seemingly remote areas of rural Greece (e.g., Smith, Wallerstein, and Evers 1984) without overlooking the counterpressures emanating from these regions themselves (Marcus 1989; Nash 1981).

Past, Present, and Ethnoarchaeology in Greece

In this final section, I consider what the above findings suggest for ethnoarcheology in Greece and for attempts to use studies of the present to inform those of the past. The work done in the southern Argolid draws much of its import from the ways in which it has helped us rethink the nature of ethnoarchaeology. One might argue that the region's modern condition is so unlike its ancient that there is little purpose achieved by juxtaposing studies of the area's past history with those of its present. I believe the situation is otherwise. The conclusion that very little of present life in the region precisely replicates the past does not negate the value of ethnoarchaeological studies, but it does make their nature more complex.

An interdisciplinary approach conjoining studies of modern Greek life with archaeological survey projects yields four sorts of benefits. First, the comparison of different phases in a region's history, when carefully done, continues to be a source of rich and provocative analogies for interpretation. Second, the interdisciplinary juxtaposition of different theoretical viewpoints reworks assumptions and redirects attention to new areas. Third, when brought together, investigations of different time periods can build a comprehensive regional history that clarifies the connection between the Greek past and present. Fourth, such joint endeavors forge a direct link between survey archaeologists and the people whose fields they walk. These four consequences of blending archaeological survey with ethnographic research are equal in importance. All are discussed in this final section. The need to connect the first point—comparison of different phases in a region's history—to the general literature on analogical reasoning in archaeology, however, will make its presentation somewhat longer than the others'.

Present-Past Analogies

Despite earlier debates (e.g., Wylie 1982), most archaeologists now accept that understandings of former times are generally based on one form or another of analogical reasoning. The past is nearly always comprehended through the concepts, patterns, and concerns of the present. The ways in which the present is used as a model for the past can, however, be less than explicit and on very different levels of abstraction. I find it useful to distinguish two types of present-past analogies. The first is a kind of *object-identification analogy*, which is directed quite specifically at determining the characteristics and uses of particular objects, especially those items of the archaeological record that are still in use and whose nature in antiquity has posed something of a puzzle. The studies by Kardulias and Joan Koster can, for example, greatly aid in identifying numerous artifacts associated with pottery workshops and household weaving operations in the past. As important as such object-identification analogies are, the work presented here has been more concerned with a second kind of analogical reasoning with a greater emphasis on context than on direct equivalencies.

This second type, which may be termed *contextualized analogy*, pursues parallels in complexes of thought and behavior, rather than in specific objects, and judges each comparison in terms of context as well as content. In this light, the inventories of material culture conducted by Kardulias and Joan Koster are pieces of much larger studies concerning the shifting conditions and practices of hand pottery manufacture and weaving. Drawing analogies between current manufacturing practices and past ones rests on more than tool identification. Contextualized analogies depend on identifying much broader parallels in the systems of economy, kinship, and community in which the tools under consideration are found. The various contributions to this volume that examine the organization and dynamics of farming, shepherding, shipping, household economy, and migration are critically important in establishing systemwide parallels for this kind of analogical reasoning. The pursuit of contextual analogies is open-ended and complex. It requires care in approaching the presence of older technologies in modern times, recognizes that the same trait can operate differently in different contexts, looks for parallel patterns even in seemingly disparate periods of Greek history, considers parallels in social relationships as well as between objects, and finds insight in difference as well as similarity.

The advent of contextualized analogical reasoning in ethnoarchaeology has been supported by two complementary lines of thought that have recently appeared in modern Greek studies in general. Each of these approaches presents new ways of thinking about the existence of older traits in modern circumstances. The first approach revolves around what is sometimes known as articulation-reproduction, a concept that Seremetakis, for example, invokes in examining the ritual laments of contemporary Maniote women (1991, 1993). Noting the presence of similar forms of mourning in antiquity, Seremetakis employs the idea of articulation-reproduction to explore the repetition of such cultural features across several historical periods. The concept suggests that various patterns of behavior and belief from one period may be consciously reproduced in later periods for purposes of either resisting or legitimating authority. Such traits do not operate in precisely the same manner as their prototypes once did, however, because they are given new meaning through their articulation with new contexts.[20] David's general assessment of ethnoarchaeology reaches the same conclusion in its recognition that the lifeways of a society at any particular moment in time represent a "borrowing, reinterpretation, inversion, montage, and jumbling of elements," some old and some quite new (1992: 346).[21]

A second development in modern Greek studies that gives insight into the existence of ancient traits in contemporary circumstances has emerged from the writings of political economists such as Mouzelis (1978, 1996), Vergopoulos (1975), Evangelinides (1979), and Hadjimichalis (1987) concerning the nature of the modern Greek economy. These analysts point both to the particular position of Greece with respect to global centers of capital accumulation and to the relative poverty of the rural Greek population to explain the maintenance of labor-intensive agricultural techniques, even among farmers producing for urban and international markets. Such theorists offer a view of the modern Greek economy that sees both small-scale, labor-intensive family farming and Athenian factories as parts of the same system. Their coexistence is not a result of traditional ways continuing until contacted by modern ones, but stems rather from the spatial inequalities of underdevelopment.

While such ideas have been developed outside the discourse of ethnoarchaeology, they strongly support the kind of contextualized ethnoarchaeological analogy presented in this volume. It cannot be assumed that the labor-intensive agricultural methods described by Forbes for modern Methana are part of an overall pattern that has remained unchanged since antiquity. Certain tools and techniques employed on Methana do have a long ancestry. Their continued usage, however, reflects the relative poverty and placement of the peninsula within the modern Greek state. This context, significantly different from those in many periods of the past, greatly affects the crops that are grown and the places they are sold. In like manner, Ioannis Sampson, the Ermioni potter, still made vessels by hand in the twentieth century, but his production levels and distribution mechanisms repeatedly shifted in response to modern conditions. Both cases indicate that a focus on the most remote and seemingly isolated areas as a source for precise parallels for the past is misguided.

Ethnoarchaeology is better served by redirecting its search for remaining bits of antiquity toward broader, more thought-provoking comparisons of different periods of Greek history. Different moments of settlement expansion, for example, may well provide informative comparisons, even when modes of transportation and construction techniques are quite different. In this regard, possible analogies may be pursued in any chronological direction, and the past may well advance understanding of the present (as with rural settlement dynamics). Such understandings additionally suggest that the differences between two periods may be as revealing as the similarities. Land use under familial ownership, for instance, may expose a great deal about land use under various forms of feudalism precisely because of the contrast.

Interesting analogies based on similarities of context (or lack thereof) may also be found in places quite distant from one another. Some scholars have noted two kinds of contextualized analogy: the direct historic analogy, which draws comparisons between earlier and later periods for the same region; and illustrative or comparative analogy, which looks for systematic parallels wherever they might be found (Stahl 1993:236). Indeed, those interested in the nature of Mediterranean seafaring before steam would do better to examine Venetian life in the seventeenth century than Kranidhiote life at the same time. Direct historic analogies are justifiably at the heart of regional survey projects, drawing their strength from the existence of certain environmental constants and the continuation (albeit in reworked fashion) of various beliefs and behaviors among people who live in an area.[22] Not all contextualized analogies, however, need be restricted to a single geographical setting.[23]

In either case, contextualized ethnoarchaeological analogies require clear definition of those parameters of contemporary life that bear on the issues of land use, settlement, and economy, which are matters of great interest to most survey archaeologists. In the modern period the population of the southern Argolid has grown, settlements have proliferated, and external economies have become significant, as shown in Petronoti's assessment of the southern Argolid's expanding economy in the nineteenth century as well as in my own examination of demographic trends in the twentieth century. The contemporary situation thus presents parallels for certain phases of the area's past, but not others. There are, for example, strikingly similar patterns in the Bronze Age, when maritime connections enabled the region to play a role in long-distance trade, a circumstance accompanied by increase in population and proliferation of settlements (Jameson, Runnels, and van Andel 1994; van Andel and Runnels 1987). Other periods of the southern Argolid's past, when population was in decline, find a better demographic counterpart in late seventeenth-century conditions, as discussed by Forbes. Such conclusions give new meaning to certain aspects of the present that initially seemed anomalous for understanding the past. The development of new communities along the coastal strip east of Ermioni, once seen as irrelevant and even contaminating for archaeological efforts, thus become a source of insight into various periods of settlement expansion, both past and recent.

Discursive Juxtapositions

The second benefit of meshing studies of the contemporary and ancient countrysides is the conjunction of different disciplinary viewpoints thus engendered, a conjunction which can rework assumptions and direct attention to new topics. Such interdisciplinary dialogue undoubtedly has changed the ways many of us approach rural Greece. The issues central to those who study the Greek past have challenged those who study the present to expand their views, and vice versa.

On the basis of their contact with archaeology, many of the essays that follow thus reassess concepts that have long guided research on the modern Greek countryside.[24] They attempt, for example, to break loose from village-bounded thinking to comprehend the breadth and complexity of rural land use, reflecting the ways in which survey archaeology has gone beyond the site in approaching the surface evidence of past periods (Jameson, Runnels, and van Andel 1994: 419–421).[25] The folds, sheds, production sites, seasonal shelters, hamlets, and similar places documented in this volume reveal a richer, and in some instances alternate, texture to rural life than emerges when one thinks strictly in terms of formal, recognized settlements.

These interdisciplinary exchanges have also encouraged us to find new ways of talking about the Greek countryside. To modify a phrase from Clifford (1988), we face a predicament of language in discussing recurrent aspects of Greek life. Standard terms such as village, region, shepherd, and dowry can evoke misleading notions of fixity. The fluid processes by which a farmer becomes a shepherd or a dowry is negotiated are replaced with a sense that shepherds have always been shepherds and dowries have always followed normative ideals precisely. The word village, for example, when used as a background given of the Greek countryside without definition or discussion, often leaves the most interesting aspects of village life unexamined. Several contributors work to broaden interpretation of the term to reflect the life history, variable boundaries, flexible membership, internal contests, and even transportable nature of villages as settlements.

The meshing of ethnographic and archaeological approaches has also encouraged us to pay greater attention to issues of meaning when interpreting the material record of the past. Settlement, economy, and land use are often approached, even in regard to the present, with standardized ideas of rationality, and little attention to the expressed motivations or meanings of various actions. While one might have expected a largely materialist volume such as this to conform to this pattern, we have generally come to see this situation in a different light. Our work relies heavily on understandings reached in conversation with farmers, shepherds, and sailors of the southern Argolid. Most of us stand somewhere on that middle ground that claims primacy for neither the ideational nor material worlds, but sees the two spheres in dynamic interaction (David 1992; Peebles 1992; Sanjek 1991). One cannot fully understand the construction of identity without reference to the demographics that underlie settlements and populations. Conversely one can make little sense of population statistics without knowing the social boundaries and subdivisions drawn by the people glossed by such numbers.

Seremetakis (1991), Karakasidou (1997), Herzfeld (1991), and others have recently made great strides in meshing material and interpretive approaches to modern Greek life. There is, however, much more work to be done. I suspect there are issues of economic rationality that we who have contributed to this volume could be confronting more clearly. I am also persuaded that many of us could usefully direct greater attention to the conceptual frames concerning settlement, land use, and economy that are employed by the people whose decision making we represent. On the other side, those pursuing interpretive approaches to Greek life could gain from the detailed assessment of rural Greek settlement and economy presented here. Forbes and Adams's examination of the ways in which normative declarations such as land tenure rules are undercut by actual practice is an apt example.

The kind of materialism found in these studies thus argues that, in weighing the usefulness of any present behavioral pattern for understanding a particular moment in the past, consideration must be given to issues of meaning and decision making. Beliefs and values are part of the analogical context that must be established. Most of us involved in this volume would also take the position that meaning is accessible in the archaeological record. It is true that ethnographers have more inputs for understanding meaning than do archaeologists (although conversations only convey values and beliefs to the extent that lines of communication are open). It is also true, however, that the material world is a rich source of meaning in ways that archaeologists such as David (1992), Ingersoll and Bronitsky (1987), Hodder (1986),

Fotiadis (in Watson and Fotiadis 1990), Melas (1989), and Morris (1994: 45) have recognized. Parallel insights have recently been drawn for the understanding of landscapes (Lagopoulos and Boklund-Lagopoulou 1992; Lawrence and Low 1990; Pred 1990).

Comprehensive Regional Histories

The third benefit of conjoining studies of the modern countryside with archaeological surveys lies in the development of comprehensive regional histories, which are worthwhile even when ethnoarchaeological analogy is not the primary goal. Chang, in fact, has become so disenchanted with distortions arising from most analogical efforts that she would rather concentrate on material culture for specific history than for universal law. On one level, such efforts to build cumulative histories of a region serve to connect modern with ancient Greece in the face of those who would disconnect them. This is particularly important, given the ease with which modern Greeks were declared to have no link with antiquity in the nineteenth century (Angelomatis-Tsoukarakis 1990; Herzfeld 1982), various tendencies to continue this thinking even now, and the element of cultural expropriation involved in such disconnections.[26] Comprehensive local histories work against such ideas by replacing crude survivalism with recognition of the mixing of peoples, cultural transformations, and political and economic shifts that have built most contemporary nations. Furthermore, the Venetian period and others that are written out of many abbreviated versions of Greek history thus regain their place in the narrative of events.

Human Linkages

A fourth benefit of such archaeological-anthropological collaborations as occurred in the southern Argolid concerns the connection between researchers and the people of rural Greece, an issue that is rarely discussed in the literature on ethnoarchaeology. Paying attention to the present condition of the area under study acknowledges the importance of contemporary Greek life, even for those whose primary research interest is in the past. Dialogue with current residents has great potential for creating productive links between those working on archaeological surveys and those whose fields they walk. It brings a human face to issues of cultural property and the impact that archaeology has on local communities. To my mind, such dialogue also contributes to the refiguring of Greek archaeology in a world where the classical period is no longer the center of attention (Morris 1994). The participation of ethnographers on archaeological projects includes modern Greece within the purview of what is significant to study, gives voice to the concerns of contemporary people, and recognizes that archaeologists are actors in the modern Greek arena. One consequence of the long-standing separation of studies of the Greek past from those of the present has been the alienation of modern Greeks from the ancient places around them (Sutton 1997). The work reported in this volume is a step toward closing this gap.[27]

These four benefits of a broad, multidisciplinary, multiperiod approach to the Greek countryside also illuminate the sometimes contentious issue of who is best suited to carry out ethnoarchaeology. Speaking generally, Longacre and Skibo (1994) favor archaeologists, who, they feel, have a distinctive appreciation for details of material culture. The papers collected here join others who argue, from a variety of perspectives, that the efforts of ethnologists, historians, geographers, and others are equally important because these give context and meaning to archaeological artifacts and sites (Gould 1980, 1990:65; Hodder 1986: 103–104; Jacobsen 1985:92). The kind of social history long pursued by the AEP (Jacobsen 1985: 93; Jameson 1976a, 1976b, 1994) is well served by a combination of perspectives on the present that mesh the study of material objects with social analysis (Pavlides and Sutton 1995). To phrase this in a slightly different way, it is a major tenet of these papers that using the present to interpret the past is best done within a full and rich ethnographic framework.

In sum, the AEP and similar surveys have provided a meeting ground for archaeology and ethnography in Greece. Early efforts to bring these approaches together aimed, in general, sometimes vaguely defined ways, at broadening conceptions of the past and affirming the importance of the present. Neither side initially understood all that was offered by the other, nor how they resonated with more general discussions of the connection between ancient and modern Greece. Twenty-five years of work in the southern Argolid have brought about significant rethinking, shaped by disciplinary shifts, increasing awareness of the political implications of various representations of Greece, and the ability of interdisciplinary exchanges to rework assumptions. The chronological depth of survey research has demanded that we explore the historical formation of present-day settlements and institutions previously taken for granted. Approaches to antiquity have gained, in turn, by recognizing the active nature of modern times. Together, they have awakened us to the texture and dynamism of the Greek countryside.

CHAPTER TWO

The Southern Argolid from Byzantine to Ottoman Times

Peter W. Topping

My aim is to sketch the history of the southern Argolid, especially of the Ermionidha, under Byzantine, Latin, and Ottoman rule, and to relate to this outline bits of evidence bearing on the human and material landscape of the region. The long period I cover encompasses the centuries of the later Roman or Byzantine Empire (from the early fourth century to 1453); the Frankish or Latin period (1212–1540: French feudal lords 1212–1389, Venetian rule 1389–1540); the Ottoman domination or first Tourkokratia (1540–1685); renewed Venetian rule (1685–1715); and the second Tourkokratia (1715–1821).

Ermioni (ancient Hermione), or what was then known as Kastri, continued to be the chief town of the lower Argolid (ancient Hermionis) in the early Byzantine era. It is found in the sixth-century *Synekdemos* of Hierokles, which lists the cities of the empire. Evstathios Stikas has also excavated a large basilica complex in the court of the Ermioni elementary school. At an early date a church clearly succeeded the sanctuary of Poseidon on Bisti promontory, and the sanctuary's wall underwent restoration. The ancient cemetery of Ermioni, on the south slope of Mt. Pron, also continued in use in Christian times (Konti 1983: 187–189).

The Slavic penetration of the Peloponnesos (late sixth century to late eighth century) apparently bypassed the southern Argolid. Byzantine naval strength was sufficient to maintain imperial authority on the eastern coasts of the peninsula. The city of Argos, to be sure, experienced a Slavic raid in the late 580s, but it was spared occupation (Yannopoulos 1980: 348–353). The paucity of Slavic place-names in the southern Argolid suggests that Slavic migrants did not settle in the district.

From the ninth century, the authority of Constantinople was reestablished in most regions of the Peloponnesos. The Argolid no doubt shared in the more prosperous middle centuries (ninth to twelfth) of the Byzantine Empire. Yet, for many decades in the ninth and tenth centuries, especially during the domination of Crete by Spanish Saracens (ca. 825–961), the Argolic coasts, like the Aegean world as a whole, were prey to constant attacks by Arab pirates. From 829, the Arabs occupied Aegina for some years. We must suppose that the inhabitants of Kastri and of hamlets or farms on the shores of the Kranidhi peninsula often withdrew to towers and inland locations to escape capture by these raiders. Nor had invasions of the Peloponnesos from continental Greece entirely ceased. The *Life* of St. Peter (Vasiliev 1947), about the bishop of Argos in the first decades of the tenth century,[1] reports a destructive attack on the peninsula by "barbarians." These were probably pagan Slavs who were led by the now Christian Bulgars. St. Peter's *Life* also tells of a violent famine in the countryside. The inhabitants ate grasses and plant roots to survive. A local tradition in Argos confirms this "three-year" affliction, which may have coincided with the descent of the Slavs (Vasiliev 1947).

New monastic foundations were one of the signs of recovery in the Peloponnesos. It is certain that the monastery of Ayios Dhimitrios of Avgho, on the mountain of the same name some three hours' walk west of the settlement of Dhidhima, was established in the eleventh century (Sotiriou 1935). Tradition has it that the monastery of Ayioi Anaryiroi, near Kastri, was also founded in the same century. It was dedicated to Saints Cosmas and Damian, renowned as the "moneyless" practitioners of medicine.

The closing decades of the twelfth century witnessed the rapid decline of imperial authority at Constantinople and in the provinces. In the Greek peninsula landed magnates (*arkhontes*) seized power for themselves. Prominent among these was Leon Sgouros, lord of Nafplio (Nauplion) in succession to his father. By capturing Argos and Corinth, Sgouros became virtual master of the northeastern Peloponnesos. He failed, however, in a grand effort to extend his rule to Athens and central Greece, and Latin knights conquered this region and much of the Peloponnesos soon after the Fourth Crusade (1204–1205). Among their leaders, Geoffrey de Villehardouin (nephew and namesake of the famed chronicler), was recognized as Prince of the Morea (1210–ca. 1228). Sgouros held out for a few years in the strongholds of Nafplio, Argos, and Corinth. At last, in despair he plunged on his mount to his death from the heights of Acrocorinth (1208).

By resisting the Franks and taking his life, Sgouros made some atonement for the many cruelties he had inflicted on his fellow Greeks. From a letter of Michael Choniates, the eminent Orthodox metropolitan of Athens, we learn that Sgouros's harshness caused many inhabitants of "Argos, Ermioni, Aegina, and Corinth" to seek refuge in nearby Latin lordships. By Ermioni, Choniates, of course, meant Kastri and its vicinity. It is probable that the tyrant's authority extended for a time to the Ermionidha and even Aegina.

After Sgouros's death, the Doukas family, rulers of Epiros, continued Greek resistance to the Franks in the Morea. Villehardouin needed help from Othon de la Roche, "great lord" of Athens and Thebes, in order to capture Argos and Nafplio (1211–1212). Geoffrey rewarded de la Roche by granting him the two places as a hereditary fief. Othon and his descendants were to hold them until 1308 (Kordosis 1986).

While the southern Argolid became part of the fief de la Roche, the Franks were not numerous in the district. Greek landowners, here as elsewhere in the Morea, accepted Frankish rule and were allowed to retain their estates and Orthodox creed. Such a Greek noble was Manuel Mourmouras who, together with his family, erected the church of Ayia Trias near Kranidhi in 1244, as an inscription attests. The painter "John of the megalopolis of Athens" (actually a small town then) decorated its walls. It is purely Byzantine in style. So, too, are the Kranidhi churches of Ayios Andreas, of similar date, and Ioannis Theologos, somewhat younger (Kalopissi-Verti 1975: 1–19).

Frankish Morea reached its zenith in the first decade of the reign of William, the third Villehardouin prince (1246–1278). The reestablishment, however, of Byzantine power in the southeastern Morea, centered at Mistra (1262), and the weakness of William's successors led to an increase of Byzantine influence elsewhere in the peninsula as well. This situation makes less surprising the granting, in April 1288, of the village of Kranidion, that is, Kranidhi, by Andronicus II Palaeologus to a Theodoros Nomikopoulos. The grant included a vineyard "in the *topothesia* (vicinity) of Gonia," very probably in the contemporary locality of this name in the Iria peninsula northwest of Kranidhi. The carefully worded chrysobull (decree) implies that Nomikopoulos was "returning" to his proper lord. Apparently he, too, was a Greek noble who had served a French baron but who now wanted to assure the possession of his estate for himself and the heirs "of his body" through a new grant from the Byzantine emperor (Dolger 1955).

We know little more about Kranidhi as a *pronoia* (the Byzantine term for an imperial grant in return for military service). Vassals of Duke Guy II de la Roche (1287–1308) must have continued to hold villages in the southern Argolid. On Guy's death, his closest male relative, Gautier de Brienne, of the great family of this name established in France and Italy, succeeded him as Duke of Athens. But he was soon to lose his life and duchy in the battle of Halmyros (Thessaly) in 1311 between the assembled chivalry of Frankish Greece and the Catalan Grand Company. The ill-fated duke's son and namesake, Gautier II, invaded Greece with large forces in 1331–1332, but he failed to expel the Catalans from Athens and Thebes. Catalan and Turkish pressures tested the loyalty of de Brienne's vassals in the Argolid. The most important of these were the Foucherolles. Writing from Avignon in 1319, Pope John XXII urged them to stand fast against the Catalans. They held the fortresses of Argos, Nafplio, Kyveri and Thermisi for Gautier II, and the four places figure in the testament he made in 1347. Prominent in the West as the tyrant of Florence (1342–1343) and constable of France, the titular duke of Athens fell at Poitiers in 1356 (Bon 1969: 201n6, 207, 236).

Gautier II de Brienne was survived by a sister, Isabelle d'Enghien. But it was her five sons who inherited his claims and far-flung possessions. Guy d'Enghien became the lord of Argos and Nafplio (1356–1377). He was married to Bonne de Foucherolles. A few surviving documents shed some light on events and conditions in Guy's domain, including the southern Argolid. When his *bailli* (bailiff), a member of the Medici family of Florence, restricted the sale of currants and figs, the Argives and Nafpliotes rebelled in protest (1360). From a document that Guy issued in Nafplio in late 1376, we can reconstruct several generations of the Foucherolles and to some extent their Argolic lands from 1309. The villages or estates that comprised their three fiefs are named. Their identification is difficult, but *Forne* is surely Fournoi, and mention is made of the agricultural district of *Castri*, that is, Kastri. The identifications proposed by Jameson are as close as we can come to understanding this obscure passage (Luttrell 1966: 50–55; Jacoby 1971: 213–215; Jameson, Runnels, and van Andel 1994: 112–126).

Guy d'Enghien was succeeded by his daughter Marie, destined to be the last French ruler of the Argolid (1377–1388). Through her marriage to Pietro Cornaro, scion of the richest family of Venice, the Enghien seigneury, including the southern Argolid, entered the sphere of influence of the Republic of Venice. Venetians (and other Italians) had long served as officials in Nafplio and Argos. Venetian merchants were active in exporting agricultural products of the

Argolid and in importing textiles. Documents of 1378 and 1384 reveal that the Venetian Senate allowed the Cornaro family to export currants, valonia dye, resin, carobs, and salt to Venice.

Pietro Cornaro died prematurely in 1388. His young widow was persuaded to sell her domain to the Republic at the end of the same year. Before, however, the Venetians could occupy Argos and Nafplio, Theodore I Palaeologus (1382–1407), the Byzantine despot of the Morea, seized their citadels. The Venetians succeeded in getting Nafplio in May 1389, but it took them five more years to persuade Theodore to surrender Argos (Bon 1969: 263–264). The despot had the backing of his suzerain, Sultan Bayezid I, in his usurpation. The Turkish pressure on Venice's new colony was incessant. In 1397, the Turks captured Argos. During their brief occupation they deported much of its Greek population. To make up for this loss the Venetian authorities settled Albanians in the territory of Argos, granting them long-term exemption from agrarian dues. The despot Theodore had set Venice an example by introducing Albanians into the Corinthia. The immigrants were herdsmen and cultivators. Along with the Greeks, they also supplied *stratioti* (mercenary light horsemen) to Venice's armies (Topping 1980).

From the beginning, the Venetians found it difficult to control the southern Argolid, in particular Thermisi castle and the salt lake on the shore beneath the fortress. In fact, the rector (governor) at Nafplio did not exercise direct authority over Thermisi, inasmuch as the French seigneurs had at an early date granted the castle to the Latin bishops of Argos-Nafplio. We learn this from a document of 1437, in which the Venetian government replied to several petitions of the bishop. One of these concerned the castle of Thermisi, described as being three days' distance from Nafplio. Greek and Albanian subjects of the despot Theodore II Palaeologus (1415–1443) were helping themselves freely to the "products of the territory and salt," depriving the church of income. Venice acknowledged the bishop's right to appoint and dismiss the castellan, provided the appointee was loyal to the Republic (Choras 1975: 106–107, 252–255).

From Senate documents of 1441 and 1444 we learn that Theodore was continuing to occupy the territory. Likewise, his brother Demetrius was committing usurpations there. This is revealed in a list of grievances that the community of Nafplio addressed to the seigniory in 1451. Not only were Demetrius's Albanian subjects obtaining salt at Thermisi without paying any tax, but both his Albanian and his Greek subjects were wintering their flocks in Venetian pastures in the southern Argolid while paying the grazing tax to his agents instead of the Nafplio regime. In addition, the community begged the seigniory's assistance to recover the lands of Castri and of the church of Sancta Marina del Didimo (Ayia Marina of Dhidhima) that Demetrius and his men had seized (Fedalto 1978: 233, 237; Thiriet 1961: 168–170; Jacoby 1971: 220–221).

In 1458 and 1460, Sultan Mohammed II eliminated the Byzantine despots as Venice's rivals in the Morea when he conquered the entire peninsula, excepting the Republic's holdings in Messenia and the Argolid. In 1463, the first of several great wars between the Porte (Ottomon government) and the Serenissima (Ventian lords) broke out. It is not clear if the Venetians had effective control of the southern Argolid during the long course of the war. When the two adversaries agreed on terms of peace (January 25, 1479), it was understood that they would define the boundaries of Venice's Argolic territories in later negotiations. We know about these from the dispatches of Bartolomeo Minio, the rector at Nafplio in 1479–1483. The Turks claimed the Thermisi, Kastri, and Iri districts. Only in April 1482, after prolonged parleys, did they acknowledge Venice's claims to all three places (Sathas 1884 6: 121–129, 137f., 141–146, 191–197).

It is clear from Minio's reports that the southern Argolid was a vital hinterland for Nafplio, the more so following the Turks' definitive conquest of Argos in 1463. The security of the colony depended a good deal on Albanian and Greek stratioti. Besides receiving allotments of wheat from the rectors, the stratioti raised cereals in the southern Argolid for themselves and their families, while their horses grazed in the Iri grasslands. By Minio's reckoning, the outlying districts constituted nearly two-thirds of Venice's Argolic possessions (Sathas 1884 6: 128).

We glimpse other details of the colony's life and trials from Minio's dispatches. During Turkish attacks, the fortress of Thermisi and the tower at Kastri were refuges for the local families. These included Albanians, other than stratioti, who lived in their own settlements or encampments (*catune* in Italian transcription; *katouna* (sing.) in Greek; *katun* in Slavic, a term widely used by pastoralists in the Balkan peninsula). Dhokos served as a refuge island for the Albanians' animals. (A later mention of Dhokos, as "a certain uninhabited rock named Docos in the Castri district," occurs in a document of 1493, whereby the Senate made a grant of it to a Nafpliote against payment of four pounds of wax annually [Sathas 1888 7: 51]). Minio reported good harvests of winter cereals in 1480 and 1481, but a very poor one for 1482. Some olive oil and wine were imported from Attica. On one occasion, the southern Argolid was a source of firewood for Nafplio; it was needed to fire a kiln there for the production of lime. Repeatedly Minio stressed the importance of the sea and of trade to the inhabitants. The sea yielded valuable products in fish and sponges. But the human cost of obtaining them was very high. On October 25, 1482, Minio reported that in the nearly four years since the peace, one hundred men—the flower of the sailing population—had been captured by Turkish pirates, and some were sold into slavery (Sathas 1884 6: 120–121, 167, 205).

In 1499–1502, Venice and Turkey fought the second of their great wars. The Republic saved Nafplio, but it had to surrender Lepanto (Naupactus) and southern Messenia (Modon, Coron, Navarino Bay)—serious losses for a maritime empire of bases and islands stretching from the north Adriatic to Cyprus. An all-out Turkish assault on Nafplio and Monemvasia, Venice's last Peloponnesian holdings, came in the third war between the two powers (1537–40). The Turks quickly seized Thermisi and Kastri. But, although Acronafplio and the rock of Monemvasia withstood prolonged sieges, Venice had to surrender them both to Turkey, an empire at the pinnacle of its strength on land and sea.

By an official census of 1530 or 1531, Nafplio had 9,431 souls. Together with the 3,868 inhabitants of the castelli, the colony's total population was 13,299. Castelli must mean the Thermisi and Kastri fortifications and their districts. It is evident that the lower Argolid was an important part of Venice's colony. The town of Nafplio was mainly Greek, and was guarded by Albanian and Greek stratioti. One rector stated candidly, in his report to the Senate at the end of his term, that Greeks did not want to serve under Albanians, while the latter insisted on serving only under captains to whom they were related. The Albanians may well have been a majority now in the southern Argolid. Bands of Albanian robbers preyed on the population in both the Venetian and the Turkish territories. One rector's allusion to "a place called Cragnidi" as the lair of one band of Albanians suggests that the Venetians did not effectively control Kranidhi, nor did they control Iri and Candia at this time. The stratioti, however, continued to sow the fields of these places, thanks to an annual payment by the Venetians to the Turkish authorities (Sathas 1884 6: 249, 253).

Two families, the Alberti and the Palaeologi, were in possession of Kastri for a number of decades, as grantees of the Venetian regime. The rectors speak of them as exploitative lords. It was they who maintained towers as refuges for the people when Turkish pirates landed. Naturally strong, Thermisi was a "true" castle in one rector's words, in contrast to Kastri's towers, and, with proper maintenance and a small garrison, might be impregnable. But it needed, in this rector's view, a captain of noble rank who would impose his authority over neighboring Kastri and the usurping Alberti and Palaeologi. Such a commandant would rightfully receive the profits "from the outside animals that came in the winter for pasture there" (at Thermisi). This income, however, did not itself suffice for a *gentilhomo* (man of noble birth) (Sathas 1884 6: 246–247).

Hemmed in by the Turkish Morea, the Nafplio colony led a precarious existence in its last decades. At any time the Turks could easily have stopped the flow of agricultural produce into the town and starved its inhabitants. Extreme shortages from the end of 1530 until the harvest of the summer of 1531 forced the Nafpliotes to mix spoiled stocks of millet with herbs or grasses for the barest sustenance. The millet must have been imported and stored for emergency use, since very little of this cereal was then being sown in the Morea (Sathas 1884 6: 251).

A rather serious weakness in the defenses was the lack of lumber to provide blocks used for the cannons. When a supply was cut on Hydra (la insula de Idres), it proved impossible to transport it to Nafplio because of pirates. The fact that light Venetian galleys did not winter in the gulf of Nafplio, so that the watch around Cape Malea was not maintained, increased the danger on the sea. Despite the risks, sailors went out in all seasons, using all manner of small craft in search of the sea's produce. Exceptionally, the salt lake of Thermisi was so productive that its yield had to be restricted. The farmer of the taxed salt was forbidden to load any vessels for his own account or send any salt abroad except to Tsakonia. An effort was made to stop both the Monemvasiotes from going to Melos for salt and the Aeginetans (likewise subjects of Venice) from going to Dhamala and Piadha in Turkish territory to obtain it (Sathas 1884 6: 248, 253–254).

From Venetian data on the Cornaro years and the period of Venice's direct rule in the Argolid we can compile the following list of products of the land that had commercial or fiscal value: wheat, barley, wine, currants, salt, raw silk, cotton, flax, resin, carobs, wax, and valonia and kermes dyes. Flocks of sheep and goats contributed to revenues, but apparently the Argolid did not export cheeses to the metropolis, as did Crete. Nor, apparently, was olive oil produced in sufficient quantity in the Argolid, at this time, for export to Venice. Crete, again, and Corfu were more important producers of oil.

The first Ottoman tax register (*tahrir defter*) of the Morea (ca. 1461) has been studied recently by scholars in France, Bulgaria, and Greece. It did not, of course, include the Venetian-held parts of the Argolid. It is of interest, nonetheless, to note a calculation of the percentages of the fiscal value of fifteen crops or products (see Table 2.1). Wheat and wine represent 81 percent of the value, while barley, raw silk, and flax together came to nearly 16 percent. These data pertain to ten districts in the peninsula, including Corinth, Vostitsa (Aigion), and Patras, all three of which had extensive vineyards. We cannot apply these figures to the Argolic colony, whose production of salt, for one thing, was exceptionally large. Wheat and barley, of course, must always have been the chief crops (Beldiceanu and Beldiceanu-Steinherr 1980: 24–37). A Greek

Table 2.1
Ottoman Tax Register for the Morea Around 1461

Products	Fiscal value	Value (florins)	Percentage (%)
Wheat	1,950,264	48,756.60	45.649
Cotton	28,280	707	0.661
Fruit	22,330	558.25	0.522
Olive oil	15,120	378	0.353
Flax	110,390	2,759.75	2.583
Mastic	110	2.75	0.0025
Honey	8,520	213	0.199
Mulberries	130	3.25	0.003
Barley	312,648	7,816.20	7.318
Vegetables	2,490	62.25	0.582
Raisins	5,700	142.50	0.133
Rice	29,300	732.50	0.685
Salt	19,844	496.10	0.464
Silk	255,550	6,388.75	5.981
Vines (wine)	1,511,590	37,789.75	35.381
TOTAL	4,272,266	106,806.65	100

SOURCE: Beldiceanu and Beldiceanu-Steinherr (1980: 30).

testament that survives from the first Tourkokratia in the southern Argolid confirms the continuing production of cotton there, and also mentions honey, olives, and wheat as products of bequeathed fields. This rare document was composed in Kranidhi in May 1634. By it a *hieromonakos* (priest-monk) Gerasimos willed various properties to a nephew, including a field at Ververonda (Lambros 1908).

Besides the defter of ca. 1461, several other detailed Ottoman tax registers for the Morea have been located in Istanbul and Ankara archives. When exploited they will provide important data on the agrarian economy and the population of the peninsula. Surviving regulations or law codes (*kanunnames*) are an important, indeed necessary, complement to the defters, recording tax rates on many products (Alexander 1974: 354–375).

Famine and disease took their toll on the defenders of Nafplio during the war of 1537–40. At its end, the town's population was further reduced by the migration of many inhabitants to other Greek colonies of the Republic, such as Crete, Corfu, Cephalonia, and Cyprus—colonies in which they were granted choice lands. Possibly some inhabitants of the southern Argolid joined this exodus, which the Ottomans had agreed to under the peace. No doubt the members of privileged families, such as the Alberti and Palaeologi of Kastri, migrated. (Early in the war four Palaeologi were beheaded by the Turks in Argos.) After a time, however, nostalgia and favorable reports received from Nafplio induced a number of the emigrants or their descendants to remigrate to the Turkish Argolid.

In the Ottoman Empire as a whole, the 16th century was one of notable increase in population and economic expansion. We may guess that Nafplio and the southern Argolid participated in this growth, thereby making up some of the losses suffered in the war of 1537–1540. Was the area's recovery held back by special factors, such as the conscription of the experienced mariners of the Argolid for the imperial navy? New sources, especially Turkish documents, may enable us to answer such a question. The needs of the Sultan's fleet were heaviest in the Turko-Venetian war of 1570–1571, during which the Ottomans conquered Cyprus but were defeated in the celebrated sea fight at Lepanto (Nafpaktos).

In contrast to the 16th century, the 17th was marked by significant demographic decline in the empire. The Morea could hardly have escaped this trend. In any case, the province suffered from the large demands that the Ottomans made on its harbors, manpower, and products during their fourth war with the Venetians (1645–1669). This, the longest conflict of the rival empires of the Levant, resulted in the loss of Crete, Venice's most prized possession, to the Sultan.

At about the end of the Cretan war, Evliya Celebi, most famous of the Turkish travelers, twice visited the Morea (1668, 1670). Despite his exaggerations and inaccuracies, his account is of value for the historical *Landeskunde* (regional studies) of the Peloponnesos. He mentions Iri and the monastery of Avgho. He stopped at Thermisi and Kastri and remarks on the flourishing vines and figs of Thermisi and on its salt—the "best tasting" in all the Morea. From the abundant ancient remains at Kastri, he imagines it to have once been a large and populous city, in contrast to the village of "three hundred houses" that he found. Evliya marvels at its several fine harbors. The gulf of Kapari-Potokia could hold one thousand ships. It was, in fact, a regular station for the Ottoman fleet that cruised the Aegean (Wolfart 1966: 101–104).

Soon after Evliya, the English merchant Bernard Randolph visited the Peloponnesos. Randolph lived in Greece during 1671–1679, observing the people and the country with keen interest. He recorded the population of Morea as 120,000, consisting of 90,000 Christians and 30,000 Turks. We do not know how Randolph arrived at these figures. The total of 120,000 is not farfetched in view of the first Venetian census of 1689 (see below). The figure for the Turks, however, is disproportionately large. It may reflect the tendency to conversion to Islam on the part of Moreote Greeks, which was quite noticeable when Randolph was visiting the Peloponnesos (Randolph 1689: 15).

In 1685–1687, as a member of the Holy League against the Ottoman Empire, the Republic of Venice retook all of the Morea (except Monemvasia, which fell in 1690). The Venetians were to hold the vast peninsula, which they called the Regno di Morea, until 1715, when an Ottoman expeditionary force quickly reconquered it. The fighting of 1685–1687, together with the plague, cost the lives of many Moreotes. The losses in the Argolid were made up, at least in part, by the influx of refugees and immigrants from several regions of Greece. The presence of refugees from Athens, Euboea, western Crete (Chania), and Chios is attested in the detailed cadastre of Romania, ca. 1705. The name Romania derives from Napoli di Romania, Naples of Greece, as the Venetians called Nafplio (see Forbes, this volume). The failure of Venetian expeditions against these places caused the exodus of many of their inhabitants. There were other newcomers as well, particularly in Nafplio (then the capital of the Morea) from the Ionian Islands, the Archipelago, and continental Greece (Dokos 1975).

When the Venetians made the first census of the Moreote population, in 1689, the total—excluding the peninsula of Mani—was only 98,885 inhabitants (Topping 1976a: 93). It is not certain if this enumeration included the first wave of refugees from Attica and Euboea.

In 1700, a more accurate and complete enumeration was made under Francesco Grimani, the proveditor general (civil and military governor) of the "Realm of Morea" in 1698–1701. Panayiotopoulos (1985) has edited this remarkable census (see Table 2.2). Under each village

Table 2.2
Grimani Census of 1700, District of Thermis

Settlement	Number of families	Ages of male population						Ages of female population					Total population
		1–16	16–30	30–40	40–50	50–60	60+	1–16	16–30	30–40	40–50	60+	
1. Cranidi	220	235	120	72	50	23	31	201	108	54	48	60	1,002
2. Castri	103	99	38	39	33	5	8	87	40	37	9	13	408
3. Boaria Illia	9	7	1	4	5	-	-	7	5	4	3	1	37
4. Castel di Termis	24	19	10	12	3	2	3	16	10	8	4	7	94
5. Aga	13	13	10	2	-	4	2	8	6	3	4	3	55
6. Boaria Lucaiti	5	5	5	1	1	1	1	-	3	-	1	4	22
7. Balabani	28	25	12	8	7	3	5	9	8	10	5	4	96
8. Dardessa	1	2	-	-	-	-	-	-	-	1	-	1	5
9. Furni	44	40	18	16	7	2	7	24	20	13	7	12	166
10. Dimo	42	45	31	10	4	8	5	38	25	10	8	11	195
11. Boaria Peligi	7	1	1	2	1	3	1	4	2	1	3	2	21
TOTAL	496	491	246	166	111	51	63	394	227	141	92	118	2,101

SOURCE: Panayiotopoulos (1985: 248).

we are given first the number of families, then the numbers of males and females according to six and five age categories, respectively. The villages are grouped under the twenty-four *territorii* (districts), into which the Venetian administration divided the Morea, and also under two smaller units or *giurisdizioni*—Porto Porro (Poros) and Termis—in the northeastern Peloponnesos. The Termis (Thermisi) jurisdiction corresponds fairly closely to the modern eparkhia of Ermionidha. In 1700, it comprised the following settlements (population given in parentheses): Kranidhi (1,002), Kastri (408), Ilia (37), Thermisi Castle (94), Agha (55), Loukaiti (22), Balabani (96), Dardhiza (5), Fournoi (166), Dhidhima (195), and Pelei (21) (Panayiotopoulos 1985:248). The families numbered altogether 496, while the males and females numbered 1,129 and 972, respectively. Termis thus had 2,101 inhabitants in 1700.

For all of the Morea, 92,314 males and 82,812 females were counted in the census of 1700, for a total of 175,126 inhabitants (Panayiotopoulos 1985: 199). There were 111.5 males for every 100 females in the Regno. In Termis this ratio was even higher—116.1 males for 100 females. Without a doubt there was undercounting of females in 1700. To make up for this Panayiotopoulos has added 10,643 females, to bring the total for the Morea to 185,769. Undercounting of females is a persistent trait of censuses in independent Greece until after 1900 (Panayiotopoulos 1985: 200–201).

The population density in Termis was 5.4 persons per km². This was in the lowest or sparsest range, which Panayiotopoulos defines as 4 to 7 persons per km². The highest density in the Morea in 1700, in the Kalamata area, was in the range of 24 to 36 persons per km² (Panayiotopoulos 1985: 175–178).

It was likewise under Grimani that a summary cadastre (*catastico ordinario*) of the territorio of Romania was made. This district comprised much of the present-day eparkhia of Nafplio and all of the eparkhia of Ermionidha. The summary cadastre records the boundaries and the extent of the arable, pasture, and unusable land of each village. It also sets down the number of families, churches, houses, wells, and animals. I copy the number of families recorded for the villages of Ermionidha: Kranidhi (227), Kastri (104), Dhidhima (42), Fournoi (41), Thermisi (25), and Ilia-Loukati (8). It is of interest to see that the total of 447 families coincides with the total derived from adding the slightly different figures for the same places found in the census of 1700. It appears that at least in the count of families, the cadastre represents a high degree of accuracy (Archival Sources: c).

About five years after the census and the summary cadastre were made, a *catastico particolare*, or detailed cadastre, of the entire territorio of Romania was completed, under the supervision of Antonio Nani, the governor of Morea in 1703–1705. In the report on his term that Nani read to the Senate in 1706, he alludes to the making of this "much needed cadastre of real property," whose chief purpose was to increase the revenue from tithes and tenancies. The Nani cadastre is a complete register, on drawings and in columns of text, of the fields and vineyards held by the inhabitants of the district of Romania ca. 1705. In principle, the heads of all households, including widows, are named in the cadastral volume. The plots bear numbers in both the drawings and the text; their precise dimensions are given, in both Greek and Italian measures. Thus the location and size of each family's holding—consisting as a rule of scattered plots—can readily be ascertained (Archival Sources a; Topping 1976a).

Table 2.3
Small Livestock in the Ermionidha, 1700–1705

	Sheep	Goats
a. Catastico Ordinario (Dated 1700)		
Ayios Dhimitrios		
of Avgho	3,000	300
Dhidhima	4,000	4,000
Kranidhi	5,500	1,200
Kastri	2,000	800
Anioi Anaryiroi	1,800	800
TOTALS	16,300	7,600
b. Catastico Particolare (Completed Around 1705)		
Ayios Dhimitrios		
of Avghou	1,550	3,900
Dhidhima	1,500	800
Fournoi	100	510
Kranidhi	1,200	7,000
Ilia	400	400
Thermisi	382	300
TOTALS	5,132	12,910

SOURCE: a. *Catastico Ordinario* (fol. 6V-7v).
b. *Catastico Particolare* (fol. 113v, 114v, 116v, 121v, 147v).

The detailed Nani cadastre gives the number of families of each village, distinguishing between the native families and the immigrants from other Greek provinces. The correspondence, however, between these figures and those of the 1700 census is less close than that between the census and the summary cadastre. Nevertheless, careful study of the lists of the possessors of fields and vineyards in the detailed cadastre indicates that the population increased somewhat between 1700 and 1705.

The Nani codex provides no data on the production of cereals and currants. However, by recording the trees of each village it gives us some notion of the variety and importance of the tree crops. Most important was the olive. No olive trees are recorded under Dhidhima, but Fournoi had 2,531, more than either of its larger neighbors, Kranidhi with 1,900 or Kastri with 2,199. But even for Fournoi, the number of trees per family was well under the number regarded as a minimum for subsistence in modern times (Forbes, this volume). It is possible that Dhidhima's olive trees were cut down during the fighting in the 1680s. Or, owing to the village's higher altitude, possibly they were frozen in a series of exceptionally cold years, 1693–1697. The local proveditor of Coron (Koroni) in southern Messenia, reporting to the home officials on June 20, 1712, alluded to "the completely sterile planting of 1693 and the four years following" (Topping 1981: 35–36). Fournoi had the greatest variety of trees besides the olive: carobs, figs, almonds, pomegranates, quinces, pears, apricots, apples, peaches, and walnuts. To be sure, Kranidhi and Kastri had many more carobs and figs than did Fournoi.

The figures in the summary cadastre suggest the importance of small livestock in the economy of the southern Argolid (see Table 2.3).[2] The higher totals for Dhidhima need not surprise us, given the village's upland location and long tradition of pastoralism. In the cadastre of 1705,

77 percent of Dhidhima's surface is described as "pasture" and as "stoney." This is close to the 82 percent of "nonarable mountainside" calculated by Koster and Forbes (this volume) for the village today.

The drawings in the cadastre of 1705 appear to be a complete record of the cultivable areas of the Ermionid villages. We must not suppose, however, that these lands were fully planted, even assuming the employment of a system of fallow. The lands granted to immigrant families were extensive, but they were in large part of inferior quality. Only a small part would have been planted, and larger stretches used as pasture.

The limited extent of viticulture in 1705 is striking. According to the Venetian surveyors' own figures, the vineyards of Kranidhi, Kastri, and Fournoi represented only about one percent of the cultivable surface of each village (Archival sources a: folios 116v, 121v, 138r; Topping 1976a: Figure 3). To be sure, the drawings by the skilled draftsmen accompanying the surveyors contradict these figures. Thus, for Kranidhi, two drawings, each entitled *dissegno di vigne* (drawing of vineyards), of the Lakkes and Flamboura localities, record the 303 plots numbered 575 to 877 (Archival sources a: folios 128v, 129r). The 303 "vineyards" are a good one-third of all the Kranidhi plots. However, in the separate list (*catalogo*) of all the possessors of the Kranidhi fields, we find that 64 of these 303 plots are labeled *terreni*, that is, fields not planted in vines. One of these, number 618, is by far the largest piece of ground on either drawing. It was assigned to a band of immigrants (Michalli Baccio e Compagni). It is evident that the Lakkes and Flamboura drawings are not a record of actual cultivation; rather, they represent the Venetians' program of vastly increasing viticulture in the future. The proveditor general Angelo Emo (1705–1708) in his relation to the Senate expressed optimism over the program's success. Heavy duties were levied on imported wines to help domestic production (Emo 1709: 693–694). The Venetians, however, were soon to be expelled from Morea. Their efforts to promote viticulture yielded substantial results only during the second *Tourkokratia*.

The Ottoman recovery of the Morea entailed severe casualties, military and civilian, at several major fortified centers where the Venetian defense was concentrated. Acronafplia and Nafplio town were among these. The southern Argolid probably was not affected seriously by the catastrophe at the capital. Such a favorable outcome would have been due, at least in part, to the pro-Turkish sentiments of the Monochartzis family of Kranidhi. Documents published by Panteleemon K. Karanikolas, a native of Kranidhi and long-time metropolitan of Corinth, establish that the Monochartzis were an important landowning family in the territory of Kranidhi since the later 17th century. Members of the family also took to the sea and, along with other southern Argolitans, served in the Ottoman navy (Karanikolas 1980: 35–37, 66, 122–123, 139).

Promptly after their reconquest, the Ottomans made a detailed defter of the Morea (1716), now preserved in Ankara. It awaits publication. In it, farmers are recorded by prenames under their villages along with the tithes and taxes that they paid for specified products. Such information from the section on the Argolid will complement the data of the Nani cadastre of a decade earlier; in particular, it will enable us to calculate the amount and value of the field crops and certain other products, a calculation that the *catastico particolare* does not permit. For the southern Argolid the defter has data on Kranidhi, Kastri, Fournoi, Dhidhima, and Thermisi; the monasteries of Ayioi Anaryiroi and Ayios Dhimitrios of Avgho; on the farms of Omani, Orlendi, and Milindra; and on the salt-tax raised at Thermisi. (Communication of J. M. Wagstaff and U. Fahri.)

Studies by Greek scholars, based mainly on French archives, have cast much light on the agricultural economy of Morea after 1715. No fewer than seventy products were exported. Two of these alone, olive oil and wheat, constituted 80 percent or more of the exports through the eighteenth century. Raw silk and animal skins followed, but on a lower scale. Olive oil was in great demand as a raw material for the soap manufactories of southern France. Currants continued in demand (Kremmydhas 1972: 198–201). For centuries, the Venetians had helped to create a demand for products like these, whether as consumers or as shippers. It is well established that they promoted the cultivation of the olive in the Morea in 1685–1715. The proveditor Antonio Nani, as we learn from his relation, urged the Senate to permit the export of more agricultural products; he names valonia, wool, cheese, silk, cochineal, olive oil, and wax. We can assume that the southern Argolid had its share in raising or collecting products like these. Nani confessed failure, however, in dealing with the superabundance of salt in the Morea, especially from the Thermisi lake. Contraband salt from Roumeli was widely sold in the Morea. To limit production, Nani closed the salt pans of Modon (Methoni) and Ververonda (Archival sources b: folios 241r, 242r–v).

The population of the Morea, by a conservative estimate, comprised no more than 200,000 Orthodox Christians on the morrow of the Turkish reconquest in 1715. Population grew slowly in the succeeding three or four decades. After 1750, however, it grew at an unprecedented rate, doubling by the year 1821, when the Greek Revolution broke out. This extraordinary increase occurred despite the loss of many lives and the flight of inhabitants resulting from the Morea's participation on the Russian side in Catherine the Great's first war with Turkey (1768–1774). It is certain that many inhabitants of the southern Argolid, especially of Kranidhi, fled or migrated in the 1770s to Spetses. They helped to make up for the severe losses suffered by this island when it was overrun by Muslim Albanian troops of the sultan (Panayiotopoulos 1985: 170–173; Orlandos 1877: 30–34).

Hydra came through the upheavals of the 1770s unscathed, having managed to keep on good terms with both the Turks and the Russians. The decades after the Treaty of Kioutsouk Kainartzi (July 1774), which concluded the Russo-Turkish war, witnessed the astonishing growth of the Greek merchant marine. The islands of Hydra, Spetses, Poros, and Psara had the lion's share in this expansion. Their inhabitants were to make an indispensable contribution to the winning of the war for Greek independence (1821–1829). The relations between the villagers of Ermionidha and the Hydriotes and Spetsiotes were very close, owing to ties of blood as well as geographical proximity. Kranidhi, Kastri, Fournoi, and Dhidhima now largely made up the district of Kato Nakhage (a hybrid Greco-Turkish name), governed by an Ottoman official. The elders of Kranidhi counted for much in the conduct of the district's affairs.

The sixteen-volume Archive of the Community of Hydra (1778–1832) records the history, at times day-by-day, of the largest of the offshore islands of the northeastern Peloponnesos in the era of its greatest prosperity and political importance. Scattered references in this collection to Kato Nakhage yield interesting data on the activities of its inhabitants. The light and fast *kaiki* (caïque), built from local timber and manned by Kranidhiotes, was indispensable to communications and transport in the Aegean Sea and up and down the coasts of the eastern Morea. A Kranidiote serving Turkish officials of Nafplio was the first to inform them that eight Russian ships had called at Kea (January 1, 1807). The messenger had learned this at Kranidhi from a fellow villager who had just visited Hydra. A few weeks later the Nafplio officials reminded the Hydra elders that they must always rush intelligence to them by the fastest caïque; in case of severe weather, however, letters should be sent by land via Kastri (Lignos 1922 3: 1, 19). When the governor of Hydra, Yeorghos Voulgaris, was summoned to Tripolitza, seat of the *Mora Vali* (Ottoman governor of Morea), he wrote from Poros (January 19, 1808) to have his brother at home send him his best clothes, including a fur coat, to Kranidhi before his arrival there (Lignos 1922 3: 221). A few months later (May 12, 1808) the Mora Vali wrote to Voulgaris, then at Kranidhi, to send two caïques with sturdy masts, one to Hydra and the other to Poros, to be loaded with cannons the Vali had bought. Voulgaris was to send the cargo, inexpensively, to the port of Kenkhries (ancient Cenchreae). The following winter (February 10, 1809), a shipment of twenty-five muskets intended for the Vali was received at Hydra via Portokheli (Lignos 1922 3: 266, 425).

On behalf of a former Mora Vali about to depart from Constantinople with his harem, the Porte sent an order to the elders of Hydra (July 23, 1802) to collect at once in Kranidhi, from the twenty or so districts (*kazas*) of the Morea, thirty master workmen who would go to Tripolitza to renovate the harem quarters. The Hydriotes were also supposed to supply the implements needed by the craftsmen (Lignos 1921 1: 304–305).

Other items from the Hydra archive illustrate agricultural activities and economic relations in the southern Argolid and on neighboring islands. Kranidhi caïques were delivering much of the wine imported by the Hydriotes in the late 1790s (dispatch of Hydra elders to dragoman of Mora Vali, November 11, 1798; Lignos 1921 1: 186). Kastri and Tsakonia were sources of wine imported by Hydra (March 26, 1803; Lignos 1921 2: 20–21). A Hydriote endowed his sister with an inherited field and its olive trees on Dhokos (June 27 and August 7, 1812; Lignos 1923 4: 251, 265). Nine Kranidhi elders, including two higher clerics and three priests, wrote to the Hydra elders (March 23, 1807) to protest against an incident at the Thermisi salt-lake. Caïques with cargoes of salt for Ottoman ports had been seized by Hydriot vessels; yet all of the Morea at the moment was "very quiet" (Lignos 1922 3: 34–35). A prominent ship-captain of Kranidhi wrote to the Hydra elders on December 8, 1807, on behalf of the Mora Vali to urge Hydriot shipowners to transport cargoes of wheat from several northern Greek ports. The writer suggested that interested shipowners should go with him to call on the Vali and reach agreement quickly on shipping charges. Since the Vali at this time was Veli Pasha, one of the sons of Ali Pasha, the tyrant of Ioannina, we may suppose that he was eager to market grain produced on his family's vast estates in northern Greece (Lignos 1922 3: 193–194). From the will, dated August 19 and 22, 1812, of Voulgaris, who served the Ottomans as governor of Hydra from 1802 to 1812, we learn of his purchase of "one garden opposite in Morea at Kastri near Ayioi Anaryiroi." Voulgaris paid 12,500 piastres for this bountifully watered property still associated with his name (Miliarakis 1886: 246). This price may be compared with the 38,480 piastres that Voulgaris paid for a one-third share in a large ship (*karavi*) built in Hydra (Lignos 1923 4: 274–278).

In January 1792, when plague had broken out in Hydra, the more prosperous of the townsmen crossed to Kastri to escape contagion. Here, however, they had the misfortune of being robbed by Lambros Katsonis, the most famous Greek sea-fighter of the time, who practiced piracy when not serving in the squadrons of Catherine the Great (Lignos 1921 1: 28–29). A pirate active in Argolic waters in 1794–1795 was Andreas Tsakonis, no doubt a native of Tsakonia. He was a scourge to the inhabitants of Hydra, Spetses, Poros, and Aegina. Dhokos was his lair. Arriving at Koiladha, "a village of Kranidhi," with an accumulation of booty, Tsakonis seized two small craft to help him transport it to Leonidhio, his Tsakonian lair in southern Kinouria opposite Spetses (Lignos 1921 1: 80–95).

The valuable farm (Metokhi) of the famous monastery of the Dormition of Hydra town, on the Argolic coast east of Thermisi, receives mention owing to the murder in 1804 of one of its sharecroppers by a Russian subject. The Porte was entitled to a fine for the crime. Men of Kranidhi raised the sum on the farm itself. Yet, it was the villages of Kato Nakhage that were collectively responsible for security at Metokhi. The Hydra elders tried to obtain compensation for the fine and for the victim's family from the Russian ambassador at Constantinople. They were concerned that the flight of the remaining sharecroppers would cause the ruin of the season's harvest, especially the grape crop. The monastery owned fields at Kastri, too (Lignos 1921 2: 168, 172–173).

The southern Argolid shared in the demographic and economic expansion that the Morea experienced, along with its larger islands, in the late eighteenth and early nineteenth centuries (Petronoti, this volume). Although many of its inhabitants migrated to Spetses in the 1770s, its population may well have doubled by 1800, going from the 2,100 of the 1700 census to 4,000 or more (Sutton, this volume). Pouqueville, the French traveler and diplomat in Greece, found "600 Christian families" in Kranidhi early in the nineteenth century (Pouqueville 1827 5: 261). If not exaggerated, this figure represents 2,400 or more inhabitants. A veritable town, Kranidhi was the seat of the national government of Greece in 1824. In 1829, it had an estimated 5,000 inhabitants.

We lack specific data on the products of Kato Nakhage. No doubt the district raised some part of the exports recorded by Scrofani, the Sicilian traveler, for the port of Nafplio in 1795 — wheat, wool, cheeses, cotton, salted butter, wax, honey, wines, and gallnuts (Scrofani 1801 3: Table 10A). Whatever its precise contribution to these exports, there is no doubt about the significant role of Kato Nakhage in ship construction, and in transportation around the sizable region made up of Ermionidha, the Argolic coasts and islands, and Tsakonia. To a lesser extent, the caïques of Kranidhi and Kastri also plied the waters between the Aegean islands. Pouqueville described Portokheli (Bizati) as the largest and most secure harbor of the gulf of Argos. One could get wood there, and the Hydriots visited it regularly to obtain the provisions needed for their voyages (Pouqueville 1827 5: 261).

In 1715, upon the Venetians' expulsion, the southern Argolid, like the Morea as a whole, had a sparse population that exploited only a fraction of its usable surface. During the second Tourkokratia there was an exceptional demand for the wheat, olive oil, and wines of the Morea, both abroad and from within the vast Ottoman Empire. The export of Peloponnesian wheat was in certain years so profitable that the peasants who produced it were threatened with famine (Kremmydhas 1972: 174–190). The growing population of the southern Argolid must have helped to meet this demand, some of it coming from the neighboring islands of Hydra and Spetses, now well populated. Was the increased agricultural production of the southern Argolid the result of more intensive cultivation of the fields and vines registered in the cadastre of 1705? It is more likely that the inhabitants cleared overgrown or wild tracts and perhaps drained coastal marshes in order to increase the cultivable area. The Venetians had begun a program of clearing and drainage in their time. Extensive farming was a ready recourse of Greek villagers throughout history. The alternate expansion and contraction of the area under cultivation, varying with the increase and decrease of the population, must have occurred many times in the long history of the Argolid and other provinces of Greece. Intensive cultivation became more characteristic of Greek agriculture after the Greek state arose (1830), a period which coincides with the modern demographic revolution.

The Agrarian Economy of the Ermionidha Around 1700: An Ethnohistorical Reconstruction

Hamish A. Forbes

This contribution is an attempt to paint a picture of the economic and social situation in the Ermionidha as it existed some three hundred years ago.[1] Materials are drawn from some of the documentary sources originating during the Second Venetian Occupation of the Peloponnesos between 1687 and 1715.[2] The documents primarily involved are the reports of a cadastral survey undertaken by the Venetians (discussed by Topping 1972; 1976a, c; this volume) and Venetian population censuses published by Panayiotopoulos (1985). The intention here is to flesh out the laconic lists of people and property contained in the documentary sources by applying ethnographic information derived from my own field research and from the researches of other ethnographers connected with the Argolid Exploration Project (e.g., Gavrielides 1976a, 1976b; H. Koster 1977; Koster and Koster 1976). Much of the resulting economic picture is, admittedly, speculative, because on occasion the approach allows more than one interpretation of the data. Further, certain interpretations may be considered debatable, since hard data generally only form the starting point for discussion. Nevertheless, given the significant level of detail of source documents, it would seem the counsel of defeat not to accept the challenge of a relatively detailed reconstruction of the agrarian economy around 1700, however preliminary and imperfect the results might be. Moreover, any picture of the state of the Ermionidha that can be built for this period provides an important baseline for discussions of later trends in the region.

The picture that emerges is of a largely inward looking, agrarian-based economy, quite different from the vibrant, maritime, trade-oriented economy of the later eighteenth and nineteenth centuries. With low population and plentiful land, economic activities concentrated on agriculture in general and on livestock rearing in particular. Much of this economic activity was dominated by owners of large estates. Besides estates owned by monasteries, a number had been owned by Turks who fled on the arrival of the Venetians. These estates controlled much of the immovable agrarian wealth (land, olive trees) and movable agrarian wealth (livestock of all sorts). They also affected the settlement pattern of the region, through their ownership of dependent settlements or estate hamlets, where those who worked the land resided. Many local inhabitants were not independent peasants, but were dependent on these estates as sharecroppers, or possibly they and their households were even tied to the estates in some semiservile status.

In this situation, most wealth was inevitably derived from agricultural production. Certain major agrarian activities, especially the keeping of sheep, goats, and cattle and the breeding of horses and possibly mules, were predominantly economic enterprises of large estates employing substantial numbers of hired or even possibly semiservile shepherds. This pattern is thus quite different from that of independent, locally based, or transhumant pastoralist households documented for the region in the twentieth century (e.g., H. Koster 1977).

Another difference is the very low level of olive cultivation found in the region around 1700. Other contributions to this book touch on the contrasting importance of olive cultivation in the region in the nineteenth and twentieth centuries. The area is plainly well suited to this activity. Its olive oil has long had a deservedly high reputation. Yet, documents show that this apparently age-old concentration had a relatively recent origin. The reasons for the development of olive cultivation and its connection with maritime activity in the centuries following the Second Venetian Occupation are dealt with elsewhere (Petronoti 1985a, b, this volume; Forbes 1993).

Despite many elements of continuity in the region over the last three hundred years, these differences are very significant. Their importance lies not least in the insight they give to the dynamism of local populations and their reaction to various stimuli, both internally and externally generated. It is further warning to those who would see the Greece of today, or at least Greece of the early to mid-twentieth century, as static, changeless, and tradition-bound.

Methodology

The extent to which we can hope to "understand" the bald figures of the census and cadastral documents depends heavily on reading back into the past from an ethnographic understanding of the present situation in the Ermionidha. Such a *uniformitarianist* approach makes two fundamental assumptions: first, that, despite all the changes over the last three hundred years, the underlying elements of continuity in the region outweigh those of change; second, that occasional major discrepancies between different communities found in the Venetian data are generally more apparent than real. In several instances, discrepancies are likely to be products of the way the survey was conducted and the data classified, rather than due to genuine major differences.

The first assumption concerning continuity is supported by a number of lines of evidence, although Sutton's strictures (this volume) about projecting the present into the past need to be kept in mind. Names of most settlements and even toponyms in use today can be found in the cadastres of 1700 and 1705, indicating that no general replacement of settlement or population has occurred. Document descriptions of the boundaries of different communities include presently identifiable toponyms such as Malavria, Korakia, Meghalovouni, and Ververonda.[3] The exploitation of the same landscape with a limited repertoire of tools and traction methods and an array of domesticated plants and animals in a manner that has altered little over many centuries (see Mansolas 1867: 52) constitutes an important brake on rapid change. The ways in which the southern Argolic peninsula is, and has been, exploited by farmers and herders have been documented by numerous ethnographic studies over the past twenty years (e.g., Chang 1981; Clarke Forbes 1976a and 1976b; Forbes 1976, 1982; Gavrielides 1976a and 1976b; H. Koster 1977; Koster and Koster 1976).

The second assumption about merely apparent discrepancies is rather more open to challenge. Yet, simple explanations are available for certain glaring discrepancies between contemporary communities in the Venetian data. By referring to patterns well documented for the region, at present or in the recent past, particularly in terms of traditional links between different communities or zones, it is possible in certain circumstances to "re-align" the Venetian data in such a way that the discrepancies largely disappear. It seems highly unlikely that the disappearance of such discrepancies when the data are treated in this manner is simply the result of coincidence.

The Venetian Documents

During the occupation of the Peloponnesos between 1687 and 1715, the Venetians undertook several censuses, all of which differed in amount of detail and probably in accuracy (Panayiotopoulos 1985: 135–148; Topping, this volume). The most detailed published census, on which this contribution relies heavily, is the Grimani census of 1700, which not only enumerates the number of families in each community, but breaks the population down by sex and age-group.[4]

During their occupation, the Venetians also instituted two cadastral surveys of the Peloponnesos, noting both real property and livestock. The background and dating of these surveys have been discussed by Topping in several publications (e.g., 1972; 1976; this volume). While analysis here focuses on transcriptions of the *catastico ordinario*, occasionally I refer to listings from the *catastico particolare* that relate to the monastery of Ayios Dhimitrios tou Avghou. The catastico ordinario is the earlier of the two documents and is considerably less detailed than the other.

The date suggested for the production of the catastico ordinario in the Ermionidha is close to 1700. In fact, comparison with evidence contained in other censuses (Panayiotopoulos 1985) suggests that the information may have been gathered a few years earlier than this date. The catastico ordinario notes that the settlement of Loukaïti, within the confines of the territory of Ilia (Iliokastro), is uninhabited. In the detailed census of Grimani, dated to 1700, however, Loukaïti is shown as containing five families and as having a population of twenty-two inhabitants (Panayiotopoulos 1985: 248). The most likely explanation for this difference is that Loukaïti had been resettled by the time of the Grimani census, making the catastico ordinario the earlier of the two documents. Other lines of evidence to support this suggestion include: (1) a significantly larger number of families recorded in the 1700 census than in the census figures of the catastico ordinario and (2) slightly lower numbers of families recorded in the 1700 census for the area's two major settlements (Kranidhi and Kastri, i.e., Ermioni), which are being more than compensated for by increases in the population sizes of smaller settlements (Table 3.1).

These observations can perhaps most easily be explained as a return to some kind of normality after the recent hostilities from 1685–1687, with an overall population increase and with

Table 3.1
Population of the Ermionidha, Late Seventeenth Century

| | Catastico Ordinario | | 1700 census | |
	Families	Population	Families	Population
Monasteries				
Ayios Dhimitrios:				
Agricultural population	10	43	7	21
Monastic population	/	32	—[a]	—
Ayios Anaryiroi	/	37	—	—
Villages				
Dhidhima	42	181	42	195
Iliokastro	8	34	9	37
Loukaiti	0	0	5	22
Fournoi	41	176	44	166
Kranidhi	227	976	220	1,002
Ermioni	104	447	103	408
Thermisi	25	108	24	94
Aga	—	—	13	55
Balabani	—	—	28	96
Dardhiza	—	—	1	5
Radho	—	—	15	62
TOTAL	457	2,034	511	2,163

NOTE: Population = families × 4.3, except for monastic populations (lay and clerical).
[a] Dash = not reported.

households returning to smaller settlements from the temporary safety of larger ones. In such a case, the catastico ordinario would have been drawn up some years prior to 1700.

However, alternative explanations are possible: for example, the catastico ordinario might have been compiled more or less contemporaneously with the Grimani census of 1700, but conducted less rigorously. In this case, a high degree of population mobility and residential flexibility within the region might explain the apparent absence of population in some small communities and the higher percentages of population in the two main population centers recorded in the catastico ordinario. Additionally, the catastico ordinario is concerned primarily with agricultural wealth, so that conceivably some of the households of nonagriculturalists might have been ignored by the census-takers.

These reservations aside, however, it is very possible that the cadastre gives a picture of the economic state of the region within a decade of the end of hostilities between Venice and Turkey. One of my aims will therefore be to examine whether any lasting economic effects of the recently concluded war are visible in these documents.

The catastico ordinario describes each community, first in terms of its boundaries, then in terms of its total land area. Area is measured in Greek *stremmata*, then glossed with the equivalent area in two other measuring systems: the *campo padovano* and the *campo trevisano* (Italian units of measurement of approximately 5,205 m² and 3,863 m², respectively). The figure for the total area is then further broken down into categories—cultivable land, pastureland, and useless land—in figures using the same three units of measure. A further unit of areal measurement, the *zapada*, is used in the catastico particolare for measuring vineyards. Description then continues with a list of real property and livestock (e.g., number of houses, of fruit trees by species—olive, pear, etc.—of plow cattle, sheep, goats, etc.). The final entry is always *famiglie del paese* (literally, "families of the country").

Two aspects of the catastico ordinario pose problems for any attempt at an economic reconstruction of the region: translation of the land measurement systems of the time into modern equivalents, and conversion of numbering of families into per capital numbering of population size. There is no indisputable answer to either problem, so that any approach must include an element of uncertainty and speculation. Nevertheless, the particular solutions chosen here correspond to the views of well-known authorities in this field (Topping 1972; 1976).

The problem of producing modern metric equivalents for the units of land measurement in the Venetian documents is related to problems the Venetians had in ascertaining the exact equivalents of Greek areal measurement systems of the time (Topping 1976a: 94). Authorities on premodern Greece generally hold that the stremma in use around 1700 in the Peloponnesos had an area of 1,270 m². Topping, however (1976a: 102, n. 7), has called this belief into question, raising the possibility that its size may have approached 2,000 m². See Appendix A for a detailed discussion of the modern metric equivalents of the Italian and Greek measuring systems in the Venetian cadastres. Here it is sufficient to state that the generally accepted figure of 1,270 m² per stremma in this period is probably the correct one.

The question of how to translate the numbers of families into approximate population figures involves assumptions about the average number of people per household. A hearth-multiplier of 4 has been used by Topping (1972: 70; this volume), rather than the figure of 5 suggested by Barkan (1957). Qualified support for the use of the higher figure as a hearth-coefficient can be found in the census of the Peloponnesos made by the French Expédition Scientifique towards the end of the Greek War of Independence (Houliarakis 1973: 32–45). The Expédition Scientifique used a hearth-multiplier of 4.75. The use of such a high figure by scholars whose views were not affected by experience of the demographic transition needs to be taken seriously, especially when the census produced *actual* average family size figures of well above 4.75 for some areas. Particularly significant is a figure of 5.19 persons per family reported from the *eparkhia* of Kato Nakhage, which comprised the area of the present-day Ermionidha plus parts of neighboring Troizinia (Houliarakis 1973: 37–38). Topping's hearth-multiplier of 4 is justifiable as a Pan-Peloponnesian figure for the Venetian period, being supported by Venetian census documents for the Peloponnesos as a whole. Nevertheless, for the province of Romania (of which the Ermionidha was a part), the Venetian census data of around 1702 indicate a mean of 4.3 individuals per household (Topping 1972: 78). This is further supported by the detailed census of 1700, which gives a per household figure of 4.55 for Kranidhi and of 4.24 for the Ermionidha as a whole (Panayiotopoulos 1985: 231–32, 248). Under these circumstances, I prefer to use a hearth-coefficient of 4.3 specifically for data of the Ermionidha.

Even though the use of a hearth-multiplier involves uncertainty, it is important to be able to generate figures of population size, rather than to rely merely on numbers of households. The figures thus generated make economic features in the Venetian period visible for comparison with their counterparts in the region today. Reference will also be made to more generalized mid-nineteenth-century figures for the *nomos* of which the Ermionidha was a part (Mansolas 1867). Comparisons of absolute figures of, say, plow cattle or olive trees in the region at different dates have much greater meaning when the actual numbers of people involved are taken into account (see, for example, Jameson, Runnels, and van Andel 1994: 285). Since the nineteenth- and twentieth-century population figures are normally on a per person basis rather than a per household basis, it is important to be able to use actual population figures from the Venetian period for comparative purposes.

A further, though relatively minor problem, which is pointed out by Topping (this volume), is the tendency for the figures given in the two cadastres' lists of real and movable property to be suspiciously rounded off for several communities. This suggests that the figures represent informed estimates by village elders and priests.[5] There are two reasons why this lack of complete accuracy in the figures should not concern us unduly. First, estimates by elders and priests probably represent as accurate a source of information as any available at the time.[6] Second, much the same practice is still used in Greece for annual reports on agriculture to the National Statistical Service. For each community, "best guestimates" are made by a small committee of individuals most likely to know, such as the village secretary, the local agricultural guard, and the agricultural extension officer. This fact should be noted because these modern data are occasionally used in this contribution as comparanda with the Venetian material; even if not completely accurate, both data sets were produced by similar methods.

An Economic Reconstruction of the Ermionidha in the Venetian Period

Economic Issues

Because of the nature of the documents at my disposal, the main focus of this contribution is on the earlier part of the Venetian occupation until about 1700. One question must be whether the documents indicate losses in population, property, and livestock as a result of the recent war between the Venetians and the Turks. Any such losses may have been compounded by the effects of famine and plague in the years 1685–1689 and exceptionally cold climatic conditions in the 1690s (Topping, this volume).

It would be reasonable to expect that the cadastre would indicate a population struggling with the economic aftermath of a series of disasters (Jameson, Runnels, and van Andel 1994: 131), although population decline may have begun much earlier than the mid-1680s (Topping 1976a: 93). Quite apart from a low human population, we would expect to find evidence for significant losses in livestock, particularly in plow cattle but also other animals, as well as possibly olive trees. Comparison with later periods can be expected to give some idea of the extent to which the area's economy had escaped, or else recovered from, any of the problems mentioned above (see Jameson, Runnels, and van Andel 1994: 285).

The Maritime Dimension

A difference between the Venetian settlement pattern and the present one is readily apparent. Neither the cadastres nor the detailed census of 1700 mention Portokheli and Koiladha, two of the region's three present major coastal settlements (see Jameson, Runnels, and van Andel 1994: 133). The third, Ermioni, which is mentioned, was the second largest settlement in the region around 1700, but whether there was any significant involvement in maritime activities is unclear from these documents. Lack of mention does not mean that the associated harbors were entirely unused, since from at least the nineteenth century on, Portokheli and Koiladha were exploited by the inhabitants of Fournoi and Kranidhi. The growth of both Portokheli and Koiladha beyond small clusters of fishermen's huts is, however, a largely twentieth-century phenomenon. Nevertheless, as far back as the early nineteenth century there may have been a village at Koiladha, apparently associated with the use of the port (Gell 1817: 199). The census taken by the French Expédition Scientifique towards the end of the Greek War of Independence (Bory de Saint Vincent 1834–36) makes no mention of a permanent settlement, however, and lists only sixteen inhabitants of the Monastère du port Kiladia[7] (Houliarakis 1973: 38). It is thus probable that Koiladha in the early nineteenth century had a cluster of huts, most of them temporarily inhabited, associated with maritime activities. The lack of evidence for any settlement at either Koiladha bay or Portokheli bay in the Venetian period suggests a genuine lack of emphasis on maritime activities. That settlements in these locations were simply missed by the Venetian surveyors seems unlikely. Elsewhere in the region (Panayiotopoulos 1985: 248), the censuses even list so-called settlements with a single family (e.g., Dardhiza), and other settlements are recorded that seem to have been composed largely or exclusively of temporarily inhabited dwellings.

Even more significant is the lack of mention of any population at all on either of the region's off-shore islands: Spetses and Hydra. They are not listed in the Grimani census under either the *giurisdizione* of Porto Porro (roughly equivalent to modern Troizinia and part of Epidhavria) or the *giurisdizione* of Termis (roughly the modern Ermionidha) (Panayiotopoulos 1985, 247–48).[8] This lack of mention is surprising, because less than a century later Hydra and Spetses, together with the island of Poros, not only dominated Greece's merchant marine, but controlled a significant proportion of the Mediterranean's maritime trade. These islands by then had populations in the thousands.

In fact, archaeological evidence suggests that a small defensive site on Spetses started in the second half of the sixteenth century, and occupation of Hydra seems to date prior to that. Both islands are recorded as being inhabited in the mid-seventeenth century, immediately prior to Venetian occupation, although apparently they were far less thriving than the nearby island of Poros, which they surpassed a century later (Jameson, Runnels, and van Andel 1994: 128n54, 129, 136, 607–8). The omission of these two islands from census records should not be dismissed as purely an oversight by Venetian surveyors leaving large populations unenumerated. The island of Poros, in fact, is listed in the Grimani census, but in this period it had a population of only seventy-one families—275 inhabitants in all. This was smaller than the town of Dhamala (modern Troizin, ancient Troezen), which Poros far outclassed in population within a century. The evidence strongly supports the implication of Jameson, Runnels, and van Andel that the populations of Hydra and Spetses were small at this time—a view shared by Koster (1977: 29–31)—and their suggestion that the islands' maritime position was exploited little, if at all (Jameson, Runnels, and van Andel 1994: 136). That the region was not entirely devoid of maritime activities is evident from the record of a powerful shipowning family in Kranidhi at the end of the period of the Venetian occupation and from mention of Hydra as being inhabited by poor fishermen in this period (Jameson, Runnels, and van Andel 1994: 135–36). Taken as a whole, however, the evidence indicates that the economy of the southern Argolic peninsula overall was largely land based at this time, while the economic contribution of maritime activities was small.

Settlement Pattern

A notable feature of the Venetian cadastres is that the present major mainland settlements of Kranidhi, Ermioni, Dhidhima, Fournoi, Iliokastro, and Thermisi are all listed. With the possible exception of Iliokastro, all seem to have been permanently inhabited. Loukaiti, today a small village located within the *koinotis* of Dhidhima, is also mentioned as belonging within the confines of Iliokastro, but as being uninhabited.[9] In Grimani's census of 1700, however, Loukaiti is shown as inhabited, containing five families, with a population of twenty-two inhabitants (Panayiotopoulos 1985: 248). This apparent rapid resettlement might suggest a temporary abandonment of Loukaiti as the direct result of hostilities: it is conceivable that the inhabitants had removed to larger settlements for the sake of safety until the disruptions of war had clearly ended. Alternatively, as a *sevgolatio* (subsidiary settlement), it might have been only seasonally occupied and recorded by census-takers when unoccupied. The village of Radho, at present within the eparkhia of the Ermionidha, close to the border of the eparkhia of Troizinia, also appears in the Grimani census of 1700, but within the neighboring giurisdizione of Porto Porro. It had fifteen families and a population of sixty-two people (Panayiotopoulos 1985: 247).

Although the major settlements of the region today are all listed in the catastico ordinario, the pattern of distribution of population three hundred years ago was very different. In contrast to the present relatively dispersed settlement pattern of the region (Sutton, this volume), the Venetian documents indicate a high degree of nucleation (Table 3.1). As Sutton indicates, 46.3 percent of the region's population was concentrated in Kranidhi alone, with a further 18.9 percent in the adjacent community of Ermioni. Thus, these two settlements, less than 10 km apart, contained some two-thirds of the whole region's population. It is noteworthy that, with the exception of the relatively densely settled community of Fournoi, each community listed in the catastico ordinario has a broadly similar total land area associated with it, although population sizes vary widely (Table 3.2).[10] Hence, outside the central Kranidhi-Ermioni sector, the region was very thinly populated indeed.

Within each community's total land area figure, however, amounts of land listed as cultivable are quite variable. Thus Kranidhi had 4,478 ha of arable land and Ermioni had 1,666 ha, whereas Thermisi, with a total land area comparable to that of Ermioni, had approximately one quarter as much arable land. But, behind this variability lurks a rough regularity: four out of the six secular communities have very similar ratios of arable land to population.

Fournoi had a high ratio of population to total land area—a feature also visible in the ratio of population to arable land. In contrast, Iliokastro had an area of arable land enormously in excess of what could be cultivated by its population of eight families, giving an extremely high ratio

Table 3.2
*Land Area, Population, and Presence / Absence
of Sevgolatio Settlements in Venetian Cadasters*

	Number of households	Total area (ha)	Pasture and useless (ha)	Cultivable land (ha)	Cultivable per Household (ha)	Sevgolatio?
Ayios Dhimitrios:						
Catastico particolare	10[a]	3,314	3,167	128[b]	12.80	yes
Catastico ordinario	10[a]	3,314	2,210	1,105	110.50	yes
Dhidhima	42	2,221	1,480	740	17.62	no
Iliokastro	8	2,872	1,917	956	119.50	no
Fournoi	41	726	363	363	8.85	no
Kranidhi	227	5,309	531	4,478	19.73	yes
Ermioni	104	2,221	555	1,666	16.02	yes
Thermisi	25	2,067	1,626	407	16.28	no

[a] Only *famiglie degl'agricoltori del paese* included.
[b] Plus 15 ha "uncultivated but cultivable," plus 4 ha vines.

of arable land to population. In other communities, ratios very similar to each other strongly suggest that it is the area actually cultivated, not the potentially cultivable area, that is documented. This suspicion is strengthened by the example of the Ayios Dhimitrios monastery, where 957 ha of land categorized as cultivable in the catastico ordinario was reclassified as "pasture land or useless" in the catastico particolare (Table 3.2): only 15 ha of the original "cultivable" figure is declared as "cultivable but uncultivated." It may not be a coincidence that the monastery's population to arable land ratio before the reclassification of its land was quite comparable to that of Iliokastro. After the reclassification it was broadly in line with that for the majority of the other communities in the region documented in the catastico ordinario.[11]

Evidently, limited amounts of arable land did not restrict the population of the area outside of the more densely populated Kranidhi-Ermioni axis, but it is not easy to explain the uneven spread of population over the region. The flat fertile plains associated with Thermisi and Iliokastro, which were quite underpopulated at this time, were notoriously malarial until after World War II (H. Koster 1977: 39; Sutton, this volume). However, this fact alone does not seem sufficient explanation for their sparse populations. The plain at Ermioni was also malarial, at least on its seaward side (Jameson, Runnels, and van Andel 1994: 131, fn 57), yet its population was relatively high for this period.

A major feature of the region in the twentieth century is the way in which commercial agriculture has taken prominence over seafaring in its economic profile. At the same time, the population has become increasingly evenly spread over the whole area (Sutton, this volume). In the nineteenth century, when population was more heavily concentrated in Ermioni, and in Kranidhi and its satellite settlements of Koiladha and Portokheli,[12] seafaring was a particularly important part of the region's economy. It is tempting to suggest that the late seventeenth- and early eighteenth-century population concentration in these two centers was likewise related to seafaring. However, as noted above, evidence for a significant involvement in maritime activities at that period is very hard to find. Ethnographic data suggest an alternative explanation.

In the late nineteenth and early twentieth centuries some inhabitants of Kranidhi and

Ermioni owned sizable tracts of land at very considerable distances from their villages—for example, close to the modern settlements of Thermisi and Iliokastro. The exploitation of such land would have involved traveling distances of up to 15 km, or even more, from the owners' villages. This pattern may well point to the way land was exploited during the Second Venetian Occupation. However, studies in many parts of the world (Chisholm 1968: 49–66) show that distant plots generally receive lower inputs of labor.[13] Distant plots produce correspondingly lower returns than those close to the village.[14] In addition, certain crops grown in Greece under traditional conditions, especially olives and cereals, tend to involve labor demands that are concentrated into short bursts of activity (sowing and harvesting for wheat; harvesting and, secondarily, cultivating for olives). Thus, as long as the bulk of agricultural operations consisted of relatively low-labor, unintensive activities restricted to short periods, such as occurs with extensive cultivation of cereals or unirrigated olives, exploitation of plots from such a distance would have been feasible.[15]

As commercialized agriculture has risen to prominence, with its emphasis on irrigation and other high inputs of labor and materials (e.g., manure and topdressings of chemical fertilizers), the exploitation of plots at such distances has become increasingly impracticable. Nowadays, exploitation of these areas is more generally from communities close by. This trend has been increased by the break-up of the large estates, which formed a significant element in the land-use patterns of the region in the nineteenth century and into the earlier twentieth century (Sutton, this volume; Jameson, Runnels, and van Andel 1994: 137–38, 412). Jameson, Runnels, and van Andel (1994: 412) also argue that the construction of motor roads in the region is another important factor. All-weather roads allow inhabitants of small communities much easier access to the major centers, where a wide range of facilities and services is available, and also allow easier access to markets outside the region.

Another reason for the ability to exploit land at such distances may be the tradition, widespread in Greece, of using field houses called in Greek *kalivia*—shelters built close to landholdings for temporary residence (e.g., Clarke 1995: 517–518, and this volume; Jameson, Runnels, and van Andel 1994: 133–134; Wagstaff and Augustson 1982, 110). Various Venetian documents relating to the area refer to the existence of kalivia, that is, huts, in contradistinction to houses, found in certain settlements. They also occur in *sevgolatia*—the hamlets associated with estates—suggesting that at least some individuals inhabited these settlements on a part-time basis. The existence of isolated structures owned by persons less well off, as evidenced on Methana and the plain of Troizin in later centuries (Clarke 1995: 517–518 and this volume; Forbes, Mee, and Foxhall 1995: 75), is highly likely, although not recorded in the documents.

Such temporary residences at a distance from the home base would be particularly necessary under the technological circumstances of the period. Cattle, the traction animals of that time, travel very slowly: at approximately half the speed of equids, that is, horses and mules (White 1966: 57–69). In comparison with mules, in particular, they are not surefooted. Thus, considerable time is lost traveling to fields, and time involved in plowing is greater than if equids are used (White 1966: 57–69). Cattle are also anatomically incapable of carrying the burdens that equids can bear (Furse 1895: 77–79, 90–91; RAVC 1986),[16] and it is therefore difficult for a farmer to transport the necessary tillage implements and seed grain to distant fields on a daily basis if he uses plow cattle. The answer to the problems of the slower and inferior weight-carrying abilities of cattle is for farmers with sizable areas of arable land far from the village to maintain a structure of some sort there. Seed grain and tillage implements may then be kept safely at the scene of operations. The farmer can also reside there temporarily during the period when plowing and sowing occur.

In this period the terms *sevgolatio/zevgolatio* and *ziogolatio/giogolatio* (derived from Greek *zevgharizo* = I plow; *zevghilatis* = a plowman; Venetian Italian *ziogo* = a yoke) are used to describe isolated hamlets containing a high proportion of kalivia. The large number of kalivia probably indicates a primary function as communities for shelter while cultivating and harvesting. Many may have been largely or completely deserted for substantial parts of the year, with the population based elsewhere. Thus, Orlendi, an estate hamlet near Ermioni with six houses and four kalivia, had no population listed in 1696 (Jameson, Runnels, and van Andel 1994: 131). Although possibly a simple oversight, it might equally indicate that at the time the census was taken, the population was resident elsewhere.

The use of multiple exploitation bases by agriculturalists has had a long history in the region. Their use is known in the medieval period (Jameson, Runnels, and van Andel 1994: 131) and still existed in the 1980s (see below, and Sutton, this volume). This practice indicates a high degree of mobility and residential flexibility in the region's agrarian population, which is paralleled by the local level mobility of the region's pastoralists (H. Koster 1977). The fact that some of the population had more than one residence should be born in mind when censuses and other documents are considered. Under this circumstance, uninhabited communities need not necessarily indicate decline: their inhabitants may have been working from another base during that season.[17] Nevertheless, they may suggest low, even if stable, populations, and a widespread reliance on low-intensity agricultural practices. As the population of the region has risen and agricultural practices have become increasingly intensive, the exploitation of plots at such distances has become progressively more impracticable. Nowadays areas like the Thermisi plain and the Iliokastro basin tend to be exploited by the inhabitants dwelling there permanently. In rare instances where large estates still exist at a distance from their owner's base, however, the system occasionally continues. One example is a large stone structure on an Hydriote monastery's estate near Thermisi, where hired laborers reside during the summer months (see Sutton, this volume).

Larger, permanently occupied settlements are defined in the Venetian documents by the term *villa* (village). But the existence of sevgolatia is a significant feature of the period's settlement pattern. As noted above, some of these may have been occupied seasonally for the purpose of agricultural operations carried out far from the main settlement, as the name suggests; others seem to have been estates of the wealthy with dependent workers (see Jameson, Runnels, and van Andel 1994: 131). The term *boaria* is also found—again, in apparent contradistinction to the term villa. Whether Loukaiti and Iliokastro were permanently occupied settlements at this time is open to question. The catastico ordinario lists Iliokastro as a villa, placing it in the same category as presumably permanently occupied settlements such as Kranidhi, Fournoi, or Dhidhima. However, the Grimani census lists Iliokastro as a boaria, along with Loukaiti and the settlement of Pelei,[18] the latter being attached to the monastery of Ayios Dhimitrios tou Avghou.

Pelei is also described in the catastico particolare as a sevgolatio, a term used elsewhere in the 1700 census, but not for any settlement in the Ermionidha: elsewhere in Venetian documents Pelei is described as a *metochio*, a term regularly used to describe outlying monastic properties. It seems, therefore, that the Venetian surveyors used the terms boaria and *sevgolatio* as essentially interchangeable in many instances. The Italian word boaria, ultimately derived from the word for cattle, has several different meanings, depending on period and region in which it was used (Boerio 1829: 57; Cotelazzo and Zolli 1979: 149; Reynolds 1962: 101). The most likely possibilities in this case are: a place where tenants or sharecroppers live or farm or a seasonally occupied settlement. None of these meanings can be completely excluded, but none satisfactorily reconciles all evidence from the various Venetian documents. From the internal evidence of the catastico ordinario it would seem that Iliokastro (and presumably Loukaiti) was a subsidiary settlement to the village of Dhidhima. However, in a roughly contemporary ecclesiastical census these two settlements are listed under Fortezza Thermisi (Jameson, Runnels, and van Andel 1994: 133). Despite the apparent discrepancies between the two documents, they both suggest that Iliokastro and Loukaiti were dependent in some way on other settlements. For this reason a meaning like "subsidiary settlement" may be preferred as an ad hoc meaning for the terms boaria and sevgolatio.

This definition works well for Pelei, described variously as a sevgolatio and a metochio (see above). Furthermore, it is probable that the "hovels of straw," which served as "habitations for the agriculturalists" listed in the cadastre as part of monastic property, were concentrated at Pelei.[19] Although there are only ten families of agriculturalists listed in the cadastre, twenty habitable houses are listed: eleven with tiled roofs and nine "of straw." In other words, there were two houses for every family. It might be argued that some of these houses were inhabited by some of the complement of the monastery, perhaps some of the servants. However, the monastery of Aghioi Anaryiroi at Ermioni, which had servants but no families of agriculturalists listed, did not possess any houses. Presumably, therefore, the houses listed for Ayios Dhimitrios tou Avghou were inhabited by agriculturalists who temporarily moved to Pelei from the monastery when necessary. Pelei in the 1980s was still a seasonally occupied settlement. Since the years between the world wars of the twentieth century, when lands originally belonging to the monastery were allocated to Dhidhimiotes, Pelei has served the villagers of Dhidhima who have gone to that area to work (Koster 1977: 153; Adams, this volume). Of the other sevgolatia mentioned in the Venetian documents, including two belonging to Kranidhi and one belonging to Ermioni (see Jameson, Runnels, and van Andel 1994: 131), there was apparently no longer any trace by the 1880s (Miliarakis 1886: 240–49). Miliarakis (1886: 241) mentions that, according to tradition, there used to be four small settlements near Kranidhi, one of which bore the name Milindhra—the name of a sevgolatio listed as belonging to Kranidhi in the catastico ordinario.

Although subsidiary settlements in the Ermioni area cannot be directly related to archaeological sites, those associated with Kranidhi (Milindra, or Melindra, and Sakofoli) have been tentatively identified (Jameson, Runnels, and van Andel 1994: 131).[20] Both are located less than a kilometer below Kranidhi and overlook the Koiladha plain. Milindra was a substantial settlement, with 106 persons (possibly 25 families)[21] in 1696.[22] This is much larger than any subsidiary settlements termed boaria listed in the 1700 census.[23] Although the nucleus of the settlement may have been formed by an estate hamlet, the large numbers of people indicate that others may have resided there, permanently or temporarily. Sakofoli, with twenty-five persons in six houses, was much smaller (Jameson, Runnels, and van Andel 1994: 131). Using Pelei as a model, there is no reason for assuming that this site was permanently occupied.

In light of previous discussion of the function of sevgolatia at substantial distances from permanent settlements, the existence of settlements called sevgolatia so close to main population centers calls for explanation. The Venetian documents are of little help on this matter. The Grimani census uses the term boaria for subsidiary settlements located at considerable distances from the major population centers but makes no mention at all of those close to them. It might be argued on this basis that settlements called boaria were different in some way from those called sevgolatia. Doubtless, subsidiary settlements took a number of forms which are not readily identifiable. The explanation for such settlements so close to the two major population centers may lie in the particular capabilities of the cattle used for plowing.

Kranidhi, set defensively on its steep-sided hilltop, is not easily accessible from the Koiladha plain below. As noted above, cattle would not be sure-footed on the steep, unevenly paved *Kalderimi* tracks, which were the main routes of the time. Thus, although the subsidiary settlements of Milindra and Sakofoli were geographically near to Kranidhi, due to a steep decline of some 60 m (ca. 200 feet), cattle would require considerable time to negotiate the route to the edge of the Koiladha plain. In eliminating the time taken on difficult terrain by locating subsidiary settlements closer to land to be worked, estate owners—and, presumably, others who owned and/or worked land on the plain—could exploit their holdings more easily and efficiently.[24]

In the case of Ermioni, one possible subsidiary settlement near the town was Orlendi, where there were six houses and four *kalivia* in 1696, although the exact location seems unidentifiable. Another was a place called Omagni in the catastico particolare. Jameson, Runnels, and van Andel (1994: 131) note the existence of a present-day area with houses and olives called Omania, which may well be the same place as the Venetian Omagni. Omania is located in the foothills on the north side of the Ermioni plain, a site which would have been considered healthfull in contrast to the plains' malarial seaward end. Although the authors do not identify the location, the description places the area approximately 3 km from Ermioni—up to an hour's travel at the normal walking speed of cattle (Furse 1895: 77–79, 90–91). Once again, the traveling speed of cattle may have been a contributory factor in the location of this subsidiary settlement.

Because of the large areas of pasture land listed in the cadastres and the importance of pastoralism in the region, it is reasonable but probably incorrect to assume that some subsidiary settlements were associated with temporary occupation by shepherds (see Jameson, Runnels, and van Andel 1994: 133). However, the terms sevgolatio and ziogolatio, based on words for yoking and plowing, are suggestive of a direct association with cultivation, which is further supported by statistics on land area in the cadastre. Not all communities with large total land areas contain sevgolatia within their bounds. All communities with large quantities of arable land do contain sevgolatia, while communities with smaller amounts of arable land do not, even if the total area is very large (Table 3.2). Thus, it is probable that these subsidiary settlements were predominantly related to the needs of agriculture and do not represent temporary shepherd settlements, either for local pastoralists or transhumants.

Status of the Agrarian Population

Besides questions of the size and distribution of the population, another important difference between today and the period under discussion is the status of the monastery of Ayios Dhimitrios tou Avghou. It is now uninhabited, and its lands have been redistributed, mainly to the villagers of Dhidhima (see H. Koster 1977: 98, 153, 461). Apart from ten *famiglie degl' agricoltori del paese* (families of farmers of the country), the catastico particolare lists sixty-six clerical and lay personnel attached to the monastery, although the earlier cadastre lists a monastic complement of only thirty-two.[25]

The status of the agricoltori del paese attached to the monastery, and, by implication, of those attached to other large estates, is of considerable interest. Little light is shed on the problem by the two Venetian surveys, but indirect evidence gives some clue. Koster notes that, although detailed entries of the catastico particolare list resident families together with land holdings for most communities, neither the peasants associated with the monastery nor the villagers of Dhidhima were deemed worthy of individual mention. From this evidence it would appear they owned no land of their own but worked that of others (H. Koster 1977, 93–94). It is possible that they were sharecropping tenants (Topping 1976a: 98; Jameson, Runnels, and van Andel 1994: 134). The impression of nonindependence is heightened by an entry in the catastico ordinario describing them as "families belonging to the metokhi": the same verb *belonging* is used elsewhere in the documents for trees belonging to a house and to a garden. The use of this term raises the question of whether these peasant households, and others associated with large estates in the region, were free peasants, or whether their status was effectively that of dependent cultivators, possibly comparable to feudal serfs.

In their recent review of this period, Jameson, Runnels, and van Andel (1994: 134) note that some subsidiary settlements that seem to be estate farms are listed as having peasants attached to them. They suggest that a considerable number of those actively working the land were sharecroppers. However, with relatively plentiful land and a low population, the arrangements under which sharecroppers would have worked would probably have been very favorable. The existence of dependent peasants (*paroikoi*) seems to have been widespread in Greece in the late medieval period. They are well-documented for monastic estates in Macedonia, as well as for the Latin possessions in the Peloponnesos: three similar nonmonastic fiefdoms of this type are documented for the medieval southern Argolid (Laiou-Thomadakis 1977; Jameson, Runnels, and van Andel 1994: 119–120). Although Jameson, Runnels, and van Andel argue that the pattern of dispersed estate farming hamlets found in the region at this time was a continuation of a pre-existing medieval pattern of agricultural estates with attached serfs (Jameson, Runnels, and van Andel 1994: 120, 124, 131), they believe serfdom had died out by the late seventeenth century.

In practice, however, some late seventeenth-century sharecroppers may have differed but little from the serfs of earlier periods. While the Venetian documents do not specifically indicate the status, rights, and duties of those who worked the land, the internal evidence of Venetian documents provides hints that some peasants were not completely free. In particular, some, like the medieval *paroikoi* and their western serf counterparts, may not have been fully entitled to leave the service of their landlord (Laiou-Thomadakis 1977: 145). A serflike status might explain why, contrary to expectation in a period of relative abundance of arable land, a significant proportion of the population continued as "sharecroppers" rather than as independent peasants who rent land from large landowners. It would also explain another feature of the Venetians' policy in the region: the preference for granting very large amounts of property—almost certainly, given their size, with dependent laborers attached—to settlers from outside the Peloponnesos. Thus, most of the large estate of Sakofoli, with possibly six dependent households, seems to have been granted to two people with the surname of Morello, one of whom received over 90 ha of land (Topping 1976a: 98–100).

These observations may help answer the question raised by H. Koster (1977: 93), why did not the Venetians give the extensive lands in the Dhidhima basin to indigenous villagers, and why did they prefer to give them to settlers from Euboea instead? If the native Dhidhimiotes were indeed legally tied to the land, the Venetians may have considered them as effectively belonging *with* the land and therefore not entitled to own it. While it cannot be proven, it is thus possible that during the seventeenth century the lands of the monastery and other large estates were worked at least in part by cultivators whose status did not differ markedly from that of their forebears on similar estates three hundred years previously.

The cadastres do not indicate the extent to which the monastery's property was worked by its own servants. Some direct involvement by its servants in agriculture seems certain, however, since the documents indicate more pairs of plow cattle than peasant families to work them. The catastico ordinario indicates twelve pairs of cattle and the catastico particolare twenty-five pairs. In both cases there were only ten peasant families (Table 3.6). Significantly, the increase in numbers of plow cattle in excess of the number of peasant families in the two cadastres (from 2 pairs to 15 pairs) is approximately paralleled by the increase in monastery servants (from 16 to 35).

Livestock

It is plain that the peasant families associated with the monastery were not exploiting the totality of the property primarily for their own subsistence. Comparison of numbers of stock per agricultural family for the monastery of Ayios Dhimitrios with the same figures derived from other communities in the region highlights the monastery's disproportionately large numbers. Stock rearing was evidently a major enterprise, both for the monastery of Ayios Dhimitrios and for the Ayioi Anaryirioi monastery. Presently and in the recent past, livestock rearing in the region (as elsewhere in Greece: Campbell 1964) has provided cash rather than direct food subsistence (Chang 1981; H. Koster 1977). The documents indicate that, for the region's monasteries in the seventeenth century, raising livestock was a form of "agribusiness."

The catastico ordinario indicates a combined total of 3,800 head of sheep and goats at the monastery of Ayios Dhimitrios. By the time of the catastico particolare the number had risen to 5,450. Comparison of the earlier figure per agricultural family at the monastery produces a family to stock ratio of twice that of even Dhidhima (still the leading pastoralist community in the region) and over ten times the ratio for Kranidhi and Ermioni (Table 3.3). This observation strongly suggests that supervision of a major portion of these flocks was under the control of the

Table 3.3
Number of Sheep and Goats in the Ermionidha,
Late Seventeenth Century–Late Twentieth Century

	Sheep	Goats	Total	Sheep and goats per family	Sheep and goats per person
Venetian Records					
Ayios Dhimitrios					
Catastico particolare	1,550	3,900	5,450	545.0	126.7
Catastico ordinario	3,000	800	3,800	380.0	88.4
Dhidhima	4,000	4,000	8,000	190.5	44.3
Kranidhi	5,500	1,200	6,700	29.5	6.9
Ermioni	2,000	800	2,800	26.9	6.3
Ayios Anaryiroi	1,800	800	2,600	—ᵃ	—
TOTAL/AVERAGE (*Catastico ordinario*)	16,300	7,600	23,900	62.4	14.5
Grazing Nexuses (*Catastico ordinario*)					
Ayios Dhimitrios	3,000	800	3,800	380.0	88.4
Dhidhima + Iliokastro	4,000	4,000	8,000	160.0	37.2
Kranidhi + Ermioni + Fournoi + Thermisi	7,500	2,000	9,500	22.4	5.2
TOTAL/AVERAGE	16,300	7,600	23,900	46.6	10.8
1860 Argolid and Corinthia					
Agricultural population	—	—	—	41.3	9.6
Total population	—	—	—	19.6	4.4*
1981 Ermionidha					
Total population	13,393	12,852	26,245		2.2*

SOURCE: *Catastico Particolare, Catastico Ordinario*, Mansolas (1867: 50-55, 88-91), Greece, National Statistical Service (unpublished).

NOTE: Population figures = households × 4.3, except figures with *, where actual population figures are used. Lay and clerical complements of monasteries excluded from calculations. The 1981 figures exclude transhumant flocks.

ᵃ Dash = not reported

monastery, and that the flocks were not simply part of local household economies. The roughly parallel increases in small stock and servants documented in the catastico particolare suggest that monastery servants may also have been involved.

It might be argued that these high figures for small stock represent the inclusion of the flocks of transhumant shepherds renting monastery land for grazing. However, the balance of probability must be against such an argument. For the monastery of Ayios Dhimitrios, the catastico particolare describes the items of real and movable property (including sheep and goats) as belonging to it. It seems unlikely that this term would be used for the flocks of any transhumant shepherds who might rent grazing for only part of the year. We may assume that the same holds true for the monastery of Aghioi Anarghiroi, as well as other communities in the region. The existence of transhumant shepherds overwintering in the region at this period seems quite possible, but the likelihood must be that they are not documented in the cadastres. Alternatively, transhumant flocks might have been included in the cadastres if they were owned by large landowners in the region. This is particularly likely in the case of monastic flocks and herds, since it is known that the monasteries of Ayios Dhimitrios owned some property in the central Peloponnesos (see Jameson, Runnels, and van Andel 1994: 134; Topping 1976a: 97–98). That

Table 3.4
Density of Sheep and Goats in the Ermionidha,
Late Seventeenth Century–Late Twentieth Century

	Sheep	Goats	Goats and sheep per total ha	Goats per ha pasture and useless land	Sheep per ha cultivable land
Venetian Records					
Ayios Dhimitrios:					
Catastico particolare	1,500	3,900	1.64	1.23	10.82
Catastico ordinario	3,000	800	1.15	0.36	2.72
Dhidhima	4,000	4,000	3.60	2.70	5.40
Kranidhi	5,500	1,200	1.26	2.26	1.15
Ermioni	2,000	800	} 2.43	2.88	2.28
Ayios Anaryiroi	1,800	800			
TOTAL (*Catastico ordinario*)	16,300	7,600			
Grazing Nexuses (*Catastico ordinario*)					
Dhidhima + Iliokastro	4,000	4,000	1.57	1.18	2.36
Kranidhi + Fournoi + Ermioni + Thermisi	9,300	2,800	1.17	0.91	1.29
1860 Argolid and Corinthia	—[a]	—	1.11	—	—
1981 Ermionidha					
Local flocks	13,393	12,852	0.60	0.62	1.08
Local and transhumant flocks	22,741	14,583	0.86	0.70	1.84

SOURCE: *Catastico Particolare*, *Catastico Ordinario*, Mansolas (1867: 88–91), Greece, National Statistical Service (unpublished).
[a] Dash = not reported

shepherds were employed by large landowners to maintain large flocks in earlier centuries is documented by Walpole (1818: 142).[26]

The numbers of sheep and goats listed in the catastico ordinario are a good example of the tendency, noted earlier, of using rounded numbers (Table 3.3; see Topping, this volume). Reference to Walpole's (1818: 142) description of sheepherding and goatherding in Attica in the late eighteenth and early nineteenth centuries suggests that these figures represent notional numbers derived from counting whole flocks, or extrapolations from counting the numbers of herders employed, rather than attempting to produce actual numbers of animals. Five shepherds were considered sufficient for 1,000 sheep, though apparently few flocks reached that number. A figure of two hundred sheep per shepherd can be extrapolated from this observation. Significantly, all but one of the figures for sheep and goats in the catastico ordinario are divisible by 200.

The breeding of non-traction cattle, listed in the cadastres as *vacche* in contradistinction to *animali d'aratro*, also seems to have been a specialist business of the region's monasteries at this time (Table 3.5)—as it was in Attica one hundred years later. These were presumably kept for their meat and hides, rather than for dairy products, which would have been provided by sheep and goats. The herd, or perhaps herds, belonging to Ayios Dhimitrios, totaling 180 beasts in the catastico ordinario, is quite considerable, even in terms of modern western European cattle keeping operations. The herd(s) had increased to 317 animals by the time of the catastico particolare. These figures contrast sharply with those for *vacche* belonging to the nonmonastic population: just 190 in the whole region at the time of the catastico ordinario.

Table 3.5
Beef Cattle in the Ermionidha,
Late Seventeenth Century

Community	Number of cattle (*Vacche*)
Ayios Dhimitrios:	
Catastico particulare	317
Catastico ordinario	180
Dhidhima	50
Iliokastro	0
Fournoi	30
Kranidhi	0
Ermioni	110
Ayios Anaryiri	150
Thermisi	0
TOTAL (*Catastico ordinario*)	520

SOURCE: *Catastico Particolare, Catastico Ordinario,* Mansolas (1867: 50–55), Greece, National Statistical Service (unpublished).

Just how distinct the two categories of cattle—vacche and animali d'aratro—were is open to some question. In the late nineteenth century on Methana, and in the 1970s in parts of Crete, cows were used as traction animals, rather than oxen (castrated bulls). Cows were put to a bull annually to produce a calf, besides being used for plowing. Most of the calves were sold for meat, though a few heifers would be kept for training as plow cattle. In such a situation, the dividing line between the two categories is a rather fine one. The fact that in the catastico ordinario identical figures for beef cattle and traction cattle are listed for Fournoi and Dhidhima (see Table 3.6) suggests that the same cattle were involved, but that there was some confusion over the category to which they should be assigned.

How cattle kept primarily for meat and hides, rather than for traction, were managed is not clear: there is no ethnographic information that helps us. The figures in the catastico ordinario show that significantly more cattle were kept as vacche than as animali d'aratro, giving a ratio of traction cattle to non-traction cattle of 1 to 1.67. By the late nineteenth century this aspect of pastoralism in the region seems no longer to have existed, because cattle by that time were associated exclusively with plowing. Miliarakis (1886) makes no mention of the keeping of non-traction cattle, although, since he makes few comments on pastoralism generally, this cannot be considered conclusive. However, Mansolas's (1867: 91–94) data indicate that the keeping of cattle primarily for non-traction purposes was not common in Greece in the mid-nineteenth century: traction cattle outnumbered cattle by more than 2 to 1.

During the eighteenth century, however, the keeping of cattle for purposes does not seem to have been unusual. Apart from Walpole's observations noted above, it is known from French sources that in the eighteenth and early nineteenth centuries cattle were one of the major export items from the Peloponnesos (Yiannakopoulou 1976: 123). At the beginning of the nineteenth century, the value of cattle exported from the Peloponnesos was approximately double that of sheep. Cattle export amounted to a minor, though significant, proportion (0.6 percent) of the value of the peninsula's total exports (Yianakopoulos 1976: 141–42). It must be presumed that this kind of cattle-keeping, in areas such as the Ermionidha, which are not at all

Table 3.6
Plow Cattle in the Ermionidha,
Late Seventeenth Century - Late Nineteenth Century

	Number	Persons per household	Land per beast (ha)
Venetian Records			
Ayios Dhimitrios:			
Catastico particolare	50	5.00	2.56
Catastico ordinario	24	2.40	46.03
Dhidhima	50	1.19	14.08
Iliokastro	4	0.50	238.93
Dhidhima + Iliokastro	54	1.08	31.41
Fournoi	30	0.73	12.09
Kranidhi	130	0.57	36.75
Ermioni	65	0.63	25.63
Ayios Anaryiroi	21	—[a]	—
Ermioni + Ayios Anaryiroi	86	0.83	19.37
Thermisi	20	0.80	20.32
TOTAL (*Catastico ordinario*)	344	0.75	29.11
1860 Argolid and Corinthia			
Agricultural persons	—	1.12	1.82[b]
Total persons	—	0.53	

SOURCE: *Catastico Particolare, Catastico Ordinario,* Mansolas (1867: 50–55, 91–93).
[a] Dash = not reported.
[b] This figure refers to sown land only.

environmentally favorable for such an enterprise, was only possible because the low human population density left substantial areas of good quality land uncultivated and thus available for grazing.[27]

The breeding of horses was probably also a specialist enterprise. The catastico ordinario lists one hundred horses as belonging to Ayios Dhimitrios (Table 3.7) (130 in the catastico particolare). This number of horses is in stark contrast to the very low numbers found in nonmonastic communities.[28] For ordinary peasant activities, donkeys seem to have been the standard pack animals. A minimum of one donkey per household is evident from the catastico ordinario data in Table 3.7: the 1:1 relationship of families to donkeys in Iliokastro and Thermisi adds emphasis to this observation. A few richer families presumably kept a horse rather than a donkey, and doubtless some households had no pack animal at all.

The cadastral documents thus strongly suggest that the monastery of Ayios Dhimitrios was the region's dominant economic power around 1700 (see H. Koster 1977: 94–5), and that one of the monastery's most important economic activities was the rearing of stock of all kinds.[29] Exactly *how* the various kinds of stock were exploited is impossible to say from these documents. Nor is it possible to say with certainty whether the major markets for the monastery's products were predominantly inside or outside the region, although evidence to be discussed below suggests a mainly extraregional market. One thing is plain, however: by comparing figures with those for nonmonastic communities, we can be certain that these activities were not simply for the consumption or work needs of the monastery itself, but represent major cash generating enterprises.

The monastery of Ayios Dhimitrios was not unique in its exploitation of stock. Much the

Table 3.7
Horses, Mules, and Donkeys in the Ermionidha,
Late Seventeenth Century - Late Nineteenth Century

	Horses	Donkeys	Horses per household[c]	Donkeys per household
Venetian Records				
Ayios Dhimitrios:				
Catastico particolare	135[a]	25	13.50[c]	2.50
Catastico ordinario	100[b]	20	10.00[c]	2.00
Dhidhima	10	70	0.24	1.67
Iliokastro	0	8	0	1.00
Dhidhima + Iliokastro	10	78	0.20	1.56
Fournoi	6	55	0.15	1.34
Kranidhi	22	210	0.10	0.93
Ermioni	10	120	0.19	1.15
Ayios Anaryiroi	20	5	—[d]	—
Thermisi	0	25	0	1.00
TOTAL (*Catastico ordinario*)	168	513	0.15	0.15
1860 Argolid and Corinthia				
Agricultural population	—	—	0.63	0.90
Total population	—	—	0.30	0.42

SOURCE: *Catastico Particolare, Catastico Ordinario,* Mansolas (1867: 50–55, 93–95).
[a] The figure in the horses column includes 5 mules.
[b] The figure in the horses column includes 7 mules.
[c] Mules are included in the horses/household figure.
[d] Dash = not reported

same practice seems to be documented for the monastery of Ayioi Anaryiroi. The catastico ordinario does not list any agriculturalist families as belonging to the monastery, so possibly some of the twenty-four *serventi* of the monastery were employed in agriculture—although some of the monastery's agricultural work could have been done by labor hired from Ermioni. Despite the small number of servants and a clerical complement of only thirteen, the monastery of Ayioi Anaryiroi owned a herd of 150 non-traction cattle and twenty horses (but only 5 donkeys). These figures are in obvious contrast to the numbers listed for the inhabitants of Ermioni: 110 cattle, 10 horses, and 120 donkeys for a community of 104 families—perhaps 450 people. The numbers of the monastery's sheep and goats were also well in excess of the numbers needed for subsistence alone: 2,600 small stock altogether, as compared with 2,800 for the whole of the community of Ermioni (see Tables 3.3, 3.4, 3.5, 3.7).

That the maintenance of flocks of animals was an important cash-producing enterprise is an observation that can be extended to nonmonastic situations: the Venetian governor Grimani noted that at this period the native Moreotes loved idleness, cultivating only enough land for their precise needs, but being inclined to maintain large flocks (Topping 1976a: 95). It is thus highly likely that at least some of the large nonmonastic estates in the region also owned substantial flocks and herds. As noted above, shepherding is nowadays practiced as a way of generating cash, and does not primarily produce food for households' own consumption: all evidence suggests that the same was true in the Ermionidha in the late seventeenth and early eighteenth centuries.

The importance of pastoralism as a cash-producing activity in Greece during the early eighteenth century can be seen from French mercantile reports dating from 1715 onwards (i.e., after the Turks had reoccupied the Peloponnesos). Nafplio, at the head of the Argolic Gulf and not far from the Ermionidha, exported more wool and cheese than any other port in the Peloponnesos at this time, so that it is quite conceivable that the Ermionidha contributed to these exports. Annual exports of wool from Nafplio were reported to have averaged between 39 and 45 tonnes in the earlier eighteenth century, and by the middle of that century its annual cheese exports were stated to have averaged 140 tonnes. It is also significant that of the Peloponnesian imports into Marseilles in the period 1715–1730, pastoral products (hides—the bulk of which were from sheep and goats—and wool and cheese) averaged 19.8 percent of the total, while all food products (exclusive of cheese) averaged only 17.5 percent (Kremmydhas 1972: 173, 192, 197, 202).[30] While these data refer to the period immediately following the Venetian occupation, there is no reason to believe that the situation was significantly different in the years preceding 1715.

Taken at face value, the figures on small stock in the catastico ordinario show no obvious pattern in terms of the density of stock for the Ermionidha as a whole. Although both local monasteries owned sizable flocks, only three village or town communities out of six had sheep and goats listed (Tables 3.3, 3.4). If we were to accept these figures as they stand, we should be presented with a picture in which the grazing resources of certain communities were not exploited at all, while those of others were exploited at very high levels—well in excess of the levels documented for Dhidhima since 1940 (Table 3.4; Koster and Forbes, this volume). By interpolating ethnographic evidence, however, it is possible to suggest that the flocks listed as "belonging" to particular villages were regularly grazed outside the bounds of those villages.

The communities of Dhidhima and Iliokastro have no really substantial barriers between them and traditionally have had close economic and social ties. Even as late as the 1880s, Iliokastro was a huddle of ten houses inhabited by farmers from Dhidhima (Miliarakis 1886: 245). Informant data from Iliokastro also indicate that the rapid growth of its population in the twentieth century is substantially the result of in-migration from Dhidhima of people who already owned land close to the village of Iliokastro. There is also considerable intermarriage between the two communities. Similarly, the present-day territorial boundaries of Fournoi, Kranidhi, Ermioni, and Thermisi all march on each other, and land communications between these communities, while not exactly easy, do not suffer from major physical obstacles. Furthermore, as noted above, oral history in the region records that in the nineteenth and early twentieth centuries, Kranidhiotes and Ermionites owned substantial holdings of land around Thermisi.

Much the same connections seem to have existed some three hundred years ago. If one combines the figures for caprovines (sheep and goats) and land areas for Dhidhima and Iliokastro, on the one hand, and for Fournoi, Kranidhi, Ermioni, and Thermisi, on the other, and compares them with the monastery, the ratios of small stock to land area make much greater sense (Table 3.4). For both groupings of villages the ratio of goats per hectare of land defined as "pasture and useless" by the Venetian surveyors falls at the bottom end of the range documented for all small stock per hectare of common land in Dhidhima since 1940 (Koster and Forbes, this volume). It would therefore seem that these two groupings represent separate *grazing nexuses*, and that the monastery of Ayios Dhimitrios represents yet a third such nexus (Table 3.4).

The treatment of the data here assumes that, by and large, sheep were not generally grazed on areas described as "pasture" by the Venetians. From the data available it is possible to suggest that a significant proportion of the land described as "cultivable" was always under fallow. With the exception of Fournoi, all villages of the region produce average figures of 16 ha or more of cultivable land per household (Table 3.2).[31] Whatever the actualities of the landowning pattern of the time, these very high mean figures contrast sharply with the figure for the Ermionidha in 1971, when a mean figure of 5.12 ha per agricultural enterprise was recorded.[32] Under conditions of low population and plentiful land, one can expect agriculture to have been unintensive, with widespread use of extensive fallow to restore soil fertility. This assumption is also supported by the comments of Randolf Bernard, who, writing on the Peloponnesos in exactly this period, notes that manuring was not widely practiced (1689: 17). The figures from the cadastres thus suggest indirectly that during the Venetian period there would have been very extensive areas available for fallow grazing, for which sheep would be better suited than goats. Differences in the two cadastral returns for the monastery of Ayios Dhimitrios corroborate the suggestion that much land listed as arable was in fact permanently or temporarily under fallow. The two cadastres give identical figures for total land area, but differ greatly in the proportions of pasture and cultivable land. In the later document a very high percentage of land previously listed as cultivable has been reclassified as pasture. This results in a 70 percent increase in the amount of land classed as "pasture" and "useless." At the same time, the numbers of goats have increased by 79 percent in the later document, while the numbers of sheep have been reduced by almost half.[33]

It is therefore possible to argue with some conviction, first, that sheep were predominantly grazed on land that is listed in the cadastres as cultivable, while goats were largely grazed on "pasture" and "useless" land. Second, it is plain that in practice the distinction between land classed as cultivable and that classed as pasture was not always clear. This latter point would help explain not only the reclassification of the bulk of the monastery's cultivable land, but also some of its anomalous stock density figures (Table 3.4). Thus, in the catastico ordinario, although the number of goats per hectare is anomalously low, the ratio of total caprovines to total land area falls between those of the other two grazing nexuses. This suggests that some of the monastery's land classed as pasture was actually used for sheep grazing. The same observation helps to explain the very high figure for sheep per hectare of cultivable land in the catastico particolare, despite the fact that the overall density of caprovines is only marginally higher than that for the Dhidhima-Iliokastro nexus derived from the earlier document.

Previously in the chapter I raised the possibility that agricultural statistics in the catastico ordinario might have been affected by disruptions caused by warfare, plague, and bad weather in the years immediately preceding the census. Livestock might have been particularly badly affected by any warfare in the area, with sheep, goats, and cattle being (at least theoretically) highly vulnerable to depredations by marauding armies for food, and with horses being requisitioned for baggage trains (see Topping 1976a: 101 for this latter circumstance even after hostilities had ended). However, analysis of the cadastre data suggests that any such effects of the hostilities were at worst rather patchy. Figures for caprovines per household and per total area are broadly comparable with data for the area from the 1860s (Tables 3.3 and 3.4): their relatively high densities suggest that flocks were not badly affected.[34] While these figures do not define real flock sizes, being simply an indicator of the intensity of caprovine grazing, they give no reason to believe that in the Venetian period flock sizes were in any way seriously depleted by the effects of hostilities.

Greater discrepancies between the Venetian and mid-nineteenth-century figures appear when we examine the numbers of plow cattle per family (Table 3.6). The figure of 1.12 cattle per agricultural family, which is extrapolated from Mansolas (1867: 50, 92), is almost twice that for Kranidhi in the Venetian period, and only the Dhidhima-Iliokastro community approaches the mid-nineteenth-century figure at all closely. Of course, not every household in the Venetian period is likely to have been primarily agricultural. Kranidhi and Ermioni, the largest communities, show the lowest ratio of plow cattle to families: they are also the communities most likely to have contained families of nonagricultural specialists (artisans, for example) in any numbers. Nevertheless, it seems likely that most of the population would have engaged in agriculture and that these cattle to family ratios may represent a genuine shortage of traction animals.[35]

The most likely explanation for any shortage of traction animals is the effect of recently completed hostilities. However, the figures for the area of cultivable land per plow animal derived from the cadastres cannot be taken as support (Table 3.6), since they seem far too large to be realistic. The only exception to this statement would seem to be the cattle to cultivable land ratio for the monastery in the catastico particolare. As we have already seen, much of the monastery's land that was originally classed as cultivable in the earlier cadastre was later reclassified as pasture. Moreover, the later cadastre also differentiated "cultivated land" belonging to the monastery from "uncultivated but cultivable" land. I am therefore inclined to believe that the land area stated as cultivated approximated reality in this particular case.

Is there any support for this belief? The extrapolated hectares to plow animal ratio is about 2.5 ha per animal, which gives a figure of 5 ha as a notional size of holding that could be managed with a yoke of oxen. Assuming approximately half that area to be in fallow annually (see H. Koster 1977: 166), this gives a figure of 2.5 ha as the area that one plow team could cultivate for cereals in a season. Data from late eighteenth-century Attica are broadly in agreement with this figure. Walpole (1818: 143) reports that four or eight cattle were sufficient to cultivate one hundred Turkish period *stremmata* (12.7 ha) of land, the number depending on whether the soil was light or heavy. Dividing 12.7 ha by four and by eight produces results which bracket the figure of 2.5 ha quite satisfactorily.

Twentieth-century observations also fall within the same range. In Messenia in the later 1960s, family farms in the region near Messeni averaged 3.4 ha in extent (van Wersch 1972: 178). Yet in one community only four of eighteen households who used cattle for plowing kept a complete team: the rest kept only one animal and used sharing relationships to arrange a team (Aschenbrenner 1972: 57). This strongly suggests that to support and employ a plow team, a holding larger than 3.5 ha is normally needed. Aschenbrenner (1972: 57–58) also estimates that an area of 0.3 ha, or a little more, could be plowed in a day with a pair of cattle. This is directly comparable with the Melian area of measurement known as a *zevgari*, which is 0.3 ha (Wagstaff and Augustson 1982: 131). Since in the Ermionidha area two plowings are normally used when sowing cereals, as they are in Messenia (Aschenbrenner 1972: 58), using the above figures, we can derive a figure of 0.15 ha of land that can be plowed and sown in a day.[36] At this rate, it would take seventeen days to sow 2.5 ha if plowing were done every day. While this is not an excessively long period, it greatly exceeds the five to six days of plowing that subsistence farmers on Methana have traditionally cultivated for their staple wheat supplies (Forbes 1982: 247). If we further exclude Sundays (traditionally kept firmly as a day of rest) and one other day every week for such imponderables as rain, a figure of twenty-four days is reached. These figures give no conclusive answer, but they indicate that half of a 5.0 ha holding would take considerable time to sow, especially in a period when weather and growing conditions might only allow a restricted window of opportunity for starting winter cereals (Aschenbrenner 1972: 50–51; Forbes 1982: 244).

In the study of ancient Greek agriculture there is a comparable issue: what size of farm would a *zeugite* (a man of a particular property class) be likely to own? Because of the etymology, it is often considered that a *zeugite* would have been wealthy enough to own a land area that would have necessitated ownership of a pair, or of a yoke (ancient Greek *zeugos* = a yoke), of oxen. One suggestion, based partly on (not entirely unambiguous) archaeological evidence, is that the minimum area would be about 5 ha (Burford 1993: 67; cf. Hodkinson 1988: 39).[37] Despite difficulties in using these data—in particular the many assumptions that must be made—it is evident that a figure of about 5 ha is neither unduly large nor too small for a holding that could comfortably be cultivated with a yoke of oxen under a two-year rotation system. More important, in the context of the discussion here, these calculations, despite the uncertainties involved, emphasize the unreality of the other hectares to plow animal ratios extrapolated from the catastico ordinario.

In contrast to cattle, equids—particularly donkeys—do not seem to have suffered any obvious depletion of numbers as a result of recent hostilities. The donkeys to household ratio for Argolis and Corinthia in the 1860s is actually lower than that for any Venetian period community in the region (Table 3.7). The reason for the large numbers of donkeys in this period is presumably that few households could afford horses or mules (the latter animals only being documented for the monastery of Ayios Dhimitrios in the catastico ordinario). Comparison of the equids to family ratios for the Venetian period and the mid-nineteenth century indicates the increased importance of horses and mules in the latter. Since horses and mules are generally more expensive than donkeys, both to purchase and maintain, differences in equid numbers between the two periods indicate the relative poverty of the Ermionidha in the late seventeenth to early eighteenth centuries.

In some respects it is easy to explain why cattle might have been more depleted as a result of hostilities than donkeys: cattle are generally considered edible while equids are not. Hence cattle might have been requisitioned for food, since they could not be moved and hidden in the mountains as easily as flocks of sheep or goats. Horses and mules, on the other hand, would be needed by armies to move men and supplies in terrain lacking roads. They might have been subject to requisitioning, while donkeys would probably have been considered too small. It is not clear from the catastico ordinario alone whether numbers of horses and mules were significantly depleted.

Olives

Information from the cadastres on olive cultivation is enlightening from a number of points of view. The most obvious feature is the small number of trees in comparison with the present situation (Table 3.8). The rise in the region's population in the nineteenth century, however,

Table 3.8
Olives in the Ermionidha, Late 17th Century–Late 20th Century

	Catastico Ordinario			1880s			1981		
	Trees	Trees per person	Oil per person[a]	Trees	Trees per person	Oil per person[a]	Trees	Trees per person	Oil per person[a]
Ayios Dhimitrios[b]	630	14.65	43.95	–	–	–	–	–	–
Dhidhima	0	0	0	3,900	3.4	9.42	30,000	18.82	56.46
Iliokastro	600	17.44	52.32				55,720	88.03	264.09
Dhidhima + Iliokastro	600	2.79	8.37				85,720	46.34	139.02
Fournoi									
"Private"	1,230	6.98	20.93				14,000	37.74	113.22
Total	2,480	14.07	42.20						
Kranidhi	1,600	1.64	4.92	84,000	12.53	37.59	276,500	43.77	131.31
Ayios Anaryiroi	450	–	–	–	–	–	–	–	–
Ermioni	3,000	6.76	20.13	75,000	36.64	109.92	106,100	44.34	133.02
Thermisi	200	1.85	5.58				175,700	150.04	450.12
TOTAL TREES	8,960			162,900			658,020		

SOURCE: *Catastico Ordinario*, Miliarakis (1886: 240–250), Greece, National Statistical Service (unpublished).
[a] Estimated annualized production (in kg) using Ermionidha rule-of-thumb: 6–7 kg/tree in alternate years.
[b] Population figures refer only to *famiglie degl'agricoltori del paese*.

makes direct comparison of numbers of trees between the Venetian period and the present problematic. A better comparison can be found in the numbers of trees per individual. Such a figure does not, of course, give any idea of the numbers of trees owned by particular households in either period; the Venetian cadastres (Topping 1976) and modern ethnographic data show major differences among households in holdings of olive trees. A count does indicate, however, that, whereas olive cultivation is presently one of the most important features of the region's agrarian economy, it has not always been so. Only three hundred years ago the olive quite plainly played a subsidiary role.

An even better indicator of change in the importance of olives in the region over the last three hundred years is the estimate of oil production per capita of population (Table 3.8). This estimate was achieved by applying the modern farmer's rule of thumb of 6–7 kg of oil per tree in alternate years (since unirrigated olives can only be expected to fruit biennially).[38] This rule was applied to Venetian nineteenth- and twentieth-century data, although the results must be considered somewhat high for the first two periods, since the rule assumes inputs of chemical fertilizers and the use of high-powered oil extraction equipment. Nevertheless, this caveat only emphasizes the low levels of olive oil production in the Venetian period. In the 1980s, typical oil consumption was 50 kg / person / year. Most of the annualized olive oil per person figures for the Venetian period fall well short of this (e.g., Kranidhi: 4.92 kg / person; Ermioni: 20.13 kg / person). Moreover, the Venetian communities that approached the modern rule of thumb were all special cases. It is quite plain that, in contrast to the present situation, during the Venetian period, olive oil must have constituted merely a minor element of the general diet. Presumably only the very richest households, such as that of the Turk, Mustafá Chiaussi of Fournoi, who had 1,025 olive trees before the Venetian occupation (Topping 1976a: 98), were in a position to sell (or even consume) appreciable quantities of oil. The fact that this individual owned so many trees helps make sense of the anomalously high oil per person figures for Fournoi. If we eliminate the 1,250 so-called public olive trees from the Fournoi total, most of which were presumably the Turk's property, we arrive at figures for trees and oil per person that are closely comparable to those for Ermioni.

Figures for trees and oil per capita of population in the Venetian period stand out as unusually high for two other communities: the monastery and Iliokastro. This high figure is immediately understandable for Ayios Dhimitrios, since it can be assumed that the agriculturalists did not own the trees. They either sharecropped the trees, or worked them under direct supervision of the monastery. Quite apart from the dietary needs of the inhabitants of the monastery, lay and religious, oil would also be needed in significant quantities for performance of religious ceremonies. Olive oil is used in the Orthodox church in several ways, notably for oil lamps in the church. It seems probable, therefore, that, although the figure for oil per capita of agricultural population at the monastery was high, the nonagricultural members' requirements for oil (both dietary and religious) meant that sale of olive oil could not have been a major source of income.

The village of Iliokastro was also credited with an anomalously large number of olive trees per capita of population, while the neighboring village of Dhidhima was registered with no olive trees at all. While the present numbers of olive trees around Dhidhima are the result of fairly recent intensive plantings, a total lack of olives during the Venetian period seems difficult to believe. If we, however, treat Iliokastro as a subsidiary settlement to Dhidhima and combine figures for the two villages, we achieve a number of trees per person broadly similar to the figures for Kranidhi and Thermisi (Table 3.8). That such an approach is acceptable is supported by arguments already presented with regard to livestock. In this case, it is not clear whether Dhidhimiotes actually *owned* the trees, but it seems probable that they at least *worked* them.

The olive is usually considered a natural choice for farmers exploiting poor soils in an area like the Mediterranean where rainfall is low and unpredictable. The evidence from more recent periods shows that olive cultivation is highly practicable and potentially profitable in the region, so the question must be asked: why was olive cultivation such a minor element in the Venetian period economy? If we ignore the Venetians' belief that the Greek population was constitutionally lazy (Topping 1976: 95), we must seek some other explanation, especially since some parts of Greece at this time were exporting substantial quantities of olive oil. It is probably no coincidence that these oil exporting regions seem to have had relatively high population levels (see Kremmydhas 1972: 152). It may well be, therefore, that a substantial concentration on olive cultivation was an indicator of agricultural intensification under conditions of increasing population pressure and/or an increasingly market-oriented agriculture (Forbes 1993: 217–218). Neither the low population levels of the Ermionidha in the late seventeenth century nor the generally inward looking nature of the economy would favor a major emphasis on olive cultivation. The extent to which olives have become a focus of agricultural activity in more recent centuries indicates the fundamental changes that have occurred in population levels and economic structures within the region (see Forbes 1993; Sutton, this volume).

Another interesting line of information to emerge from the Venetian cadastres is an indication of the approximate capacity of the olive milling machinery of the period. A number of olive mills are listed in the cadastres, including two at Thermisi reported as ruined in the catastico ordinario. These latter might indicate some of the aftereffects of recent hostilities. It is a fairly safe assumption that the Thermisi mills were constructed to process olives from trees in that area. It also seems likely that some olives from neighboring parts of the territory of Ermioni were processed there as well: Gell noted the existence of "the mills of Kastri [i.e., Ermioni]" located close to Thermisi about a century later (1817: 197). If we accept these two assumptions, the ratio of olive trees to mills becomes remarkably consistent for all communities in the Ermionidha. The numbers of trees per mill fall quite neatly into the range of four hundred to six hundred, with a maximum of 630 trees per press in the territory of the monastery (Table 3.9).

The relative lack of variability in the ratios of trees per mill in different parts of the Ermionidha suggests that recent hostilities had little effect overall in terms of destruction of olive trees. The one possible exception to this inference is the destruction of mills in the Thermisi area, where a fortress overlooked the important salt pans on the coast. Any military activity during the recent war could well have been concentrated around this defensive installation. Whatever the reason for the ruinous state of the two mills there, the fact that they had not been rapidly put to rights may well be significant. Neglect of the mills could indicate that a substantial number of trees had been destroyed, or that economic disruption caused by the war had made it difficult to find money and/or craftsmen to make the necessary repairs.

Table 3.9
Olive Presses in the Ermionidha, Late Seventeenth Century

	Presses	Trees	Trees per press
Ayios Dhimitrios	1	630	630
Dhidhima	0	0	0
Iliokastro	1	600	600
Fournoi	6	2,480	413
Kranidhi	4	1,600	400
Ermioni[a]	4	3,450	863
Thermisi[b]	2	200	100
Ermioni + Thermisi	6	3,650	608
TOTAL	17	8,960	

[a] Olive trees from the monastery of Ayioi Anaryiroi are included in the trees column.
[b] Both the olive presses in Thermisi are described as ruined in the *catastico ordinario.*

The extrapolated figures for the ratio of olive trees to milling establishments also allows speculation concerning the possible effect of the period's simple milling technology on the numbers of olive trees that could be grown. Olive processing equipment seems to have been a major capital investment in every period, so that ownership seems always to have been restricted to relatively few individuals (see Forbes and Foxhall 1978). This observation seems to hold true for the Ermionidha in the Venetian period: no less than three out of seventeen mills directly mentioned in the catastico ordinario are listed as public, presumably indicating property confiscated from major Turkish landlords (see Topping 1976a: 98). Yet, if the numbers of trees per person in the Venetian period had been similar to the figure for the region today (Table 3.8), it would have been necessary to have approximately one olive mill for every four people. Therefore, any consideration of olive growing in the region in the late seventeenth century must include the possibility that the comparatively small numbers of trees owned were not simply the result of political insecurity or economic underdevelopment. Although these factors were undoubtedly involved, the low capacity of the milling technology of the period might also have limited the sizes of olive holdings.[39]

Summary

This preliminary analysis of Venetian documents gives a detailed economic picture of the Ermionidha from a period well before the inception of the industrial revolution and the demographic transition. The possibility, raised at the beginning of this chapter, that the situation documented by the catastico ordinario might be unrepresentative of normality because of economic disruption directly caused by the recently concluded hostilities between the Venetians and the Turks seems largely not to be the case. While some evidence can be explained as the result of the war, there are few immediate signs of major economic disruption. On the whole, the low population levels and economic stagnation visible in the documents is more likely to have resulted from long-term political and economic stagnation and/or mismanagement.

For these reasons, the picture produced here, however impressionistic and incomplete, provides a necessary baseline for discussions of more recent trends and developments in the region.

While similarities are plainly visible between the late nineteenth century and the late seventeenth century, there are also considerable differences. Those of particular interest in the context of the history of the last three centuries are as follows.

Maritime Activities

The Venetian documents give no indication that maritime activities played any significant role in the region's economy in the late seventeenth century. This is in sharp contrast to the importance of the merchant marine for the region and its offshore islands since the later eighteenth century. Much evidence for the idea that maritime activity was negligible in the Venetian Ermionidha is negative, and therefore needs to be treated with caution. Nevertheless, two arguments have been presented above to suggest that negligible maritime activity is the correct conclusion to be drawn from such documentary silence. The chronology of the rise of the Greek merchant marine in general, and particularly maritime development of the islands of Hydra, Spetses, and Poros, is well documented. French sources especially show that Greek vessels began to play an important role in Mediterranean shipping only from about the mid-eighteenth century (de Jassaud 1809: 17–21; Kremmydhas 1972: 298–318). Of major significance are comments in French sources on the participation of *albanais* (meaning, for example, Idhriotes, Spetsiotes) from the 1750s onwards (Kremmydhas 1972: 307–8). These comments, as well as those of Pouqueville (1806: 99), indicate that the powerful fleets of Hydra and Spetses of the later eighteenth and nineteenth centuries had no antecedents in the period of the second Venetian occupation of the Peloponnesos.

Olive Cultivation

For the last 100 to 150 years, ethnographic evidence indicates that olive growing and olive oil sales have been a major feature of agriculture, due to the dry climate and poor soils of the Ermionidha (Forbes 1993). The catastico ordinario, however, shows that olive cultivation was not a major economic activity—much less a major cash generating enterprise—in preceding centuries. It may be surmised that low population density and economic underdevelopment were major factors in leading landowners to prefer pastoral activities to olive cultivation as a principle method of gaining an income. Furthermore, the fairly standard ratio of trees to olive mills, as documented by the Venetian records, suggests that major war losses were not to blame for the situation. The small numbers of trees in the Venetian period may be related in part to low population densities in the region, but the possible limiting factor of the inefficiency and small capacity of preindustrial olive mills, constructed primarily of wood and stone, should not be ignored.

Pastoralism

There are several aspects of the particular economic activity of pastoralism about which the catastico ordinario is completely silent. In particular, there is no evidence that the flocks of transhumant pastoralists, who have been a significant element in the region in the recent past, are included in the figures. It is highly likely that suitable grazing niches for overwintering trans-humants existed in the region at least as abundantly then as now. Moreover, Nafplio, located close to the migration route between the southern Argolic peninsula and the upland regions of Arcadhia and Corinthia, was the prime exporter of pastoral products from the Peloponnesos. On both counts it is tempting to assume that transhumant pastoralists exploited the region in considerable numbers in the late seventeenth century. Yet, oral histories of neither of the two transhumant groups who now overwinter in the Argolic peninsula (Sarakatsani and Valtetsiotes) have a time depth that reaches back to the Venetian period. Indeed, the oral history of the Valtetsiotes, the transhumant group that overwinters in the Ermionidha itself, gives an early nineteenth-century origin for their presence there (Koster 1977: 78). Any suggestion that certain features of the Venetian period should be associated with transhumant pastoralism must therefore be made with this caveat in mind.

Whatever the answer to the problem of transhumant pastoralism in the Ermionidha in the Venetian period, the importance of pastoralism generally as an economic activity stands out. Considering major differences in the human population of the late seventeenth century compared with the later twentieth century, it is all the more surprising that densities of caprovines per hectare show such relatively minor differences across this time span. This observation suggests, first, that shepherds and goatherds have been carefully managing their animals' numbers so as not to do permanent damage to their grazing resources. This issue is tackled elsewhere in the present volume (see Koster and Forbes). Second, the evidence presented in this chapter also indicates that pastoralism in its various guises may be one of the most enduring economic activities in the Ermionidha.

The Documents Themselves

Finally, in any investigation of the situation during the Second Venetian Occupation, it is important to consider the circumstances in which the documents were produced. That the Venetian administrators inevitably put a gloss on the documents emphasizes their domination of the process by which the population and wealth of the new province were enumerated, and thus could be controlled, for taxation and other purposes. Yet, in the course of these investigations, it has become apparent that the indigenous population was heavily involved both in measurement of the region's wealth and in such surveying of the land area as may have taken place. This can be seen in apparent misunderstandings by the Venetians of Greek terminology and, even more important, in fundamental flaws in the translation of Greek areal measurement into units understood by the Venetians (see Appendix A). Thus, rather than being passive bystanders to the Venetians' administrative process, the Greeks were active, even if probably unwilling, participators. They should therefore be considered to have had a level of input and control over the information that was much higher than might otherwise be presumed.

Social and Economic Formations in Kranidhi (1821-1981): A Preliminary Investigation

Marina Petronoti

By the middle of the nineteenth century, Kranidhi, the principle settlement of its region, had emerged as a center of remarkable maritime and commercial power, having departed from its land-based, pastoral economy, which, as Forbes (this volume) describes, dominated the southern Argolid in the early eighteenth century. Political and economic changes in Greece and other parts of the Mediterranean, however, caused the Kranidhiote economy to shift yet again after the mid-nineteenth century. This chapter investigates the impact that certain aspects of the town's postrevolutionary commercial growth had upon local economic and social formations throughout the nineteenth century and up to 1981, when this research was carried out (Petronoti 1985a, 1985b). More particularly, the chapter explores the degree to which local economic initiatives have interacted with national and even international forces to give Kranidhi the distinctive social character it has exhibited at various points in time.

This analysis examines the articulation of commercial activities with processes of social mobility and with factors accounting for survival of the local stratification system, even when Kranidhi lost its maritime prominence. Especially noteworthy in this respect are the commercial enterprises Kranidhiotes developed, both within and outside the geographical boundaries of the Argolid, as they shifted capital from one sector of the economy to another and exploited opportunities provided at national and international levels. The shifting and transitory nature of these enterprises and their penetration into a wide variety of contexts urge us to investigate how such activities effected the social and economic structures of Kranidhi.

This discussion also responds to the contemporary anthropological concern that too rigid a focus on small communities bypasses the intermingling between local and national and sacrifices complementarity and interdependence to a dichotomous sense of opposition. Although small communities exhibit cultural idiosyncrasies often labeled as "traditional," they have also been constantly and repeatedly absorbed into economies on a larger scale.[1] Analysis of the repercussions such processes have on community life does show that sometimes local groups are unable to respond quickly to changes and that control is removed from them and relocated at higher echelons, or captured in specialist markets (Herzfeld 1987: 8–12). At the same time, however, it is clear that those variously described as villagers, peasants, or rural people perceive, interpret, and contest hegemonic ideologies and values in multiple ways and are by no means isolated bearers of tradition (e.g., Cowan 1990; Dubisch 1986a; Kenny and Kertzer 1983). Ethnographic representations of such groups thus increasingly emphasize their imaginative and active contribution to the transformation of both local and national structures through the strategies with which they pursue wealth, the initiative they take to improve their life standards, the maintenance of extended social networks, and the flow of goods between rural and urban areas.

In order to understand the origins and development of social and economic formations in Kranidhi, I review the basic features of the town's economy at the time when commercial operations were at their highest growth—the mid-nineteenth century. The end of this period coincides with the last decades of the nineteenth century and is characterized by contradictions and ambiguities associated with the prolonged engagement of many Kranidhiotes in an unstable and risky combination of different kinds of activities. Nonetheless, certain aspects of the town's commercial boom in the nineteenth century led directly to the successive economic innovations that have taken place in the surrounding area, the progressive changes in people's occupations, and the emergence of new social strata.

These issues have been approached through the collection of personal accounts,[2] as well as through the analysis of archival material (register books, marriage contracts) and secondary sources. This combination of methodological tools provided a comprehensive view of factors and processes related to my inquiries. Needless to say, it proved very difficult to obtain precise figures about economic transactions during the nineteenth century. Narrators also had a tendency to project current beliefs and ideas related to their own experience into their accounts of the past. While this tendency may have distorted some events, it was of great analytical use, in identifying the meanings currently attached to these events.[3] While additional sources would certainly yield a more detailed description of the former nature of the local economy, the material presently available was sufficient for establishing the basic framework of Kranidhiote life in the nineteenth century.

Shipbuilding and Commercial Enterprises During the Nineteenth Century

During the first part of the nineteenth century, the Greek economy was influenced by a series of international events of both economic and noneconomic importance (see also Topping, this volume).[4] Many developments were related to the Treaty of Kioutsouk Kainartzi, such as protective, as well as restrictive, ties, which were enforced upon the circulation of goods, a growing demand for various agricultural products in Europe,[5] and an increase in the price of these products.[6] The interaction between these political and economic factors enhanced the significance of several Greek commercial and maritime centers and determined their economy in the decades following liberation from Turkish rule. The subsequent expansion of the Greek merchant marine brought about an unforeseen increase in the investments made in shipbuilding and maritime enterprises. The impressive development of certain islands (such as Hydra and Spetses) reflects the magnitude of sea trade and further suggests that the growth of this sector of the economy had a strong and unavoidable impact on the economic life and organization of surrounding regions.[7] Indeed, formal documents clearly manifest that these maritime centers provided jobs to both skilled and unskilled workers from Kranidhi and even attracted entire families for permanent settlement (Kremmydhas 1976–77: 144; Hatzianargirou 1925: 26; see also Topping, Forbes, Sutton, this volume). Equally if not more interesting are the instances of migratory movements towards Kranidhi. Although such movements were comparatively few, they allow us to assume with reasonable certainty that this town, too, developed a wide range of activities that served as major economic incentives to individuals and families from neighboring areas.[8]

Sources are inadequate for verifying how much Kranidhiotes contributed to the development of national commerce during the early postrevolutionary period.[9] Yet, it seems analytically safe to draw a number of conclusions. Most important, Kranidhi experienced a noteworthy economic growth that remained closely linked to the expansion of Greek external trade and exercised great influence on the formation of the town's social stratification during this time. According to written documents and the oral narratives of elderly people, during the nineteenth century many shipowners and captains from Kranidhi traveled as far as Odessa, Romania, Trieste, North Africa, and Asia Minor.[10] Judging from these testimonies, I am inclined to believe that the percentage of shipowners reached 2 or 3 percent of the town's population. The Merchant Shipping Registers at the islands of Spetses and Hydra shows the large number of vessels built by Kranidhiotes between 1848–1908 (see Figure 4.1).[11] The information provided by these Registers further highlights the location of shipbuilding operations, the number of people who shared the ownership of each vessel, and finally, that, with only one exception, shipowners were also sailors themselves.[12]

Also deserving further exploration concerns the means by which Kranidhiotes accumulated capital for shipbuilding. It is clear that the first shipbuilding operations were based on a cooperative system in which landowners, captains, shipworkers, and lumber dealers shared both expenses and profits. The type of partnership exhibited in the Merchant Shipping Registers indicates a preference towards cooperation among individuals related by blood or affinity, something which can be inferred by the fact that most owners have the same surname.[13]

Throughout the nineteenth century, agricultural production and sea trade were closely interdependent. The interests of shipowners, captains, and sea traders were connected to those of landowners; in fact, many Kranidhiotes engaged in both types of activity. According to oral accounts of the descendants of several wealthy families in Kranidhi and Fournoi, it was quite common for wealthy merchants and landowners to invest the money they earned from olive oil trade in shipbuilding and the transportation of merchandise (sermaya). The town's economic growth was therefore favored, as well as limited, by the ability of landowners to extend their enterprises beyond the local market and to finance sea trade with agricultural capital.

The striking point here concerns the position landowners occupied with respect to resources and competitors. Landowners sought to exploit an environment they knew nothing about (sea trade), with relatively few assets in terms of capital, skills, and claims. The essence of their activity was the discovery and exploitation of possible new channels of profit. The choices they made and the risks they took in their effort to invest capital formed by agricultural activities in other spheres of the economy is in line with the meaning Barth (1963) has given to the

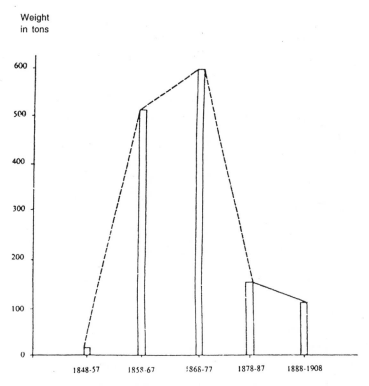

Weight
in tons

600

500

400

300

200

100

0

1848-57   1858-67   1868-77   1878-87   1888-1908

Figure 4.1.   Ships of all types built by Kranidhiotes, 1848–1908. From shipping registers of Hydra and Spetses.

concept of the entrepreneur.[14] The entrepreneurial pursuit of the maximization of profits and goods pertaining to social rank and power differentiates these Kranidhiotes from others who remained faithful to traditional statuses and acted according to institutionalized roles.[15] The content and density of the entrepreneurs' economic networks dissociated them from the limits of the local economy and generated linkages with markets in different parts of the nation.

The interdependence between Kranidhi's agricultural and commercial operations cannot be described with accuracy because of the scarcity of the available data. Judging from what we know about the goods shipped from the Argolid in general, however, it appears that such exports derived mostly from the cultivation of land throughout the nineteenth century. Especially in the southern part of the region, the main export commodity was olive oil; of lesser significance were cereals (mostly wheat), wine, and carobs, none of which demanded great care or rich soil to grow. Commercial pastoralism continued to dominate in the northern Ermionidha (see Forbes, Koster, this volume). The degree to which the nature of local production was influenced by the demands of the national market and the means by which Kranidhiotes traded local crops are facets that have been described by several authors. For instance, Kremmydhas (1980: 158) notes that in the beginning of the nineteenth century a sharp decline in the cultivation of olive trees throughout the northwestern part of the Peloponnesos was accompanied by a remarkable increase in both the production and trade of olive oil in southeastern lands (i.e., around Kranidhi).

The variable evidence we have about prices of local products, the ways in which these were channeled to Greek or international markets, and the proportion of tradable quantities within total agricultural production hinders the construction of a full picture of economic processes in Kranidhi. Still, we can be certain, as I have already mentioned, that the majority of captains and shipbuilders were also owners of large landholdings with olive trees, cereals, and vines. These holdings were attended by peasants who worked for daily wages and normally belonged to poor and landless strata. Some even came from neighboring areas, such as Tsakonia. Manpower was also sometimes hired on the basis of the *gemouro* system, in which workers submitted to landowners a specified amount of produce, regardless of the total yield of the season (Sakellarios 1978: 51). This system predominated among landless peasants and small landowners. Other methods of hiring laborers included rent and, not of least significance, the *misiako*, whereby landowners covered part of the expenses required for planting and purchase of seeds and tools, while workers provided labor and skills. The latter method was used particularly in the cultivation of cereals and the harvest of olives, in which workers were rewarded with half the produce.

Since very little is known about the economic power and composition of wealth among Kranidhiote landowners and sea traders, this discussion intends to draw attention to, rather than arrive at, final conclusions about their enterprises. Nonetheless, it would not be presumptuous to say that during the nineteenth century, economic organization and development in the Ermionidha lay in the hands of only a few landowners and sea traders whose power derived from their systematic engagement in the collection and distribution of local crops.[16] Such engagements placed Kranidhi within a wider economic framework—a process which encouraged the dependence of local agricultural production on national and European markets, thus making possible the appropriation of agricultural produce by local merchants, who transported and traded it to other Greek cities and markets abroad.

Import Trade and Social Characteristics of the Town

Kranidhiote sea traders who traveled abroad brought back various commodities: wheat,[17] raw materials, lumber, fabrics, carpets, sugar, and so forth. As a rule, these commodities were sold to wholesale traders in Piraeus or other Greek ports; some even went as far as Constantinople and Smyrni. The remainder of the imported goods was destined for general stores of the Ermionidha, as well as for the traders' own families. Indeed, it is still possible to see balconies and terraces paved with tiles from Malta, floors made of lumber from Trieste,[18] and numerous decorative items of European origin; all constitute reliable evidence of the luxurious lifestyle of sea-trading families at the time. Moreover, the construction of three large churches in Kranidhi (Kato Panayia, Ioannis Prodhromos, and Ayios Yeorghos at Bardhounia) was financed by captains who thereby introduced a new architectural style in the town, inasmuch as two of these churches were built according to Italian plans.[19]

The houses of these sea traders were originally located in Bardhounia, a hilly area overlooking the rest of the town of Kranidhi. Similar clusterings occurred among other social groups. The neighborhoods of Sarandaspita and Grammatiko, for instance, attracted people who were almost exclusively devoted to the cultivation of land, whereas the majority of those working in crafts and construction were concentrated in Roumania and Lainadhika. Such preferences reveal a residential division of the town that gradually brought about the creation of a series of neighborhoods with dissimilar social features. Kranidhi was thus internally differentiated into better and lesser sections: status distinctions that are less apparent to the outsider today. Only the elderly now emphasize the social prestige once accorded to different neighborhoods or associate them with the inhabitants' economic position and activities.

During the first half of the nineteenth century, housing arrangements were further affected by the practice of *patrilocality*. The male members of the family often settled in the same or a nearby neighborhood, forming a large kinship group with a common patrilineal ancestor. These neighborhoods became known by the relevant patronym—for example, Yeorghopouleika after Yeorghopoulos. Today, it is uncommon to find members of adjacent generations in the same part of the town, and it is very rare for male kin all to be addressed by a nickname based on a modified form of their father's surname. Since both customs once reflected the close cooperation of patrilineally related men who lived, worked, and administered material possessions together, there is no doubt that their absence points to a recent transformation of local economic relations.

The patrilineal aspects of past social and economic organization in Kranidhi are nevertheless still manifested in religious practices. Many inhabitants attend mass celebrations and liturgies in the church of their father's neighborhood, even if they belong to another parish. These practices may be regarded as a symbolic sign of the ties binding men together at a time when productive relations relied on the collaboration of male kin living as close as available space allowed.

Manufacturing and the Local Market

The importation of raw materials from outside the region fostered the development of workshops by skilled workers and craftsmen, as well as the establishment of specialty shops and general stores. Most important were grocers, blacksmiths, tailors, furniture makers and shoemakers—those working on the basis of personal orders.[20] In addition to such operations, the majority of these craftsmen and proprietors also cultivated small fields and sometimes engaged in wage labor on fishing or sponge-fishing expeditions. The goods they produced were distributed throughout the Argolid. Fabric merchants, for instance, supplied neighboring villages with commodities by transporting their merchandise on donkeys or selling fabrics to lesser traders or peddlers. With the exception of a few merchants who continued to market goods in Koiladha and Dhidhima until the 1980s, salesmen and craftsmen stopped such itinerant peddling when good public roads were constructed in the middle of the twentieth century.

In spite of such activities, however, craftsmen in Kranidhi had limited outlets for distributing their products. As a corollary of low productivity rates and high interest, investment in agriculture and manufacturing remained low in Greece throughout the nineteenth century (Panayiotopoulos 1979: 471). The enterprising spirit of many Kranidhiotes was restricted by national as well as international circumstances that played a key role in defining the content and duration of local activities. Thus, a general crisis in the Greek merchant marine, which was due to a decrease in fares and isolation from Russian markets during the Crimean War, and an inability of Kranidhiotes to raise capital and buy steam vessels (Leontaritis 1981: 64–65) combined to cause a steady and continuous decline in the Krandiotes' commercial and maritime enterprises in the late nineteenth century.

Maritime Activities During the Twentieth Century

As Kranidhi ceased its large-scale economic activities, it turned to shipbuilding and maritime operations carried out at a local and regional level. Although the specific Greek ports with which Kranidhiotes maintained connections are difficult to identify, it is clear that such operations involved trading of a coastal nature, as well the intensification of fishing and sponge-fishing expeditions.

Because of the scarcity of available sources, we know very little about the number of Kranidhiotes who engaged in shipbuilding, the extent to which they considered it to be a full-time job, and the profits they made. Published texts and oral testimonies manifest that the majority of maritime families were normally led in the direction of sea trade by one of their more innovative members and consequently remained focused on sea trade for one or two generations. The members of the third generation then often pursued university studies in Athens and were occasionally involved in politics.

At the end of the nineteenth century, shipowners in Kranidhi met the same difficulties and adopted a similar economic policy as their counterparts in other parts of the Peloponnesos. On the one hand, shipowners focused on transporting various commodities to Greek islands and ports,[21] and on the other, they decreased their investment in foreign merchant ships and cargoes. Some also bought, or participated in the purchase of, sponge-fishing boats (*ghaghaves*) that traveled to North African shores, or of fishing boats (*kaikia, trekhandhiria*) that did business in the Aegean Islands, Piraeus, and Patras.

Captains and shipowners in Kranidhi not only transformed local maritime activities at this time, they also liquidated a large part of their landed property, in a manner similar to that of merchants and migrants in the years that followed. The ways in which they invested their capital were ruled by three main principles. First of all—and this is evident in numerous dowry contracts and wills—they made investments in real estate in the Ermionidha and bought apartments in Piraeus (where Kranidhiotes usually migrated) or Athens. Second, they conducted retail or manufacturing operations in Kranidhi or major Greek cities. Some established shops or groceries that typically sold a great variety of items, such as olive oil, flour, fabrics, and dyes. A most characteristic case is that of the Panoutsos family, who purchased a cylinder mill and a grain mill in Piraeus and a ceramics factory in Thessaloniki. Although I have not been able to trace the amount of money invested in these operations, or how difficult it was to sell their commodities, it is clear that these enterprises existed alongside and complemented the cultivation of olive orchards in the area around Kranidhi. For this reason, merchants who lived in Piraeus and Athens functioned as absentee landowners in Kranidhi, maintaining their estates and returning to supervise the cultivation of land and the harvest of olives. The multiple ties they created in the cities where they lived strengthened communication, as well as political and economic bonds, between these urban centers and their place of origin.

The third way in which sea traders and landowners (absentee or other) used their capital concerned loans. At a time when the national economy was especially rigid and the outlets for getting secure, well-paid jobs were few, only a small number of people could finance private enterprises or public works. As one might expect, there are no written accounts about lending processes in Kranidhi, possibly because the promissory notes were destroyed by debtors as soon as debts were paid. The narratives of elderly people suggest that moneylenders (*tokoglifoi*, as they were called) made loans to small landowners, sailors, poor peasants, and families in need who often lost "a house for a bottle of olive oil." [22] The archives I located at the local notary's office further reveal a considerable number of mortgages, loans, and auctions that, until recently, only added to the circulation of money among members of the privileged strata. [23]

Social and Family Formations

In previous sections, I emphasized that fundamental changes in the form and content of economic formations in Kranidhi had a dominant impact on the social stratification of the town during the postrevolutionary period of the nineteenth century. Members of the upper classes were in a position to accumulate significant wealth, yet constituted only a small section of the population composed of merchants, landowners, shipbuilders, and captains. The middle stratum included lesser merchants, landowners, and captains, [24] while the socially and economically lower, but largest, part of the population was comprised of landless families and those who worked for wages in the merchant navy and in agriculture.

Variations in the organization and relationships of families within different social strata were significant. The primary socioeconomic unit today is the nuclear family, which comprises a separate household, except when one of the two spouses brings in his or her parents, thus creating a small stem family. [25] Until the 1950s, however, a larger, extended family type dominated among the lower strata: a married son lived and worked under his father's rule. This type of residence and collaboration was less common among the upper strata. In this class, both male and female children tended to set up separate households at marriage, except for the youngest son or daughter, who inherited the paternal house and lived with his or her parents until their death. [26]

Kranidhiote women were given dowries of real estate or capital throughout the period I am concerned with. As a matter of fact, parents gave priority to their daughters' marriage arrangements (Meremiti 1953: 13), and young men often migrated or joined the merchant marine in order to obtain dowries for their sisters. This practice enhanced the sisters' prestige, as well as their own, and increased the chances brothers had to claim a wealthy bride. [27] At the start of the 20th century, the descendants of wealthy families practiced class endogamy, or chose spouses of higher status. In time, however, the growth of the merchant navy and increasing internal migration have made possible upward mobility through marriage.

Differences in socioeconomic status and family structure have been intimately associated with variations in the process of social integration. The narratives and documents I have collected leave no doubt about the heterogeneous ways in which different groups participated in community life, social gatherings, and festivals in Kranidhi. Wealthy captains and landowners were the first to send their children to local schools or place them under the supervision of priests who guided their moral and musical instruction. In the years that followed, young people of this

Figure 4.2.   Portrait of Kranidhiote family. From author's files.

social group completed their university education in Athens and then returned to Kranidhi to work, supplying the town with politicians, doctors, and lawyers. Moreover, merchants and sea traders offered significant amounts of money for the construction of community works, schools, and churches. These sectors were responsible for the replacement of the traditional *vraka* (baggy pants) with the so-called *frangika*, that is, European style clothes.

One more symbolic sign of the high status that sea traders and landowners enjoyed in Kranidhi concerns women's activities. The female members of affluent families abstained from agricultural tasks, hired domestic servants, and occupied themselves with charity. In contrast, the wives of migrants and wage laborers worked in the houses and fields of the town's wealthiest inhabitants. Especially during the early part of their marital life, when migrants or sailors left for longer periods of time, these women were in charge of the money their husbands sent home and oversaw the running of the household themselves.

Most Kranidhiote women today abstain from almost all agricultural activities. Only a few elderly women and some from landless or very poor families continue to work in the olive groves and fields. The marked decrease in female participation in hard manual labor is a consequence of improved standards of living, technological specialization, and the creation of jobs in offices, stores, shops selling tourist items, and other jobs open to women with low educational qualifications.

Migration

As I have repeatedly stressed, the growth of commercial operations in nineteenth-century Kranidhi mirrored the economic orientation of the surrounding region. A combination of national and international forces had brought about new investment and commercial policies in northeastern Europe. These forces also encouraged various forms of migration from the area, both temporary and of some duration. Technological projects such as the opening of the Suez Canal (1858–1869) attracted many seamen and farmers from Kranidhi who settled in Egypt and worked as foremen or commercial agents even after the Canal's completion.

Likewise, a couple of years later (1880–1883), a serious economic crisis hindered the industrial growth of Syros, which was then succeeded by Piraeus as a commercial and industrial center that attracted migrants from many parts of Greece. In 1891, yet another project, the opening of the Canal at Corinth, absorbed laborers from the Ermionidha. When this project was over, some returned home after having accumulated a considerable sum of money with which they bought land, set up small restaurants, or engaged in manufacturing. The ways they made use of their capital depended on international factors, as well as local opportunities for productive investments. The extent of the entrepreneurial activities of Kranidhiotes is evident in the development of the town's economic life.

By the turn of the century, sea trade and transportation were no longer regarded as the most significant sector of the local economy. At the same time, the economy of the Peloponnesos at large provided few outlets for engagement in profitable occupations. An immediate consequence of these factors was the migration of many peasants to the U.S., Canada, and other countries.[28] Such migratory flows took on the character of mass movements between 1890–1910. Many male migrants left after the wedding; others returned home and married local women after a prolonged absence. Women and children migrated less often than men. They usually stayed in Kranidhi in order to attend to family land, depending on remittances and revenues from fields and olive groves for their living.

Capital accumulated by these migrants did not contribute significantly to the differentiation of the local economy. Their entrepreneurial spirit and orientations were restricted by the limited prospects of the area, while their skills and capabilities were insufficient to develop commercial operations or transform agricultural production. There has been a conspicuous absence of investment in industrial works and manufacturing. Those who returned from abroad tended to invest their money in land and new houses, while a very small group bought stores, fishing boats, or olive presses.

Halfway through the twentieth century, certain factors combined to lead to a further expansion of migratory flows from Kranidhi. Unlike many of their predecessors, however, mid-twentieth-century migrants generally left together with their families and did not return to invest in the cultivation of land or trade in the town. Such practices must be interpreted with reference to the scarcity of local resources and low productivity rates. The constant search by smallholders and the landless part of the population for seasonal and supplementary work at maritime, agricultural, construction, and tourist enterprises in the region lead to the same conclusion.

Socioeconomic Organization Today

The impact of vigorous migratory movements has caused a serious population decline in Kranidhi, a process that acquires even greater importance in comparison with the population growth in nearby villages and towns (Sutton, this volume).[29] This growth in communities near Kranidhi is proportionate to the expansion of arable land in the outer parts of the Ermionidha and is in itself a concomitant of the creation of new settlements in areas with nonarable land (Flamboura), or of the completion of land improvement projects (Thermisi).[30] A third type of economic activity, which secures material benefits while maintaining or even increasing the local population, is the development of certain communities into fishing or touristic centers (e.g., Koiladha, Ermioni). In contrast, Kranidhi failed to survive as a sea-trading center. The commercialization of agricultural production during the nineteenth century did not bring about conditions that might have positively transformed the economic functions of the town.

The increasing lack of manpower in conjunction with low agricultural surplus in Kranidhi—both of which relate to the absence of stable employment—prevented the development of local production, so that agriculture came to be an auxiliary and secondary occupation that depended on, rather than supported, other economic activities. The limits of agricultural development were set by the movement of the population towards the sea and cities. The deterioration of local cultivation was a corollary of the growth of other, more profitable economic sectors, since the inland of the Ermionidha does not easily support the cultivation of cash crops. The abandonment of agricultural production further reveals that the composition of the local economy and the prospects for market expansion in Kranidhi were determined by the Kranidhiotes' transactions at a national or international level.

The absence of agricultural cooperatives in Kranidhi is due to the limited amount and quality of arable land in the area. The town has only one olive oil cooperative, which supplies fertilizers but does not deal with the collection and sale of olive oil. The strong competition among landowners is caused by the scarcity of the region's resources—an insuperable obstacle to agricultural and industrial growth—as well as its narrow range of commercial operations and entrepreneurial profits. It is worth mentioning that throughout the period examined, mutual assistance and informal collaboration in everyday life predominated among small landholders and cultivators. This type of collaboration was less common among wealthy Kranidhiotes, whose ability to liquidate their capital allowed them to hire peasant labor for their farming and other operations.

Indeed, the sale of olive oil proved highly profitable for only a small number of landowners in Kranidhi. For the majority of the population, the main source of income has derived from employment in the merchant marine.[31] Hence, since 1960, young men have tended to embark on merchant ships or fishing boats, traveling eight to twelve months a year. These activities have enabled them to save money within a relatively short period of time, much of which is now invested in their children's education, new dwellings (preferably in urban centers), and luxury items. Such things are perceived as undeniable proof of high social status, just like the size of landholdings and number of olive trees in the past. To a lesser degree, some sailors use their profits for the establishment of restaurants, confectioneries, or shops or the purchase of buses and taxis in Kranidhi.

Investment in Greek cities or abroad by Kranidhiotes has combined with their engagement in the merchant marine to undermine previous social and economic inequalities in the town. By the middle of the twentieth century, commercial operations had lost the concentrated nature that had accounted for the appearance of a small but powerful group of merchants and landowners, partly because usury was no longer a realm of private investment. Wealthy Kranidhiotes were deprived of the control they once enjoyed in the organization of production and economic relations in the Ermionidha. Athens and Piraeus emerged as poles of attraction for cultivators and their produce. Since small-scale farmers are increasingly represented by agricultural and animal-breeding cooperatives, their entrance into urban markets is not controlled by merchants. As a corollary of the absence of a regional market in the Ermionidha, contemporary landowners trade olive oil through networks of personal relationships, rather than with the mediation of wholesale traders.

The appropriation of agricultural production and the formation of economic ties with other areas, both inside and outside Greece, are no longer exclusive prerogatives of great landowners and merchants. The middle strata—composed of small landowners, civil servants, technicians, and small traders—are growing in size as well as in power. In contrast to the situation prevailing at the start of the twentieth century, when the means of production belonged to a small group of privileged Kranidhiotes, socioeconomic inequalities today depict differences in the quantity, rather than quality, of material possessions.

Conclusions

This brief outline of social and economic formations in Kranidhi has been only a preliminary attempt to raise questions about the town's integration into national markets. Significant issues remain unresolved, such as the size of landholdings that shipowners and merchants possessed during the nineteenth century and the exact range of fluctuations in land use. Such information demands the search for more precise accounts in order to clarify and interpret the evidence already available.

In spite of these inadequacies, however, the material collected thus far helps us to construct a good picture of the development of the town's socioeconomic characteristics and enables us to make certain assumptions about the origin and meanings of the entrepreneurial behavior of its inhabitants. Socioeconomic life in Kranidhi has been approached in terms of wider political and economic forces. The variable ways in which Kranidhiotes have organized their lives challenge any view of the region as a marginal "static island community" cut off from the rest of the Peloponnesos. As many authors now stress, there is no sharp division between local and national, rural and urban, traditional and modern, since these symbolic oppositions coexist and incorporate elements of each other (e.g., Kenny and Kertzer 1983: 10; Herzfeld 1987: 65; Mouzelis 1978).

In this sense, the analysis of Kranidhiote shipbuilding and trading activities highlights the repercussions that the broader economic and historical framework had on social life and economic relationships at the local level. The sources I have examined leave no doubt that the factors determining the form and content of the town's organization are inherent in the articulation of events that took place beyond the southeastern Peloponnesos. They point out that Kranidhiote involvement in such events was also connected to acceptance of significant changes in community life and organization.[32] Kranidhiotes altered local modes of production and social institutions with a series of deliberate choices in the process of negotiating their position in the economy. Their occupational mobility was intimately linked to shifts in the local market, as well as prospects for investment in various sectors of the economy. Since the basic products of the area (olive oil and cereals) did not demand constant attention, landowners were not altogether tied to the cultivation of land but searched for additional jobs and complemented their agricultural income with earnings from maritime or other occupations. The economic development of the town during the nineteenth century coincided with the expansion of sea trade, the engagement of its inhabitants in shipbuilding, and the commercialization of local agricultural products. These activities demonstrate the dependent and circumstantial nature of the town's economic boom and urge us to reflect on the influence that fluctuations in national and European markets had on transformations taking place in the Ermionidha.

The longitudinal perspective employed in this paper also raises serious doubts about survivalistic assumptions of a uniform and stable past. The recent dominance of the service sector and the absence of significant industrial and agricultural development have been preceded by an altogether different period during which Kranidhi experienced important growth and functioned as a center of commercial and maritime operations. Kranidhi's distinctive features relate to the use landowners made of agricultural capital invested in shipbuilding, sea trade, and education, the combination of which enabled them to exploit opportunities and extend their sphere of activity far beyond the physical boundaries of the town. Such dynamic practices call for further exploration and comparative analysis of the complex web of changes and transformations, continuities and adjustments in successive phases of the history of small Greek towns and rural communities.

CHAPTER FIVE

Liquid Landscapes: Demographic Transitions in the Ermionidha

Susan Buck Sutton

The national census of Greece counted 12,222 people for the *eparkhia* of the Ermionidha in 1981, and 13,404 in 1991.[1] Among those represented by such statistics was Tassos Franghos, an elderly man who regularly moved back and forth between the large upland village of Iliokastro and the nearby hamlet of Tsoukalia during the 1980s. In Tsoukalia, he and his wife made cheese, which they sold in regional markets, and tended fields, flocks, and house, often spending the night. Tassos's family was the last to live—even if only occasionally—at Tsoukalia, a settlement attested by travelers as early as the first decade of the nineteenth century (Gell 1810: 168–69). Never very large, Tsoukalia's other residents have gradually left, and its houses stand abandoned or turned into seasonal work space.

The Botsaris family was also reflected in the census figures. During the 1980s, they moved into the new *sinoikismos* of Kritselaika, located east of Thermisi along a coast booming with commercial agriculture and touristic enterprises. Former shepherds from the Arcadian village of Valtetsi, following World War II the family strengthened ties to these shorelands, which they had long used for winter pasturage. As marshes were drained and land made available, they bought fields and settled with five or six other families along an open stretch. Because Kritselaika is too small to be identified in census reports, it is included in the numbers for nearby Metokhi. This latter settlement is the estate of an Hydriote monastery—now rented and farmed by a family who hires laborers from as far away as Thessaly for the summer months.

These census counts also encompassed Stamatina Iatrou and her son, Angelos, residents of the harbor village of Koiladha on the western side of the eparkhia. Stamatina's husband was born in Koiladha, but she came from the nearby market town of Kranidhi and still considered herself something of a *Kranidhiotissa*. As a young woman, she spent a year as a seamstress in Athens, but then returned to the area, married, and settled in Koiladha. Over the years, she and her husband operated several fishing boats, which they eventually sold to purchase a general store, which, in turn, they converted into a small hotel. Operating alone after her husband's death, Stamatina rented rooms to occasional tourists, former villagers, and those members of the Argolid Exploration Project who also were present during this period—even if not counted in official statistics.

The stories of others resident in the eparkhia during the last decades take us on still other trajectories. These narratives speak of those who have always lived there and those who have just arrived, those who worked solely as farmers, shepherds, or sailors, and those who did all these things combined or in sequence. Such stories invite us to understand this region as one in flux; to examine its demographic history with an openness to growth as well as decline, national markets as well as traditional technologies; and to consider the ways in which local and more distant processes have coexisted and shaped each other.

This complex understanding of the region has emerged from the particular kind of anthropological-archaeological collaboration that has characterized the Argolid Exploration Project.[2] I joined the AEP in 1982 with the goal of conducting an ethnographic study of modern settlement patterns that articulated with the archaeological survey work being done on earlier periods of the region's history. In this endeavor, I was determined to remove the area's residents from an imagined land before time by considering events such as Stamatina's renting rooms to us to be illuminating rather than contaminating. I wanted to bring the richness of contemporary ethnography to the emerging field of ethnoarchaeology and resisted efforts to look at the present only for examples of archaic technology. While none of us knew exactly where this collaboration would lead, we agreed to take the modern period on its own terms before making comparisons with the region's past. What I only dimly realized at this point, however, was the reverse impact that the chronological depth and regional perspective of survey archaeology would have on my own comprehension of the area's contemporary circumstances.

The result was a more complex settlement history than any of us had anticipated, one revealing a series of demographic transitions that involved settlement rearrangement and proliferation,[3] inward as well as outward migration, economic diversification, and long-term articulation with distant markets. The story of the southern Argolid still argues for understanding contemporary Greek life as the product of contemporary history but gives a more active nature to this history than we had expected. While I had conjectured a straightforward and linear process of rural depopulation, the Ermionidha emerged as one of a few areas of the Peloponnesos that maintained their population levels in the twentieth century. This is not because it has been subject to different forces from other areas but because its particular points of articulation with these forces have allowed more opportunities. The story of its demographic success thus also contains the story of decline in other regions. It is a tale that says much about the ways Greek villagers have negotiated the conditions of their lives, and the varied settlement decisions they have made.

It is in such light that this chapter presents a demographic analysis of changing settlement patterns in the Ermionidha since 1700.[4] The activities of the seemingly most westernized and most remote villages within this region are seen as intrinsically linked, with shifts in the population size of one linked to parallel shifts in the other. The demographic accounts that summarize these changes are themselves analyzed as products of various definitions and assumptions and are shown to derive new meaning from our ability to juxtapose them with the decisions and actions of individual people like Tassos Franghos, the Botsaris family, and Stamatina Iatrou. Understood in this manner, these demographic narratives reveal the historical fluidity of the rural Greek landscape and suggest a rethinking of the ways we conceive villages, sites, and the interconnections among them.

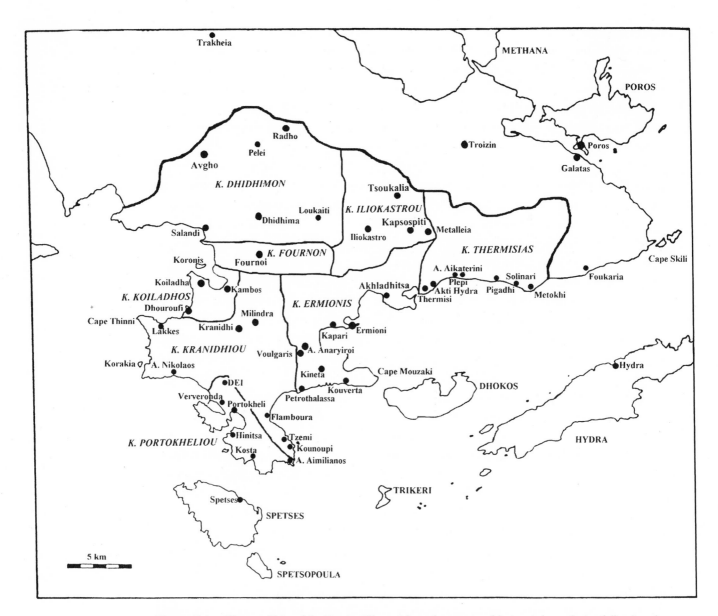

Figure 5.1.   The eparkhia of the Ermionidha, with settlements and koinotis boundaries following the reorganization of 1956. From records at National Statistical Service, Athens.

I begin with some epistemological issues in demographic analysis, outline the shifting economic and political situation for the Ermionidha over the last three centuries, then focus on the settlement history accompanying these changes. The discussion concludes with thoughts on what this regional study suggests for anthropology and archaeology in rural Greece.

Ghosts in the Numbers

Population figures are the kind of data often associated with a crude positivism. Careful demographers, however, approach them differently (Newell 1988: 13–21; Thomlinson 1965).

Such numbers guide our comprehension of a situation only to the extent that we understand what they can and cannot tell us. The recognition by many archaeologists that empirical observations are units constructed, rather than things simply observed, sounds the same theme (see David 1992: 331). Demographic statistics indicate what patterns emerge among large groups of people. They can even indicate, if we are careful, contestation and variation in these patterns. They also contain, however, their own ghosts and the ability to appear more real than they are. If we are not attentive, they fix our thoughts and limit our conceptions in ways that do an injustice to the people they represent.

This analysis is based primarily on figures for de facto population, or the number of people resident in an area at a particular moment in time.[5] These figures are compiled and referenced in Appendix B. Most derive from national census reports for 1851 through 1991.[6] Those for earlier periods are based on the Venetian census of 1700 (see Topping and Forbes, this volume) and the report of the French Expédition Scientifique de la Morée for 1829 (Bory de Saint Vincent 1834–36, 2: 65–84).[7] These figures were also placed against the backdrop of accounts and descriptions by various travelers and topographers, although relatively few ventured into this area compared to some other Greek regions.[8] The Ermionidha neither lay on major land routes nor offered the decayed ruins, wild landscape, and timeless folk sought by the Romantic imagination (Angelomatis-Tsougarakis 1990: 1–24; Eisner 1991: 81–104, Tsigakou 1981: 21–62). Its antiquities were ground level or below, its landscape cultivated, and its peasants capitalized.

The population figures gained from such sources were supplemented with my own visits to all major settlements, and 90 percent of the smaller ones, in the eparkhia. In all instances, I discussed settlement and population issues with local residents and officials, and in the cases of Koiladha, Kranidhi, Portokheli, Thermisi, and Iliokastro I consulted the *dhimotoloyia* (continuous population registers) maintained there as well. While this differed from the methodology standard in village ethnography, it also pursued a different, more regionally based set of questions.

The figures thus produced, as with all such figures, contain ambiguities. There are, first of all, obvious and important ambiguities concerning accuracy. Population size, for example, can be over- or underreported for various reasons, as in the persistent undercounting of women in Greek censuses until the twentieth century,[9] or the official desire to inflate a region's population for tax or voting purposes.[10] Census forms may be misunderstood or improperly filled out by those charged with completing them. Settlements change names or are reclassified from one administrative region to another. Fourkaria, for example, was included in the eparkhia until 1920, while Radho was excluded until this time. The coastal settlement of Dardhiza is now listed under the new name of Akhladhitsa, Sambariza under Pigadhia, Avgho under Pelei, and Karakasi under Iliokastro. At one point, Metalleia shifted from the *koinotis* of Thermisi to Iliokastro, while Dardhiza was reclassified under Ermioni.

Beyond these toponymic and administrative issues, however, there are ambiguities inherent in reducing social processes to single numbers. Such figures freeze population at one moment in time and one spot on the landscape. If we take this too literally, we miss the dynamics of migration and multiple residence, the existence of dispersed housing and smaller settlements, and the gradual nature of demographic change. The same individual may have two or more bases, may be in the process of migrating, or may live in one place but still feel attached to another. Where he or she is found on the day of the census is but one dimension. Whether a settlement is occupied year-round or seasonally can also be disguised (see Forbes, this volume).

Such figures also mask small outlying settlements and scattered housing of the sort discussed by Clarke, and by Murray and Kardulias in this volume. Unless and until they reach a critical size, numbers for such localities are embedded in figures for larger settlements. In other cases, total population for a string of hamlets is listed first for one then another—as happened for the small communities of the Thermisi coast during the nineteenth century. Indeed, the same small settlement sometimes appears, disappears, and then reappears in census reports. While this may indicate periodic lack of habitation, it can also mean that the settlement was lumped with a nearby village during its absence from the reports, confounding figures for both.[11] Diffuse settlements such as Kineta or Kambos are given a seeming nucleation by their condensation into a single figure, while others—such as Petrothalassa—can be double-listed because they straddle the boundary between two municipal divisions.[12]

Finally, there is ambiguity as to how much each of the three demographic processes of natality, mortality, and migration have contributed to overall population levels. The relative weight of these forces is masked by summary population figures, a circumstance that thus hides the formative demographic processes at work in an area. An increase in de facto population does not necessarily mean, for example, an absence of outward migration if it occurs during a time of high birth rates. Such appears to have been the case during several periods in the recent history of the Ermionidha. Migrants were indeed leaving the region but their number was exceeded by that of births among those who were staying.

While the following analysis is based squarely on various figures for de facto population, it is thus also something of an interpretive exercise. Understanding whether a particular census count represents a permanent, seasonal, compact, or dispersed settlement is, for example, dependent on analysis of various bits of documentary evidence, local knowledge, and the life histories of those who lived there. The figures for particular points in time are better understood if placed against general trends that illuminate the dynamic processes at work.

In conducting this interpretation I approached most figures as covering at least some outlying settlements, and thus as describing an area rather than a precise spot.[13] To underscore this perspective, the tables that accompany this text report data either on the eparkhia level or according to the general regions of the three *demoi* into which the Ermionidha was divided in the nineteenth century. While I could have adjusted for various kinds of undercounting, I decided against this to insure comparability with figures from other regions of Greece. The data therefore should be seen as general guides to the magnitude of growth or decline, rather than as precise accountings. Finally, I attempted to identify the role of migration in such growth or decline through standard demographic formulas. Using national birth and death rates for the last 160 years, the volume of net migration (the balance between inward and outward migration) was thus derived for each intercensal period.[14]

Politics and Economy in Recent History

Such demographic reckonings gain greater significance, of course, when placed against the circumstances shaping them. I am among those who feel too much migration theory reflects simplistic assumptions of economic maximization by individuals of totally free will (Jobes, Stinner, and Wardwell 1992; Kearney 1986). Kinship networks, emotional attachments, the role of place in identity formation, political constraint, and variable conceptions of what is a worthwhile life surely also enter into migratory decision making. With such caveats in mind, the present analysis is nevertheless directed towards understanding the connection between historical shifts in opportunities for cash production in the Ermionidha and the migratory and settlement trends that have characterized the eparkhia over the last two centuries. Occupational changes are relatively accessible in historical records and survey archaeology, amenable to regional comparisons, and—most significantly—the factor most frequently mentioned by the residents of the Ermionidha in explaining their own settlement shifts.

This approach also connects my analysis of changing settlement patterns in the southern Argolid to more general discussions of the semiperipheral nature of the Greek economy and the highly centralized character of its national systems. The decentralized, regionally based networks of the late Ottoman period in Greece have given way to ones focused more squarely on national centers and international markets (see Kayser, Pechoux, and Sivignon 1971; Hadjimichalis 1987; Mouzelis 1978). The declining importance of a broad network of evenly spaced regional centers, as a result of Greece's increasing involvement in international political and economic systems, is much more important in understanding the settlement shifts of modern Greek history than forces such as population pressure. While Greek rates of natural increase accelerated in the nineteenth century, they have declined steadily ever since (Valaoras 1960). Population pressure has not driven economic and political life in ways suggested by either Malthus (see Thomlinson 1965) or Boserup (1965).[15]

How economic opportunities have rearranged themselves over the landscape in the last three centuries is thus intimately connected to population levels and migration streams into, out of, and within the Ermionidha. Before exploring the region's recent demographic patterns, therefore, this section briefly recounts its political and economic history since 1700. My goal is to identify the evolving position of the Ermionidha within the emerging systems of the modern Greek state.

Around 1700, during the brief Second Venetian Occupation of the Peloponnesos, the area's economy was based primarily on farming and pastoralism, with some maritime activity at Kranidhi and Ermioni, and salt-panning at Thermisi (Forbes and Topping, this volume; Gavrielides 1976b: 157; Jameson 1976a: 82; Jameson, Runnels, and van Andel 1994: 126–135; Karanikolas 1980). The century that followed brought dramatic changes. There is growing recognition of the importance that long-distance trade had for many Greeks, both rural and urban, during the eighteenth century (e.g., Angelomatis-Tsougarakis 1990; Anoyatis-Pele 1987; Beopoulou 1981; Hadjimichalis 1987; Kremmydhas 1972; Mouzelis 1978; Zakynthos 1976).[16] Consumption of British and French goods was on the rise throughout the Ottoman Empire, matched by increasing western European demand for such Greek products as currants, olives, dyes, and textiles, as well as Russian grain transported by Greeks. The Turkish defeat of Venice left a vacuum in shipping networks serving this trade, a gap soon filled by the spectacular rise of Hydra and Spetses. Semi-independent due to both geographical isolation and concessions granted by the Sultan, the coastal traders of these islands quickly expanded their operations to command a central role in Mediterranean shipping (Kriezis 1860: 38; Michaelides 1967: 12–16; Petronoti 1985a: 64, and this volume; Thomas 1977: 4–6).

Separated by only a few kilometers of sea and connected by long-standing ties of kinship to Hydra and Spetses,[17] the Ermionidha participated in this economic boom (Jameson, Runnels, and van Andel 1994: 136–139; van Andel and Sutton 1987). As Topping points out in this volume, small vessels built in the Ermionidha were quite important for coastal and Aegean trade during this period. Some Kranidhiotes also owned and captained larger ships, which traveled to the Black Sea, North Africa, and Asia Minor (Forbes 1993; Petronoti 1985a: 65–66, and this volume). The situation provided multiple opportunities for men to sign on as sailors for ships departing Hydra and Spetses as well.

Growing seafaring populations of this region also appear to have stimulated agricultural production on the mainland in the eighteenth century (Gavrielides 1976a: 273; Jameson 1976a: 77; Koster and Koster 1976: 281; Petronoti 1985a: 67, and this volume). Oil production in the Kranidhi area was animated by the desire of local shippers to use it as trading capital on their voyages (Forbes 1993). Also, Hydra and Spetses were not suited for the kind of farming necessary to provision ships and feed the inhabitants of their port towns. Some of the wealthiest families and monasteries on these islands consequently initiated agricultural operations along the coasts of the Ermionidha. The Hydriote monastic Metokhi on the Thermisi coast, the Voulgaris estate near Ermioni, and Spetsiote estates near Kosta were in place by the time of the Greek Revolution (Kriezis 1860: 7; Halioris 1929; Miliarakis 1886: 226; Paraskevopoulos 1895: 52; Topping, this volume).

Although affected by the decline in grain prices in Europe after 1815, Hydra and Spetses were still major shipping centers when the Greek Revolution erupted in 1821. They contributed vessels to the cause, and their leaders represented a major faction in struggles to oversee the war and organize the modern Greek state. The Ermionidha was a close ally of these islands. Ermioni, Kranidhi, and the monastery of Avgho were all, at various times, revolutionary centers (Antonakatou and Mavros 1973: 139–145; Jameson, Runnels, and van Andel 1994; Karanikolas 1980: 19; Petropulos 1968: 35).[18]

Establishment of the Greek nation, however, changed the fortunes of the region yet again (see also Jameson, Runnels, and van Andel 1994: 139–148). The importance of Hydra and Spetses as shipping centers declined, as first Syros and then, by 1870, Piraeus became the chief Greek ports (Kolodny 1974, 1: 103–112, 192–99; Petronoti, this volume). Centralized administrative structures and dependent economic relations created a primate city. The economic and political life of the country came to revolve around Athens and its harbor Piraeus. As a consequence, although Hydra, Spetses, and Kranidhi remained active in shipping throughout the nineteenth century, they did so with fleets that were smaller and traveled shorter distances than before (Karanikolas 1980: 20; Mansolas 1867: 195–96; Orlandos 1877: 39; Paraskevopoulos 1895: 37–46; Petronoti 1985a). Although sailors from the region continued to predominate in the Greek merchant marine, comprising one-quarter of all Greek sailors in 1879 (Kolodny 1974, 1: 348), they increasingly worked on ships based outside the region. When Athenian fleets converted to steam in the late nineteenth century, Hydra and Spetses were essentially eliminated as bases for international shipping (Karanikolas 1980: 20; Kolodny 1974, 1: 328; Orlandos 1877; Paraskevopoulos 1895: 37–39; Petronoti 1985a: 72).

This decline in long-distance shipping led many in the region to turn to other maritime activities in the mid-nineteenth century. Kranidhi and its surrounding ports continued to manufacture small wooden ships similar to those still sometimes assembled in Koiladha and Ermioni. Some six hundred ships from these shipyards appeared in the harbor registers of Hydra and Spetses at the peak of this construction around 1870 (Petronoti, this volume). Many of these vessels were used to transport Peloponnesian produce to Athenian markets, and to serve the area's growing sponging industry (Karanikolas 1980: 34; Kriezis 1860: 197; Miliarakis 1886: 241; Paraskevopoulos 1895: 32; Petronoti 1985a: 72).

Indeed, the region became second only to the Dodecanese in the harvesting of sponges in the late nineteenth and early twentieth centuries. Many inhabitants of Hydra, Spetses, Kranidhi, Ermioni, and Fournoi turned their seafaring skills and equipment toward the sponge banks off North Africa in response to increased northern European demand (Miliarkis 1886: 241; Paraskevopoulos 1895: 48; Georgas 1937; Kolodny 1974, 1: 309–323). The opening of sponge beds in the Americas and the development of synthetic sponges eventually ended this trade. Commercial fishing has proven more durable. In the late nineteenth century, ships from the area began going after octopus, mullet, pelamyd tuna, and other fish—as far away as Evvia and the Cyclades (Bintliff 1977; Petronoti 1985a: 72). By mid-twentieth century, the Argosaronic area commanded over 15 percent of Greek fishing production (Kolodny 1974, 1: 302). Much of this catch was regularly sent to Athens. Some is now also diverted to local restaurants serving the tourist trade.

This diversification of maritime activities, despite the drop in long-distance shipping, accounts for the Ermionidha's occupational profile in the late nineteenth century. At that time, Kranidhiotes still had over 100 ships, both large and small, which they sheltered in various harbors in the region (Paraskevopoulos 1895: 46). The 1879 census recorded that 36 percent of the Ermionidha's working population was engaged in maritime activities, while only 27 percent was listed as farmers and shepherds (Greece 1880).[19] The ratio varied within the region, however, since no seafarers were counted in Dhidhima, while over half of the Ermioni population was so classified. Dhidhima, on the other hand, housed almost as many shepherds as the rest of the area combined.

This profile of the Ermionidha gradually shifted as commercial agriculture took prominence over seafaring in the area's economic base. By 1951, 61 percent of the region's population was engaged in agriculture, including 40 percent of the inhabitants of Kranidhi (Greece 1955, Kranidhi dhimotoloyio). Only 16 percent worked in maritime activities. Agricultural production had, as already mentioned, been initially stimulated by the shipping boom. As shipping declined, the area found itself in a good position to produce for the growing markets of Athens. Some wealthy families turned greater attention to their agricultural estates (Petronoti, this volume). Much of this development, however, was undertaken by ordinary villagers, especially as fields became available to them, either through distribution of the National Lands (McGrew 1985) or the break-up of large estates. Much property controlled by the Avgho and Ayioi Anaryiroi monasteries was distributed or sold during the early twentieth century, as were the Voulgaris and Spetsiote estates. The Metokhi of Hydra is now rented to private individuals. Considerable territory described as uncultivated in the nineteenth century was thus opened to agriculture in the twentieth, so that as early as 1928, 86.6 percent of those engaged in farming owned at least some land of their own (Greece 1938).

As these agricultural changes occurred, olive oil from areas around Kranidhi became the most important cash crop, accompanied by wine, cheese, honey, carobs, and resin (Miliarakis 1886: 230; Paraskevopoulos 1895: 49). Although Kranidhi oil is still considered of high quality in Athens, its relative importance in the area has been supplanted (Petronoti 1985a: 79). Citrus orchards began appearing near Ermioni in the late nineteenth century (Paraskevopoulos 1895: 49; Philippson 1892: 48) and were extended to Kineta in the 1920s, Fournoi in the 1930s (Gavrielides 1976a: 266), and the Thermisi plain when it was drained following World War II. Increased irrigation, improved roads, and expanded tourism have further stimulated commercial agriculture and have encouraged garden farming of fruits and vegetables.

Tourism has played an increasing role in the region throughout the twentieth century. Wealthy Athenians started building summer houses on Hydra and Spetses in the 1880s, and the economy of these islands came to revolve almost entirely around the tourist trade after World War II. By the 1960s, this development spilled onto the mainland as large hotels began to appear near Portokheli. Others now dot the entire coast from Portokheli to Ermioni and northward past Thermisi. Much land in these coastal regions has recently been sold for vacation houses, causing an upsurge in construction trades. While the large hotels are generally not locally owned, they employ residents from the area for housekeeping and waiting tables. Workers are brought in daily by truck or bus, even from such upland villages as Radho and Iliokastro. Small hotels, rooming houses, restaurants, tourist shops, and yacht facilities have sprung up around the large hotels.

The 300 years of regional history just recounted indicate that, while Spetses and Hydra followed much the same trajectory as the Ermionidha during the eighteenth century, developments on the islands and the mainland have progressively differentiated ever since. This was formally marked when the eparkhia of Spetses and Ermionidha split after World War II. With limited possibilities for agricultural development, the economic base of Hydra and Spetses is now almost exclusively tourism, while the inhabitants of the mainland pursue a more diversified economy. The capital accumulated during the shipping boom has been redirected toward other pursuits. The Ermionidha clearly looks toward the power and wealth now concentrated in Athens. Its proximity to the capital and the multiple opportunities available within its borders have combined to place it in a more favorable economic position, however, than much of the rest of the Peloponnesos.

There is thus little sense in representing the Ermionidha as an area cut off from recent history. During the last three centuries, farmers, shepherds, sailors, and others resident in the area have participated in economic and political networks that stretch well beyond Greece.[20] Households have relied on juggling multiple economic strategies that shift and change during the course of a lifetime. Gavrielides has documented, for example, how Fourniotes combined fishing, sponging, shepherding, cash cropping, pine tapping, seafaring, and cyclical migration to provide a flexible base of operations during the nineteenth century (1976b: 143). It is currently common for young men from Kranidhi, Ermioni, Koiladha, and Portokheli to work in the Greek merchant marine before returning to invest in new houses and economic operations in the area. Even the transhumant shepherds, whom one might imagine as carrying on self-sufficient lives, have depended on marketing their produce to others for some time (Forbes, this volume).

The Demographics of Kinisi

The demographic trends which grew out of this economic history condense around a word used repeatedly to explain why people chose to stay in the Ermionidha or what they liked about the area. That word is *kinisi*, and it is multivocal. It appeared in a man's explanation of why he often sat in the evening in front of his new house on the main road south of Ermioni: he enjoyed watching the passing cars. It surfaced in the hopes of a young couple in Porto-kheli that their small shop would see increasing tourism come into the area. It emerged in official statements about migrants entering the region from other areas. And it was used to describe the travel that befalls members of the merchant marine. Kinisi variously conveys motion, traffic, migration, sociability, commerce—or some combination of these. It runs through the recent population history of the Ermionidha, for if nothing else, this has been a landscape in motion.

The first row of Table 5.1 initiates our demographic journey with the region's population in 1700 (see also Topping and Forbes, this volume). Even though Hydra and Spetses were probably no longer as thinly inhabited as they were a century before (Kriezis 1860: 15; Thomas 1977), the mainland Ermionidha still registered more residents than either island.[21] Inland and centrally located, Kranidhi was the major town in the Ermionidha, housing slightly under half of the area's population, and constituting the kind of regional market center typical of the Peloponnesos at this time. Other settlements, listed in descending order of size, were Ermioni, Dhidhima, Fournoi, Thermisi, Radho, and several small hamlets whose exact nature is not clear from the evidence (see Forbes, this volume; Jameson, Runnels, and van Andel 1994: 608). Very small shepherding and farming settlements, which were at least seasonally occupied, existed at

Table 5.1
Hydra, Spetses, and the Ermionidha: De Facto Population

Date	Hydra	Spetses	Ermionidha	Kranidhi region	Ermioni region	Dhidhima region
1700	1,480	900	2,163	1,168	603	392
1829	22,000	15,000	6,968	4,985	1,429	584
1851	12,301	8,929	10,510	8,252	1,395	819
1861	9,666	9,843	9,763	7,175	1,659	902
1870	7,428	8,443	11,501	8,439	2,011	1,051
1879	7,342	6,899	10,020	6,705	2,047	1,268
1889	6,478	5,192	10,151	6,442	2,396	1,313
1896	7,177	4,432	12,666	8,236	2,802	1,628
1907	5,542	4,290	11,803	7,588	2,620	1,595
1920	3,409	3,218	10,037	5,962	3,081	1,464
1928	3,729	3,661	9,893	5,813	2,361	1,719
1940	3,780	3,633	11,906	6,523	2,868	2,515
1951	2,843	3,172	11,903	6,267	3,322	2,314
1961	2,794	3,378	11,958	6,024	3,507	2,427
1971	2,538	3,469	11,794	6,055	3,341	2,398
1981	2,732	3,729	12,222	6,368	3,600	2,254
1991	2,373	3,621	13,404	7,599	3,653	2,152

SOURCE: Panayiotopoulos (1985: 247–248), Houliarakis (1973–76: 40), Kriezis (1860: 15–17), Pouqueville (1826: 304), Bory de Saint Vincent (1834–36: 62–77), Rangavis (1853: 285–286), Greece, National Statistical Service (1872, 1880, 1890, 1909, 1921, 1929, 1946, 1955, 1962, 1972, 1982, 1992).

Iliokastro, Loukaiti, Tsoukalia, and a few places along the Thermisi coast. It is even more likely that four small places listed near Ermioni and Kranidhi were used only seasonally. Koiladha and Portokheli seem to have been port facilities with little if any year-round habitation. There were also four monasteries, including the powerful Ayios Dhimitrios tou Avghou above Dhidhima, Ayioi Anaryiroi near Ermioni, the much smaller Zoodochos Piyis at Koiladha, and Ayios Ioannis at Salandi.

As Table 5.1 shows, by the time the French Expédition Scientifique assessed the area's population in 1829, it was a much-changed place. Rather than demographic retreat in the late Tourkokratia, there had been remarkable growth. The Ermionidha more than tripled its population, while Hydra and Spetses rose fifteenfold. While this was a particularly dramatic increase, it nevertheless reflected general trends. Even though some areas were abandoned in the eighteenth century (McGrew 1985), others grew. The Greek population as a whole was on the rise and on the move (Beopoulou 1981; Frangakis and Wagstaff 1987, 1992; Panayiotopoulos 1985: 170–171; Spiridonakis 1977; Wagstaff 1982; Zakynthos 1976: 88–89).[22] The total Peloponnesian population doubled from 176,444 to around 350,000. The proportionately greater increases experienced by Hydra, Spetses, and the Ermionidha indicate how much of a magnet this area became for a mobile rural population.[23]

The nature of this growth is revealed by its concentration within particular areas of the Ermionidha. Virtually every part of the region gained population, but Ermioni and Kranidhi outpaced all other settlements. Both were directly involved in seafaring, and their populations swelled with those who came to participate in the boom. Ermioni grew almost three times in size, while Kranidhi increased almost five times. Equally telling, Kranidhi, which oversaw several harbors along the southern and western coast, now contained a full 70 percent of the total population of the Ermionidha.

The subsequent collapse of the region's prominence in long-distance shipping presaged, of course, further demographic shifts. Table 5.1 and Figure 5.2 give an overview of what has happened since establishment of the modern Greek state. This most recent phase began with Hydra the most populous, Spetses second, and the Ermionidha a distant third. The situation is now reversed. Hydra is but 11 percent of its size at the time of the Revolution, Spetses only 24 percent, but the Ermionidha has grown by almost 650 percent. These figures reveal the progressive economic differentiation of the mainland from the islands.

Such demographic growth also differentiates the Ermionidha from much of the Peloponnesos, especially in the last half century. The Peloponnesos in particular, and the Greek state in general, gained population in the nineteenth and early twentieth centuries as rates of natural increase accelerated with relative peace, freedom, economic opportunity, and the inward migration of Greeks from outside the nation (Baxevanis 1972; Mansolas 1872: 11; Panayiotopoulos 1985: 172).[24] The decline late in the nineteenth century in the international market for currants combined with several other fiscal crises to incite the first large waves of emigration from the Peloponnesos (Petronoti, this volume). As the twentieth century progressed, this outward movement increased while birth rates declined (Valaoras 1960). From 1940 to 1971, the absolute population level of the Peloponnesos fell by 15 percent, and only three *nomoi* held stable: Achaia, the Corinthia, and the Argolid, to which the Ermionidha belongs (Baxevanis 1972: 11–26).

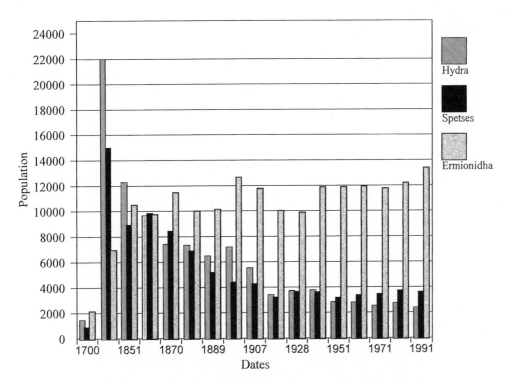

Figure 5.2. Shifting population levels for Hydra, Spetzses, and the Ermionidha.

Even as the Peloponnesos has steadied somewhat in the last two decades, the Ermionidha has showed above average demographic health (Greece 1982, 1992).

The general population loss of the countryside is a frequent topic of public discussion in Greece. The semiperipheral nature of the Greek economy has encouraged international emigration and has also caused many staying in Greece to concentrate around the single settlement of Athens (Hadjimichalis 1987; Mouzelis 1978). The capital city has attracted one-third of the national population. Life in all areas of Greece has been affected by this centralization of political power—bureaucracy, industry, health care, higher education, and even the sense of what it means to be modern; all center around Athens (Kayser, Pechoux, and Sivignon 1971). The demographic health of the Ermionidha takes on heightened significance precisely because it differs from the common pattern. To explore why this happened, we need to look beneath the regional level of the eparkhia's population history.

Subregional Variations

The last three columns of Table 5.1 reveal differences among the three major subregions of the Ermionidha. Tables 5.2, 5.3 and 5.4 examine each of these three areas, revealing significant variation within the eparkhia. All three subregions have gained in comparison with their 1829 populations, but not at the same rate. The Kranidhi area grew one and one-half times, the Ermioni area grew two and one-half times, and the Dhidhima area three and one-half times. The Kranidhi subregion today is still considerably more populous than the other two, but the gap has narrowed.

Table 5.2
Kranidhi Region: De Facto Population

Date	Kranidhi region	Kranidhi town	Fournoi	Koiladha	Portokheli	Other Settlements
1700	1,168	1,002	166			
1829	4,985	4,813	156	16		
1851	8,252	7,987	265			
1861	7,175	6,639				
1870	8,439	7,185				
1879	6,705	6,359	176	113	57	
1889	6,442	5,500	347	354	241	
1896	8,236	6,937	269	464	501	65
1907	7,588	6,033	448	641	406	60
1920	5,962	4,384	470	566	470	72
1928	5,813	4,214	403	631	517	48
1940	6,523	4,456	463	815	585	72
1951	6,267	4,280	432	866	520	169
1961	6,024	3,942	422	884	690	86
1971	6,055	3,657	372	983	885	158
1981	6,368	3,794	371	1,062	754	386
1991	7,599	3,962	367	1,044	1,233	993

SOURCE: Panayiotopoulos (1985: 247–248), Houliarakis (1973–76: 40), Kriezis (1860: 15–17), Pouqueville (1826: 304), Bory de Saint Vincent (1834–36: 62–77), Rangavis (1853: 285–286), Greece, National Statistical Service (1872, 1880, 1890, 1909, 1921, 1929, 1946, 1955, 1962, 1972, 1982, 1992).

The Kranidhi Area

Further variation exists within each subregion. When the Greek state began, the town of Kranidhi was the dominant settlement of its vicinity, which included a small village at Fournoi, beachheads at Portokheli and Koiladha, a few scattered agricultural estates, and a small monastery at Koiladha (Table 5.2). With some ups and downs, Kranidhi gained population through 1896, showing the greatest increases in the mid-nineteenth century when still active in shipping. Its population has steadily declined ever since. Most of the area's wealthy families have moved to Athens. Its seafaring functions have declined. The growth of agriculture in the area, the widespread availability of land, and the collapse of local hierarchies of power worked to erode Kranidhi's prominence.

While Kranidhi declined in population, the small bases of Koiladha and Portokheli became bustling coastal towns, each now larger than Kranidhi had been during the Venetian occupation. Both grew dramatically as long-distance shipping—once dominated by the captains of Kranidhi, Hydra, and Spetses—was gradually replaced by sponging, fishing, coastal trading, and the building of small boats, activities that could be carried out as family operations, or by hiring a few workers. Such occupations brought seafarers away from the dominance of Kranidhi and down to the harbors themselves. Portokheli's recent development of tourism gave it an additional demographic boost.

The impact of tourism is also reflected in the growth of other settlements in the Kranidhi region, particularly those on the southern coast. Early census accounts often glossed over these coastal settlements, most likely numbering only two or three, and totaling around 65 souls in the late nineteenth century. By 1991, however, there were at least fifteen shore communities with 993 year-round inhabitants and many more residents in the summer. Agriculture in this south-

Table 5.3
Ermioni Region: De Facto Population

Date	Ermioni region	Ermioni town	Thermisi coast	Thermisi town	Other settlements
1700	603	408	195	94	
1829	1,429	1,157	227	12	45
1851	1,380	1,294	86		
1861	1,659				
1870	2,011	1,819			
1879	2,047	1,850	183	114	14
1889	2,396	2,070	300	157	26
1896	2,802	2,512	263		27
1907	2,620	2,240	331		49
1920	3,081	2,164	786	233	131
1928	2,361	1,922	417	197	5
1940	2,868	2,212	305	239	112
1951	3,322	2,239	931	519	152
1961	3,507	2,297	692	490	234
1971	3,341	2,186	1,017	412	138
1981	3,600	2,104	1,245	437	251
1991	3,653	2,395	968	467	290

SOURCE: Panayiotopoulos (1985: 247–248), Houliarakis (1973–76: 40), Kriezis (1860: 15–17), Pouqueville (1826: 304), Bory de Saint Vincent (1834–36: 62–77), Rangavis (1853: 285–286), Greece, National Statistical Service (1872, 1880, 1890, 1909, 1921, 1929, 1946, 1955, 1962, 1972, 1982, 1992).

ern area has been almost totally supplanted by vacation housing. The northern village of Fournoi, on the other hand, continues its strong agricultural orientation. If the nearby new agricultural settlement of Kambos is included, the population around Fournoi has remained remarkably steady.

The Ermioni Area

Ermioni, the major town of the eastern subregion within the Ermionidha (Table 5.3), experienced neither the dramatic increases nor losses of Kranidhi. Ermioni also grew until the late nineteenth century, but has undergone minimal decline since. Never as dominant as Kranidhi, Ermioni had less to lose. Its economic base remains a mix of farming, tourism, and seafaring. Substantial and relatively sustained growth has occurred, however, in surrounding parts of the Ermioni area.

The coastal area stretching eastward from Thermisi contained perhaps six small settlements in 1829. None even reached a population of 150; most had only a family or two, and some were only inhabited seasonally. Travelers and geographers throughout the nineteenth century remarked on the uninhabited nature of the area, its difficult marshes, and the Arcadian shepherds who tended flocks there in the winter (Gell 1810: 124; Curtius 1852: 453; Philippson 1892: 48; Pouqueville 1826: 257; Miliarakis 1886: 248–249; Rangavis 1853). Two small but stable points on this coast were Thermisi at the west end—with its old *kastro* (fortress) and salt flats—and the Metokhi of Hydra at the east. The coastal area gained significantly, however, as transhumant shepherds began settling there year-round, particularly after the government drained marshes and sprayed for malaria in the 1950s. Commercial agriculture and tourism have since developed, causing several older settlements to relocate from slightly inland positions to coastal ones.[25] By 1991, eight major settlements and several smaller ones reached a combined population of just under 1,000.

The southern part of the Ermioni subregion has also gained population. At the start of the nineteenth century, its population was composed primarily of the agricultural estates of the monastery of Ayioi Anaryiroi and of the Voulgaris family of Hydra. These estate lands were gradually given or sold to families moving into the area. Five rather diffuse agricultural settlements arose in the vicinities of Kineta and Kouverta as citrus orchards and other cash crops spread. Tourist operations have also recently appeared along the southern shoreline of this area.

The Dhidhima Area

The northerly area around Dhidhima has shown the greatest rate of population increase, although it is still smallest in absolute numbers (Table 5.4). The town of Dhidhima doubled in population during the nineteenth century when it was a farming and shepherding center that both supplied its own needs and sold produce to the seafaring populations elsewhere in the eparkhia. Its population has remained rather steady throughout the twentieth century, while the two satellite settlements of Loukaiti and Iliokastro have grown. These communities had long been seasonal habitations for people from Dhidhima. Around the turn of the century, many families decided to stay in them year-round, although they remained closely connected to Dhidhima in terms of economy and kinship (Vellioti 1987). The largely seasonal village of Pelei also grew as land from the Avgho monastery was distributed. The mining operation at Metalleia created a short-lived settlement that faded by the mid-twentieth century.

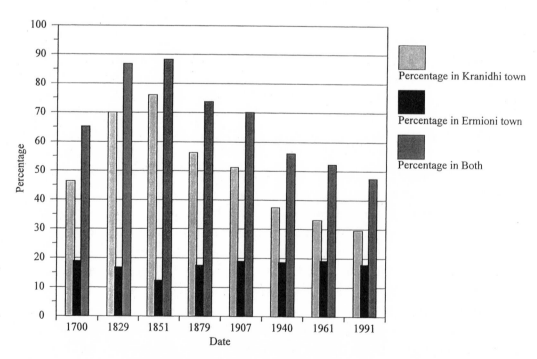

Figure 5.3. Proportion of population in Kranidhi and Ermioni towns, 1700–1991.

Table 5.4
Dhidhima Region: De Facto Population

Date	Dhidhima region	Dhidhima town	Iliokastro	Loukaiti	Metalleia	Other settlements
1700	392	195	37	22		138
1829	584					48
1851	809					32
1861	902					25
1870	1,051					25
1879	1,268					25
1889	1,313					12
1896	1,628					25
1907	1,595	1,171	307	44		73
1920	1,489	861	340	181		107
1928	1,731	1,017	395	145	17	157
1940	2,515	1,217	572	174	184	184
1951	2,314	1,170	631	224	114	175
1961	2,427	1,198	665	284	79	201
1971	2,398	1,252	706	278	4	158
1981	2,254	1,217	633	241		163
1991	2,152	1,189	611	252		100

SOURCE: Panayiotopoulos (1985: 247–48), Houliarakis (1973–76: 40), Kriezis (1860: 15–17), Pouqueville (1826: 304), Bory de Saint Vincent (1834–36: 62–77), Rangavis (1853: 285–86), Greece, National Statistical Service (1872, 1880, 1890, 1909, 1921, 1929, 1946, 1955, 1962, 1972, 1982, 1992).

Table 5.5
The Ermionidha: Population Concentration

Date	Kranidhi town (%)	Ermioni town (%)	Both (%)
1700	46.3	18.9	65.2
1829	70	16.8	86.8
1851	76	12.3	88.3
1879	56.2	17.5	73.7
1907	51.1	19	70.1
1940	37.4	18.6	56
1961	33	19.2	52.2
1991	29.5	17.9	47.4

SOURCE: Panayiotopoulos (1985: 247–248), Houliarakis (1973–76: 40), Kriezis (1860: 15–17), Pouqueville (1826: 304), Bory de Saint Vincent (1834–36: 62–77), Rangavis (1853: 285–286), Greece, National Statistical Service (1872, 1880, 1890, 1909, 1921, 1929, 1946, 1955, 1962, 1972, 1982, 1992).

The Changing Settlement Hierarchy

While Kranidhi declined and Ermioni held steady over the last one hundred years, most other places in the eparkhia gained. The result is a flattening of differences among settlements and a loss of settlement hierarchy. Table 5.5 and Figure 5.3 show that the two towns of Kranidhi and Ermioni housed over 88 percent of the area's population in 1851 (with Kranidhi alone containing 76 percent), but today they hold less than half, with more people outside Kranidhi and

Table 5.6
The Ermionidha: Settlement Size and Number

Date	Total number of settlements	Settlements over 1,000	Settlements 500–999	Settlements 100–499	Settlements under 100	Average settlement size
1700	14–16	1	0	3	10–12	125–143
1829	16–18	2	1	1	11–13	529–625
1851	18	2	1	1	14	584
1879	20	3	0	4	14	501
1907	21	3	1	4	13	562
1940	23	3	3	7	10	518
1961	23	3	3	7	10	520
1991	39	5	1	6	27	344

SOURCE: The data on individual settlements collected in Appendix B.

Ermioni than within. Indeed, much of the population of the other settlements ultimately derives from Ermioni and Kranidhi. Table 5.6 examines the issue in another way. The increase in the eparkhia's population has been matched by an increased number of settlements, with the greatest gain for settlements over 1,000.

The issue of settlement hierarchy illuminates the subregional variation within the eparkhia. Kranidhi is still the capital and major commercial center of the area. However, while Kranidhi was among the fifteen largest Peloponnesian settlements in 1700 and among only six of these remaining in the top fifteen in 1879, by 1991, Kranidhi was far down the list (Panayiotopoulos 1985: 189). Kranidhi is no longer as dominant a center for the region as it once was, a circumstance made ironically clear in construction of the bypass road around it in the 1980s. Kranidhi's fate echoes a common theme in modern Greek history: the disintegration of local hierarchies of power as national life has come to center around Athens. Many early political struggles of the emerging nation were connected to the onset of this centralization (Petropulos 1968). As the administrative structures of Athens gained greater power, local political leaders often found themselves moving there. This phenomenon was compounded in the Ermionidha as wealthy shipping families also saw their economic life shift to Piraeus (Petronoti, this volume). The decline and distribution of monastic land added to the forces flattening local class structures and favoring small family farms and enterprises.

As shown in Table 5.7, this collapse of settlement hierarchy was accompanied by significant change in municipal organization in the Ermionidha. During the nineteenth century, the eparkhia contained variously three or four demoi, including the nearby island of Spetses, which served as an even higher regional center than Kranidhi. As the national government grew, the Greek state placed increased emphasis on smaller municipal divisions with fewer functions (McGrew 1985: 103–114; Meynaud 1965; Petropulos 1968). Sweeping changes in 1912 shifted the nation from a system of few but relatively large demoi to one dominated by many smaller units, each known as a *koinotis* (Drakakis and Koundhouros 1939: 6–10). The four demoi of the eparkhia became eight koinotites, and then seven when Spetses was reallocated to the nomos of Attica after World War II. The number expanded to eight again when Thermisi hived off from Ermioni in 1956. In 1998, under pressure to bring its municipal organization in line with the rest of the European Union, the Greek nation took steps to reverse the proliferation of small ad-

Table 5.7

Municipal Organization of the Ermionidha

1834–1899, 1909–1950: Nomos of the Argolid and Corinthia

Eparkhia of Spetses and Ermionidha

1834–1840, 1866–1912:	Demos of Spetses
	Demos of Masitos (Kranidhi)
	Demos of Ermioni
	Demos of Dhidhima
1840–1866:	Demos of Spetses
	Demos of Kranidhi
	Demos of Ermioni
1912–1950:	Koinotis/Demos of Spetses
	Koinotis of Kranidhi
	Koinotis of Koiladha
	Koinotis of Portokheli
	Koinotis of Fournoi
	Koinotis of Ermioni
	Koinotis of Dhidhima
	Koinotis of Iliokastro

1899–1909, 1950–present: Nomos of the Argolid

1950–present: Eparkhia of the Ermionidha

1950–1956:	Koinotis of Kranidhi
	Koinotis of Koiladha
	Koinotis of Portokheli
	Koinotis of Fournoi
	Koinotis of Ermioni
	Koinotis of Dhidhima
	Koinotis of Iliokastro
1956–1998:	Koinotis of Thermisi added
1998–present:	koinotites consolidated into
	Demos of Ermionis

NOTE: See Drakakis and Koundhouros (1939) and Houliarakis (1973–76) for further discussion of such changes, both in this region and more generally.

ministrative units.[26] All koinotites in the Ermionidha were combined into a single demos known as Ermionis. How much this is a genuine move toward the reestablishment of strong regional administrative structures, however, remains to be seen.

Net Migration

Demographic variation within the Ermionidha is also reflected in changes in different subregional migration patterns. National rates of natural increase were used to calculate the approximate net migration experienced in the Ermionidha during each intercensal period.[27] Table 5.8 summarizes the results for Hydra, Spetses, and the Ermionidha; Table 5.9 treats the three subregions of the Ermionidha. The calculations are necessarily rough and are not broken into annual rates, which would give them greater weight than they deserve. Even in this crude state, however, they indicate the general role played by birth, death, and migration in particular population changes for particular areas. The figures derived by these calculations correspond in general magnitude to records from several censuses showing differences between de facto and de

Table 5.8
Hydra, Spetses, and the Ermionidha: Net Migration

Date	Ermionidha: net migration since last date	Ermionidha: change due to migration (%)	Hydra: net migration since last date	Hydra: change due to migration (%)	Spetses: net migration since last date	Spetses: change due to migration (%)
1829						
1851	1,328	19.2	−16,346	−74.3	−10,603	−70.7
1861	−2,099	−19.9	−4,217	−34.2	−235	−2.6
1870	−13	−0.1	−3,920	−40.6	−3,166	−32.2
1879	−3,203	−27.8	−1,198	−16.1	−2,808	−33.2
1889	−1,572	−15.7	−2,112	−28.8	−2,880	−41.7
1896	1,367	13.5	−33	−0.5	−1,347	−25.9
1907	−2,858	−22.6	−2,766	−38.5	−840	−19
1920	−3,440	−29.1	−2,920	−52.7	−1,680	−39.2
1928	−980	−9.8	36	1.1	175	5.4
1940	752	7.6	−424	−11.4	−495	−13.5
1951	−1,534	−12.9	−1,423	−37.6	−928	−25.5
1961	−1,105	−9.3	−326	−11.5	−103	−3.2
1971	−1,173	−9.8	−492	−17.6	−194	−5.7
1981	−440	−3.7	7	0.3	5	0.1
1991	555	4.5	−499	−18.2	−299	−8

SOURCE: Panayiotopoulos (1985: 247–248), Houliarakis (1973–76: 40), Kriezis (1860: 15–17), Pouqueville (1826: 304), Bory de Saint Vincent (1834–36: 62–77), Rangavis (1853: 285–286), Greece, National Statistical Service (1872, 1880, 1890, 1909, 1921, 1929, 1946, 1955, 1962, 1972, 1982, 1992).

Table 5.9
The Ermionidha: Net Migration

Date	Kranidhi town	Rest of Kranidi region	Ermioni town	Rest of Ermioni region	Dhidhima region	Dhidhima town	Rest of Dhidhima region
1829							
1851	1,720	169	−213	−253	59		
1861	−2,375	237	199	−114	−22		
1870	−645	622	−138	251	19		
1879	−2,633	−364	−241	−24	60		
1889	−1,549	146	−95	96	−171		
1896	815	250	208	−75	164		
1907	−1,997	49	−668	45	−289		
1920	−2,504	−198	−394	304	−357	−476	119
1928	−535	399	−422	−555	133	84	49
1940	−295	264	45	161	577	70	507
1951	−749	−346	−258	341	−524	−204	−320
1961	−755	−99	−106	21	−113	−86	−27
1971	−618	141	−305	−157	−234	−47	−187
1981	−132	−1	−243	230	−20	−127	107
1991	−27	932	183	−315	−219	−90	−129

SOURCE: Panayiotopoulos (1985: 247–248), Houliarakis (1973–76: 40), Kriezis (1860: 15–17), Pouqueville (1826: 304), Bory de Saint Vincent (1834–36: 62–77), Rangavis (1853: 285–286), Greece, National Statistical Service (1872, 1880, 1890, 1909, 1921, 1929, 1946, 1955, 1962, 1972, 1982, 1992).

jure population (Table 5.10).[28] No less than 1,100 of the Ermionidha's legal members were living outside the eparkhia at the time of each census.[29]

Indeed, one of the most significant implications of the migration levels shown in Table 5.8 is that while the Ermionidha has grown in absolute population since 1829, there has nevertheless been fairly constant migration away from it. It has not lost as greatly or steadily as have Hydra

Table 5.10
The Ermionidha: Comparison of
De Facto and De Jure Population

	1879	1907	1928	1940
Ermionidha				
De facto population	10,020	11,803	9,893	11,906
De jure population	11,788	13,487	11,235	13,069
Kranidhi region				
De facto population	6,705	7,588	5,813	6,523
De jure population	8,267	9,533	7,149	7,880
Ermioni region				
De facto population	2,047	2,620	2,361	2,868
De jure population	2,227	2,306	2,301	2,904
Dhidhima region				
De facto population	1,268	1,595	1,719	2,515
De jure population	1,294	1,648	1,785	2,285

SOURCE: Greece, National Statistical Service (1880, 1909, 1921, 1950).

and Spetses, but inward migration has exceeded outward for only three intercensal periods. On balance, the Ermionidha has lost more migrants than it has gained, although this loss has not been so great that it outpaced natural increase. The area has thus not experienced the absolute population decline of the rest of the Peloponnesos. Dhimotoloyia records and interviews indicate that the flow of outward migration has been primarily in the direction of metropolitan Athens, with the areas around Poros and Nafplio as secondary destinations.

While newcomers are fewer than out-migrants, net migration rates nevertheless indicate a steady stream of migrants to the Ermionidha during the last century. Listings in dhimotoloyia of nonlocal birthplaces often confirm movement into the area from other parts, with the Argolid, Arcadia, and Tsakonia figuring most prominently.[30] The 1907 census shows all demoi in the area having some nonmembers present, ranging from 1.2 percent of the total population (Dhidhima) to 23.7 percent (Ermioni). Similar figures are given in the 1928 census (Greece 1909, 1933). In our conversation, the president of Fournoi characterized the origins of his village as *anamikhto* (mixed up), a statement reflecting this long-term pattern of inward migration. It remains clear, however, that after attracting large numbers of migrants in the eighteenth century, the Ermionidha has since drawn considerably fewer and has lost more than it gained, a strong indication that, even in this region of relative demographic health, the force of Athens is still present.

The impact of this outward migration has been differentially felt across the area (see Table 5.9). The town of Kranidhi has sustained greater migratory losses than the rest of the eparkhia. Its total negative net migration is ten times that of all other settlements combined, which is further evidence of the loss of settlement hierarchy in the region.[31] This loss reflects the movement of Kranidhiotes to other communities within the eparkhia, such as the seafarers who moved to coastal villages, as well as a large number of young people moving to Athens.

Closer scrutiny of the eparkhia's patterns of net migration reveals the kinetic nature of the region's population dynamics. In working with similar figures for three other areas of Greece, I have not seen such striking ups and downs.[32] The eparkhia, both as a whole and in its component parts, has repeatedly alternated between positive and negative rates of net migration. There is no single direction to what has occurred. This is a region in motion, and the shifting population levels of its settlements signal strategic moves in response to varied and fluctuating opportunities within it.

Perspectives on the Modern Greek Countryside

The demographic history just recounted lies somewhere between single-village studies and national-level statistics. It has aimed at bringing these two perspectives together in ways that might illuminate both and that might enliven our understanding of the Greek countryside. Too much emphasis on single sites has caused larger systems to be dismissed or treated in formulaic fashion (Marcus 1989; Wolf 1982), while too much on sweeping trends has removed agency and variation from our understanding of local systems (Nash 1981; Seremetakis 1991). Over the last fifteen years there has been increasing interest in intermediate views revealing how global systems are locally experienced and modified, how local institutions reflect more distant processes, and what comes from focusing on the margins rather than the center (D. K. Forbes 1984; Kearney 1986; Shanin 1988; C. Smith 1985; N. Smith 1984). As this study has shown, it does little good to reduce rural Greece to a land of long-lived and inward-looking villages now uniformly dying and depopulated. The situation is, and has always been, more complex.

As Gledhill (1985: 53) says, when looking at small-scale farmers, we need to move beyond static typology to "specific historical models of the formation, transformation and recreation of rural society in regional settings" (see also Netting 1993). As a minimum, the present regional history suggests factors that can sometimes stabilize population in rural Greece: multiple economic opportunities for cash production, easy access to national markets, significant capital accumulation within the last few centuries, and the availability of land. Certainly, the image, amenities, and social connections accompanying the area's development as a center for Athenian vacation housing also played a role.

To view the Ermionidha's history as merely a demographic success story, however, overlooks the internal variations that have led to a loss of settlement hierarchy in the region. Because weak regional centers have long been seen as characteristic of underdeveloped economies (Johnson 1970), some neoclassical planners have harbored the belief that stimulating development would lead to a landscape of strong regional towns in developing nations. The case of the Ermionidha confirms instead the suggestion of Friedmann (1988) and others that involvement in worldwide markets often precipitates the reverse: collapse of local centers toward a primate city (see also D. K. Forbes 1984: 115; C. Smith 1976: 31; N. Smith 1984; Timberlake 1985). Lack of a strong regional hub in the present-day Ermionidha indicates that the real center is offstage, some 90 km to the northeast. This situation underscores the precarious nature of the region's prosperity, if only because there is so much beyond its control.

The present account also supports the idea voiced by Hadjimichalis (1987), Mouzelis (1978), and Vergopoulos (1975) that uneven regional development in Greece does not reflect two separate economies, the developed and the traditional, but rather the different roles played by various regions within the same economy. For centuries rural Greeks have gauged their actions according to external markets. However rustic and remote the Ermionidha once may have seemed to some of us, over the last two centuries its inhabitants ferried the wheat of Russia and the sponges of northern Africa to western Europe. Greece's semiperipheral agricultural role in the global economy has predicated approaches to farming that combine long-standing, labor-intensive technologies with modern market production. The cheese hanging from the ceiling of the Franghos' house in Tsoukalia still finds its way to the shops of Athens.

Greek villages have not been still since antiquity, however they may appear. The goal of which I have been most conscious in this study has been to move beyond exotic, traditional, even cyclical images of Greek villages in order to place them in the stream of history affecting us all. One of the greatest contributions of survey archaeology and historical demography to Hellenic studies has been clear demonstration of the rise and fall of villages throughout Greek history (Panayiotopoulos 1985, Antoniadis-Bibicou 1965, Wagstaff 1982, Wagstaff and Cherry 1982, and Laiou-Thomadakis 1977).[33] The present account and Clarke's contributions in Chapters 6 and 9 of this volume document this process in the southern Argolid.

Such work has enabled a nonessentialist view of villages to emerge. The existence and internal characteristics of these settlements have become variable and contingent, matters for investigation rather than assumed homogeneity. The centuries-old village, a place of cohesive year-round habitation, is but one element in rural Greek landscapes. There are also seasonal and exploratory settlements, dispersed homesteads, abandoned villages, and newly created ones. The history of any particular settlement moves from neutral background to shaping force, providing a window on its articulation with broader economic and political events, and raising new questions on issues long central to village studies. Identification of recent migration into a settlement, for example, can illuminate economic forces at work in that area and also clarify local social relations by focusing attention on the interaction of older and newer residents. In such ways, villages are returned to historical time and active choice and agency to those who reside within them.

Ethnoarchaeological Implications

The information which built this analysis of recent settlement in the Ermionidha parallels that available to survey archaeology concerning past periods: placement and dating of settlements, approximate population size, nature of economic activities, and contacts with more distant areas. The success of any survey project lies in its ability to generate coherent and defensible interpretations of such information concerning past periods. Modern patterns such as are described here can, of course, suggest possibilities. Their ability to do so, however, is unnecessarily limited if they are treated as static templates, with each settlement array deemed to represent one and only one economic and political configuration (Kroll and Price 1991). They are also overly limited if explained by ecological or locational factors alone (van Andel and Runnels 1987). The Ermionidha and its island neighbors of Hydra and Spetses share a common location but very different demographic histories.

Settlement patterns in the present demonstrate complexity and fluidity; those in the past did so as well. Pursuing such themes requires close readings of changes in the sites identified by survey work. The intricacy of recent settlement in the Ermionidha directs archaeologists to scrutinize their data for evidence of expansion, abandonment, use, and reuse of particular locations, as well as what other sites existed in the area during each of these processes (Cameron and Tonka

1993; Horne 1993; Rossignol and Wandsnider 1992). For example, not every phase of a site may be a stand-alone settlement. Seasonal habitations, work stations, even culturally significant features of the natural landscape must be considered (Chang 1992). Tacit assumptions that sites and residential settlements are always the same should also be discarded (Dunnell 1992; Fotiadis 1992).

The present does not precisely repeat the past, and each phase of the past has its own character. Attempts to use any period as a complete analogue for another mask these differences. There is increasing interest, from a variety of philosophical positions, in approaching the complexity of particular places and times on their own terms (David 1992: 342; D. K. Forbes 1984: xii; Hodder 1989: 71; Pred 1990; Stahl 1993). In this light, it is likely that only bits and pieces of present-day patterns will suggest parallels for only bits and pieces of moments in the past. Particular elements acquire new meaning through juxtaposition with other features distinctive to each period. To expose the structures and decision making that are characteristic of a particular time, it is necessary to analyze the full range of settlement and land use in conjunction with such items as land tenure, political organization, trade, kinship structures, ethnic relations, and environmental features (Crumley and Marquardt 1987).

In this light, the recent settlement shifts of the Ermionidha seem most apt for providing interpretive guidance for those periods of the past that witnessed a proliferation of sites and decline in site hierarchy. The disintegration or disappearance of a strong local elite, the availability of land to family farmers, and the existence of a powerful center outside the area become matters worth considering in such cases. In reverse fashion, Jameson's argument (1994) that whenever land was concentrated in the hands of a few in antiquity, most farm laborers lived in towns, provides parallels for understanding the seventeenth and eighteenth century concentration of population in Kranidhi. The analysis of modern times given here also encourages some meeting of the minds between archaeological theories emphasizing local structures and those stressing contact with distant centers (Champion 1989; Kohl 1987; Renfrew 1984; Shortman and Urban 1987). Neither the florescence of Hydra, Spetses, and the Ermionidha in the eighteenth century, nor the events that followed, can be understood without reference to both local and global forces.

This discussion also relates to a theme driving this volume as a whole. When those seeking ethnoarchaeological analogies in the Greek present focus exclusively on the most isolated villages and long-standing technologies, they do so at some risk. Greek rural life has not stood still; those elements which are of considerable antiquity take on new meaning with each context in which they appear (Fotiadis 1995; Gledhill 1985; Stahl 1993; Turner and Brush 1987).[34] A truly isolated village in contemporary Greece would be strange indeed and not necessarily equivalent to a typical Bronze Age village. The maintenance of older production technologies must similarly be seen in light of the semi-peripheral economic relations in which they now exist. The recent settlement and migration history of the Ermionidha offers many possibilities for understanding the past, but isolation and stasis are not among these.

CHAPTER SIX

Changing House and Population Size on Methana, 1880-1996: Anomaly or Pattern?

Mari H. Clarke

The ethnoarchaeology of *fit*, that is causal relationship, between material culture and socio-economic organization, or more specifically, between house size and form, is the focus of this chapter.[1] I examine fit in terms of the membership, residence patterns, and economic activities of smallholding households. Based on the premise that material culture reflects the social and economic order of society, archaeologists have long used site and house area to extrapolate community and household size in the past (Weissner 1974). The spatial distribution of structures within and outside houses has provided the basis for interpretation of economic activities and residence patterns. More recently, ethnoarchaeologists have demonstrated that the relationship of the size and structure of houses to the number, social organization, and economic activities of the householders dwelling therein is replete with anomalies and subject to debate.[2]

Ethnoarchaeological research has shown that simply equating people and social units with floor space and numbers of rooms often results in serious misinterpretation of population size and residence patterns. Research has also demonstrated pitfalls in extrapolating economic activity from structures and artifacts. For example, in the early 1980s, Kramer found that dwelling rooms of the same size in Aliabad, Iran, housed anywhere from two to nine individuals. Numbers of ovens and bins also proved to be misleading indicators of numbers of families in a compound, while such important places as threshing floors and cemeteries were situated outside the bounds of the settlement (Kramer 1982: 86, 120). More recently, Horne has documented reuse of buildings and lack of fit between house structures and households in Bagestan, Iran; twenty-six out of thirty-three households owned and used one or more rooms at some distance from their living quarters (Horne 1994: 1987). Similarly, Chang has shown that herd numbers in a contemporary pastoralist site in Greece were not directly related to the area of pens or folds (Murray and Chang 1986; Chang 1984, and this volume).

Building on this ethnoarchaeological literature, this chapter documents changes in smallholder settlement and house structures on Methana between 1800 and 1996. It traces the ways in which these aspects of material culture are related to certain organizational and economic changes, which are described in more detail in my other chapter in this volume. Over this period, as income from wage labor and business has become increasingly important, smallholders have transformed their houses from shelters that were base units for production into "villas" that are now units for consumption.[3] My analysis identifies and explains four key anomalies in any attempt to directly equate house structure and size with number of householders, residence patterns, and household activities:

1. Changing house size has been inversely related to changing population size.
2. Individual households have owned and used noncontiguous house, shelter, and other structures.
3. Households have shared ownership of houses and other structures (e.g., cisterns, threshing floors).
4. Functions of houses and rooms have changed over the domestic cycle of the household.

I focus here on smallholders—farmers who practice intensive, diversified agriculture on relatively small farms in areas of dense population, relative to the carrying capacity of the land.[4] The smallholder's family, or household, organizes labor and manages resources and consumption. While smallholders produce a significant amount of their food, they also participate in the market, selling farm produce, crafts, and labor (Netting 1993: 2). Smallholders thus live and work at the margins of power and wealth and respond adaptively to these influences, just as they attempt to make the most of the physical environment in which they are situated. Their dwellings are relatively small, and domestic spaces are often multifunctional. Because they have tenure to the land they cultivate, inheritance and residence patterns make a significant imprint on domestic structures and their uses.

To address the issue of fit and particularly the assumption of a direct equation between house size and householder numbers, it is important, given the nature of smallholder life, to focus on the dimensions and spatial arrangement of house structures in relation to the economic activities and social organization within them, to the local environment, and to the larger political economy and ideology in which the smallholders are embedded. It is even more important to consider what aspects of social and economic organization are hidden, or ambiguously reflected, in house form and arrangement and hence to look for ways in which this fit may not be as direct as often assumed. Several elements are necessary for an ethnoarchaeology of smallholder house form and function:

1. using regional analysis to examine the "big picture"—the larger political economy and ecological context;
2. tracing change over time using historical documents and ethnohistorical technique;
3. eliciting and observing the perspectives, decision making, and behavior of individual householders, including both economic strategies and cultural constructs; and
4. analyzing material aspects of the house for how they affect, and are affected by, the social organization, mode of production, cultural constructs, and wider political economy.[5]

Using this approach, I begin with highlights of scholarship on house and settlement form in Greece and then briefly summarize the settlement history of one village on the peninsula of

Methana.[6] I follow this summary with a detailed history of one specific house between 1800 and 1996. I offer hypotheses about the apparent anomalies in fit between house size and householder numbers on Methana. I then conclude with the suggestion that this type of in-depth analysis of the key elements of this relationship in specific contexts is needed for a more accurate interpretation of smallholder structures in the archaeological record.

Studies of House and Settlement Form in Greece

In Greece, there has been a long history of analyses of the relationship between house form and function by archaeologists, architects, folklorists, and, more recently, anthropologists and geographers. While architecture was always a central concern of classical archaeologists in Greece, only in recent decades have the humble houses of ancient villagers been regarded as seriously as temples and other major public structures.[7] Rather than archaeologists, it was Greek folklorists and architects who conducted many of the earliest studies of domestic architecture. They often stressed the ancient origins of house forms as evidence of the continuity of contemporary national identity with classical Greece. For example, Megas's classic study, *The Greek House* (1951), presented detailed typological diagrams showing the evolution of contemporary house forms from ancient models.[8]

Later work in architecture,[9] folklore,[10] and sociocultural anthropology[11] continued this examination of the social and economic facets of domestic architecture. Anthropologists have also studied the symbolic use of space and the cultural rules ordering the arrangement of houses, objects, and people in space.[12] Pavilides and Sutton (1995) recently synthesized the insights of both architects and anthropologists regarding the built environment in Greece, concluding that

> historical reconstructions of architecture and social relations require attention to oral histories, archival material, and dating of buildings through visual examination of their features and accounts of their construction. The local system exists in a framework of regional, national, and international systems. This observation directs attention to the kinds of economic, political, and cultural links existing at various points in time, such as critical moments of encounter and transformation, changing avenues for information exchange, evolving schools of architectural thought, and building technologies and codes (1995: 286).

Geographical studies of rural Greek settlements up to the late 1960s presented house and settlement typologies based on characteristics of the landscape (Wagstaff 1969: 308). More recent work takes a general systems approach, in the context of interdisciplinary work examining political and economic, as well as physical factors, affecting settlement (e.g., Renfrew and Wagstaff 1982).[13] Anthropologists working with regional archaeological surveys have examined house and settlement form as one of the adaptive strategies used to make a living from the environment through farming and herding.[14]

The most promising results in Greece have been produced from such interdisciplinary collaboration between anthropologists, archaeologists, geographers, architects, and others in regional survey projects, starting with the Minnesota Messenia Expedition in the 1960s (McDonald and Rapp 1972; McDonald and Aschenbrenner 1980) and followed by similar work in the southern Argolid (Jameson 1976; Jacobsen 1985; Jameson, Runnels, and van Andel 1994), as well as other parts of Greece, including Kea, Nemea, Corinth, Boeotia, Crete, and Grevena (Cherry 1994; Keller and Rupp 1983; Kardulias 1994; Renfrew and Wagstaff 1982; Cherry, Davis, and Mantzourani 1991; Watrous 1982; Snodgrass 1987; Chang and Koster 1986). These regionally focused projects facilitated the analysis, beyond disciplinary boundaries, of rural Greek domestic architecture and use of space. For example, Aschenbrenner examined changing contemporary house form and settlement pattern as a part of the Messenia Expedition (1972, 1976), while Jameson combined archaeological and ethnographic data to trace various factors affecting the use of space in classical Greek domestic architecture (Jameson 1990).[15]

Such studies of domestic architecture and settlement patterns in Greece have documented great variety in the form and use of human shelter. They suggest that domestic space is shaped by the political economy, the local economy, and ideology—through effects on the standard of living, markers of prestige, style and local tradition, as well as the resources and constraints of the physical environment. These studies provide a wealth of description with potential for comparative purposes. The features described and the detail provided differ among scholars, however, often limiting comparative analyses that could offer insights for archaeological interpretation. There is thus a need for systematic approaches to the ethnoarchaeology of house form and function, such as the one presented at the beginning of this chapter.

Changing House and Settlement Pattern

The changing house and settlement pattern in Liakotera[16] falls into three periods that are based on the building activity of householders, which, in turn, reflects major changes in the larger political economy: (1) the late Turkish period, (2) Postindependence, and (3) post-World War II. These periods are congruent with divisions Liakoterans use when they describe events and experiences in the past—*epitourkokratia* (during Turkish rule), *prin apo to polemo* (before the war, implying World War II), and *meta apo to polemo* (after World War II and the Greek Civil War that followed).

During the late Turkish period, the settlement consisted of a line of nine or ten tiny, one-room, mud-roofed shelters hidden in the bushes along the path that connected villages on the peninsula. The linear settlement pattern was oriented to the landscape and the paths across it. Two or three smallholder families constructed the dwellings as bases for their near subsistence farming and livestock raising on the flat areas near the village and nearby hillsides. Although the houses were small structures (roughly 8 m long, 2.4 m wide, and less than 2 m high), they had many occupants. Figure 6.1 shows the exterior of a mud-roofed house still in use in 1974. Liakoterans constructed these dwellings using local stone, mud, wood, and other materials. Unlike the mud roofs of the Cycladic islands, which were supported by vaulting (Kenna 1995), the weight of this heavy, flat mud roof was carried by very thick stone walls (just under 1 m thick) and twisted juniper boughs mounted across the walls. The smallholders placed a layer of heather and seaweed between the wood supports and the mud roof. Figure 6.2 shows these wood supports for the roof. After each rainfall, smallholders used a heavy stone roller to smooth the mud roof. Walls consisted of two courses of stone with rubble between them. Mud was used for mortar. The fireplace was built in the middle of the long wall of the house. The chimney was a hole in the roof protected from the wind by a few stones.

Figure 6.1. Mud-roofed house, Methana.

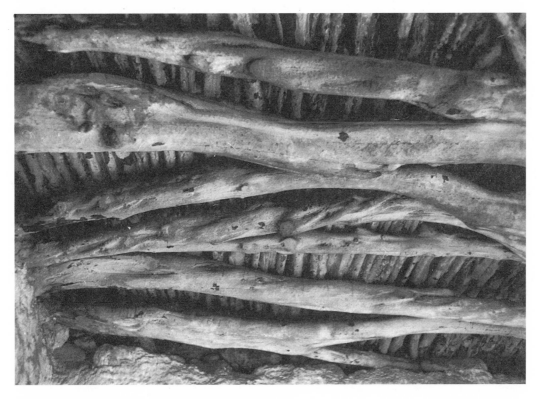

Figure 6.2. Ceiling of a mud-roofed house, Methana.

Figure 6.3.   Room space of a mud-roofed house, Methana.

Shelter and food storage for people and animals were the main functions of housing at this time. Figure 6.3 shows the simple, utilitarian furnishings of a mud-roofed house. Comfort and appearance were not major concerns. Instead, smallholders directed their energy toward construction of cultivation terraces and paths. There was no public space in the village, except in the chapels and the cemetery at its edge. Business, men's daily drinking, and celebrations took place in and around the house. Men and women spent most of their time working in the fields. Women also spent long hours spinning cotton, flax, and wool with drop spindles, as well as weaving on pit looms to produce clothing and blankets.

After Independence, the village did not start expanding significantly until the 1860s. In 1851, an estimated 39 households with 7.8 persons per household lived in Liakotera and the neighboring hamlet (Rangavis 1853). From 1850 through 1900, Liakoterans constructed 27 new two-room, two-storied houses, 12 of which were built in the 1870s. These houses were more than shelters; they were part of an estate, which also included farm land, for sons. Smallholders continued to construct terraced fields. They also dug many cisterns and built stone threshing floors. During this period, Liakoterans also relocated the cemetery on another site outside the village.

In another burst of building activity in the 1900s, ten additional houses were built, as well as a large village church. By 1911, the village had reached its present nucleated form; most of the contemporary buildings had been constructed. The village population reached its peak around 1911 with 239 inhabitants in 50 households—an average of 4.8 people per household. Liakotera maintained a steady size until the end of World War II.

The predominant house form during this second period was the two-room, two-storied, low-pitched tile-roofed house, roughly 10 m by 6 m in size (see Figure 6.4). Local builders and itinerant masons from northern Greece and the central Peloponnesos constructed these houses using local stone and mud as well as imported lumber and ceramic tiles. Such lumber enabled Liakoterans to build wider houses with more windows. No longer concerned to hide their dwellings from raiders, they whitewashed the walls inside and out.

The central frame for the low pitched roof of these prewar houses consisted of a central beam on top of two wooden triangles. Two beams stretched from the base of each triangle to one corner of the house. Builders placed wooden struts from the center beams onto the walls. On the struts they placed boards or locally grown canes. Figure 6.5 shows an interior view of this type of roof. Figure 6.6 shows the recent retiling of a roof, as well as basic roof construction and placement of ceramic tiles. In this type of house, the fireplace was on the short wall of the house, and a ceramic chimney was added. Householders purchased construction materials and labor using profits from sales of olive oil and, to a lesser extent, wine, almonds, and lambs or kids, as well as using wages earned in distant lands and in the Greek merchant marine. Furnishings remained simple.

Although social life and business still centered in the house at this time, a public space appeared around the large, new village church. It was not by accident that the new Orthodox Church claimed the center of Liakotera and other villages in newly independent Greece. Other than construction of the village school in 1930, there was little building activity in Liakotera between 1911 and the end of the Greek Civil War. A number of Liakoterans were directing their

Figure 6.4. Tile-roofed house, Methana.

Figure 6.5. Ceiling of a tile-roofed house, Methana.

Figure 6.6. Retiling a roof, Methana.

resources elsewhere. By the 1880s, some Liakoterans had invested in land on the nearby plain of Troizinia and in farmland outside of Athens, in what is now the suburb of Brakhami. Around the turn of the century, Liakoterans also purchased land in the port town and constructed houses to be rented to the people who came from Athens and elsewhere to take mineral baths at the health spa, which opened in 1887.

In the postwar period, new house styles began to appear as houses became units for consumption at the same time as smallholder incomes increasingly came from wage labor and business. Up to this period, the design and layout of houses in Liakotera were fairly uniform, with the exception of one elaborate house, which by the 1970s was being used only for storage. With greater access to cash to purchase goods after the war, women stopped weaving household clothing and blankets (J. Koster, this volume). In the 1960s, three new single-storied houses were built for nuclear families along the vehicle road, which had reached the village in 1958. Two were stone houses with low-pitched tile roofs. One was a brick house with a flat, concrete roof. These houses had three rooms and a hall. Around the same time, two stores opened and a tiny governmental office was constructed on the square around the church.

By 1972, there were 40 houses in Liakotera, occupied by 161 people, with an average of 3.4 people per household. Thirty percent of these households were stem households, including more than one generation of adults and their children. From the 1970s through the present, there has been a great deal of house remodeling, facilitated by the arrival of electricity in 1971, running water in 1972, and the asphalt road, surfaced in 1972.

By the end of the 1980s, nearly half the village householders had added special purpose rooms, bedrooms, kitchens, and bathrooms—in brick or cement block. These houses and their furnishings displayed socioeconomic status, so that Liakoterans called the fanciest of these houses villas. Figure 6.7 shows two "villas" quite different in design. Liakotera's population declined significantly during this period. As the port town expanded and people continued to migrate to Athens, Methana's mountain villages shrank. By 1987, there were 42 houses with 118 householders in Liakotera—an average of 2.8 people per household. Houses thus had more space and more rooms, but fewer people.

In the 1980s, a new type of house appeared on the edge of the village: the holiday house. These were built not by contemporary Liakoterans but by former Liakoterans, or their descendants, who wanted a place of their own with modern conveniences for their visits to the village. A house was also built by a man from Crete, the first of the non-Methanites to own land in the village. There was also remodeling of parental homes by migrant children who had married spouses from other parts of Greece with different traditions in domestic architecture. Migrant children also wanted to provide more comfort for their elderly parents, who were tilling the soil without their help, and to make their parents' houses more attractive for their own visits to the village. By 1996, there were thirty occupied houses in Liakotera, with a total of seventy-two full-time residents, a total of 2.4 people per house, and only five stem households. In addition, there were ten empty houses and fifteen holiday houses.

House remodeling, addition of stucco to the outside walls of the village church, and introduction of marble tombstones in the cemetery reflect the influence of Athenian styles and consumerism, as well as the effect of migration to Athens, Piraeus, and the port town. The square

Figure 6.7. "Villas," Methana.

formed by the stores and government office, with the church at its center, concretely reflects growing Liakoteran involvement in, and subjection to, the larger political economy. With the holiday houses, not only had Athenian and other regional styles affected the form of Liakoteran dwellings, but Athens itself had invaded the village at the same time as the port town was beginning to look and function like an Athenian suburb.

A House History

Just as the configuration of the settlement changed from linear to nucleated over time, the shape of most buildings also changed with remodeling over the years. Not all houses changed in the same way or at the same time. Some people were quicker than others to adopt new techniques and styles. Every householder with a flat, mud-roofed house eventually demolished and rebuilt the house or raised the height of the walls and replaced the roof with a low-pitched tile roof. Some householders created houses for sons by making additions to storage sheds, leaving little of the original structure. Not all householders added extra rooms, and those who did differed in how elaborately they furnished and decorated the rooms. Examination of the history of one house, and the generations of householders that resided therein, reveals in greater detail some of these changes. It also demonstrates how individual and family decisions have shaped changing house forms and responded to a variety of influences.[17]

I selected this particular case because it shows the transformation of an older, mud-roofed house into a low-pitched, tile-roofed dwelling and the addition of rooms serving different functions. It also documents a decrease in the ratio of residents to floor space over time. Such changes characterize the shift from houses as units for production to houses as units for consumption. The case also illustrates a common pattern of owning two houses that serve different functions at different points in the domestic cycle. It also shows how structures are shared with other households. This history further documents the disappearance of a house through reuse of the wall stones in construction of several other structures, including a paved path. The remaining rubble was removed to a refuse site.

The case house belongs to a smallholder household that had minimal income from wages throughout the period described here. The cash for house remodeling came primarily from crop and animal sales and, in the last three or four decades, from the sale of herbs, noodles, and other produce in the summer street market (Clarke, 1997). Kinsmen also donated skilled labor for various tasks (H. Koster, Forbes, this volume). By 1995, the adult sons, who had migrated to Athens and Khalkhidhiki, had begun to contribute remittances and labor for additional house refinements. Some of the other householders expanded their dwellings earlier and more elaborately, using additional income from wages or businesses in the port town of Methana and apartments rented out in Athens. Figure 6.8 graphically summarizes the transformation of this house and household from 1900 through 1988.

Apostolis was born in 1819 in a village near Liakotera.[18] He was the first Velioti to live in Liakotera, and all of the Veliotidhes in the village are his descendants. Apostolis married into Liakotera as a *soghambros*, that is, he moved into the house of his wife's family. They lived in a small, flat, mud-roofed house, among the bushes in a string of similar houses along the path that connected the villages on the peninsula. The house was roughly 8 m by 2.5 m and 1.75 m in height, with one room and few furnishings. Apostolis's in-laws had constructed the house from local stone, wood, and mud around 1800, or possibly earlier.[19]

There was storage space under the lower half of this house, because it was built against the mountain slope. The house and storage areas were full of wine barrels, vessels for olive oil, a large wooden grain chest, and other goods. The household also stored grain and oil in round stone structures on the mountain, away from the house, to protect their food supply from raiders who came by sea. They kept their livestock in a walled enclosure roughly 5 m from the house in fair weather and in the storage area under the house in bad weather. They built a cistern near the house and a threshing floor on the slope opposite the village; both structures were later shared by Apostolis's sons.[20] They also constructed high terrace walls to carve fields out of the mountainside. They also built a small shed, with fireplace, high on the mountain (around 500 m in altitude), near their grapevines, with a *patitiri* inside the shed for pressing their grapes there (see Figure 6.9). The cows that served as beasts of burden moved very slowly (Forbes, this volume), so that it was more efficient to stay on the mountain during the harvest and transport only the grape juice back to their wine barrel in the village. The family also remained on the mountain to guard their grapes against theft by people from other villages on the peninsula.

One of Apostolis's sons, Paraskevas, born in 1853, remained in the house and brought his wife there from another village, about one and a half hours' walk away. In 1885, when she arrived, aged 24, she found a tiny village with many mud-roofed houses hidden among tall bushes. The house had not changed since Apostolis had arrived years before (see Figure 6.8a). It sheltered Paraskevas, his parents, and his wife and eight children. Only five of Paraskevas's eight children

Figure 6.8. The changing Velioti household, Methana. From architectural drawing of house remodeling, Village Register, author's census. Dates in parentheses are birth dates.

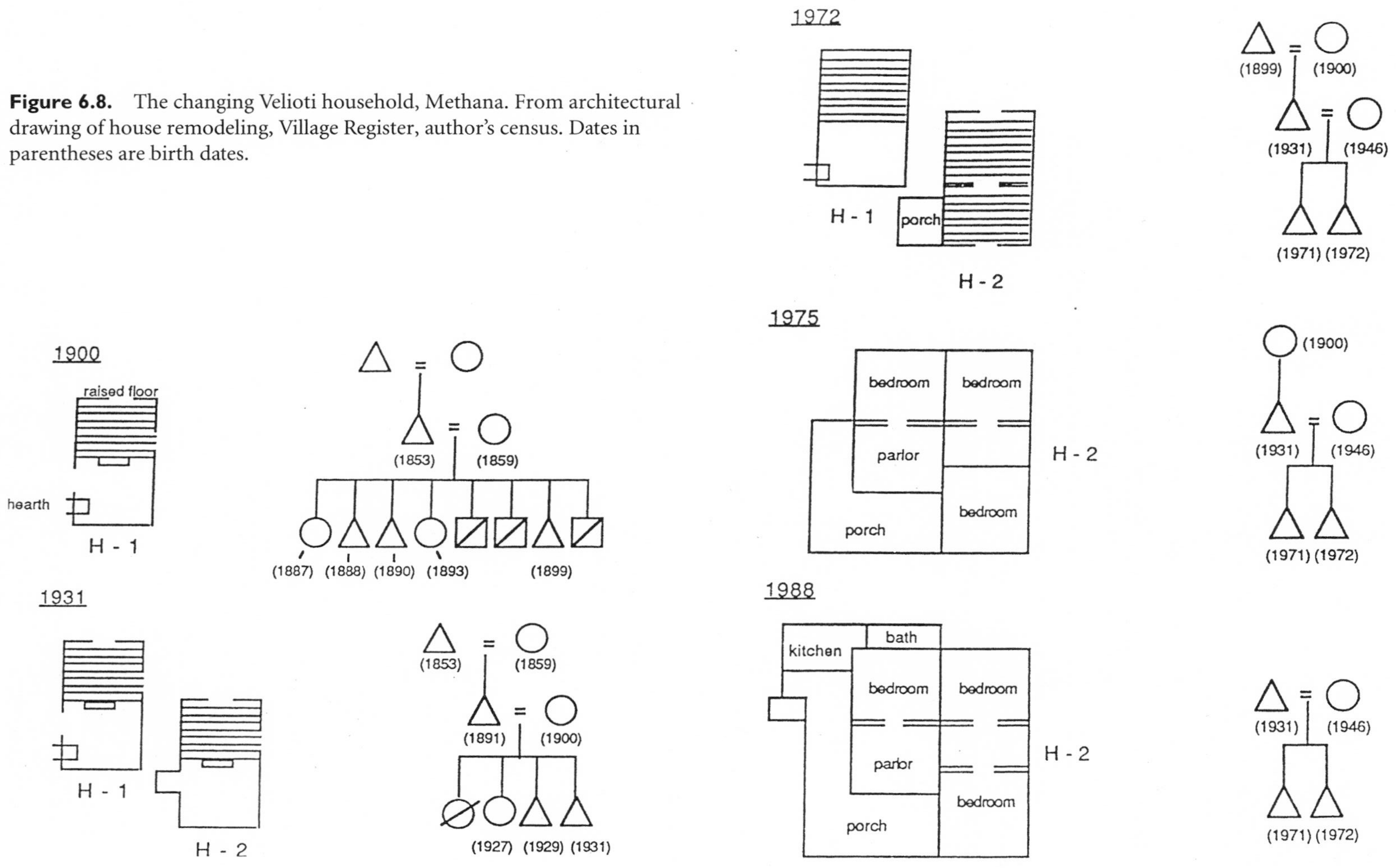

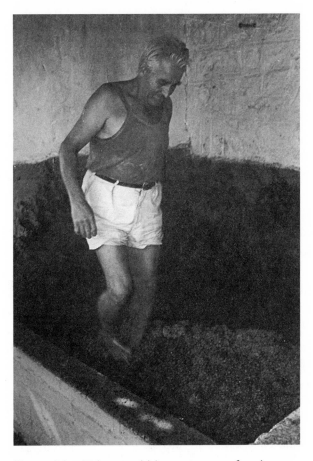

Figure 6.9.   Using a *patitiri* to press grapes for wine.

survived to adulthood. Their youngest child, Ulysses, born in 1899, stayed in the household, helping his parents till the soil. In 1926 he brought his Liakoteran bride to live there.

In 1925, Paraskevas purchased the adjacent house, a larger mud-roofed house (12 m by 3.7 m), from another family in the village (see Figure 6.8b). They used the second house for storage of the big grain chest, and other goods, leaving more living space in the original house. Ulysses and his wife, Afrodhiti, put glass in the windows and replaced the mud-roofs of both houses with cement in 1927. They raised the house walls when they did this. Because they had purchased enough pack animals to carry grapes relatively quickly down to the village for pressing, they constructed a patitiri in the storeroom of the house and no longer stayed on the mountain during the grape harvest. They also assisted Afrodhiti's sister and her husband, who lived in an adjacent house, in replacing their flat mud-roof with tiles and a pitched roof. They purchased the tiles and lumber in Piraeus, transporting the materials by a small trading vessel to the coast below the village, where they were loaded onto donkeys and mules. Afrodhiti recalled carrying lumber on her shoulder up the steep path, a forty-minute walk from the village.

In 1931, Ulysses lent their second house to the village to use as a school until a school building was completed. Ulysses and Afrodhiti had three children, a daughter born in 1926, and two sons born in 1929 and 1931. The daughter married a carpenter in Methana's port town, the younger son went on to high school and became a government employee in Aegina, while the oldest son, Aryiris, remained in the household, helping his parents cultivate the land. Ulysses' parents lived with him and his wife—his mother until she died at the age of 105, his father, Paraskevas, until he died at the age of 90.

In the early 1960s, when Aryiris was still a bachelor, he raised the roof of the second house even higher and replaced the flat roof with a low-pitched tile roof. The flat, cement-covered mud roof had been falling down, chip by chip, so that he decided it should be changed. He also realized that he would not find a bride willing to live in the house as it was. His father, his brother-in-law (a carpenter), his distant cousin (a roof tiler), and a builder from the port town helped him. Aryiris paid for the building costs from the sale of livestock and crops and from wages paid him for work for other smallholders and on construction of the road. He also dug out the area under the upper room that backed against the mountain slope, thus doubling the storage area under the house. Aryiris built a wooden partition separating the house into two rooms and added ceilings below the rafters in all the rooms (see Figure 6.8c). His was one of the last flat mud roofs in the village to be converted to tile.

Aryiris's bride came from central Greece. Her father, who was a trader and farmer who traveled to Methana regularly, arranged the marriage with Aryiris's parents. After the wedding, Aryiris and his wife, Lucia, slept in the second house with the tile roof, while his parents, Ulysses and Afrodhiti, stayed in the remaining mud-roofed house. Both couples prepared meals and worked in the fields together. Lucia delivered sons in 1971 and 1972. As babies they slept in their parents' room, but later they slept in their own room with individual beds. Lucia took the boys to visit their grandparents in central Greece at least once a year.

In 1975, Aryiris and Lucia added an extension of 4.2 m by 9 m to the second house. This created two new rooms: a bedroom for Aryiris's parents and another room for guests (see Figure 6.8d). They also extended the porch. Aryiris decided the mud roof in the old house was getting weak; he feared it would collapse on his parents. Many years ago a mud roof had fallen in on another family during an earthquake. Lucia also wanted an extra room she could set aside for guests and eventually furnish as a parlor (saloni), as people did in central Greece where she grew up.

Aryiris partially demolished the old house to get stones for the room extension. By 1978, he had reused the rest of the good stones in construction of animal shelters on the slope above the house. He also paved the yard with stones so it would not be muddy in the rainy winter. He hired a truck to carry off the remaining rubble to a nearby dry riverbed, where the villagers dumped the scraps from their remodeling efforts.

In 1983, Aryiris added a kitchen (4.2 m by 2.6 m) with a fireplace at the end of the house. He used cement blocks that he had made himself by pouring cement into wooden forms. For the sake of economy, he put a corrugated fiberglass roof on the kitchen. By 1993, he had installed running water in the kitchen and had added an indoor bathroom (2.5 m by 1.9 m) with a flush toilet and shower. Earlier they had only a water spigot in the yard near the kitchen and an outdoor pit toilet. By 1995, their sons had left the village to pursue livelihoods in the city, leaving only the parents in the large house that had been constructed on top of the small house where nine people had resided in 1900, and even more people earlier.

Today the house has a refrigerator, a woodstove, built-in wooden cupboards and drawers, a bed for every member and two for guests, a standing wooden wardrobe, a sewing machine, the trunks moved from the old house, three tables and numerous chairs, as well as cooking utensils and a bottled gas stove. The guest room has carved wood decorating the base of the ceiling light. Shelves display good dishes and items collected on visits to various saint's day celebrations beyond the peninsula. The saloni doubles as a workroom for noodle production for the summer street market. The bread oven in the yard, opposite the site of the old house, is covered, so that rain does not prevent bread making, but increasingly they buy bread from the bakery truck that passes through the village.

Figure 6.8 summarizes the transformation of the Velioti house and household between 1900 and 1988. Today no trace remains of the mud-roofed house. The stone threshing floor, like those of other families, is covered with grass. It was last used in the early 1970s. All that remains of the shelter on the mountain is only a trace of wall foundations, as is the case for other mountain shelters. Many of the terrace walls have fallen down as well; the fields are overgrown with brush. These crumbling artifacts of intensive labor starkly reflect the transformation of the household economy and houses from units for production to units for consumption.

The Velioti case also illustrates the strong association of the house with residence and inheritance patterns, as well as with parental responsibilities to provide estates, including houses, for their children and with children's responsibility to care for parents in their old age.[21] The purchase and remodeling of the second house prior to Ulysses' marriage had clearly been intended as investments for his future, just as the later remodeling prior to Aryiris's marriage was intended for his future. Expansion of the house provided for the well-being of the elder parents as well as the young sons.

This case does not show, however, the postwar trend for many Methanites toward provision of urban real estate rather than of farmland as inheritance for the futures of sons and daughters. Parents who had the economic means to do so purchased apartments in the Greater Athens area for children, but they referred to them as houses (*spitia*) rather than apartments (*diamerismata*). The Velioti family lacked the means for such investments. Instead, they gave their sons a higher education, so that they could earn salaries and build their own houses in the future.

The creation of more living space, with special purpose rooms and the increase in material goods, was influenced by styles from Athens and other regions, as well as greater access to cash and consumer goods, even for full-time farmers with limited wage income. Aryiris said that his remodeling design copied the style of a relative's house in Piraeus that he liked. Elder Liakoterans often talked about past days, when everyone slept on the floor together in one room "like sardines." Based on that experience, they insisted that it is much better for different generations to sleep separately in beds, since it is more comfortable, healthier, and better for household relations. A few people even commented: "in those days, we lived like animals, now we live like humans."

Anomaly or Pattern? The Fit Between Houses and Householders

Analysis of the "big picture"—the larger political economy of the region over time—and of the physical environment, as well as an understanding of the house construction, destruction, and remodeling decisions made by smallholders, and careful observation of architectural features have enabled me to identify critical influences on house size and form on Methana during the time period considered in this chapter. This identification of influences, in turn, revealed that the apparent anomalies in regard to the commonly assumed direct fit between house size and household size were actually frequently occurring patterns in which the relationship between these variables was indirect and complex.

Changes in Liakoteran house form and function reflect ongoing changes in the political economy of Greece. Liakoterans dwelling in tiny shelters during the late Turkish period were part of a market and administrative system very different from the centralized system of today—one based on island sea powers, trade, smuggling, and tribute—all working unofficially within the Turkish empire. With Independence of the Greek state and expansion of the market economy, Liakoterans gained access to national systems and resources, as well as a greater degree of physical security, but at the cost of increased control of the state over them, in the form of taxes, price controls, and the registration of property, births, deaths, marriages, and migration.

Throughout this early period, the settlements of Methanites were relatively near the centers of power and commerce in Greece, but Methanites never had much share in the wealth and prosperity associated with these centers. Methana remained part of a class system extending beyond the peninsula, with its elites located first in Hydra and Poros and later in Piraeus and Athens. Methanites remained in a lower class—neither serfs nor gentry, just poor smallholders with determination to improve their lot. This status and their pragmatic tactics were reflected in local architecture. There was a marked absence of large, elaborate houses constructed in the villages of Methana in the late nineteenth and early twentieth centuries. Even in the port town, people invested in commercial hotels and stores, rather than private mansions. In contrast, in the regional centers of power, such as Hydra, Poros, and Kranidhi, shippers and traders constructed elaborate mansions (Arnaoutoglou 1986, Michaelides 1967, Stamatiou 1937, Stavrolakis 1979, Petronoti, this volume).

For more than half the period examined (roughly 1800–1911), smallholder houses were modest shelters protecting residents, food, and animals from the elements and from raiders who came by sea in the unruly days of the late Turkish period. Houses that were constructed from materials found in the local environment blended nearly imperceptibly into the landscape. The resources and constraints of their rocky environment led villagers to construct houses on the flanks of the mountain to preserve precious, tiny flat areas for cultivation and to build stone walls for terraces on the mountainside for cultivating the rich volcanic soil.

As cultivation expanded to new areas, higher on the mountain, smallholders constructed simple stone shelters for use in cultivating and defending these crops. It is important to keep in mind that house construction may have been of no more importance than the building of terrace walls, threshing floors, cisterns, and hidden storage areas. All were essential for smallholders to survive and to expand their areas of production. The conditions that can be associated with tiny houses and emphasis on construction of other buildings despite large households during this period were an expansion into new environments with no constraint on moving into unoccupied territory and a loose administrative system that provided no protection from brigandage.

The larger, tile-roofed, white-washed houses using purchased lumber and builders from outside the peninsula coincided with Greek Independence, development of a centralized market economy, faster sea transportation, and a more secure countryside. Expansion into new environments and building of new shelters continued, reaching even into the malaria-ridden plain of Troizinia and farmlands outside of Athens. Growth of the national economy developed new markets for agricultural products but at the same time provided other sources of income which, in time, superseded agriculture. Many sons of smallholders became small businessmen, skilled workmen, sailors, and bureaucrats off the peninsula. Some Liakoterans began to arrange the marriages of their daughters with men who were not farmers. Key elements associated with the appearance of larger houses and large households were the growing economy and transportation system and improved security. Over time, however, these same elements led to continued growth in the size of houses, but decrease in the size of households. Limited infrastructure, particularly lack of roads, still provided some constraint on house construction.

In the post-World War II period, increased cash, significant outmigration, and urban styles influenced house construction as people moved back and forth between Athens and Methana and children married spouses from other parts of Greece. A more developed infrastructure greatly facilitated the expansion of houses. Greater access to cash enabled consumerism, leisure time, holiday houses, and travel to other parts of Greece to see different architectural styles and collect artifacts to decorate houses. Key features associated with this phase of house development were continued economic growth, a strong central state, infrastructural development, leisure time, migration, and intermarriage with people from other regions.

At no time during the entire period examined did the houses in Liakotera fully reflect the economy of the householders dwelling therein. Even during the Turkish period, shelters and storage structures beyond the settlement were important parts of the livelihood. Thus, viewed in this broader historical and political economic context, the seeming anomalies to a direct fit between houses and householders make sense and even emerge as more common than not. The inverse relationship between floor space and household size reflects the transition from a period of insecurity and of expansion of agricultural production into new resource areas to one of security, economic growth, expanded infrastructure, and nonfarm opportunities that enabled the construction of villas rather than units or shelters to support production.

Ownership of noncontiguous houses and other productive buildings was part of a strategy of agricultural expansion later redirected to urban areas. Patterns of dowry and equal partible inheritance also yielded ownership of noncontiguous structures and land holdings (Clarke 1988, 1998; Adams, Forbes, this volume). Shared buildings resulted from such inheritance patterns as the population expanded and parents passed on productive resources to their children.

The changing functions of structures over time, with the same building operating as dwelling, storage area, and/or animal shed, were related to stem household structure and residence patterns. A number of stem households, from the past through the present, have used two houses even though they functioned as one household. The way these two dwellings were used, however, changed over the course of the domestic cycle. The second house often served as a storage area until the son married, and often until his wife had a child. Then the younger family started using the second house for sleeping but continued meals and farming tasks together. In some cases, meals were prepared separately or the younger woman cooked and carried food to the elders' house. When one or both of the elders could no longer manage to care for themselves, they moved into the younger couple's house.

Changing house form in Liakotera may reflect a pattern common for smallholders in many areas of Greece in the past, and potentially other parts of the Balkans and Mediterranean, where smallholders were part of an economic system focused on external centers of power. For example, elsewhere in the Argolid in the nineteenth century, one finds single-room, mud-roofed structures, both in Dhidhima (Koster 1977) and Fournoi (Gavrielides 1976c). The simplicity of such house forms and the sparsity of possessions sharply contrast with the picture painted by Petronoti of Kranidhiote houses adorned with European furnishings (this volume).

It appears that, like the Methana smallholders at that time, Dhidhimiotes and Fourniotes were part of a larger system that gave them little access to the wealth and power held by its elites. At the same time, construction of multiple dwellings in different areas of cultivation may reflect a pattern of expansion into new resource areas in which elites had no interest or control. Some shelters developed into full-blown settlements, as was the case with Liakotera; others lacked suitable resources or location and were abandoned, such as those near the vines higher on the mountain. Such expansion into new areas seems most likely to take place under weak administrative systems and/or with the availability of newly opened land.[22]

Clearly there is value in ethnoarchaeological work that takes into account the macrolevel of political economy, environmental constraints, and historical shifts as well as the microlevel of household decision making in order to interpret the relationship between the architectural form and the size of smallholder houses. Hopefully other scholars will be inspired to follow suit and engage in a comparative analysis of the many patterns that suggest a less than direct fit between house size and household size. The increasing understanding of the complexity of this relationship could form the basis for the kind of flexible and contextualized archaeological interpretation suggested in this volume.

The Material Culture and Settlement History of Agro-Pastoralism in the Koinotis of Dhidhima: An Ethnoarchaeological Perspective

Claudia Chang

More than twenty years ago I spent thirteen months collecting ethnoarchaeological data on the architecture, construction, and spatial arrangements of animal folds (*mandria*) found in Dhidhima.[1] These data made up the bulk of a doctoral thesis in which I explicitly set out to provide a number of ethnographic comparisons about village animal husbandry that would serve as "analogies" for examining animal husbandry in ancient Greek economy (Chang 1981). The ideas spawned from this doctoral research and my subsequent publications had their origins in these fieldwork data collected during 1978 and 1979. The world has changed over these last two decades, both in how archaeologists integrate ethnographic data into their archaeological research projects and in how Greek farmers and herders have been affected by Greece's entry into the European Community in 1982. Dhidhima herders who once stayed overnight in huts next to flocks sheltered in folds now travel twice daily between their village homes and these folds. Although herding continues to be a low status occupation, recent subsidies and agricultural policies have allowed most Greek herders to live a life with as many amenities as their urban relatives. In twenty years we have seen, in both the people we have studied and in our own discipline, tremendous strides toward the recognition of a fully integrated, global economy where the practice of animal husbandry is not isolated from larger market forces (Koster and Chang 1994). The goal of this chapter is to present my original fieldwork data in a brief synopsis and synthesis. This synthesis then allows for an opportunity to explore the changes taking place in the Greek countryside and its people, and to relate how social scientists like myself account for such changes, as well as how we undergo "paradigm shifts" as a response to a nonstatic world.

I began my work labeling myself as an ethnoarchaeologist. My objective was to use ethnographic descriptions of the pastoral architecture of Dhidhima herders as the basis for studying animal husbandry in ancient economies. Over the years there has been considerable debate about how ethnoarchaeologists use ethnographic data to make archaeological arguments. After all, the past is not the present, nor vice versa. Twenty years ago, however, I simply began with the understanding that my fieldwork contributed both to archaeologists who wished to reconstruct prehistoric economies based on animal keeping and to ethnographers who examined land use practices of farmers and others in contemporary rural communities. The nature of the academic enterprise back then, however, was such that my fuzzy notions of how my research contributed to two different disciplines placed me and the work in the category of "neither fish nor fowl." My main objective in revisiting these fieldwork data almost twenty years later is to provide an honest evaluation of where contributions were made on both sides of the ledger—archaeological and ethnographic—and of how I might suggest new directions for Greek ethnography and archaeology. My analysis accounts for the tremendous changes in what social scientists observe and describe in the lives of Greek rural villagers.

When I revisit my thoughts, ideas, and cherished hopes for what appeared to be the promising field of ethnoarchaeology in the late 1970s, I find that three major areas of interest for reconstructing a pastoral economy formed my thinking. These areas continue to represent my main focus points, but the way I approach them has evolved. They include: (1) how the planning and construction of the animal fold reflect herd numbers and composition, as well as a symbolic view of the pastoral world in village thought; (2) the study of rural animal husbandry practices in an agro-pastoral setting; and (3) the decisions made by herders in locating their animal folds at places where critical resources such as pasture lands and agricultural fields can be easily reached. I have based my discussions on two assumptions: first, the Dhidhima animal fold is an *artifact* of the economic, social, and symbolic aspects of village herding in rural Greece; and second, the Mediterranean landscape is a geographic feature that shapes the herding and farming activities practiced by smallholders,[2] so that the locations of animal folds are a result of how herders lay territorial claims to pasture resources.

The Dhidhima herders who kept sheep and goats in a village context in the late 1970s were enmeshed in a complicated system of land tenure that included cereal farming, olive cultivation, orchards, and small vegetable gardens. Their participation in intensive agriculture as well as village herding is of special importance to both archaeologists and ethnographers. Animal husbandry practices that do not fit into the more exotic categories of nomadic pastoralism or the Western versions of ranches have often been overlooked. The frequent response to my doctoral research was that Dhidhima herders were not nomadic pastoralists and therefore, the suggestion was often made, my case was an inappropriate analogy when used to describe the typical animal husbandry systems found among ancient rural populations. By the mid-1980s, based partially on the work reported here, we (Chang and Koster 1986) were able to expand the category of pastoralism in archaeological studies to include village herding in the continuum of pastoral adaptations in the Mediterranean. More recently, especially for archaeologists and ancient historians working in Greece, the issue has even become whether *pastoral transhumance*, the seasonal movement between winter and summer pastures, served rather as an exceptional pattern of pastoral mobility, while mixed herding and farming communities predominated during ancient and historical periods (Cherry 1988, Halstead 1987, 1990).

In 1978 and 1979, 10 percent, or 160 households, participated in keeping flocks of sheep or goats. The main artifacts of their animal husbandry system were mandria, or animal folds made of brush, stone, concrete, or tin, usually located away from the main residential area of the village. One of the goals of my initial research project was to establish a series of material correlates from these herding sites that could then be applied to the archaeological study of pastoral architecture and sites. In that stage of regional archaeological studies in Greece, ethnoarchaeologists such as myself were often included as part of multidisciplinary projects. Although my ethnoarchaeological study of animal folds was seen as important to the Argolid Exploration Project, it nevertheless remained at first a peripheral endeavor, not fully integrated into the goals and objectives of the larger survey and excavation activities. There were several reasons why this was the case: (1) the ethnographic work on Dhidhima herders done by Koster and Koster (1976) was the documented case of herding in a village economy, and (2) no explicit links were made between the "site data" I collected and the archaeological data collected by the AEP. In the early 1980s, information gathered on contemporary mandria was not considered archaeological but analogical, in a very abstract, nonmaterial sense. Archaeological settlement patterns were described using the criterion of the site as the primary, even exclusive marker of material evidence of human behavior on the physical landscape (see Cherry 1994: 93). The *new wave* approach to regional survey (Cherry 1994), where archaeologists conduct surface surveys that record artifactual distributions as well as sites, has given new credibility to the material study of Dhidhima animal folds as artifacts and not merely as minor parts of possible, generalized analogues for how pastoralism may have operated in the ancient past.

Let me spell out what I see as the difference between looking at the animal fold exclusively as part of an analogy for past behaviors and as an actual artifact on the archaeological landscape. If the animal fold is used simply to build analogies between past and present systems of animal herding, then by extension it can easily become a timeless "object" suspended in air without regard to context, time, or place. If the animal fold is first and foremost an artifact, and if modern history is accorded as much importance as ancient, then a fold represents a recent landscape *signature* that, like other surface indications of human activity such as artifact scatters, shrines, paths, homesteads, field houses, terraces, and settlements, is part of a historical pattern of land use by humans over the last eight thousand years.[3] The Dhidhima animal fold can be used as both an analogy and as an artifact; the problem is that we must not confuse the two levels of discussion. Whenever possible throughout this chapter, I will point out when I refer to the animal fold as an artifact and when I make analogies or comparisons between Dhidhima herding and prehistoric or ancient pastoral economies. In the late 1970s when I conducted this research, I saw the animal fold as a "production site" that could be used to make analogies between the past and the present; almost twenty years later I view the animal fold as an artifact on a landscape that may be compared to features found on ancient landscapes, but only when considered as an artifact and not as a disembodied object without context, and only when not placed within a misconstrued "evolutionary" sequence of changing human economies. I focus now on the ways in which the material culture of animal folds can illuminate recent change and thus complete the long-term regional history arising from a comprehensive surface survey of past periods. The animal fold is an object, not an idea.

In the late 1970s, when I first designed my research project to study the material culture of contemporary animal husbandry systems in a Greek peasant village, there was still considerable debate about what constituted "pure" pastoralism or nomadism. Here my study became the prototype for a new "analogy" of how animal husbandry systems were organized across landscapes. The Kosters, who had already done the bulk of the ethnographic research on land tenure and pastoralism in Dhidhima throughout the 1970s, were able to demonstrate that the herding of sheep and goats was fully integrated with a cereal cultivation system (H. Koster 1977). Yet, archaeologists working in areas like the Dei Luran Plain in Iran (Hole 1978; 1979) still argued for the origins of early pastoralism as early as the Neolithic Period and drew frequent analogies between contemporary groups of nomadic pastoralists and the archaeological record of early animal domestication in the Near East. These arguments began to find their way into the literature about prehistoric and ancient periods of Greece, suggesting that ethnoarchaeology could be used as an explicit methodological and theoretical means for drawing a comparison between the herding system found on the modern-day landscape of Greece and the origins of pastoralism during prehistoric periods (for criticisms of this approach see Halstead 1987; 1990).

The analogies I hoped to make between present and past herding systems in Greece depended almost completely upon the ecological models for mixed herding and farming systems in Dhidhima already developed by the Kosters (Koster and Koster 1976; H. Koster 1977). By examining how herders managed their flocks—the amount of fodder, forage, and animal feed consumed by the flock—and, in turn, the milk and meat yields from the flock, the Kosters (Koster 1977) defined the household as the primary unit of production and consumption in the village (see Netting 1993, Wilk 1991). The invaluable information provided by the Kosters was due to their attention to a conceptual framework in which the Dhidhima herding household functioned as the key locus for economic and ecological decision making.

By defining the household first, it was then possible to consider how competing households engaged in economic activities that altered the physical landscape of fixed resources. Furthermore, the household was also affected by its own domestic cycle of births, deaths, marriages, and retirement. These events shaped the daily routines and organization of labor within the larger village and regional contexts. A herder reaching his middle age was compelled for social and economic reasons to provide an adequate dowry for his daughter—a dowry that included part of an animal flock, as well as items such as linens, blankets, and field property. An object or artifact such as an animal fold also could reflect the processes of a domestic cycle that a given household might undertake over the course of several generations. The modern-day fold, however remote and distant it was from the herder's residence in the village, was as much an artifact of the household unit as the household residential compound, and thus changeable and variable as the houses discussed by Clarke in this volume.

While the Kosters did not predict that a decade later all village economies in Greece would be fully integrated into regional, national, and international contexts through the European Community, their research provided archaeologists and ethnographers with the baseline for observing how individual households were the key decision-making units for shaping land use.[4] The impact of Greece's entry into the European Community in 1982 on rural production systems such as village herding could then be traced by examining how individual households adjusted their land use practices to new market supports, subsidies, and credit. Although many other anthropologists noted the changing social structure and ideological tensions emerging in the new Greek state (e.g., Herzfeld 1987; Dimen 1986), those of us working within an ecological paradigm witnessed significant changes affecting the human-land relations visible on the Greek landscape. Such changes included continued migration out of rural communities, changing household structure, the appearance of peasant commodities in larger regional and national markets, and improved conditions for herders through better subsidies, price supports, and credit arrangements through the European Community.

It is an important intellectual exercise for anthropologists such as myself to activate historical hindsight and return to a "simpler, happier time" when the ecology of a herding or a farming system within the context of a peasant community was neither "pristine" nor "timeless," yet still remained untouched by the agricultural policies of the European Community. Ecology as a concern within sociocultural anthropology and archaeology has waned and waxed as fashionable over the past two decades; those of us subscribing to the ecological perspective argue that a rural landscape cannot be fully appreciated without first unraveling the complex set of relationships between the herders and farmers who inhabit these rural places and the land itself.

The Material Culture of Dhidhima Pastoral Sites

In the late 1970s, Dhidhima animal folds were constructed of stone footings with brush and pole lean-to construction and often with a concrete or stone stable incorporated into the brush design. These animal folds were situated on valley, plateau, or hilly areas away from the main village settlement of Dhidhima. The mandri (animal fold, sg.) often housed from twenty to one hundred head of sheep or from sixty to three hundred head of goats. The folds sheltered flocks during the winter and spring months at night and during rainy and inclement weather. Associated with the folds were *strungas* (milking pens), *kalivas* (herders' huts), and *mandras* (stone or brush fence enclosures). The animal fold was the nexus from where herding, pasturing, watering, and milking of the household herd were organized on the rural landscape. Each of the herding households in Dhidhima during 1978 and 1979 owned, or had access to, at least one animal fold. My original sample of herding sites was based on a total of fifty-eight of these sites; forty-one were situated in the Dhidhima Basin, which is the enclosed geographical concavity surrounding the village residential areas.

Herd Management Strategies
Reflected in Fold Architecture

The design of the folds reflected herd management practices. A herder, when he gathered the flock into the fold at night, directed animals to different sections. The shepherd kept all the flock members (lactating ewes, lambs, first-year replacement females, barren females or castrated male animals, and rams) as one herd unit during the day; at night he separated the flock into these fold sections: (1) the *galaria* (ewe section), (2) the *tsarkos* (lamb pen), and (3) the *sterpha* (remaining flock members' section) (Figure 7.1). The ewes were separated from their lambs to ensure maximum milk production, and the rest of the flock was usually given shelter of a secondary quality.

In contrast, the goat herder practiced different grazing strategies during the late winter and early summer months (February through March) that were also reflected in fold layout. The lactating does and newborn kids were grazed on more productive grasslands, where green fodder,

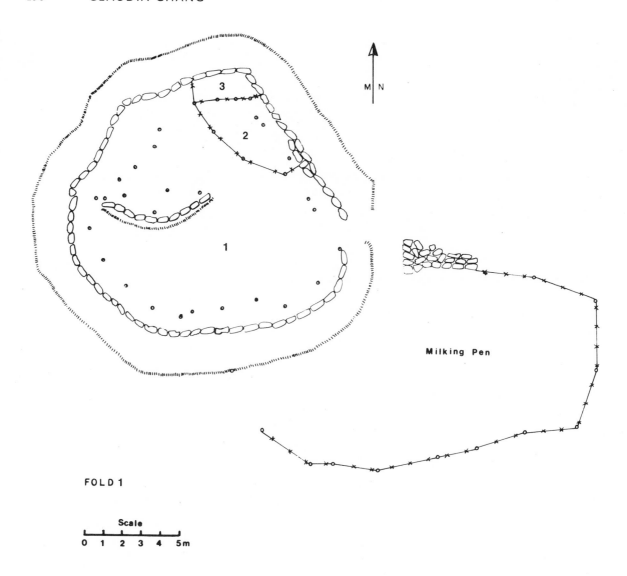

Figure 7.1. Layout of a sheep fold, Dhidhima.

such as oats of vicos, a legume, were cultivated. The animals of the sterpha (first-year female replacements, barren females, castrated males, and bucks) were grazed on shrub and uncultivated grasslands. The goat fold reflected these management strategies by having a minimum of at least four sections (Figure 7.2). The sections included: (1) the galaria (roofed stable area for lactating does); (2) the *proiema* (section for the first group of kids born from November to January); (3) the *opsima* (section for the second group of kids born from January until May); and (4) the outside section (the sterpha), for remaining flock members.

In Dhidhima, herders depended on their flocks for milk, meat, and wool production. Milking animals represented their most valuable stock, since the ewes and does produced both milk and young animals fattened for meat. In the 1970s, herders still concentrated their efforts on producing milk, which meant that lactating animals had to graze on high quality green fodder

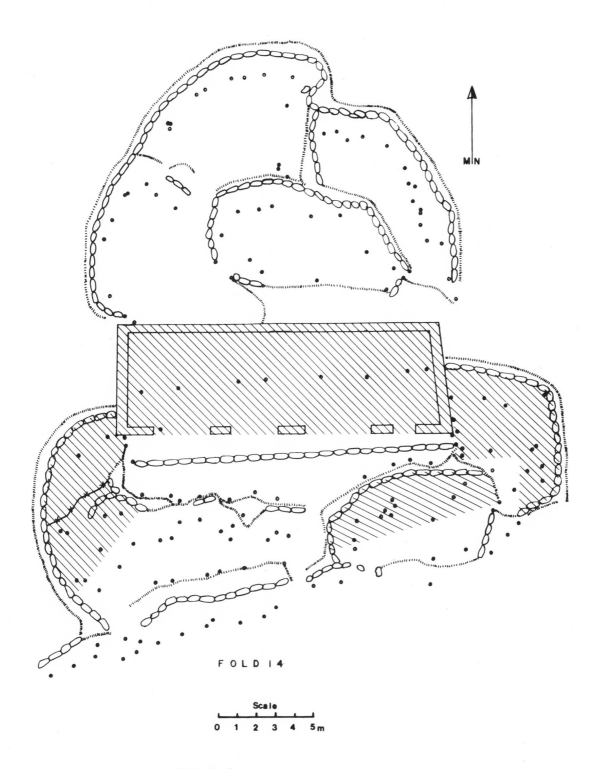

F O L D 1 4

Scale

0 1 2 3 4 5m

Figure 7.2. Layout of a goat fold, Dhidhima.

and pasture, as well as supplementary feed. The milk produced by herd animals was taken to the village cheese merchants twice a day until the months of July and August, when most ewes and does were dried up, and milk production dwindled to that remaining for the household production of cheeses and other dairy products.

The use of milk, meat, and wool products in the Dhidhima system that we observed in the 1970s gave Harold Koster and myself considerable reason to question archaeological assumptions about the origins of Old World pastoralism. Under these assumptions Sherratt (1981) and others speculated that animal domestication first began as meat-based, or carnivorous, pastoralism and then later evolved to a dependency on "secondary products" of milk, wool, and work as draught animals (in the case of cattle). In 1986, a coauthored review article on the archaeology of pastoralism questioned the assumptions inherent in the "'secondary products' revolution argument" (Chang and Koster 1986). While we never explicitly claimed that contemporary Dhidhima animal husbandry represented a "prototype" of Neolithic village herding, many of our arguments against prevailing archaeological notions of pastoralism were drawn from our own work, as well as contemporary pastoral systems throughout the world. Milk production could have been easily carried out in conjunction with killing herd animals for meat; one type of pastoral production did not exclude the other type. The evolutionary ghost that remained hidden in so many archaeological explanations of the origins of pastoralism seemed simply wrongheaded. It was only the logic of possibilism that led archaeologists to argue that prehistoric peoples progressed from hunting animals, which they killed for meat, to herding animals that they also used only for meat. In this case, we used our rich knowledge of the ethnography of village herding to provide archaeologists with "alternative" explanations, although not a direct, one-for-one analogy.

Flock Numbers and Fold Sizes

Dhidhima folds were used to shelter flocks of either sheep or goats. Sheep folds were smaller in dimensions, conforming to the smaller herd numbers (20 to 100) and only having two to three interior sections. Goat folds were larger in dimensions, conforming to larger herd numbers (60 to 300) and having from four to thirteen sections. Statistical data demonstrating the relationship between fold dimensions and flock sizes have been published elsewhere (Chang 1984). Both sheep and goat folds had a crescent-shaped construction plan and consisted of stone footings and a brush lean-to structure supported by upright beams. Masonry or concrete stables often were at the core of the animal folds. The entrance to the fold usually faced down slope so that the flock was driven uphill into the various sections or partitions of the folds. Most folds were situated on the south- or east-facing slopes, thus maximizing radiant heat and protecting animals from a prevailing northerly wind.

Associated Features

Associated with the folds were the herder's hut, the milking pen, feeding troughs, windbreaks, open-hearth areas for making cheese and boiling milk, and the manure piles that were just outside the folds. At many fold locations were long wooden trough areas for animal feed. The troughs were supported by small posts set into the ground. Livestock were fed supplemental grain and cottonseed cake on a daily basis. Tree or plant prunings were often tied to the inside of the animal fold for additional fodder. Watering basins of metal or stone were situated just outside the fold shelter. While activities such as cheese making, feeding and watering stock, and even organizing the flock for herding took place at the fold, for the most part, animal butchering occurred in areas distant from the animal fold. Therefore, there was little to no evidence of butchered remains in the immediate vicinity of the animal fold. Other features at the pastoral site were upright posts used for tethering pack animals and hanging saddlebags, blankets, and milking and cheese-making equipment. Some animal folds also had accompanying mandras for cultivated fodder or for penning young lambs.

The Fold as a Symbol of the Pastoral Worldview

The brush animal folds blending into the limestone cobbled slopes of Dhidhima Basin often appeared to be in direct contrast to the neatly constructed whitewashed villages of stone, plaster, and concrete housing so typical of the southern Argolid. The folds themselves were part of the wild and lawless world of the *vouna* (mountains), a world where single women, like myself, were often questioned for traveling there beyond the boundaries of the settled community. Village people spoke about the animal folds as places where "theft" or "violence to the flock" took place. The typical village house was rectangular or square in plan; the stone and brush animal folds were round and crescent shaped in appearance. Any interpretation of the symbolic intent of the builders of both houses and animal folds led to the conclusion that a boundary existed between the world of animal keeping and the tamed domestic life of households in the village. In an earlier version of this chapter, I argued that the sheltering of animals in circular or crescent-shaped structures was an attempt to enclose and protect animals from their inherent "wild" and uncontrollable state. The entrances to all animal folds faced toward the village, where the civilized world carried on everyday life. Reflecting on my earlier structuralist approaches to the "code of meaning" behind Dhidhima folds, I found an even more important point to be made—one that tied the symbolic and cognitive dimensions of pastoral architecture to the economic and material life of animal husbandry in Dhidhima and other rural Greek communities.

In other areas of Greece I noticed that when a herder was with his flock on the hillside he had a particular identity distinct from his village persona. At home with his flock in the remote areas away from the village, he was free to exercise movement and cross boundaries between areas of cultivated and natural lands. The shepherd living in this broader, more expansive geographical territory than that of his farmer neighbor developed different sets of social relations and mental templates concerning the use of space. If this principle were applied to the Dhidhima fold and its crescent shape, then the animal fold was a special place where humans and animals were mutually dependent. The pastoral world was not the opposite of the farmer's world; these were, rather, worlds apart. A farmer who toiled on his fields and returned year after year to reap his harvests had permanently carved out a piece of property through his manual labor. The herder who viewed the extent and nature of his pastures—some on actual plots of owned or rented land, and some at places of uncultivated land—left his signature on the landscape by building an animal fold. When he moved from place to place in search of greener pastures, his fold represented the one fixed place embodying his household's commitment to animal husbandry. What happened in the pastoral world of the mountains was of a different magnitude and nature than what happened within the confines of the village. The pastoral and agricultural worldviews differed because herders evaluated pasture areas and moved from place to place, while farmers were tied to a bounded area.

All herders continually evaluated their pasture areas and where they traveled with their flocks of sheep or goats. This was especially true of dairy-based systems, where herders relied on the high quality of grazing and fodder for producing high yields of milk from lactating animals. According to H. Koster (1977, Koster and Forbes, this volume), it was for these very reasons that Dhidhima herders maintained the quality of the common lands, rather than overgrazing these open areas. The location of an individual household's animal fold marked this territorial claim to a particular area of grazing, whether owned, rented, or part of the maquis common lands. The vertical zones of Dhidhima land use were such that the lower elevation lands in the Dhidhima Basin were irrigated for potato and vegetable cultivation, the slopes and foothills were designated for cereal and olive cultivation, and the wild maquis of the hillsides were used for wood collecting, grazing, and foraging of wild greens. The shepherd, who needed to organize his flock movements throughout all the major vertical zones, situated his animal fold either in the wild maquis or at its edge. He had his own cognitive and symbolic map for planning and scheduling of flock movements and manipulating social networks between other herding households in neighboring areas.

From an ideological perspective, the animal fold, with its circular structure, represented another worldview, a day-to-day existence by which the herder was dependent upon the abilities and skills of household members to maintain animal flocks and protect them from theft and predation. The pastoral worldview, as represented by fold architecture and spatial arrangements, was an alternative perspective by which a herder and his family were "masters" in their mountain refuge. The organic nature of the housing, the brush lean-to structure with rounded corners and circular shapes, represented a separate view from the confinement of rectangular buildings and protected courtyards of the village. Here was the mountain refuge, the shelter for flock animals, and a place for pastoral activities. The use of space in the mountains was unrestricted and unfettered by the regulations of domestic village life. In the following section, I will fully articulate how it is that the location of the animal fold became the vantage point from which herders coordinated their daily activities with neighboring households.

The Pastoral Site and the Domestic Household Cycle

Elsewhere I have demonstrated how the animal fold can be considered a living artifact reflecting flock numbers in floor plans and dimensions (Chang 1981). As Stenning (1958) pointed out, the developmental cycle of a pastoral household often dictated the demographic structure of individual Fulani cattle herds in West Africa. In the late 1970s, I also collected extensive data on the life histories of fold facilities in Dhidhima. A domestic household cycle would often follow this pattern: (1) a shepherd at the time of marriage owned a small flock of twenty sheep, part of which came from his wife's family as dowry; (2) as the shepherd and his wife had children, and these children reached the age of six or older, when they began contributing to household labor, the flock increased to sixty animals; (3) when the man was expected to provide a dowry for his daughters or some form of partible inheritance for his sons, his flock continued to increase to a maximum of one hundred sheep; and (4) as the shepherd reached retirement, the flock would be reduced in size to thirty or less. The household going through this developmental cycle had to provide adequate shelter for its flock. The rule of thumb was that each sheep needed about 0.5 m^2 of floor area in the animal fold. Since an animal fold was not a balloon that could expand or contract to fit a given spatial requirement, the household was faced with two alternatives: (1) to overcrowd a flock into a small facility, counting on the eventuality that the flock would diminish in numbers; or (2) to find an abandoned facility that was larger in size, remodel, or build a larger facility. The usual practice for Dhidhimiote herders was to predict how large a facility would be required over the course of a domestic cycle and then to build a structure reflecting the prediction. When I set out to make statistical comparisons between flock numbers and floor areas of individual folds, at best I only found rough correlations. Life's chances were unpredictable in some cases, so that herders found themselves forced to build new facilities over the course of a lifetime, or to remodel existing ones.

During the period of a developmental cycle, Dhidhima households went through changes in household composition. The changing household composition was tied to herd demography (Barth 1961) and hence influenced whether or not a given animal fold was half empty, packed, or overpacked. For goat husbandry, the changes in the developmental cycle did have considerable implications for changing floor plans. Goatherds increased the overall floor area of their animal folds by: (1) adding new sections to the exterior of the structure; (2) keeping the same floor area but increasing the number of internal sections, thus allowing for more lean-to space; and (3) modifying the internal section walls.

Archaeologists usually think of "households" within the context of the actual residential living structure or compound identified as dwelling units. It is unusual for them to think about the spatial planning of outlying production units, such as animal shelters, as also embodying a "concept of the household." Because individual households were the very unit of labor and primary decision making for the economic activity of animal husbandry in the village of Dhidhima, one must assume that the pastoral site itself would embody some "concept of the household." The importance of pastoral household organization as reflected in the use of space at animal folds shall be highlighted further in my discussion of pastoral settlement patterns in Dhidhima.

Vertical Zones and Pastoral Site Location

The *koinotis* of Dhidhima, a 400 km^2 region of hilly limestone terrain, has been described as a classic example of vertical zones of resources by Dhidhima farmers and herders (Koster and Forbes, this volume). The situation described here represented the ecology of Dhidhima during the late 1970s. The irrigated valley floor was used for the cultivation of olives, potatoes, and vegetable gardens. The next elevation zone of the slopes of the Dhidhima Basin was terraced and planted in tree crops, wheat, barley, and other dry crops including legumes of vetches and vicos, often raised as green fodder for animal flocks. The wild maquis zone included species of juniper, pistachio, wild olive, arbutus, cistus, hermes and holm oak, and perennial grasses (Koster and Koster 1976). This upland zone was used for animal grazing, firewood collection, and foraging of wild greens. H. Koster (1977) described village agro-pastoralism in Dhidhima as consisting of two management strategies: (1) a system of *intensive* labor input whereby sheep flocks were herded in areas of agricultural stubble and wastage, green fodder, and maquis vegetation; and (2) a system of *extensive* labor input, whereby goat flocks were herded in areas of fallow fields, cultivated green fodder, and maquis vegetation. The intensive management system, which required more careful herding of smaller flocks, was used primarily in the irrigated valley floor and the slopes of the Dhidhima Basin. The corresponding extensive management system, which required a lower ratio of personnel to flock (but more energetic herding), was used primarily on the slopes of Dhidhima Basin and in the wild maquis zones and mountainous areas. Dhidhima herding was defined as agro-pastoralism, because usually herders were also farmers; moreover, all herding activities were coordinated in conjunction with farming activities.[5] Flocks of sheep grazed in harvested areas, leaving their manure on these fields; herders cultivated green fodder for their animals and owned olives, cereal fields, and vegetable gardens as well.

Of the forty-one animal folds found in the Dhidhima Basin in 1978 and 1979, the majority of the sheepfolds (28 total) were found at the lower elevations of the slopes of Dhidhima, while the goat folds (13 total) were located in the maquis zone (Figure 7.3). When herders were asked how they chose their fold locations they gave the following explanations: (1) they had inherited a given area, even though claim of common lands is by use rights and not by principles of land tenure; (2) their fold location was close to their agricultural holdings of olives and cereal fields; and (3) they had easy access to grazing lands that could be rented from others. Herders who had disputes over grazing areas often retaliated by setting fire to an opponent's brush fold (Koster and Koster 1976). All households owned their folds, whether on common lands or not. Some fold locations were passed down over a period of five generations, giving these families plenty of opportunity to consolidate fields, pasture areas, and olives in close proximity to the fold itself.[6]

The Pastoral Site Location
as a Claim to Grazing Territory

The Dhidhima animal fold was also a claim to grazing territory. In my doctoral dissertation (Chang 1981) I was able to apply the statistical analyses of the spatial arrangements of Dhidhima Basin animal folds to the amount of available grazing territory. Each sheep or goat in the Dhidhima system required from 1 to 2 ha of grazing area over the time period of 1940 to 1975 (Koster and Forbes, this volume). The forty-one fold locations found in the Dhidhima Basin represented a circular pattern of points surrounding the main village residence. Using a model of concentric rings, I suggested that each fold location represented " a wedge" in the overall system of land use patterning. A fold, which also to some extent represented a given commitment to a certain flock size, could expand, but not if there were insufficient grazing resources available for a household's flock. The between-site spacing of folds in this concentric ring system meant that folds with

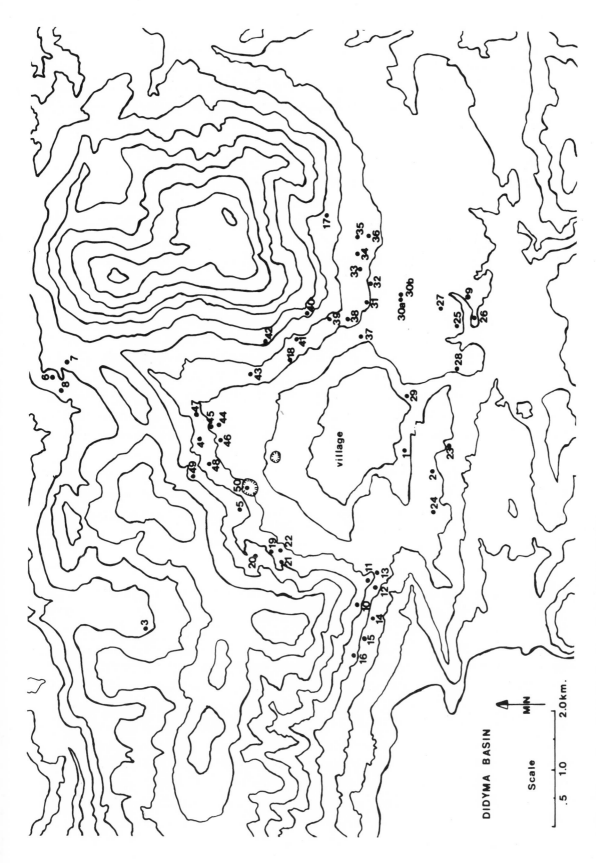

Figure 7.3. Geographical distribution of animal folds, Dhidhima.

larger dimensions should have larger grazing areas and greater between-site spacing, while folds with smaller dimensions should have smaller grazing areas and less between-site spacing. In general, my quantitative methods proved these assumptions to be the case for Dhidhima fold site locations. When the quantitative methods did not prove these assumptions, it was possible to return to earlier arguments that the choices individual pastoral households often made to overpack a given facility during certain peak demographic periods of the flock numbers might falsify the relationship between actual fold floor area and flock size.

These quantitative analyses were significant for several reasons: (1) the relationship between herd demography, household domestic cycle, and size of grazing areas suggested that the Dhidhima herding system operated in such a way that grazing lands were "fixed resources" for which individual households competed; (2) herders had to maintain flock numbers below the carrying capacity of the pasture areas; and (3) each individual household anticipated and predicted its own domestic cycle in relationship to the larger aggregate system, so that if one herder was getting ready for retirement by decreasing his flock numbers, a neighboring herder began to increase his flock in anticipation of the greater availability of grazing lands.

Early in this discussion I outlined the symbolic and cognitive nature of herding in the Dhidhima as represented in the plan of the animal fold. The animal fold also marked the territory used by a herder for his flock and other agricultural pursuits. The locations of these folds on the contemporary landscape provided the herder with a vantage point from which to evaluate his place in the entire village system of land use. From the hillside location of his animal fold, the irrigated and agricultural fields were visible, as were the higher areas of maquis common lands and olive groves cultivated with vicos and vetches. A herder watching the world go by could organize how he would best take advantage of the agricultural fields below for the stubble and fodder, as well as compare how other herders used their grazing areas. This vantage point also was used to schedule daily movements from the fold to the pasture areas. A herder watching his neighbor's two hundred goats leave the animal fold was able to schedule his own path up the mountainside, following his neighbor's flock but occupying a swath of ungrazed territory.

New Directions for Land Use Studies in Archaeology and Ethnography

In the early 1980s, archaeologists subscribing to settlement archaeology continued to rely on "ideal" site types and hierarchical systems of places based on Christaller's (1933) central place theory. The animal fold as an artifact on the contemporary Greek landscape would have been overlooked in favor of residential sites such as hamlets, villages, or cities. The key items used for identifying ancient pastoral systems were animal bones and not artifacts or architecture associated with animal husbandry. The spatial analysis of sites specifically used for production purposes, such as animal folds, had not yet entered the archaeology of pastoralism (Chang and Koster 1986). Furthermore, archaeologists had borrowed from anthropologists, especially those working in the Middle East, a particular definition of pastoral systems as commitments to a type of livestock husbandry in which herders moved from place to place in search of adequate pasture and water resources. This meant that the wide range of economic forms of animal keeping, from nomadic pastoralism to dairy farming or Western ranching, was ignored in favor of those groups fitting this narrow definition. Only more recently have archaeologists come to see ancient Greek animal husbandry systems in which animal herds were kept as ranging from mixed farming and herding systems to specialized palace economies (Cherry 1988). It has thus become increasingly clear that the facilities used to shelter animals can range from barns and stables to folds and corrals; some might be attached to major residential centers, while others might be found in areas distant from villages or towns.

The Dhidhima example of animal folds in outlying zones surrounding the residential village showed that animal husbandry practices took place away from the main village activity of farming. The location of animal folds in elevations above the village settlement was a result of herders' decisions to situate their animal shelters in the ecotone, the edge between cultivated lowlands and the maquis hillsides. The "particularism" of this kind of land use, whereby herding was fully integrated into an intensive agricultural system, could be seen as a cautionary tale for archaeologists seeking to draw analogies between the present and the past. If the animal fold was viewed by the archaeologist as an object or artifact on an evolving landscape, then the location of the animal fold represents the last or most recent human episode of land use. The most recent episode of land use is important to the history of land use in Greece, because it lies on the top of previous episodes and thus influences how we reconstruct earlier landscapes. We must refine new wave regional surveys to include all forms of modifications on landscapes, both human and natural. Ethnoarchaeology may contribute directly to this end in a far more useful way then the often spurious analogies and just so stories that have sometimes been perpetuated about the origins and development of ancient economies. The animal folds of Dhidhima were signatures and artifacts on continually changing landscapes. The comparisons between a pre-EC Greek village herding system and what existed in the past can be used to make "fast and loose" analogies that must in the end be proven by the interpretation of actual archaeological data. Since I have yet to be informed by any archaeologist working in Greece that a prototypical Dhidhima fold has been identified at an archaeological site, I must assume that most archaeological comparisons drawn from this research remain in the category of such fast and loose analogies.

The ethnoarchaeological research on Dhidhima folds showed us how an "object," in this case a building used to house sheep and goats, could embody key principles of the land use system operative in Dhidhima during the late 1970s. The domestic household cycles, the size of herding facilities, and the demographic pressure of herds on the carrying capacity of a fixed land base were key aspects of the Dhidhima land use system. An ethnographer might need to know how land, terrain, and natural vegetation were used over the last one hundred years. Even in the absence of written documentation, the animal fold is an enduring artifact that can be used to study such changing patterns of land use. For each one of the animal folds I studied, I also collected a life history of ownership and construction dates. Such historical information could be quite useful for tracing the history of pastoral land use in Dhidhima, thus giving greater time depth to previous studies.

It is perhaps obvious that change is the normal state of the world today. When the circumstances of the people and village have changed and the framework of our disciplines has undergone revisions, what end products might we reasonably expect? Let me trace some future directions that I see emerging out of the research I did in Dhidhima and point to where I think archaeologists and ethnographers are headed almost two decades later. First, the disciplinary boundaries between ethnography and archaeology need to be rethought. Pigeonholing academic specialties into even more tightly confined slots narrows our scope; what the Dhidhima case demonstrates is the necessity for a blurring of disciplinary boundaries and for seeing the landscape, whether in the recent past or in the ancient past, as part of a larger picture.

Just as the herders of Dhidhima were not timeless peasants representative of a way of life that would endure for the following decades, neither must the investigators remain committed to static models and interpretations. The European Community caused a new form of large-scale market integration that crosscut national and regional boundaries and allowed Dhidhima herders to benefit economically in the same ways that other urban and rural workers had under previous forms of administrative support. The changes in the daily lives of herders also influenced their organization and management of animal herds over the landscape.

The animal fold has remained a key artifact on the Dhidhima landscape, but now continues as such in competition with modernized methods of stock raising and agriculture. Over the intervening years I have come to focus on the animal fold as an artifact of landscape use, and not as a generalized analogy for all ancient pastoralism. This shift in my perspective refocused my attention on archaeological and ethnographic problems specifically dealing with long-term land use. It may be that, in a philosophical sense, some form of analogy hunting will always be at the heart of archaeological interpretations (Wylie 1985), but what might happen if we in fact placed ourselves squarely in the realm of doing long-term history in which ethnoarchaeology remained the last step of tracing out historical changes on a landscape? The chance to trace out changing land use through an artifact such as an animal fold, an agricultural terrace, or a field house is even more exciting when combined with the opportunity to trace out the domestic cycles of households (Clarke, this volume) and the life histories of property ownership (Forbes, Adams, this volume). My one last plea is that we begin to take our disparate specialties and weld them together in new and creative ways, knowing that the answers to any worthwhile question are far more complicated than a single perspective, methodology, or theoretical framework might suggest.

The Present as Past: An Ethnoarchaeological Study of Modern Sites in the Pikrodhafni Valley

Priscilla M. Murray and P. Nick Kardulias

In the summer of 1982, as part of the Stanford University Archaeological Exploration Project of the Southern Argolid,[1] a modern site study was undertaken. All modern structures and features in one valley within the survey area were classified by function and characterized by location, site, and material content. The purpose of the study was twofold: (1) to conclude the culture history of the valley with information about man-made structures, features, and artifacts from the recent past and the present, and (2) to collect a body of data that could form the basis for hypotheses about site functions in the past.

The results of our study are offered here in hopes that they may be of use to others who are conducting archaeological surveys and who are faced with trying to understand what activities occurred in the past at the sites they discover. We offer a possible method for hypothesizing about ancient site functions.

Ethnoarchaeology and the Modern-Site Survey

We define ethnoarchaeology broadly as the study of contemporary behaviors and their material correlates for the purpose of aiding in the interpretation of archaeological material (Gould 1990; Stanislawski 1974; Schiffer 1978). Information about the present is used in two ways: (1) as the basis for hypotheses about relationships between materials and behaviors in the past, and (2) as a test of assumptions that have been used by archaeologists in interpreting the archaeological record (Isaac 1968). The present study concentrates on the formulation of hypotheses for ancient site functions based on material definitions of those for modern sites.

One thrust of ethnoarchaeological research has been concerned with the formulation of "middle range theory" (Binford 1977), or the study of site *formation processes* (Schiffer 1972), emphasizing the exploration of human depositional behaviors, that is, discard, loss, or abandonment (e.g., studies by Binford 1978; Cameron and Tomka 1992; Hayden and Cannon 1983; Yellen 1977). By contrast, this study, with several exceptions, does not focus on human depositional processes. We were primarily concerned with studying the repertoire of objects functioning in their systemic (modern behavioral) contexts; in only two cases (i.e., in our observations of abandoned features and garbage middens) did we look into the processes that transfer materials to archaeological contexts. Thus, this research is similar to an effort by Frank Hole (1979), in which he endeavored to identify, on the surface, ancient pastoral sites by reference to modern pastoral site locations and material inventories (see Horne 1993, Kent 1987 for parallel studies).

Explicitly ethnoarchaeological research has been undertaken in Greece for two decades. Aschenbrenner (1976a) used analogies from the modern village of Karpofora in southwestern Greece to suggest interpretations of features encountered in the Nichoria excavations nearby. Chang (1981, 1992) has defined modern pastoral sites both in the area around Dhidhima and in Grevena according to their architecture, size, and locations, and correlated these attributes with herding behaviors. Murray and Chang (1981) studied discard and storage behaviors at a contemporary herder's site in the Argolid, and Runnels (1981) used information about modern millstone manufacture and distribution on Aigina to form the basis for hypotheses about ancient decision making with respect to ground stone tools. Gallant (1991), Halstead (1990), and Forbes (1992) have drawn analogies for ancient agricultural practices from contemporary ones, while Wagstaff (1982), Sutton (1994), and Whitelaw (1991) have explored the ethnoarchaeological implications of current settlement patterns.

The present study adds to this corpus of ethnoarchaeological research in Greece. It is a survey of a variety of habitational and nonhabitational modern sites for the purpose of augmenting and aiding in the interpretation of material collected during the course of an archaeological reconnaissance in the same valley. Because of its scale, it must be viewed as only a pilot project for future efforts. Recently, Whitelaw (1991) conducted a more thorough study of the sort we envisioned.

Research Setting: The Modern-Site Survey
as Part of the Stanford Survey

The Stanford archaeological survey was conducted from 1979 through 1981 (Jameson, Runnels, and van Andel 1994). The study area encompassed almost the entire Ermionidha. In all, 20 percent of this region (or 44 km²) was explored. Sample areas were chosen so that every type of landform in the study region, from coastal plain to upland plateau, was investigated. Field teams walked systematically in a line over the chosen sample areas. When concentrations of cultural materials, called *sites*, were discovered, they were mapped and a collection of artifacts and ecofacts was taken. Sites were sampled by laying out random transects and picking up everything within these meter-wide strips. In addition, "grab samples" were taken so that very good examples of datable materials outside the transects could be added to the overall collection. Sites identified in the surveyed areas represented periods of occupation from the Middle Paleolithic through the Turkish era.

In the 1982 field season, the emphasis was on the analysis of the data collected in the previous seasons. One problem that needed to be addressed was how to determine the functions of all of the sites that had been discovered. The Modern-Site Survey was conceived as one means of approaching this issue.

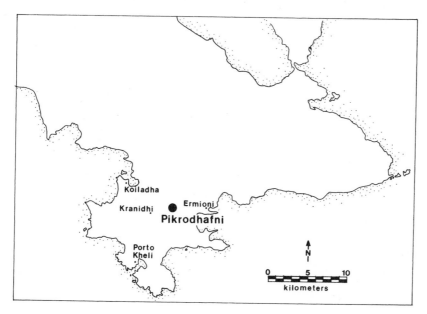

Figure 8.1. Location of Pikrodhafni.

When faced with having to interpret the archaeological record, archaeologists have always drawn upon their knowledge of the present, whether explicitly or not. Our goal in doing the Modern-Site Survey was to make use of the present in a less informal way, and to structure our observations so that they would bear directly on the specific archaeological problem at hand.

We chose to do our research in the same areas as the archaeological survey because we wanted the past and present situations to be directly comparable. We assumed that at least some of the environmental variables that at present challenge the user of the study area had also to be faced by some of the past inhabitants. Yet, we agreed with Watson (1979: 3): "logically speaking the source of any specific analogy has no significance whatsoever. It makes no difference where the hypothesis comes from, what matters is whether or not it is confirmed in appropriate tests" (see Fotiadis 1995 for similar sentiments).

From the beginning, the scope of the Modern-Site Survey was limited by time factors. The 1982 field season was planned to last just six weeks, and other fieldwork had to be done.[2] Opportunities for transport into the field were limited to a few afternoons each week. Since it was not feasible to examine all areas covered by the archaeological survey, we elected to do just one valley, Pikrodhafni. It extends from the upland region near Kranidhi down to the sea near Ermioni (Figure 8.1) and thus provides a characteristic profile of the variety of topographic conditions common to the project study area as a whole. We examined every man-made structure in the valley that fell within the bounds of the intensive archaeological survey done there in 1981. These structures were first located through close scrutiny of 1:5,000 maps and then visited. In addition, other modern sites not included on the maps but encountered during our field trips were recorded. Only wells were excluded from our attention because a thorough study of those present in the project study area had already been done (Harper 1976).

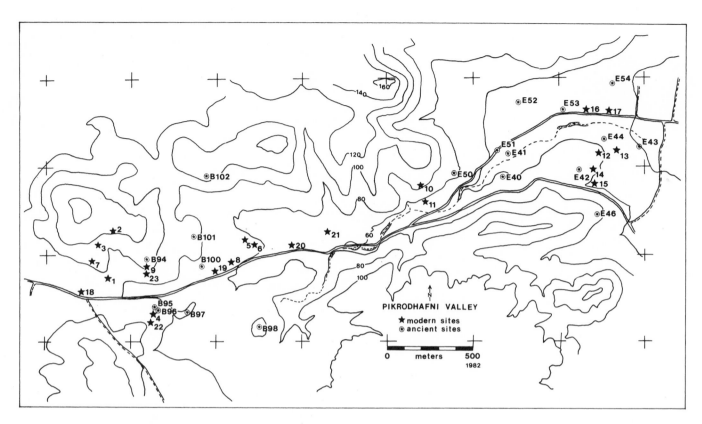

Figure 8.2. Modern and ancient sites, Pikrodhafni.

Methods

In all, twenty-three modern sites were studied in the Pikrodhafni area (Table 8.1). These may be divided into two categories: (1) those that can still be viewed on the landscape, but are no longer in use and are becoming archaeological sites, and (2) sites actively in use and continuously maintained. The sites included in the first category are limekilns, threshing floors, hearths, and one abandoned farmstead. The sites in the second category are farmsteads, storehouses, animal folds, roadside shrines, animal keeps, two chapels, and a garbage dump by the road.

At all of these sites, our focus was on the material aspects (objects and construction materials) as they related to site function. To facilitate the recording of data, forms were devised before entering the field. In the field, the questions on the forms were answered by our own observations or by informants, or both. Our queries were based on our conjectures as to what we would find in the field. These conjectures had their foundations mainly in previous informal observations of modern sites and behavior in Greece and elsewhere.

In applying our forms to the field situation, certain arbitrary decisions had to be made. Selecting the correct form to fill out required a decision as to whether the site to be observed was (1) a structure (habitational or not), (2) a large feature, or (3) a structureless site. There was a problem in some cases in deciding which sites would be classified as features and which would be classified as structureless sites. Information about animal folds was included on the form for

Table 8.1

Summary of Data on Modern Sites

Site number	Site type (function)	Site location	Distance to water (m)	Features	Associations: Structures	Associations: Animal	Associations: Plant	Feature, structure size (m²)	Site size (m²)	Artifacts	Ecofacts	Construction material
3	lime kiln (reused)	hillside	225			sheep, goat	olives, wild	15	200	domestic animal related	lime, boulders, bone	durable
8	lime kiln	low rise (side)	75	road			olives, grains, wild	6.4	6.4		lime	durable
12	lime kiln	hillside	200				olives, wild	4.5	4.5			durable
15	lime kiln (reused)	hillside	20	road			olives	15.9	225	domestic		durable
4	threshing floor	hilltop	325	hearth			olives, carob	353	353			durable
5	threshing floor	low rise (top)	60	fold	house, animal keep		grains	314	314			durable
2	hearth	hillside	250				olives, wild	5	5		ash	nondurable
22	hearth	hilltop	325	threshing floor			olives, carob	8.75	8.75		ash	nondurable
23	hearth	hillside	150				olives, carob	6	6	ash		nondurable
11	fold	low rise (side)	60	threshing floor	chapel		olives, carob, wild	243	243	domestic animal related	dung	nondurable
13	fold	low rise (side)	200	fence			wild	1,800	6,750	domestic animal related	dung	nondurable
14a	fold	hillside			storehouse		olives, wild	48	1,800	animal related	dung	durable, nondurable
6c	fold	low rise (side)	60	threshing floor	house, animal keep		grains	90	658		dung	nondurable
6d	fold	low rise (side)	60	threshing floor	house, animal keep		grains		658		dung	durable
18	shrine	flats	300	road			olives, wild	.35	.55	domestic, religious		durable*
20	shrine	hillside	75	road			olives, carob	.29	.29	domestic, religious		durable*
21	chapel	hilltop	120	hearth			olives, carob	44	448	domestic, religious, manufacturing		durable*
9	chapel	hilltop	150	dirt piles, hearth			olives, carob	54	100	domestic, religious, manufacturing		durable*
10	storehouse	hillside	175	metal, wood pile			olives, fruit	20	57	agricultural, manufacturing		durable
14b	storehouse	hillside	210	fold			olives	10	1,800	domestic, animal related, manufacturing		durable

Table 8.1 *Concluded*
Summary of Data on Modern Sites

Site number	Site type (function)	Site location	Distance to water (m)	Features	Structures	Animal	Plant	Feature, structure size (m²)	Site size (m²)	Artifacts	Ecofacts	Construction material
17b	storehouse	flats	10		house, pump	sheep, goat, horse, rabbit, turkey, pigeon	citrus, vegetables	ca. 9	ca. 700	domestic, animal related, agricultural manufacturing		durable
7	animal keep	low rise	200			pigeon, goat, sheep, dog, pig, pig, chicken, rabbit, turkey	olives	120	960	domestic, animal related, agricultural manufacturing	dung	durable
6b	animal keep	low rise (side)	60	fold, threshing floor	house		grains	163	658	domestic, animal related, agricultural manufacturing	dung	durable
17a	house	flats	ca. 20	oven, road	storehouse, pump	sheep, goat, horse, rabbit, turkey, pigeon	citrus, vegetables	ca. 50		domestic, manufacturing		durable
16a	house	flats	50	road	garage, shed animal keep	dog, cat, chicken	citrus	55	ca. 750	domestic, manufacturing		durable
6a	house (side)	low rise	60	fold, threshing floor			grains	92.5	658	domestic, manufacturing		durable
1a	farm (side)	low rise	30	oven, outhouse		sheep, chicken	citrus, vegetables, fruit, olives	ca. 260	1000	domestic, animal related, religious, manufacturing, agricultural manufacturing	dung	durable*
16b	workshed	flats	50	road	house, garage	chicken, dog, cat	citrus	ca. 10	750	manufacturing		durable
16c	garage	flats	50	road	workshed, house	chicken, dog, cat	citrus	ca. 10	750	domestic		durable
1b	outhouse (side)	low rise	30	farm		sheep, chicken	citrus, vegetables, fruit, olives	.5	1000			durable
19	garbage midden	flats	50	road			wild	500	500	domestic, manufacturing		

NOTE: The site number contains both site and structure/feature designations. In this table, each structure or feature is considered individually, even if part of a complex of structures and features. If structures/features were parts of such complexes, they were designated as follows: first, the site number (for the complex as a whole), and then a letter for the structure/feature designation. 16b, for example, is structure b at site 16. Structures or features that have only a numeric designation are unrelated to other man-made structures or features.

* = Decorations present

Table 8.2
Sample Modern Site Form, Pikrodhafni

A. Inhabitant:

B. Owner:

C. Location:
   1. Area_____ Map#_____
   2. Situation:
     ____low rise ____flatlands ____hilltop ____seaside
     ____mountaintop ____mountainside ___view of sea ____upland plain
   3. _____m.a.s.l.
   4. Proximity to population concentration

D. Associated water source:
   ____well ____spring ____lake ____river ____stream ____none
   distance to:

E. Site size   Site density
   Length: Center:
   Width: Periphery:
   Area:

F. Site composition:
   1. Structures:
     ____habitation ____religious structure ____animal stable/fold
     ____storehouse ____outhouse ____manufacturing center ____tomb
     ____unidentifiable ____special purpose:
   2. Features:
     ____well ____oven ____hearth ____fence/wall ____garden/yard
     ____vat ____garbage midden ____garbage fan ____threshing floor
     ____kiln ____road/path ____cistern ____patio ____quarry
     ____mine ____mill ____pit ____bridge ____terrace ____dam
     ____irrigation channel ____other:
   3. Outdoor artifacts/ecofacts:
     ____present ____absent

G. Associated animals:
   ____sheep ____goat ____cattle ____horse ____chicken ____rabbit
   ____dog ____cat ____other:

H. Associate cultigens:
   ____olives ____vines ____grains ____fruit ____vegetables
   ____other:

I. Photographs:

J. Notes:

structureless sites, for example, although the large feature form would have served just as well. In future studies, the forms will be revised in light of these problems (see Tables 8.1 and 8.2 for sample forms).

We had hoped when we began our investigations that we would find at every modern structure or feature informants who would explain the various site activities to us, thus elucidating the relationship between material culture and behavior at each place. In fact, we encountered informants only at three occupied farmsteads, one fold/storehouse complex, and at one animal

Table 8.3

Sample Modern Habitation Form, Pikrodhafni

A. Habitation type:
____farmhouse ____town/village residence ____summer house ____hut

B. Habitation status:
____permanent ____seasonal ____uninhabited ____months/year inhabited
____good condition ____disrepair ____ruins

C. House ownership:
____resident owns ____resident rents ____sharecropper

D. Number of people: ____kin ties: _____

E. Exterior house parts: ____ledges ____porch ____balcony ____1st storey
____2nd storey ____decoration

F. House dimensions:
____m. long × ____m. wide

G. Date built_____ house cost_____

H. Construction materials:
____mudbrick ____brick ____stone ____tile ____wood ____glass ____plaster
____cement ____terrazo ____metal ____cardboard ____particle board

I. Foundation footers: ____depth; where dirt?_____

J. Number of rooms: ____all rooms in use? _____

K. Room types: ____kitchen ____living room ____bedroom ____bathroom ____storeroom

L. Facilities: ____toilet ____sink ____bathtub ____shower ____fireplace
____heating device ____water holding tank

M. Appliances: ____stove ____refrigerator ____gas burner ____other:

N. Furniture: ____table ____chair ____stool ____shelf ____lamp ____bed ____sofa
____dresser ____chest ____wardrobe

O. Cooking and serving aids: ____pots ____pans ____crockery ____glassware
____utensils ____food

P. Storage containers: ____jar ____basket ____bag ____box ____can ____bottle
____pithos ____jug

Q. Personal sanitation items: ____mouth ____body ____hair
drugs/other medicines: ____present ____absent

R. Cleaners and cleaning aids: ____present ____absent

S. Leisure items: ____TV ____radio ____books/magazines ____games

T. Decorative objects: ____pictures ____vases ____other:

U. Cloth: ____clothes ____bedclothes ____curtain ____towels

V. Associations: features and locations _____
structures and locations _____
outdoor artifacts and locations _____

keep. We questioned these people not only about the sites they owned or used, but about other sites in the valley as well. The result was that, with the addition of data from informants outside Pikrodhafni and from the ethnographic literature on modern Greece, we were able to associate a set of behaviors with each of the modern sites in Pikrodhafni.

When we investigated a site at which an informant was present, we began with an explanation of our project and an assurance that any information given to us would be used in a discreet manner. Thereafter, we perused the structure or feature interior and then examined the surrounding grounds, making note of all material elements. During the examination of both the interior and exterior, the informant was consulted as to the functions of various items, rooms, or features, and was tactfully questioned about the practices that led to the existing array of artifacts on the property. Beyond this, our discussions with various informants dealt with a variety of topics, including the means by which the property was acquired, the age and construction technique of the building involved, personal data on family history and occupation, and any knowledge about the use of traditional tools in agricultural or industrial practices. Much of this information was not directly relevant to the present study as it later evolved, but rather to archaeological problems in general.

Field Observations

Only selected characteristics of modern sites were recorded. We concentrated primarily on those site attributes that, for the sake of comparison, could also be observed in the archaeological record. We were further restricted by our interest in surface manifestations of ancient sites. Thus, our focus was on site location, site size, and the materials that characterized each modern site. These were the same attributes recorded about ancient sites during the archaeological survey of the valley.

The modern data are summarized below. We observed and recorded site location, dimensions, and material content. Information about site function (i.e., behaviors associated with each site) was taken principally from Greek informants, except where indicated.

Limekilns

Limekilns (Figure 8.3, upper right), which are large circular pits lined with worked stone blocks, were used until the early 1950s to manufacture lime by burning limestone. Lime was used locally in house construction or for other building projects. A substantial amount of lime was also shipped out of the region, providing a ready source of cash. The modern cement plants to the north (in Nafplio) had no significant effect on this local industry until a paved road running the length of the Argolid was built in the 1950s. With cheap bagged cement and concrete blocks easily acquired, the economic viability of local lime production was undermined and rapidly declined.

The primary determinant of limekiln location was availability of fuel, largely juniper wood, rather than easy access to limestone. Kilns were built as close to wooded areas as possible because of their voracious fuel requirements: a typical three-day firing could use as much as 100,000 kilos of wood (Forbes and Koster 1976:123).

Figure 8.3.   Some modern features, Pikrodhafni: *upper left,* overgrown threshing floor; *upper right,* abandoned lime kiln; *lower left,* garbage along road; *lower right,* inside a fold.

The limekilns in Pikrodhafni range in diameter between 2.5 m and 4.5 m. When they have not been reused as garbage dumps, so that there is no scatter of materials around them (see MS#8 and MS#12), total site size is quite small (4–7 m^2). For those kilns (see MS#3, MS#15) that have been reused as dumps, site size is as much as 225 m^2.

Threshing Floors

Up until thirty years ago, the preparation of harvested grains in the southern Argolid required a special circular floor for threshing and winnowing purposes (see Figure 8.3, upper left). In certain other parts of Greece, Cyprus, and Turkey (Bordaz 1969), the usual method of threshing involved hitching a draft animal to a sled on whose underside a number of flints or metal fragments had been imbedded to cut grain stalks. In the Ermionidha, by contrast, a team of horses was tethered to a pole in the center of the floor. As the horses swept out a radial path, their hooves chopped the stalks to the appropriate length for winnowing. Threshing floors were abandoned with the beginning of mechanized agriculture in the area. The movement of agricultural products, tractors, and associated machinery and the transport of fuel to run them were facilitated by the construction of the paved Argolid road mentioned above.

Both threshing floors studied are on open spots at elevations where there is a breeze for winnowing. One floor (MS#5), situated on a low rise in the midst of grain fields, is closely associated with a farmstead, which it presumably served (no informants were found to confirm this). The other floor (MS#4) stands alone on a hilltop that is 350 m from the nearest farm (MS#1). The farm's owners built the floor for their own use.

The threshing floors in Pikrodhafni are built of concrete and stone and have no associated artifacts. Compared with other sites in the valley, they are medium-sized (diameter 20 m).

Hearths

Hearths, consisting of small burned areas located high on cultivated or uncultivated hillsides, have no associated artifacts; they consist only of ash and burned pieces of wood. No informants could be found to explain these features satisfactorily to us. We thought that they might be the remnants of burned prunings. Hearths, with diameters of only a meter or two, are, except for shrines, the smallest sites in the valley.

Folds

Chang (1981, and this volume) has noted for the Dhidhima area north of Pikrodhafni that goat folds tend to be built on the upper elevations of the hills surrounding the basin there, and that sheepfolds occupy the lower elevations adjacent to cultivated land. Since all of the folds recorded in Pikrodhafni (see Figure 8.3, lower right) are also situated on the lower elevations of the valley near the farmland, it is likely that they house only sheep, and not goats. An informant confirmed this for two (MS#13 and MS#14a) of the five folds visited; informants were not identified for the other three sites, MS#6c, MS#6d, MS#11.

MS#14a is used in the winter months and consequently consists of a roofed shelter in addition to a low brush corral. It is likely that MS#6d, which is a reused one-room structure, is also used in the winter because it is roofed. At least part of MS#6b, classified as an animal keep (see below), may in fact be a winter sheepfold as well, because in addition to being a large dung-filled area, it is partially roofed. MS#11, MS#13, and MS#6c, on the other hand, consist solely of low brush walls forming animal corrals, and are probably used in the summer. MS#13, because it allows ample space for fenced-in animals to roam, is the largest site in the entire valley; the other folds are smaller (ranging in size from small to medium).

Normal fold activities include "herding activities such as feeding, watering, milking, birthing, tethering, and housing animals" (Chang 1981: 68). Artifacts within the folds are not plentiful, but in part reflect these activities: many (though not all) are animal related, including feed troughs and water barrels (water sources are not on site at MS#11, MS#13, MS#14a).

Chapels

Chapels (see Figure 8.4, upper right) are small, one-room religious structures, very commonly found in the Greek countryside (Dubisch 1995b; Hart 1992; Kenna 1976; Stewart 1991).

Figure 8.4. Some modern structures, Pikrodhafni: *upper left,* farmstead; *upper right,* chapel; *lower left,* shrine; *lower right,* isolated storehouse.

Each is dedicated to a particular saint, though icons of other saints may also be housed in the structure. Unlike churches, chapels do not have priests permanently assigned to them and do not see regular weekly services. Priests visit the structure only on special occasions, such as the festival of the saint to whom the chapel is dedicated.

In regular everyday use, occasional visitors come to pray or to leave offerings. "According to circumstance, the faithful invoke the saint who has the power to help them in their predicament and try to propitiate him with prayers and offerings" (Megas 1958: 13–14). Chapels are most often privately financed. Such a display of religious faith is often seen as a way of assuring good fortune because the saint for whom the structure is built will then be well disposed toward the builder.

It has been observed in the Argolid and elsewhere in Greece that chapels often incorporate antiquities into their decor or walls and/or are built on ancient remains. Both of the chapels studied in Pikrodhafni conform to this pattern. MS#9 sits in the center of an archaeological site

(B94) that has components ranging from at least the Middle Byzantine period to modern times. The other chapel (MS#21) is a medieval structure that has been continuously maintained and used right into the present. Fragments of stone work of classical times were found in association with this building.

It seems that sacred significance has been associated with particular chapel locales perhaps because of a continuation of pagan traditions and values into the Christian era (Lawson 1910: 36–64). Dyer (1891: 88–89) suggests that certain places retained "through many centuries . . . a dread and most religious sanctity," which was not obliterated by the success of the new faith. In fact, early Christians acknowledged the sacred nature of certain spots by erecting churches in such places (Hyde 1923: 55). Lawson (1910: 46, 63) argues that this was an intentional campaign to get people accustomed to the new faith by continuing to use places where the populace had traditionally worshipped. The widespread practice of transforming temples into churches is another example of this phenomenon (Hyde 1923: 61–62).

Both chapels sit atop small knolls (on plateaus) and are not associated with other modern structures or features. They are built of durable materials and are decorated with religious symbols. Their orientation is east to west (as versus the southerly exposure of all other structures in the valley), with the apse at the eastern end. Many of the artifacts, but not all, associated with these structures can be classified as religious, including such items as candles and candlestands, icons, and altar cloths.[3] Compared to the other sites in the valley, the chapels are medium-sized. They are, for example, larger than roadside shrines but smaller than farmsteads and folds.

Shrines

Shrines (*proskinitaria*) are very small religious features commonly found along paved or dirt roads throughout the Argolid as well as the rest of Greece (see Figure 8.4, lower left). The two included in the present study (MS#18, MS#20) are located on the north side of the unpaved road that dissects the Pikrodhafni valley. These small enclosed repositories contain mostly religious artifacts, for example, icons, incense, and *kandhilia* (glass with water, oil, floating wick). They are made of durable material (metal or stone) and have crosses decorating their exteriors. They are the smallest sites in the valley.

Neither of the shrines in Pikrodhafni was apparently built to mark the site of an accident or successful avoidance of one, as shrines elsewhere in Greece often do. MS#20 presumably allows a passerby to light a candle or burn some incense without having to climb the steep hill to MS#21, a chapel, which is just to the east. The reason for the building of MS#18 is less clear. It may have been built by a private individual as a reflection of his religious faith, just as chapels are.

Storehouses

Both storehouses studied have walls of cement block, heavy corrugated roofs, stout locked doors, and barred windows. One (MS#10) is located by itself (Figure 8.4, lower right) in an olive grove on a high terrace and contains implements and containers used in olive cultivation and harvesting, including a metal plowshare, ladder, rakes, crates, and a reed basket.[4] MS#10 is rather small in size compared with the other sites in the valley.

The second storehouse (MS#14b) is a shearing station directly associated with an animal fold located on a low rise. In the recent past, it also served as the winter shelter for an itinerant herder. The only visible contents of the storehouse are sacks of clipped wool.

It appears that field storehouses such as these provide convenient repositories for items that are too cumbersome to haul constantly between home and field, which can be far apart. Through this expedient, equipment is readily available in the locale where it is utilized.

Animal Keeps

The one isolated animal keep recorded (MS#7) is a building of solid cement block construction with a metal roof. Associated with it is a large fenced-in area for corralling animals of all kinds (e.g., chickens, goats, pigs, rabbits) and for a small amount of olive cultivation. Animals are housed, fed, and otherwise maintained throughout the year. They or their products are periodically sold for cash. The site is medium-sized and is located on the lower slopes of a hill. Certain objects associated with this site are animal related, for example, feed troughs and containers, and cages.[5] Other artifacts can be classified as domestic or manufacturing, including such items as building materials and machines (from a recent construction episode), brooms, and water jars.[6]

The other animal keep we recorded (MS#6b) is associated with an abandoned farmstead. It consists partially of a roofed stone structure containing large built-in, waist-high feed troughs. This structure is connected to a dung-strewn area partially roofed on two sides by open-sided shelters. One of these shelters has wall niches suitable for pigeons or hens. It seemed likely that the large feed troughs were for horses or cows, thus making the roofed structure a stable. It is possible that the attached dung-filled area is a sheepfold; it has characteristics of winter folds elsewhere (Chang 1981). No informants could be found to confirm these notions. Since more than one kind of animal seemed to be housed at this locale, the label animal keep was given, though at least part of the complex is probably a fold.

Farmsteads

Farmsteads (see Figure 8.4, upper left) in Pikrodhafni consist minimally of a habitation whose residents engage in agricultural activity as well as animal husbandry (see also Whitelaw 1991). The habitation may be a house whose occupants are people only, or a farm. A farm contains agricultural or other storerooms and/or animal keeps and the structure inhabited by humans—all under the same roof. All four farmsteads observed in Pikrodhafni (MS#1, MS#6, MS#16, MS#17) are found just north of the road that runs through the valley; and all consist of a number of structures in addition to habitations: sheds, garages, animal shelters, outhouses, and so forth. The farmsteads are built on, and are surrounded by, arable land. They are located in only two sections of the valley: the far western and the far eastern. This is because the land in these two areas is relatively flat and open, permitting the cultivation of various crops, primarily cereals and citrus. In addition, the water table is presumably more easily tapped by wells in those areas, as opposed to the steep, hilly central section of the valley (Harper 1976).

Farmsteads make use of the following classes of artifacts: domestic, religious, manufacturing, animal related, and agricultural. The house, or inhabited portion of the farmstead, contains most of the domestic and all of the religious artifacts. Including the scatter of organic and/or inorganic garbage around the buildings, farmsteads are today medium to large in size.

All the habitations within the farmsteads studied are built of substantial materials and have a southern exposure in order to take maximum advantage of solar heat during the winter. Three of the four have trees or grape trellises that protect their front doorways from the intense summer sun. MS#1, which is occupied seasonally (the other three are occupied year-round), has no cover to provide shade.

Garbage Dumps

Garbage middens (dumps or concentrations, see Figure 8.3, lower left) in Pikrodhafni are located on property not assigned other functions. They are usually some distance from habitations. Owners of the farmsteads in the eastern part of the valley (MS#16, MS#17) regularly dump trash in the streambed, which is within easy walking distance (ca. 60–70 m) to the south of their front doors. The river channel is cleaned out seasonally by winter rains. The owner of MS#1 in the western end of the valley hauls his refuse by car to the municipal dump some kilometers away.

Two of the kilns studied contain refuse, though only one is systematically reused as a dump. MS#15 is located adjacent to a road that facilitates access to it. As a result, it is nearly full of trash (containers, bottles, paper, food scraps, etc.), much of which is fragmentary and is contained in the blue plastic bags ubiquitous throughout Greece. Nuns from the Ayioi Anaryiroi monastery, the owners of the large tract of land on which the kiln sits, collect trash discarded in the area by visitors; it is placed in the kiln and periodically burned when the kiln is full. MS#3 contains the remains of five or six goats and is therefore not a typical refuse pit.

The last midden of note is MS#19, located on the flats beside the road that runs through the valley. It is an extended scatter containing substantial amounts of broken building materials, torn clothing, and fragmentary kitchen residues. The nearest modern site is MS#8, an abandoned limekiln about 100 m away from the midden (the nearest habitation is ca. 300 m away).

In addition to the middens noted above, all of the sites studied in the Modern-Site Survey, except threshing floors, hearths, and unreused kilns, have light garbage scatters surrounding the features or structures.

Site Locations

In summary, the farmsteads in Pikrodhafni are located on the flatlands in the eastern end of the valley, or on the lowest elevations of the gentle slopes in the western end. Generally, they have water sources (wells) on site and are closely associated with grain fields or citrus groves. The only other sites in the valley that are found on flat ground are MS#19, a garbage midden, and MS#18, a shrine. Flat ground, however, does not appear to have been a factor in the location of these last two sites. Rather, the road, which passes through the valley and runs next to these sites, seems to have been the sole determining factor in their placement. Shrines are always beside roads (the other shrine, MS#20, located on a low rise, is also beside the road). The garbage was probably dumped directly from a vehicle.

Chapels, threshing floors, and hearths are all located fairly high above the valley floor on the tops and sides of hills. Factors other than proximity to water or arable land have determined their locations. Threshing floors must be located where there is a breeze for winnowing, and chapels seem to occupy traditionally sacred spots. Another kind of site also occupies the upper elevations in Pikrodhafni. Ms#10 is an isolated storehouse situated in an olive grove. The contents of the structure serve the owner of the trees in maintenance and harvesting tasks.

Limekilns are also found in the upper elevations of Pikrodhafni, but they can be located on the lowest portions of hills and low rises as well. Their proximity to adequate fuel resources (mostly juniper trees) is the primary determinant of their location.

Lastly, besides kilns and the farmsteads mentioned above, folds and animal keeps are also located on low rises or the lowest elevations of hillsides. Though water is not on site, it is not distant (60–200 m away).

Site Size

Table 8.4 contains a site-size continuum based on our approximations of feature/structure size plus the object-scatters around them. The smallest sites in our study are roadside shrines and hearths; the largest is a fold that contains relatively few artifacts but is great in horizontal extent. Farmsteads tend to be toward the medium to large end of the site-size scale (or greater than 650 m^2).

Table 8.4
Modern Site Size, Pikrodhafni

Site no.	Site type	Site size (m^2)	Relative size
18, 20	shrines	0.29–0.55	small
2, 22, 23	hearths	5.0–8.5	small
8, 12	lime kilns	4.5–6.4	small
10	isolated storehouse	57	small
9	chapel	100	medium
3	reused lime kiln	200	medium
15	reused lime kiln	225	medium
11	fold	243	medium
4, 5	threshing floors	314–353	medium
21	chapel	448	medium
19	garbage midden	500	medium
6	farmstead	658	medium
16, 17	farmsteads	700–750	medium
7	animal keep	960	large
1	farmstead	1,000	large
14	fold, storehouse	1,800	large
13	fold	6,750	very large

Materials at Sites

In recording modern artifacts, our concern was not with whether they were preservable; perishable artifacts today may have durable ancient equivalents and vice versa. Our focus was on artifact purpose rather than composition when hypothesizing based on the present was applied to ancient situations.

When reviewing the lists of objects present at the Pikrodhafni sites (see Table 8.5 for an artifact inventory), one is struck by the fact that domestic artifacts are not confined to domestic contexts. That is, objects that are common to the domestic activities of cooking or cleaning, for example, or that would be at home in a bedroom or linen closet, are often found at nonhabitation sites. Olive oil bottles and aluminum foil were found at one chapel, for example, and some clothes and a box of detergent were seen at one fold. We saw a man's sock and some other domestic trash in the middle of an animal keep. In fact, domestic artifacts were found at fifteen of twenty-three modern sites in the Pikrodhafni valley.

Objects commonly associated with habitations appear at nonhabitation sites for at least two reasons. First, the objects in question may serve a variety of purposes in a variety of contexts. For example, olive oil is used in lamps in chapels as well as for cooking in homes. Second, domestic objects discarded as a group may find their final resting place at an activity area no longer in use: garbage is dumped into abandoned kilns, for example. Domestic objects also become part of the light garbage scatter associated with nonhabitational sites, such as animal keeps and cultivated fields. We do not fully understand the processes that lead to this kind of deposition. One possibility is that kitchen refuse (which may be inorganic as well as organic) is used as fertilizer.

Although domestic objects are found commonly in nondomestic contexts, it may be that the proportion of these goods with respect to other objects present at the site would be small, unless the domestic artifacts have multiple functions. Though domestic artifacts are found at religious structures, for example, they do not seem to dominate the assemblage there as do religious objects such as icons, votives, and so forth. By the same token, religious objects in habitational contexts seem to form a very small percentage of the total domestic assemblage. These ideas will require further testing in the future.

Farmsteads have a greater quantity and variety of artifacts than do other sites in the valley. At the other end of the scale, the threshing floors, hearths, and a couple of the limekilns are completely devoid of artifacts. All of the structures and built features at the sites examined are assembled of durable materials, such as bricks, stones, and cinder blocks, except circuit walls of some folds, which are made of brush. Only religious structures and some habitations have any kind of architectural decoration.

Archaeological Site Functions in Pikrodhafni

The information collected about the modern situation was applied to the archaeological data of the valley in the following way. Location, size, and material attributes for each modern site function are summarized in Table 8.1. For each archaeological site in Pikrodhafni

Table 8.5
Inventories of Artifacts/Ecofacts on Modern Sites

Site	Appliances	Furniture	Food related	Containers	Personal Sanitation	Cleaners	Leisure	Decoration	Cloth and clothing	Other Domestic	Religious	Agricultural	Animal related	Manufacturing	Ecofacts
1	kerosene lamp	table, bed, chair, shelf, stool, chest, wardrobe	crockery, glasses, utensils, pots, food	jar, basket, bottle, jug, pithos	comb, brush, back scratcher, medicine	present		pictures	clothes, towels, bedclothes, curtains	plastic pieces, umbrella	icons	basket, tools, ladder, crates, oil vat, chains, insecticide vat, wheelbarrow	feed pans, bridles, feed bags, perches	tile pile, brick pile, wood pile, tin roofing	
2															rubble, burned brush
3															lime, animal bones
4															
5															
6				plastic bottle					shoe	paper piece		plow, crates	feed bags	metal pile, wood pile	
7				can, water jar		broom			sock	paper and plastic pieces		shovel, rake, ladder, crates	feed troughs, feed cages, feed container	saw, bricks, building materials, wood containers, metal containers, cement mixer, metal barriels, wood	dung
8															
9		table, chair	oil	bottle cap, can, match box, ash can, ashtray, bottle		broom, rags	cigarette butts		table cloth, curtain	matches, paper and plastic pieces, cardboard	cross, icons, chanters' chairs, book stand, iconostasis, oil lamps, votives, candles, incense burner, candelabra, wreaths of paper and plastic, coals			bricks, plaster pile	
10		stove pipe	tray	can											
11		chair seat			sponge, detergent				cloth piece, towel, sack, trousers, shirt	shotgun shell		ladder, crates, baskets, rakes, plowshare	bucket, shepard's staff	wood pile, brick pieces, nails, metal hoops	
12															dung

Table 8.5 Concluded

Site	Appliances	Furniture	Food related	Containers	Personal Sanitation	Cleaners	Leisure	Decoration	Cloth and clothing	Other Domestic	Religious	Agricultural	Animal related	Manufacturing	Ecofacts
13				plastic bottle, cans, plastic bag			cigarette box, pen			paper pieces			feed troughs	wood pieces, barrels	
14				glass bottle, cans		bleach bottle			cloth pieces, trousers, belt, shoes	plastic pieces			feed troughs, burlap sacks filled with wood, chicken wire	brick pieces, concrete block, wire, wood pieces	dung
15				plastic bag, plastic bottle, can, glass containers			magazines, newspaper			telephone book					
16	stove, gas burner, refrigerator	table, chair, lamp, bed, sofa, chest, wardrobe, dresser	pots, pans, crockery, glasses, utensils, food	jar, bag, box, bottles, cans, pithos, barrel, bucket		washtub, bleach, detergent	ashtray, T.V., radio, games	pictures, vases, clock	clothes, bedclothes, curtains, towels			crates		metal, glass, wood	
17	stove, washer, refrigerator	table, chair, dresser, bedstead	pots, pans, crockery, glasses, utensils, food tray	pithos, can, wood, box, canvas sack, plastic bag, barrel, jars, watering can		broom	T.V, comic book		clothes, cloth pieces	paper, wood, glass		plow, ladder, crates		shutters, tires, pipes, metal, boxes	
18			fruit peel, oil	glass and plastic bottles, money can, wood box, match box, glass and plastic jars, chalice		brush, rags	newspaper			matches, tissues				tiles	
19	gas canister	straw mats	knife	bags, boxes, flower pot, glass bottle, sacks, cans		paper towels, steel wool, dish drainer	toy pipe		clothes, carpet, shoes, boots, tablecloth	curtain rods		rubber hose		wood, wire, tin, plaster and marble pieces, screens, paint	
20			oil, plate, saucer	bottles, money box, glass box											
21		table, candle	ceramic pieces, bottle caps, candy box and wrapper, sardine can	bottles											
22															wood, ash
23															wood, ash

Table 8.6
Modern Site Characteristics by Function, Pikrodhafni

Site type (function)	Location, surface configuration	Total site size	Artifacts	Ecofacts	Decoration, construction materials
lime kiln	hillside, unrelated to other features, structures	small	none; domestic if reused as dump	lime in soil; bones if reused as dump	durable; worked stone
threshing floor	hilltop, on flat spot; can be associated with farmstead	medium	none	–	durable; worked stone
hearth	hillside	small	none	ash	none
fold	hillside or low rise; can be associated with associated farmstead	small if associated with farmstead; large if isolated	mostly animal related; some domestic	organic soil	durable and nondurable
chapel	hilltop, on locus with previous occupation	medium	mostly religious; some domestic, manufacturing; artifacts from earlier periods	–	durable; embellishments
shrine	on road; unrelated to other features, structures	small	mostly religious, some domestic	–	durable; embellishments
isolated storehouse	hillside	small	mostly agricultural; some manufacturing	–	durable
animal keep	hillside or low rise, can be associated with farmstead	small if part of farmstead; large if isolated	mostly animal related; also manufacturing, agricultural, domestic	organic soil	durable
garbage midden	unused areas; along road in streambed, in abandoned feature	small to large	mostly domestic; manufacturing	organic material	–
farmstead: (includes the following:)	flats or low rise; on or adjacent to arable land; water on site; access to road	medium to large	domestic; religious; agricultural, animal-related, manufacturing	organic soil	durable; embellishments
farm	flats or low rise; on or adjacent to arable land; water on site; access to road	small to medium	domestic; religious; agricultural, animal-related, manufacturing	organic soil	durable; embellishments
house	flats or low rise; on or adjacent to arable land; water on site; access to road	small to medium	mostly domestic; religious; manufacturing	–	durable; embellishments
storehouse	flats or low rise; on or adjacent to arable land; water on site; access to road	small	domestic; animal related; agricultural, manufacturing	–	durable
special-purpose structures	flats or low rise; on or adjacent to arable land; water on site; access to road	small	manufacturing	–	durable

(Table 8.7), the repertoire of ancient materials, site size, and site location was compared with that expected, based on our modern observations for each site function. When concordance was evident, that site was classified as to its ancient function. These classifications were seen as hypotheses only, to be tested when more information becomes available in the future.

In the translation from the modern situation to the ancient, certain adjustments were made. Because artifacts with the same function can look very different through time, expectations as to the nature of the artifacts in the past were kept general. We expected artifact classes, like religious or domestic, not specific items. Also, expectations as to ancient site size were made on a relative scale. Based on our knowledge of modern sites, we expected ancient chapels to cover a smaller area than ancient farmsteads, isolated storehouses to be about the same size as habitations, and so on.

It was also necessary to make a number of assumptions about the uses and use contexts of certain ancient artifacts. Though many of these assumptions are untested, particularly concerning the use of items in the Bronze Age and earlier, many of our ideas about how analysis of object functions, especially for the historical periods, should be based on accumulated knowledge from written records and excavations have a firm foundation.

Most pottery, both coarse and fine, was seen as primarily for single-family domestic use (for cooking and/or for serving). Large pottery storage jars were for domestic and/or agricultural use (e.g., to store grains for sowing, etc.). Millstones were used in domestic contexts as food-processing appliances (e.g., flour manufacture) and may also have been used in processing agricultural products (sometimes on a large scale or at an industrial level). Chipped stone (including flakes) were multipurpose tools meant for domestic, agricultural, and manufacturing use. Large machine parts like *trapeta* (press blocks) were used for processing agricultural products.

In order to apply the above procedure, several assumptions were made about the natural and human processes that contributed to the content and configurations of the ancient sites in Pikrodhafni. As was pointed out above, our primary purpose was not to look into the depositional processes that formed the archaeological sites in the valley. We can, therefore, offer no hypotheses as to why most of those sites contained the materials that they did. It is safe to say that a myriad of cultural and natural processes structured not only the actual content of the sites, but also their observed surface manifestations. It is also safe to say that the depositional scenario for each ancient site studied was different. Ethnoarchaeologists have only recently begun to document site formation processes (using data mostly from parts of the world other than Greece). There is an enormous amount of work to be done before such information can actually be used in archaeological interpretations.

In order for our study to proceed, therefore, we assumed that the ancient sites in Pikrodhafni contained most of the artifacts that had been used there in the past and that the sample from the surface was representative of that assemblage. We also assumed that the size of the surface scatter at any one locus was representative of the size of the ancient site. In light of our scant knowledge about site formation processes in general, these assumptions were naive. Yet, without any specific knowledge of how sites had been transformed since the time of their use, we could do no more than to make those assumptions. We are well aware, therefore, that our thoughts about site functions in ancient Pikrodhafni are open to further testing.

The determination of site functions required comparison of both the ancient and modern

Table 8.7

Summary of Data on Ancient Sites and Hypothesized Site Functions, Pikrodhafni

AEP site number	Location, and surface configuration	Site size (m²)	Artifacts	Construction materials	Function (site type) per period
B101	hillside; hilltop just above site	hilltop has same diameter as modern threshing floor 1,191	agricultural (chipped stone) = threshing sledge flints?		threshing floor: period?
B102	chert outcrop	very large 10,976	domestic, agricultural (chipped stone, undiagnostic sherds)		quarry: Roman period?
B94	hilltop; in line with two medieval chapels on north side of the valley; on earlier site	medium 4,834	domestic (pottery), religious (perirrhanterion), agricultural[a] (chipped stone)	embellishment (marble)	chapel: medieval
E50	hilltop; in line with two medieval chapels on north side of the valley; on earlier site	very large[a] 14,710	domestic, agricultural[a], manufacturing[a] (chipped stone, pottery)	embellishment (frescos, column) durable (walls)	chapel: medieval
E46	hilltop, on earlier site	medium 1,546	domestic (chipped stone, pottery)	embellishement (frescos, stone fragments)	chapel: medieval
E51	flats, along road; away from contemporary sites	very large 23,173	domestic, agricultural, manufacturing (chipped stone, pottery, loom weight); in worn, small pieces		garbage midden: classical to modern periods
B95/96	hilltop[a] and hillside; easy access to arable flatlands	medium 3,345	domestic, agricultural (millstones, pottery)	durable (worked block)	farmstead: classical-Hellenistic
B97	hilltop[a]; easy access to arable flatlands	medium 1,173	domestic, agricultural, manufacturing (pottery, millstones, chipped stone)	durable (walls)	farmstead: Bronze Age and medieval
B100	low rise; on arable land	very large 16,674	domestic, agricultural, manufacturing (pottery, millstones, chipped stone)	durable (walls, stone block)	farmstead: classical-Roman and medieval Turkish
B94	hilltop[a]	medium 4,834	domestic, agricultural, manufacturing (chipped stone, pottery)		farmstead: Turkish
B98	hilltop[a]	medium 2,310	domestic, agricultural, manufacturing (pottery, millstones, chipped stone)	durable (stone block)	farmstead: Bronze Age and medieval Turkish
E40	low rise; easy access to arable flatlands	medium 4,533	domestic[a] (pottery)		farmstead: Bronze Age-medieval

Table 8.7 *Concluded*

AEP site number	Location, and surface configuration	Site size (m²)	Artifacts	Construction materials	Function (site type) per period
E41	flatlands, by the road	medium 2,085	domestic[a] (pottery)		farmstead: classical–modern
E52	flatlands; on arable lands	small[a] 501	domestic[a] (pottery)	durable (walls, blocks)	farmstead: classical–Hellenistic
E53	flatlands; on arable lands	medium 4,703	domestic, agricultural, manufacturing (pottery–mostly large storage containers[a], chipped stone)		farmstead?: Roman modern
E54	flatlands; on arable lands	small[a] 274	domestic (pottery), agricultural (press block)		farmstead: classical–Roman
E43	flatlands; on arable lands	small[a] 297	domestic, agricultural (pottery, millstones)	durable (rubble walls)	farmstead: classical–Hellenistic
E44	low rise	medium 1,798	domestic[a] (pottery)	durable (stone blocks, wall?)	farmstead: classical–Hellenistic
E53	flatlands[a]; on arable lands beside road	medium 4,703	domestic, agricultural, manufacturing (pottery–mostly large containers, chipped stone)		storehouse?: Roman–modern
B97	hilltop	medium[a] 1,173	domestic, agricultural (pottery–large containers)		storehouse: classical Hellenistic
B98	hilltop	medium 2,301	domestic, agricultural, manufacturing (pottery–mostly large containers, millstone, chipped stone)		storehouse: classical–Roman
E42	hillside[a]	medium 2,301	domestic, agricultural, manufacturing (pottery, millstones, chipped stone)		farmstead: medieval
E46	hilltop	medium 2,301	domestic, agricultural, manufacturing (pottery[a], millstones, chipped stone)		storehouse: classical–Hellenistic

[a] Does not conform to prediction for designated function.
NOTE: No ecofacts are reported for this table.

sites. Sometimes the expectations as to ancient site characteristics based on the modern data were met and sometimes they were not. In considering the disconfirmed hypotheses, new hypotheses as to site functions emerged. Ancient site functions and the logic that led to their determination are presented below.

Chapels

The easiest site functions to identify were those of sites E50 and E46. The plans (arrangement) of their still visible walls, combined with the fresco fragments and other architectural embellishments associated with the walls, identified the sites as chapels used in the medieval period. The chapel at E50 sits in the middle of a rather large scatter of archaeological material. The scatter is larger than what one would expect to have come from simply one structure; perhaps there was a small medieval village surrounding the chapel.

Not so easy to identify is a possible third medieval chapel (B94), beneath the modern chapel of Ayia Panayia (MS#9). The pottery found at the site could be labeled domestic, but we know from the modern-site data that domestic artifacts are a part of religious assemblages. The marble pieces found at B94 were perhaps architectural decoration, a characteristic one would expect at a religious structure. The few premedieval artifacts (classical and Roman), most notably a perirrhanterion base (a religious object in classical times), found at the site are consistent with expectations for a medieval religious structure. The geographical position of B94 was also a factor in hypothesizing its religious function. Two other chapels, E50 and a medieval chapel that is still in use (MS#21), are situated on hills on the north side of the valley, as is B94. Adding B94 to these others would result in three chapels on the same side of the valley, approximately equidistant from each other.

An alternative hypothesis for the function of B94 is that it was a medieval farmstead. Its domestic/agricultural artifacts and hilltop location are congruent with our observations at other hypothesized medieval farmsteads.

Threshing Floor and Quarry

The scatter of lithics that forms site B101 perhaps represents the residues of threshing activities from an unknown period. The diameter of the hilltop just above this site matches the diameters for modern threshing floors, suggesting a buried threshing floor lies there. The lithics might be debris from the use of threshing sleds on the floor, the material having subsequently washed a short distance downhill. Lithic analyses to date, however, have not confirmed this surmise, even though recent studies (Anderson-Gerfaud 1992; Ataman 1992; Kardulias and Yerkes 1996) have identified a specific microwear signature for threshing sled flints.

Farmsteads

It appears that most (13 out of 23) ancient sites in Pikrodhafni were farmsteads. Like their modern counterparts, the hypothesized ancient farmsteads are located in the far western and far eastern ends of the valley, though not exactly on the same spots as the modern farmsteads.

To be labeled unequivocally as farmsteads, ancient sites had to meet the other criteria (i.e., location, size, and material content) for modern farmstead sites. Besides being located on flatlands or low rises, modern farmsteads, medium to large in size, are made of durable materials, can consist of a complex of buildings in addition to a house, and make use of the following classes of artifacts: domestic, religious, manufacturing, animal related, and agricultural. Only one ancient site, B100, fully met these criteria. It is situated on a low rise at the western end of the valley on arable land, and has some preserved ancient walls. Agricultural, domestic, and manufacturing artifacts form the bulk of the material assemblage. The wide horizontal extent of the scatter and the long period of time represented by the artifacts (classical-Roman, medieval-Turkish) suggest a lateral association with some overlap as opposed to a direct vertical superimposition of successive site components.

Three sites, E52, E54, and E43, were probably farmsteads as well, for they are located on the flats in the eastern part of the valley and have domestic/agricultural artifacts. The sites are much smaller than expected, however; in fact, they are the smallest archaeological sites in the valley. Perhaps their small size is accounted for by the fact that they are essentially one-component sites (classical-Hellenistic) and are located on land that is not easily affected by erosion. E52, besides being small, has only domestic artifacts, not the variety expected for farmsteads. Its location, however, makes it seem unlikely that E52 was simply a house (versus a farm or farmstead). The visible architectural remains at E52 are also comparable to those at hypothesized ancient farmstead sites known elsewhere in Greece, such as the Vari house (Jones, Graham, and Sackett 1973) and surface sites in Attica (Young 1956).

Located on a low rise not far from E43, E44 meets the criteria for a farmstead except that it, too, does not have a variety of artifacts, but only domestic pottery. Perhaps E43 and E44, assuming both were occupied at the same time and were connected in some way, were being used for the same purpose at slightly different times, or for slightly different purposes at the same time.

E40, located on a low rise on the edge of the eastern flatlands, may have been a farmstead, though only domestic artifacts are found there. It is interesting to note that E40 produced the only evidence for Geometric-period (ca. 1100–750 B.C.) activity in the Pikrodhafni valley. The site spans the periods from early Helladic (3rd millennium B.C.) through the medieval. During the classical-Hellenistic and Roman periods, E40 had a very close neighbor, another possible farmstead, E41 (which also produced only domestic artifacts). Perhaps E40 and E41 were closely related in the same ways hypothesized for E43 and E44.

E53, also situated on the flat agricultural land in the eastern end of the valley, was perhaps a farmstead from Roman to modern times, though the domestic pottery found there consists mainly of large storage vessels. An isolated storehouse is an alternative hypothesis, though the location of the site, as well as its size, would then not fit the expectation for isolated storehouses. Perhaps this site had a function for which there are no modern examples: a small country store, for example.

The last five sites in Pikrodhafni that might be called farmsteads do not meet one important criterion. Their locations are not those expected for farmsteads (i.e., flats or low rises) but are, rather, hillsides or hilltops. E42, situated on a hillside on the south side of the eastern part of the valley, was occupied during the medieval period. Despite its location, its size and artifact assemblage fit those expected for farmsteads. Perhaps it was characteristic of the medieval-Turkish inhabitants of the valley to occupy more out-of-the-way spots, as opposed to the more open locales chosen by the classical Greeks or modern peoples. This argument gains strength as one examines the other possible medieval-Turkish farmstead sites and finds that they are all situated on hilltops (B98, B94, B97). It appears that the Bronze Age inhabitants of B97 and B98 also preferred hilly locales.

B95/96 seems to have been chosen as a farmstead site in the classical-Hellenistic period despite its hilltop location; that is, other classical-Hellenistic farmsteads are located on flatlands on cultivable land. B95/96 has easy access to such lands and therefore is perhaps not so different; it also has domestic/agricultural artifacts and is medium in size, thus meeting other requirements for a farmstead.

B97 and B98 were hypothesized above to have been farmsteads during the medieval-Turkish period, but they were also in use during the classical-Hellenistic period. Their hilltop positions, however, make it seem unlikely that they were farmsteads during this latter period, a postulate that is strengthened by the apparent preference during the classical-Hellenistic period (see observations above) for locating farmsteads on arable flatlands or low rises. Since most of the classical-Hellenistic pottery at sites B97 and B98 consists of large storage containers, the function of isolated storehouse is suggested for those sites during the classical-Hellenistic period, though the sizes of these sites exceed those expected for storehouses. Perhaps the later components of these sites, being larger, mask much smaller classical-Hellenistic components. E46, another hilltop site occupied during the classical-Hellenistic period as well as during the medieval period, seems to fit the same pattern suggested for sites B97 and B98 and thus was perhaps a classical-Hellenistic storehouse, although only a few domestic sherds and no storage vessels from that period were found.

Garbage Midden

Site E51 consists of a very large scatter of domestic, agricultural, and manufacturing artifacts. The scatter is situated on the flatlands on either side of the modern road that runs down the center of the valley. One might be tempted to call this site another farmstead (dating from the classical period to modern times) because of its location on cultivable land and its artifact assemblage. The problem is that most of the artifacts at E51 are quite fragmentary and worn, a condition not encountered at the other hypothesized farmsteads. An alternate explanation is that the site represents an ancient dump similar to MS#19, which is also located, like E51, on unused arable land beside a road. E51 is near sites E41 and E40, but far enough away that it could have served them as a dump beginning in the classical period. E50 and E52, as well as the rest of the farmsteads at the eastern end of the valley, could also have used this location to deposit unwanted articles of all kinds.

Changing Function Through Time

Another significant result of the project was the information on formation processes gained by examining abandoned sites. The rapid decay and/or obscuring of limekilns and threshing floors, and the paucity of artifacts associated with them, suggest that certain significant features from the past may be difficult to interpret if analysis is based solely on surface indications, and thus these features may be underrepresented in the sample of archaeological sites. Information was also gained relevant to the reuse of sites and artifacts through time. With regard to several kilns, some deserted homes, and certain objects in occupied sites, a process of degradation of function was noted. This process saw structures and artifacts pass through a series of stages from initial function to ultimate nonuse or discard. Limekilns serving ultimately as repositories for refuse and abandoned houses transformed into goat or sheep pens are examples of the degradation of structural use. With certain artifacts the process is even more elaborate. Large oil storage jars, or *pithoi*, for example, underwent secondary use as water containers, followed by a tertiary use either as decorative pieces if they remained whole or terrace wall components if they broke. Only when the object, or parts thereof, were seen as totally useless were they discarded—the final or most degraded stage. The overall impression from these observations is that pithoi, and other artifacts, must be viewed as progressing through a sequence of functional phases through time, from the highly pragmatic to the ornamental. The overabundance of certain items in the artifact inventory of archaeological sites may in part be attributed to the maintenance of such specimens in a nonutilitarian mode after their pragmatic value has been exhausted. Once again, the problem of discerning such episodes in the career of artifacts collected from the surface is considerable. An awareness of this phenomenon, though, does at least permit the archaeologist to hint at the complexity of forces that created the surface scatter one encounters.

Conclusions

In conclusion, a few general statements concerning modern sites and ancient sites in Pikrodhafni are in order. First, all modern sites are situated at places devoid of archaeological material, with two exceptions. MS#9, Ayia Panayia chapel, is on top of B94, and MS#4, a threshing floor, is superimposed on B95/96. The location of the former may have been deliberate (see above), but the location of the latter seems to have been fortuitous. That is, the builders of the site had no prior knowledge of ancient remains on their building site. Though ancient site locations are mostly different from modern ones, they are in some cases similar. Ancient sites that are hypothesized to have been classical-Hellenistic farmsteads, for example, are located in general areas and on specific spots similar to those chosen for modern farmsteads.

Estimations of ancient site size are, on the whole, larger than those of modern site size (see Tables 8.4 and 8.7). It appears that natural and cultural forces may have spread ancient materials over greater areas than they originally occupied.

There are some modern sites in Pikrodhafni for which we found no ancient analogs. We found no evidence for ancient limekilns, shrines, isolated animal keeps, small hearths, and folds. Because we expect hearths and some folds to have been made from nondurable materials and to have contained very few, if any, artifacts, it is not surprising that no surface indications of these kinds of sites were detected, though it would be difficult to believe that they were never previously extant in the valley. That we found no isolated animal keeps is a bit more surprising. Animal-related artifacts from the past may not have preserved well, or perhaps they have not been properly identified as such. We expect ancient shrines, if they are like modern ones, to have been very small, and therefore would not be easily seen on the surface today. Shrines are perhaps modern structures only, and thus we would not expect to find them in the archaeological record. The same is perhaps the case for limekilns.

Finally, there is at least one kind of archaeological site in Pikrodhafni for which there are no modern counterparts. Site B102 was apparently an ancient chert quarry. There are no chert quarries in operation today, of course, because the need for this commodity has ceased.

The Modern-Site Survey afforded us the opportunity to focus on ancient site usage by examining contemporary contexts. We have used this information to formulate hypotheses about site functions. In addition, our observations have led to the formulation of a number of cautionary statements, as follows:

1. One must consider the possibility that a substantial number of sites, especially in higher elevations, represent storage or special activity loci rather than residences, thus decreasing the population figures and number of autonomous sites for any particular period in the past (but especially for those times in which agriculture is the primary subsistence form).

2. Since domestic items may well be present in considerable amounts in various kinds of sites, one must not hasten to categorize all sites with such material as farmsteads or residences based simply on a presence/absence scale.

3. Certain sites of some economic importance today (e.g., goat/sheep folds) contain few artifacts and are often constructed of nondurable materials that will leave behind little evidence of their function in the future. Postulating a similar situation for antiquity, and there is no reason to believe that many ancient animal pens were any less flimsy than their modern counterparts, we can expect to have a minimal record of a site type that in truth formed a vital link in the economic network.

4. There are certain modern sites with no known ancient analog. If the converse is true, we are again faced with an unbalanced view of site diversity.

5. If ancient sites were as frequently reused as are modern ones, the precise nature of a multicomponent site in terms of functions may be much more complex than would be implied by considering the components simply as successive periods of on-site habitation.

6. Since certain artifacts tend to be utilized well beyond the time when their initial function has ceased (through the process of degradation of function), employing such items as temporal indicators may give a false impression of a site's age.

It has been our intention to demonstrate the utility of ethnoarchaeological research as a supplement to archaeological survey work. Since the latter must focus on data extant on the surface, explanatory models concerning ancient behavior tend to be somewhat limited. Any technique that can provide a more developed exegetical framework can contribute to a clearer understanding of site function. Although still in a nascent stage, the method outlined in this essay has attempted to provide such assistance.

CHAPTER NINE

The Changing Household Economy
on Methana, 1880-1996

Mari H. Clarke

The countless rows of stone walls supporting terraced fields of grain and olives on Methana's mountainsides and the farmers plowing those fields with mules, cutting wheat with sickles, and digging vines with hoes gave the casual viewer in the 1970s and 1980s a false impression of isolation and traditional self-sufficiency. The peninsula appeared to be far removed from the economic and social changes that had transformed nearby Athens into a noisy, crowded, international city over the past century. Looking beyond Methana's traditional technology, necessitated by the mountainous terrain, to the history of trade, travel, and especially population movement—between Methana and other parts of the Argolid as well as Piraeus, Attica, and the islands of Aegina, Poros, Hydra, and Syros—reveals that Methanites have been significantly affected by the same economic forces that created modern Athens in the nineteenth and twentieth centuries.

In the following pages, I examine the transformation of the household economy on Methana over the past century (1880–1996).[1] I argue that in order to explain this transformation it is necessary to examine both the larger economic, ecological, and historical context in which Methana participated and the corresponding social and economic dynamics of particular households. My analysis draws on the analytical frameworks of cultural ecology (Netting 1977, 1993; Wilk 1989), family history (Kertzer 1984), and the feminist critique of the neoclassical approach to household economics (Folbre 1984). This approach also reflects the growing sense of both anthropologists and historians that household history must move away from counting numbers of static household types to examining the processes of change in the activities pursued by the individuals within households. Household history should also present the cultural values and meanings that often underlie the persistence of particular household forms (Netting, Wilk, and Arnould 1984).

A number of scholars concerned with household dynamics and the economic position of women have emphasized the need to focus on individuals as primary units of analysis, rather than on households, in order to examine carefully the transfer of goods and services both between and within households. By investigating the activity spheres of individual household members, it is possible to specify which activities characterize the household and which link individuals or households to other groups. Folbre, an economist who has analyzed data from the

Philippines, has focused on household decision making in terms of the negotiation of individual interests (1984). She has thus demonstrated how the ability of individuals to control the outcomes of household decision making was directly related to their control of valued resources (land, houses, etc.) and how the "negotiating power" shifted for some individuals due to greater involvement in the market economy.[2]

Folbre's notion of negotiating power also provides a useful tool for explaining some of the changes in relations between generations, from the Turkish period to the present, in Methana's stem households (married, adult children, and at least one parent living and working together for at least one phase of the domestic cycle).[3] My approach differs from a strictly economic analysis, however, because I situate households in ecological, economic, and political contexts and account for cultural values and other factors affecting the individual decisions and household negotiations. Thus, my approach includes factors that have changed household form and function over time. I have used oral history to ask what values concerning "family" and "household" have affected economic behavior and what economic factors have affected family and household form and activities over time.

This chapter is organized in terms of continuities and changes during two key periods of economic development for Methana—from 1880 to the Second World War, and from the postwar period to the present. The first period spans many years but shows relatively few changes, although it does show the seeds of changes that occurred later. In my other chapter in this volume, I discuss the earlier period in more detail, distinguishing between the Turkish period and the period between Independence and World War II. I based the starting date of 1880 for the earlier period on the limits of reliability of oral histories and the scarce availability of older documents. Given such factors, discussion of the first period should be viewed as a sketch that sets the scene and suggests the origins of the developments that followed in the postwar period.

The division between these two periods reflects the insistence of Methanites that major changes in their lifestyle occurred after World War II, a view affirmed by evidence from Methana and other areas of Greece. Within each period, I examine the linkages with the region and the nation. I discuss as well demographic trends, the changing local economy, and household form and activities. Throughout I emphasize the relationship between the transformation of the national economy and the transformation of the household economy on Methana.

Ecological and Cultural Continuities

Certain constant features of life on Methana are a necessary part of the explanation of what has changed and why. These include the rugged landscape, the smallholder agricultural livelihood, and the value placed on family and household.

The Landscape

Methana is a mountainous volcanic peninsula in the Saronic Gulf. It is attached to the rest of the Greek Argolid at a narrow isthmus. Methana's steep hillsides, combined with a Mediterranean climate of winter rainfall and summer drought, necessitated construction of terraced fields (see Figure 9.1) to create arable land and reduce soil erosion.[4] Cultivation terraces stretch

Figure 9.1. Terraced fields, Methana.

from sea level to roughly 700 m, near the top of the peninsula. Today the steeper and less productive terraces have been abandoned and are overgrown with scrub.

Water has always been a limiting factor on Methana. Only one village has a spring. Until recently, other villages depended on rainwater for farming, drinking, cooking, and watering livestock. When cisterns ran dry, people had to carry water from somewhat brackish wells near the sea. People also used these wells for irrigation of nearby fields. In the early 1970s, piped water from the nearby plain of Troizinia began to provide a steady year-round water supply. Unfortunately, the cost was too high for profitable use in irrigated farming.

There are ten nucleated agricultural settlements on Methana. Loutrapolis (Figure 9.2), the present port and administrative center, developed mainly in the twentieth century with growth of the sulfur spring health spa starting in 1870 (see Clarke 1995, this volume). The plain of Troizinia has been an important part of the landscape also because Methanites owned and cultivated land there throughout the period from 1880 to 1986. While the climate, soil, and slope thus remained the same, what changed over time was the amount of landscape cultivated by Methanites.

Smallholder Agriculture

Methanites' economic livelihood is best described as smallholder agriculture. Following Netting (1993: 2),

smallholders are rural cultivators practicing intensive, permanent, diversified agriculture on relatively small farms in areas of dense population. The family household is a major corporate

Figure 9.2. Loutrapolis, 1920. From author's files. Reproduction by C. Mouzy.

unit for mobilizing agricultural labor, managing corporate resources, and organizing consumption. The household produces a significant part of its own subsistence and generally participates in the market. Smallholders have ownership or other well-defined tenure rights in land that are long-term and often inheritable.

On their mountainous terrain Methanites have combined farming with livestock raising. Basic crops have included wheat, barley, oil olives, legumes, wine grapes, vegetables, carobs, and, in the past, cotton and flax (see Joan Koster, this volume). Local farmers also grow almonds, figs, pears, other tree fruit, and hay. Each family maintains a few chickens, sheep, and goats and one or two mules or donkeys. Methanites have selectively cultivated their terrain, matching soil composition, altitude, and slope with temperature and moisture needs of specific tree and field crops (see Clarke 1976a, 1977, Forbes, this volume). They interplant tree crops, such as olives, with field crops, such as wheat, on the same terraces.

Because of this diversity of crops, Methanites must coordinate several tasks at any one time. For example, in March farmers must hoe the soil around the grapevines, weed or spray weed killer on the wheat, plow the summer vegetable gardens, and begin harvesting peas. It is important to bear in mind that the scheduling of tasks changes from year to year with variations in rainfall, temperature, and the care of biannual crops such as olives, which require harvesting only in alternate years.

In addition to scheduling a variety of farming tasks over the year, it is also necessary to coordinate those activities in space because landholdings on Methana are scattered. Most fields range from five minutes to one hour in walking distance from the villages. Some are as far as three hours away. Most villagers own twenty-five to fifty-five separate plots. These plots range in size from a few square meters to five *stremmata* (about .5 ha) of adjacent terraced fields. This fragmentation of landholdings is a result of dowry and inheritance patterns (see Clarke 1998; Adams, Forbes, this volume). It is possible that the irregular nature of the terrain also contributes to the fragmentation of landholdings (Wagstaff 1986). While such smallholder agriculture has persisted over time, what has changed is its importance in the national, local, and household economy.

The Value of Family and Household

Following Wilk and Netting (1984), I use the term *household* as a unit of activity distinct from the term *family*, because the latter is a unit of kinship that is not necessarily localized.[5] It is important to understand the meanings and values that Methanites associate with these terms in order to assess the ways in which these cultural constructions have affected changes in the household economy and have been affected by them. In discussing the meaning and value of family and household on Methana, it is important to bear in mind the Albanian heritage of Methanites, even though it is difficult to assess the extent to which it might have affected them.[6]

Methanites frequently use the terms house (*spiti*) and family (*oikoyenia*) interchangeably. The house as a physical structure is viewed as a reflection of family prosperity.[7] The behavior of the house as a group of people who live and work together reflects family honor and worth.[8]

When asked who the members of a family were, most Methanites replied, "the mother, father, and children who live together." When questioned about elders in the stem household, everyone also included them as part of the family. Furthermore, when they described family photographs and gatherings and visits by family members, the family included people outside of the household and even outside the village. The term *soi* (line of descent) was also used in instances where family or kin (*sinyenis*) would generally be used in English. For example, a villager explained that there were many guests at a recent wedding because the bride's mother has a large *soi*.

Local ideals associated with family emphasize the responsibilities of family members. These include carrying on the family line through offspring, providing for the basic needs of family members, maintaining and increasing the family estate, providing for the future of one's children, and caring for aging parents. While the family and household continue to be valued, what has changed over time is the ways in which family members carry out such family responsibilities and the kinds of places where they reside.

The Changing Household Economy:
1880 to World War II

The period from 1880 to World War II was one of ongoing economic growth as the new Greek nation continued to develop an infrastructure of roads, communications, administration, and education—an infrastructure that had been neglected during the period of Turkish rule.

Links with the Region and the Nation

In the nineteenth century Methanites looked to Poros as a trade center as well as administrative seat. Poros was an important maritime hub, even though it lacked a large fleet (Stamatiou 1939, Stavrolakis 1979).[9] The early traveler Dodwell described Poros town, opposite the plain of Troizinia, as a thriving settlement of prosperous traders in the early 1800s (1819: 274–75). Until construction of the health spa in the 1870s, the area that is now the town of Loutrapolis had only cultivated fields and a *kafeneio* (coffee house) at the harbor. Methanites went to Poros to buy shoes, weaving supplies, salt cod, and for simple legal matters. As Piraeus grew into a commercial center and steamships greatly reduced travel time, Methanites increasingly looked toward the national capital *also* for trade and employment.

In the past, the sea was the major link between Methana and other areas. In the nineteenth century, cargo boats driven by sail and later by motor carried olive oil, figs, pears, and almonds from Methana to Athens, Poros, Hydra, and later to Syros and brought other goods back to Methana. Most cargo boats were owned by men from the nearby islands of Aegina and Poros; few Methanites engaged in this trade.[10] By 1918, a steamer made regular trips between Piraeus, Aegina, Poros, and Methana (Great Britain 1918: 118). In the days of travel by sail, the journey of 52.8 km from Methana to Piraeus took five to eight hours depending on the wind. The same journey by steamship took three hours.

During this period there were no roads on the peninsula, only steep, stony paths leading from villages to tiny ports, docking places, villages, and the plain of Troizinia. By mule or by foot, travel from the villages to the port took one to three hours; the journey to fields on the plain was five to eight hours; a trip to Nafplio required over a day.

Despite the lack of roads and vehicles, Methanites's economic ties also stretched overland through participation in trade fairs on the plain of Troizinia, connections with itinerant craftsmen such as stonemasons and tinsmiths, and exchange of goods between transhumant shepherds and farmers (Harold Koster 1977, this volume; Koster and Koster 1976; Petronoti 1985c). In the winter, Methanites rented their fallow fields on the plain to transhumant shepherds from the mountains in Arcadia who brought their flocks to graze in lower pastures. Many Methanites took their wheat to a water-driven mill on the plain of Troizinia. They also purchased mules and donkeys there since no one raised them on the peninsula. Serious legal business such as court cases required a journey by mule to Nafplio, the capital of the Argolid, the administrative unit for Methana until the late 1920s.

The plain of Troizinia played an important role in Methana's economic history because many Methanites cultivated land there when they did not own enough on the peninsula to grow wheat without fertilizer. Lacking fertilizer and quality seeds, wheat yields were low. Methanites bought or rented fields on the plain in the sparsely populated area between Metamorphosis and Ayios Yeorghios.[11] In the 1880s, the geographer Miliarakis described the plain as uncultivated and full of scrub except for the lemon orchards and other crops near the village of Troizin and the gardens around the villas of estate owners (Miliarakis 1886: 195).

The history of changing political boundaries reflects a shift in Methana's external ties from the Argolid region to the greater Athens area. In 1879, Methana was part of the *nomos* (department) of the Argolid and Corinthia and lay within the *eparkhia* (county) of Hydra and Troizinia.

Its capital was Nafplio (Houliarakis 1974, 2:58–61; Sutton, this volume). By 1928, Methana was a part of the *nomos* of Attica and Boeotia and lay within the eparkhia of Troizinia. Its capital was Athens (Greece, National Statistical Service 1935: 48–53).

A similar reorientation of administrative seats also took place within the peninsula of Methana. In 1851, the administrative center was Megalokhori on the western side of the peninsula, facing the rest of the Argolid (Rangavis 1853: 283). By 1881, the village of Kounipitsa, on the eastern side of the peninsula, looking toward Piraeus, had become the seat (Houliarakis 1973: 61). And by 1928, Methana's port town was the center of local administration (Greece, National Statistical Service 1935: 68).

Demographic Trends

The population of Methana increased steadily from 1,644 inhabitants in 1851 to 2,747 in 1940. However, population growth was not even throughout the peninsula. The port town grew from 114 inhabitants in 1896 to 789 in 1940. The population of most mountain farming villages remained constant with the exception of the highest settlements. One small settlement was abandoned. Two others shrank from 192 inhabitants in each in 1851, to 138 and 101 inhabitants respectively in 1940.

On the plain of Troizinia in 1851 only the village of Troizin had a population over 300. Other settlements ranged from scattered farmhouses to clusters of three to 37 houses (Rangavis 1853: 282). Most settlements on the plain increased in size rapidly.[12] The village of Taktikoupolis increased from 11 inhabitants in 1851 to 381 in 1940. Troizin increased in population from 334 to 531 during the same period. The overall population on the plain increased from 524 to 2,805 (Ragkavis 1853: 282, Greece, National Statistical Service 1950: 78).

The lack of population growth in Methana's mountain villages from 1850–1940, as compared with the growth on Troizinia, can be explained by migration of many Methanites to the port town, Piraeus, Athens, and overseas as well as a reduction in family size toward the end of the period.[13] Methanites contributed to the growing population of the greater Athens area which expanded from 36,594 (3.5% of the total Greek population) in 1853 to 1,124,109 (15.3%) in 1940 (Ward 1963: 66).

In the early part of the twentieth century, some families sold land on Methana and purchased cheap, poor quality farmland in what are now the districts of Dafni and Ayios Dhimitrios in Athens. Many boys left Methana in their early teens seeking work as shop boys, waiters, and servants. Migration of females to Athens was mainly through marriage, adoption, or working as live-in maids with the understanding that the house owners would provide their dowry. Toward the end of the period more girls went to Athens or Piraeus to learn to be seamstresses, living with relatives already based there.

The Local Economy

By the second decade of the twentieth century, Methana town had expanded to a full row of shops and hotels along the seaside; included were a pharmacy, rooming houses, a post office, a bakery, a butcher's shop, a fruit store, coffeehouses, and a dry goods store. The growth of the port town also stimulated development of a street market, which started with the sale of fresh milk and eggs by women from mountain villages to visitors staying in rooming houses.[14] Village boys earned money as waiters in the *kafeneia* and restaurants. From around 1910 through the end of the period, men in a small settlement on the isthmus of Methana engaged in trapping fish with nets.

In the early decades of the twentieth century, some village men went to Athens to work seasonally in the salt flats. In the 1940s men went to Koropi and Markopoulo in Attica to earn wages hoeing, harvesting, and pressing grapes. In addition to coastal trade of goods, there was increasing employment in the merchant marine. This was most common in villages with "connections." As sailors left, wives, children, and parents remained behind to till the soil. On the plain of Troizinia, owners of large holdings hired workers for harvesting grain, olives, and citrus crops.

From the 1870s through World War II, most Methanites, like most Greeks, were farmers. Farming on Methana largely served family needs, but there was also sale of surplus wheat, olive oil, almonds, and fruit. Local people insist that the agricultural technology and standard of living in the villages on the peninsula did not change until after World War II. They emphasize the poverty of the past, the difficult, rocky terrain, dependence on rainwater, the lack of access to cash, and the need to work dawn to dusk to provide for family needs. Their descriptions of the lifestyle of their parents and grandparents are similar to historians' accounts of the conditions of Greek farmers during the Turkish period—near self-sufficiency; a spartan diet of barley bread, olives, and legumes; homemade clothing and tools (McGrew 1985: 5).

Conditions on Methana fitted these descriptions very closely. Houses were simple. Clothing was handmade, and few people wore shoes. They rarely ate meat or sugar or drank coffee. Until about the 1920s, men on Methana plowed with wooden plows pulled by locally raised cows. Mules, purchased from other areas, were used only as pack animals. Gradually everyone sold or butchered the cows and plowed with mules and donkeys (see Figure 9.3). Even though this required a greater cash investment, the mules and donkeys were more efficient. Methanites threshed grain on circular stone threshing floors, first with cows and later with mules and donkeys (see Figure 9.4). When they still used cows to plow, they pressed their grapes on the mountain in *patitiria*, small buildings constructed for this purpose, and carried the wine must in goatskin bags (*touloumia*) by mule to the village. Before the start of World War II, villagers had already started carrying the grapes in baskets on mules to the village for pressing.

During the Turkish period, people pressed olives in small, hand-driven stone presses. Later they used donkeys to turn the stones. For limited irrigation along the coast, they drew water from wells by hand or with the aid of a forked stick with a weight at one end to lift a bucket of water at the other end. In the late 1920s, they began using the Persian well (a series of small buckets connected by a chain to gears which were turned by a mule) to provide a steady stream of water.[15]

Many families owned twenty to fifty sheep and the same number of goats—all were grazed on the mountainside. No one grew hay or other fodder for the animals. Sheep and goats provided important products for subsistence and trade. The wool was essential for making clothing and the milk for preparing cheese. People used the manure from animal sheds to fertilize their grapevines and vegetable gardens. There was not enough manure for wheat and other crops, and chemical fertilizer was not available. They sold lambs and kids to the butcher in the port town.

Figure 9.3. Sowing and plowing wheat by mule, Methana, 1985.

Figure 9.4. Threshing barley, Methana, 1974.

They also raised chickens, which roosted in trees and wandered in and out of houses. Their pigs roamed the paths of the villages scavenging for scraps of food.

It is important to keep in mind that the spartan existence of Methanites prior to World War II was in part due to frugality rather than dire poverty. People ate simply and spent little on consumer goods in order to build up capital from surplus crop sales and seasonal wage labor to invest in land and businesses on Methana, the plain of Troizinia, Poros, Aegina, and in Piraeus and Athens.

For most of this period there were no trained health professionals on the peninsula. More infants and young children died than was the case in later years. Children and adults died of conditions that are easily treated or prevented today such as diarrhea, tetanus, smallpox, and influenza. More women died in childbirth.[16] Local healers treated broken bones. Untrained local midwives and neighbors delivered babies. When there were complications in delivering a baby or serious illnesses, people traveled to Poros to get a doctor. Because cash was scarce, people sometimes had to borrow money at high rates of interest to pay for medical care. The state established an outpatient clinic with a nurse on the peninsula in the decade before World War II.

Before the turn of the century, there were only two primary schools on Methana. They were in the two villages that shared the status of administrative capital. In the early twentieth century the state built schools in two other villages. Many children had to walk several kilometers to attend school. Until about 1930, parents rarely sent girls to school. Instead, girls tended sheep, goats, and small siblings and performed other farm tasks. Parents occasionally took boys from school for farmwork. Parents' rationale for educating only boys was that males needed to learn to read and write in order to buy and sell goods when they headed a household, whereas females would become farmers' wives and perform tasks they could learn from their parents.

This selective schooling was particularly significant on Methana because school was the only place to learn Greek. The first language was Greek-Albanian (*Arvanitika*). Thus most women were unable to converse in Greek, let alone read or write. Elsewhere in Greece as well, the education of girls lagged behind that of boys.[17] Higher level education was costly and carried prestige that was seen as wasted on a girl unless she was an aristocrat.

Most Methanites insist that it is inaccurate to talk about class differences on the peninsula during this period. Everyone was poor except the successful cargo boat owners, and they were few in number. The class distinction they recognized was between the farmers of Methana and the Athenians who visited. Athenians generally were more educated, did not work with their hands, and had access to cash and thus luxuries that Methanites had no hope of buying. Many Athenians also employed servants, including some Methanites. No one on Methana had either servants or hired hands for farmwork. Household members performed all tasks in the house and in the fields.

The Household Economy

Household Form.   During this period the stem type of household predominated because it was the most efficient means for allocating labor and resources for farming, serving the needs of family members, and providing a small surplus for sale in an economic environment with few wage earning opportunities and no pensions for the elderly. In the nineteenth century, some-

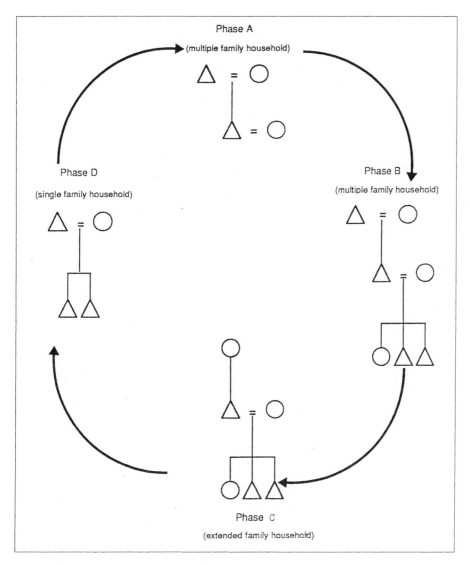

Figure 9.5.   The domestic cycle, Liakotera.

times two or three brothers lived together with their brides in their parents' house for part of the domestic cycle. More commonly one son, usually the youngest, brought his bride to live and work within his parents' household. The duration of joint residence depended on the number of other sons bringing wives to join the household, as well as economic opportunities for couples to establish separate households. Economic cooperation with the husband's family continued after residential separation.

Figure 9.5 presents the domestic cycle on Methana during this period. The figures show one generation moving through the cycle. Usually the son who resided with and cared for his parents inherited the house and a larger share of land. When there were no sons, or all sons had migrated, parents kept one daughter with them and arranged her marriage with a man willing to join the household as a *soghambros*. Childless couples informally adopted children, often "borrowed" from siblings or ritual kin. When parents had more than one son but only one son lived with them, to the extent that their resources allowed, they assisted the other sons in acquiring houses and land to support their own families. Migration to nearby Athens provided a residential solution for "extra" sons who did not "fit" in the stem household; in the past these would have stayed with the parents, established separate households in the village, or married elsewhere as *soghambroi*.

During this period most marriages were arranged (*me proksenio*) by parents of the couple through a third person who negotiated the match. Some couples eloped because one set of parents did not accept the match or, more frequently, the dowry negotiations. Later in the period the younger generation had more voice in the decision about when and whom they married.

Unmarried females were closely chaperoned until their wedding. Parents did not even allow a girl to meet alone with her fiancé. Females wore long skirts, long-sleeved blouses and covered their heads with large white scarves. Sisters married in order of age. Only the eldest attended saint's day celebrations and other festivities, where marriage arrangements were often initiated. Brothers sometimes delayed marrying in order to help parents acquire adequate dowry for their sisters.

Both female and male children received a share of the family estate. Parents strove to provide each child with dowry (*proika*) or inheritance (*klirinomia*) in the form of land of comparable quality as well as equal quantity. They tried to give each child pieces of land suitable for different uses, such as vineyards, vegetable gardens, and grain crops.[18] Olive, almond, and fig trees sometimes passed to daughters as dowry without ownership of the fields on which they were growing.

Women generally took their share of the family estate as proika when they married. People viewed the dowry as a means to provide the daughter with an economic base and status within her husband's family as well as a source of security if her husband died, deserted, or divorced her. Some people insisted that families in the past often sought a bride with a small dowry for their son so that they would have more control over her. Others emphasized past competition to "catch" brides with large dowries in order to increase the family estate.

Household Activities.   The household was the basic unit for smallholder agricultural work on Methana during this period. There was also labor exchange (*allilovoithia*) between households (Harold Koster, this volume). In general the heavier agricultural work in the fields, such as plowing and hoeing, was the responsibility of the younger men and women. Older adults and children did lighter tasks such as herding sheep and goats. The entire household helped with the wheat, grape, and olive harvests.[19]

Men in each family spent long hours building and repairing terraced field walls, mainly in the summer and early autumn, which was a slack time in the agricultural cycle. Work groups of men from several families constructed and repaired paths that led to fields on the mountain and by the sea. Men fished for family consumption from the shore or in boats. A few sold fish within their villages and to the port town.

Three or four times weekly, women and girls climbed in a forty minutes' to one hour's journey up the mountain to cut green leafy branches for the sheep and goats to eat in the evening and for later use as firewood. They carried the branches back to the village on their backs. Farmwork, not housework, was a woman's first priority in the household economy. Women did little housework other than cooking and laundry. Laundry was a labor-consuming task for women.

Figure 9.6.   Drawing water from a cistern, Methana.

They carried heavy clothing, rugs, and blankets forty minutes' journey by mule to the sea, where they used stone basins and well water for washing. Water for cooking and cleaning had to be carried from cisterns and wells (see Figures 9.6 and 9.7). In addition to work in fields and house, women spent many hours spinning and weaving locally grown wool, linen, and cotton (Joan Koster, this volume). All day long, while girls tended the animals they were spinning cotton, wool, and linen thread for weaving.

Because migration and demographic chance increasingly left some families without sons or spouses, some women did work considered "men's work." When there was no son in the village, daughters helped their father in the fields. Wives plowed when their spouses were sailing in the merchant marine. Widows went out with their children to work the soil. Nevertheless, it appears that many families were large enough and work demands were great enough to favor specialization of male and female tasks in the activities just described—a distinction that diminished over time with increasing cash income and migration.

Age, gender, and control of farmland were the key factors determining the household

Figure 9.7. Washing laundry in a stone quern, Methana.

authority structure. The elder generation managed the household estate—land use, labor allocation, food distribution, marketing, and transmission of resources to the next generation. The elder man in the household was manager of the land and field work, in consultation with his wife. The elder woman in the household was manager of the household tasks and, if a widow, manager of the family estate. A *nifi* (daughter-in-law) coming into her in-law's house had a low status and little voice in household decisions, except indirectly through her husband. A nifi was "like a slave," said village women, recalling their youth. A nifi was expected to do, without question, whatever her *pethera* (mother-in-law) and husband told her to do. Similarly, children were supposed to obey parents and grandparents without a word or face a beating. All household members worked the elders' land, slept in their house, and ate meals from their produce.

The proika lands and trees brought to the household by the nifi, however, were managed by her and her husband. They worked the proika land, harvested, and sold the produce separately. This division of resources within the household gave the younger couple the means to start providing for their own children and reduced conflict over authority between father and son and, to a lesser extent, between the nifi and her pethera (see Sutton 1986). In some instances the older couple controlled all the resources, particularly when the nifi's dowry was small. In most cases, when the elders could no longer work in the fields, they passed on the management of most or all of the household resources to their son.

The distribution of products of family labor on Methana was publicly managed by men. In most cases, however, the actual economic decision making was made jointly by men and women. Wives influenced major decisions about capital expenditures, crop sales, and labor exchange, as well as land use and the marriage of children.[20]

Saint's day celebrations (*paniyiria*) on the peninsula and the plain of Troizinia were the important social and marketing events during this period. People arranged marriages, sold land, made small purchases, and exchanged information on these occasions. These celebrations also allowed parents to visit children married in other villages and attracted migrants to visit the home community. Each Saint George's Day, the Methana Migrant's Association in the Athens area, established in 1905, rented a boat to carry members to attend the festivities (see Kenna 1983, Sutton 1983).

Every evening in the village in the nineteenth and early twentieth century, groups of six to eight men gathered in houses to drink, talk, and dance. The women of the house served wine and *meze* (snacks) but did not participate in the merrymaking. Around 1910, men started gathering in a newly established general store with a few items and ample wine. Women did not socialize in the evenings. They stayed in their own houses cooking, sewing, and caring for children, after working all day in the fields.

The Changing Household Economy: World War II to 1996

The period of World War II and the Greek Civil War was a time of hardship throughout Greece. Greece emerged from the wars facing starvation and political strife, with most of its productive capacity destroyed and disorganized. Most Methanites were hungry, but few died of starvation. They subsisted on wild greens, carobs, and a little bread, olives, and beans. Athenians came to Methana's villages, and other areas, begging to trade sewing machines, copper dishes, and other goods for flour and oil so that their families would not starve. Some Methanites made charcoal from the branches and roots of wild scrub.[21] The charcoal was sold in the city for cash because changes in currency had left them penniless.

With foreign assistance in aid and loans along with foreign investment in Greek industry, the economic picture changed. The housing and service sectors expanded rapidly as Athens grew. Tourism, shipping, and remittances from emigrants overseas made considerable contributions to the economy. From the 1960s through the 1970s, Greece experienced great economic growth in terms of the gross national product and exports, but it still remained on the periphery of the world economy. Starting in the 1980s, Greece began to face serious economic problems—high inflation rates, rising unemployment, and stagnation of productive investment (Ioakomides 1984).

Links with the Region and the Nation

Most local people insist that the opening of the road at the end of the 1950s was the most important factor changing the lifestyle of Methana's mountain villages. By 1976, all villages on the peninsula were accessible by road. Villagers could travel on the local bus or with four local taxis, which significantly reduced travel time from the villages to the port town and plain. By vehicle, the trip to the port town took only fifteen to thirty minutes; to the plain, twenty to forty-five minutes; and to Nafplio, about 3 hours. The expansion of the national road system increased the importance of trucks for carrying freight and selling goods and made it possible

Figure 9.8. Transporting wheat by mule, Methana.

Figure 9.9. Transporting wheat by truck, Methana.

for Methanites to trade with Argos, Nafplio, and Tripolis (see Figures 9.8 and 9.9). The road also offered an alternative route to Athens when the sea was rough.

Even though the road expanded links with the Argolid, Methanites became even more enmeshed in the economic and social networks of greater Athens as more Methanites lived and worked there and more Athenians visited Methana. As in other parts of Greece, patronage ties with Athenians provided some Methanites with better hospital care, jobs, building permits, and other opportunities (Allen 1976, Dubisch 1977, Kenna 1983, Sutton 1983). The boat services expanded, making it possible to travel to Athens for business and return in the same day. The hydrofoil, introduced in the early 1980s, reduced the trip to Piraeus to forty-five minutes. The ferry boat enabled trucks and cars to travel between Methana and Piraeus more quickly than by road. Poros continued to play a role as local administrative center and regional office of the Agricultural Bank,[22] but most people looked toward Athens and Piraeus to purchase clothing, furniture, appliances, and real estate.

Demographic Trends

During this period the population of Methana decreased from 2,315 inhabitants in 1951 to 2,088 in 1981. The port town of Loutrapolis increased from 848 in 1951 to 988 in 1981.[23] The population in agricultural villages decreased an average of 45 percent over this period, ranging from a 30 percent to a 59 percent decline (Greece, National Statistical Service 1952, 1982).

In mountain villages, the increasing ratio of elders over sixty years of age to younger inhabitants created an inverted population pyramid. This was not the case in Loutrapolis or the plain of Troizinia, where the population pyramid maintained a substantial base of young people. As in the preceding period, the population decline of the agricultural villages was the result of migration to the port town, Athens, and out of Greece, as well as smaller family size.[24] Methanites continued to migrate to the greater Athens area as it expanded from 1,852,709 inhabitants in 1961 to 3,027,331 in 1981.

The plain of Troizinia showed steady population growth, from 3,026 inhabitants in 1951 to 3,611 in 1981. In the early 1950s, a government project drained the marshes and eradicated malaria there, increasing the amount of inhabitable and cultivable land and thus stimulating expansion of settlements. Most population growth on the plain is a result of the economic growth that I will discuss shortly (Greece, National Statistical Service 1980: 17).

The Local Economy

On Methana, the 1960s initiated more rapid technological change and increasing access to the conveniences enjoyed by city dwellers. Wage and enterprise income superseded agriculture in economic importance on the peninsula even though many families continued to pursue near-subsistence agriculture along with other activities. By the end of the period, the basis of wealth had shifted from agriculture to trucking, other enterprises, and wages earned in the port town, Athens, Troizinia, or the merchant marine. It was increasingly difficult to sell terraced agricultural land on the mountainside at any price. Those who had capital built rooming houses in the port town and established businesses there.

As the Greek economy improved and more people could afford to visit the health spa, the port town expanded physically and economically. The number of stores, hotels, and rooming houses increased to fill three streets parallel to the sea and the borders of the road leading to the next village. This expansion created business and employment in the building trades, trucking service businesses, and commerce, which, in turn, required more civil servants employed as postal and telephone workers, police, harbor officials, teachers, and administrative clerks.

Most wage earning positions—waiters, cooks, civil servants, builders, electricians, plumbers, carpenters, and truckers—were filled by men. Local women worked selling goods in family businesses, sewing as seamstresses, and cleaning family-owned or others' rooming houses. By the 1980s, a few women worked in civil service positions, and four women had opened their own businesses—three beauty salons and one notions store. Women from the mountain villages produced homemade noodles in increasing amounts to be sold, along with other village produce, in the summer street market.

Unlike local people in many tourist areas in the Argolid and other parts of Greece, Methanites have retained ownership of most businesses in the port town, with the exception of one or two large hotels (see Stott 1985). Also unlike many resort areas, most visitors here have been Greeks, attracted by the sulfur baths, rather than vacationers. It is perhaps for this reason that no local craft production has developed for sale to these visitors. This also may be one reason why the port town resembles a suburb of Athens or Piraeus more than a tourist resort.

After World War II there was growing demand for fresh fish, fruit, and vegetables to feed tourists in the restaurants of Methana, Aegina, and Poros, as well as ever-expanding greater Athens. More Methanites thus pursued fishing, and some moved into cash crop farming on the plain of Troizinia. Intensified cultivation on the plain by others also provided agricultural wages for men and women from Methana. Flower cultivation there for national and international markets became a growing source of income. Small factories on the plain, involved in such activities as cutting marble and packaging fruit for export, also offered employment opportunities.

Although limited by steep mountainsides, farming technology changed considerably after the road opened, making farming less labor-intensive than in the past. With the road came the itinerant threshing machine that reduced days of wheat threshing and winnowing to a few hours. The road made the way for electricity and piped water in the early 1970s.[25] By 1986 all villages had electricity, and by the mid-1990s most houses had telephones. Olive oil presses were motorized in the 1950s, and some were replaced by more automated electric facilities in the 1970s. By 1985, a fully automated press in the port town reduced labor and processing time dramatically. This took business away from the small press owners in the villages, so that by the 1990s they had closed.

Construction from the 1970s into the 1990s of roads to fields by the sea and grapevines high on the mountain enabled trucks to transport tools, seed, fertilizer, and produce to and from the fields. By the mid-1980s, roughly one-fourth of the households had farm trucks. In the 1950s, families started plowing grapevines to break up the soil before digging them by hand. By the mid-1980s, a few families had started using small, motor-driven hand tillers to cultivate the vines.

Chemical fertilizer, more productive strains of seed, weed killer and other sprays to reduce crop loss, and assistance from agricultural extension officers enabled fewer people to produce larger crop yields. Since there was no shortage of land per household, families concentrated their efforts on the most productive land. They abandoned the more distant, narrower, rockier terrace fields with poorer soil and concentrated their efforts on the nearer, flatter, wider, richer fields accessible by truck. By the mid-1990s, only a small portion of land was still cultivated—the grapevines near the village and flatter lands near the road. Most fields and vineyards on the mountain had been abandoned.

Villagers also reduced their herds of goats because young girls, the former herders, were fewer in number and were attending school rather than tending animals. Most people stopped raising sheep because they no longer needed the wool for weaving (see J. Koster, this volume). Instead, they kept one or two Swiss goats, because they produced more milk for cheese than sheep and the local breed of goats. In addition, the demand for lamb in the Athens market had decreased with awareness of and concern about cholesterol. By the 1980s, only two families on the peninsula continued to specialize in herding, and these were growing more fodder for the animals than before and spending less time grazing their herds on the mountainsides.

The decline in importance of agriculture on Methana is part of a national trend occurring in areas that cannot be mechanized and irrigated (Baxevanis 1965, 1972: 46). While Methanites did not abandon smallholder agriculture, they decreasingly viewed it as the major source of income. Most households in the mountain villages continued to cultivate some wheat, hay, olives, grapes, and vegetables.

Government programs offering loans for construction, subsidized seed and fertilizer, pensions for farmers, free health services, and low cost medicine provided more security for Methana's farmers, particularly the elderly. By the early 1980s, every farmer and farming wife over sixty years of age received 7,000 drachmas per month (about $53). Pensions for sailors, construction workers, civil servants, and others were higher. Elders felt less dependent on their children, and children felt less burdened by the care of elderly parents. The older generation said that it was no longer necessary to keep a married child in the house to look after them. They still expected attention and assistance from their children but not necessarily coresidence.

Increasingly in the 1980s and 1990s, as salaries rose more rapidly than the price of wheat and pension checks arrived monthly, households reduced or even abandoned wheat cultivation. They offered the rationale that the cost of fertilizer, weed killer, threshing, and milling, along with losses in bad years and damage from rats and insects, made it more economical to buy flour with their wages than to produce it themselves on Methana's terrain. By the mid-1990s, households that had produced two tons of wheat in the early 1970s produced 400 kg at most. More households were often purchasing their wheat and bread.

Starting in the late 1960s and continuing through the 1980s, many of those who remained in the mountain villages started remodeling their spartan two-room houses to add separate kitchens, indoor bathrooms, and more furniture (Clarke, this volume). Even before the 1970s, many houses had two-burner bottled gas stoves. By the late 1970s, some had water heaters, wood or electric stoves, and washing machines, and most had refrigerators. This remodeling provided better sanitation, more comfortable living conditions, and more prestige. Many people said that they remodeled so their children in the city would visit more often. Athens-based children sometimes paid for this remodeling to make their aging parents' lives easier and to have a comfortable place to visit. Local people referred to the more elaborately remodeled houses as "villas." By 1996, more households had been refurbished, and some Athens-based children had built Athens-style living accommodations in, or on top of, their parents' village house, or nearby.

The postwar years brought another new house form to Methana—the summer cottage. Methanites living in Athens built cottages for use during their annual leave and for longer stays after retirement. They wanted the conveniences of the city and preferred not to impose on relatives for food and lodging. Almost all of these cottages were owned by people with roots in Methana. Methanites were extremely reluctant to sell land to outsiders.

By the mid-1970s, village women were no longer producing handmade textiles other than rag rugs. Young girls preferred machine-made blankets for their trousseaux; and they purchased most clothing ready-made in Piraeus in the latest styles. They used the time thus freed to clean, organize, and decorate the house and prepare sweets (*glika*) to serve to guests—activities neglected in the prewar days of labor-intensive farming. By the mid-1980s, none of the women were weaving. Instead, they did embroidery, crocheting, and prepared noodles and other items to sell in the street market in the port town.

After World War II, health services also improved on the peninsula.[26] Virtually all women went to hospitals in Athens or Aegina for prenatal care and to deliver their babies. They often stayed in the city with relatives while they recovered. By the 1970s the state was paying a doctor to visit Methana's villages once a week to provide free health services.

By World War II parents on Methana had started sending both girls and boys through at least six years of primary school. Since the late seventies, all children were required by Greek law to attend nine years of public school. Since that time, students have attended the first three years of secondary school in the port town. Prior to that, students had to travel to Aegina, Poros, or Athens and to pay for boarding costs as well as books and clothing. Farming families strove to provide a better life for their children through education. They sought to give their offspring access to more prestigious and more economically rewarding vocations than farmwork. Sons who dropped out of school were encouraged to learn a trade rather than to farm.

By the 1980s, girls who had passed the qualifying exams were attending university and taking positions in teaching, accounting, pharmacy, and other professions, mostly in the greater Athens area. By that time, having an education offered a girl the kind of security that a good dowry with ample farmland had offered in the past. There was a growing notion that, with the high rate of inflation, even daughters that married in Athens might have to work as well as their husbands to provide an adequate standard of living for their family. As parents looked at increasing divorce rates in Athens, they no longer viewed marriage as an entirely certain future for their daughters. Some said, "Marriage is like a lottery; you never know if the spouse will be a good one these days."

With mechanization of grain threshing and textile production, the acquisition of electricity and running water, and the expansion of roads, farming and household chores took less time. Both women and men had more free time to spend on nonfarm work and on leisure. According to most Methanites, life in the mid-1980s and 1990s was much easier than before World War II, and the standard of living was much higher. They ate more meat, purchased foods, clothing, and other consumer goods, and had more leisure time than they had had even in the early seventies. Most people had television sets and cassette tape players. Some had videos and CB radios. Children had numerous toys, whereas the children in the past had had only sticks and stones to play with. Many people said, "Now we have leisure time. In the past we married one day and worked in the fields the next."

This change in lifestyle also reflects a change in values regarding the use of household resources. A thirty-year-old smallholder observed, "In the past our parents scrimped and saved to buy land for the future; we want to enjoy some comforts now." His words characterize the shift from frugality to consumerism that took place during this period. Villagers expected to live more comfortably and have leisure time for activities such as television, video, embroidery, shopping trips to Piraeus, and traveling to distant shrines and saint's day festivities. Younger people and educated elders read magazines and newspapers.

In rural Greece as a whole between the 1960s and 1970s, there was a widespread shift in spending patterns from frugality to consumerism. By 1970, rural consumption patterns were similar to those of Athens. These changing rural expectations were not, however, supported by better prices for farm goods, but rather by intensification and diversification of the rural family's labor (Karopostolis 1983). This has been the case on Methana.

Even though life was easier, Methanites insisted that farmwork remained very hard because of the terrain and the dependence on rainwater for crops. They also said that the availability of cash was still limited compared to its accessibility in Athens and Piraeus. Changes in the activities of the Methana Migrant's Association in Athens illustrate this disparity. The Association no longer needs to charter a boat to attend the Saint George's Day celebrations because most people drive in their own cars. Association members donated funds to erect at the site of the celebration a monument honoring a Methana war hero, as well as to support small improvement projects on the peninsula, such as cementing the village paths. Instead of Saint George's Day, the main event of the Association was a dinner dance held in an Athens nightclub.

During this period, there was still a reluctance to recognize wealth differences in the villages. People usually insisted that everyone was about the same. The only real wealth and class difference that they recognized was between Methana farmers and those who had "done well" in the city or the port town; that is, a person who had a steady civil service salary or business, owned a nice house with luxurious furnishings and appliances, had a car, and was educating children through college.

The Household Economy

Household Form.   Between 1974 and 1986, in the mountain farming community with the lowest rate of population decline, the number of stem families decreased by 30 percent, while the number of nuclear households consisting of old couples whose children had migrated or set up separate households increased by 28 percent. The number of nuclear households with resident children also decreased. By 1996, only five stem households remained, and three of those had only a widow or widower in the elder generation. None of the children planned to stay in the village and cultivate the land.

Figure 9.10 presents the impact of these changes in terms of the domestic cycle. The pattern of the previous period, shown in Figure 9.5, continued in only a few families that combined wage earning or business with farming. The broken cycle, shown in Figure 9.10, represents households in the majority of farming villages on Methana. The demographic and economic trends already discussed have been breaking down the cycle, reducing the number of stem households, and increasing the number of households consisting of old couples, widows, and widowers living alone. In the port town, the majority of households were nuclear. Elder parents resided with their children, rather than the reverse; in most cases it was a widowed parent who could not manage alone in the village.

Earlier incentives for the stem household had disappeared, largely because the younger generation sought a livelihood away from the farm. Girls did not want to marry farmers, leaving some dutiful sons to become aging bachelors living with their parents in the village. Young men refused to become soghambroi. With smaller families, there were fewer "extra" children for childless couples to "borrow."

Children also had more voice in the choice of mates, although most village marriages were still arranged by parents through the 1970s. Some young men asked for the hand of the future spouse themselves. A few young couples eloped when parents failed to agree to the match. Those who migrated to Athens generally found their own spouses, usually from other areas of Greece (see Sutton 1983). Young people remaining in the village in the 1980s and 1990s expected to find their own spouses and move to the port town or Athens.

Unmarried females had much more freedom than their prewar predecessors even though many parents did not allow them to go on "dates" in the port town. They wore jeans, fingernail polish, and makeup. Some even smoked cigarettes, copying the style of behavior in Athens. Many young women traveled to Athens unchaperoned or joined friends in groups at the disco and *kafeteria* in the port town (see Cowan 1990).[27] Some of these women said that in Athens they were free to do what they wanted because no one from the village could see them. They

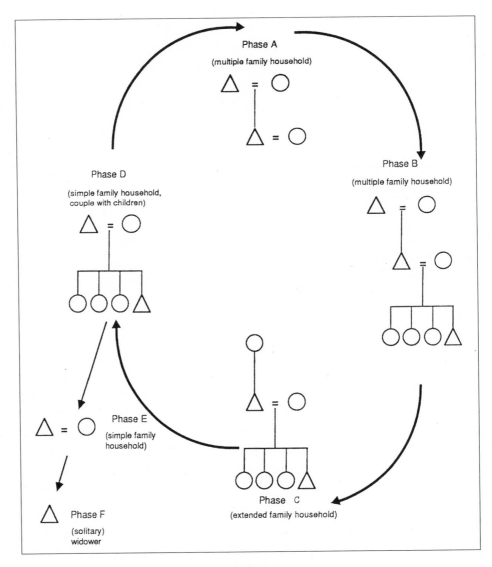

Figure 9.10.   The broken domestic cycle, Liakotera.

suggested that their parents were more concerned about what people said—about gossip—than their actual behavior, as long as they did not get into trouble.

Dowry increasingly took the form of real estate during this period—usually an apartment in Athens or the port town. As in the past, parents with adequate means provided apartments for sons working in the city as well. Even though the Greek Civil Code changed in 1984, eliminating the legal requirement for fathers to provide dowry for daughters "according to their means," many parents strove to give each child an apartment or house in the city as a gift, although fully recognizing it as proika. Parents often said that urban rent was so high that a young couple living on wages could barely get along if they did not own housing. Young men from Methana who lived and worked in Athens often said that they did not care whether or not their future wife had any dowry, they just wanted a good woman. Their mothers advised them to find young women with houses so they did not have to pay rent. Young women who married on the peninsula rented their houses in Athens for income.

Household Activities.   In the postwar years, the household continued to be the basic unit of production on Methana, but its activities changed considerably. There was much less allilo-voithia because most of the people needing labor were elders who could not return it. Some older couples hired younger people to do farmwork. Mechanization of agriculture eliminated the need for outside labor in tasks such as threshing grain, which had been a major time of allilovoithia in the past.

The decline in family size in the farming villages on Methana due to increased participation of farm residents in wage labor and more years of education for children caused a sharp reduction in the farm labor force. More women regularly did tasks considered men's work because their husbands were absent earning wages. Many elderly couples were left to tend family fields as best they could with occasional help from their migrant children. When fathers had good wage incomes, teenage girls seldom helped mothers in the fields with men's work, and only reluctantly took goats to graze. Instead, they tended the house and helped with harvests, preparing to become housewives, not farmers' wives.

Scheduling of household labor has increasingly required consideration of the summer "tourist" season and working hours of wage laborers. For example, in a single spring day in the life of a certain stem household, the younger male worked in a marble factory on the plain of Troizinia from seven until three, his parents planted tomato seedlings in their small irrigated vegetable garden one hour's mule ride from the village, and his wife took animals out to graze while their two sons attended school.

Within the stem households that remained, there was a shift in authority structure from domination by elders to negotiation between generations or even domination by the younger generation. As the basis of wealth moved into the market economy, limited education left the elders at a disadvantage. While most elders were reluctant to learn to drive farm trucks, their sons eagerly acquired and used the skill. The elders' negotiation power, which had been based on control of farmland, dwindled with the value of such land, unless they had also purchased land in the port town, the plain of Troizinia, Athens, or other growing areas. Younger people no longer wanted Methana land but rather jobs, cash, urban real estate, and businesses.

As negotiating power shifted in the household, mothers-in-law complained that the nifi "doesn't listen; she does whatever she wants and complains too much." Similarly, parents complained that their children "didn't listen" to them. Even small children made fun of grandparents and refused to obey parents. On the other hand, people of all ages commented on how much cleverer today's children were than they themselves had been.

Intertwined with these changes in negotiating power between generations have been significant changes in values associated with the relations between the generations. There has been increasing recognition that the younger generation "know something." The essence of this shift was expressed in a conversation between a man in his seventies and a woman in her early fifties while waiting for their hay and grain to be threshed. Standing near the threshing machine, the old man yelled at his son about the way he and the two grandsons were unloading wheat from their truck. "The young people don't know anything," he muttered. The younger woman commented, "Don't you know that it is not that way anymore? The young people know everything. We're the ones who don't know anything."

In the past, most people believed that elders were a source of wisdom based on experience. Young people were not considered capable of making their own decisions with so little experience in life. Thus most people accepted arranged marriages and elder management of farming activities as necessary parts of life. By the 1980s, the younger generation openly questioned their elders and even ridiculed them, saying they were "backward" and "stupid." By the mid-1990s many of these elders had passed away, leaving the aging middle generation in charge with no younger generation in line to carry on the family farm.

Men still gather in the village store in the evenings to talk and drink, but their numbers are shrinking as young men go to the port town to socialize with people their own age. Women visit other women in the evening to watch television and talk, no longer fearful of the authority of the pethera. The local cultural organization in the port town organizes bus trips to different parts of Greece, which many villagers, particularly women, eagerly take.

Household Transformation:
Two Cases from Methana

The histories of two households show ways in which individuals on Methana participated in the changes in the larger society and in their local economy. The first case illustrates the evolution of the most common pattern today—old couples living alone after their children have migrated to pursue nonfarm employment. The second case shows the development of a contemporary stem household that combines farming with business. Both households originated from a single household three generations ago.

In the 1880s, the Petronoti[28] household consisted of a couple and their five children—four boys and one girl. The parents arranged marriages in other villages on Methana for one son and the daughter. The oldest son, Spiros, brought his bride to live in his parents' home. The parents built a second house on land next to the first and moved there with the other two sons. Sotiris, the first of these two to marry, brought his bride into his parents' new house. When the second son married, he and his bride lived on the lower floor of the new house until his father bought him a shed, which he and his wife enlarged into a house. Case One and Case Two present the subsequent histories of Sotiris's and Spiros's households.

Case One: Decline of the Stem Household

Sotiris, the brother who lived with his parents, gradually took over management of the family farm. He and his wife, Froso, had three daughters and two sons. One son was killed in World War I. The other went to America and was never heard from again. Since they had no sons to live with them, they arranged a marriage for their youngest daughter, Zoi, with Chronis, who came from a poor family in another village. His father had persuaded him to leave sailing and join the Petronoti household as a soghambros. The Petronoti parents arranged marriages for their other two daughters in the village, with small dowries because the parents retained most of the land (40 stremmata) to attract the soghambros.

Chronis, the soghambros, had spent his youth in Pireaus working and later sailing. When he was about ten, an acquaintance of his father had come to his village looking for a boy to help in his painting business in Piraeus. He said the boy would learn the trade and receive food, clothing, and education. Seeing this as an excellent opportunity, the father sent Chronis to Piraeus. The man did not live up to his promises, however, and soon offered the job to a relative who needed work. Chronis found other work in food stores, coffeehouses, and *souvlaki* shops until 1928, when he started working as a sailor in Greek waters. Chronis's father soon advised him to leave the sea and marry Zoi because her family had ample land and her dowry was large. He insisted that the sea was dangerous and the work was not steady. Chronis reluctantly followed his father's advice.

Chronis and Zoi had a daughter and two sons. They arranged a marriage for their daughter, Antigoni, to a man in the port town whose father ran an oil press. After briefly living with the man's parents, the young couple set up their own household and engaged in summer work, housecleaning, and cooking for a restaurant, as well as cultivating the little land they owned. By 1986, their son and daughter were in their early teens. Antigoni's father-in-law resented their departure from his household because he lost control over his son and his son's labor and blamed Antigoni for this separation.

In contrast to their sister, Antigoni, the two sons went to Athens, shared an apartment, and worked with an uncle laying parquet floors. The eldest brother, Sotiris, had first gone to Athens in the 1950s to attend secondary and technical school. Despite his degree in engineering, he found that he could make more money laying floors with his uncle. Like many other Methanites, once Sotiris left the village to study he never returned there to live, only to visit. He married a woman from Mytilene and lived in his wife's dowry house in Athens, where they raised a girl and a boy who both went on to attend the university.

The younger brother, Angelos, and his Chiote wife went to seek their fortune in the United States, where her brother was already working. After ten years there, Angelos managed to save enough money to return with his wife and four children to Methana in 1979, to buy land, and to build a house and woodworking shop in the port town. Angelos said that he did not want his children to grow up in America amidst crime and drugs. His wife said she preferred to stay in America because she felt that they all would have a better life there.

Before Angelos left Boston, Chronis spent a year, from 1973 to 1974, working with his son. Zoi flatly refused to go to America. She said, "I do not want to leave my own hearth." She added, "I do not enjoy going to Athens, why would I want to go a foreign country?" Chronis earned enough American dollars to demolish his old two-room house in the village in 1975 and build a new one with five special purpose rooms and other modern conveniences. Soritis helped with both money and labor, but Chronis and Zois lived alone there. Chronis gave the house to his older son, Sotiris, with the explanation that none of the children would care for the house if they all owned it.

Antigoni, Sotiris, Angelos, and their spouses and children all helped the parents during harvests; and they visited regularly. Both sons had cars. Antigoni visited by bus and sometimes helped with laundry and bread making. Otherwise, Chronis did these tasks because Zoi could not manage. In the early 1990s, Zoi passed away and Chronis lived alone. He continued to plow fields and hoe grapevines, to provide food for himself and to share with his children, even though they insisted it was not necessary.

Case Two: Adaptation of Stem Household Functions

Spiros headed the household next door to the one just described. He and his wife, Kalliopi, had four sons. One son married on the island of Poros, where his father had purchased land for him. Another son married in Ayios Demitrios in Athens, which was then still farmland. The two youngest sons, Panos and Erasimas, remained with their parents.

So that Panos and Erasimas would each have a house, Spiros purchased a second house nearby from a man who sold all his holdings to move to Athens. Spiros's family moved to the newer, larger house and used the older house as a storeroom for hay and animals. Spiros also purchased land on the plain of Troizinia around the same time. Panos, the elder son, married Lucia, who came from a family in the village with four daughters and two sons. Her dowry included fields, olive trees, and grapevines. Panos and Lucia had two sons, Spiros and Thomas.

Erasimas stayed on in the house for over ten years after his brother Panos's marriage. Then he decided to go to Athens in 1960, where he worked as a construction worker. He married a woman with a dowry house there. She had been born in Kalamata and had come to Athens to live with her brother while she learned to be a seamstress. Her brother arranged her marriage. Erasimas and his wife had no children. When Erasimas retired, he and his wife moved to his house in the village, which Panos had been using for storage. Erasimas replaced the roof, expanded the terrace, built a modern, separate bathroom and installed a solar heater. In 1996, they returned to Piraeus to live in the dowry house, visiting their village house only to collect olives and for holidays.

When Panos took over management of his parents' household, he invested in land on Aegina. In the early 1960s, he sold that land and reinvested in a rooming house in the port town. He sent his eldest son, Spiros, to secondary school. Spiros became a civil servant in the port town and married a local girl with a dowry house there.

Thomas, the younger son, did not enjoy school. He preferred to work with his parents on the farm. He married Ioanna and had three children. Ioanna came from the same village as Chronis, the soghambros in Case One. In fact, Chronis arranged the match (*ekane to proksenio*), and Zoi was Ioanna's godmother. Ioanna had a dowry house in Athens which her father had built, hoping she would find a husband there. Her father had worked many years in the merchant marine to provide his two daughters with real estate in the city. The other daughter married a schoolteacher and lived in Piraeus on this land until 1994 when they sold it and purchased another, larger house to accommodate their three children.

By 1986, Thomas, aged forty-two, was running the family farm. Panos, aged seventy-two, helped as best he could despite his arthritis, as did Kalliopi, aged seventy-three. The household estate included fifty-one stremmata of good land on Methana and seven stremmata on the plain of Troizinia. The crops grown on this land fed the family, provided wine and oil for Spiros and his family in the port town, and provided cash from the sale of peas, figs, wine, olive oil, and straw. They were the first in the village to remodel their original three-room house to add a separate kitchen and indoor bathroom. They were also among the first to purchase a television set, washing machine, water heater, and a farm truck.

By the late 1970s, Spiros and Thomas owned Panos's rooming house and ran it, together with their wives, in summer. In 1986, Thomas built a three-story apartment building in Piraeus, where his own eldest son lived while attending secondary school. Thomas planned to establish a *kafeteria* on the ground floor of the building for his two sons (aged 17 and 14) to run. He and Ioanna also rented her dowry house for income and sold olive oil, wine, noodles, and *rigani* to guests in the rooming house. They both spent a considerable amount of time away from the village—roughly four months of the year. During the summer they stayed in the rooming house in the port town and in fall and winter visited the son and worked on their building in Piraeus.

In the early 1980s, Thomas and Ioanna made plans to live in Piraeus in their apartment building for a year to establish the *kafeteria* business. However, they intended to return to the village for permanent residence. Thomas said that he could not abandon his aging parents, insisting that Panos and Antigoni would never join him in the city. Ioanna, aged 36, said she preferred the clean, open air of the village and saw it as a better place to raise her daughter, Kalliopi. She hoped that Kalliopi, who was an excellent student, would continue to do well in school and go on to the university. She wanted Kalliopi to be able to do whatever she wanted with her future. In the mid-1990s, Ioanna began to plan to live in Piraeus if her daughter was accepted for university study.

By the early 1990s, when the sons were old enough to run the coffee shop, they wanted to pursue other careers. One son apprenticed as a plumber in Piraeus and developed his own business. The other son attended secondary school and worked in advertising for a travel agency in Piraeus. The sons lived in apartments their parents had built for them. Thomas and Ioanna rented out the store space intended for the *kafeteria*. They had remodeled their rental rooms in the port town and continued to cultivate smaller portions of the land. In 1996, Thomas's mother Kalliopi passed away, and Panos was nearly bedridden with arthritis.

The two household histories illustrate a range of responses to the social and economic changes discussed in the preceding sections. Clearly not all individuals had the same choices, abilities, or preferences in responding to opportunities created by the expanding market economy. Gender, birth order, wealth of parents, success in school, connections, personality, and preferences affected personal choices and fates.

Explaining Household Transformation on Methana

In the late nineteenth and early twentieth centuries, male elders within stem households largely controlled the productive resources (farmland) and household decision making on Methana. As market employment expanded and the basis for wealth shifted from farmland to cash, the negotiating power of the younger generation increased, giving them more authority in stem household affairs and more opportunities to establish separate houses, particularly after World War II.

Education also played an important role in these changing relations of authority. Until recently education was the basis for differential access to the opportunities of the market economy. This problem of access was compounded by class and later by gender. Stem households decreased in number, and the number of old couples living alone in Methana's mountain villages increased. Stem households that persisted combined business or wage income with agriculture.

Methana's external links shifted from a Poros-focused regional orientation in the nineteenth century to an Athens- and Piraeus-focused national orientation in the late nineteenth and twentieth centuries. The mountain villages shrank as the port town expanded due to business from the health spa. Despite emigration, migration, and decreasing family size in some areas, the overall Methana population remained steady throughout the period. The nearby plain of Troizinia grew in population as the economy expanded with cash crops and tourism (see Sutton, this volume, for comparison with the rest of the southern Argolid).

Methana's economy grew with that of Greater Athens. The local economy was transformed from a frugal existence with near subsistence agriculture and limited trade to a cash-based economy with growing emphasis on consumerism. There was a shift from arranged marriages to marriage by choice. Dowry changed from farmland to urban real estate for sons as well as daughters. With increasing involvement of men in wage labor, women took over more of the heavier farmwork. Young women moved on to higher education and professions and had fewer constraints on their activities.

Throughout this period the household remained the basic unit of production and the basis for individual articulation with the larger society, even though household forms and functions changed. Basic values regarding responsibilities of household members remained constant even though the ways in which they were carried out changed considerably. The most critical change for the household economy was the shift in the economic and social relations between generations and the values associated with them. Gender, birth order, wealth of parents, success in school, connections, and preferences affected individual opportunities, choices, and fates—all of which in turn reshaped family form and activities.

Continuity and Change in the Household Economy

There was both continuity and change in the transformation of the Methana household economy. Changes in household form did not necessarily translate into changes in all household functions, although there were modifications in how household activities and responsibilities were carried out. Children in other households in the village, the port town, and Athens continued to provide assistance to their parents. Instead of living with parents and working on the family farm, many children helped in the fields only at harvest time and gave their parents gifts of clothing, food, appliances, and money to pay laborers and make house improvements so that these elders could live more comfortably. Although children were willing to extend this help to coresidence in the city, most elders refused to leave their hearth and the familiar life of the village to enter this unknown and noisy terrain, particularly older women who were illiterate.

There was significant change in the activities and authority structure of the stem household in the postwar period. For example, in some of the stem households that combined farming with business, the younger couple engaged in "transhumance" to the resort town in the summers to run their businesses and to Athens in the winter to collect rent and visit children there. At the same time, they still participated in agriculture in the village. They were absent from the village four to five months of the year, leaving the older couple to tend the house and animals.

The Ecological, Historical, and Economic Context

It is important to make clear that the pattern described for Methana is not presented as a standard for the transformation of rural households in Greece. It provides one model for analysis of such changes. As I stressed at the outset, however, changing household form is only meaningful when considered in the context of specific historical, ecological, geographical, and economic shifts. The diverse household forms in contemporary Greece, analyzed in terms of their wider context, provide strong support for this point. For example, in nineteenth-century Kranidi, both nuclear and extended families occurred on a class-segregated basis in an agrarian and sailing-based mercantile economy, whereas in 1981 the nuclear family prevailed in an economy supported by olive cultivation, work in the merchant marine, and tourism in nearby seaside resorts (Petronoti, this volume). In nineteenth-century Mykonos, nuclear families were the basic units of production in a seafaring economy and persisted as such as as Mykonos changed to an economy based on tourism (Stott 1985). On early twentieth-century Cyprus, the nuclear family continued as the basic social and economic unit in an economy based on subsistence farming and livestock raising (Loizos 1975).

Along with differences in household form, the nature and apportionment of dowry and inheritance in Greece have also varied across areas and over time. On Cyprus the transfer of houses shifted from males to females due to greater involvement in the cash economy, while on the tiny island of Meganisi in the Ionian sea, there was a shift from stem to nuclear families, although parents continued to transfer houses to males (Just 1988). On many islands in the Aegean, where nuclear households predominate, houses are passed from mother to daughter, not father to son as is the case on Methana (Galani-Moutafi 1993, Hoffman 1976, Dubisch 1973, Kenna 1976, Sutton 1978). On Karpathos, a form of primogeniture was practiced so that the oldest son inherited all the land from his father, the oldest daughter inherited the house from her mother, and other children inherited nothing (Vernier 1984). In the past, in parts of Greece, bride-price was given to the parents of the bride to compensate for the loss of her labor (Alexakis 1984).

There also has been considerable variation in the sexual division of labor throughout Greece wherever different tasks, crops, degrees of mechanization, and involvement in the market economy have created different labor demands and expectations.

Recognizing this diversity in the dynamics of household transformation in Greece, what then is significant and unique about the situation of Methanites? Four factors stand out: location, ecology, history, and economic diversity. The first three factors brought about the fourth. The proximity of Methana to Athens enabled Methanites to participate in the growth of the market economy of Greece at an early date. Proximity also facilitated continued contact by migrants with the home area and easy access for Athenians to visit Methana's health spa. Contact helped establish patron-client relations that assisted Methanites in getting jobs in the city. Today this proximity means that Methana is within commuting distance from Athens, and the port town resembles and functions somewhat like a suburb of Athens.

The island-like nature of Methana and its early sea-trading connections also directed Methanites toward Piraeus and Athens. Similarly, the steep, rocky terrain and dependence on rainwater led them, like islanders elsewhere in Greece, to look outside Methana for other sources of livelihood at an early date. The presence of the sparsely populated, well-watered plain of Troizinia nearby enabled Methanites in the nineteenth century to extend their zone of arable land to the adjacent plain, as people on the islands of Hydra and Poros had done in the past.

The significance of Methana's location and ecology was enhanced by historical factors. Methana was on the periphery of the commercial growth of Hydra, Spetses, Kranidhi, and Poros and at the edge of the later rapid economic expansion of Athens and Piraeus. Because of such factors, Methanites have been able to pursue a variety of diversified economic strategies allowing them to overcome the physical limitations of their dry, rocky terrain and to use the "city as a resource" rather than simply becoming a resource for the city (see Dubisch 1977).

Rather than specializing in tourism or cash crop farming, Methanites have been able to do "a little bit of everything" (*ligho ap' ola*), a local phrase that Forbes (1976a, this volume) sees as characterizing a risk-reducing crop blend in farming on Methana. The phrase actually applies more widely than crops. One can also interpret it as an entrepreneurial strategy of not only avoiding putting all one's eggs in one basket, but also of trying to get as many baskets of eggs as possible. As Methanites say, "*apo ligho ligho yinete poli*" (lots of small efforts can produce something large).

The four factors above also provide the backdrop for understanding how household transformation on Methana has played out differentially for different individuals. Gender, birth order, wealth of parents, success in school, connections, personality, preferences, and luck have affected individual choices and fates. Panos Petronoti's household, in the second case above, is an excellent example of a diversified economic strategy. In this case, the resource base encompasses the port town, Athens, Piraeus, and the plain of Troizinia as well as Methana's mountainsides and supports a blend of business, farming, rentals, civil service, and the production of foods, such as noodles, for sale.

Comparing Panos's strategy with that of his brother Erasimas illustrates how some Methanites have been better entrepreneurs than others. While Panos was successful in buying and selling property at the right time, establishing a rooming house when the health spa was just starting to expand, and setting up his two sons on equally successful paths in investment, Erasimas did not fare so well. He delayed marrying, had no children, and has only his monthly pension check to show for his years of effort on the family farm and construction work in Athens. He even left behind his remodeled house in the village to return to Piraeus.

Examination of such transformations on Methana sheds new light on the nature of the stem household in Greece and possibly elsewhere. In contrast to the strong value for the corporate extended family described in Campbell's study of the Sarakatsani pastoralists of Epiros in the 1950s (1964), on Methana in the 1980s I did not find the extended or stem family to be an ideal, nor was it considered to have been one in the past. Instead, people described it as a practical and less-than-desirable solution to the problem of fulfilling basic and highly valued family responsibilities.

The separate control of the dowry resources within stem households on Methana belied the high value placed on nuclear units even in the past. This type of stem household economy in which the wife's dowry lands were managed separately from the parental estate reduced somewhat the inevitable conflict over authority between generations in the stem household. Inquiry into possible separation within the internal budget of the stem household in other parts of Greece and in other countries is still needed. As I have argued elsewhere and in arguments others have made, it is possible that emphasis on the solidarity of the Greek family as the basic unit of society has led scholars to overlook the significance of individual concerns and of conflict of interest within families (Clarke 1988, 1989, Loizos and Papataxiarchis 1991, Sant Cassia 1992, Seremetakis 1991).[29]

Dowry and Inheritance: Their Relationship to Land Fragmentation and Risk Reduction on Methana

Hamish A. Forbes

The argument that holdings of widely scattered plots are a major impediment to farm efficiency is too well known by now to need much documentation: some aspects of this argument are explored by Adams (this volume), and the issue has been discussed in a wider context by Bentley (1987b: 31–34, 42–47). The opposition that traditional farmers frequently show towards official attempts to consolidate plots has generally been considered by those who wish to increase consolidation to be merely irrational conservatism. An extreme viewpoint sees land fragmentation as "the blackest of evils, to be prevented by legislative action as one would attempt to prevent prostitution or blackmail" (Bentley 1987b: 31). In the context of Greece, Thompson's work (1963) taking a comparable line, though using less colorful language, is something of a classic, although others have expressed a similar point of view (e.g., Campbell and Sherrard 1968: 329–33; Tsaousis 1976: 455–56).

A number of observers, however, particularly those whose academic traditions emphasize cultural relativity, have questioned the received wisdom concerning the inefficiency of farming scattered holdings and the supposed causal relationship between fragmentation and partible inheritance. Several writers have noted that division of farms in the Alpine zone of Europe tends to occur only when the viability of the farm allows it, and farmers find ways to avoid breaking up individual plots, even where partible inheritance exists (Weinberg 1972; Cole and Wolf 1974: chap. 4; Wolf 1970; Netting 1972; Netting 1981: chap. 8). Similarly, in Mexico, a minimum plot size has been noted, below which division seldom takes place (Downing 1977: 240). In other words, there is evidence that farmers do not irrationally continue to subdivide farms when it is against their perceived interests.

It is also clear that even in places like post-famine Ireland, medieval England, and Spain, where impartible inheritance was the rule, fragmentation has occurred (McCloskey 1975; Homans 1941; Douglass 1969: 88). My own experience from living in a rural area of the Midlands of England, where consolidation by parliamentary legislation (the "Enclosure Acts") occurred in the last few centuries, is that many farmers do not work fully consolidated holdings. The vagaries of the land market mean that frequently it is smallish, isolated acreages that become available for sale or rent. Additionally, when farms are sold, the land of large, reasonably consolidated, farms is often sold in two or more separate lots. This means that the original large farm is broken up and other farms may acquire separate parcels, which may or may not be contiguous to their own land. Expanding one's acreage therefore often necessitates purchasing or renting land in small parcels at some distance from one's other fields—an observation that holds good in other parts of England (Edwards 1978), and in the U.S. (Smith 1975) and Canada (Carlyle 1983). On the other side of the same coin, Adams (this volume) indicates that the level of fragmentation that he documented in Dhidhima was not caused by the workings of partible inheritance. Since he critically discusses the literature on farm fragmentation in Greece and uses cross-cultural comparanda to indicate some of the problems with these arguments, it is unnecessary to go into further detail here.

In addition to questioning the supposed links between fragmentation and inheritance systems, scholars studying indigenous agrarian systems in Alpine environments *sensu lato* have for some time argued that the farming of scattered plots has a number of beneficial effects (J. Friedl 1973; Rhoades and Thompson 1975: 539; Netting 1981: 42–69). More recently it has become apparent that household ownership of fragmented, scattered holdings can be beneficial, even in parts of the world with a less spectacular altitudinal and environmental range than Alpine zones and in situations other than subsistence farming. Galt's (1979) discussion of land fragmentation among market-oriented farmers on the Italian island of Pantellaria and McCloskey's (1975; 1976) analysis of fragmentation in the medieval English three-field system are both comparable to the Greek situation in many aspects.[1]

In this contribution I argue that the ownership of scattered holdings of small plots has been, despite the frequently discussed disadvantages, an effective way for households on Methana to minimize the risks of total, or near total crop failure.[2] Within the discussion I use the terminology and definitions set out by Adams (this volume). In particular:

1. *Fragmentation* defines the combined effects of the subdivision of plots and the dispersal of individual plots on a farm.
2. *Subdivision* describes the division of a plot into two or more smaller plots, resulting in use-access to the different plots resting with more than one person or household.
3. *Dispersal* indicates the spatial scattering of a household's noncontiguous plots over the landscape.
4. *Consolidation* defines the reverse process to subdivision.
5. Finally, Adams observes that ownership (i.e., legal) data suggest higher degrees of fragmentation than do operational (i.e., actual use) data; in this contribution I use operational data.

A number of studies of the phenomenon of fragmentation have used quantified data or mathematical models. Such approaches allow claims to be verified more readily than those using anecdotal or unquantified informant data alone. Mathematical models are more frequently applied to issues involving the sizes and distributions of plots (cf. Bentley 1987b: 32–34) or measures of increased or decreased fragmentation over time (e.g., McCloskey 1975; Adams, this volume). Many studies of fragmentation by anthropologists have been marked by careful description but little quantification (Bentley 1987b: 54). Claims that land dispersal and fragmentation have positive adaptive advantages have frequently been based more on theoretical considerations, backed by unquantified informant evidence, than on actual quantified data. Although these theoretical discussions are important, they have been widely rehearsed (see, e.g., Forbes 1976a: 236–38; Bentley 1987b), and I will not review them in detail.

In this contribution I present a case study of a community on the peninsula of Methana to support the idea that land fragmentation had a number of beneficial aspects for indigenous farmers at the time when fieldwork was undertaken. Some aspects of the situation will be discussed in theoretical terms, but, in light of the comments made above, I intend to concentrate where possible on presenting quantified data to demonstrate the way in which the actualities of a real life situation relate to theoretical concerns. Needless to say, unquantified informant data are used where they are relevant.

The Ethnographic Location

The peninsula of Methana, barely attached to the rest of the Argolic peninsula by a narrow isthmus, and jutting out into the Saronic Gulf, is markedly different in a number of ways from the adjacent mainland. Geologically, the largest and agriculturally most productive part of Methana is volcanic in origin, whereas the nearby area of the mainland is dominated by schists and limestones. The result of the volcanic activity has been a landscape that is much more precipitous and complex than that of the mainland, with a maximum height of about 740 m (2,400 ft.) in a landmass barely 10 km across. Despite this, the productivity of the volcanic soils and, in former times, the safety from attack (Forbes and Foxhall 1997: 82–83) afforded by the rugged landscape have traditionally made Methana an attractive place for settlement.

All ten of the small agricultural settlements on Methana are situated at some distance from the sea, typically close to, or above, the 200 m (650 ft.) contour.[3] According to villagers, these elevated locations were chosen to afford protection against seaborne raiders (Forbes 1976a: 238; Clarke, this volume). In addition to providing protection, these locations have also allowed villagers access to land spread over a wider altitudinal range than would have been the case for coastal settlements. Administrative units on Methana (*koinotites*), each composed of two to three villages, controlled approximately wedge-shaped sectors of the peninsula, running from the coast to the highest parts in the center of the landmass. Similarly, households on Methana typically exploited plots of land scattered over a wide altitudinal range: the strategic locations of their villages, approximately one third of the way up the sides of the peninsula, allowed relatively easy access to the land below them as far as the coast, as well as to the land above. In the period of study, and even more so in the past, some villagers exploited a vertically distributed "archipelago" of holdings from virtually sea level to over 700 m (2,275 ft.) altitude. Most of the households of the village of Liakotera (pseudonym), where research was concentrated, exploited parcels of land from near sea level to over 500 m (1,625 ft.), and their agricultural holdings were frequently forty-five minutes and more walking distance from the village.

Apart from mechanized grain threshing, mechanical pumps, and modern oil presses, agricultural operations on Methana in the early 1970s depended on human or animal power. The repertoire of tools employed was correspondingly simple, but the knowledge of the ways in which this repertoire could be employed was frequently very complex. The management of crops on Methana has been similarly complex, reflecting the considerable range of microenvironmental factors involved in the exploitation of households' widely scattered holdings in a topographically diverse landscape. Such factors include insolation (i.e., exposure to sunshine); shelter—or lack of it—from strong drying winds; the depth, fertility, and porosity of the soil; altitude, and so forth. Distance from the village also affected crop management practices.

The lack of mechanization in the second half of the twentieth century has been a direct result of the extreme ruggedness of the agricultural landscape. Virtually all agricultural land was terraced, with the vast majority of terraces being under 4 m wide: some as narrow as 1 m across were cultivated during the early 1970s, though narrow terraces were generally less highly favored for cultivation. Access to these terraces has traditionally been mostly via steep, narrow, winding mule tracks (*dhromi; kalderimia*), or paths (*monopatia*). Under these circumstances even the simplest mechanization of agricultural tasks was impossible.

The dominant feature of Methana's climate is its low rainfall, with the annual mean being under 40 cm. It is concentrated in less than fifty rain-days, which occur almost exclusively during the winter and early spring months. High temperatures in the summer months increase the aridity due to high evaporation rates. With a low annual average rainfall and a mean temperature of 18.5°C (Kayser and Thompson 1964, 1: 4), Methana fits squarely in the band of environments defined as semiarid, with all the special agrarian problems such environments present (Bailey 1979: 79, 93; Bowden 1979: 65–71; Carter and Konijn 1988: 61–62). These factors by themselves are important for populations making a living by agriculture, but they are associated with two further variables.

The first is the range of variability in annual rainfall amounts. It is well known that on a global scale interannual rainfall levels are generally most variable in areas where rainfall is least abundant (Ricklefs 1980: 847–48; Carter and Konijn 1988: 61–62). Thus rainfall on Methana is both low in average terms and highly variable from year to year: drought conditions can be expected relatively frequently (Forbes 1982: 35–37, 200–201). The second factor is the effect of the timing of both individual falls of rain and the onset of the period of hot, dry summer weather on wheat especially, but also on barley and olives. Rainfall events on Methana are least dependable, and amounts of rain tend to be lowest, at the beginning and end of the winter rainfall period. Coinciding with the end of the rainfall period, temperatures tend to rise rapidly in the two months prior to the cereal harvest, which occurs in June (Forbes 1982: 453–54). These factors of low rainfall at sowing time and in the two months prior to harvest—combined with high preharvest temperatures, especially if associated with drying winds—are liable to induce poor wheat yields (Leonard and Martin 1963: 285–86; Stoskopf 1985: 118; Gusta and Chen 1987: 124–27). Likewise, Methanites say that a fall of rain in September also helps improve yields of the olive, a staple almost as important as wheat, helping to reduce premature fruit-drop and to swell retained fruit (see also Pansiot and Rebour 1961: 19–20, 186). A significant rainfall at this time of year, however, is not at all a dependable event.

In terms of agriculture, these factors had a number of significant effects:

1. Considerations of rainfall variability and soil moisture tended to dominate agricultural decision making (Forbes 1982: 200–29).
2. Variations in altitude affected evaporation rates, which in turn affected plant growth. Higher altitudes had significantly reduced evapotranspiration rates, largely as a result of lower temperatures.
3. The high interannual variability of both the amounts and the timing of rainfall would have made a dependence on agriculture very risk-prone if certain risk-minimization strategies, including plot fragmentation, were not practiced (Forbes 1989).

The Property-Transfer System: Dowry and Inheritance

In the early 1970s, as observed during the main period of field research on Methana, the expectations of both men and women were that they would eventually all receive equal shares of their parents' estate. This expectation was in line with the stipulations laid down in the Greek civil code. The share received by women, called *proika* in Greek and translated 'dowry' in English, was often understood by Greeks as being given to a daughter at her marriage.[4] On Methana some property was indeed normally transferred to a daughter on marriage, but often her full share was not handed over until the deaths of both her parents. Furthermore, in some circumstances she might be deemed to have received some, possibly most, of her patrimony even before marriage (see below). By definition, sons expected to inherit their portion of their parents' property only after their parents had died. However, they frequently had the use of, if not the title to, some of their patrimony while their parents were still alive.

The ideal of equal shares for all children could include equivalent values of different types of property. Hence some children (of either sex) might receive money, whereas others received education or training in a skilled trade, and still others received agricultural property. The provision of a secondary education in particular was traditionally considered as largely fulfilling the obligation of parents to provide a livelihood for a child: an educated child normally could expect little more from the parents' estate. But for those children dividing up property on the death of parents, all types of property were considered as separate resources.

When the agricultural resources of an inheritance were divided up among those children who were due a portion, there was a marked ideal that each inheritor should have equal shares of all categories of agriculturally productive resources (e.g., different types of land, crop trees, vines, etc.). In an agricultural landscape in which the growing of arable field crops (e.g., cereals and legumes) was practiced under crop trees (particularly olive, almond, and fig trees) the equitable subdivision of land inclusive of trees was virtually impossible. Not all trees were of the same size or productiveness; they were not evenly distributed on a plot; and the land in which they grew might be very variable. It was thus frequently impossible to divide a plot in such a way as to give equitable division of trees and land at the same time. Since under this sort of polycropping regime both the land and the trees were separate productive resources, however, all

Table 10.1
Land Fragmentation in Liakotera and Elsewhere

	Mean holding (ha)	Mean number of plots	Mean plot size (ha)
Liakotera	3.309	20.135	0.182
Peloponnesos	3.880	6.260	0.620
Greece	3.520	6.530	0.540

SOURCE: Forbes (1982: fig. 11).

species of crop tree could be inherited independently of the land on which they grew (Forbes 1982: 312–23).

Similarly, some plots of land were more accessible, fertile, and so forth than others. Also, for reasons that I have documented elsewhere (Forbes 1982: 221–29), all farmers in Liakotera synchronized their cereal and legume crops in different sectors of the countryside in alternate years as part of the rotation cycle. An inheritor therefore needed to own an even spread of plots across the landscape so that each year he or she could grow cereals in some and legumes in others. In the case of vines, the moisture retentiveness of the soil and relative openness to sunshine and drying winds of the different locations where vines grew were critical features; distance from the village was another important criterion.

The answer to all these problems was to treat each category separately: different varieties of trees, individual plots of vines, and the different plots of land were all considered as separate entities. They were divided so as to provide as equitable a transfer of all productive resources as possible. In most cases, where it was practical, individual plots of land and vines were equally subdivided between all inheritors. Similarly, a tally was made of all crop trees by species, and they were then divided equally among the heirs so that each received both productive and less productive trees. It was also quite common to give a dowry of trees only, especially if a daughter was moving to another village upon marriage and would therefore be living at a considerable distance from her dowry.[5] The system resulted in situations where the owner of a plot might not own the trees that grew on it, and vice versa. Rights of ownership of trees growing on another person's plot only existed while those particular trees were growing: owners of trees had no rights to replace trees that had died with new young ones. This meant that on any plot, divided ownership of land and trees had a long but finite duration, since trees such as almonds and figs do not normally live longer than approximately a century. Once trees had died, the owner of the land could replant trees for his own use. Olive trees were the only exception to this rule, since their life span extends for centuries, at least.[6]

Liakoterans were of the opinion that the operation of this system on Methana over the generations had led to the level of land fragmentation that they experienced. It was quite extreme in comparison with the average for Greece, as shown in Table 10.1. Other communities on Methana had comparable levels of plot fragmentation, with mean plot sizes ranging from 0.175 to 0.342 ha (Forbes 1982: fig. 11).

The farm of Liakotera household 2 is an example of how this system worked out in practice (Figure 10.1). The total area that the household farmed was about twenty stremmata (2 ha), divided into eighteen separate plots.[7] Plot sizes ranged from about 100 m^2 to about two strem-

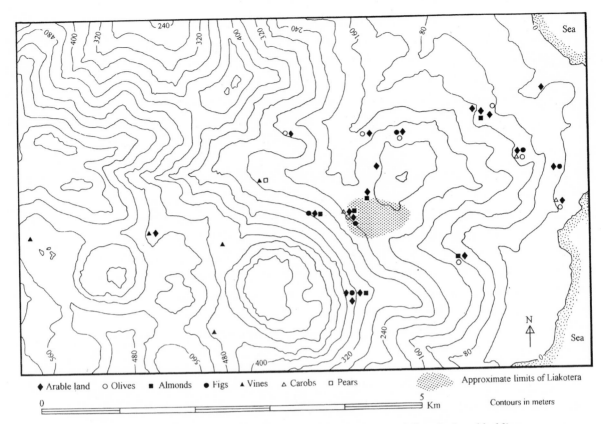

Figure 10.1.   Household 2, Liakotera: Approximate locations of all agricultural holdings.

mata.[8] The largest single holding of olives owned by the household was 8 trees: but out of a total of forty-four olive trees owned, at least eleven (25% of the total) were on land owned by another household. The whole property was distributed over a distance of about 3.5 km, and ranged in altitude from some 30 m to about 400 m above sea level.

With a mean plot size of 0.11 ha per plot, the degree of property fragmentation that this example represents was far greater than the Greek national average (0.54 ha per plot), but not much greater than the Liakotera average (0.18 ha per plot). Methanites themselves complained that land fragmentation was uneconomical in terms of time spent traveling from one plot to another. They considered that the equal inheritance system was at the root of the phenomenon, but said that since this was the way the property transfer system worked, they had to put up with it. Nevertheless, various measures were taken by Methanites to ensure that further fragmentation was kept to a minimum: occasionally consolidation of property could be achieved (e.g., Forbes 1982: 151). Furthermore, although they complained about some aspects of fragmentation, evidence given below illustrates that households recognized the benefits of dispersed holdings. On occasion they took measures to ensure that their plots remained dispersed over different microenvironments.

In many cases the family's cash surplus was used to provide an education for one or more children so that the other(s) might receive more land. The provision of a house or house site in

Athens, or money for such, by way of dowry, was another way of ensuring that the family's land resources were not divided among too many heirs. Especially when there were no daughters, sons might also be given money in lieu of land. This too might be invested in a house or business, or used to buy more land.[9]

A number of observers of modern Greece have commented somewhat unfavorably on the way in which cash generated from the agricultural enterprise was traditionally often spent on a dowry house or house site in a large provincial town or in Athens (E. Friedl 1962: 67–68; Campbell and Sherrard 1968: 338). This has been seen as drawing off cash derived from the agricultural enterprise for the least desirable and least productive forms of investment, thus depriving agriculture of cash that could have been reinvested in the family farm. The cash generated from the agricultural enterprise itself mostly came from the urban centers, however, since it has been largely urbanites who have bought farmers' products (Forbes 1975). This has certainly been true for Methana and has probably applied to most other rural Greek situations in recent generations. Furthermore, on Methana there has historically been very little in which the farmer could invest to increase the efficiency and productivity of the farm, since mechanization and extensive irrigation are impossible there. When a relatively large capital investment has been needed, it seems to have been made. Ironically, the main problem, at least in the present century, seems to have been to find a suitable safe channel for investment within agriculture (Forbes 1982: 153–54).

On the other hand, whether money was spent on a child's education, buying agricultural land elsewhere, or providing a dowry house in Athens, the expenditure of cash can be seen as a conservation measure: it ensured that the subdivision of a family's agricultural land was kept to manageable proportions. Nevertheless, despite the important caveat presented by Adams (this volume), it is hard to counter the argument that the scattering of small plots across the countryside has been at least in part the result of the operation of the legally institutionalized system of property transfer over the generations, however much Methanites attempted to mitigate its more extreme effects. Within Greece, various official attempts have been made to encourage or facilitate the consolidation of holdings in order to reduce the apparent waste of time in traveling between widely scattered plots. In particular, during the period of field study the Greek government published various pamphlets setting out the advantages of land consolidation. Nevertheless, Methanites did not follow the suggestions set forth in the pamphlets.

Settlements and Landholdings

Like Liakoterans, a number of scholars have commented unfavorably on the time spent traveling from farmhouse to plot under conditions of land fragmentation (Bentley 1987b: 42–44). Thus Thompson (1963) calculated very large distances that a farmer would have to travel annually to visit each field from the farmhouse for each cropping activity. As Bentley (1987b: 43) points out, however, Thompson is assuming that farmers always return to the home base before visiting the next field. He does not calculate the time economies of visiting two or more fields on a single trip. Furthermore, Bentley (1987: 43) notes that under Thompson's calculations a farmer averages about twenty minutes to arrive at his work—a traveling time that many urban commuters would envy.

Throughout the now extensive literature on land fragmentation and plot dispersal, little attempt has been made to link the phenomenon with aspects of settlement size and distribution.[10] When discussing the issue, many North American scholars tend to think of their own rural landscape, which typically consists of isolated farmsteads set in their own consolidated landholdings. On a worldwide scale this pattern is atypical, and is the result, at least in part, of the particularistic circumstances of the sudden (in human historical terms) imposition of an intrusive population onto a landscape where the settlement pattern of the indigenous population was largely ignored. Elsewhere in the world, rural settlement is usually nucleated to some degree, whether this be in small villages, or larger but still agriculturally based towns, such as the agro-towns of parts of the Mediterranean (e.g., Chisholm 1968: 55–59).

Where concentration of population into villages or towns occurs, it is virtually impossible for all, or even most, owners of small farms to own consolidated holdings contiguous to the settlement. In a situation where farmers live in a nucleated settlement and own consolidated holdings, some holdings would be close to the settlement, whereas other farmers would be forced to travel considerable distances to reach their land. European farming demands the storage of a wide variety of commodities, tools, and equipment (Forbes and Foxhall 1995: 72–73). In the hypothetical situation outlined here, those farmers who had distant consolidated holdings would have two unenviable choices: either to incur considerably increased costs in travel time and the necessity of transporting all equipment and commodities between dwelling and farm, or else to construct on the holding secure storage facilities to house these items and to avoid the risk of theft. In addition, environments are not usually completely uniform: even those areas not definable as mountainous have lands of greater and lesser desirability, by reason of soil quality, access to water, proneness to flooding, and so forth. Farmers whose holdings contained a high percentage of low productivity and/or high risk land would be unlikely to stay in business very long—and in premodern conditions, "business" might be equivalent to "life." Under such circumstances, one obvious way of ensuring a reasonably fair distribution of land of all types in a nucleated community is to allocate it in smallish parcels of each type spread over the whole community territory.

The alternative approach is to spread settlement over the consolidated landholdings—to produce a dispersed settlement pattern. This is the pattern familiar to many who live in North America. It is also the pattern being aimed at in several parts of the Mediterranean region and elsewhere (e.g., Chisholm 1968: 113–21) by governments who wish to improve the efficiency of farming. It is developing independently, to a limited extent, not far from Methana, on the Plain of Troizinia and in parts of the Ermionidha, but primarily in the flat, low-lying lands of the Thermisi plain, where settlement has only become fully feasible since the eradication of malaria in the 1950s (Jameson, Runnels, and van Andel 1994: 145–47; Sutton, this volume). Here isolated dwellings are springing up on small intensively worked farms specializing in irrigated crops such as citrus fruits.

It is important to note that, on a worldwide scale, most of the examples of land consolidation and the associated development of a dispersed settlement pattern that have occurred in recent times are the result of modern developments in technology and market integration. They are also generally associated with the least variable types of terrain. Furthermore, they are associated with the introduction of features like year-round irrigation and the construction and maintenance of all-weather roads. The latter allow communication with isolated farms and the transport of farm produce to external markets. However, in a number of instances, there has been a resulting removal of a resource (e.g., grazing land) that had been widely used by a large number of households prior to the development (Bentley 1987b: 55–61; Chisholm 1968: 113–21).

In most cases, therefore, the only alternative to the ownership of dispersed holdings by farmers who live in consolidated (i.e., nucleated) communities is consolidated holdings in dispersed communities. This fact emphasizes the costs, both social and financial, that arise from the development of consolidated holdings. The costs of installing mains for electricity and water to a number of widely scattered dwellings rather than to a single tightly clustered community must be added to the costs of the roads that link the isolated dwellings. The costs for farmers of communicating between the farm and the wider community are increased. The loss of regular daily social intercourse with kin and neighbors means that it is harder to pool labor or exchange equipment among farmers, or to indulge in the constant small acts of borrowing, lending, and exchange of produce and so forth that occur in many rural communities (H. Koster, this volume). There is also an increase in the loneliness experienced by those living on isolated farms; this is likely to be felt particularly keenly by members of societies, such as those of the Mediterranean, whose cultures place a high value on life in large nucleated communities. Additionally, village communities act as foci of information exchange, on such matters as current commodity prices, opportunities for sales of produce or purchase of important items such as land or machinery, new developments in agriculture, government schemes, life crisis rituals of community members, and even such details as at what time the Sunday church service will take place.[11] Finally, in many government-instituted consolidation schemes, the wealthiest members of the community tend to benefit at the expense of the poorest (Chisholm 1968: 121–23; Bentley 1987b: 55–58).

Agrarian communities on Methana have been in most aspects at the opposite extreme from the situation associated with dispersed settlements and consolidated holdings. Thus:

1. A major aim of Liakoterans and most inhabitants of other villages on Methana has been subsistence—that is, production for direct household consumption, rather than market-oriented production. Conversely, the broken landscape makes the mechanization of agricultural operations associated with market-oriented production extremely difficult.

2. The brokenness and vertical range of the landscape have yielded immense variability in the landscape, and therefore have provided every reason why farmers would wish to disperse their holdings over it, especially in the context of the production of a wide range of crops for direct household consumption.

3. The ruggedness of Methana has also made communication across the landscape difficult, despite the network of paths and mule tracks. For the same reason, construction of all-weather roads to connect isolated farmsteads would be difficult and time-consuming, demanding much blasting, the construction of many culverts where the road crosses seasonal watercourses, and additional length for hairpin turns, and so forth.

4. In a highly broken topography like that of Methana there have been a relatively restricted number of locations in which it has been possible to build a house: it is quite

conceivable that a consolidated landholding in this environment would not contain a suitable house site.

5. Finally, the religious dimension is often forgotten when considering the needs of communities. In a devout population, nearness to place of worship may be an important consideration that may work in opposition to economic ones.[12]

Scattered Plots: Practical Considerations

The reality of the significant inefficiencies supposedly entailed in ownership of scattered plots has not been widely discussed. Apart from Bentley's observations (see above), McCloskey (1975: 78–80) has shown that the time spent traveling between plots in medieval England has been exaggerated. On Methana a number of factors also combined to reduce time spent in traveling between plots. First, distances between plots were often fairly small. For household 2's holdings the average direct distance between a plot of land (or a tightly packed group of plots) and its nearest neighbor was 0.8 km. Even if the farmer's day involved work on as many as four neighboring plots, the total direct distance traveled between plots would have been less than 2.5 km, or about a forty-five minute walk—probably no greater an amount of walking than what many people who work in large buildings cover during the course of a day. Obviously, such simple calculations do not take account of a number of problems. For instance, rarely did paths lead directly between plots; and a short distance traveled might still have necessitated loading the equipment onto the mule or donkey and off-loading it at the next plot. Nevertheless, these calculations do indicate that time spent in traveling between plots was not as great as might be imagined.

Other factors involved in the way Methana farmers scheduled their work also reduced the time spent moving between plots. Frequently more than one task was undertaken on a particular plot at any one visit—another factor that Thompson failed to consider. Thus, although a farmer might state that he intended to sow cereals, he might actually start by picking up windfall olives on the plot, then complete the final stages of *perikopsimo* (field clearing) or rebuild a portion of the terrace wall that had collapsed before the main task of sowing his crop. Brushwood was frequently cut from nearby scrubland, to be transported on the pack animals at the end of the day (the leaves to be used for fodder for sheep and goats and later the wood to be used for fuel), as part of a day's activity out in the fields. By undertaking several tasks in the course of a day's work at a single location, farmers decreased travel time between scattered plots and eliminated the need to make a special journey to a single plot for relatively minor maintenance tasks.

This is not to claim there were *no* disadvantages to plot scattering on Methana. Undoubtedly some time was lost in travel, even if less than is often claimed. Some land was lost because of the numerous paths allowing access to large numbers of plots in separate hands. Where paths did not exist, access to one person's plot across that of another could cause problems to the owner due to trampling of crops, and so forth. When trees and land were owned by different households, the owner of one resource might be less than scrupulous about the needs of the other owner. Thus, trees on land owned by someone else might not be cultivated because the owner of the land did not wish to sow arable crops there; arable land might be plowed before another's windfall olives were gathered; or a young cereal crop might be trampled by uncaring olive pickers who did not own the land and the crop.[13]

Background to the Problem:
Climatic and Topographic Variation

The pattern of small, highly fragmented plots on Methana did not, however, arise merely as a dysfunctional result of recent social trends in the transfer of rights to productive resources: the system of dowry and inheritance in use seems to have had an extremely long history. Much the same legal intentions as those laws on dowry/inheritance current at the time of fieldwork (though differing in legal structure) seem to be detectable in ancient Greek legal texts (i.e., inscriptions and courtroom speeches: Foxhall 1987; Hodkinson 1986). One of the earliest documents in which these rules were laid out is the Gortyn code of about the mid-fifth century B.C. from Crete (Meiggs and Lewis 1969: 95–99). The fragmentation known to exist in the landholdings of ancient Greek households has likewise been considered to be the result of these rules and has been directly linked to the need for diversity in agricultural production strategies (Osborne 1987: 37–39; Foxhall 1986); however, this observation does no more than agree with Igbozurike (1970: 323—quoted in Bentley 1987b: 34) that land fragmentation would not have existed for so long if it were not functional in some way. In order to substantiate the claim that fragmentation on Methana had similar adaptive advantages it is necessary to view the data against the background of the environment in which Methanites operated.

One of the most fundamental features of any community's natural environment is the climate. It is, however, frequently forgotten in theoretical discussions of small-scale agriculture that "climate" is not merely average weather conditions punctuated by periodic "hiccups" of particularly good or disastrous years. Even without taking into account freak good or bad years, which may be expected to occur as little as once in a lifetime, the assorted factors that constitute climate vary markedly from year to year. Agricultural productivity therefore varies as well. As noted below, a community cannot afford to adjust its mechanisms for coping with the environment to the "average" climate. In such a case, starvation would be as common as sufficiency. Moreover, traditional agrarian economies must be able to cope with the kinds of freak conditions already mentioned. Such variations in the natural environment are expectable but not predictable,[14] and it is against this background that the cultural coping mechanisms of farmers on Methana are discussed.

> All ecological systems are influenced by variables which, while expectable sooner or later, are not predictable as to exact time or place. Some of these variables are of nonhuman origin such as fluctuating weather patterns, while others which are conceivable, such as conquest, are of human origin. Agricultural systems must contain mechanisms which allow for survival during periods of crop failure and then for recovery afterwards. . . . In areas of the world such as the Mediterranean, which are characterized by extreme year to year variability of climatic factors such as rainfall (cf. Walker 1964, 30), mechanisms which allow the system to "roll with the punches," so to speak, are likely to be quite important (Galt 1979: 98–99).

With regard to coping with climatic variability, the most important fact for farmers, particularly if practicing subsistence or semisubsistence agriculture, is not the average or even the maximum yield. It is the yield in poor years that is most crucial. After all, average or maximum yields well above subsistence needs are of little benefit to a farmer if yields in poor years are inadequate to feed the household. Land fragmentation on Methana was one method of ensuring that minimum yields were kept as high as possible: the maximization of productivity and labor efficiency were less important considerations in a situation where survival might possibly be at stake. Such a minimax strategy, as it is sometimes called, functioned to reduce the below average "dips" in productivity rather than to increase the above average peaks (see Gould 1963).

In the highly broken terrain of Methana, there are considerable variations in the environmental factors that affect plant growth and therefore crop productivity. The following four factors are most important:

1. *Altitude* affects not only temperature and evaporation rates but also soil moisture— higher elevations have lower evaporation rates and moister soils on average.
2. *Soils*, in particular, their moisture retention capacity, are important, although factors of plant nutrients, and hence fertility, are also involved.
3. *Aspect*—that is, the particular direction that a location faces (north, south, etc.)— affects the amount of sunshine received, and the extent to which the location is affected by winds.
4. *Topographical features* such as exposed or sheltered locations that also affect factors like sunshine, wind, evaporation, and so forth.

Agricultural fragmentation ensures that each household exploits plots over a wide altitudinal range with a variety of soil types and considerable differences in other environmental factors. The ways in which ownership of small sectors of a wide range of microenvironments on Methana has spread the risk of crop failure under any particular set of annual climatic conditions are indicated in the following sections.

Cereal Cultivation

The reduction in fluctuation of a household's crop returns due to ownership of widely scattered plots can be documented by quantified data from Liakotera. Tables 10.2 and 10.3 indicate a single household's wheat production (both in numbers of sheaves and in total yield in wheat) for individual plots over a period of eleven years.[15] Because arable crops were grown under a two year crop rotation regime, wheat was only sown in any particular plot in alternate years—hence the need for two separate tables.

During odd numbered years this household sowed wheat in a maximum of twelve plots averaging 1.46 *stremmata* (0.146 ha) per plot. More than half of the plots (7 out of 12) were under the 2.0–2.5 stremmata size that most Liakoterans reckon to be able to plow in a day. During even numbered years this household generally sowed wheat in a maximum of fifteen plots averaging 1.59 stremmata per plot. Again, of these plots more than half (9 out of 15) are smaller than the 2.0–2.5 stremmata regarded as plowable in a day. In this instance, the smallest plot was estimated by the household as being one-third of a stremma—0.03 ha, or approximately 1/20 acre. The degree of fragmentation of this household's land holdings was not unduly large for Liakotera, where the mean agricultural plot size was 1.82 stremmata (Greece 1971).

The claim that fragmentation of holdings reduces total harvest fluctuation is based on the assumption that the fluctuation of productivity from year to year in any single plot is likely to

Table 10.2
Annual Production of Wheat in Liakotera by Plot: Even Year Rotation

Plot number	Plot size (stremma)	Productivity (sheaves per stremma) 1962	1964	1966	1968	1970	1972	1974	Coefficient of variation
1	2.0	37.0	46.0	28.0	28.0	57.0	48.0	42.0	24.21
2	2.5	– [a]	43.2	36.0	40.8	52.0	42.0	52.0	13.22
3	1.0	33.0	54.0	54.0	10.0	60.0	44.0	54.0	36.66
4	1.5	–	24.0	18.0	–	24.7	–	17.3	15.96
5	1.5	52.0	42.7	25.3	24.0	20.0	–	18.7	40.88
6	0.5	22.0	34.0	–	18.0	–	–	–	27.56
7	0.5	40.0	44.0	36.0	36.0	44.0	52.0	36.0	13.47
8	4.0	8.3	11.0	13.5	24.5	20.5	19.0	10.5	36.56
9	0.5	28.0	24.0	24.0	8.0	42.0	32.0	36.0	36.27
10	0.3	30.3	39.4	42.4	30.3	45.5	45.5	27.3	19.32
11	1.5	10.7	22.7	19.3	23.3	34.7	25.3	17.3	31.4
12	2.0	18.5	14.0	24.0	–	26.0	16.5	17.0	22.03
13	1.0	21.0	20.0	14.0	24.0	17.0	–	10.0	26.28
14	2.0	22.0	18.0	13.5	16.0	22.5	–	7.0	32.07
15	3.0	–	6.7	6.7	7.3	12.0	13.3	–	31.2

Mean of coefficients of variation of all plots: 27.14

| Total harvest (sheaves) | | 511 | 600 | 501 | 462 | 713 | 489 | 493 | |

Coefficient of variation for harvest (sheaves): 16.11

| Threshed wheat (kg) | | 1,132 | 1,861 | 1,471 | 786 | 1,908 | ? | ~1,500 | |

[a] Dash = not reported

Table 10.3
Annual Production of Wheat in Liakotera by Plot: Odd Year Rotation

Plot number	Plot size (stremma)	Productivity (sheaves per stremma) 1965	1967	1969	1971	1973	Coefficient of variation
1	2.0	30.5	31.5	24.0	24.0	5.0	41.45
2	1.0	30.0	52.0	66.0	66.0	38.0	28.88
3	1.5	18.7	13.3	35.3	14.7	14.7	42.39
4	2.0	34.0	30.0	33.5	48.0	– [a]	18.93
5	1.0	116.0	110.0	118.0	66.0	78.0	21.93
6	2.0	49.5	45.5	55.0	46.5	40.5	10.08
7	1.0	67.0	60.0	46.0	71.0	25.0	31.09
8	1.0	40.0	32.0	34.0	48.0	16.0	31.13
9	3.0	38.0	36.0	30.7	23.3	21.0	22.55
10	1.0	57.0	35.0	34.5	22.0	24.5	35.70
11	0.5	–	–	144.0	196.0	160.0	13.05
12	0.5	–	16.0	8.0	30.0	12.0	50.25

Mean of coefficients of variation of all plots: 28.95

| Total harvest (sheaves) | | 737 | 674 | 779 | 737 | 468 | |

Coefficient of variation for harvest (sheaves): 16.30

| Threshed wheat (kg) | | 2,530 | 2,190 | 1,741 | 1,780 | 1,713 | |

[a] Dash = not reported

be greater than that of the overall harvest figure over the years. This is because, under particular weather conditions, adverse reactions of a crop in one area with one combination of soil, altitude, and so forth are likely to be counterbalanced by increased productivity—or at least not as severe a reaction—by a crop in another area with a different combination of microenvironmental factors. In other words, theoretically, if the household under discussion had grown all of its wheat in a single large plot in any one of the widely scattered places in which it had small plots, there would have been no plots in other areas with differing environmental features to counterbalance on the occasions when that particular plot yielded poorly. Thus, in order to indicate that fragmentation of land holdings could reduce variability of total yield, it must be demonstrable that over time fluctuations in the harvests of individual plots are greater than those of the aggregate of plots that made up the total harvest.

The quantitative data in Tables 10.2 and 10.3 provide such demonstration. The *coefficient of variation* section indicates the degree to which productivity varies, higher figures indicating greater fluctuation.[16] In Table 10.2 the mean of the coefficients of variation for individual plots is 27.14, whereas the coefficient of variation for the total harvest is only 16.11. In Table 10.3 the mean for the individual plots is 28.95 whereas the coefficient of variation for the total harvest is 16.30. In both sets of years, therefore, the mean variability in the productivity of individual plots was considerably higher (59.4% and 56.3% respectively) than the variability of the total harvest. Furthermore, the closely comparable results of the statistics from the two quite separate sets of plots—and years—further validate the argument that a range of widely scattered small plots is likely to ensure greater stability of harvests.

There are, however, four plots out of the total 27 (14.8%) in which individual coefficients of variation were notably lower than those of the total harvests. This highlights another aspect of the dowry and inheritance system as practiced on Methana. It had a tendency to act as a leveling mechanism, which ensured that a large number of people had access to both more and less favorable productive resources.[17] If households had exploited one, or even a few consolidated landholdings, it is possible that a favored group would have owned the land with the most dependable yields. This would have left the majority with land whose productivity was considerably more variable and would therefore have necessitated a larger area per household under cultivation to ensure adequate returns for survival in poor years. In other words, a property transfer system that allocated to the whole community a good "mix" of better and poorer land over a wide area may well have allowed a greater population density than a system of single, large landholdings in which a majority of people owned land whose productivity was highly variable. The association of high levels of fragmentation with high population levels has been noted in many parts of the world; it may well be that widely dispersed plots may be one of the better coping mechanisms that humans have devised for supporting high levels of population by agriculture (Bentley 1987b: 36, 40–41).

Vine Cultivation

The degree of fragmentation of plots of vines has been even more extreme than that for wheat. Since vines have generally been spaced at approximately 1 m intervals, it will be apparent from

Table 10.6 that many households had plots of vines of about 300 m^2 (i.e., 0.03 ha / 0.3 stremma) or less. Of all the multifarious tasks associated with vines, the most critical has been digging. Since an adult male took a full day to dig approximately three hundred vines, even a plot of as little as 200 m^2 (0.02 ha / 0.2 stremma) has entailed most of a day's work. Thus simple measures of plot size do not always accurately indicate the "inefficiency" of a particular level of fragmentation: plot size must be related to the labor-time needs of the crops involved.

The comments and actions of informants, together with data on holdings of vines per household, suggest that the effects of fragmentation on yield stability for vines were similar to those for wheat. There were far fewer areas of vines than arable terraces, however, since deep soil suitable for vines is not particularly common on Methana. Each of these areas of vines experienced differing combinations of microenvironmental conditions. The most important factors involved were: (1) The water-retentive qualities of the soil: some soils were light and readily drained, while others were heavy, water-retentive clays. (2) The degree to which these areas were open to sun and drying winds: some areas were very open and thus dry, while others were in enclosed locations (volcanic caldera features, re-entrants on the hillsides), thus sheltered from the wind and experiencing relatively greater amounts of shade.

In the case of Liakotera these two factors frequently combined to produce noticeably dry or noticeably damp conditions. In a dry year, vines in drier areas did not produce particularly well, whereas a good crop was to be expected from those in damper locations. Conversely, during years with unusually damp conditions, the vines in wetter locations suffered from excess moisture, while those in drier locations were expected to produce well. During the period from 1972–74, weather conditions were at opposite extremes. In 1972, it rained briefly on several occasions shortly before the grape harvest. There were substantial losses due to various forms of rot in the damper locations, but vines in the drier locations were relatively unaffected. In a particularly sheltered location, one informant estimated that nearly half his grape crop was destroyed by rot and mildew. In the following year there was a period of intense heat and very low humidity in July. Shade temperatures rose to 46°C (117°F), exacerbated by a strong, dry wind. The combined effects of heat and wind dried up and destroyed a considerable percentage of the grape crop in the relatively dry areas. In locations with damper soils and more shelter from sun and wind, the grapes were not so badly affected, and some produced very well.

Another environmental hazard for vines has been occasional summer hail storms, which do considerable damage to grapes. These storms and their effects can be severe but very localized.[18] Thus, in 1972 direct observation at harvest time indicated that one area of vines had been significantly affected by hail, while other areas 600–700 m away were barely touched. Ownership of widely scattered plots of vines therefore helped reduce the risk that the total crop would be devastated by such events that, while expectable, were not predictable as to year or location. The yield from a consolidated holding in any specific area of vines would probably have been very good in one of these two years (1972 and 1973) and very poor in the other, depending on the particular soil and exposure conditions involved. On the other hand, a mix of vine holdings, with some holdings in damper areas and some in drier, would have shown substantially less environmentally caused fluctuation of yield.

It is also significant that a mix of grapes from different locations on Methana is thought to

Table 10.4
Liakotera Vineyard Areas:
Moisture Values for Soils and Location Exposure

Toponym	Moisture indices (1.0 = wettest; 7.9 = driest)		
	Exposure	Soil	Combined
Khiroma	5.0	7.0	6.0
Lakateime	5.0	7.0	6.0
Korthi	2.0	2.0	2.0
Skala[a] above Korthi	5.0	5.0	5.0
Groshnjeze	2.0	2.0	2.0
Krishtenja	7.0	3.0	5.0
Kjefanderi	6.0	3.0	4.5
Gouri Lazeri	6.0	3.0	4.5
Khiromeze	5.0	5.0	5.0
Lakhora	5.0	3.0	4.0
Lakateime/Gouri Lazeri	5.5	4.5	5.0
Kjafa	1.0	2.0	1.5
Stravolongos[b]	1.5	1.5	1.5
Stravolongos[b]	2.0	2.0	2.0

[a] A *skala* is a vertical block of terrace.
[b] Different parts of this location have different moisture values.

produce a better wine. Vines in drier locations tend to produce fewer but sweeter grapes than those in damper microenvironments. Wine made from grapes from damper locations with a lower sugar content tends to be very dry, with a rather low alcohol content, whereas wine made solely with grapes from drier locations is generally considered too sweet for village palates. It is particularly important to ensure a reasonably high alcohol content in a wine produced by fermentation and storage in the same barrel, since a low alcohol content significantly increases the risk of spoilage of the wine.

Full lists of the locations of their holdings of vines were obtained for thirty of the forty-four households in Liakotera. Of these, only one had all its holdings in one place: this was an anomalous household of three unmarried sisters. All other households in Liakotera for which data were obtained had vines in two or more different locations. Of these households, however, because of the way property was acquired and divided via the system of dowry and inheritance, not all had vines in locations at both drier and wetter ends of the spectrum. Even when they did, some had much larger holdings of vines in a location at one end of the spectrum than they did in a location at the other. A number of households also had vines in locations that were approximately intermediate in terms of soil moisture retention and exposure between the wettest and the driest. Nevertheless, twenty-four households were identified that owned plots of vines in one or more of both the wettest and the driest vine locations, as opposed to only four households that were identified as owning vines in two of the wettest or two of the driest locations but without vines in locations at the opposite end of the spectrum to counterbalance them.

Table 10.4 sets out the relative dampness or dryness of the various places where vines were located by assigning numerical values to each for both water-retentive qualities of the soil and degree to which these areas were open to sun and drying winds.[19] These measures represent the

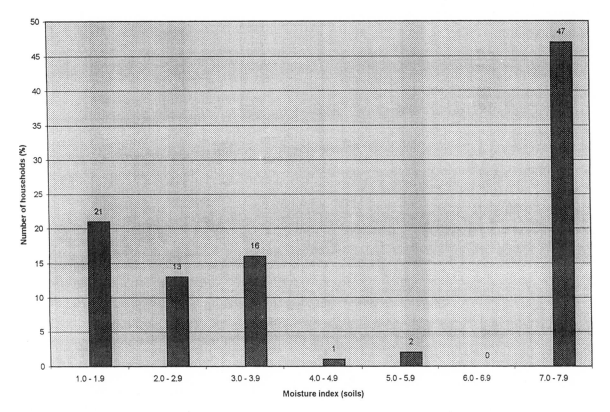

Figure 10.2. Distribution of total vine plots recorded (in percent) over moisture index for exposure, Liakotera.

result of repeated direct personal observations of the factors in question at different times of year. They have been assigned numerical values on a scale of 1.0–7.9. I refer to these values as a *moisture index*: 1 represents the dampest conditions, whereas higher values represent progressively drier conditions.[20]

Table 10.5 presents the data on holdings of vines for the thirty Liakotera households for which complete data on locations of vines were recorded. The combined effects of soil and exposure on the overall dampness or dryness of each location are indicated by the mean of the two numerical values.[21] No information on the actual sizes of each holding is presented, since data of this level of detail were obtained for only a few households. Nevertheless, despite their relative crudeness, the data indicate the advantages to Liakoterans of owning plots of vines in several locations.

Figures 10.2 and 10.3 indicate the distribution over the moisture indices of all plots recorded in Table 10.5. It will be noted that the distribution of these plots tends to be concentrated at the wettest and driest extremes of the moisture indices, indicating that most households owned individual plots of vines at one or both of the extremes of the moisture index, but few owned plots in the intermediate range.

Figure 10.4 illustrates the effect of owning vines in a variety of locations: for each household the moisture index scores of the locations in which they owned vines have been averaged to produce an aggregate numerical value for all its plots of vines. The distribution of these mean

Table 10.5
Holdings of Vines by Household in Liakotera, Showing Moisture Indices

Household	Vine location	Combined moisture index	Mean household moisture index	Household	Vine location	Combined moisture index	Mean household moisture index
1	Khiroma	6.0		22	Khiroma	6.0	
	Lakateime	6.0	6.0		Lakateime	6.0	
2	Khiroma	6.0			Stravolongos	1.5	4.5
	Korthi	2.0		23	Khiroma	6.0	
	Krishtenja	5.0			Korthi	2.0	
	Lakateime	6.0			Stravolongos	1.5	
	Stravolongos	2.0	4.5		Lakateime/		
3	Khiroma	6.0			G. Lazeri	5.0	3.6
	Korthi	2.0		24	Khiroma	6.0	
	Krishtenja	5.0			Kjafanderi	4.5	
	Stravolongos	1.5			Lakateime	6.0	
	Lakateime	6.0	4.1		Stravolongos	1.5	4.5
4	Khiroma	6.0		25	Khiroma	6.0	
	Korthi	2.0			Krishtenja	5.0	5.5
	Lakateime	6.0		27	Khiroma	6.0	
	Stravolongos	1.5	3.9		Groshnjeze	2.0	
6	Khiroma	6.0			Lakateime	6.0	
	Korthi	2.0			Stravolongos	1.5	3.9
	Kjafanderi	4.5		28	Khiroma	6.0	
	Groshnjeze	2.0	3.6		Lakateime	6.0	
8	Khiroma	6.0			Stravolongos	1.5	4.5
	Korthi	2.0		29	Khiroma	6.0	
	Lakateime	6.0			Korthi	2.0	
	Stravolongos	1.5	3.9		Stravolongos	1.5	
9	Khiroma	6.0			Lakhora	4.0	3.4
	Korthi (skala)	5.0		30	Khiroma	6.0	
	Stravolongos	1.5	4.2		Gouri Lazeri	4.5	
11	Khiroma	6.0			Stravolongos	1.5	4.0
	Kjafanderi	4.5		31	Khiroma	6.0	
	Krishtenja	5.0			Kjafa	1.5	
	Stravolongos	1.5	4.3		Stravolongos	1.5	3.0
13	Khiroma	6.0		34	Krishtenja	5.0	
	Khiromeze	5.0			Lakateime	6.0	
	Korthi	2.0			Stravolongos	1.5	4.2
	Lakateime	6.0	4.8	35	Krishtenja	5.0	5.0
14	Khiroma	6.0		37	Khiroma	6.0	
	Lakateime	6.0			Korthi	2.0	
	Stravolongos	1.5	4.5		Gouri Lazeri	4.5	3.5
15	Khiroma	6.0		39	Khiroma	6.0	
	Stravolongos	1.5	3.8		Lakateime	6.0	
16	Khiroma	6.0			Stravolongos	1.5	4.5
	Stravolongos	2.0	4.0	42	Korthi	2.0	
17	Khiroma	6.0			G. Lazeri	4.5	3.3
	Krishtenja	5.0		43	Khiroma	6.0	
	Lakateime	6.0			Kjafanderi	4.5	
	Stravolongos	1.5	4.6		Stravolongos	1.5	4.0
21	Khiroma	6.0		44	Khiroma	6.0	
	Groshnjeze	2.0			Stravolongos	1.5	3.8
	Lakateime	6.0					
	Stravolongos	1.5	3.9				

Table 10.6
Detailed Breakdown of Vine Holdings in Liakotera:
Mean Moisture Indices for Selected Households

Household	Vine locations	Number of vines	Household total	Mean household moisture index	Mean moisture index from table 10.5
1	Khiroma	500			
		200			
			700	6.0	6.0
2	Khiroma	200			
	Korthi	200			
	Krishtenja	200			
	Lakateime	300			
	Stravolongos	300			
			1,200	4.2	4.5
13	Khiroma	400			
	Korthi	300			
	Khironmeze	2,950			
	Lakateime	300			
			3,950	4.9	4.8
21	Khiroma	200			
	Groshjneze	1,000			
	Lakateime	700			
	Stravolongos	700			
			2,600	3.3	3.9
31	Khiroma	650			
	Kjafa	1,600			
	Stravolongos	1,300			
			3,550	2.3	3.0
42	Korthi	350			
	Gouri Lazeri	800			
			1,150	3.7	3.3

plot location scores for household holdings in Figure 10.4 clusters about the middle (3.0–4.9) of the range of the moisture index. This is in sharp contrast to the dispersion of all plots recorded (Figures 10.2 and 10.3), which has concentrations around both extremes of the range. In this way it is possible to illustrate graphically that most households in the sample had an approximate balance of vines in locations tending towards both the wetter and the drier ends of the possible range.

The evidence presented here merely concerns the various combinations of *plots* of vines held by households. A more accurate picture would be produced if more detailed data on the actual *sizes* of holdings in each location were included. As noted above, however, these more detailed data were available for a few households only, and thus could not be used to give a particularly meaningful picture of the overall situation. Nevertheless, they provided a check on the data just presented. Table 10.6 demonstrates the extent to which addition of more detailed data on holding size affects the mean moisture index data for six of the households documented in a rougher way in Table 10.5. It will be seen that although the use of more fine-grained data causes some changes in the index, none are over 10 percent, and in only one case (household 31) would an adjustment to the graph in Figure 10.4 be necessitated. Thus the detailed data support the results of the more coarse-grained data reflected in Table 10.5.

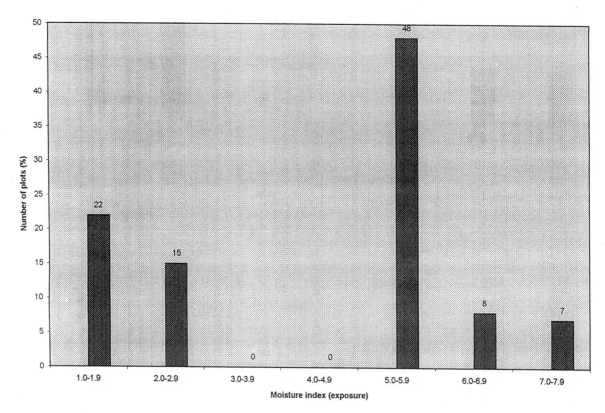

Figure 10.3. Distribution of total vine plots recorded (in percent) over moisture index for soils, Liakotera.

The combined effects of the chances of dowry and inheritance, as well as demographic factors such as number of heirs, meant that not every household obtained the best possible blend of vine plots in areas having very different microenvironmental conditions. Nevertheless, the demonstration that a high proportion of families had a good, even if not always optimal, balance of vines in both wet and dry areas is highly significant, as is the fact that in the sample of Liakoteran households, only one owned vines in a single location. This observation suggests that although villagers complained about scattered holdings, they also appreciated the beneficial aspects of the phenomenon. The actions of individuals further strengthen this belief. For example, the head of household 4 gave as dowry to his daughter his vines in two locations—Lakateime and Stravolongos—while keeping for himself vines in two other locations—Korthi and Khiroma (see Table 10.5). It is noteworthy that:

1. After division of the property, both he and his daughter had vines in both wet and dry locations.
2. Because of the preexisting scatter of vines at several locations with different conditions, it was unnecessary to subdivide the plots still further.
3. The vines kept by household 4 were closer to the village. It was considered that the elderly parents should own vines that did not entail too much travel when work on them was needed.

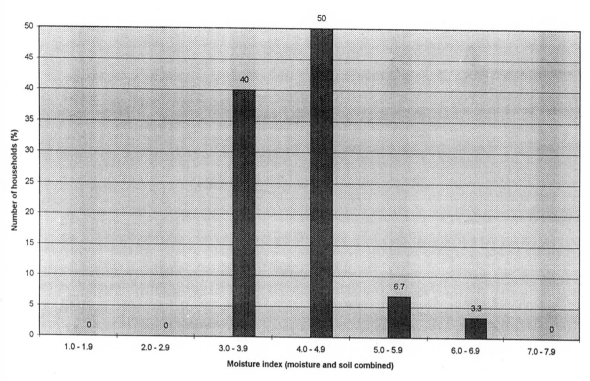

Figure 10.4. Holdings of vines (by percent of households): mean scores for exposure and soil moisture combined, Liakotera.

Scheduling

Another important function of fragmented land holdings in many parts of the world is facilitation and orderly scheduling, over several microenvironmental zones, of agricultural tasks that might otherwise demand more labor at any one time than a household's own resources could provide. In environments without much microenvironmental variability, households often need to organize work groups that include nonhousehold members. These extra hands must be recompensed by payment in cash, kind, food, alcoholic beverages, or a combination of these. All represent a drain on a household's resources, including the household's labor involved in food and beverage preparation (see Stone, Netting, and Stone 1990). In some parts of Greece, certain agricultural tasks have traditionally been undertaken by groups with more participants than could be provided by the nuclear family (see Bialor 1976: 231–32, H. Koster, this volume): a traditional Greek saying equates the cereal and grape harvests with war in their need to mobilize large numbers of people: "*Theros, trighos, polemos . . .*".

The association of dispersed holdings with crop scheduling is well known in Alpine environments *sensu lato* (Netting 1981: chap 2; Cole and Wolf 1974: 127–36; J. Friedl 1973; Rhoades and Thompson 1975: 539). It may be as important, however, in environments far less varied than those of major mountain chains. Galt (1979: 101–2) has documented, for the small Mediterranean island of Pantellaria, the way in which holdings planted in vines and capers that are dispersed in small plots across a variety of microenvironments can be worked with family labor, whereas larger, more consolidated holdings demand hired labor at critical times of year. In a similar vein, Fenoaltea (1976) has claimed that the scattered strips of land worked by medieval English farmers in open field systems also helped to spread out the work load, allowing them to minimize the amount of nonfamily labor required.

It is unfortunately not possible to provide quantified data, of the kind presented above, to support the argument that dispersed holdings on Methana facilitated scheduling of agricultural tasks: the nature of the argument itself makes it difficult to generate such data. Other evidence, however, strongly supports the idea that the pattern of dispersed holdings in a "vertical economy" relieved some of the pressure of work for the family labor force at crucial points in the agricultural cycle. In the early 1970s, virtually every household in Liakotera had enough land, crop trees, and vines for its own subsistence. This fact, and the existence of more lucrative employment outside agriculture, meant there were then no families with an inadequate land base who could depend on agricultural wage labor as a normal part of their income (see Clarke, this volume). Furthermore, since almost all household economies in Liakotera were subsistence oriented and cash poor (Forbes 1982: chap. 6), every attempt was made to keep cash outlays to a minimum. Agricultural labor had to be provided almost exclusively from within the household. Members of different households did occasionally cooperate and exchange labor for certain agricultural chores, particularly for digging vines and harvesting grapes. For the grape harvest, however, the main reason for cooperation was the pooling of a large number of pack animals to facilitate transportation of baskets of grapes back to the village, rather than increase in the number of hands involved in the harvest. On occasion, kin or neighbors might lend pack animals but not participate in the harvest, especially if the animals were relatively docile, and/or the owner was old and not particularly energetic. The bottleneck in the work was less in human labor resources than the number of animals that were mobilizable.

Work groups were also formed for digging vines, generally taking the form of ad hoc mutual labor agreements. Their main function seemed to have been to cement social relationships (see H. Koster, this volume), since contributing households ended up digging the same number of vines, either individually or as a cooperating group. The hard work of digging vines is more pleasurable and goes more quickly if several friends work together. Under stress conditions, however, the system of work groups tended to break down. Thus in one year, adverse weather conditions that delayed the digging of vines at the normal time (the earlier part of March) were immediately followed by a sudden warm spell that made the buds on the vines suddenly start to swell and soften. Once the buds had softened, they were particularly prone to being knocked off by careless work during digging. Each bud thus destroyed meant a whole fruiting branch of grapes lost. There was therefore a general rush to dig vines as quickly as possible, before their buds softened any further. Because no household was prepared to suffer a few days' delay while members first helped other households, every family was forced to rely entirely on its own labor resources. Despite the slow, arduous nature of the work, the vertical distribution of vines mitigated the worst of the labor bottleneck. Households dug first their plots in lower locations where vines had started to shoot earliest and then worked their way through progressively higher, later, locations.

In contrast to work on vines for which certain tasks needed concentrated effort over a very short period, there was no general pattern of mutual help for sowing or harvesting cereals or other arable crops. Because of the high level of dispersal of plots, a household's holdings of arable land were spread over a wide altitudinal range. For wheat, grown as a staple for home consumption by all independent Liakotera households, the normal practice was to start sowing in plots at higher elevations and work progressively lower, since the higher zones tended to have lower evaporation rates and were considered moister than lower zones. Apart from ensuring a longer growing period, because at higher elevations cereals take longer to develop and mature, the fact of lower evaporation rates in those zones was an important consideration. Under normal circumstances, the earliest substantial rainfalls in this part of the Mediterranean can be expected in late October or the earlier part of November. It is a frequent occurrence, however, that the earliest substantial rainfalls of autumn, when the main cereals (especially wheat, but also barley and oats) are sown, are followed by prolonged rainless periods (e.g., Forbes 1982: 453–54). In this situation, much moisture in the soil, which is usually still only in superficial levels, might be lost by evaporation before the next rainfall (Forbes 1982: 242–47). Under these circumstances Methanites reduced the risk of serious losses of crops from a long dry spell following the early rain by sowing cereals first in those areas where evaporation was lowest, and only sowing more evaporation-prone areas later, when there was a better chance of further rainfalls. In any event, since wheat sown as late as early December could be expected under normal conditions to mature satisfactorily, there was no real urgency to sow in late October.

For the harvest, wheat growing on the lowest land, close to the sea, could be expected to ripen at least three weeks before that which Liakoterans would harvest in the highest elevations that they were exploiting. This meant that households started reaping cereals close to the sea while those at higher altitudes were still unripe. This harvest was a time of hard work on Methana, but it was spread over a considerable period as each household reaped its cereal plots progressively up the mountainside. Indeed, many households had spells of relative inactivity during the period, their cereals at lower elevations having been harvested while plots at higher elevations were still maturing. Except in unusual cases, there was no necessity to employ labor from outside the household for the cereal harvest.

The hay harvest was a situation directly comparable to wheat. It occurred in spring and involved predominantly autumn-sown vetch. For optimal returns of high quality hay, vetch had to be cut before the seed started to mature, since after that point its nutritional value for the animals was markedly reduced. On the other hand, overall quantity would be reduced if the crop were cut too early. In addition, besides the necessity of cutting the crop, it had also to be turned to accelerate the drying process, then made into bundles or bales, and brought back to the village—all before prolonged exposure to the sun reduced its quality. There was thus not only a considerable labor requirement for the hay harvest but also a restricted time period for producing both optimal quality and quantity. It is doubtful whether households could have balanced the competing needs of high labor inputs and a limited harvesting period using only their own labor if all land had been in a consolidated holding. Unlike several other legume crops that were less cold-tolerant (e.g., peas, broad beans), however, vetch was sown over a wide altitudinal range. That at lower elevations matured first, and so, as with cereals, the harvest of vetch hay was a steady process, starting close to the sea and continuing progressively up the mountainside.

Fig picking, too, was staggered over a considerable period of time. Not only did Methanites grow several varieties of figs with different ripening times, but fig trees were also located at varying altitudes, particularly in the area between the village and the sea. From the 1930s onward, relatively few figs were picked for dried fruit. The majority were picked fresh and transported to Athens for sale in the wholesale market. This meant that they had to be picked as they ripened. Since a fig tree ripens most of its fruit over a relatively short period (about two weeks), with the limited labor force at the disposal of a household, it was most economical to own fig trees situated at different altitudes so that only a few trees would be ripening their fruit at any one time. In this way, a household avoided a glut of figs that it could not pick before they became unsalable. The earliest ripening figs on Methana fetched the best prices because traditionally they were some of the first available in Athens, and demand was high at the beginning of the season. Nevertheless, because of the bottleneck produced by limited household labor supplies, Liakoterans did not concentrate all efforts on growing such very early figs on lands closest to the coast. Secondarily, concentrating production in a single area would also have left them open to substantial financial loss if localized adverse conditions (e.g., hailstorms) with a significant effect on fruiting occurred. Liakoterans were prepared to accept a dispersed holding of fig trees, with the inevitably reduced prices received for figs sold later in the season from trees at higher elevations, because in this way they spread the labor requirements involved in the picking over a longer period and also reduced the risk of near total crop losses.

Egalitarianism

A number of scholars have argued that fragmentation is the result of a strong cultural ethic of egalitarianism winning out over practical rationality. Even some who have seen the beneficial aspects of the phenomenon have likewise noted that scattering of plots has an egalitarian element to it (e.g., McCloskey 1975: 113–19; also see above). Regions such as the European Alpine zone, the Andes, and the Himalayas, besides sharing the tendency to a high level of plot dispersion, also all have societies that emphasize egalitarian concepts and a high degree of community cohesion (Rhoades and Thompson 1975: 541–42, 545–46). Similarly, it was noted above that plot fragmentation in Liakotera acted as a leveling mechanism: without it there would likely be only a few households controlling the most desirable land, leaving the majority to farm land more prone to the risk of crop failure.

The existence of fragmentation in a highly diverse vertical landscape that allows households to schedule tasks in succession might well also be seen to be related to a widespread egalitarian ethic in Alpine environments, *sensu lato*. It could be argued that since scheduling allows households to make a living using almost entirely their own labor for normal agrarian tasks, there is no need in these environments for a separate class of agricultural laborers. In addition, the existence of strict cultural controls over the numbers of children in families in some of these environments (e.g., Galt 1979: 102–5; Netting 1981: chap. 8; Rhoades and Thompson 1975: 541) means that high levels of plot subdivision, with the near destitution of siblings in large families, are minimized. Thus there are relatively few nearly landless individuals who would be dependent on agricultural wage labor for a living.

These observations notwithstanding, there is no provable general correlation between communities with high degrees of plot fragmentation and developed egalitarian ideals. Still less is there any reason to consider that egalitarianism is the cause of fragmentation; McCloskey (1975: 88–93) specifically rejects this argument in the context of the medieval English open field system. It was noted above, for the sample Liakotera household whose wheat yield was discussed (Tables 10.2 and 10.3), that some plots had a high degree of dependability in production. Thus, if a few households were able to monopolize land with such high dependability, the rest would be placed at greater risk of harvest failure. In this particular case, however, only about 15 percent of the plots showed significantly above average dependability, and they were scattered widely enough that it would be hard to concentrate a whole farm, or even a substantial part of one, on an area of higher than average dependability. Although there are areas of highly desirable arable land on Methana that are relatively flat and have deep soils, they are few in number and relatively small (usually no more than 2–3 ha) in size, and ownership of a plot on them was not essential for survival. In light of these observations, it is clear that the advantage to a household of owning a single substantial holding in any one part of Methana would have been relatively small.

On Methana, despite the existence of a high degree of plot fragmentation, there is no evidence of an enhanced egalitarian ethic, nor a particularly marked sense of community cohesion of the kind discussed by Rhoades and Thompson (1975). In Liakotera at the time of fieldwork, the population was almost entirely composed of independent small farm households, with enough land to make a living by agriculture, although a few (less than half a dozen) supplemented their agriculture with some paid employment. Yet, Liakoterans reported in the past that there were people in the community who did not have "a handsbreadth" of land of their own, who had rented land or worked as wage laborers (see also Clarke, this volume). With the rise of employment opportunities in Athens/Piraeus over the last century or so, many of these people left Methana to work in the city. In addition, it was frequently stated that in the earlier part of the twentieth century a number of families who were quite well-to-do sold all their possessions and also left, because there were better opportunities for the investment of their wealth in the metropolis.[22] Thus, the present situation with regard to wealth distribution is not the result of the playing out of some egalitarian ethic associated with fragmentation, but the steady draining away of those who did not fit the "small family farm" category. Those not in this category often left for what they perceived as better opportunities elsewhere. In this case, all that can be said is that this pattern of differential emigration suggests that small farm units, dependent almost exclusively on family labor, seem best suited to the exploitation of highly diverse landscapes with extremes of plot fragmentation.

Conclusions

The system of dowry and inheritance as practiced on Methana in the 1960s and earlier 1970s (and indeed in many parts of the Greek mainland at that time—Campbell and Sherrard 1968: 329; E. Friedl 1962: 48–74) was associated with an extremely diverse series of microenvironments and an unusually high level of land fragmentation. Although Methanites believed that fragmentation was caused by the working out of the dowry and inheritance system over generations, from the work of Adams (this volume) and the preceding discussion, it is plain that agencies other than the property-transfer system may have been at least partly responsible. Although not advocating environmental determinism, this chapter has noted that the rugged and highly diverse landscape put a premium on spreading one's landholdings over a wide range of micro-environments, while it simultaneously restricted the number of possible settlement sites.[23] In this situation, and given the cultural emphasis in Greece and elsewhere in the Mediterranean on nucleated communities, it is hard to see how else a community could organize a household land ownership system except in dispersed pockets, exploited from a common village base.

Despite the fact that fragmentation of landholdings on Methana entailed an element of travel between separate plots, it was noted that the actual amount of "dead" time involved in travel from plot to plot was less than might have been expected from the pronouncements of those who favor enforced consolidation. This was because farmers, conscious of the potential problem of time wasted in travel, employed various strategies to reduce this. On the other hand, ownership of plots scattered across a highly varied landscape has been an effective way of maintaining at least a moderate level of productivity in the face of the risk of crop failure in an unpredictable climate, especially (in the Methana case) in terms of annual rainfall. At the same time it enables households that are mostly composed of nuclear or stem families to be almost entirely self-sufficient in labor supplies.

It is important, moreover, to view dowry and inheritance as important elements within the wider culture of Methanites. These elements link the human population with its productive resources. The fragmented holdings owned by each household have had to be passed to the next generation in such a way as to enable it, in its turn, to own a suitably wide range of different environmental niches across the landscape to balance the twin problems of a restricted land base and a variable, unpredictable semi-arid climate. This is not to deny that scattered holdings did not increase the labor costs of production. In an agricultural system in which time was inevitably expended in traveling between scattered plots but where every year some crops in some areas were almost certain to give poor yields, overall productivity per person-hour could be expected to compare unfavorably with other farming methods. This loss of efficiency can best be viewed, however, as an "insurance premium," paid to ensure self-sufficiency in agricultural labor and a reasonable supply of food even in unfavorable years.

Essentially similar arguments have been advanced for communities with fragmented holdings in other parts of the world (for a review of many of these, see Bentley 1987b). The value of this study of the situation on Methana lies less in the corroboration of these observations than in the detailed and quantified data to support what has generally been an argument based primarily on theory and logic.

Epilogue

These observations on land fragmentation emphasize its importance in the context of a cash-poor, subsistence-based, agricultural regime. Its main energy inputs were the labor of a family and its draught animals, and one of its primary aims was minimization of the risk of hunger from crop failure. The opposition of such a regime to the aims of commercialized agriculture, in which farmers concentrate on a limited range of products to be sold for cash and in which major emphasis is on maximizing yields, has been obvious, if not explicit.

In the past, the rugged but fertile environment of Methana attracted settlers who valued not only the security against crop failure provided by the varied landscape but also its safety from attack (Forbes and Mee 1996: 81–86). Memories of former periods of instability (such as World War II) have now receded, and the population of Methana has been increasingly drawn into a cash economy and the world of consumerism. With this increasing integration into a cash economy it would have been interesting to see whether Methanites reacted to the demand for specialized, mechanized cash cropping by consolidating their holdings into larger but fewer plots. This trend is what might have been expected if fragmentation were primarily linked to subsistence concerns. But the peninsula's ruggedness and broken topography, for so long a positive advantage under conditions of subsistence agriculture, are insurmountable obstacles to mechanization.

For successful small-scale commercialized agriculture, soil fertility by itself is not enough. The bulk of the arable landscape of Methana is composed of steep, terrace-covered hillsides, yet commercial plots must be large enough to accommodate the economies of scale and mechanization. It is impossible to create large plots out of a series of narrow terraces, even if an access road can be bulldozed to them. In the Mediterranean region, irrigation is almost a sine qua non for small-scale, intensive, commercialized agriculture. Unfortunately, Methana has only limited supplies of (mostly brackish) groundwater, restricted to parts of a narrow band close to the coast.

Many younger Methanites, unprepared to continue the subsistence-oriented lives of their parents, have left for employment in urban centers, primarily Athens/Piraeus, while those who remain have increasingly been drawn into employment in the tourist industry in the peninsula's spa town. Many older farmers have now reached pensionable age. In either case, many villagers have become essentially part-time farmers (see Clarke, this volume). In this situation, ownership of land has become increasingly irrelevant. Only those plots both with easy access to a road and propinquity to the coast generally have any real value—as potential sites for holiday homes. In the case of families where all children have left the peninsula, the necessity to pass on a widely scattered productive resource to the next generation exists only in theory. The house may be a valued part of the inheritance as a vacation home, but increasing sectors of the landscape now consist of abandoned terraces covered in scrub or pine trees.

CHAPTER ELEVEN

Mutable Boundaries: Subdivision and Consolidation in a Greek Village, 1936-1978

Keith W. Adams

One single-born son would be right to support his
father's house, for that is the way substance piles up in
the household; if you have more than one, you had
better live to an old age; yet Zeus can easily provide
abundance for a greater number, and the more there
are, the more work is done, and increase increases.
—Hesiod, *The Works and Days*

With the modern economy of Greece, a new rural landscape has emerged from the old.[1] This is a human landscape, inescapably historical, forming and reforming in response to both endogenous and exogenous social, economic, and legal pressures. As with most subjects of analysis, descriptions of landscapes depend on the observer's point of view, but it is the perspective of the Greek farmers and pastoralists that has shaped the rural landscape of Greece. Convention has depicted "peasants" as out-of-date, conservative, inwardly focused, and unresponsive to changes in a modern world.[2] But could it be otherwise? It is perhaps the outside perspective of the observer and the constrained structure of the model that are at fault here for the ahistoric notion of the "peasant" as marginal, solely defined in opposition to national and world political and economic forces. By contrast, examination of the Greek village of Dhidhima shows a people engaged with socioeconomic contingencies, participating in the politics of Greece and Europe, and creatively reformulating an historically rooted landscape. Peasants, or, as they are better labeled, smallholders,[3] are not solely defined in opposition to the larger world. Land use and landscapes constantly form and reform as smallholders themselves negotiate and reformulate their relationships in a worldview that includes local, national, and world community identities.[4] Patterns of land tenure, like landscapes or land use, are not stable.

Social, economic, and political changes since the original 1936 distribution of land in this case study have been many and far-reaching. Increased access via new roads, changes in the relative importance of crops together with the introduction of new crops, access to larger national and European markets, changes in the politics and policies of Greek agriculture, and changes in the traditional relationships between herders and farmers are all factors that have acted to mold the new landscape. Not only has the perspective of researchers and policymakers changed, but (contrary to much published opinion) the perspective of the Greek farmer has changed in response to new social, economic, and political conditions. The following case study investigates the problem of farm fragmentation in Greece by discussing subdivision and consolidation of landholdings in light of changes, specifically with regard to land valuation (productivity).[5]

The Study Area

This analysis involves a part of the landholdings of the town of Dhidhima, located in an alluvial basin in the central highlands of the southern Argolid (see Chang, Harold Koster, Joan Koster, and Koster and Forbes in this volume). Access to the town is by an asphalt road built in 1953 (since improved) that connects Dhidhima to nearby Kranidhi and to the larger towns of Nafplio and Argos. This road also allows access to the landholdings that lie to the north of Dhidhima near the small village of Pelei. These landholdings are considered in the analysis below. Prior to 1953, products were carried out on donkey and shipped to markets by ferryboat. Recently constructed agricultural roads have further improved access to fields.

Although Pelei has some year-round inhabitants, most of the hamlet has long served as a temporary residence for Dhidhimiotes cultivating landholdings in the area (see Forbes, Sutton in this volume). With the advent of easy access to this area the nature of this temporary occupation has changed. Seasonal occupation has changed to a pattern of occasional overnight stays. The ability of those with landholdings in the study area to move on a daily basis between field and village has brought a concomitant change in perspective, an increased participation in the daily life of Dhidhima.

The traditional economy of this region was based on the stereotypical Mediterranean agricultural mix of wheat, olives, and grapes and on a complex social, economic, and ecological integration with pastoralism.[6] Although this basic pattern has been considerably altered by recent economic development, its continued importance should not be underemphasized, even with the addition of such new items as fruit orchards, fodder, cash crops and fish farming. Risk reducing practices such as polycropping and the dispersal of holdings,[7] as well as factors such as soil fertility and the availability of irrigation water, have also acted to form the landscape typical of southern Greece.

Demography

With a population of 1,688 at the time of the study, the *koinotis* of Dhidhima was typical of many of the settlements of Greece, of which over 40 percent had a population between 200 and 1,999. The population density of Dhidhima, however, was low.[8] For the total land area, it was 14 persons per km^2. For arable land, the density was 99 persons per km^2. The latter was less than the average density for arable land in the Argolid region (128/km^2), and also less than that for Greece as a whole (221/km^2). Historically, the population density of Dhidhima rose from a low of 3.45 per km^2 in 1829 to a high of 13.83 per km^2 in 1971 (based on total land area; Houliarakis 1973: xx–xxi).

There has been a decline in both fertility and mortality within the koinotis of Dhidhima in the twentieth century; there has also been a decrease in the total number of siblings per family. The fertility and mortality statistics for Dhidhima were comparable to Greece as a whole, showing a slight lag in the 1940s and 1950s.

Another major demographic phenomenon in Greece has been out-migration from rural areas to urban centers, particularly Athens (Kayser et al. 1971, Sandis 1973; see also Sutton 1983, 1988, 1994). This has been paralleled by emigration from Greece to more developed areas of the world. Dhidhima has been no exception. The effect of this net loss of rural population has been to reduce pressure on local resources. In many instances the out-migrant population has also made a considerable contribution to the local economy, in the form of remittances.

The Landholdings

The landholdings that constitute the basis for this analysis resulted from the reform of the lands of the monastery of Ayios Dhimitrios tou Avghou. The first mention of the monastery is found in the *catastico ordinario* ordered by the Venetian proveditor general Antonio Nani in 1703 (Topping, Forbes this volume). At that time the monastery was among the smaller ones in Greece, with only thirty-one brothers, thirty-five servants, and ten tenant families. Nevertheless, the monastery had an impressive list of properties: 2,215 ha of grazing land; 217 ha of tilled land; 1,550 sheep; 3,900 goats; and 527 cows, beef cattle, and draft animals. Land tenure was under the manorial system throughout the period between 1699 and 1715 (Sanders 1962: 63). Under Turkish rule, it is likely that by extension of Koranic law and the system known as *Wakf* the monastery was able not only to keep but to enlarge its landholdings.[9]

The history of the monastery after the brief mention by the Venetians is obscure. It is certain that the monastery was not active after the beginning of the twentieth century. The mother house, on Mount Athos, still managed the land just after the turn of the century. The buildings have now gone out of use and are abandoned, and the landholdings were turned over to the Greek state in 1934 under the land reform laws of 1917 and 1925.

In 1936 when reform of the monastery lands was carried out, fields were apportioned to the landless population of Dhidhima, Radho, and Pelei on the basis of need. Great care seems to have been taken to make an even allocation of these resources. A committee was formed that was responsible for determining the quality of various areas of land, surveying the land, and dividing the land equitably. In dividing the land, great care was taken to insure two things: (1) that the total land allocated to each recipient provided a subsistence base; and (2) that some land from each type was given to each recipient. Land was classified according to soil quality, availability of water, and its potential use (e.g., herding, dry farming, or irrigated garden).

The landholding pattern that resulted from this redistribution was one of scattered small plots whose size depended on their quality as classified by the committee. There is evidence in the records and in oral history of some inequities in the classifying of the quality of land and in the determination of who received land. Even so, interviews with those recipients still alive in the

1980s indicate that the goals of equitable distribution and the insurance of basic subsistence were met and that Dhidhimiotes were satisfied with the results of land reform.

The research reported here deals with the spatial history of these holdings after 1936. From 1936 to 1980, approximately one thousand transfers of ownership took place among the eight hundred parcels. Some of these transfers resulted in the division of parcels into smaller units, while other transfers resulted in the consolidation of parcels. The following analysis shows how a single variable, land value, affected the propensity toward subdivision or consolidation.

The Analysis of Land Fragmentation in General

Discussions of land tenure in Greece have usually centered on the problem of subdivision and plot dispersal. These discussions, along with those dealing with other areas of the world, have often lacked clear definition of terminology. According to Van der Meer (1975a: 15), imprecise analysis caused by ambiguous definition has led to erroneous conclusions about the causes of fragmentation. Bentley's review (1987a, b, c) of the literature supports Van der Meer's conclusion, while discussing the decidedly different perspectives of the disciplines involved.

Development agencies have often seen farm fragmentation as an outright evil. Economists and Europeanist geographers usually portray it as once adaptive but now outdated. And anthropologists, though they have not commented as often on farm fragmentation, tend to find it ecologically adaptive or a risk reducing strategy (Bentley 1987b: 31–32). Bentley notes that the failure to comment on fragmentation by anthropologists "perhaps reflects a functionalist bias that assumes rationality in a stable pattern of land tenure." Perhaps also, whether evil or adaptive, many of these perspectives on fragmentation share and are bound up in the ahistoric notion of the "peasant" as solely defined in opposition to national and world political and economic forces.

The data most easily available (and most often used) for studies of fragmentation are normative statistics provided by agricultural census authorities. The exclusive use of these statistics continues a top-down perspective of analysis. These data generally, but not always, reflect ownership and do not necessarily reflect the operational aspects of land tenure, thereby skewing the picture of land fragmentation. Ownership data generally suggest greater land fragmentation than do operational land tenure data (Van der Meer 1975a: 14). I have argued elsewhere that this distinction between legal and operational data extends to other terminology, such as holding, farm, or plot (Adams 1981: 45–49). In this study operational data are thus emphasized.

In order to determine operational land tenure and whether or not subdivision or consolidation obtained, the following set of definitions was employed.

1. *Land tenure* is the right of access to a unit of land, which can be defined either in terms of ownership or operation.
2. *Ownership* is the legal right of access to a unit of land as defined by title or deed.
3. *Operational tenure* is the right of access in order to use a unit of land by formal or informal agreement between owner and user.
4. A *plot* is all contiguous land under legal or operational tenure to an individual (or family).

5. A *holding* is the total of all land under the ownership of an individual (or family).
6. A *farm*, in contrast to a holding, is all of the land under operational tenure to an individual (or family).

The term fragmentation has been used in some literature to mean the division of plots, as well as the dispersal of the plots making up a farm or holding. According to Van der Meer, however, "fragmentation, having the capacity to mean both subdivision and dispersal and to apply equally to farms and holdings, can generate faulty reasoning" (1975a: 15). These and related terms are defined below:

1. *Fragmentation* refers to the combined effects of subdivision and dispersal.
2. *Subdivision* is the division of a plot into two or more smaller plots, such that access to and use of the resulting plots rests with more than one individual or family.
3. *Dispersal* is the spatial scattering of noncontiguous plots in a holding or farm.
4. *Consolidation* is the reverse of subdivision, such that the resulting plot is larger in size and resulting access and use rests with the same individual (or family).
5. *Transfer* means the conveyance of the rights of access or use, either by deed, rentall or other measure, from one individual (or family) to another.

Subdivision has been thought to be one of the main causes of the dispersal of farm plots (Van der Meer 1973: 1). Subdivision has also been seen as the major factor in the formation of excessively small holdings (e.g., Binns 1950: 14; Jacoby 1953: 22; and Nylon 1959: 361). Busch and colleagues have also considered subdivision caused by equal partible inheritance to be a factor in the creation of smaller farm plots and hence of smaller landholdings (1979: 40). Before getting to the analysis at hand, it is necessary to briefly discuss the relationship of subdivision and consolidation to the literature on land tenure and agrarian structure, both generally and within Greece.

Land tenure has often been discussed in the context of agrarian structure and land reform. Discussions of agrarian structure, in turn, have often centered on landlessness, security of tenure, and those holdings that are too small to support a family under current land use. Agrarian structure is closely interrelated with land use. Some time ago, Van Wersch demonstrated that land use, to a measurable extent, determines land ownership patterns and that the converse is also true—land tenure arrangements restrict the degree to which any given land use can be adopted (1969). He also argued that this relationship affects rural development. The latter statement assumes that the system of landholding is inflexible and cannot adapt to new land uses and economic conditions. Under such assumptions, the only means of adjusting to such changes becomes the wholesale realignment of agrarian structure known as "land reform."

In a discussion of the social aspects of agrarian structure in Mexico, Stavenhagen noted that constitutional land reform achieved the breakdown of *latifundismo*, the sociopolitical system of the large holdings known as *latifundia* (1970: 226). He also argued, however, that Mexico did not subsequently solve all of the problems that had prompted such reform, and that the continual process of change that has resulted constitutes a state of "reforming land reform" in which Mexico's leadership has not always been conscious of the historical goals and purposes involved.

Greece, like Mexico, initially concentrated on the elimination of large landholdings with the land reform laws of 1917 and 1925 (Sanders 1962: 66; Varvaressos 1950: 180). A change of policy after the end of World War II, however, led to a series of legislative schemes promoting consolidation. This legislation has met with varying success (Keeler and Skuras 1990: 74–75). Much of it came in response to a large body of development literature calling for the consolidation of landholdings to facilitate a modernization of agricultural production. In any case, the changing economic conditions of Greece have led to moves, similar to those of Mexico, for reforming land reform.

Although the concept of *minifundia* (excessively small landholdings) is intuitively simple,[10] it is difficult to identify at what minimum size of landholding minifundia exists. The difficulty lies in prescribing a minimum size suitable for all variety of land uses (Binns 1950: 18). For example, the goal set by the European Economic Commission for the minimum size of Greece's farms was 30 ha. In some areas, however, a much smaller holding will provide an adequate living when cultivating irrigated cash crops.

In discussions of minifundia, the landscape is often said to appear fragmented,[11] a static visual impression that parallels ahistoric views of the smallholder. This may be seen, for example, in the following: "Viewed from a vantage point, and in the clarity of its celebrated light, the Greek landscape contains much to charm and interest the observer. . . . Most striking, perhaps, is the fact that the arable land generally presents the aspect of an intricate mosaic of tiny fields set in a matrix of roads, paths, and field divisions" (Thompson 1963: 1).

Binns was one of the first to characterize smallholdings as a problem (minifundia) and to systematically list a variety of conditions that encourage minifundia through "fragmentation" of landholdings,[12] including growing population, land shortage, equal partible inheritance, long histories of cultivation, and nuclear settlement patterns (Binns 1950). Most of the literature that followed emphasized only one of these as the chief cause of minifundia: equal partible inheritance (Benito 1976; Fitzgerald 1951; Jacoby 1953; and Thompson 1963, for example). They usually cited Binns as the authority, but their statements oversimplified both Binns' argument and the decisions involved in the inheritance of land.[13]

Arguments citing inheritance practices as the cause of subdivision have often concluded that the customary practices of inheritance should be altered legislatively (for example, Jacoby 1953). As noted by Van der Meer, "The implications of altering millennia of refinement of traditional customs by a stroke of the pen are obviously colossal" (Van der Meer 1975a: 15). Farmer argues against the legislative control of inheritance because it would reduce the flexibility of land management decisions (Farmer 1960). In a discussion of a different part of the subdivision problem, Binns made a point worth considering here: "that regulation [legislation] cannot move much in advance of public opinion" (Binns 1950: 18). Finally, the legislative restriction of partible inheritance does not address the causes as outlined by Binns. A careful reading of Binns indicates that he saw partible inheritance simply as the agent of subdivision, and that a number of other factors could be causes of minifundia and fragmentation (1950: 10–11). In fact, Binns argued that "fragmentation is not . . . a necessary consequence of such a right [equal partible inheritance] which may equally facilitate the growth of large estates, nor is fragmentation unknown where this right does not exist" (1950: 10).

Downing, in a study in Oaxaca, Mexico, provided one of the first empirical examinations of landholding subdivision not based on a deterministic relationship between partible inheritance and subdivision (1977). A model based on the ratio of subdivided to nonsubdivided fields provided a *probabilistic* rather than deterministic framework for the analysis of factors that may "affect the propensity of a field to be divided into two or more parts when it is being transferred to co-heirs" (Downing 1977: 235).

Hypothetically, starting with one hundred parcels of land, with two heirs per inheritance and assuming the deterministic relation above, with just three transfers for each parcel, one hundred parcels become eight hundred, and after six transfers 6,400 parcels exist. In the Oaxaca study, however, Downing found that over time a roughly equal number of parcels were transferred intact and subdivided (1977: 239). Since the hypothetical scenario above is based on a geometric progression, the increase in the number of parcels resulting from roughly one-half the rate of subdivision greatly reduced the number of expected subdivisions.

Questions about the spatial pattern of subdivision were moot under the assumption of a deterministic relationship between partible inheritance and subdivision. By assuming the probabilistic model proposed by Downing, one is able to ask the question, which fields are more likely to be subdivided? Put another way, what characteristics of the landholding or of the landholder affect the subdivision of the transferred land? The effect of land value on this issue is given greater perspective by some of the factors proposed by Binns as affecting subdivision: (1) an increasing population or a shortage of land ("population pressure"); (2) strong microecological variation; (3) little nonagricultural employment; and (4) land as the principal object of investment (Binns 1950). Only the first two have been the object of significant research.

When rural population pressure is great and few alternative sources of livelihood exist, demand for land increases, and thus the opportunity for dispersal increases (Van der Meer 1973: 182). This has also been found to be true of subdivision (Downing 1977: 241–42). The specific link that ties population pressure to subdivision is the number of children (potential heirs) per family (Downing 1977: 242; Van der Meer 1973: 182). It has also been noted that permanent emigration may retard subdivision by reducing the potential number of heirs (Downing 1977: 242). This, however, is not the case when the emigrating population retains rights to the landholdings. In Epiros, Yotopoulos found that small landholdings may result from land speculation by absentee landholders (1965: 79).

Galt, with a perspective based in the anthropological tradition of human ecology, has argued that population control and environmental variation on the Sicilian island of Pantellaria combined to achieve an ecological balance (1976). Galt found that dispersal was used by small proprietor households to adapt to climatic conditions and the high cost of labor (1976: 93). He also argued that some subdivision was necessary for the "diachronic parceling of land among productive units such that each such unit receives enough land to operate at a level of comfort as locally defined" (1976: 98). By this statement, then, Galt recognized that at different stages of the life cycle a family required different amounts of resources, including land (see Chang, this volume, for parallel statements on animal folds). As stated above, Galt saw population control as the mechanism that allowed an agricultural system to maintain ecological equilibrium.

Three more factors affecting subdivision can be added to those mentioned by Binns. These are (1) the development of new infrastructure, such as field boundaries or terrace walls, the addition of new roads, or the introduction of irrigation canals; (2) the effects of previous land reforms aimed at the equitable division of land based on ecological factors; and (3) the value of the land itself, whether measured as productive potential or as a monetary worth. The development of new infrastructure has been given only passing comment in the literature, but may become increasingly important with agricultural mechanization (Van der Meer 1973: 35, Busch, Busch, and Uner 1979: 43).

The early literature on subdivision did not mention the effects of previous land reform on present conditions. This was perhaps because most of these studies were carried out in northern Europe, where land reforms occurred at a considerably earlier date. The effect of land reform may be seen in a study of farm plot subdivision and dispersal in Turkey (Busch, Busch, and Uner 1979). The authors found that only four of seventy-two extremely small plots resulted from inheritance, but sixty-four "were created by the government when village pasture land was distributed after irrigation waters were provided" (1979: 41–42). Pechoux also found that the various land reforms that resulted from the constitutional changes of 1917 and 1925 in Greece left a landscape of small privately owned farms, most too small for the present European economic environment (1975). This is supported by data on the average holdings created by the land reform in some regions of Greece (Varvaressos 1950: 180–81). It would seem that one must understand how much of a landscape resulted from previous land reform and how much stems from other factors before drawing conclusions regarding subdivision or dispersal.

Farmland can attain value for many reasons, including (1) high fertility or productivity, (2) suitability for important cash crops, and (3) proximity to sources of irrigation water. Variations in the size of parcels apportioned in Greek land reforms aimed at achieving landholdings of roughly equal value as measured by productivity. Downing's study of a Mexican village tested for the effects of several measures of land value on subdivision and concluded that variation in cropping was the most significant factor (1973: 126). To phrase this in more general terms, competition for scarce or valued resources tends to increase the subdivision of more prized land. For example, in Greece access to irrigation sources has often been closely guarded by heirs, with land around the irrigation source becoming greatly subdivided.

Consolidation is the opposite of subdivision and represents a situation in which two or more contiguous farm plots are brought together under a single owner or operator. As already stated, many authors have proposed a determinant relationship between inheritance and subdivision, yet if this relationship indeed held, many more plots would have to exist than is often the case. Faced with this evidence, some authors have offered consolidating factors, such as the purchase of land. Downing, however, pointed out that under a probabilistic model of subdivision (assuming fewer subdivisions in the first place), consolidating mechanisms have less work to do (1973: 122). Downing found that in the Mexican village of Diaz Ordaz, consolidation occurred, but infrequently. Some of the mechanisms of consolidation mentioned by Downing were (1) selling land, (2) exchanging land, and (3) joint tenancy. He suggested that "the strong Zapotec principles stressing individual household economic independence and minimal sibling solidarity" were related to the lack of consolidation.

Although consolidation is thus noted in some studies, none of the literature considers the possibility of trends toward consolidation. Below I expand the concept of a probabilistic model to include both consolidation and subdivision as possible trends in a changing landscape. Thus, a landscape might, as a whole, be consolidating, subdividing, or in some equilibrium state. This implies that the traditional system of landholdings involves self-regulation of subdivision, a suggestion supported by findings of Downing and Galt (Downing 1977, Galt 1976).

Subdivision and Consolidation in Greece

In successive modifications of the Greek Constitution, from the turn of the century to about 1950, Greece attempted to produce an equitable land ownership pattern. These reforms aimed to break down large holdings, such as those of monasteries and nunneries, and to eliminate tenant farming. By 1950, a new tenure policy began to emerge, a redirection greatly affected by the U.S. economic development plan for Greece. In fact, the first published statements of the new policy appeared in the U.S. Department of Agriculture periodical *Foreign Agriculture* (Whipple 1943, 1944; Varvaressos 1950). This new policy promoted consolidation to combat what American agronomists saw as the inefficiencies of small landholdings. The perception of what constituted a sufficient quantity of land per holding thus changed. In an extensive study of the potential for economic development on Crete, for example, Albaugh remarked on the small size of holdings, stating that "there is a slight tendency for the percentage of farms of 12.5 to 49.9 acres (5.1 to 20.2 ha) to increase and above 50 acres (20.2 ha) to decrease" (1953: 250). While Albaugh emphasized the importance of capital investment in such things as irrigation, processing plants, and research on pest control, he also mentioned the need to reduce land fragmentation (1953: 285). It is not clear whether he meant dispersal, subdivision, or both.

Papageorgiou was among the first to make land fragmentation in Greece the major topic of his presentation (1953). His approach was indicative of the direction soon taken by most research on farm fragmentation in Greece. He concluded that the "causes" of fragmentation were twofold: (1) physical and economic, and (2) social (Papageorgiou 1953: 545). Although he reiterated factors mentioned by Binns, such as long-established cultivation, land scarcity, and population pressure, Papageorgiou placed greatest emphasis on unrestricted rights of transfer (implying partible inheritance). On this basis, he recommended legislative action to prohibit the division of land for inheritance by more than one person.

In 1963, Thompson published the results of a field investigation of land fragmentation in various settings in Greece, following up on an earlier piece of research (Peplasis and Thompson 1959). He collected data on such issues as accessibility to plots, use of plots, and origins of holdings (Thompson 1963: 3). A basic failure of the investigation was that resource limitations (a two-person team and nine months' time) limited the actual extent of the sample (1963: 4). Only three hundred interviews were conducted in eleven villages, for an average of less than thirty interviews per village. This was an inadequate sample size in light of the very low frequency of subdivision and dispersal. The sample included only one village in the Peloponnesos and only one in Epiros and was thus statistically and spatially unrepresentative, lacking sufficient numbers of either individuals or environmental settings.

Despite these shortcomings, Thompson's work remains notable as the only systematic attempt to gather empirical data on land fragmentation in Greece. Thompson also recognized that trends of industrial expansion and low population growth might make consolidation a less important issue in the future. It was unfortunate therefore that he carried out the study with considerable bias toward partible inheritance as the prime cause of fragmentation.

The growing literature on Greek agricultural policy came to emphasize national self-sufficiency in agricultural production, expansion of exports, and harmonizing of farm policies with those of the European Community, including consolidation of landholdings (Frink 1973: 6;

Peplasis 1976). Peplasis explicitly voiced his feeling that too much government financial assistance was spread over a number of short-term measures without solving the real problem of small landholdings (1976: 2). Weintraub and Shapira (1975) reflected the opinions of the European Community and the U.S. Department of Agriculture when they concluded that little had yet been achieved by Greek policy towards consolidation of holdings. Thus, their comments: "The major impetus in this [consolidation effort] was provided by outside help and pressure, the participation of the Greek partners involved was not commensurate," and "It is clear that it [refragmentation] seriously undermined the program [of land reform]" (1975: 52). The Greek Five-Year Plan of 1975–1980 correspondingly addressed the issue of fragmentation in some detail.

In a more recent summary of attempts at consolidation in Greece, Keeler and Skuras have continued this line of thinking, concluding that success of the 1948 law was "inhibited by suspicion," lack of publicity, reliance on the voluntary action of farmers, and an unsystematic approach to land subdivision (1990: 75). They also noted that "the socio-cultural factors which result in fragmented landholdings" were not addressed, thus eroding any gains in consolidation.

In the absence of any systematic study of the processes of fragmentation or refragmentation, it is difficult to understand how such conclusions have been justified. Indeed there have been two major failings in virtually all studies of Greek land fragmentation. First, most analyses have lacked precise definition of terms relating to this issue, a circumstance that has led to inconsistent word usage and the erroneous equation of certain types of data with subdivision or fragmentation (e.g., small farm size equals a process of fragmentation). Second, most of the literature has implicitly assumed that fragmentation was a function of time, yet did not gather longitudinal data suitable to an analysis of process.

While consolidation of landholdings makes little sense, especially for the purposes of mechanization in countries with an abundance of rural labor and few alternative sources of livelihood, this is not the case for Greece. Out-migration and the growing availability of alternative employment have forced Greek agriculture to deal with a dwindling labor supply. The consolidation of agricultural lands might be one way to deal with this problem. For this reason, it is hoped that the research on the relationship of land value to subdivision and consolidation presented here imparts a better understanding of the process by which landholding patterns adapt to changing agricultural economic conditions.

The Case of Dhidhima

It is immediately evident from the Dhidhima data that subdivision was not a frequent occurrence in that area. Of the 800 plots comprising the study area, 563 were transferred at least once between 1936 and 1976, but 237 were never transferred. Furthermore, of the 959 transfers between 1937 and 1976, only 80, or 8.3 percent, resulted in subdivision. While these subdivisions all involved transfers by inheritance, there were 620 other transfers by inheritance that did not involve subdivision.

These statistics show that subdivision did occur in the Dhidhima area, and that it had some connection with partible inheritance. It is also clear, however, that this relationship was not necessarily a causal one. Indeed, even though the mean number of children (potential inheritors) has been declining in Dhidhima, there was potential for much more subdivision than appears

Table 11.1

Total Plots by Class and Period, Dhidhima

	Class I[a]	Class II[b]	Class III[c]	All
1936	272	320	208	800
1936–38	270	319	206	795
1938–48	281	311	201	793
1948–58	280	299	194	773
1958–68	284	287	186	757
1968–78	288	271	179	738

NOTE: Land class is a proxy for value. Figures listed are for the end of each period.
[a] Class I: High value, fertile, irrigable.
[b] Class II: Moderate value, fertile, not irrigable.
[c] Class III: Low value, less fertile.

in the data. The Dhidhima situation thus contrasts greatly with Binns' statement that "once the process of fragmentation is begun, it is accelerated with each succeeding generation in a geometrical progression, so that in a very few generations quite a remarkable number of parcels may be formed" (1950: 14).

The two strategies most often involved in circumventing the subdivision of plots by inheritance were joint ownership and cash sale with the proceeds divided equally among the heirs. Another factor that retarded the frequency of subdivision was out-migration. Dhidhimiotes who migrated often either gave up their share of inheritance or allowed it to be used by those heirs who remained in the area. While these actions did not always act as consolidating mechanisms, they limited the occurrence of subdivision.

What then of the occurrence of consolidation? Of the previously mentioned 959 transfers, 144 led to consolidation of plots. This represents 15.0 percent of the total number of transfers between 1936 and 1978. Of these, 116, or 80.6 percent, occurred since the end of the Greek Civil War. Although some consolidating transfers were accomplished by inheritance (a total of 26, or 18.1%), the majority were by means of cash purchase or rental. Cash transfers (permanent rental or sale) were a negligible part of plot transfers until after 1948 when greater access to capital was available.

As a result of the combination of subdivision and consolidation, the total number of plots decreased during the period in question by 8.75 percent, with the majority of this decrease occurring after 1948. From the original 800 plots by 1980 there were 738. This reduction has not been equally distributed either spatially or with regard to the characteristics of the plots. As can be seen from Table 11.1, the effects of subdivision and consolidation have varied across land classes.

In order to illustrate better the relationship between land value and the processes of subdivision and consolidation, a consolidation index was devised to provide a shorthand summary. The index used the ratio of consolidated to subdivided plots for each time period, and was calculated as follows:

$$CI = (Cp/Sp)/Tp;$$

where CI = Consolidation Index; Cp = the number of consolidated plots in a given period and class; Sp = the number of subdivided plots in a given period and class; and Tp = the total number of plots in existence for that class and period.

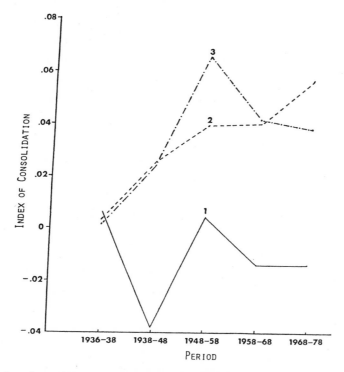

Figure 11.1.   Index of consolidation by class and period, Dhidhima. Class 1: High value, fertile, irrigable. Class 2: Moderate value, fertile, not irrigable. Class 3: Low value, less fertile.

Three ordinal classes of land determined by such factors as accessibility, slope, fertility, and availability of irrigation water were used as measures of potential productivity (see Table 11.1). These classes were employed in the original cadastral survey for the land reform of 1936 and are still used for quick evaluation of land value in Greece. The infrequent nature of land transfers was overcome by aggregating the data roughly into decades.

Table 11.1 shows changing consolidation indices for the three value classes over time. It indicates a general trend toward consolidation for Classes II and III. Class I plots, however, vacillated between subdivision and consolidation, with the cumulative effect being an increase in the number of plots. There was thus a distinction between irrigated and nonirrigated land (Class I versus Classes II and III). Class II plots declined in number by forty-nine (15.3%), while Class III plots declined by twenty-nine (13.9%). The differences revealed in Figure 11.1 indicate a relationship between the subjective valuation of land and the processes of subdivision and consolidation. In a very general sense, this relationship adheres to the following pattern. With higher-valued land, there is a greater occurrence of subdivision, which tends to offset any consolidation. With lower-valued land, consolidation occurs more frequently, yielding a reduction in the number of plots.

One might interpret the general trend toward consolidation as resulting from changes in government agricultural policy. As Peplasis pointed out, however, most economic aid to agriculture during this period was in the form of price supports, technological improvement, and other issues unconnected to the problem of small landholdings (1976: 2).

The trend toward increasing consolidation by cash purchase after World War II seems more likely to have reflected the improving regional economy. There was an increase in available capital for the Argolid region resulting from expanding nonagricultural employment, tourism, cash crops, and remittances (see Sutton, this volume). Poor accessibility of some Class I land in Malavria, the southern part of the study area, also depressed the market value of these plots, and some were purchased for growing fodder crops by herders utilizing nearby slopes.

The purchases of land were not evenly distributed through time. The peaks in frequency correlated, given some lag, with infusions of capital into the Dhidhima community. For example, a peak from 1967 to 1970 corresponded with the sale of land to the west of Dhidhima, on Salandi beach, to a hotel developer. This episodic pattern of plot purchases was, in large measure, a result of the interaction of the high cost of land suitable for new uses with periodic availability of investment capital. In the study area, the pattern of investment was one of initial rental and later purchase when enough financial resources were available.

By way of another example, as noted above, the consolidators in the Malavria section were goat herders whose *mandria* (folds) were located on the mountain slopes above. They consolidated plots in Malavria for growing fodder crops and assured access to winter grazing in response to changes in the relations between herders and farmers (see Chang, H. Koster, this volume). An increasingly cash-crop orientation reduced the degree to which herders could rely on access to other fields for winter grazing.

It thus becomes clear that partible inheritance did not "deterministically" cause subdivision in Dhidhima, and that subdivision is but one outcome of such inheritance on a continuum with consolidation. Land value greatly influenced this outcome. Overall, holdings in the area consolidated at a slow rate between 1936 and 1980, with greater consolidation in low-valued plots and greater subdivision in high-valued ones. The latter process reflected at least three factors: (1) a higher market price for such land with relatively little capital available to purchase it; (2) greater competition among heirs over such plots due to land speculation; and (3) the farming of certain cash crops on this land, which required relatively little acreage to yield a profit.

I have applied a spatial and explicitly historical approach to the changing structure and pattern of landholdings in Dhidhima. In doing so, I acknowledge a return of ethnography, with its attention to local experience, to the center of anthropological and geographical endeavor. Theoretically informed, but diverted from a subordination to overly broad models, our understanding of land tenure and land use becomes complicated and is richer for it. This ethnographically centered approach, coupled with more detailed data than usually assembled for discussions of fragmentation in Greece, provided a point of departure for modeling processes of land tenure change. This model, in turn, yielded a very different perspective from the usual top-down approach, a perspective acknowledging the power of the smallholder to form and reform community and landscape. It is a perspective that also recognizes that in matters of land tenure, it is the smallholder who indeed has the vested interest.

CHAPTER TWELVE

Neighbors and Pastures:
Reciprocity and Access to Pasture

Harold A. Koster

In his model of the "dyadic contract," Foster long ago identified two major channels of nonkin social relations within peasant villages, distinguished from one another by the relative socioeconomic status of the persons involved and the nature of their reciprocal bonds (Foster 1961: 1174).[1] It is interesting then that only one of these, the "asymmetrical dyadic contract" or patron-client relationship, received concentrated attention in the early ethnography of the Mediterranean coast of Europe (e.g., Blok 1969; Boissevain 1966, 1969; Campbell 1964; Kenny 1960; Pitt-Rivers 1954). There has been, until relatively recently, little focused theoretical discussion of the "symmetrical dyadic contract" in this same geographical zone. This situation pertained even though the careful studies of those such as Brandes (1973, 1975), Dimen (1970), Filipovic (1970), Freeman (1970), Friedl (1962), Sanders (1962), and Silverman (1968) early on noted various nonkin bonds among socioeconomic equals based upon "complementary reciprocity."

Thus it was that much ethnography of Mediterranean rural society came to focus on patterns in which villagers displayed feelings of severe distrust of one another that were accompanied by intense family loyalty. Patterns of relationships displayed generally asymmetrical bonds outside the family. Such work has been stimulating because it is descriptive of an important facet of interpersonal relations in the region, but it has been at least partially contradicted and certainly softened by growing recognition of other sorts of ties.[2] Within Greece, the folklorist Petropoulos (1943–44) provided an early discussion of customs of collaboration, whereas Sanders (1955, 1962) examined patterns of rural cooperation in the postwar period. More recently, Herzfeld (1987) has interrogated the perspectives underlying such characterizations of Greek life; Papataxiarchis (1991), Hart (1992), and Kennedy (1986) have explored the bonds of friendship that clearly exist alongside patron-client ties; Dubisch (1986a) and Seremetakis (1991) have refigured Greek social relations from the viewpoint of women; and others have documented the conflicts that arise in families (Loizos and Papataxiarchis 1991), as well as the bonds of mutual obligation that appear among Athenian migrants from the same rural area of origin (Kenna 1983; Sutton 1978, 1983), among residents of the same neighborhood (Hirschon 1989), and among members of marginal ethnic groups (Karakasidou 1992).

This essay joins in such discussions by considering the role of symmetrical bonds of mutual obligation for local economic integration in Greece. It asks how important such ties of neighborhood and friendship might be in the operation of village economies. By addressing this question with information drawn from Dhidhima (Adams, Chang, J. Koster, Koster and Forbes, this volume), I intend to demonstrate that the intensive pastoralists of this village have utilized reciprocal relationships to adjust the volatile needs of their flocks to fixed and restricted ownership of land and to maximize grazing on local fields while minimizing the cash drain incurred by short-term pasture rentals.[3] Under conditions of agricultural and pastoral intensification in this village, processes associated with increasing diversification of household subsistence activities, mutual obligation among neighbors and friends has been an important strategy employed by herders to survive in a market economy.

This analysis thus also connects to the often cited and significant example of the village of Ambelakia, an important production center for fine textiles in the seventeenth century whose commercial affairs were run corporately by an efficient cooperative association (Georgios 1951; Koukkidi 1948). Such formal institutions of economic cooperation, which also include the cooperative movement and credit unions, have played an important role in both local and national economic spheres, but it is not the purpose here to analyze their operation. I turn rather to a discussion of less formal reciprocity in the context of the village economy in Dhidhima, particularly as this is revealed in close examination of detailed figures of expenditures for the early 1970s graciously provided by one Dhidhiomiote household, here referred to as the family of Nikos Tzanos (a pseudonym).

Intensification and Pasture

The two factors of (1) splitting available labor between both pastoral and agricultural tasks, and (2) maximizing production from smaller flocks have continually led intensive shepherds directly to a major dilemma that must be faced and surmounted. The problem has been how to maximize access to the more productive fields and pastures near the village, thus allowing shepherds both to use their labor force efficiently and to maximize the production of their flocks. These fields have usually carried a high cash rental value. Since shepherds' familial cash reserves have generally been low, it has been uneconomical to rent these valuable lands regularly through cash contract.

As with most other features of both the local and national economies, land prices and land rentals have displayed extreme inflation in recent decades. Two aspects of land in Dhidhima have been particularly important in determining land value—location and agricultural potential. The latter has long been judged in terms of soil fertility, drainage, slope, aspect, and so forth. In assessing location, the first question has been whether the land was near the village and accessible to motorized vehicles. A second and more recent feature of land prices in relation to location has resulted from speculation for tourist development. Land within sight of, or with access to, the sea and connected by paved roads is now highly valued, regardless of its distance from the village (which has little or no attraction for tourists) and its agricultural qualities. This aspect of land price and value, however, has had little direct impact on pasture rental values.

Figure 12.1.   View of Dhidhima, looking north to Megalovouni.

The relative rental value of winter fallow (*herso*) in the vicinity of Dhidhima for 1971–1972 is plotted in Table 12.1. The lowest rental values were in areas so distant from principal settlements and fields that to use them required a full-scale allocation of labor to herding, making it more difficult to split limited labor resources between herding and farming tasks. Rental of prime cereal fields in the Dhidhima Basin within thirty minutes' walk of the village has been most valued, although the case of land in the Fournoi Valley presents an apparent anomaly. This land is an hour's walk from Dhidhima, but Dhidhimiote flocks have competed in this valley with local Fourniote and some Valtetsiote flocks, for whom these fields have had high value because of proximity to both their homes and fields. Shepherds from Dhidhima using the grazing on the ridge separating Fournoi from Dhidhima have generally located their folds on the south slope of this ridge within the territory of Fournoi. These fields still allowed them to graze their flocks within a radius of one-and-a-half-hour's walk from their home base.

The pressure placed upon intensive pastoralists to avoid cash rental of pasture can be illustrated with reference to Tables 12.1–12.3. The total value of milk sales in 1971–1972 of the Tzanos' family flock, was 18,804 drachmas ($627). With the total value of pasture used in the same year fixed at 13,958 drachmas ($465), it is apparent that the family could not have afforded to pay cash to rent a high percentage of pasture and hope for any margin of profit. A further constraint was imposed by the local pattern of land tenure. With a family's plots scattered throughout the arable land, if shepherds were to form parcels large enough for efficient grazing, they had to come to terms with several owners in any given location.

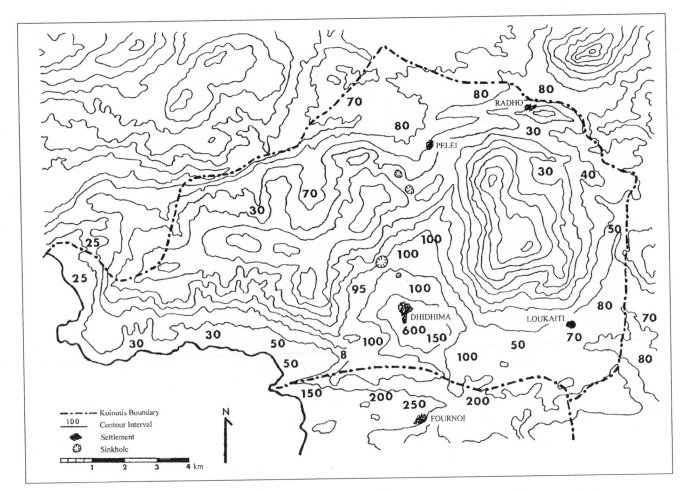

Figure 12.2.   Map of winter fallow rental prices, Dhidhima, 1974–75, in *drachmas* per *stremma*.

Tables 12.1–12.3 also reveal what strategies herders have used to gain access to nearby fields. As can be seen in these charts, Nikos Tzanos owned some fields and obtained grazing privileges in others through short-term rentals. The bulk of his grazing, however, was obtained through informal contract, through patron-client ties, and especially through a network of mutual exchange or obligation. The percentage of land controlled by large landowners in the 1970s was not sufficient to meet the needs of all the flocks. It seems likely that if a greater proportion of the land had been in the hands of large landowners, the use of patronage by both shepherds and landlords might have been higher.

A Continuum of Reciprocity

It may be instructive to view these relations between households to obtain grazing land as a continuum, with informal contract and a generalized "neighborliness" at opposite poles of the sequence. Informal contract represents a binding verbal agreement between two parties for exchange of specified goods and services of equivalent value within an agreed period of time. It has not normally involved the transfer of cash, a process which even in the 1970s was increasingly

Table 12.1

Grazing Used by Nikos Tzanos, Dhidhima, 1971–1972

Land type	Stremma	Number of plots	Cost (Dr)	Value (Dr)	Method of payment
Winter fallow	28	3	—[a]	1,400	Owned
	49	11	2,850	3,175	Patron-labor
	4	1	—	200	*Tramba*
	35.5	5	1,120	1,475	*Allilovoithia (labor)*
	34.5	9	1,312	1,350	*Allilovoithia (goods)*
	37.5	5	1,298	1,875	Cash Rental
Total Winter fallow	188.5	34	6,580	9,475	
Summer fallow	28	3	—	700	Owned
	0.5	1	20	25	*Allilovoithia (labor)*
	27	6	167	675	*Allilovoithia (goods)*
	15	1	—	38	Cash Rental
Total	70.5	11	187	1,438	
Planted vetch and green barley	8	1	—	100	Owned
	8	2	800	800	Patron-labor
	3	1	—	300	*Tramba*
	8	1	800	800	*Allilovoithia (labor)*
	9	1	900	900	Cash Rental
Total	37	6	2,500	2,900	
Grazing stubble	7	2	—	325	Owned
	44	5	1,950	2,200	Patron-labor
	6	2	—	150	*Tramba*
	34	8	1,201	1,213	*Alliloivoithia (goods)*
	10	2	350	400	Cash Rental
Total	101	19	3,501	4,288	
Commons	—	—	1,190	1,190	Cash Rental
TOTAL	396	70	13,958	19,291	

[a] Dash = not reported

accompanied by written receipt. To understand such informal contracts better, let us examine the adaptive strategy of the Tzanos household in greater detail.

Nikos Tzanos used the method of informal contract in payment for a large sector of winter fallow. These plots were all contiguous, and formed an excellent block of grazing. They were attractive to him due to their proximity to his winter sheepfold, used in protecting the animals from the elements, and because they were planted with olive trees to be pruned that winter. Olive prunings provide a good source of feed for sheep. In return for these grazing rights, Tzanos agreed to plow the land after finishing grazing in April, a necessary activity in the process of olive cultivation. Plowing increases water retention in the summer months, cuts down on the presence of nutrient-robbing weeds (as do the sheep by grazing), and works in manure left by sheep, as well as chemical fertilizers the olive grower may also spread.

Table 12.2
Grazing Used by Nikos Tzanos, Dhidhima, 1974–1975

Land type	Stremma	Number of plots	Cost (Dr)	Value (Dr)	Method of payment
Winter fallow	55	5	—[a]	5,500	Owned
	46	11	6,050	6,700	Patron-labor
	21	3	—	2,100	*Tramba*
	14	2	1,350	1,400	Allilovoithia (labor)
	36.5	7	3,550	3,650	Allilovoithia (goods)
Total	172.5	28	10,950	19,350	
Summer fallow	55	5	—	1,100	Owned
	16	2	—	320	*Tramba*
Total	71	7	—	1,420	
Planted vetch and green barley	15	2	—	1,500	Owned
	38	7	2,400	3,350	*Allilovoithia* (goods)
	10	1	1,000	1,000	Cash Rental
Total	63	10	3,400	5,850	
Stubble	11	2	—	550	Owned
	18	1	1,800	1,800	Patron-labor
	8	1	300	400	Allilovoithia (goods)
Total	37	4	2,100	2,750	
Commons	—	—	1,900	1,900	Cash Rental
TOTAL	343.5	66	18,350	31,270	

[a] Dash = not reported

This exchange took place in terms of current market rates for such plowing and pasture, and was in marked contrast to similar exchanges with patrons who often commanded a much lower rate. For example, Tzanos plowed the olive orchards of a wealthy miller for seven days in return for a pasture area worth only four days' plowing. He did this to gain consideration with the miller, who owns a fenced fold area within two hundred meters of Tzanos' house and *perivolia* (irrigated fields). Tzanos rented this facility in the summer at the going rate, and wished to secure his claim by plowing the olives at a below market rate. This fenced area was particularly useful as his location for organizing household labor during the summer when irrigation and hoeing of cash crops were in progress and sheep had to be kept closer to the home fields.

The other end of the continuum of reciprocity was encompassed by a general norm of neighborliness and friendliness. *Yeitones* (neighbors) maintained positive relations by engaging in a regular system of redistribution of temporary surpluses of goods and services not overtly calculated. One of the worst things that could be said about neighbors was that they were *tsinghounides* (penny pinchers) who hoarded their assets and refused to participate in such neighborly exchanges. Neighborliness and friendship were also expressed in a system of both formal and informal visits. This system of exchanges was not, of course, limited to nonkin, but overlapped a similar ethic of "natural" exchange among households linked by descent, affinal, and spiritual kin ties.

Table 12.3
Summaries of Grazing Used by
Nikos Tzanos, Dhidhima, 1971–1972 and 1974–1975

Method of Payment	Stremma	Number of Plots	Cost (Dr)	Value (Dr)
a. Method of Pasture Acquisition (1971–1972)				
Owned	71	9	—	2,525
Cash Rental	71.5	9	2,548	3,213
Patron-labor	101	18	5,600	6,175
Tramba	13	4	—	650
Allilovoithia	44	7	1,940	2,300
Allilovoithia	95.5	23	2,680	3,238
Commons	—	—	1,190	1,190
TOTAL	396	70	13,958	19,291
b. Method of Acquisition (1974–1975)				
Owned	136	14	—	8,650
Cash Rental	10	1	1,000	1,000
Patron-labor	64	29	7,850	8,500
Tramba	37	5	—	2,420
Allilovoithia	14	2	1,350	1,400
Allilovoithia	82.5	15	6,250	7,400
Commons	—	—	1,900	1,900
TOTAL	343.5	66	18,350	31,270

Allilovoithia: Mutual Obligation

Neighborliness, as expressed through mutual assistance, is termed *allilovoithia*. This context of positive social relations among households includes those exchanges that directly fit Foster's category of complementary reciprocity central to this discussion. In other words, bonds of mutual obligation have generally been understood and discussed within the idiom of the spirit of neighborly cohesiveness, friendship, and goodwill. It has not been proper to admit of any economic calculation in these exchanges. When informants were pressed as to the economic effects of these transactions, however, they readily admitted the necessity of not being taken advantage of. If, after a period of time, the exchanges did not appear to be achieving a rough balance, the economic relationship was quickly terminated, although positive social relations frequently continued.

It has been crucial to this form of distribution that the norm of outward neighborliness be maintained with no hint of economic manipulation, thus avoiding overt calculation, which would lead to direct haggling over value. An example of how fragile this fiction can be involved a shepherd who served in the previous year as a wedding sponsor (*koumbaros stefanos*) for a younger farmer, recently returned from Germany, who had invested his foreign earnings in a large tractor. This sponsorship placed the two within a relationship of ritual kinship. Several months later, the young farmer's mother came to the shepherd with several lambs her son had purchased. She asked if he would he keep these lambs with his flock for several months and fatten them on the milk of his ewes and on his excellent grazing. "Of course," he answered, "hadn't they always been good neighbors, and now they were *koumbaroi*, and what were a few lambs to him, anyway?" In fact, fattening lambs was a very valuable service for the shepherd to provide. It involved the loss of milk, an extra number of animals on his pasture, an increase in labor (lambs being the most difficult animals to work in the flock), the risk of the possible loss of the farmer's lambs, and some disturbance of other animals in his flock. This household was, however, within the shepherd's network of friends and neighbors and was now within the circle of ritual kin as well.

Several months later, when the shepherd was transplanting and grafting new olive trees for his daughter's dowry, he went to his koumbaros and asked him to bring his tractor and water wagon to haul water to the new trees. When the young man had finished watering the trees, he immediately asked for the standard rate of cash payment for the service he had provided. He was paid. After this incident, relations between the households, although not broken off, were strained, and the economic relationship was terminated. The shepherd argued that he had been treated shabbily, and that the young man was "mean" because he had demanded cash payment for his services. He had not done the neighborly thing; that is, to engage in allilovoithia. This behavior was attributed to the fact that the young man "had been to Germany and thought he was very modern." It was also the case that with the capital he had earned in Germany he was more easily able to run his farm with a lesser degree of dependence upon other members of the *koinotis*.

Mutual obligation must not be confused with a simple barter system. An element of synchronic exchange has long been implicit in most definitions of barter (Mauss 1967: 35). Mutual obligation, or balanced reciprocity as it might also be labeled, is instead a system through which individuals, and the households to which they are attached, develop a credit network through exchange of goods and services over an extended period of time on a roughly equivalent basis. Barter belongs to the realm of the marketplace: it is an overt business relationship. Mutual obligation is set in a matrix of noneconomic, ongoing social relations. Perhaps the differences between barter and mutual obligation can best be explained through illustration. Barter occurs when a woman from a farming family comes to the home of a shepherd asking for several kilos of wool for her daughter's dowry blankets, offering an equivalent value of potatoes in return. The transfer is agreed upon and made later that day. In a case of mutual obligation, a farmer, who is a pensioner and no longer able to do the heavy work of plowing, asks a neighboring shepherd to plow his field for the planting of a new crop of potatoes. This is done. Several months later, the shepherd asks his older neighbor if he will do him the favor of allowing him to graze his flock on the potato greens before the crop is harvested. The old man agrees, without mentioning that this balances the work of plowing already done by the shepherd. If the shepherd wants to keep the economic tie active, he may continue the relationship with the neighborly act of sending the women of his household to assist the older man's family in the harvest after the greens had been grazed, thereby keeping the old man in a relationship of obligation. This establishes another credit that the shepherd may be able to call in by making a neighborly request at some future time.

In Dhidhima, intensive pastoralists have made greater use of the system of allilovoithia than have their extensive pastoralist neighbors. Greater use can be seen in the percentage of grazing land and in the value thus gained through the system of mutual obligation, as well as the value of the labor exchanged (see Tables 12.1–12.3). Besides having a wider range of needs due to their diversified subsistence, intensive pastoralists also possess a greater variety of seasonal surpluses of goods and services of value to other members of the village. This does not imply that mutual obligation is utilized predominantly by such herders, or that they are more neighborly than other members of the koinotis, but rather that a higher percentage of economic exchange occurs within the ambience of "friendly" and "neighborly" relations for intensive pastoral households than for extensive ones.

Mutual Obligation and Pasture

In securing access to grazing through mutual obligation, a seemingly endless variety of transactions has been used. The intensive shepherd has generally been faced with a patchwork quilt of possible grazing resources in constant flux due to the rotation of crops, transfer of ownership, condition of the pasture, and arrangement of competing flocks on the pasture. From this exceedingly complex situation he has had to organize sufficient pasture to match the changing needs of his flock. The total annual grazing used by an intensive pastoralist's flock has generally been composed of many individual units of land. In the case of Nikos Tzanos, the flock grazed seventy discrete parcels of land in 1971–1972 (see Table 12.1), which included the common pastures of both Dhidhima and Fournoi and involved relations and separate agreements with forty-three different households. The variety of these exchanges may best be illustrated through a series of seven instances of mutual obligation commonly employed by intensive shepherds in acquiring rights to pasture.

This network of reciprocity has been used not only in securing grazing privileges, but also in assuring rights of *access* to the grazing through the adjacent fields of neighbors. Many times a herder has paid cash for a parcel of grazing, only to find that he would be denied passage to it by owners of surrounding fields. Unless he could activate his network of mutual obligation to obtain such right of passage, he had little recourse but to attempt to trade the grazing through *tramba* (exchange), trespassing (with its risk of court proceedings), or just absorbing the loss.

1. *Exchange of grazing lands between two herders.* This has been a very common method used by herders when shifting from the use of one year's set of lands to another. In one case a shepherd traded six stremmata of high quality fallow land in the vicinity of Pelei, at a distance of eight km from the main village. This land had been planted in olive trees several years earlier. It was exchanged for three stremmata of planted vetch in the basin near Dhidhima and the herder's irrigated fields. The other man was an extensive shepherd who kept his flock in the vicinity of Pelei throughout most of the spring months. Such an exchange (*tramba*) favored both shepherds.

2. *Exchange of grazing lands between three or more herders.* Another instance of informal exchange is the transfer of temporary grazing rights among more than two households. For example, in attempting to assemble a unified good area of grazing in the summer stubble, Nikos Tzanos traded one of his wheat fields to Kostas Bozis, who owned a field adjacent to it. Use of the Tzanos field allowed Bozis to unify and consolidate the two wheatfields for an area of summer stubble. Tzanos made the transaction with Bozis because he knew that he would receive in exchange from Bozis a field that bordered on the wheat stubble of Dimitrios Andrakis. Tzanos

then traded the field he received from Bozis to Andrakis in return for one of Andrakis' fields adjacent to another wheat field owned by Tzanos, which he in turn planned to use for his summer stubble. This arrangement allowed all three shepherds to unify a larger and consolidated set of fields for grazing. Such complex exchanges were made throughout the year in as casual a manner as possible, so that agreements were generally phrased in terms of kinship, neighborhood, and friendship rather than in the idiom of the market.

This mechanism has frequently been used to circumvent a recalcitrant landowner who refused to rent pasture or demanded an exorbitant price. The mechanism has often also involved relations between herders and cheese merchants, which partially explains why such a high percentage of shepherds have taken their milk to the merchants, rather than selling to the Cooperative as have most goatherds. A merchant who has been crossed by a shepherd may hold land in the vicinity of the shepherd's *livadi* (pasture area). He would then be in a position to make life difficult for the shepherd by blocking access to grazing in that area and/or claiming damages to his holding from the shepherd's flock.

Merchants have not only been aware of the nature of this game of trading pasture to avoid difficult owners, but have themselves been consummate players. They, too, have traded land to gain a parcel that would block a shepherd, thus frustrating him and leading to expensive damage suits. They have been well placed within the network of landowners to effectively manage such a strategy in maintaining control over their clients. In Dhidhima, the cheese merchants have not themselves been the largest landowners, but they have maintained close ties with such families, and have been connected by bonds of kinship, marriage, and spiritual kinship. The two Dhidhima merchants have been closely related to the operators of the village threshing machines. Because of their occupation, and because they held large units of land themselves, these two men were, in turn, in positions of influence with other landholders who would refuse to rent to a particular herder upon the specific request of a merchant channeled through these social links.

3. *Exchange of agricultural products for grazing privileges.*   Intensive pastoralists have temporary agricultural as well as pastoral surpluses that they have sometimes chosen to circulate within the local network of reciprocity. For example, a herder with a reputation for raising excellent potatoes heard that one of his farming neighbors was in need of seed potatoes for the next crop. This neighbor had been depending upon receiving seed potatoes from the Agricultural Cooperative, but they had not yet been distributed, and rumor had it that when they did arrive the potatoes would be of poor quality. The shepherd told his son to deliver 100 kg of seed potatoes to the farmer. Of course, he was "being a good friend and neighbor." They had always had good relations in the past, and he voiced the sentiment that he expected nothing in return. Several months later, when the shepherd requested use of five stremmata of good fallow land that the farmer owned, he, in equally neighborly fashion, returned the gift.

4. *Exchange of raw wool for grazing privileges.*   There have been, of course, many pastoral products that a shepherd could also distribute in the system of mutual obligation. One of these is wool. This has often been exchanged with those who owned no sheep and required wool for

weaving their daughters' dowry goods (see J. Koster, this volume). Goatherds who owned some wheatland in the basin have been prime movers in this practice. They could not easily graze the wheat stubble with their own animals, because in the summer they have generally moved their goats to the highest pastures. Also, when goats were brought down into the arable they were much more likely to be charged with causing damage. A goatherd, who was returning one winter evening in the company of an intensive shepherd whose winter fold was adjacent to his own on the mountainside, told the shepherd that he planned to sow wheat in a particular field, and that after the harvest the shepherd was welcome to graze the stubble. Later, after the spring shearing, the shepherd's wife took 1½ kg of clean wool to the goatherd's wife for her to spin into yarn for her daughter's dowry blankets. She, too, was just being neighborly. "What is a kilo of wool to us?" And, knowing that "with goats there is only rough hair for rugs," she felt she would "give her friend a bit of wool for her loom."

5. *Herding animals in the flock in exchange for grazing.*   An example of this practice has already been mentioned, the incident between the two koumbaroi. Lambs have frequently been brought to run with a good flock to fatten as milk lambs. Milk lambs have been more highly prized than those fed from an early age on a diet of grain and kept with the house animals. It has also been a common practice for a farmer to bring one of his house sheep to be run with the flock and served by the shepherd's ram.

6. *Exchange of cheese for grazing privileges.*   In Dhidhima, shepherds make their own cheese for household consumption in June, after the cheese merchants closed operations. Although most households kept some milk animals, there was still a high demand for this homeland cheese, *tirovoli*, in the village. It was common practice for the widows of herders who still owned fields to exchange the rights to grain stubble for this cheese.

7. *Exchange of milk for grazing privileges.*   Raw milk has been an essential in the diet, particularly during the last week of *Apokries* (the Carnival preceding the Lenten period) or "Cheese Week," and especially on "Cheese Sunday." During this week dairy products form the central constituent of the diet—large milk pies in particular are made by all self-respecting households. Another time when a high ritual demand for milk is felt throughout the community is the Feast of St. George. At such times herders have severely limited the amount of milk delivered to cheese factories, and indeed these factories have closed their doors on Cheese Sunday and St. George's Day, because their operators knew they would not receive enough raw milk to make operations worthwhile. On these days herder families have busily carried gifts of milk to a widespread network of neighbors, friends, and kin. These gifts have allowed herders to reinforce feelings of goodwill with other households and sometimes to ask for a parcel of grazing along the way.

Advantages of the System of Allilovoithia

These examples demonstrate the importance of maintaining sufficiently positive relations so that mutual exchange with as many people as possible may be viable for Dhidhimiote herders.

The question that becomes obvious at this point is: when herders have indeed exchanged the equivalent value of their *livadi* in goods and services rather than cash, does any advantage accrue? The fact is that these exchanges for pasture were not always strictly equivalent. Nikos Tzanos consistently underpaid in terms of value for pasture he acquired through patron-client ties and through the system of mutual obligation (see Table 12.3). In the case of patron-client ties in which the shepherd household exchanged labor in return for pasture, this discrepancy was understandable. Although wages for the plowing of orchards and collection of olives—and for agricultural labor in general—have risen, this has not been work with much appeal to the rural population, for several reasons. First, it is day labor rather than salaried. More importantly, it is agricultural work, work with one's hands in the soil and under the hot sun, which is associated with the past. Dhidhimiotes do not yet romanticize the drudgery of peasant life. A final factor that contributes to a scarcity of agricultural field labor is the fact that alternatives have come to exist. Manual work can be found in the region in the marble quarries, textile factories, construction business, and tourist facilities. Although such work is not generally salaried, it is associated with modernity—and not with being relegated to a stifling backwater.

Such values were evident in a case that affected Dhidhima in 1975. The canneries operating in the Argos plain, at a distance of roughly two hours from Dhidhima by truck, could no longer find for their orchards and factories workers who were willing to work for the offered wage. These factories had at first drawn their manual labor force from the population of the surrounding plain, but every year they were forced to search further afield in their effort to find a cheap source of labor. Finally, the radius of willing labor was extended to include Dhidhima. Almost immediately, women and girls who had not participated in agricultural field labor for wages (either cash or kind) rushed to work in Argos and Nafplio. The trucks daily carried loads of from sixty to one hundred men and women to make the four hour round-trip to work in the Argos-Nafplio canneries. This principle was especially visible in the preference of most girls for work in the canneries on the production line over work in the cannery fields and orchards, even though the fieldworkers received a higher wage. The work inside the cannery with dangerous machinery was considered modern. Suddenly, girls who had balked at collecting olives or at reaping in their home village or in adjacent villages for wages leaped at the opportunity to do very similar work (see Lambiri-Dimaki 1959, Sutton 1985, 1986). In this case, however, they would not be under the direction of fellow villagers, nor would they have to fear that potential village husbands would believe they were so poor that they had to work as day laborers performing the hated agricultural tasks of olive and grain harvesting (which had long been the lot of many Dhidhima families who worked as day laborers both within the region and beyond).

It is not surprising that in such a situation it has become increasingly difficult for the larger landholders and orchard owners to locate sufficient cheap labor to collect their produce. This is one of the most often heard complaints among wealthier landowners in the southern Argolid. Thus, when an olive orchard owner has found a shepherd willing to plow his olives in return for the prunings and grazing rights, he has not been inclined to press the shepherd for full value.

By the same token, by not paying full value for pasture in the system of exchange, herders have been placed in debt to such people. This has been to the advantage of both parties—but the herder could not take extreme advantage by exchanging goods and services far below the

Figure 12.3.   Threshing, Dhidhima, 1972.

accepted value of pasture. In the case of Nikos Tzanos, in 1972, 87 percent of the value of his pasture acquired through methods other than ownership or tramba was paid (see Tables 12.1 and 12.3). In 1975, this figure reached 91 percent (see Tables 12.2 and 12.3). This system allowed Tzanos to cut pasture costs by 9 to 13 percent of their cash value.

There have been other advantages in this system for herders that remained even when they gave full value in goods and services for pasture. Perhaps the most important aspect of such a system for households with low cash reserves has been the ability to reimburse the pasture owner with goods and services at a time *convenient* for the herder, thus minimizing the problem of cash flow. For example, when plowing olive orchards in exchange for grazing under informal contract, the herder would sometimes agree merely to plow a certain number of olive groves in April at the end of the winter grazing period. No day or hour was fixed for the plowing. The herder could thus afford to fit this work into his schedule (within a period of several weeks) at a time convenient to him in terms of the overall labor demands within the household.

One might ask why the herder did not just ask for cash for the plowing. Several advantages would be lost in such a strategy. First, by exchanging labor for pasture he was able to contract for grazing in September or October, but could have the use of that pasture until May, when he finally resolved the debt by plowing. This allowed him to defer payment, and it also did not require him to have cash available to rent the pasture in autumn. Also, in an inflationary economy he might have earned 5,000 drachmas for plowing in April, only to find that, although this sum was sufficient for the previous year's pasture, it would not purchase the same amount in the next season.[4] Allilovoithia has held other advantages for the herder. By exchanging goods and services in a context of mutual obligation, he could form what Bailey (1971: 6) called a "multiplex tie," or what Wolf (1966: 81–85) termed a "many-stranded coalition." Not only have such ties allowed herders to maintain wide fields of favorable social relations, insuring sufficient alternative sources of pasture, but they have also reinforced the ability of herders to defer payment when necessary or acquire goods and services through the security of a tie reinforced through manifold relationships. Relationships have been a source both of strength and weakness for such ties, because what was gained in security was potentially lost through decreased flexibility (Wolf 1966: 81). The clear advantage of cash exchange has been that it allowed the parties to operate outside other relationships that might bind them. In Bailey's (1971: 290–295) metaphor, the single-interest relationship involved in cash transaction circumvented the multiplex ties that might otherwise link the participants.

Another advantage to herders in exchanging goods and services rather than cash for pasture has been that they have often received more than market value. This fact may be illustrated by the example of tirovoli, the traditional homemade cheese of this hot, semi-arid region. Tirovoli is made from milk that is not readily marketable. After the merchants close their factories, the shepherds still have milk that they cannot readily sell to the Cooperative, so that it has to be converted to some other form to retain value. Tirovoli serves this purpose. These cheeses, however, are not readily marketable beyond the village except at a loss. The herder does not have sufficient volume, nor has there been an adequate demand to attempt to market directly in the regional towns. This rough cheese cannot compete beyond the village orbit with commercial *feta*.[5]

What is the herder to do with this product? His family often consumes 50 percent of it, but even here there are limitations. He exchanges it with those families who do not have small stock and cannot make cheese. This, however, has always been done within the context of non-monetary exchange for pasture. As the local economy became increasingly more involved in a cash economy, these products remained outside the open market in Dhidhima. Along with wool, they are solely available within the networks of allilovoithia, or as direct exchange for pasture through informal contract. Thus, if one asked the price for *tirovoli* in Dhidhima in 1975, the quote would have been 50 drachmas, but this was not a market price, even if spoken of in such a way. This was the exchange value used by herders and landowners in their computations of cheese for pasture. If a villager wished to purchase tirovoli with cash, he might have gone to a herder with an offer of 50 drachmas per kilo, but unless the herder was kin or bound by some other reason to him, it would have been unlikely that a sale would result. At 50 drachmas the herder could use the cheese to acquire pasture through a multiplex tie within his network of allilovoithia. He had a product for which there was sufficient *local* demand, and by exchanging cheese or wool within the context of allilovoithia he maintained the relationship fixed in a matrix of neighborliness with all of its powerful symbols and sanctions, rather than as a mere commercial transaction. By distributing cheese and wool in this fashion the herder also gained value by saving the costs of retailing the cheese (either by selling to a local wholesaler, or by directly retailing the produce). Thus, tirovoli's "true" or net market value would have been less than 50 drachmas if it had indeed been placed in market circulation.

Herders have also preferred to exchange goods and services rather than use cash for pasture because they have viewed produce and labor as separate from cash and have attached very different values to these categories. Cash has had the most fluid value they could acquire, with the possible exceptions of high quality olive oil and butter. Labor and household produce have generally been viewed as expandable within the household economy (see Clarke, this volume). Families could engage more intensely in "self-exploitation" in the fashion described by Chayanov (1986). Wool and cheese were valuable, but they could not purchase as wide a range of goods and services as money. Household members did not view the labor of a young woman collecting olives as equivalent in value to the 250 drachmas that her labor could have acquired. After all, she could always work a bit harder, but 250 drachmas were 250 drachmas. Needless to say, the young woman was less likely to adopt this view herself. She might have attempted to minimize such work in an effort to avoid a reputation as one who must do *merokamato* (day labor). This resistance to day labor has conferred another advantage to the household for exchanging goods and labor rather than cash. In such an instance, the father could contract for two days of olive collection and tell his daughter that they had to honor the contract. If she balked, as she would likely do if he suggested that she collect olives to supplement household income, he could simply say that if she valued her *prika* (dowry), she had best remember that it consists of sheep, and sheep need pasture. That this contract obtained the necessary grass would be an argument she would find difficult to contest.

It is apparent that there have been definite advantages for shepherds in the system of allilovoithia, but why have others not attempted to incorporate products such as tirovoli and wool into the normal cash circuits of exchange that flourish in the village? The first answer to this question is that it has been difficult for individuals to breach this system. One could purchase these items only by offering above the "quoted price." Why follow this course of action, when one could simply exchange grazing land at the quoted price either through allilovoithia or informal contract? A person who attempted to purchase tirovoli or wool was not interested in multiplex ties, and was, thereby, of little use to the herder. The latter would generally prefer to locate a landowner who could make him a better offer within the context of a many-stranded relationship.

Not only has it been difficult for consumers to bring these items into the local marketplace,[6] but they, too, have found advantages in multiplex ties. A relationship of allilovoithia has increased the likelihood that they could acquire wool, cheese, milk, labor, and other items, when needed. This advantage has been reinforced by the difficulty of locating these items in the market. By embedding this exchange in a matrix of friendship and neighborliness, the consumer has also been assured of better quality. The shepherd family has been less likely to provide green or undersized potatoes, poor quality cheese, thinned milk, belly wool wrapped inside a fleece, or inadequate plowing, because the relationship was more personalized than it would have been in a commercial transaction. The consumer also has had recourse to the sanction of public opinion on appropriate behavior governing such a relationship, in contrast to the attitudes concerning commercial transactions, which are best summarized as *caveat emptor*.

That these goods and services have become less valued has been a growing problem for Dhidhimiote herders. Both wool and tirovoli have been losing their appeal (as goat hair already had), although prices have continued to rise with general inflation. Both are elements associated with an ancient lifestyle. Today, most families aspire to diets with plenty of meat, purchased pasta, and the whitest bread possible. The cheese they desire is not tirovoli, but commercial (and therefore, "modern") *feta*. Wool obtained in the village must be spun and woven. Many girls prefer synthetic materials and have little desire to occupy their hours with these activities (see Joan Koster 1976, this volume). In such a situation, these people have been uninterested in the shepherd's offer of wool or cheese for pasture. They have felt too constrained by attempts to bind them with appeals to neighborhood, friendship, or even kinship in such a context, and have endeavored to move toward single-interest and strictly commercial relationships in this regard. This process has, in fact, been on the increase in Dhidhima. As it becomes more difficult for herders to locate grazing that can be obtained in exchange for goods and services, it is likely that either they will have to accept a lower profit margin and purchase the pasture at full value, or they will have to alter their system of herd management.

As has now been suggested from several different points of view, it is a mistake to expect a uniform knee-jerk reaction to market penetration on the part of smallholder communities (e.g., Blaxter 1971, Brandes 1975, Kearney 1986, Netting 1993). In many cases, the reaction to considerable depopulation and marketization has been an increasing utilization of "traditional" patterns of adaptation such as reciprocal farm labor. Dhidhimiote herders have found their old system of allilovoithia to be quite an effective mechanism in adjusting their changing system of herd management to increasing levels of production and a cash economy. The fact that they have been well aware of this situation is attested by Tables 12.1 and 12.2. In comparing methods of pasture acquisition used by Nikos Tzanos in 1972 and in 1975, it can be seen that he succeeded in lessening the role of cash purchase. Indeed, in 1975, of a total pasture area of 345.5 stremmata, only 10 stremmata of high quality vetch were purchased with cash—representing only 5.5 percent of the total cost of grazing.

These data also indicate that this same shepherd succeeded in decreasing the percentage of purchased grazing and also dramatically lowering the percentage of pasture value actually paid from 72.5 percent in 1972 to 58.7 percent in 1975, although this was principally achieved by increasing the percentage of pasture *owned*. Purchase has been, in fact, the best method of minimizing grazing costs. The question then arises, if land has had such increasing value as pasture, why have shepherds not simply sold off their flocks and lived from the proceeds of pasture rentals? Indeed, where alternative work has been both preferable and available, some shepherds have so chosen. Such herders have, however, been quickly replaced in the Dhidhimiote system. If a significant number of herders followed the strategy of shifting from using pastures to renting them out, herding in Dhidhima would rapidly become uneconomical, so that the demand for these lands as pasture would drop and rental values plummet.

Intensification and Labor

Because members have provided the major source of labor for the running of household economies, much pressure has been exerted on those living in intensifying pastoral households to perform a wide range of activities throughout the calendar year (see Clarke, Forbes, this volume). The daily round for these families has required a constant shuffling of family personnel in matching a variety of seasonal tasks.

Table 12.4
Herding Effort Distribution for Tzanos's Flock, Dhidhima, 1971–1972

	Dec.	Jan.	Feb.	Mar.	Apr.	May	June	July
Nikos Tzanos (father)	75	260	190	115	70	80	78	60
Ionanna Tzanos (mother)	130	15	230	387	233	105	130	168
Tula Tzanos (daughter)	20	7	30	23	28	—	25	22
Kristos and Panos Tzanos (sons)	115	118	38	45	210	45	128	10
Kinsmen	—	6	—	12	2	—	—	—
Neighbors	—	3	28	7	10	18	12	22

NOTE: Effort is shown in hours per month.

The nature of these fluctuations may be demonstrated through the labor allocation in the Tzanos household graphed in Table 12.4. It will be noticed that a heavy portion of the herding tasks fell to Ioanna, Nikos' wife. This was due to factors such as the number of herders available, the age structure of the household, and Nikos' abilities as a plowman. In March, Ioanna worked 387 hours with the sheep. This was a key month for flocks in grazing and milk production, as well as in agriculture for plowing. The coincidence of these activities placed a severe strain on the Tzanos family's labor supply. At this time, Nikos was busy plowing olive groves for landholders in Fournoi in return for rights to graze sheep on their olive prunings and fallow. He also plowed for several larger olive owners in Dhidhima, as well as friends, neighbors, and kin in return for grazing. In the following month of April, Ioanna was assisted for two weeks by her son, Panos, who regularly attended the high school, but who was on vacation. Nikos was then busy with the grafting and planting of new olive tree for his daughter Tula's dowry and with plowing for the summer crop of irrigated potatoes. Ioanna, rather than being freed from the tasks of shepherding simply to relax at home, instead assisted her daughter in the preparation of seed potatoes and their planting. Throughout the year the daughter, Tula, ran the house—preparing meals, cleaning, feeding and caring for the house animals, washing clothes, and baking bread. She also bore the responsibility of representing the family at numerous ritual events.

The strain on the household labor pool was greatest in the wet months from December through May when shepherding tasks were heaviest and were accompanied by tasks of crop farming such as plowing and sowing of winter cereals, harvesting, pruning and cultivation of olives trees, and planting and hoeing of potatoes and garden vegetables. For intensive pastoral households, the work shifted in the dry months to the grain harvest, threshing, and the intensive cultivation of irrigated crops of potatoes, cauliflower, and cabbage. Throughout dry months the sheep made use of stubble from the newly harvested grain fields and of greens from the irrigated crops.

Mutual Obligation and Labor

Pasture has thus not been the only resource with which intensive shepherds have had to be concerned. Heavy pressure has been placed on the household's labor. It is apparent in Table 12.4 that neighbors have not provided very much in the way of total labor input, but these gross statistics do not reflect the importance of this help. Neighbors have assisted one another in times of crisis. Help in the form of allilovoithia has often been offered by neighbors in pastoral and agricultural activities, as well as the bulk preparation of staples.

Examples of mutual aid and obligation in pastoral activities have been quite common. At regular points in the pastoral round, herders who were on good terms would assist one another—for example, when milking duties were heaviest or in shearing. Shearing has generally been done in May, when the shepherds were fairly certain that the hot, dry weather had set in. A group of shepherds would be invited to assist in the work by a shepherd who was ready to shear his flock. A day would be appointed. A lamb would be slaughtered to provide a festive meal for the occasion. After the shearing was finished, all assembled shared in the meal. When the other shepherds were, in turn, ready to shear their animals, the first shepherd would reciprocate by assisting his neighbors.

Shepherds who for reasons of insufficient labor found it inconvenient to wean their lambs by herding them in a separate flock would frequently exchange their suckling lambs for purposes of weaning. These lambs were rejected by the ewes in the new flock, and after sufficient butting they became accustomed to grazing, at which point they were returned to their owners.

Unpredictable crises calling for reciprocal labor can easily arise during the normal pastoral round. For example, one shepherd was taken seriously ill and was forced to go to Athens for an operation. During the two months that he was incapacitated another shepherd family pooled his flock with their own, sharing all costs and resources until he was sufficiently recovered to once again work his flock (a practice known as *smiksimo*). Several months later when this friend was taken to court over a boundary dispute, the shepherd who had been ill went as witness, affirming his friend's position in the dispute.

Other crises can occur—ritual events such as baptisms, weddings, and funerals in which a shepherd family must fully participate. When a herding couple received the sudden news that their daughter, who lived in a more isolated mountain hamlet, had lost her second child (delivered prematurely several months earlier), it was necessary for immediate neighbors and friends to assume the responsibility of managing the flock, allowing the family to rush to the funeral. This was done, it was said, within the "normal course of things."

Labor assistance has been just as important in agricultural activities as in herding. At many points in the cultivation cycle of irrigated cash crops, friends and neighbors aid one another. When potatoes are to be planted, a family might announce to friends and neighbors that they are cutting seed potatoes and would be ready to plant in a day or two. Some neighbors and friends would then come to assist in the cutting. When a field is prepared for planting, the women whose families own potato fields, as well as some whose families do not, might come to the aid of their neighbors. When this is done, the women retire to a private feast, very much like that of the men after shearing, with plenty of good food and wine provided by the hostess. This form of allilovoithia may be repaid in a variety of ways. In some cases, the family will send women to help neighbors plant their potato fields. In others, when a neighbor needs potatoes she need only ask her friend for a full basket, or if she wishes fresh greens or other garden produce, she need not ask her neighbor for the privilege to go into her garden and cut what is required.

Work groups are formed in similar fashion for the harvest of cash crops. When buyers stop in the village to offer a price higher than the current wholesale price on the Athenian market (which frequently occurs in this region because potatoes and cauliflower are usually early and of high quality), a sudden pinch is felt for labor to fill orders. Members of the household may not be available because they are performing tasks away from the house, or there may simply not be enough of them to meet the buyer's schedule.[7] At this time, friends and neighbors who are available will pitch in. In one such case, a farmer who was rushing to harvest cauliflower had a work group of eleven men and women from five different households assisting him. At the same time, the flocks of three of these families were all gathered on his land and grazed in common by one family while others cut and bagged the cauliflower. It is this kind of behavior that lends credence to the village aphorism, "neighbors are more important than kin, because when you are in need of help they can never claim that they didn't see this need," as can kin who may live in another neighborhood of the village or elsewhere.

Mutual Obligation and Food Preparation

The system of allilovoithia has also been used by women in the preparation of certain staple foods. This has been most common for foods such as *hilopittes*, egg noodles, and *trakhanas*, a kind of bulgur made from milk and coarsely ground wheat. In the summer it has been common to see women carrying short tables, rolling sticks, and a basket of eggs hurrying on their way to prepare egg noodles. Five or six women would thus gather enough eggs to do a day's worth of noodles. They would each roll out one thin sheet of noodles after another that would then be laboriously cut into small squares for drying. When one house was provided for, the women would begin saving eggs for the next neighbor in turn. This group preparation has been more efficient both in labor and in accumulating the perishable resources of eggs and milk in sufficient bulk.

The preparation of trakhanas has required a group to take turns in the heavy work of turning the stone quern and roughly grinding the wheat. This is very heavy work. The men say, "when one hears the hand mill (*heromilo*) turning, it is also the sound of the Devil's Mill." Because there are only several hand mills in each neighborhood, they have also served as an important focus in the local system of reciprocity.

Conflict and Cooperation

Although I have intended to establish the importance of the institution of allilovoithia in the operation of the local economy of Dhidhima, I have not wished to convey an impression of a community distinguished by completely harmonious relations. Conflict and intense competition have also been very real features of the society. Sheepfolds have been burned on the mountainside, and valuable property has been destroyed. Numerous instances could be cited of whole households refusing to speak to one another. In short, many of the patterns long described for the Mediterranean apply to the local interaction and politics of Dhidhima. It is worth noting, however, that very close alliances must be maintained with some neighbors as long as hostile relations with others are kept up.

Furthermore, the institution of mutual obligation has functioned to integrate the local economy within an idiom of "natural" neighborliness. The fiction of not calculating every transaction due to factors of neighborhood and friendship has been crucial to the health of the system (Gouldner 1960, Plattner 1989). When this mask has sometimes been removed (as in the

Table 12.5
Annual Income for Tzanos Flock,
Dhidhima, 1972–1975

Source	1972 (Dr)	1975 (Dr)
Milk		
Home	1,050	1,000
Exchange	858	1,300
Sold	18,804	50,860
Cheese		
Home	6,400	6,500
Exchange	2,400	5,000
Butter		
Home	60	140
Meat		
Home (lambs)	2,825	2,500
Exchanged (lambs)	4,825	6,000
Sold (lambs)	16,237	25,000
Sold (culls)	4,500	6,900
Lamb Subsidy	539	1,000
Wool		
Home	1,000	2,000
Exchange	2,600	4,000
Manure		
Home	1,800	2,600
Totals		
Gross income	63,898	114,800
Total costs	28,850	48,300
Net income	35,048	66,500
Profit margin	54.85%	57.93%

NOTE: Income includes only that which was incurred directly in flock operation.

Table 12.6
Annual Expenses for Tzanos Flock,
Dhidhima, 1972–1975

Source	1972 (Dr)	1975 (Dr)
Seed	2,553	7,900
Plowing	1,150	800
Feeds		
Cottonseed cake	8,050	12,000
Sugarbeet cake	—	2,800
Maize	—	3,500
Wheat, barley, oats	900	—
Salt	50	100
Damage suits	300	500
Wormers	300	700
Vaccinations	539	130
Other veterinary costs	200	500
Equipment	200	400
Hay	500	900
Pasture		
Winter fallow	6,580	10,950
Summer fallow	187	—
Planted grazing	2,500	3,400
Stubble	3,501	2,100
Commons	1,190	1,900
Total	28,850	48,850

NOTE: Expenses include only those which were incurred directly in flock operation.

case of the koumbaros with the tractor), cash has quickly become a more critical exchange element, because it is the most convenient measure of value.[8] This fiction has also lent a certain fluency to the flow of goods and services, effecting an efficient redistribution of temporary local surpluses. It has been economically necessary for households to maintain as wide a field as possible of positive, or at least neutral, relations with others in the village. These relationships have been reinforced best through the reciprocal movement of goods and services. A norm of overt sociability has been very helpful in supporting this economic system.

Neither should the inference be drawn that all neighborly behavior and friendship have been simply of a calculated, economic nature. It appears best to view these types of transactions as a continuum. Many simple exchanges of goods and services have been just that—uncalculated gifts between friends and neighbors. Structurally, however, even these exchanges have served to support the idiom of friendship and neighborliness upon which so much of the local economic behavior of Dhidhimiotes has been predicated.

For intensive pastoralists, the economic importance of maintaining a widespread network of mutual obligation ties can once again be illustrated through the example of the Tzanos household (see Tables 12.5 and 12.6). In 1971–1972, this family failed to meet their milk contract with their cheese merchant by only 300 kg (about ten days' production). In the same year, they distributed well over 300 kg of fresh milk within their mutual obligation network. They were well aware that if they failed to meet the contract they would be bound to the merchant in the coming year, and this caused them great anxiety. The reinforcement of the ties of positive affect created through mutual obligation took precedence, however, and milk was used in this fashion. Without a wide range of friends to draw upon for pasture and access to pasture, there would have been little point in being free to choose a cheese merchant, for there would have been little milk to sell. Without friends and neighbors to rely upon in times of crisis, the diversified household economies used as insurance against climatic and market variation might quickly fail (see Forbes, Clarke, this volume).

In conclusion, interhousehold networks of mutual obligation have played key roles in the economic integration of Dhidhima, particularly for intensifying pastoralists. With restricted access to pasture due to dispersed land ownership and local ecology, the system of allilovoithia has served to maximize grazing in fields near the village, while averting the cash drain that would have resulted from renting these fields. Mutual obligation has also provided the extra labor required at critical points in the productive cycle and has served the local economy by efficiently redistributing temporary local surpluses of goods and services. Although interfamilial competition adequately describes many attitudes of the shepherds of Dhidhima, it has been through active mutual obligation with neighbors, friends, and kin that these herders have most effectively exploited their social environment in assuring economic success.

The "Commons" and the Market: Ecological Effects of Communal Land Tenure and Market Integration on Local Resources in the Mediterranean

Harold A. Koster and Hamish A. Forbes

The Mediterranean landscape has experienced severe ecological change at the hands of humans. The fact that over the course of at least ten millennia these lands have been so closely molded by human action is, perhaps, of importance to an audience beyond those directly interested in the region. Indeed, because of the long course of pressure which Mediterranean natural resources have endured, it may not be unreasonable to view the use of this environment by humans as paradigmatic of the ecological crisis facing the contemporary biosphere.[1]

Excesses of woodcutting, burning, mining, grazing, the extension of agriculture, and climatic fluctuations—all have been advanced as principal causes of deforestation and erosion in the Mediterranean and in the Near East, and we have addressed these issues before (e.g., Forbes 1983, Forbes and Koster 1976, Forbes, Koster, and Foxhall 1978).[2] An examination of such proximate agents of environmental change is necessary and useful, but we should be reminded that where humans are involved, causation may be viewed at another and less direct level. Two themes commonly proposed as critical forces in the mismanagement of resources are first, what Garrett Hardin (1968a, b) termed the "tragedy of the commons," and second, the factor of external demand on local resources exacerbated by market integration. We propose to investigate the effect of these forces on local resources in the Mediterranean, with specific reference to data from the southern Argolid.

What is the "tragedy of the commons," and how might it apply to Greece? The essence of Hardin's concept was presaged by Aristotle: "What is common to the greatest number gets the least amount of care. Men pay most attention to what is their own; they care less for what is common" (*Politics*, 2.3). When a resource is held in common, according to Hardin's thesis, it is to the advantage of every individual to exploit the resource as thoroughly as possible under the assumption that others will do likewise. The nature of the tragedy lies in the remorseless deterioration of the resource occasioned by the inability of individuals to look beyond their perceived self-interest.

Hardin's type case was that of herders overgrazing their flocks on village common grazing lands. He described Sahelian drought and famine as an example of the model in practice (Hardin 1977). While this interpretation of recent African events has not gone unchallenged (Brokensha, Horowitz, and Scudder 1977; Franke and Chasin 1980; Hasler 1996), Hardin's general thesis has remained a key element, sometimes supported, sometimes debated, in most discussions of common lands throughout the world to the present (Keohane and Ostrom 1995; Ito, Sai Jo, and Une 1994; Stevenson 1991; Soden 1988; Swanson 1996).

The second major force that we will consider with respect to environmental degradation is that of the role of human populations, linked through political and market mechanisms, in the abuse of local resources. Essentially, this is a problem of carrying capacity—defined as the maximum number of a species that may be supported indefinitely by a habitat, allowing for seasonal and random changes, without degradation of the environment. Carrying capacity has presented problems as a theoretical construct in biology, and when extended to the human species it has been particularly fraught with difficulties. Among these is the fact that a habitat's resources are often utilized by more than the resident population. In such cases, obviously, carrying capacity must not be defined simply in terms of the local population, but rather with reference to the total set of populations dependent on the habitat. An unfortunate consequence of such political and economic integration is that nonresident consumers often have little interest in, or information about, such resources. Examples of such behavior are all too familiar. When an international corporation clear-cuts pulp wood in central Newfoundland to produce newsprint for the *New York Times* or the *Washington Post*, few readers in Brooklyn or Silver Spring will be aware of what is happening, or will care.

For several reasons, Greece is a most appropriate place to investigate Hardin's thesis. As we have noted, there is considerable evidence in this region for a long history of exploitative human behavior. Pastoralism has formed an essential component in the economy from the Neolithic period to the present, and these activities have often depended upon common pasture. Also, Hardin's concept should have a familiar ring to students of Mediterranean ethnology as a scholarly sibling of the concepts of "amoral familism" and the "image of the limited good," which have misguided the study of smallholders for several decades, particularly when applied in blanket fashion by national level planners and economists (see Netting 1993; Sutton, Introduction to this volume). Banfield and others argued that the behavior of southern European peasants might best be explained as if they conformed to the following rule: "maximize the short-term advantage of the family, assuming that all others will do likewise" (e.g., Banfield 1958, McNall 1976). Foster's "image of the limited good" (1965) posited a generalized peasant worldview of a fixed set of resources. Those resources used by one person were taken at the expense of all others, so that it behooved individuals to look to their own best interest in the belief that others would do the same. While such formulations tapped certain aspects of village social relations, they overlooked and distorted others, a point that has become increasingly clear over the years (see DuBoulay and Williams 1987; Gallant 1991; Hart 1992; Herzfeld 1985, 1987 for discussion of this point for Greece). Clearly, Hardin's formulation was little more than a paraphrase of these rather problematic characterizations of peasant values, which, because they were often used to describe Mediterranean folk, would lead one to expect such people to comfortably fit the model of the "tragedy of the commons."

The assignment of land—variously described as marginal, forested, or waste—for common use has been a widespread practice with a long history in the Mediterranean. The description recorded in A.D. 1070 of the Customs of Barcelona is typical: "Flowing water, and springs, meadows, grazing grounds, forests, garigues and rocks belong to barons not to be held *en alleu* (that is, in disregard of any rights but their own) or as part of their demesne, but in order that their people might enjoy them at all times" (cited in Bloch 1966: 283). Bloch has, in his unique style, summarized the critical role of such resources to the rural populace: "By his fields alone the peasant literally could not have lived. . . . These moors and marshes and forests did not merely furnish necessary food for his cattle. His own nourishment depended on them—for wild vegetables and fruits were even more important in his dietary than wild game" (Bloch 1966: 281). The importance of these lands and resources to the Mediterranean peasantry has often been noted, and it is reasonable to assume that the widespread appropriation and sale of common lands in the eighteenth and nineteenth centuries, often in the name of liberal reform, contributed to the process of social differentiation and to the growth of a rural proletariat (e.g., Gilmore 1977; Sarti 1985). The abuse of these commonly held resources has also often been cited as a reason for the overexploitation and decline of the Mediterranean landscape. As a Serbian adage has it: "It belongs to everybody, and therefore to nobody. In the common everybody reaps, and nobody sows" (Tomasevich 1955: 161).

In Greece, the dedication of common grazing lands around villages was encouraged by various policies and laws concerning disposition of what were called National Lands after the Revolution (McGrew 1985: 121–124). As the forces of modern Greek history have subsequently unfolded, however, a variety of legal land tenure arrangements have arisen. Within the southern Argolid, we find very different patterns for the rural communities of Dhidhima and Methana, located a scant twenty kilometers from one another in a straight line. In Dhidhima, the most important single economic activity is the herding of sheep and goats for the sale of milk, meat, and wool, with a third of the households significantly involved in pastoralism (Chang, Adams, J. Koster, H. Koster, this volume). On Methana, herding is a minor activity, with the cultivation of tree crops, vines, and grains taking precedence (Clarke, Forbes, this volume). The two areas stand in stark contrast with respect to land tenure. In Dhidhima, 82 percent of the village's surface area consists of nonarable mountainside, all of which is held as commons by the residents. Arable land comprises the bulk of the remaining territory, so that here individual or private tenure is the rule. On Methana, all land, both mountain and terraced arable land, is in private hands.

An old anthropological question concerns how clearly actual behavior matches formal systems of social rules and legal prescriptions. As is often the case, we found that for a variety of reasons, in both Dhidhima and Methana there is in fact a system of variable access to resources mediated by both communal and individual norms of tenure. The divergence between the system on Methana and that in Dhidhima is not as great as it initially appears. This point is of particular importance for those of us interested in interpreting, through historically specific documentation, the role of communal tenure as it has affected the physical environment.[3]

Dhidhima exhibits a classic example of Hardin's type case of common pasture on which village herders depend for pasture for their animals. All herders in the *koinotis* are assured access to the commons pasture after the payment of a small per capita fee. This fee is doubled on every animal above a flock size of 150. The animals of nonresidents are admitted to the com-

Figure 13.1. Brush fold in vicinity of a previously burned fold, Dhidhima, 1972. Note the bright white cluster of limestone which has been transformed by the heat.

mons upon the decision of the village council and the payment of a double head tax. As can be seen in Figure 13.1, nonresident flocks have not been permitted access to the Dhidhima commons since 1965.

The civil law states that all residents of the koinotis may keep as many animals as they choose on the common land. Each shepherd or goatherd who has paid the grazing tax is free to go as he pleases and to graze his animals wherever he chooses in the common lands. The only restriction placed upon this freedom of movement is a legal proscription upon the grazing of goats in areas of fir forest (which do not exist in Dhidhima) or the grazing of flocks on recently burned mountainside. Local practice is not, however, congruent with codified law.

The customary law of herders in Dhidhima recognizes personal territories within the communal mountain pastures. These are linked to *mandria*, or sheep and goat folds (Chang, this volume) and are heritable rights in conjunction with these shelters. There is flexibility in the system. For example, a goatherd will allow another the right of passage through his core grazing area, but if the herd traversing his territory dallies and grazes intensively, this might lead to difficulties between the herders. These territories often follow natural boundaries such as a ridge line or a ravine, although in many areas the line is not so clear. In fact these territories are characterized by clearly defined core zones surrounding the folds and by peripheral areas that are less easily demarcated. These territories are linked closely to home range behavior among the animals herded (Koster 1977: 286–90).

There has been no fixed number or pattern to the territories existing within the Dhidhima common lands over time. Just as with houses, fields, and other holdings, they have been constantly reshuffled into new patterns. Individuals enter and leave herding as an occupation. If one is to begin successfully in—or later return to—herding, access to both a fold site and a grazing territory is required. The situation is reminiscent of that reported among the lobster fishermen of New England and the Maritime Provinces who require both an anchorage and a fishing territory for successful operation (Acheson 1972, 1975; Bowles 1972).

In the past, when state controls were not as effective at the local level, if a family had numerous sons and close kinsmen, it was in a favorable position to compete for grazing with weaker neighbors. This competition was often a source of conflict. Even in recent years, force has been used to test the ability of potential competitors, in ways strikingly parallel to the more general contests of manhood that Herzfeld (1985) has described for herders on Crete. The most frequent form this takes is the "stealing of grass," in which one herder intentionally grazes his flock on the pasture of another. A more drastic action is to burn a competitor's fold or to steal his animals. Instances of fold burning have recently occurred, but to judge from informants' statements, not with the frequency of earlier years (Koster and Koster 1976). These grazing territories within the communal pasture serve to control effectively the total number of animals that can be herded in the koinotis. The tragedy of the commons is avoided by each herder's maintaining his right to a core area and in turn being limited by the boundaries of his neighbors' grazing lands.

Focusing on statistics for the period from 1940 to 1975, it appears that this common pasture supported between 9,500 and 19,000 head of sheep and goats, with from 110 to 179 herders depending on these flocks (see Figures 13.2 and 13.3). The density of mature animals on the commons fluctuated between 1 and 2 head per hectare, but in more than three-fourths of these years the density was between 1 and 1-1/2 head per hectare. It is of interest to note that the highest densities were achieved in the years following the mass destruction of the Civil War, but after peaking in 1953 at 2 head per hectare, the densities stabilized at much lower levels in a pattern of tracking fluctuations in market prices and in grazing conditions.[4] It should also be stressed that these densities do not include inputs from supplementary feeds, which increased dramatically in availability during the 1960s, nor do they consider the contribution of the arable and fallow land to the feeding of the flocks. In discussions of Mediterranean pastoralism, the degree of interdependence of the pastoral and agricultural sectors is all too often overlooked. Mountain grazing and water are not the only limiting factors in Mediterranean pastoralism. Access to, and quality of, fallow agricultural fields are equally critical factors in the adjustment of flock sizes.

From these data we can see that communal tenure as it has operated in Dhidhima has evolved into a less formal system of territories defined by quasi-proprietary rights of usufruct. The development of individual grazing territories allows the close monitoring of the quality of pasture by herders, and pressures these families to manage mortality in their flocks, in attempts to adjust animal numbers to fluctuations in the resource level. As Hart (1992: 171–192), Herzfeld (1985), and Gallant (1991) have noted in discussing intravillage competition in other parts of Greece, the pursuit of family interest ultimately requires a recognition of community interest as well. In this recognition of community interest lie the limitations of the concepts of amoral familism and the inevitably tragic use of common lands.

Grazing land on Methana is formally in private hands, as are agricultural fields. Here too, however, the formal rules have not adequately described behavior. In the period following the

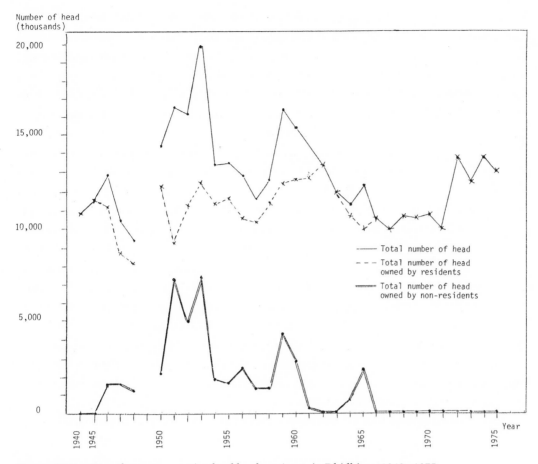

Figure 13.2. Use of common grazing land by sheep/goats in Dhidhima, 1940–1975.

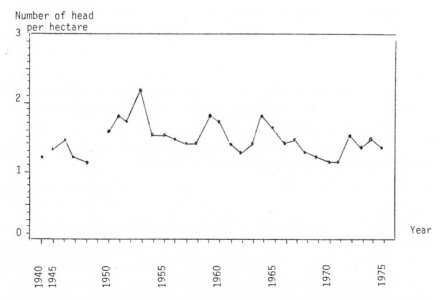

Figure 13.3. Density of sheep/goats per hectare on common land, Dhidhima, 1940–1975.

harvest, villagers have been free by customary law to graze their household animals on the stubble or fallow land within the community that has not been specifically marked off for the owner's use. Stubble and fallow vegetation have remained free goods until the first major autumn rains, when the fields are once again prepared for planting. These customary rights have not been unimportant in the local domestic economy, because, in contrast to Dhidhima, there have only been several large flocks, and most houses have maintained a small group of sheep and goats to supply their family needs for milk, cheese, and meat.

But what of resources other than grazing? Firewood continues to provide a basic source of energy for much of the world's population. In the 1980s, the average family of four in the southern Argolid required 2 t (metric tons) of firewood and brush to meet its annual fuel needs for heating, cooking, and for other household purposes. Some of these needs were met from the prunings of cultivated trees, but the bulk of the supply was drawn from the mountainside vegetation.

In both communities the customary rules regarding such behavior were again not so different, although a polar divergence existed between the formal rules. On Methana, brush and firewood were free goods, as long as an individual did not overexploit these resources in the view of the owner. People were well aware of the limits and how far they might be stretched. The less fortunate, including the elderly, the poor, and widows, were more likely to achieve free access than were those who were better situated economically and socially. As with grazing land in Dhidhima, although in theory all wood and brush in the commons was freely available to residents, a less formal level of quasi-proprietary rights developed. Brush could be collected as a free good, but it was necessary for the collector to remain aware of the limits of exploitation and to respect the rights of the herder who used that area.

Earlier we quoted Bloch with respect to the importance of gathered resources in smallholder subsistence. This continues to be true of the southern Argolid. In both Dhidhima and Methana, as Clarke has demonstrated, wild greens (*horta*), when they are growing during the winter and spring months, form an integral part of the diet (Clarke 1976a, 1976b, 1997). Regardless of whether these grow on communal or private land, in both communities they are freely accessible to all residents. Only village gardens and fenced fields are off limits to the horta collectors, although again, the village poor or disabled are often free to collect wild plants even in these places as a gesture of charity. On Methana, another collected resource, wild oregano, is an important economic asset that is sold to both local and national markets (Clarke, this volume). Interestingly enough, wild oregano on private lands is freely available to all residents in the eastern half of the peninsula, but not to those in the western villages. This is presumably due to the capital investment made in the oregano crop in the west, where many of these plants are fertilized by individual plot owners.

The limitation of numbers of caprovines on the noncultivated landscape of the Ermionidha in recent generations means that some sectors of the local community have been excluded from pastoralism as a way of generating cash. One traditional alternative for those with a restricted arable base was to exploit other aspects of the noncultivated landscape. The extent of activities such as woodcutting for lumber and firewood, the tapping of pine trees for resin, and the exploitation of the maquis and garrigue areas for charcoal burning and lime burning in earlier years

Figure 13.4. Juniper pruned for firewood and construction materials, Dhidhima.

is well documented in the Forest Service records in Kranidhi.[5] Like shepherding, these activities have been claimed by a number of authorities as a major cause of the erosion that has occurred in the Mediterranean. Also like shepherding, these activities produced cash, not food for home consumption. Moreover, again directly comparable with pastoralism, the bulk of the production has traditionally been sent out of the region. Forest Service records for the area note that in the 1930s most of the lime was shipped to the town of Nafplio, while virtually all the charcoal and firewood were shipped to the capital (Athens/Piraeus) to provide the fuel needs of the expanding urban population.

Lime burning was a major source of cash for many families in Dhidhima through the nineteenth and the first half of the twentieth centuries. The village had a ready supply of the three elements necessary for such a toilsome industry: limestone, brush, and poor and needy laborers. In most cases lime was burned in Dhidhima as a source of supplementary income, although several professional lime-burning crews did operate on a full-time basis. These crews often burned a kiln monthly. After the stone had been collected from the mountainside and piled in the kiln, juniper was cut from the communal land. When this was done, however, the herder

Figure 13.5.   Old limestone kiln, Dhidhima, 1972.

who depended on this area for grazing either did the work himself or was provided a commission by the crew. The kilns had to be fired for three or four days and were stoked continuously during this period to maintain the intense heat necessary to decompose the crystalline rock. This activity had a particularly marked, although localized effect on the vegetative cover, and, indeed, it is still possible to observe the scoured sites on steeper mountain slopes where such cutting was concentrated.

Traditionally in the southern Argolid the exploitation of forest products for a livelihood was a very low-status occupation, lower even than pastoralism. It was practiced largely as a part-time specialization by poorer farmers and laborers who needed more cash than their cultivation enterprises could provide. The use of brush, roots, and wood from the noncultivated areas of the Ermionidha for charcoal burning and lime burning was finally banned by the Greek government late in the 1970s, but by that time these activities had largely been abandoned. Forest Service records for the area are supported by the comments of the local population. The production of both charcoal and lime rose sharply during the 1930s. In 1931 (the date when the records begin), 382 t of charcoal were produced, and 667 t of scrub were cut for lime burning. Charcoal production peaked at 805 t in 1937, and 940 t of brush were cut for lime burning in the peak year of 1938. By 1958, charcoal production was down to only 80 t, and 635 t of brush were cut for lime burning. By 1970, only 10 t of brush were cut for lime burning—and none thereafter—and production of charcoal from noncultivated sources averaged 44 t in the years 1970 and 1971.

There are two reasons for the drop in these products. First, the introduction of fossil fuels largely replaced demand for charcoal from the maquis and garrigue. Kerosene and, later, bottled

Figure 13.6. Modern limestone kiln, Nafplio, 1972.

gas largely supplanted charcoal as the fuel for heating and cooking in urban areas; and petroleum oils, gas, and industrialized methods are generally now used for burning lime. Second, other, much more desirable (and higher status) methods of earning cash are available, particularly in the merchant marine, house construction, or tourist industries in the region. The rapid, large-scale development of the region's tourist economy in the later 1960s has been particularly important. The entry for 1969 in the Forest Service records specifically links the drop in forest products to the sharp increase in tourism. The disappearance of long hours of backbreaking, smoky, dusty work involved in lime and charcoal burning is not lamented.

The value of forest products produced annually in the Ermionidha in the 1930s, as documented in the Forest Service records, was considerable and represents almost entirely cash income rather than home consumption. Comparison with today's prices is difficult. But if the price—quoted from memory for wheat in the first half of the 1930s—of two drachmas per *oka* (1.6 drachmas per kilo) is correct, the combined values of firewood, lime, charcoal, and resin produced in 1931 would have been equivalent to approximately 790 t of wheat. Using the same price figure for wheat, the value of these products in 1935 would have been equivalent to almost 1,870 t of wheat—or equivalent to 1,840 t of wheat after subtracting dues to the Forest Service for rights to exploit forest products. This last figure is in excess of the total estimated annual wheat consumption for the whole of the Ermionidha.[6]

Why would these same herders tolerate the potentially drastic long-term effects of brushcutting activities on the commons vegetation of Dhidhima while they were demonstrably sensitive to problems of over-stocking on these pastures? To answer this question, we must return to a closer inspection of Hardin's model and the problem of integration as it affects local carrying capacity.

One difficulty with Hardin's model is that it fails to place equal emphasis on the forces that might encourage equilibrium and on those causing overexploitation. As Clark (1973), Fife (1971), Keohane and Ostrum (1995), and others have suggested, Hardin presumed that herders must be ruined by the destruction of the commons, and that herein lies the tragedy of the process. What if, however, the local population is *not* dependent upon the common resource, or has the ability to kill the goose and shift easily to a new pattern of exploitation? We are all too familiar with such behavior on the part of major corporations, which can often overexploit a common renewable resource and through diversification or reinvestment of capital shift to a different economic activity. Indeed, the scholars mentioned above have argued persuasively that this would be the most economically "rational" course of action for a firm attempting to maximize profit.

Hardin aimed at consideration of the effects of communal use of resources; however, he failed to distinguish such resources with regard to the nature of their physical distribution. Where resources may be localized or easily bounded, it is possible for small-scale populations, as in Dhidhima, to develop conservative strategies of management through the appropriation of rights of usufruct by individuals or groups. It should be emphasized, however, that this is done within a formal system of social rules that retains common rights and responsibilities. Hardin's thesis appears most applicable to common resources that cannot so easily be bounded, as, for example air, the oceans, the overall hydrologic cycle, or truly widespread pasturelands. This is rarely the case with grazing land in the Mediterranean, where even transhumant flocks traversing hundreds of kilometers from summer mountain pastures to winter in the lowlands generally depend on the long-term use of the same set of local pastures.

Another problem with Hardin's model is that he was not very sanguine about the ability of humans to adjust to what is obviously a disastrous situation. His herders are literally trapped and driven like actors in a Greek tragedy by the *hubris* of failing to move beyond the economically rational goal of short-term personal profit.

The case of grazing in the Dhidhima commons has demonstrated that herders, even in Hardin's type case, are capable of developing mechanisms enabling them to avoid the logic of the tragedy of the commons. These same herders, however, coincidentally overexploited the local vegetation by burning lime. How can this inconsistency be best explained? To answer this question it is necessary for us to consider the constraints of the "stick" and the "carrot"— coercion and profit or market demand. It must be stressed that such constraints may act to encourage *either* sustainable conservation *or* abuse of resources. The proximate decision to overexploit or conserve local resources is most often in the hands of the resident population, although this decision is obviously heavily influenced by the possibly conflicting pressures of coercion and market demand.

In the case of common pasture, Dhidhima herders are, and have been for centuries, concerned with the marketing of the products of their flocks. This was especially so in the past, when cheese was more readily stored and transported to external markets than was meat,[7] and remains true even today, as milk products continue to form the keystone of the pastoral economy.

Hardin would ask why a herder faced with the need to maximize his profit and respond to market demand would not simply increase his flock size. When queried as to why he did not increase his flock from one hundred to two hundred sheep, a Dhidhimiote shepherd answered that he would get an equivalent amount of milk from the larger flock, and of course more meat—for a year or two. Soon after, however, it was obvious that his flock's milk yields would decline drastically as the pasture suffered. Asked why he could not expand his grazing area, he smiled and pointed to the white scar of a burned fold site on the limestone mountainside. He could hardly expect his neighbors to acquiesce to his usurpation of grazing that they required for their flocks.

But why would the same herder sell, or himself cut juniper on the pasture land that he used, for the production of lime? Once again, the herder was responding to the force of market demand for lime, that is, the requirement of human populations in the Mediterranean far removed from his village. Juniper is ubiquitous in Dhidhima and is not a highly valued species as browse for the sheep and goats. He recognized that cutting so many trees from the vicinity of the kiln would have an effect on the condition of the soil and subsequently on plant cover in that spot. The effect, however, was extremely localized and patchy. It did not extend to his entire territory in the manner that an increase of flock size would and thus had limited effect on the general condition of pasture for the period of his use.

Such effects were incremental and limited in scope. Thus, it is likely that the impact of such localized vegetation removal would not have a rapid or dramatic result. If, for example, the cutting required for a single firing of a limekiln caused an annual decrease in the total available vegetation by one or two per cent in a herder's territory, it would take as long as twenty to thirty years for this to be translated into a significant decline in the milk production of the flock depending on that territory. If, at such a point, the herder did recognize a clear link between woodcutting and pasture decline, he would be faced also with the fact that just as the pressure on his pasture had been established on an incremental basis, so too would the regeneration of vegetative production be a slow process. By not cutting brush in that year he could only improve his pasture by one or two per cent in the instance cited. Also, over such a long period the regeneration of vegetation would be proceeding on previously cut-over areas, and this would contribute to the amelioration in the decline of pasture production. The herder would also be faced with the loss of cash income from woodcutting for charcoal and lime production. Such cash losses would have to be balanced against the slow improvement in milk production, and, indeed, there would be no guarantee of a milk increase in the short run, as such small improvements could easily be negated by changes in other variables, such as those of weather, disease, labor, and market price.

Since herders did continue to allow or to participate in such exploitation until it declined for the reasons noted earlier, it appears that in this case the element of short-term profit outweighed the concern for the long-term condition of the vegetation, a response that certainly can be documented repeatedly in the Mediterranean and elsewhere. It should be stressed, however, that there is little direct and quantifiable evidence in Dhidhima of the actual effects that such activity has had during the last century. In this regard, it is of interest to note that Dhidhimiotes claimed in 1978 that the *venya* (juniper) was generally growing taller than in the previous decade, and they asserted that this change was directly attributable to the dramatic decline in the cutting of wood and brush for lime burning and charcoal.

In conclusion, Hardin's thesis of the tragedy of the commons does not adequately explain the role of communal tenure in the conservation or abuse of local resources in Greece. It fails to consider the possibility of the appropriation of rights in the commons by individuals or groups; nor does it recognize the possibility that individuals may not be ruined by the destruction of the commons, because they are not dependent upon the resource. Such people, motivated by the desire to maximize short-term profit coupled with little concern for the environment, can hardly be viewed as suffering tragically.

If we are to understand the use of local resources in the Mediterranean, we must focus on the nature of the resident population's dependence on, and commitment to, these resources. What demands are placed on these resources by external populations, and what is the nature of these demands? What levels of coercion are exerted by nonresident populations to ensure the extraction of these resources, or alternatively to support their conservation against the efforts of *local* groups in attempts to profit from market demands? We may expect that in areas in which resources may be localized or bounded and in which a high level of dependence on the resources exists among the resident population, *local* measures will be taken to avoid crippling destruction of these necessary resources. When the residents have been unwilling or unable to respond to disequilibrium in the local ecosystem, it is most likely that the prime culprit will not be the direct agency of their overcutting of wood or overgrazing of goats, but rather will be the indirect demands of external populations.

CHAPTER FOURTEEN

The "Traditional" Craftsman as Entrepreneur: A Potter in Ermioni

P. Nick Kardulias

This brief study is an attempt to record some of the basic techniques employed by a potter in Ermioni.[1] The purpose is twofold: (1) to document the activities of this craftsman as a means of preserving a portion of a rapidly disappearing craft, and (2) in a manner similar to J. Koster's analysis of weavers in Dhidhima (this volume), to outline at least part of the decision-making process that has been instituted over the past two decades in an effort to meet the changing circumstances of an economy in flux.

The use of ceramic vessels has been one of the constants in Greek life for a number of millennia. Only in the twentieth century has their importance been diminished by the introduction of newer, cheaper, and in some ways more durable materials such as plastic.[2] Thus, the potter's trade has long been an important one in the Argolid and elsewhere in the country.

In the post-World War II years, the Greek economy has undergone considerable change, moving in the direction of increased industrialization and mass production. One result of this process has been the gradual reduction in the role played by those individual entrepreneurs who produce handmade wares. As mass-produced objects have encroached on their markets, their contribution to the national economy has been reduced. The part they play on the local level has also been adversely affected in many cases because centralized factories can provide larger quantities at lower prices. With improvements in the transportation system, these manufactured products can reach even the most remote villages and thus undercut the local craftsmen. Small workshop operators have had to adapt to these changes. Willett and Brachner's (1983: 44–45) examination of folk pottery in the American South suggests the decline of this industry was due in part to the influx of cheaper mass-produced wares from Ohio and other northern states. A similar situation seems to have been the case in postwar Greece.

This study was conducted in conjunction with an ethnoarchaeological examination reported elsewhere in this volume (see Murray and Kardulias), and the basic definition of ethnoarchaeology presented therein holds in this case as well. I would, however, like to augment that definition by considering Hodder's (1983: 38) functions for this subdiscipline. In addition to the construction of analogies explicitly for the purpose of strengthening inferences about past behavior, he suggests another important goal is to record pertinent information concerning social practices that are disappearing in what we sometimes call their traditional form. Recording such practices and their material paraphernalia has become a matter of some interest in Greece, as reflected in the efforts of the National Folklore Museum and the Peloponnesian Folklore Foundation. Such work has an obvious humanistic element but also provides an inventory of behaviors and artifacts to which future scholars can make reference. Another aspect of ethnoarchaeology is a concern with modern material-culture studies, which analyze objects for what they can tell us about the present (Leone 1981: 6–7). The current study encompasses such an objective in its effort to delineate basic spatial attributes of the pottery workshop in question, as well as the sources of raw materials, the functioning of various structures and features, and the disposition of finished products.

Tradition and Economy in the Southern Argolid

The present study stresses the active role played by inhabitants of the southern Argolid in the vibrant economy of the region, and, in this sense, parallels Petronoti's analysis of Kranidhi shippers (this volume). Specifically, my concern is with a potter who recently operated in Ermioni. My goal is to present this individual in light of the "liquid landscapes" to which Sutton refers (this volume). The activities of this potter contrast strongly with the image of the "developmentally delayed subsistence farmers which held sway in studies of rural Greece until recently" (Sutton, this volume). Instead of peasants locked in the unyielding vise of tradition, the contributors to this volume view the people of the Ermionidha as decision makers who have participated actively in the myriad forces that have enmeshed their social lives (see Kardulias and Shutes 1997). The production of pottery is one of the many strategies residents of the Ermionidha have followed in the effort to cope with the shifting economic tides in the modern era.

At a general level, it is my goal to position the work of the potter, Ioannis Sampson, in the ceramic production that, while changing in some specific ways to accommodate new economic realities (varying demand for wares, the tourist trade, the introduction of plastic containers), has also been one of the durable elements in the rather volatile employment curve in the southern Argolid over the past one and one-half centuries. While the relative status of maritime occupations has fluctuated significantly (Topping, Forbes, Petronoti, Sutton, this volume), certain trades, that of the potter among them, have maintained a steadier presence. While the merchant marine, agriculture, and sponging have witnessed dramatic rises and falls in the number of participants, certain crafts (e.g., pottery production, carpentry) have comprised a constant small percentage of the total employment in the region. It is in this sense that I suggest the local ceramic industry has witnessed less volatility than these other, major occupations through time. The work of the Ermioni potter, Ioannis Sampson, thus represented important aspects of both continuity and flux, issues that were clearly reflected in the production choices he made.

The present study also provides data useful to analyses that make use of world systems theory (Wallerstein 1974; Chase-Dunn and Hall 1991, 1993). Greece illuminates well the processes of incorporation into the modern world system, something amply demonstrated by the southern Argolid's involvement with national and international commerce during the last two centuries

(Petronoti, Sutton, this volume). In world systems terms, the Ermionidha has served as a semi-periphery to the Western European capitalist system; the region offers both basic products (e.g., olive oil, fruits, and vegetables) and major services (cargo shipping, tourist facilities). This information expands our understanding of several issues within world systems theory. As Petronoti also stresses (this volume), incorporation is a dynamic, two-way process in which all concerned play an active role (Hall 1986). There is a need to substantiate the claims of world systems theory on the local level, that is, to demonstrate the links between specific ethnographic data and macroscale theory (Nash 1981; Hall 1995; Shutes 1996). Analysis of local craft production, such as pottery manufacture, thus both gains from and contributes to these discussions.

Studies of Pottery Production

From the outset of anthropological inquiry, there has been considerable archaeological and ethnographic interest in pottery production. We see this interest reflected in the work of Bunzel (1929), Tschopik (1941), Plog (1980), Nelson (1985), and Rice (1987), among others. In Greek archaeology, Matson (1972, 1973) has provided a comprehensive approach to ceramic studies. Beazley's work (1942, 1956) is perhaps the best example of the classic approach, which, while still valuable, has limited possibilities for socioeconomic analysis.

In like manner, ethnoarchaeologists and ethnohistorians have also focused considerable attention on ceramics (Deetz 1965; Longacre 1991a; Stanislawski 1973, 1977, 1978). Studies in many parts of the world have documented the life span of various ceramics, household variation in pottery consumption, the role of ceramics in local and interregional trade, and the significance of stylistic elements (Longacre 1991b: 5–6). The interplay of archaeology and ethnography now has a significant history in Greece (Aschenbrenner 1976a; Chang 1981, 1993, 1994; Jacobsen 1985; Murray and Chang 1981; Murray and Runnels 1984; Sutton, this volume). While a number of these Greek ethnoarchaeological projects have focused on pottery production, relatively few of these ceramic studies have been published (see Vitelli 1984). Blitzer's (1990) recent work thus has considerable bearing on the present study.

Methods

The presentation below follows a technological format. The whole process of manufacturing and distributing finished pottery is discussed, with commentary on some of the decisions that affect this process interlacing the description. By laying out the data in this manner, an effort is made to point out how decision making has altered the form of the craft as practiced by this individual. Thus, the term traditional artisan should not be seen in this context as referring to an inflexible system followed by the craftsman. Instead, operating in a period of transition, he adapts his work to changing circumstances, primarily economic.

The subject of this study is Ioannis Sampson, a man in his mid-sixties when this research was done. The information for this report was obtained by means of several visits in 1981 and 1982 and a lengthy formal interview in 1983. Sampson was born and raised on the Cycladic island of Sifnos, noted for its potters (*pilouryoi*). Sifnos has been a source of both pottery and craftsmen; many of the latter have migrated to various parts of Greece, establishing themselves in Messenia, Amaroussi (outside Athens), Chalkis, and Aegina (Matson 1972: 213). Traditionally, the trade passed from father to son. For Sampson, both his father and grandfather were potters, and he learned the craft from them on the island. As an adolescent in the 1930s, he moved to the mainland, eventually coming to Ermioni during the Axis occupation and establishing his shop in its present location in the fertile valley on the western fringe of the town. To his knowledge, in the 1980s he was the only individual currently plying his trade in the region. Since no candidates for apprenticeship have yet appeared, he may also have been the last such artisan to operate in the southern Argolid.

The Workshop

Sampson's workshop lay at the edge of a moderate-sized citrus grove in the fertile valley at the western edge of the town of Ermioni. The complex was originally a farmhouse with associated structures. These were modified and expanded in order to accommodate ceramic production. Figure 14.1 presents the layout of the complex, including location of the kiln, storage rooms, work area, and settling pools. Sampson built the kiln, the wood shed, and two pottery storage rooms, giving the complex an agglutinative appearance. The courtyard served as a place for newly formed vessels to dry to a leather-hard condition, after which they were stacked in one of the storage rooms. In general, the workshop resembled those in Messenia studied by Matson (1972: 214) and Blitzer (1990: 689, 694). A large electric pump had been installed in the enlarged wellhouse to draw up groundwater, but this seems to have been as much a consequence of the need to irrigate the citrus trees as it was to provide water for pottery-related activities.

Procurement of Raw Materials

When asked about local clay sources, Sampson indicated there were several in the area. At one time he used to collect his material from these sources. No money was expended for this clay, but its procurement involved considerable effort in extracting, transporting, and preparing the material (see Blitzer 1990: 680). By the 1980s, he had long since abandoned this practice, opting instead to purchase prepared clay. This material was mined near Khalkhis on Euboea. It was then taken to factories in the Athens vicinity for processing. This clay was of high quality and required only minimal preparation by the potter. Every one to one and one-half months, as he acquired *kefi* (the spirit or desire) to do work, Sampson traveled to factories in Piraeus that sold construction materials. He then purchased three to four tons of clay, depending on how much work he intended to do. This amount was less than he had required when he was engaged in full-scale production, and he anticipated it to continue to decline as he got older. There were numerous indications that, by the time I spoke with him, he was engaging in his trade more as a matter of interest than economic necessity and so was no longer overly concerned with the level of his production.

The price paid for the clay varied from two drachmas per kilo to as high as fifteen drachmas per kilo in 1983.[3] There were yet more expensive clays, but he did not bother with these. A typical load cost him 6,000–8,000 drachmas for the cheap clay and 45,000–60,000 drachmas

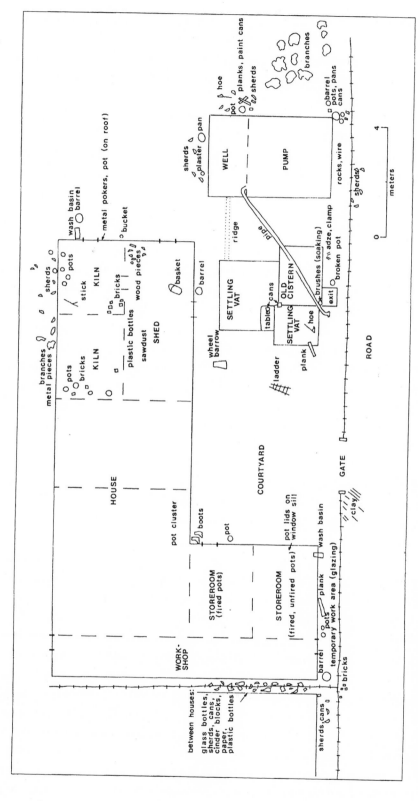

Figure 14.1. Plan of potter's workshop, showing location of production facilities, associated artifacts, and debris, Ermioni.

for the better quality material. His order was usually brought in by truck and only occasionally by boat; this did not seem to add any further cost to the price paid. Once it arrived, it was divided into small allotments and placed in plastic bags that could be brought out as needed. No other preparation was required since the clay was ready for utilization as it arrived.

The concrete basins in the courtyard had once been used to prepare locally extracted clay by allowing the heavier sediments to settle out. These basins were still employed in the 1980s, as witnessed by the presence of dried clay cut into squares. Material derived from mistakes in the forming process was tossed into the basins, allowing the clay to soften again for reuse. Such clay was ready to be used in several hours, but Sampson often let it sit for a day or more, depending on his immediate need. The quality of the clay precluded the necessity of any temper.

Vessel Formation

The moistened clay was taken to the long, narrow workroom where it was kneaded on a low stone bench that projected from the south wall (see Figure 14.2). Kneading the clay brought it to the right consistency, depending on the type of vessel intended. For Sampson, there was no set time for this process, as it was a matter of touch for him. While throwing pots on the wheel, he periodically interrupted this activity to knead the clay before extracting an amount to use. From a technological standpoint, kneading uniformly distributed moisture and inclusions, and helped to eliminate air bubbles and voids, all of which could adversely affect vessel survivability during firing (Rye 1981: 40).

Pots were thrown on an electrically powered wheel. An old kick wheel stood nearby in the workroom, but served only as a radio stand. Forming of vessels was accomplished by use of hands, a small, flat rectangular piece of wood, a sponge, a piece of wire, and a comb, the first three of which were regularly dipped into a bowl of water. A string was used to cut away bases from the rotating wheel and completed the list of accoutrements.

To determine a basic work rate, I inquired how long it took for him to throw a pot and checked this against earlier observations. A large water jug with a single handle took approximately four to five minutes, smaller vessels only several minutes each. At one sitting, he made only five to twenty pieces, again depending on his desire to work. There was obviously no longer a pressing economic need for him to produce in large quantities. His children were adults and on their own, and the citrus grove provided an independent income. In a purely economic sense, ceramic work was thus a secondary pursuit now, although it was still the means by which he was identified in the community. This reduction in production level was largely due to his age, but the impact of mass-produced vessels, both ceramic and other, could not be ignored. The degree to which such products affected his output, however, was difficult to assess. I was given to believe that if an apprentice were available, the workshop would have been producing more pottery. Sampson's schedule might not have changed radically, since he wanted someone to take up the slack rather than becoming fully involved again, as he once was, in all phases of the operation. It seems to have been more the lack of an apprentice than the changing economic situation that contributed to his lower work pace; demand for his products still remains rather high, but we were unable to determine how this level compared with the past in any truly quantitative sense.

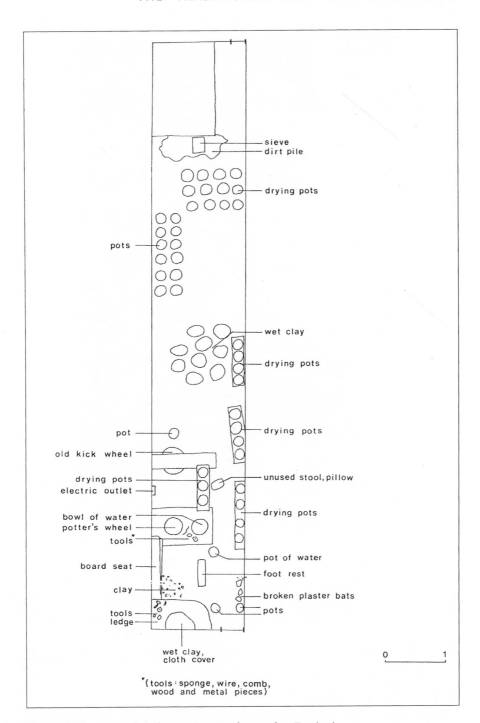

Figure 14.2.   Plan of workroom in potter's complex, Ermioni.

The situation in the 1980s contrasted with his early career when he estimated he averaged 200 pieces per day, with variations from this mean depending on the types of vessel manufactured. As a young man, he could produce 400 to 500 small pieces or 125 to 150 large vessels per day. Using 200 vessels and four to five minutes per piece as standards, one derives an average work day of 13.3 to 16.7 hours. His work pace may have been more rapid in past years, thus

Figure 14.3.   Ioannis Sampson forming a coin bank (*koumbara*) on the electric potter's wheel, Ermioni.

reducing this figure. These production figures can be compared with data obtained from studies of other individual potters. In Georgia, an exceptional worker could produce 400 one-gallon jugs in a day; a typical workday in the late nineteenth century was eight hours in winter and ten hours in warmer seasons (Burrison 1983: 31, 86). A ceramic artist in South Africa threw 30 casserole dishes in a one-half hour work period (Clark and Wagner 1974: 17). Such work rates do not seem to be the norm but rather fall on the high end of the scale. For Sampson, such a level of production does not seem to have been a sustained effort, but was instead somewhat sporadic. A ten-hour workday seems to be a much more reasonable estimate as the norm. In addition, various other chores that required attention would preclude the continuous output of such large numbers of vessels. Since he had been the only potter in the region for a substantial time, it is conceivable that he sometimes maintained high production levels to meet local demand. In addition one must consider that not every day was spent solely in throwing pots. Nonetheless, a long workday (perhaps ten to twelve hours) is clearly attested. By the time of my interviews, Sampson spent no more than four or five hours per day at his trade. This drop had less to do with a decline in demand for his wares than with other factors and is discussed below.

Figure 14.4. Ioannis Sampson in the process of glazing a water pitcher (*kanata*).

Once formed, the vessels needed to dry for one day to reach leather-hard texture, but they would often sit longer, until he accumulated enough pieces to fill the kiln. In the leather-hard condition, pots could be handled with less risk of misshaping them. It is in this state that the vessels were glazed. This process involved buying a white base mixture that was combined with water in a large ceramic basin. Using a soup ladle, he poured the mixture into a pot then swished it around to get even coverage before pouring out the excess. Turning the piece upside down, he then dipped it into the basin, covering minimally the top one-fourth and up to the entire outer surface except for the base, depending on its height. When fired, this glaze took on a deep reddish-brown hue, with drip lines and fingerprints evident. It took five to ten seconds to do a small piece, such as a yogurt bowl, and twenty to thirty seconds for larger pots. The prepared vessels were placed in one of the storage rooms to await firing.

As an entrepreneur attuned to the demands of his market, Sampson produced a range of wares (see Figure 14.5). He asserted there was no one particular type that predominated, but simply that the variety of types reflected local needs. One of the most common types was the flower pot (*glastra*), which came in assorted sizes. The largest of these was formed in two parts and subsequently joined in the middle. The water jugs (*stamnes*) also came in several sizes and functioned well in keeping water cool. Small and large lidded jars (*kioupia*) could be used for storing olives and other foodstuffs. Low bowls with flat bases and straight sides (*yiouvetsia*) were commonly used in making yogurt; these and the *kioupia* had glazed interiors. Specialty items included censers (*thimiata*) and domed coin banks (*koumbaradhes*). There were variations, in terms of body and rim ornamentation, on certain basic shapes among all of these types. There was no evidence that Sampson made wine jars (*vikia*), large soup vessels (*kapaklia*), or large storage pots (*pithoi*), all of which were commonly manufactured in Messenia in the 1960s (Matson 1972: 220–223). Blitzer (1990: 683–693) has also documented a broad range of wares, including eight types of *pitharia*, in Messenia.

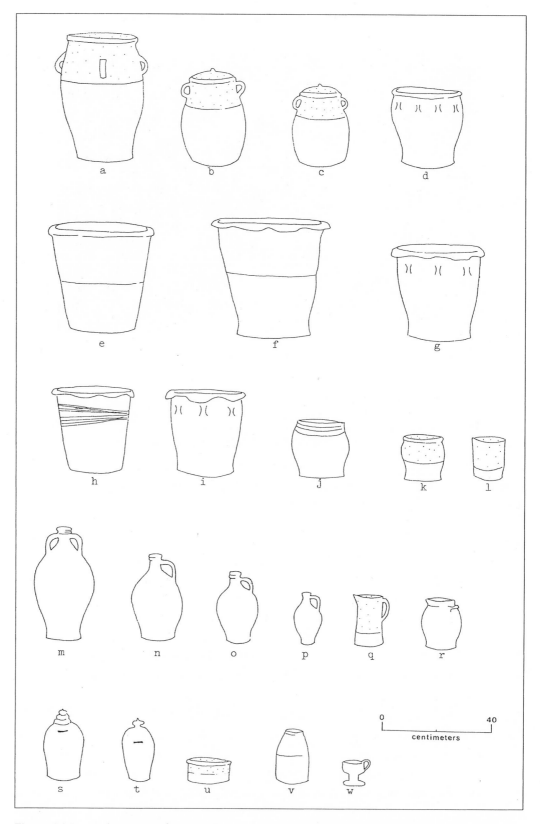

Figure 14.5. Various types of pots produced at Sampson workshop, Ermioni. Stippling indicates glaze. *a*, small storage pot (*pithari*); *b–c*, lidded storage jars (*kioupia*); *d–j*, flower pots (*glastres*); *k–l, r, v*, various unlidded storage jars (*vaza*); *m–p*, water jugs (*stamnes*); *q*, pitcher (*kanata*); *s–t*, coin banks (*koumbaradhes*); *u*, yogurt bowl (*youvetsi*); *w*, censer (*thimiato*).

Firing

The kiln was located in the northeast corner of the building complex, furthest away from the workshop where vessels were shaped. In form, it was an updraft kiln, with the firebox immediately beneath the chamber and separated from it by a perforated brick floor that permitted the entry of both heat and gases that reacted with the vessels. There were several disadvantages to such a system. A reducing atmosphere was difficult to obtain, and there was often an uneven distribution of temperature, with the bottom of the chamber getting much hotter than the rest, resulting in overfiring and the creation of many wasters. Nonetheless, it was a relatively efficient system and was widely used in the Mediterranean region (Rye 1981: 98–100).

Firing the pottery was a demanding task. In order to exploit efficiently each firing episode, Sampson waited until he had made enough vessels to fill the kiln (approximately 500 pieces) before proceeding with what he described as his least favorite aspect of the craft. The fire required constant monitoring for some ten hours in order to maintain a steady even heat that assured a

Figure 14.6. Updraft kiln, Sampson workshop, Ermioni. The opening to the firebox is in foreground, and several pots and brick separators are visible in the chamber.

sound final product. At his then rate of production, it could take him up to five weeks to accumulate a sufficient number of pieces to warrant use of the kiln. In the past, with much higher output, firings could have occurred as frequently as twice a week, but he gave no clear indication of this. In Messenia, the average firing also included five hundred vessels, but assistants, not the potter himself, tended the kiln (Blitzer 1990: 695–97).

The kiln required prodigious amounts of fuel to accomplish its task. When asked where he obtained the requisite amount of wood, Sampson answered that he got it all locally from wherever he could. A perusal of the storage shed adjacent to the kiln revealed the presence of a considerable amount of wood shavings, sawdust, and small pieces of particle board, all obviously collected from a local carpenter. In addition, in the orchard behind the pumphouse was a large stack of tree prunings awaiting use in the next firing episode. Thus, he evidently acquired most of his fuel from some commercial source and supplemented this supply with twigs and branches from his property and perhaps that of his neighbors (see Blitzer 1990: 696).

In the process of firing there was a certain amount of loss as a result of vessel deformation through overfiring and other factors. The percentage of such wasters could vary dramatically. Sometimes very few pieces were ruined, while at other times a substantial number were lost. Sampson did not specify what factors influenced this process one way or the other. Blitzer (1990: 697) noted that breakage averaged about 3%, but could be as high as 40% if a major problem occurred during firing. Sampson collected the wasters and disposed of them in various areas at some distance from the shop. He vaguely indicated the upper part of the Ermioni Valley as a general location. Observation of the grounds, however, revealed a substantial number of sherds scattered around the periphery of the buildings.

Distribution

The matter of dispensing the finished products was the final concern. As with most other facets, Sampson dealt with this aspect basically on his own. He generally sold his pots personally, most often when people came to his shop. On occasion, he traveled to local villages, hawking his wares in the street from the back of his kamikaze vehicle. Sales in larger quantities were made to several merchants in Kranidhi, but these seemed to be the only intermediaries. This situation contrasted with that in Messenia where potters sold their wares directly to truckers who often placed orders well in advance and distributed the wares to a variety of village general stores; the wider network in that region involved captains of caïques who made purchases at Koroni and disposed of the merchandise during their commercial trips to various islands and coastal areas of the mainland (Matson 1972: 220; Blizter 1990: 698–704).

The prices Sampson charged for his vessels were arranged according to the general expenses he encountered. Prices for materials, electricity, and other items had risen dramatically in the past ten years, and he adjusted his accordingly. Although he could not or would not specify the exact procedure for fixing prices, he did seem to have a clear sense of the vagaries of a market economy. With the shift to clay purchased from factories and increased mechanization (electric water pump, electric wheel, motorcycle for transport), he had more cost outlays than when he began working in the area, but these must be balanced against the amount of time and effort conserved and the enhanced efficiency of the operation. By making such adjustments, Sampson maintained a profitable enterprise even though his level of production had dropped considerably. When asked how the volume of his business had changed over the years, he said that it had fluctuated, but remained at a good level overall. He was certain that he could sell everything that he made and much more, but preferred to maintain a slower pace because he was getting tired and did not have any help. He noted that there was a great demand for certain types of items in the tourist trade, but his pots were not intended for that market, being essentially utilitarian in nature. Nonetheless, local demand was such that he could maintain a full-time status if he so desired.

Archaeological Implications

From the standpoint of physical layout, this study suggests the self-contained nature of a potter's workshop. All of the necessary facilities exist in a rather confined space: a compound with settling basins to prepare the clay, work shed to house the wheel, storage areas for unfired pots and fuel, and a kiln. Voyatzoglou (1979: 46) asserts that virtually all ceramic workshops in Greece are similar in layout; the work areas possess all of these features, and are also associated directly with the artisan's home. Work areas are often just rooms in a domestic structure, as is the case in rural Pakistan (Rye and Evans 1976: 168). The archaeological identification of such complexes should be a relatively easy matter, providing ample evidence for craft specialization. The exact nature of this specialization would be more difficult to ascertain. The presence of animal pens and agricultural fields in direct association with the workshop/home may provide some difficulty in interpreting the extent of specialization vis-à-vis agricultural and/or pastoral activities. Perhaps the size of animal pens or visible field markers can assist in determining whether raising food was a supplemental or primary activity. This combination of pottery workshop and facilities for other economic pursuits may be seen as symptomatic of an individual craftsman's strategy of risk reduction. An urban artisan with a larger clientele and involvement in a large-scale entrepreneurial enterprise would have less to fear from concentrating solely on his craft, and his household may reflect that in its lack of diversity, that is, less space allowed for nonceramic economic activities.

A major focus in this study has been the adaptation of the craftsman to shifting economic circumstances. A key question thus becomes how this change might be reflected in the material record at the Sampson workshop. One significant change was in the procurement of clay, with the adoption of factory-prepared material. This was reflected in the absence or lack of tools for extracting clay, such as picks, shovels, and various large containers. In addition, the need for processing clay in settling basins had been minimized, and thus this facility was less utilized. Over time the basins may fall into complete disuse and deteriorate, reflecting the shift in acquisition of raw materials.

The presence of two wheels indicated the adoption of a more efficient technology. The electric wheel enhanced production levels, allowing Sampson to increase his pottery output or to turn the extra time to other pursuits. In either case, the use of the electric wheel spoke of a desire to adopt innovations when some advantage was clearly envisioned. It thus seems too simplistic to suggest that "traditional" potters were by nature conservative, as stated by Foster (1965: 48), without due consideration of the extenuating circumstances that formed the basis for various decisions.

Another significant feature in the workshop complex was the large pumphouse with electric motor for drawing up groundwater. Water is certainly a necessity in pottery production, but the size of the unit seemed to have a strong relationship to the cultivation of citrus fruit in the field adjoining the work area. The prodigious water requirements of citrus probably necessitated the large pump; it certainly provided much more than the basic requirement for the making of pottery. As in the other cases, this item reflected a change in economic strategy, with the de-emphasis of pottery production in more recent years as a key component.

The present study also has implications for the understanding of regional and national economies. Blitzer (1990: 708) points out that a centralized administration is not necessary to regulate trade that reaches even far beyond the local area. She demonstrates how Messenian potters, tradesmen, and ship captains produced and distributed various ceramic wares to take advantage of commercial opportunities created by international conditions in the nineteenth century. Ioannis Sampson exhibited similar tendencies; his decisions about ceramic production could also illuminate how past potters structured their activities in response to market changes in the ancient Ermionidha.

These several elements do not exhaust the possibilities for deriving archaeological inferences. One important question that could not be fully addressed with the information available was whether the material evidence reflects the status and financial well-being of the potter and how these may have changed as he altered his operation through time. This and other problems would benefit from additional studies stressing the link between behavior, social position, and their material correlates.

Conclusion

This brief account has presented some of the basic technological aspects of pottery production for an individual craftsman. In addition, an effort has been made to describe some factors that influenced the operation from an economic standpoint over the years. Since this attempt necessarily involves viewing the artisan as making decisions in a formalist economic sense, there is the implication that the term traditional does not tie one to an unvarying, monolithic set of cultural procedures. Instead, the potter was envisioned as an active participant in the changes going on around him that influenced his craft. It was true that he practiced his trade largely within the parameters laid down for him by convention. This was evident in the general techniques he employed and in the types of vessels produced. However, he also demonstrated an awareness of factors that had altered the potter's trade from what it was when he produced his first vessels. He has made conscious choices about the level of production he wished to maintain. A combination of factors conspired to make him opt for a slowdown in his work level. These elements include his age and the lack of willing individuals to become apprentices. As a young man, Sampson was a full-time specialist operating in all seasons, but by the 1980s he had adopted a much laxer schedule in a state of virtual semi-retirement. By following a more passive marketing strategy, he was able to spread out his sales over a longer time span and thus maintain a consistent, but low, level of business.

In the long run, the inability to attract any apprentices will spell the end of this particular role on the local level, with Sampson's products being replaced by vessels produced in factories some distance from the southern Argolid. It is in this sense that traditional pottery production is nearing elimination in the region, as the result of an expanding economic network with a modified set of incentives making people look elsewhere for their livelihoods. It is important to understand, however, that there has been no set pattern to this traditional production, but rather a constantly (although often gradually) changing array of behaviors, economic and otherwise. By recording any economic activity at one point in time, we are taking a slice of life that artificially freezes in place what is truly a dynamic process. Perhaps the best we can hope for is to observe as much of the variability as is possible and thus lend greater credibility to our explanations of cultural interplay. As Stanislawski (1978: 226) has stated, a key goal of ethnoarchaeology should be to garner data on the possible range of variation and thus make us aware of alternative ways of doing things. This examination of the work of Ioannis Sampson provided a glimpse into this process, with tradition proving to be a fluid thing, some might even say expendable, when confronted with other necessities.

CHAPTER FIFTEEN

"Nobody Weaves Here Anymore": Hand Textile Production in the Southern Argolid

Joan Bouza Koster

Why has the hand processing of household textiles persisted in the southern Argolid in face of major historical changes in technology and market integration that have occurred in Greece since 1800? Cross-cultural research indicates a strong association between agricultural intensification and the specialization of craft production. Why then, in a context of increasing agricultural intensification occurring in villages like Dhidhima in the southern Argolid, do some residents continue to perform all the steps in the elaborate process of converting raw fiber to cloth, when specialists for many of these processes have long existed? Why do they continue to produce low value, utilitarian fabrics, when since the nineteenth century manufactured yarn and cloth have been marketed at their doorsteps?

The southern Argolid provides an excellent location in which to study such questions. Although it appears to be a physically isolated peninsula, it has an extended history of connection with outside markets and has been exposed through trade to potential sources of external textiles. It is ethnically diverse, and textiles have been produced in the region from the level of the household to that of the modern factory. In recent decades, agricultural and pastoral production have intensified through much of the region (H. Koster 1977, 1996). Ethnographic data on hand textile production have been collected in this region over the last twenty-five years, providing a unique view of changing practices.[1]

This paper analyzes the hand production of textiles in the context of social and economic factors that have enabled this production to persist or be abandoned over the last one hundred years.[2] Through such analysis, those factors that have encouraged or discouraged textile self-sufficiency in the southern Argolid are defined. The variables of class status, household developmental cycle, fiber availabilty, occupational textile needs, ethnic identification, time and labor, and the dowry system are examined in terms of the changes brought by the industrialization of textile production that has recently taken place in Greece. From these data, I construct a model suggesting which kinds of households continue to hand produce textiles in post-industrial contexts. Such an analysis should prove useful not only to textile specialists interested in how and why such textiles are made, but also to historians studying the effects of industrialization on household economies, and to archaeologists interested in labor expenditures required for the hand production of cloth.

The Survival of Hand-Produced
Textiles in Modern Contexts

With the invention in the eighteenth century of the spinning jenny, a revolution began in the mass production of textiles. In the century that followed, new and improved machines such as the cotton gin and the Jacquard mechanism fostered the rapid introduction and use of manufactured cloth throughout the world. Between 1821 and 1887, English factories alone produced over one hundred million miles of cloth (Baity 1942: 268), so that the English, faced with textile production capacity that far outstripped domestic needs, actively exported manufactured cloth to countries such as India that had previously been an exporter of textiles (Fox 1985: 16). By the twentieth century, the use of spinning wheels and handlooms had moved to the status of quaint customs in northern Europe and America.

Yet, throughout the world, including the developed nations of Europe and North America, some people continue to hand produce textiles using slow, tedious, and ancient methods. Such fabrics, produced from raw fibers by a household for its own use, represent a class of textiles widely produced throughout the world, but rarely analyzed. Much of the literature of anthropology and folklore has focused on more elaborate textiles with ceremonial or symbolic forms and meanings, and on those that represent commodities. A body of research, for example, discusses the effects of tourism on the form and function of traditional crafts (Graburn 1976) but ignores textiles that have not been affected by commoditization. Textile specialists have written a great deal about the techniques and tools used to create these textiles, but much less about why such simple forms endure.[3]

In a world of looms that can weave faster than the eye can see, the survival of such crude methods remains a paradox. It is commonly assumed that mechanization of textile production is cheaper and more efficient. Therefore, if hand production persists, it must be because the people are ignorant of improved methods or lack sufficient capital for mechanization.

Petty Commodity Production

There is, however, a growing anthropological literature describing the competitive efficiency of petty commodity producers in the face of industrial competition (Kahn 1980; Long et al. 1986; Netting 1993; Smith 1984; Swallow 1982). In some cases hand production methods have persisted as cherished relics of the past, performed in museum settings or relearned from historical records by people in search of cultural roots. Hand methods may also survive because they lend intrinsic value to textiles that have been commercialized, such as Oriental carpets, Navajo rugs, or Harris tweeds (Spooner 1986: 224). In other cases, hand methods persist where labor is cheap or can be exploited to produce textile commodities with high labor input and low capital investment. This is the basis of many cottage industries, ranging from North American "designer" handwovens to simplified reproductions of traditional textiles, intended for the tourist trade, such as the Mexican "wedding dress" (Waterbury 1989).

Many subcontracting systems continue to flourish even where sufficient capital exists for the construction of fully mechanized plants, because it is more cost effective to require the peasant household to meet the costs of social reproduction. Such systems also offer the entrepreneur greater insulation from the vagaries of fluctuating market conditions, as the factory owner has less capital tied up in physical plant and often a reduced social commitment to peasant subcontractors (Swallow 1982: 133).

Domestic Production

Petty commodity production is not the only way in which handmade textiles continue to be produced. They may also be made by household members for their domestic consumption. A degree of textile self-sufficiency is found in communities in such diverse geographic locales as the Andean Highlands and Iran (Casagrande 1977; Martin 1986; Orlove 1977; Zorn 1979). Such production was common in the Appalachian Mountains in the eastern United States and in the Canadian Maritime Provinces as late as 1950.[4]

Similarly, textiles produced by hand today in the southern Argolid are not intended for any market. They represent part of a "hidden" production and are neither notable for their design or construction nor easily visible to strangers passing through the communities. Unlike other areas of Greece, such as Metsovo or Eressos (Pavlides and Hesser 1986), the majority of textiles produced in the southern Argolid have not been intended for household decoration or market and so do not feature elaborate patterns, complicated tapestry inlays, or traditional stylistic symbols that might attract the attention of textile connoisseurs. Instead, these have been productive textiles serving practical uses in the herding and agricultural systems of the region. Rough and coarse, these homespun textiles are, for example, walked upon with muddy feet, thrown on the ground for the noonday meal, or used to wrap a fresh cheese being transported down a mountainside.

Not only are these textiles in essence invisible, but so are the spinners and weavers. It is quite possible to walk through a village in the southern Argolid and find no looms, nor anyone who professes to weave. "Nobody does that anymore" is a common statement heard about weaving in these villages. But once in a while, one stumbles across an old woman spinning or someone weaving rag rugs or saddlebags at a loom set up in some low, roofed shed or storehouse. These instances provide a glimpse into activities that when analyzed prove to have been, and in some cases continue to be, an integral element of the economic and social life of the Argolid.

Preindustrial Textile Production in the Southern Argolid

In the preindustrial society of early nineteenth century Greece, hand-processing methods provided the fabrics necessary for supplying warmth and comfort in a rugged existence. These fabrics also performed important roles in the technologies of cheese making, oil pressing, and herding. In addition, homespun, handwoven fabrics were featured in the local costumes worn throughout Greece as late as the 1940s. Before the industrialization of textile production in the second half of the nineteenth century, such textiles were produced in Greece either in the home or by a small class of professional weavers and spinners.

Following Goody's model, three levels of commodity production may be identified as existing in Greece during this period—"cottage craftsmen," "cottage laborers," and "small factories" (Goody 1982: 12). Cottage craftsmen, or professional weavers, produced cloth for payment.

Loukopoulos found that in Aetolia one or two fine weavers wove professionally in every village (Loukopoulos 1927: 23). In the southern Argolid independent artisans worked in their homes, often on a part-time basis, to supplement their incomes (Petronoti, this volume).

Cottage laborers worked for a merchant who provided the raw fiber and then marketed the finished fabrics paying on a piece basis. These people also performed various stages of textile production for wealthy households that furnished the fiber. This work was often performed on the basis of patron-client ties in which peasant women spun for a landowner upon whom they also depended for agricultural day labor.

Small factories or workshops also existed in which merchants gathered together tools and employees under one roof and where many or all of the processes were done. A few specialized weaving establishments were located in Kranidhi. These workshops produced sailcloth, yardage for garments, sacks, blankets, and rugs. Raw materials were purchased or imported and the resulting fabric marketed locally to particular social groups (Petronoti 1985b: 265, this volume).

Alongside this preindustrial textile market-production system, agricultural and pastoral families produced a range of fabrics required in daily life such as knitted sweaters and socks and woven blankets, rugs, sheets, and towels. Herding families also wove specialized fabrics related to their occupation such as hut coverings, mats for the floor of their huts, capes, and saddlebags. These items were produced only for use within the home, often in the context of providing a young woman's dowry.

All these levels of production were serviced by a class of specialized artisans. Often itinerant, these craftsmen offered specialized services or sold and repaired the tools required for hand textile production. For example, the *lanaras* was a craftsman who traveled through villages in the summer months repairing and replacing carding cloth and wool combs. In addition, there were professonal dyers, tailors, reed makers, and fullers.

Industrialization of Textile Production

In the late nineteenth century, textile production became one of the first sectors of the Greek economy to be mechanized, leading it to be by 1964 "the most productively organized manufacturing activity in the country" (Kayser and Thompson 1964). The earliest factories were small, family-owned establishments, making simple fabrics and threads, principally of domestic cottons, and in Macedonia, of finer wool (Kyriakidou-Nestoros 1983: 7). Marketed throughout Greece by means of small shops and itinerant merchants, the manufactured cottons were a tremendous success. Major growth in this industry occurred during the 1920s, stimulated by the influx of refugees and their capital from Asia Minor, many of whom established larger textile factories, drawing upon cotton grown in the productive plains of northern Greece (Hirschon 1989).

By 1927, hand processing of cotton had disappeared from many parts of Greece (Loukopoulos 1927: 7–9), and by the 1970s, the Greek textile industry had a few large modern textile mills such as Piraiki-Patraiki, employing one thousand workers in Patras, and many small mills employing from one to ten workers (see Table 15.1).

In 1970, Greek manufactured cottons were the most common fabrics offered for sale in stores and by peddlers throughout the southern Argolid. By 1975, imported fabrics were far

Table 15.1

Weaving Factories and Number of Employees in Greece, 1978

Number of employees	0–4	5–9	10–19	20–29	30–49	50–99	100+
Number of factories	3,272	787	414	156	139	117	164

NOTE: Greece, National Statistical Service (1985: 190).

more prevalent and competed directly with the Greek cotton yardage. Today, with membership in the EU, market penetration for all kinds of fabrics is complete. Manufactured yarns and fabrics from around the world are found in virtually all Greek homes.

The Demise of Cottage Weavers and Laborers

The professional cottage craftsmen and laborers have largely disappeared from the southern Argolid.[5] Professional weaving, often a supplementary occupation at best, became unviable in the region by the 1940s and 50s. By this time, the extensive yardage required for traditional dress was no longer needed,[6] and the textile needs formerly fulfilled by the professional could now be met through purchasing manufactured cloth. The two professional weavers in the *koinotis* of Dhidhima, for example, both abandoned their craft during this period. One, a landless woman, emigrated to Athens in 1940. The other, a weaver of garment yardage living in Radho, became a full-time farmer and shepherd. Corresponding declines can be seen in other craft specializations, particularly those relating to garments (see Petronoti, Kardulias, this volume). The Dhidhima *dhimotoloyio* lists twenty-three shoemakers, seven tailors, and eight seamstresses in 1955. Twenty years later there were only one shoemaker, two tailors, two seamstresses, and no professional weavers in trade.

Although in some regions of Greece, such as Crete, professional handweaving has been stimulated by the tourist economy, international tourism came too late to stimulate a similar market for the indigenous textiles of the southern Argolid. Coarse and plain, the locally made saddlebags and blankets offered for sale by a few merchants in Kranidhi were described by tourists as "scratchy" and "crude," and soft, colorful products woven in Crete and northern Greece from imported fibers were purchased instead.

Weaving for pay has always been considered a low status occupation, and the decline in professional weaving also reflects the availability of higher status sources of income such as working in the region's hotels or the factories of Nafplio. In Aetolia, Loukopoulos recorded a saying that reflects the low view held of weaving for money: "Weaving for strangers in order to live, how poor you are!" (Loukopoulos 1927: 24). Weaving for cash payment is still disparaged in the village of Dhidhima. Women state with great pride that they do not "sell" their textiles.

Mechanization of Textile Workshops

Growing out of the preindustrial workshops, small textile-related enterprises continue to operate in the Argolid region. These factories provide such services as spinning yarn, carding wool, and fulling handweavings. Although hand methods are no longer used, many of these family firms utilize early industrial technology. Turn-of-the-century mule spinners and "sample" carding machines discarded by northern European industry have replaced the hand labor of the preindustrial workshop. Most of the wool carded in the region is done by small mills in Kranidhi, Methana, and Ligourio. In Kranidhi, a family owned and operated business runs a small, belt-driven, vintage carder. Residents from the surrounding villages send their washed wool to the carding mill by bus or truck and pay a relatively small fee for the service.

Custom weaving is also available. Factories located in Argos and Tripolis send trucks throughout the region collecting orders and yarn and delivering finished goods. In these small family-owned factories employing only a handful of workers antique Jacquard looms are used to weave heavy woolen blankets (*kouvertes*), pictorial cotton/woolen coverlets (*heramia*), and tapestry woolen rugs (*kilimia*) using purchased cotton warps and domestic homespun, wool weft yarns provided by the customer. In the southern Argolid these Jacquard weavings are a relatively recent introduction dating from the late 1960s. Although the factories have been in operation much longer, some from soon after the Greek Civil War, it was not until the economic advances of the 1960s that the inhabitants of Dhidhima and neighboring villages in the lower pennisula had enough disposable income to afford the weaving fee and that factories could afford to expand and truck so far from their home base.

These Jacquard mills, although mechanized, are not small factories in Goody's terms, but rather fill the role of the cottage craftsmen, utilizing the dyed yarn brought by the client and exacting a fee for the weaving service. The final product belongs to the client or peasant family.

Handmade Textiles and Social Differentiation

As demonstrated in other articles in this volume, the southern Argolid supports a mixed economy based upon agriculture, pastoralism, sailing, day labor, mining, artisanal activity, and tourism, with the development of class differences. Important factors determining which families continue to weave are the family's main occupation and social class.

The Wealthy

Wealthy landholders specializing in olive cultivation raise thousands of trees, whereas other well-off inhabitants of the region have been involved in shipping, sponge fishing, and small businesses (see Petronoti, Sutton, this volume). The wealthier households of the southern Argolid have never had to weave. In the nineteenth century these households provided the market for much of the handwoven production of local cottage industries and professional handweavers and later were able to purchase manufactured luxury fabrics imported into the region during the heyday of the Kranidhiote shipping industry (Petronoti 1985b: 270, this volume). Today this group has the resources to buy any textile produced in the world.

The Bourgeoisie

During the nineteenth century, the upwardly mobile class of small shopkeepers and tradesmen often had excess cash with which to purchase handwovens or, if financially limited, were able to put out parts of the process, such as spinning or dyeing, to poorer relatives or professionals. Bourgeois women, however, had the free time available to devote to the textile arts, so that they were among those most likely to make decorative textiles. With the introduction of manufactured cloth this group could more easily emulate the wealthy. Today they view hand-weaving as a relic of the past that is rapidly disappearing from the Greek landscape. Family handwovens tend to be those done by mother or grandmother. Daughters are not taught weaving skills but may be quite skilled at the higher status textile activities of embroidery and fine crochet.

The Poor

There has always been a rural class of landless poor and other very poor who have scratched out a meager existence by working at seasonal day labor in agriculture and construction, by exploiting the environment in charcoal and lime making, and by providing cheap labor for the local mine and quarries. Although in the nineteenth century the poor and landless as cottage laborers provided much of the labor force that spun and wove for the rich, they themselves produced few textiles of their own. Poor families, because they lacked the land to devote to cotton and flax or the capital to raise sheep or goats, were compelled to meet their domestic textile needs through cast-offs, by purchasing a few woven goods from the local, professional weavers, or by accepting fiber as payment in kind for their day labor and processing it themselves.

When cheap manufactured cloth became available, poor families could use some of their small income to purchase limited quantities. Today, with the general economic growth in the region, as well as the earlier redistribution of monastic lands (see Adams, this volume), there are fewer abjectly poor. Those households more heavily committed to day labor, however, do less weaving than agricultural or pastoral families in the region.

Smallholders: Agriculturalists and Herders

In the past, the group most heavily involved in textile production for home use was that of small-scale agriculturalists and herders. Most families are, and have been for the nineteen century, small producers who attempt to raise a subsistence crop with some surplus to sell in good years. Many locally based herders have also practiced agriculture, as have many of the transhumants who used the region for winter pasture. These smallholders (Netting, 1993) produced finished textiles from the raw fiber, doing most of the processing tasks themselves. They did not have ready cash to purchase sufficient quantities of professionally handwoven cloth, nor to put out all the processing tasks, yet they required many textiles for specific agricultural and herding activities.

Although in recent decades the region has experienced a growing cash economy, costs and perceived needs have also increased. This means that, although most households may have more cash, many still do not have enough to readily purchase all of their textile needs. For example, smallholders raising cash crops must invest in water pumps and irrigation equipment. Shepherds intensifying their flocks' milk production must purchase more supplementary feeds (H. Koster 1977: 241–242). As cheap manufactured cloth has become available it has been substituted whenever economically possible for some of the traditional fabrics. Those textiles that cannot be economically or functionally replaced by manufactured cloth, however, continue to be woven.

Since weaving is related to class and occupation, it will not be found distributed evenly throughout the region, but rather predominantly in those areas with high proportions of small-holders and especially where households emphasize herding, whether local or transhumant. For the period of 1970 to 1995, the highest amount of textile production occurred in the upland communities of Dhidhima, Loukaiti, Radho, Karakasi, Ano Fanari, Trakheia, Karatza, Bafi, Skapeti, and in the coastal communities with higher populations of herders from Arcadia and Corinthia. Agricultural households were more likely to weave if they resided in communities with a larger commitment to pastoralism, because they were not only surrounded by active weavers among the herders but also had readily available wool.

The Survival of Domestic Production

Changes in regional textile production reflect changes in the region's economy. Textile production no longer is practiced on the same level as at the beginning of the twentieth century. In agricultural and herding households where hand-produced textiles continue to be made, several factors influence the family's decision to use the labor intensive preindustrial technology of drop spindle, wool combs, and counterbalanced loom in order to create purely domestic textiles.

Availability of Raw Fibers

In the preindustrial past agriculturalists raised cotton, flax, and hemp for their own use. These crops were grown in small plots throughout the region as early as the seventeenth century. Cotton was one of the main exports for the region listed by the Venetians (Topping, this volume), and Miliarakis listed a small amount of production of cotton for the *demoi* of Ermioni, Kranidhi, and Dhidhima, noting that this was for local use (1886: 214). Elderly inhabitants remember flax and cotton being grown in small plots in the Dhidhima basin for family use. Women in their eighties still know how to hand process and spin cotton, even though they have not done so in years. By 1973, only a few families continued to work with flax and cotton, as in Methana where locally grown flax was retted in the sea and handpicked cotton, obtained by families with ties to northern Greece, was still being spun and woven by hand (Clarke 1987: personal communication; Forbes 1982: 164).

Neither flax nor cotton are particularly suited to the climate of the southern Argolid, so when machine-woven cloth and yarn became available, it was not surprising that fiber cultivation was terminated and the land planted in more productive crops. No longer did land have to be devoted to a crop that was uncompetitive beyond the region and that provided the family with neither food nor cash. Valuable agricultural land could now be dedicated to food and cash crops alone. With the disappearance of plant fibers many inhabitants also stopped weaving the traditional cotton and linen towels and swaddling cloths.

The competition of plant fibers with other agricultural crops is in direct contrast to the status of animal fibers in the Argolid. Wool and goat hair are essentially by-products of the primary production of the herd—milk and meat. Wool and goat hair have always been an important, but secondary, product of the pastoral economy. The southern Argolid has generally supported a large number of sheep and goats kept principally for their milk and meat (Forbes, H. Koster, this volume). These animals, however, also provide a ready supply of fibers that both are easier to hand process than flax or cotton and have the qualities of durability and high insulation value.

The durability, strength, and water resistance of goat hair has made this fiber extremely useful to shepherds and goatherds. The small, hardy goats, kept in flocks of from one to five hundred, are, like sheep, primarily producers of milk and meat; each goat produces, in addition, a small quantity (from 1/4 to 1/2 kg) of hair, which is clipped annually from the back and flanks of the animal. Goat hair customarily has been used in large part by shepherds and goatherds for fabrics essential to their occupation. The durability and water resistance of goat hair fabrics is exceptional (heavy capes made of goat hair have traditionally been used in Greece, not only by herders but also by mariners and soldiers, for protection from the elements). Hut coverings, mats, and rugs for hut and house floors, herders' capes, ropes, and saddlebags, especially those for collecting carobs, were the principal domestic uses for goat hair in the past, and to some extent these uses continue today. Goat hair has also been traded for wool between herding households so that goatherding families regularly have wool to use and sheep herders have goat hair.

Commercial uses for goat hair have also existed. Until 1941, goat hair was used in Kranidhi workshops for the weaving of *tserges* (Petronoti 1985b: 270, this volume). This enterprise collapsed when sufficient supplies of goat hair could not be obtained because of the war (Petronoti 1985b: 71, this volume). The strength of the fiber made it suitable for use in the manufacture of special bags (*sfridhes*) into which mashed olives were placed preparatory to being squeezed in the press.

With replacement of the traditional olive press by modern machinery, the market for goat hair all but disappeared. In 1974, goat hair could be sold to buyers from Nafplio for 11 drachmas per kilo. The goatherds complained that at this price, which represented a steep decline, it was not even worth the labor involved in shearing, transport, and storage. Today goat hair is no longer viewed as a commodity for marketing, but as a subsidiary product to be used by the family if needed or abandoned at the fold if not (see Chang, this volume).

The wool produced in the southern Argolid comes mainly from local varieties of a breed of sheep known technically as the Mountain Zackel. This small, hardy animal is eminently suited to producing quantities of milk on dry, rugged pasture. Wool has always been viewed as a minor product compared to the milk and meat produced by the flocks, so unlike the northern European wool breeds, many unwanted fleece characteristics have not been bred out of these sheep. The coarse, low crimp wool has a five to six inch staple, often contaminated with short black or white hairs (kemp), which do not dye. In addition, parti-colored sheep are found in all flocks, making it difficult to sort fleeces by color.

These characteristics make the wool most suitable for rugs and carpets and give it a low value in the world market. Even in Greece the market for domestic wool is limited. In 1982, for example, the Greek textile industry used 4,950 t (metric tons) out of a domestic wool production of 10,213 t in the traditional shaggy pile *flokati* (blankets or rugs) and in the Jacquard woven runners, rugs, and blankets. In addition, 10,322 t of wool were imported (Greece, NSS 1985: 170, 214, 292). The larger textile firms and many smaller producers, whose products are aimed at the tourist market, are major consumers of imported wool, particularly from Australia and New Zealand (Hellenic Bank 1970).

The price for raw wool has remained rather stable over the last twenty years, while milk and meat prices have risen. In this period Dhidhima shepherds, for example, have been receiving about 20 to 30 drachmas per kilo for their raw fleeces and from 15 to 20 drachmas per kilo for their shorter, dirtier belly wool from buyers in Argos. For example, the production of a sample flock of sixty sheep for one year produces an income of $120 for the shepherd, at 2 kg per head of raw wool. This level of compensation pales before the returns for the sale of milk of $628, and of $691 for meat sales from the same size flock. It is not surprising that some villagers opt for utilizing the wool for their own, more local purposes rather than marketing it extraregionally. "We have the wool, so we must use it," shepherds commonly reply when queries as to why labor-intensive hand processing of wool persists in their households.

Textile Requirements of Herders

Since it is the herding households who are most likely to have a surplus of raw fiber in the southern Argolid, hand textile production has been found to be most commonly done by those households that keep sheep, and to a lesser extent households with goats. These households also have particular textile needs owing to the necessity of working outdoors and using more primitive shelters while on pasture. Transhumant herders and most extensive local herders, who fold their flocks often at distances of over two hours' walk from the village base, require textiles to cover the floor of their *kalivia* (huts) and to wrap and carry their belongings.

Transhumant households have traditionally woven fine goat hair coverings for their huts (*tentes*) and heavy felted mats (*velentza yidhino*) for the floors. In bad weather the herder would huddle under a heavy goat hair cape (*kapa*). Village-based herders, on the other hand, preferred layers of *leopannes* (woolen blankets) for flooring their huts and for wrapping items to be carried on the pack animals. All herders also used the multipurpose saddlebag (*tagari*). These sturdy bags, utilized for carrying a wide variety of items, have been an important part of the transport system.

There are few manufactured textiles that match the unique qualities of these handwoven ones. Attempts to substitute plastic for hut coverings are less than satisfactory, because the woven goat hair fabric, unlike plastic, allows fresh air to pass through while maintaining water resistance. Plastic bags can replace saddlebags, but woven bags last longer, carry heavier weights (up to 15 kg), and are easier to fasten securely to pack saddles. As long as a herding family maintains a hut as a living area they will continue to need these textiles. In the last five years, however, the bulldozing of rough roads to the upper pasture areas and the increasing ownership of small trucks have begun to eliminate the need for comfortable living conditions on pasture as transportation enables herders to easily commute to the mountain pastures daily from their homes in the village.

Ethnic Differentiation

In the southern Argolid there are three pastoral ethnic groups: the Arvanites, who form the majority of the population and keep their flocks within the region, and two transhumant groups, the Sarakatsani (or Roumeliotes as they are known locally), who graze their herds in the Argolid in the winter and in the mountains of Corinthia in the summer, and the Valtetsiotes and other Arcadian herders, who pasture in the Argolid in summer (Koster and Koster 1976).

Differentiated by language, customs, and heritage, these groups also have divergent weaving traditions. Ethnic differences are found between the Arvanites and the transhumants in the way that yarn is spun and in weaving techniques. Both transhumant groups use the unweighted horizontal spindle. This technique can be used for spinning all kinds of yarns but is best suited for loose, low-twist bulky yarns of wool and goat hair. These yarns are commonly used in the heavy goat hair mats and capes, as well as in handwoven blankets (*velentzes*). The Arvanites, in contrast, profess a distinct inability to spin this way, so that none of the Arvanite textile types display this kind of yarn but instead feature much higher twist yarns that are often tightly plied as well.

The tagari typifies the difference in weaving styles among these groups. An Arvanite tagari is all wool and very tightly beaten with a unique finger woven edging (see J. Koster 1981 for a complete description). Transhumant tagaria combine a cotton warp and wool weft and so are less dense than the Arvanite design. They usually feature brighter colors, however, and more complicated patterns and motifs. In tapestry work the Sarakatsani and Valtetsiotes use the interlock method to join areas of different colors, whereas the Arvanites use the slit method. It is not a case of ignorance of the technique that prevents the other group from using it, but rather the strongly held belief that an Arvantissa or Sarakatsanissa does not do it that way.

In discussing weavings done by another ethnicity, women often disparage the other group for using an inferior technique. The Arvanites say that the interlock method looks "sloppy," and the transhumants say that the slit method "leaves holes." There is no doubt in the minds of the weavers that the weavings of their own ethnic group are superior. The Sarakatsani pride themselves on weaving a great variety of fabrics, including the durable goat hair mats, the light, airy goat hair tentes, *flokates* and colorful *velentzes* (blankets). They feel they have the advantage in producing fulled fabrics because the fulling mills are located in their home villages. The Arcadians are proud of their complex and individualistic tapestry designs. The Arvanites believe that they excel at weaving because their pieces are tight and durable.

The traditional forms of dress that differentiated these ethnic groups might be gone, but through household weaving, members of these groups have been able to continue to distinguish themselves. While a plastic bag may serve to carry a herder's lunch, the ethnic identity of a shepherd with a tagari over his shoulder can easily be determined, even from a distance.

Division of Labor

Casual visitors to most rural Greek villages often assume that hand production no longer exists because they do not see anyone spinning or weaving. Although hand textile production

Figure 15.1. A Sarakatsanissa weaving a *flokati*, Dhidhima. Note wedding *tagari* hanging on the loom.

using preindustrial technology requires major investments in time and labor, much of the work is seasonal. At any particular moment, to expect to find numerous people weaving in their living quarters ignores its periodic occurrence in the pattern of rural life in this region. Weaving has never been a constant occupation among the smallholders of the Argolid. When not in use looms are disassembled into nondescript piles of rough timbers and stored in some dark corner of the storeroom or shed. When they are put together, they are almost never set up in the main living quarters of the home, where space is always at a premium, and the copious dust produced as well as the associated skeins of yarn, yarn winders, and shuttles would clutter the limited living space. Looms and their associated equipment are not viewed as aesthetically pleasing furniture, but rather as agricultural tools in the same class as plows, sickles, and storage containers.

Since weaving is not a constant activity, it is often easier, especially if space is constrained, to utilize a neighbor's loom (J. Koster 1976). Hence, relatively few families own looms of their own, and the number of looms in a village does not accurately reflect the actual number of weavers. In addition, these few looms are set up for only limited periods, usually one or two months at a time. Among the agriculturalists of the southern Argolid this is usually in late winter when storerooms are empty of grain and space can be found to place the loom. On the other hand, the transhumant herders—Sarakatsani and Valtetsiotes—almost always set up their looms on their summer pastures. Their weaving is done during the summer months, and their spinning is done during the winter in the Argolid.[7] It would be highly unusual to find a loom in the southern Argolid among the members of these groups who remain transhumant.

Table 15.2
Domestic Tasks Performed in a Household of Four, Dhidhima, 1971

Activity	Average (minutes)	per unit of time	Hours per year
Breadmaking	150	weekly	130
Carrying water	30	daily	182
Child care (grandchild)		variable	36
Collecting firewood	90	weekly	78
Collecting wild greens	75	60 days/year	75
Cooking	150	daily	913
Dishwashing	30	daily	183
Intra-village shopping	60	weekly	52
Ironing	30	130 days/year	65
Noodle making	240	4 days/year	16
	15	10 days/year	8.3
Sweeping	20	daily	122
Tending chickens	10	daily	61
Tending fires	15	daily	91
Tending house goats	15	daily	91
Trakhana making	360	1 day/year	6
Washing clothes	120	130 days/year	260
Whitewashing	90	6 days/year	9
TOTAL	6.5	hours/day	2,373

In addition, among those families who process raw fiber, spinning and weaving occupy only a few distinct periods in a woman's life. Traditionally many women have woven for their dowry during adolescence, although this has never been a universal practice because the wealthier families could always hire out the work. After marriage a woman might need to weave replacement rag rugs or saddlebags several times in her lifetime, depending upon the wear received, or she might occasionally choose to weave for a daughter or a granddaughter's trousseau. Women with no children rarely have a need to weave after marriage. Those with only sons might occasionally weave a piece for the boy's *proika*, that is, a contribution to household furnishings, but this is an exceptional occurrence. At any given time the actual number of weavers in a village and the amount of time they spend in fiber activities depends upon the age and sex structure of the households in that village, as well as upon their class and the availability of raw fiber.[8]

Time and Labor

In the southern Argolid almost all activities related to textiles are performed by women. This work is in addition to the domestic tasks required to keep a household clean and its members fed, as well as labor required for herding or agricultural tasks. Table 15.2 lists time spent on domestic tasks for a selected village family in Dhidhima. In comparison, time spent on textile-related activities by the same family for the year is listed in Table 15.3. In this household domestic tasks averaged 6.5 hours a day, whereas textile activities averaged 1.5 hours per day, or about one-twelfth of the total domestic labor. It should be remembered that not all of this work is performed by one woman, but is divided among all female members of the household, with neighbors and relatives offering assistance as well.

Table 15.3
*Time Expended on Textile-Related
Activities in a Household of Four Dhidhima, 1971*

Activity	Amount	Hours per year
Carding wool	15.2 kg wool	22
Combing wool	4.3 kg wool	12.5
Dyeing	15.2 kg wool	10.5
Knitting[a]		210
Sewing and mending		72
Picking wool	19.8 kg wool	58
Spinning	15.2 kg wool medium singles	64
Spinning and plying	4.3 kg wool two–ply fine	69
Washing wool	38.6 kg wool	20
Weaving[b]		32
TOTAL		570

[a] Knitted items produced: 5 sweaters, 3 pairs of socks, 2 undershirts, 1 pair of long johns.
[b] Woven items produced: 2 two-panel *leopannes*. Also, 10 kg of spun, dyed yarn was sent to a Jacquard mill.

The conversion of raw fiber to finished textile involves a series of specialized and time-consuming processes. As Table 15.4 shows, the time required to process wool from unwashed fleece to a condition ready for spinning involves not only the actual manipulation of the fiber, but many auxiliary tasks such as collecting firewood or heating water. Within each activity, individual choices can be made that lengthen or shorten the time needed. Each choice also affects the resources needed and the end product obtained. A Dhidhimiote family, for example, may choose not to wash their wool in the sea, thus saving the travel time. Since fresh water is very limited, however, only a few families have sufficient well water to wash a large amount of fleece, and the family may decide to wash only a small amount of wool for that year.

There is no fixed time during which any of the processes must be done; only their sequence is predetermined. Washing the wool requires a full day, so this is usually planned for a time when agricultural or herding tasks are few. Picking, however, can be done at random intervals. Washed wool is usually spread in the courtyard of the home and handfuls worked any time a woman finds herself sitting nearby. Visitors routinely join in this activity as well. Carding and combing can be done as needed on a daily or weekly basis to provide the wool for spinning. It is because of the flexibility of these activities, and the fact that wool does not "spoil" but can be worked when the woman is ready, that hand processing may be fit into the pattern of labor demands made upon a household pursuing agricultural or herding activities.

Carding wool is rarely done by hand today in the southern Argolid. It has become almost impossible for the domestic producer to obtain carding cloth for repairing hand carding boxes (J. Koster 1979a), and machine carding at one of the local carding mills saves approximately ninety minutes per kilo. No transportation time is required as wool can be shipped via the local bus system. Saving time is more important in the contemporary ecomony in which many women labor by irrigating market crops or working at the hotel resorts on the coast.

Saving time, however, is not a consideration in the decision whether to card or comb the

Table 15.4
Time Required for Selecting
Handprocessing Techniques, Dhidhima, 1978

Process	Associated tasks	Hours washing (per kg)
Wool	Fetching water	0.5
	Collecting firewood	
	Boiling water	
	Soaking fleeces	
	Loading on pack animals	
	Transport to and from sea	
	Washing in sea	
	Spreading to dry on beach	
	Reloading pack animals	
	Unloading pack animals	
	Fetching fresh water	
	Rinsing in fresh water	
	Turning to dry	
Picking	Sorting by color and fineness	3
	Opening fleece to remove debris	
	Packing in bags	
Dyeing with synthetic dyes (optional)	Winding skeins	1
	Fetching water	
	Collecting firewood	
	Boiling water	
	Dipping skeins	
	Hanging skeins to dry	
Carding	Unpacking wool	1.5
	Separating	
	Using carding box	
	Rolling into bat	
Combing	Unpacking wool	3
	Separating	
	Using combs	
	Rolling into roving	
Spinning	Tying wool to distaff	4
Leopanna type	Spinning and winding onto spindle	
Medium wool singles	Winding yarn into ball to set twist	
Plying	Winding two balls together	16
Fanella type	Plying onto large spindle	
Two–ply worsted	Winding into ball to set twist	

wool. The long, hand-forged, spiked wool combs are far more durable than carding cloth, so wool combs are still commonly found in villages. Usually one pair of combs is shared throughout a neighborhood. Combing separates the longer fibers from the shorter ones. This produces roving that is used to spin the fine, two-ply, worsted yarn used in undergarments (*fanelles*), sweaters, socks, and wool warps for saddlebags. Although carding is twice as fast as combing, the woolen-type yarns produced are too rough for use in garments. This contrasts with woolen-type yarns that are spun from more finely fleeced breeds of sheep (e.g., Merino), which are generally softer and are preferred for garments. The coarse Greek wool, when spun from carded batts, has short, stiff hairs (kemp), which protrude and would be extremely uncomfortable in garments worn next to the skin. The tightly spun worsteds produced from combed roving provide a smoother surfaced garment that also has the advantage of water resistance, an important feature in sweaters worn to work outside in the rainy winter season.

Spinning, on the surface, is the most time-consuming process.[9] Although it represents almost a quarter of the total time needed to convert raw fiber into yarn, spinning, unlike the other steps in fiber processing, can be done at the same time that a woman performs other tasks, such as herding a flock, watching a child, or visiting with neighbors or kin. It is not necessary for the spinner to give full attention to this habitual process. In addition, it is common for families, especially those working on a dowry, to also have kin and neighbors help with the spinning when necessary.

After the yarn is spun, the women have the option of dyeing it. Dyeing involves winding the yarn into ½-kg skeins, fetching water and firewood, heating the water, the actual dyeing, and the final rinse of the yarn, first in the sea "to make the color fast" and then again in fresh water. Dyeing adds approximately one hour of labor to every kilo of yarn.

Women claim that, although natural dyes were used in the past, they required a much greater input of labor than the commercial synthetic dyes. Only one pot of water is heated when using synthetics. Colors are obtained by starting with yellow, exhausting the bath, and then proceeding in an orderly progression of colors, ending in black. These dyes, although they save labor and fuel and add vivid color to the weavings, have the distinct disadvantages of bleeding, cracking, and fading rapidly in the Greek sun. Even so, they are very popular, and women do not often use the more time-consuming natural dyes. Before natural dyes could be used, they had to be collected, prepared by crushing or chopping, and then boiled to release the extract. After all this work only a limited range of colors could be obtained—mostly browns and yellows.

Synthetic dyes have been available since the First World War. Almost all existing Dhidhimiote pieces dating from the period between the wars, however, feature designs created with natural colors, with an occasional small band of red as a design element. This reflected the paucity of funds with which to buy dyes, and perhaps a lack of time for the more frivolous aspects of textile creation. Today, being able to create eye-catching multicolored pieces reflects not only the creativity of the weaver, but also the greater economic security of her family.

Weaving is the other time-consuming process. Each kind of textile requires varying amounts of time at the loom. Table 15.5 lists times for selected textiles. Based on the processing, spinning,

Table 15.5
Weaving Times for Selected Handwoven Textiles

Greek Name	Use	Weave	Warp	Weft	Size	Production
Leopanna	Blanket	Plain	Cotton	Wool one–ply	one panel 66 by 235	8
Velentza or *Velontza*	Blanket	Plain	Cotton	Wool bulky one–ply	one panel 65 by 209	3
Flokati	Blanket Rug	Plain with looped inlays	Wool two–ply	Wool two–ply	one panel 78 by 212	6
Tagari	Saddlebag	Plain	Wool two–ply	Wool two–ply	45 by 94	2
Sendhoni	Sheet Day cover	Plain	Cotton fine one–ply	Wool Fine	one panel 63 by 252	15
Herami	Blanket	Plain	Wool	Wool	one panel	6

NOTE: Includes warping, loom setup, and bobbin preparation

Table 15.6
Labor Input Required to Produce a Minimum Supply
of Handwoven Textiles for an Arvanites Family of Four

Article	Quantity	Size	Total Labor Input (hr)
Blankets (*leopanna*)	1	Three panel (full-size)	69
	2	Two panel (twin-size)	92
Heavy Blanket (*kherami*)	2	Three panel (full-size)	226
Sheets (*sendhonia*)	1	Three panel (full-size)	69
	2	Two panel (twin-size)	92
Towels (*petseta*)	10		15
Rag Rugs (*kourelou*)	10		15
Cotton Swadling (*panni*)	1	Ten meter length	35

TOTAL WEAVING TIME: 613

and weaving figures, it is estimated that it would require 613 hours of labor to produce a supply of handwoven textiles for a family of four, assuming that cotton warp yarns would be purchased (see Table 15.6). Traditonally much of this weaving has been done by young, unmarried girls who are preparing their trousseaux.

The Dowry and Its Impact on Textile Production

The dowry must be viewed as a core institution of Greek life. Not surprisingly, research on dowry practices has engendered a large anthropological literature (Forbes, Clarke in this volume; Dubisch 1986a; Du Boulay 1983; Friedl 1959; Herzfeld 1980a; Hirschon 1989; Lambiri-Dimaki 1972). The relationship between the loom and the dowry is a strongly held tradition in the Argolid, as it is elsewhere in rural Greece. Today the larger part of most dowries is the financial arrangement bestowed upon girls at marriage in the form, for example, of cash, livestock, motor vehicles, trees, and land or buildings in the village or in a city. However, most dowries also continue to include a trousseau or *proika*, which consists of the bride's clothing and household furnishings.

In the past, the dower textiles (*ta proikiatika roukha*) represented a much larger percentage of the actual prika. For example, in Dhidhima many turn-of-the-century dowries consisted of much less real estate and rarely included cash. One old woman, who was married in 1914, was given four olive trees, a plow animal (a cow), and a plow for her dowry. In addition she brought a lifetime supply of handmade textiles to her mother-in-law's home in which she and her husband took up residence.

A marriage without roukha was literally "a cold one." While wealthy families could afford to purchase textiles when needed, poorer families who relied on time-consuming hand methods had to plan textile production into the already burdened labor cycle of the household. A married couple required their blankets from the day of marriage, whether they moved into a new home or in with kin. A new bride had little time for weaving because she was heavily involved in domestic chores, in her family's herding or agricultural enterprises, and soon in caring for her children. Rather it was the practice for unmarried girls from the age of ten until marriage to be freed as much as possible from agricultural and herding chores and to be given mainly domestic tasks about the home and thus to be encouraged to produce a lifetime supply of textiles. In this way families could "preserve" their daughters' beauty, by keeping them out of the intense sun, which rapidly dries and ages skin, as well as their reputations, by limiting their contacts with strangers.

Customarily women were expected to be proficient spinners and weavers, their skill attested to by the quantity and quality of the textiles that they could weave for their trousseaux. Actually, the type and quantity of textiles produced more accurately reflects the age and gender structure of the household and the occupation and economic status of its members. In Dhidhima trousseaux varied from "I had no proika—my family was very poor and I wove everything after marriage" to "My proika had forty pieces—we hung them all over the sides of the truck that brought the wedding goods to Dhidhima."

The prika, or rukha, remains one of the fundamental symbols of a young woman's social competence. It provides a test and demonstration of her capability and readiness for marriage. It is a manifestation of her ability, and that of her natal family, to prepare, create, and assemble the materials appropriate and necessary to the establishment and maintenance of a new household. The careful display of the trousseau—first in her home of origin, then en route, and finally in her new home—remains a custom practiced widely throughout the region, as it is in much of Greece. Relatives, friends, and neighbors view each piece carefully, evaluating its quality and worth.[10] As Salamone and Stanton found in northern Greece, even when the roukha is largely bought, it remains a demonstrable measure of the equally important skill of managing consumer purchases (1986: 111).

The occasion of the display of the proika is invested with great significance (simasia) for the bride and the concerned families. The concept of simasia has been thoughtfully explored and developed by Herzfeld (1985) in his analysis of the meaning of the Cretan shepherd's action and performance. Just as the manhood of these shepherds is established through appropriate behaviors of sheep theft and distich singing, so also one of the principal arenas of contest and meaning for women in the Argolid continues to be the production, assembly, and wedding display of an appropriate proika.

One of the crucial elements that lends the trousseau simasia is the demonstration of competence with loom and needle, but not simply that; it is of equal significance that the sum of the work be appropriate to the purpose and to the bride's social position. As Campbell (1964: 306) has observed for the Sarakatsani of the Zagori, displays of pride should have a basis in reality, but where such pretension lacks sufficient verity, derision is the inevitable consequence. Thus, the proika may be viewed as the manifestation of the tension between a girl's aspirations and her pragmatic expectations.

The roukha should be seen as being addressed as a social statement to at least one of several possible audiences. Most Dhidhimiote girls are wed in their home village regardless of their ultimate place of post-nuptial residence. A Dhidhimiotissa can safely anticipate that her proika will be displayed at least for her fellow villagers and judged accordingly. She must also gauge whether it will be deemed an acceptable and honorable collection for her circumstances, whether she marries a herder in the village, a townsman, or an Athenian.

If a girl chooses not to prepare a proika, she is clearly breaching the village moral order. This is an option that young women from upwardly mobile farm families who have been educated outside the village often take. By announcing their intention of not bothering with a proika these girls support their decision to be new or modern women who reject the "backward" customs of the rural Greece in which they were raised in favor of metropolitan and western values. As economically comfortable young women who have been educated in Athens or abroad, they fully expect that their futures will be lived beyond the orbit of the village. There would be no rude village husbands for them. At the same time that such declarations of independence are made, however, some mothers quietly work on the provision of respectable trousseaux that can be displayed to satisfy the village audience with whom they will contend after their daughters have left.

The practice of women working on a proika for their sons has also emerged in recent years.[11] The most common articles produced are commerically woven flokates and kouvertes from the Jacquard mills made with hand spun and dyed wool. Although for most families it remained a burden simply to produce the necessary proika for their daughters, those women who could found it amusing and a measure of economic progress that they were now in a position to provide for their sons as well as their daughters.

Factors Influencing the Composition of a Proika

The quantity and type of pieces a girl chooses to place in her proika demonstrate how the factors of economic status, fiber availability, time expenditure, number of siblings, and beliefs about the occupation of the future husband interrelate with each other. Tables 15.7, 15.8, and 15.9 list the textiles, both handmade and purchased, belonging to three unmarried girls in 1973. These have been selected because they clearly illustrate how the above factors determined the resulting proikas of that period.

Proika A (Table 15.7).   This proika belonged to a seventeen-year-old Sarakatsanissa, Ioanna, who was the only daughter of a wealthy shepherd. Her family's flock provided an ample supply of fiber. Her dowry linens, therefore, had a large quantity of woolen blankets and rugs from the Jacquard mills, which had required heavy outlays of wool (280 kg washed). Both she and her mother had plenty of time to spin the large quantity of yarn needed for these pieces while herding the flocks on winter pastures in the southern Argolid. Because Ioannna had two older brothers, she did not often participate in herding activities in the summer pastures of the Central Peloponnesos and was able to devote herself to dyeing yarn and weaving at the loom.

Ioanna's proika contained many items relevant to a herding life, such as saddlebags and a goat hair mat. She did not know if she would marry a herder, but felt that the items would be useful regardless of what her husband's occupation might be, and she was proud of every piece she had made. At seventeen, she still had several more years to add to this already impressive textile collection.

Proika B (Table 15.8).   This textile collection belonged to a twenty-year-old girl from Dhidhima. Athanasia's family were village-based shepherds herding a flock of about sixty head.

Table 15.7

Proika A, Dhidhima

Quantity	Article	Wool washed (kg)	Cotton purchased (kg)	Labor input (hour)
22	Jacquard blankets (*kouvertes*)	129	—	1,237
34	Jacquard coverlets	131	—	1,261
18	Jacquard runners (*kilimia*)	35	—	342
3	*Flokates* (3 panels)	26	—	301
10	Saddlebags	4.75	25	70
1	Goat hair mat (*Velentza yidhino*)	4.75 (goat hair)	.25	52
2	Blankets (*leopanes*: 3 panels)	9.40	9.40	138
4	Blankets (*velentzes*: 3 panels)	15.60	.80	188
1	Heavy rag rug	—	.50	3
3	Purchased tablecloths	—	—	—
10	Sets of purchased sheets	—	—	—
2	Purchased wool acrylic blankets	—	—	—
12	Assorted purchased towels	—	—	—
1	Wedding bread bag, gift from mother's dowry, woven by father's aunt			
	TOTAL	350.75 wool 4.75 goat hair	35.95	3,592

Table 15.8

Proika B, Dhidhima

Quantity	Article	Wool (kg)	Cotton (kg)	Labor Input (hour)
13	Jacquard blankets (*kouvertes*)	76	—	728
11	Jacquard coverlets	42	—	407
6	*Leopannes* (4–2 panel; 2–3 panel)	22	1.0	322
1	*Flokati*	9	—	101
1	Crocheted rug	1.25	—	8
6	Crocheted pillowcases	1	—	24
2	Purchased tablecloths	—	—	—
2	Sets of purchased sheets	—	—	—
15	Assorted purchased towels	—	—	—
5	Hand embroidered table runners	—	—	—
1	Goat hair rug, gift from mother's dowry, woven by grandmother			
	TOTAL	151 wool 4.75 goat hair	1	1,655

They also owned several grain fields, a number of olive trees, and a small *perivoli* or plot of irrigated land. Athanasia's fiber resources were more limited than Ioanna's, not only because of her family's smaller flock, but also because Athanasia had a sister, two years older than herself, who had just married and taken a similar but slightly smaller proika with her to her new home in a neighboring village.

The total wool needed for the two trousseaux was approximately 300 kg washed. The annual wool clip from Athanasia's flock was 126 kg raw wool. Of this total, 46 kg a year were devoted to payments for pasture rental. Another 10 kg were used for knitted garments for the family. This left only 70 kg of raw wool or thirty-five washed to be used for the two girls' dowries each year.[12] It would require eight and one-half years to obtain enough for both dowries.

When the two sisters were living at home together, they helped each other with the domestic tasks as well as with much of the fiber preparation. Washing, picking, carding, and spinning were all done on a communal basis. Once the yarn was dyed, however, it would be designated for a specific woven project. Since it was a strongly followed practice to marry daughters off in order of seniority, most pieces produced first were for the older sister's proika. Even so, older sisters usually had smaller textile collections, as the younger siblings got at least a year or two of less contested access to the fiber resources, the loom, and the labor of kin and neighbors. In addition, as children married out, the household got smaller, and the younger sister had fewer domestic chores and more time for fiber activities.

Athanasia was responsible for all the handwoven pieces in her dowry. Her actual weaving time was limited because her loom could only be set up three months in the winter when their small storeroom was free of the family's grain stores and agricultural produce. Because it was damp and dark in the storeroom, she could weave only one or two hours in the morning when sufficient sunlight shone through the door. Since many of her chores also had to be done in the morning, her time was even further constrained. Her proika represents 130 hours of weaving as compared to 220 hours of weaving for Ioanna's.

Time could more easily be found by Athanasia for the crocheted and embroidered pieces because she could work on them in odd moments during the day. However, these items required outlays of cash and a trip to Kranidhi for necessary supplies. Each purchase involved consultation at the family table and was counted as a financial contribution to her dowry, all of which was precisely kept track of by her younger brother.

Adamantly stating that she would never marry a shepherd, Athanasia refused to weave saddlebags and other herding textiles. Instead she concentrated on weaving *leopannes* (blankets), feeling they would be useful regardless of the occupation her future husband might follow. Indeed, it was a matter of considerable pride when, after her marriage to a local trucker, she was able to use the vibrantly colored blankets to cover the seats of her husband's truck when using it to transport friends and relatives to local festivals.

Proika C (Table 15.9).   This proika provides an interesting comparison to the other two as it represents the minimal quantity of textiles sufficient to be considered a proika by village standards. Neighbors would have commented that she had nothing. The youngest of five children, all of whom were married or had emigrated, Dina lived with her elderly parents who received a minimal stipend from the government. Her father had worked as an agricultural day laborer and was landless until the land redistribution of the properties of the Monestery of Avgho (Adams, this volume, H. Koster 1978, personal communication). Only a small amount of this land remained after dowries had been provided the older daughters, so that on this remaining land they grew their supply of wheat. It was reserved as proika for Dina when she married,

Table 15.9
Proika C, Dhidhima

Quantity	Article	Wool (kg)	Cotton (kg)	Labor (hour)
10	Saddlebags including one wedding bread bag	5	—	130
2	*Leopannes* (1–3 panels; 1–2 panel)	7.8	.33	115
10	*Kourelou* (rag rugs)	—	1.00	20
1	*Panni* (30–foot length of cotton cloth)	—	2.00	30
10	Cotton towels (*Petsetes*)	—	.50	15
2	Purchased synthetic blankets	—	—	—
1	Purchased tablecloth and napkin set	—	—	—
2	Purchased sets of sheets	—	—	—
1	Crocheted blanket of purchased wool yarn			
6	Assorted purchased towels			
2	*Tsouvalia* (flour sacks) A gift from mother's dowry, woven by her mother			
	TOTAL	12.8	3.83	334

but at twenty-two she was beginning to worry whether with such minimal assets she would find a husband.

Dina did not have a loom of her own. In return for weaving one or two weeks a year on an older neighbor's loom, Dina made bread and fetched water for her. She had no source of wool, so in order to obtain fiber she exchanged her labor—doing agricultural tasks for neighboring farmers and herders in exchange for wool. Because her parents were so old and were unable to do much heavy work, she was limited in her ability to maintain a mutual exchange network based on her labor alone. As an unmarried girl her status and her marriage potential decreased the more she worked in the fields. It was with great embarrassment that she admitted to having paid to have the warp wound on the beam in a neighboring village because she did not have anything she could use within the mutual exchange network of Dhidhima.

She also found it easier to buy some of the wool she needed, purchasing it in the same neighboring village, because it was too embarrassing to buy it in her own village. Even so, Dina's proika contained only 12.8 kg of wool. Because cotton yarn could be purchased relatively cheaply and without reflecting on Dina's pride, it is not surprising to find a larger percentage of cotton items in this textile collection. She is the only one of the three girls to have woven the traditional swaddling cloth (*panni*) and cotton towels (Table 15.9). Rag rugs also required minimal cost. Dina carefully saved all her family's worn clothing items from which to cut the weaving strips. Rag rugs could also be woven quickly during her limited time at the loom. These bulky rugs helped add height to her stoiva (her pile of dowry).

Of the three girls, Dina had the most carefully made pieces. Although she did domestic tasks, she had time because her home was small, and her mother, who did little agricultural work, helped considerably. She had much more time for textile production than did the other two girls, but few raw materials and limited time at the loom. Consequently, she spent time weaving precisely, such as in her beautiful fine panni or in creating elaborate tapestry designs. She was

Figure 15.2. Weaving an all-cotton *panni*, Dhidhima.

the only one of the three who had woven an originally designed wedding bread bag. All of her pieces had elaborate fringes and finishes with carefully sewn hems.

Hand Textile Production in a Growing Economy

As these three cases indicate, the type and quantity of textiles produced in the 1970s bore a close relationship to the amounts of fiber and labor available to a household. In the 1970s and early 1980s, increasing opportunities became available for girls and women from Dhidhima to work for cash outside the village. Dina was one of the first to work in the orchards and canneries outside of Nafplio. The long truck journey (over 1½ hours in one direction) meant that she had very little time for working on woven textiles. Instead, she used some of her new cash income to purchase embroidery supplies and machine-made linens for her proika.

Previously the only way poorer girls could earn money was through agricultural day labor in their home village or neighboring villages. Although it lowered their status and marriage possibilities, many girls and married women, due to economic necessity (*anangi*), did such work as picking olives or reaping grain. The addition of cannery employment provided work during the slack agricultural season of late summer and early fall. Surprisingly, many girls who, because of their status, would not do local day labor found working in the canneries acceptable as it involved going in a truck to a major population center, which seemed a "modern" thing to do (see Cowan 1990). Working in the cannery itself was of higher status than picking fruit outdoors, even though it paid less, because once again it was considered more modern to work in a factory. Over the last fifteen years this form of day labor has been replaced with employment opportunities as domestics in the many tourist facilities that have grown up on the coast (Sutton, this volume).

This first foray by unmarried girls from a wide range of households into the wider economic offerings of the region changed village attitudes and expectations about day labor for young girls (see Galani-Moutafi 1993; Lambiri-Dimaki 1959; Sutton 1985). Unmarried girls, who had previously been kept close to home, now made daily "commutes" to more populated areas where they were in constant contact with strangers. This challenge to village practice was outweighed by the need for cash. Families intensifying agricultural and herding operations needed cash to purchase modern pumps, fertilizer, and supplementary feeds (H. Koster, 1977). Generally the income earned by girls doing day labor was considered theirs to spend as they wished, although they usually allotted it to their dowries. This relieved some of the family's burden toward supplying the dowry and allowed many families to use their agricultural cash income in other ways.

Working girls no longer had to fight and wheedle parents and siblings for a bit of cash to purchase items for their dowries or fancy clothes to catch the eye of a potential mate. Girls vied with one another for the prestige of making a purchase from one of the peddlers or gypsies who passed through the village on a regular basis. Purchased textiles were selected on the basis of their brightly colored patterns rather than their qualitiy. It was widely recognized in the village that handwoven textiles were far more durable and would "last a lifetime," while purchased pieces would soon fall to pieces under the heavy use of the household. An investment in less durable manufactured fabrics meant the girls believed that they would have a regular cash income throughout their married life, insuring funds for replacement of items. This contrasted with the experience of their parents and grandparents, who had suffered great economic deprivation through much of their lives.

The three proikas discussed previously were created at the turning point in traditional practice. Ioanna's textile collection was the largest because it represented the production from a large flock in a situation where labor demands on an only daughter were few and no competititon with siblings for textile resources existed. Given the huge amount of fiber available it was not deemed necessary to spend cash income on purchased items, especially when the cash was better used to provide Ioanna with a large cash dowry since she would bring neither house nor land to her marriage. The household intensifying agricultural and herding operations as represented by Athanasia had little cash free to use for textile acquisition, but it produced its own raw fiber and could muster sufficient labor to produce a reasonable quantity of handmade textiles despite competition between two sisters close in age. Dina's proika reflects the use of a small amount of cash to provide the materials needed to produce a meager but respectable collection of textiles. If the cash spent on fiber and yarn had been spent on an equal value of manufactured items, it would have afforded only a few of the cheapest kinds. As Dina entered the working world outside the village her cash income increased, however, while the time she had free to weave decreased. It was no longer economical for her to weave the textiles, but she could purchase more manufactured ones instead, even if of lesser quality. Based on this, it would seem to predict that as households acquired more cash income, there would be a decline in hand-produced textiles and a corresponding rise in purchased linens for the dowry.

The Transition from Utilitarian
to Decorative Textiles, 1985–1995

Looking at dowry textiles of the last ten years, one sees a significant shift from utilitarian weaving and knitting to decorative embroidered and crocheted pieces.[13] In the southern Argolid, knitted and woven items have traditionally served useful purposes, although there is nothing inherent in these processes that determines use. Examples of purely decorative weavings abound both in Greece and elsewhere, and embroidery and crochet can be applied to useful household pieces.[14] In the southern Argolid, however, embroidery and fine crochet tend to be found most often on display pieces that have only nominal use, such as furniture covers, doilies, nonfunctional pillow cases and lacy trimmings at windows and counters.

In many regards this evolution from utilitarian to decorative textiles is reminiscent of a similar transition in late nineteenth century Sicily (Schneider 1980). As in Sicily, embroidery in the southern Argolid has been considered a textile art form of the wealthy and a way of storing wealth. Because of the historical use of embroidery on folk costumes,[15] the needle arts have generally had a higher monetary status value than handwoven or knitted goods. In the southern Argolid elegant embroidered silk *pietes* (head and shoulder coverings) were made and were considered an important part of the trousseau (Petronoti 1985b: 271, this volume). These highly decorated costumes were a visible expression of wealth and status worn on public occasions. That they were also stored wealth is apparent in the fact that, even after they were less fashionable, many were sold or stolen during the difficult years of the economic depression and war.

When traditional costumes went out of favor, wealthy girls could direct more of their efforts from embroidering their garments to small-scale needlework for household decoration. Poorer girls had less time for needlework of any kind because they also had to weave the utilitarian fabrics required in herding and agricultural life—saddlebags, hut coverings, mats, and rough rugs. These fabrics, although carefully made and often creatively designed, were held in the same low esteem as the occupations for which they were required.

Embroidery and fine crochet have continued to retain their high value today. It has become a matter of prestige for upwardly mobile agricultural and herding households, who would previously have produced mainly utilitarian weavings, to emulate the wealthier households and produce decorative needlework for the proika. Activities such as handling raw fleece or picking dirt from wool are replaced by working with clean, fine cloth and silky threads. Girls aspire to life in the mainstream Greek culture, which includes a *saloni* (formal parlor) decorated with fine needlework. This is what they observe in wealthy village homes, in Athens, and on television. Such homes are now within the realm of possibility for many rural families because mortgage availability and new materials have enabled the construction of homes with more than the traditional two rooms. Moreover, western influences are encouraging the growing trend toward special use rooms (Clarke, this volume; Pavlides and Hesser 1986: 88; Sutton 1995).

In addition, as in Sicily (Schneider 1980: 337–339), time spent on embroidery isolates unmarried girls further from public view than does handwoven production. Needlework on purchased cloth and with manufactured threads separates girls from low status tasks such as washing the fleece on public and often tourist-filled beaches. The one public task associated with needlework, purchasing cloth and threads, is also a high status one. *Voltes* (excursions) to

Kranidhi and other larger population centers allow village girls to dress in their best town clothes and to be "seen" in town. There they rub shoulders with other upwardly mobile women making similar purchases. The Kranidhi stores that carry embroidery supplies, special yarns, and threads are some of the busiest in town.

Relative to the rest of Greece, the southern Argolid does not have a rich tradition of embroidery (Patrakis 1977). The pieces currently being created by rural girls are imitations of designs copied from passed around patterns and books rather than from scarce local heirlooms. Even so, these pieces are accorded a value not given to the handwovens, which truly represent the creative local textile tradition. Embroidery, however, is considered a nationally recognized art form, a part of the ethnic heritage of the Hellenes. In creating their decorative pieces girls feel more in touch with the mainstream of Greek culture while creating something of value for their own home. They also believe that this handiwork will increaase in value with age. The old embroideries and costumes are still being collected and purchased throughout Greece and are prominently displayed in major museums such as the Benaki in Athens and the Museum of the Peloponnesian Folklore Foundaton in Nafplio.

Even at the basic commodity level, embroidery and crochet are accorded a higher monetary value than handweaving or knitting. Handcrocheted tablecloths, probably of Chinese origin, have been sold by gypsies for up to $100. Such a purchase is often far beyond the means of many village girls and cannot help but add value to their own creations. Although handwovens have always been marketable within the communities and to gypsies and merchants and so could be sold when families were in great need, they were usually assigned a lower value. Gypsies, for example, might trade an inexpensive but colorful synthetic blanket for a leopanna (woolen blanket) instead of offering cash. These handwoven pieces then end up in tourist bazaars where they may sell for from 300 to 600 drachmas.[16]

Defining the Hand Producer in Modern Contexts

Within the total regional population of the southern Argolid, only the agricultural and herding sectors have carried the tradition of hand production into the twentieth century. The extremely wealthy and the abjectly poor both abandoned handcrafted textiles for manufactured ones long ago. Within the class of small farmers and herders a group of interwoven factors have determined which households continue to handweave, create fine needlecraft, or abandon domestic handwork altogether. As shown in Table 15.3, four basic factors have determined which families persist in carrying out the elaborate steps of turning raw fiber into cloth and which have shifted to the more modern but equally time-consuming needlework.

Fiber Availability

First, raw fiber must be available in sufficient quantity at little or no cost. The southern Argolid continues to produce a quantity of coarse, low value wool and goat hair as by-products of flocks kept principally for milk and meat. Families with a surplus of fiber are likely to use it. If the same fiber were to become valuable on the open market, then cash hungry households

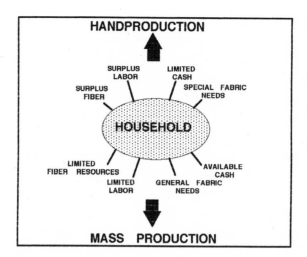

Figure 15.3. Factors determining textile acquisition: a model.

would sell their fiber and make do with cheap manufactured cloth. Agricultural families without ready access to fiber abandon wool processing before their pastoral neighbors.

Labor Resources

In addition to fiber, the household must have sufficient labor resources. If the labor involved in hand textile production was paid at the rate prevalent for day labor, the textiles would be prohibitively expensive. In the southern Argolid, however, household labor is not assigned a cash value and therefore not added into the cost of the textile (see Cavounidis 1983; Sutton 1986). Additional labor is obtained by performing fiber processing tasks at the same time as agricultural or pastoral activities, such as spinning while herding. When labor resources within the family are insufficient, many families can draw on the strong mutual exchange networks existing in the villages (H. Koster, this volume). If household labor and mutual exchange networks can be utilized in ways that return more value than textile production, it is likely that households will forego self-created textiles. As in the case of Dina, when Dhidhimiote girls find acceptable day labor jobs that rob them of time to weave, they are more likely to purchase materials for needlework or manufactured fabrics.

Limited Cash Reserves

The third factor is the limited cash fund of households involved in textile production. When cash income is limited, households must make often difficult decisions about purchases. Agriculturalists and pastoralists intensifying operations are more likely to invest in labor reducing pumps, tractors, or modern fenced sheepfolds than in fancy purchases for their daughters' trousseaux. If they do expend cash on their children's dowry, it will more often be in the form of investment in land, olive trees, or a cash dowry. Hand textile production, a remnant of the earlier subsistence economy, is one way that cash-strapped families have produced a large quantity of high quality textiles with little or no cash outlay. As families obtain higher cash incomes, they shift to the Jacquard blankets and needlecrafts that require more cash outlay and replace formerly woven items such as sheets with manufactured ones.

Social and Utilitarian Needs

Textiles for which there is no manufactured equivalent, as well as those that have high social significance, will continue to be made longer than those that can be replaced with purchased ones. In the southern Argolid, the tradition of ethnic differentiation through spinning and weaving styles, specialized herding textiles, the wearing of knitted woolen underwear, and the necessary provision of a textile trousseau for unmarried daughters have all contributed to the persistence of spinning and weaving by hand up to the present.

Conclusion

The southern Argolid has maintained a constant and integral pattern of textile production by hand over the last hundred years. Despite early availability of manufactured fabrics, agriculturalists and pastoralists maintained traditions of spinning and weaving by hand as the most economical way to provide ultilitarian textiles for their families. As these families intensified production to meet the needs of an expanding market for their products, they continued to minimize cash expenditures on textiles by using surplus fiber and available labor to produce a large part of their textile requirements. In addition, these textiles continued to provide one of the last visible signs of ethnic identity in a multiethnic context (Koster and Koster 1976), as well as offering young women a symbolic way to prove their social competence in the creation of their trousseaux.

In the last ten years, changes in economic opportunities, occupational patterns, and social behavior have strongly affected the kinds of textiles being produced. In the southern Argolid, for example, new occupations and more economic security have meant that some families have sufficient cash to purchase less durable manufactured textiles as needed, rather than to believe the trousseau must represent all the blankets and rugs they will ever own and need in their lifetime. As village house forms have changed, new heating sources have become prevalent, and sleeping arrangements have altered, families no longer need woven woolen sheets. The addition of a saloni requires more needlework for decoration and fewer rag rugs. Long hallways provide a place for Jacquard woven runners. The abandonment of sleeping at folds removes the requirement for heavy mats and goat hair hut coverings. All these changes have fostered a shift from handweaving to needlework and to acquisition of Jacquard woven products and purchase of commercial cloth.

In the southern Argolid, simple handmade fabrics created from local fibers have provided warmth and comfort in a harsh existence for hundreds of years. Handmade textiles are replaced by cheap, mass-produced textiles only when there has been a corresponding structural change in the needs of the household. Those families that have continued to spin and weave have done so not because they are backward or bound by tradition, but because it has made economic and social sense for them to do so.

Appendixes

Land Measurement in the Peloponnesos During the Second Venetian Occupation

Hamish A. Forbes

The basic unit of measurement used by the Venetians in both of their cadastral surveys of the Ermionidha was the *tavola* (pl. *tavole*), which is used to define a number of larger units of areal measurement. These are the *campo padovano*, the *campo trevisano*, the *stremma*, and the *zapada*.

Both the *campo padovano* and the *campo trevisano* are Italian units of areal measurement; the *stremma* is a Greek unit of areal measurement. The *zapada* also seems to be a Greek unit of measurement: it is used exclusively for areas of vines, the Italian *zappa* and the Greek *tsapa* both denoting a vine-digging hoe. This unit is presumably related in concept to the modern Greek "day" (*mera*) of vines—the amount that can be hoed in a day (Forbes 1982: 259–60; see also Topping 1972: 78).

In theory it should be a straightforward matter to discover the modern metric equivalent to the area of a *tavola* and then convert all the other units accordingly. In fact the definition of the modern equivalent for this unit seems extremely difficult.

From the internal evidence of the cadastres referring to the Ermionidha and from the work of Topping (1972: 78) we can define different units of measurement in terms of numbers of *tavole* as follows:

1 *campo trevisano*	1,250 *tavole*
1 *campo padovano*	840 *tavole*
1 *stremma*	625 *tavole*
1 *zapada* (the Ermionidha; Fanari district)	156 *tavole*
1 *zapada* (Gastouni district)	266 *tavole*

As noted by Topping in 1972 (78), and by Malcolm Wagstaff (letter of October 27, 1986), the Greek *stremma* of the Venetian and Turkish periods is generally considered to have consisted of ca. 1,270 m^2. This would give a *tavola* of 2.032 m^2. The latter figure, if applied to the *zapada* of Gastouni, produces an area of 540.5 m^2. Topping (1972: 78) notes that this size of *zapada* is consistent with the situation in Elis and Messinia today, where a laborer can hoe 500–550 m^2 of vines in a day. A figure of 2.032 m^2 to the *tavola*, if applied to the Ermionidha *zapada*, would produce an area of ca. 317 m^2 of vines. This is consistent with the present-day rule of thumb used on Methana in the Argolic peninsula of 300 or slightly more vines per "day," with a spacing of approximately 1 vine per m^2 (see Forbes 1982: 259–60).

However, doubt has been cast on the view that the *stremma* in use at this time was 1,270 m^2. It has been pointed out that a unit of this size, when applied to the Venetian figure for the total land area of the village of Fournoi in the Ermionidha, did not produce a figure in any way comparable with the present territorial area of the village. Instead, Topping (1976a: 102n7) has suggested a *stremma* perhaps approaching 2,000 m^2, though he also notes that the village's territorial boundaries may have changed.

In order to solve this problem I sought information from scholars who might have knowledge of old Italian land measurement systems. I am particularly grateful to Cecil Clough (University of Liverpool), Peter Laven (University of Kent at Canterbury), Professor Brian Pullan (University of Manchester), and Malcolm Wagstaff (University of Southampton) for providing crucial information and leads. The following metric equivalents for a number of different old Italian land measurement systems are derived from a variety of sources they provided, including Molinari (1873: 45), Instituto Centrale di Statistico (1950), and a list of metric equivalents for measurement systems in use in the sixteenth century provided by Laven. By and large, there are few hints of any change in the sizes of these land measurement systems from the sixteenth century on.

Campo trevisano
   1 *campo trevisano* = 5,204.69 m^2 = 1,250 Trevisan *tavole*
   Hence 1 *tavola* = 4.163752 m^2 = 25 Trevisan square *piedi*
   Hence 1 linear *piede* = 0.4081054 m

Campo padovano
   1 *campo padovano* = 3,862.6 m^2 = 840 Paduan *tavole*
   Hence 1 *tavola* = 4.5983333 m^2 = 36 Paduan square *piedi*
   Hence 1 linear *piede* = 0.357395 m

Campo veneziano
   1 *campo veneziano* = 3,656.6 m^2 = 840 Venetian *tavole*
   Hence 1 *tavola* = 4.3530952 m^2 = 36 Venetian square *piedi*
   Hence 1 linear *piede* = 0.347735 m

It is plain that each of the different *campi* used a different sized *tavola*—and, indeed, a different sized *piede*. Yet internal evidence of the cadastres strongly suggests that the same size of *tavola* was used to produce the figures for all four larger measures of area: *campi padovani*, *campi trevisani*, *zapade*, and *stremmata*. Which particular *tavola* they used is not immediately clear, however. Since there is a 10.5% difference between the Trevisan and Paduan *tavole*, this is a significant problem. Moreover, the use of any of these *tavole* to compute the size of the *stremma* produces a figure more than twice that of the normally accepted area of this period's *stremma*. Even the use of the smallest *tavola* (the Trevisan) produces a figure well in excess of the 2,000 m^2 hypothesized by Topping (1976a: 102n. 7). Similarly, the use of any of these *tavola* figures also causes the computed sizes of the *zapada* to fall well out of line with the presently accepted sizes of a day's hoeing.

A further difficulty is that the figure of 625 *tavole* per *stremma* derived from internal evidence in the cadastres does not tally with other Venetian documentary evidence. Domenico Gritti, governor of the province, calculated as early as 1691 (or even before) that 88 *campi padovani* were equivalent to 120 Greek *stremmata* (Topping 1976a: 92–94). If we accept that 840 *tavole* = 1 *campo padovano*, then 1 *stremma* would comprise 616 *tavole* of the same size, not the 625 *tavole* of the cadastres.

The problem of making sense of all the discrepancies seems to be solved by concentrating on the Greek *stremma* and using the generally accepted area of ca. 1,270 m². The evidence that the Venetians, for whatever reasons, made their actual measurements in *stremmata* of this size seems very strong: it would appear that their translations into *campi padovani* and *campi trevisani* were in error. The first line of evidence in support of a 1,270 m² *stremma* derives from agricultural practicality. As noted above, *zapade* of 156 and 266 *tavole* tally closely with their modern counterparts ("days" of vines) if a figure for the *tavola* derived from a *stremma* of 1,270 m² divided into 625 *tavole* is used. Second, for the period of Turkish reoccupation of the Peloponnesos, following the second Venetian occupation, we have the testimony of Mansolas (1867: 137–41), who tabulates the metric equivalents of a wide variety of Turkish period weights and measures. The figure given for the Peloponnesian *stremma* is also 1,270 m².

The likelihood that the same size of unit was in use in the preceding Venetian period is strengthened by Wagstaff's observation: "In looking at the general area of the Peloponnesos, I found that the use of the "old" or "Morean" *stremma* of 1,270.2 m² gave the closest approximation to the result obtained by my measurements (21,330 km²) and by the official figure published by the National Statistical Survey (21,354 km²). There is a difference of about 4.3% which may be an acceptable level of tolerance" (letter of October 27, 1986).

If we accept that a Venetian period *stremma* of 1,270 m² best fits the evidence, how can we explain the mismatch between Greek and Italian measures? The first part of the answer can probably be related to the great difficulty that the Venetians had in defining the Greek land measurement known as the yoke of oxen. It was described by one governor, Domenico Gritti, as an obscure term, subject to infinite diversity. Yet, without a standard definition of it the cadastre could not be made. By experimentation in the Gastouni plain of Elis, Gritti determined that a yoke equaled 120 Greek *stremmata* or 88 *campi padovani* (Topping 1976a: 94). The fact that this equation produces a *stremma* of 616 *tavole* rather than the *stremma* of 625 *tavole* later used in the cadastres is a likely indication that Gritti's experiment did not produce a definitive answer. Even more important is the fact that the cadastre could not proceed without a definition of the Greek units of areal measurement. This need suggests that either the Venetian surveyors depended quite heavily on local Greek estimates and statements of area rather than conducting a full survey themselves or the survey was conducted by Venetians depending heavily on the local Greek units of measurement. If either alternative is the case, then statements of area in Trevisan and Paduan *campi* may be simple translations based on original calculations in Greek units.

This suspicion is strengthened by what seems to have been a misunderstanding of the difference between linear and square measurement. The Trevisan (square) *tavola* of 4.163752 m². comprises a square with sides 2.0405273 m long (i.e., the square root of 4.163752). Multiplying 2.0405273 by 625 (the number of *tavole* in a *stremma*) produces a figure of 1,275.3295. This figure is only 0.42% greater than that generally quoted for the number of square meters in the old Peloponnesian *stremma*. If we multiply 2.0405273 by the number of *tavole* in the two different *zapade* in use, we derive figures of 542.78 m^2 for the Gastouni *zapada* and 318.32 m^2 for the Ermionidha *zapada*. In both cases these computed sizes are directly comparable to their modern equivalents.

The calculation of the *stremma* using the square root of the Venetian *tavola*, rather than that of the Trevisan *tavola*, produces a figure 2.68% greater than 1,270 m^2, and a calculation using the square root of the Paduan *tavola* produces a figure 5.53% greater than 1,270 ^{2}m.

Two conclusions follow from these observations. (1) In trying to understand the Greek mensuration system the Venetians seem to have confused statements of a square of so many *units on each side* with a statement of so many *square units* (the equivalent of assuming that "4 square meters" = a square 4 × 4 meters in area). (2) The Trevisan *tavola* is most probably the unit used as standard by the makers of the Venetian cadastres in the Peloponnesos: its square root generates a figure for the *stremma* exceptionally close to that generally accepted.

Finally, we often think of Venetian surveyors undertaking the actual work of land measurement. However, the facts documented here suggest otherwise. The native Greek *stremma* was used as the basic unit when surveying was undertaken: the Venetians seem to have simply translated measurements employing this unit into those with which they were familiar. They understood so little about what this unit of measurement represented that they incorrectly translated the term, which suggests they had little direct involvement in the work. We must therefore consider seriously the possibility that the local Greek population of the time had a much greater sophistication in the ability to survey large land areas accurately than they are commonly credited with.

Population and Settlements of the Ermionidha

Susan Buck Sutton

1700: *Grimani census of the Peloponnesos undertaken by Venetian administrators.* The figures from this census are presented and discussed in Panayiotopoulos (1985: 247–48), Pacifico (1704), Jameson, Runnels, and van Andel (1994: 127–37), Topping (this volume), Forbes (this volume).

> Ristretto Giurisdzione di Termis (population in parentheses): Cranidi (1,002), Castri (Ermioni) (408), Furni (166), Dimo (Dhidhima) (195), Castel di Termis (Thermisia) (94), Boaria Illia (Iliokastro) (37), Boaria Lucaiti (22), Boaria Peligi (Pelei) (21), Aga (55), Dardessa (Dardhiza/Akhladitsa) (5), Balabani (96).

> Listed under the Ristretto Giurisdzione di Porto Porro: Radu (Radho) (pop.: 62).

1829: *Figures recorded by the French Expédition Scientifique de Morée.* These numbers were based on a combination of local records and interviews with local officials. They are given in Bory de Saint-Vincent (1834–36, 2: 67–84) and Houliarakis (1973: 40).

> Eparkhia of Kato-Nakhage (population in parentheses): Kranidhi (4,813), Kastri (Ermioni) (1,157), Dhidhima (536), Fournoi (156), monastery of Ayioi Anargyroi (29), monastery of Ayios Dimitrios (18), Monastery of port of Koiladha (16), monastery of Ayios Ioannis (Salandi) (16), Metokhi of Hydra (26). [Gell (1810: 132) also mentions Portokheli—as does Pouqueville (1826, 5: 261)—and Koiladha as ports at this time.]

> Listed under the Eparkhia of Nafplio: Thermisi (12), Plepi (18), Sambariza (Pigadhia) and Solinari (159), Dardhiza (Akhladhitsa) and Foukaria (12). Places listed with no population given: Balabani, Tsoukalia, Kapsospiti, Stailia, Loukaiti, Karakasi (Iliokastro). [Gell (P1810: 168–69) and Pouqueville (1826, 5: 257) also list Tsoukalia and Iliokastro as small settlements at this time. Yiannaropoulos (1974: 122) gives locally reported figures for the number of families in the following settlements in 1830: Metokhi of Hydra (10 families), Sambariza (15 families), Plepi (3 families), Thermisi (12 families), Dardhiza and Balabani (5 families).]

> Listed under the Eparkhia of Corinthe: Radho (7 families).

1834: *The settlements of the four original demoi of the new Eparkhia of Spetses and the Ermionidha,* as reported in Kladhos (1837: 202) and Houliarakis (1973–76).

Demos of Spetses.

Demos of Masitos (Kranidhi): Kranidhi, monastery of Koiladha, harbor at Kheli, Fournoi.

Demos of Ermioni: Ermioni, monastery of Ayioi Anaryiroi, Thermisi, Sambariza (Pigadhia), Plepi, Metokhi.

Demos of Dhidhima: Dhidhima, Karakasi (Iliokastro), Tsoukalia, Kapsospiti, Loukaiti, monastery at Avgho, Stailia.

1851: *National Population Enumeration,* as reported in Rangavis (1853, A: 284–86).

Eparkhia of Spetses and the Ermionidha (population in parentheses):

Demos of Spetses (8,929).

Demos of Kranidhi (8,061): Kranidhi (7,987), Fournoi (265). Also lists Koiladha, Portokheli, Kosta as ports, but gives no population. [Curtius (1852, 11: 461) also mentions the harbors of Koiladha and Portokheli at this time.]

Demos of Ermioni (2,182): Ermioni (1,294), Sambariza (Pigadhia) (86), Dhidhima (777). Also lists the following as "places of little habitation": Thermisi, Plepi, Metokhi, Balabani, Dardhiza (Akhladhitsa), lliokarakasi (Iliokastro), Kapsospiti, Tselivines. [Curtius (1852: 453) mentions a farmstead at Metokhi and pier at Fourkaria, but nothing else along the Thermisi coast at this time.]

Listed under the Eparkhia of Hydra and Troizinia: Radho (pop.: 32).

1861: *National Census of De Facto Population,* given in Mansolas (1867: 29) and repeated in 1907 census report, Houliarakis (1973: 139).

Eparkhia of Spetses and the Ermionidha (population in parentheses):

Demos of Spetses (9,843).

Demos of Kranidhi (7,175): Kranidhi (6,639). Other places listed for demos, but no population given: Fournoi, Koiladha, Portokheli, monastery at Koiladha.

Demos of Ermioni (2,561): Ermioni (1,659). Other places listed for demos, but no population given: Dhidhima, Sambariza (Pigadhia), Metokhi, Salandi, Loukaiti, monastery at Avgho, Karakasi (Iliokastro), Tsoukalia, Thermisia, Plepi, Balabani, Fourkaria.

Listed under the Eparkhia of Hydra and Troizinia: Radho.

1870: *National Census of De Facto Population,* repeated in 1879 census report.

Eparkhia of Spetses and the Ermionidha (population in parentheses):

Demos of Spetses (8,443).

Demos of Kranidhi (8,439): Kranidhi (7,185).

Demos of Ermioni (2,011): Ermioni (1,819).

Demos of Dhidhima (1,026).

1879: *National Census of De Facto Population,* repeated in Miliarakis (1886: 225–58.)

Eparkhia of Spetses and the Ermionidha (population in parentheses):

Demos of Spetses (6,899).

Demos of Kranidhi (6,705): Kranidhi (5,983), sailors and fishermen (397), Koiladha (96), Portokheli (53), Fournoi (166), monastery of Koiladha (10).

Demos of Ermioni (2,047): Kastri (Ermioni) (1,850), Thermisi (14), Sambariza (Pigadhia) (69), monastery of Ayioi Anaryiroi (14). [Miliarakis (1886: 245–49) also mentions settlements at Plepi, Metokhi, and the Voulgaris estate and says Sambariza is largely deserted.]

Demos of Dhidhima (1,243). [Miliarakis (1886: 242–44) says Dhidhima is the only village in the demos but that the hamlet of Karakasi (Iliokastro) is forming.]

Listed under Eparkhia of Hydra and Troizinia: Radho (pop.: 25).

1889: *National Census of De Facto Population.*

Eparkhia of Spetses and the Ermionidha (population in parentheses):

Demos of Spetses (5,192).

Demos of Kranidhi (6,442): Kranidhi (5,500), Koiladha (348), Portokheli (241), Fournoi (347), monastery of Koiladha (6). [Paraskevopoulos (1896: 43–56) and Philippson (1892: 50–51) list these same settlements.]

Demos of Ermioni (2,396): Ermioni (2,070), Thermisi (157), Sambariza (Pigadhia) (143), monastery of Ayioi Anaryiroi (26). [Paraskevopoulos (1896: 51–55) also mentions estates of Voulgaris and Oikonomou. Philippson (1892: 48–49) also mentions Metokhi.]

Demos of Dhidhima (1,301).

Listed under Demos of Driopis: Radho (pop.: 12).

1896: *National Census of De Facto Population,* as listed in Noukhakis (1901: 456–65) and repeated in the 1907 census.

Eparkhia of Spetses and the Ermionidha (population in parentheses):
Demos of Spetses (4,432).

Demos of Kranidhi (8,236): Kranidhi (6,937), Fournoi (269), Koiladha (464), monastery of Koiladha (0), Portokheli (501), Ormos Kheliou (with lighthouse) (43), Kheli (5), Ormos Kranidhiou (17).

Demos of Ermioni (2,802): Ermioni (2,512), monastery of Ayioi Anaryiroi (27), Thermisi (263); lists but gives no figures for Sambariza (Pigadhia), Metokhi, Fourkaria.

Demos of Dhidhima (1,603): lists but gives no separate figures for Dhidhima, Karakasi (Iliokastro), Loukaiti, Tsoukalia.

Listed under Demos of Driopis: Radho.

1907: *National Census of De Facto Population.*

Eparkhia of Spetses and the Ermionidha (population in parentheses):
Demos of Spetses (4,290).

Demos of Kranidhi (7,588): Kranidhi (6,033), Fournoi (448), Koiladha (641),

Portokheli (406), Metokhi (60). [Great Britain (1918: 412–18) lists same settlements except Metokhi.]

Demos of Ermioni (2,620): Ermioni (2,240), monastery of Ayioi Anaryiroi (49), Thermisi (331). [Great Britain (1918: 412–18) also mentions Metokhi and Sambariza (Pigadhia).]

Demos of Dhidhima (1,543): Dhidhima (1,171), Karakasi (Iliokastro) (307), Loukaiti (44), Tsoukalia (21).

Listed under Demos of Driopis: Radho (pop.: 52).

1920: *National Census of De Facto Population.*

Eparkhia of Spetses and the Ermionidha (population in parentheses):

Koinotis of Spetses (3,218).

Koinotis of Kranidhi (4,384).

Koinotis of Ermioni (3,279): Ermioni (2,164), monastery of Ayioi Anaryiroi (9), Kineta (122), Thermisi (233), Dardhiza (Akhladhitsa) (5), Sambariza (Pigadhia) (259), Metokhi (289), Fourkaria (198).

Koinotis of Dhidhima (1,123): Dhidhima (861), Loukaiti (181), Radho (81).

Koinotis of Karakasi (Iliokastro) (366): Karakasi (340), Tsoukalia (26).

Koinotis of Koiladha (566).

Koinotis of Portokheli (542): Portokheli (470), Kosta (41), Metokhi (31).

Koinotis of Fournoi (470).

1928: *National Census of De Facto Population.*

Eparkhia of Spetses and the Ermionidha (population in parentheses):

Koinotis of Spetses (3,661).

Koinotis of Kranidhi (4,214).

Koinotis of Ermioni (2,361): Ermioni (1,922), monastery of Ayioi Anaryiroi (5), Thermisi (197), Metalleia (17), Pigadhia (220).

Koinotis of Dhidhima (1,273): Dhidhima (1,017), Loukaiti (145), Radho (98), Avgho (Pelei) (13).

Koinotis of Iliokastro (446): Iliokastro (395), Tsoukalia (24), Kapsospiti (22).

Koinotis of Fournoi (403).

Koinotis of Koiladha (631).

Koinotis of Portokheli (565): Portokheli (517), Kosta (38), Metokhi (10).

1940: *National Census of De Facto Population.*

Eparkhia of Spetses and the Ermionidha (population in parentheses):

Demos of Spetses (3,633).

Koinotis of Kranidhi (4,588): Kranidhi (4,456), Kambos (132).

Koinotis of Ermioni (2,868): Ermioni (2,212), monastery of Ayioi Anaryiroi (12), Kineta (100), Thermisi (239), Dardhiza (Akhladhitsa) (31), Pigadhia (67), Metokhi (207).

Koinotis of Dhidhima (1,575): Dhidhima (1,217), Loukaiti (174), Radho (97), Avgho (Pelei) (87).

Koinotis of Iliokastro (756): Iliokastro (572), Metalleia (P184).

Koinotis of Fournoi (463).

Koinotis of Koiladha (815).

Koinotis of Portokheli (657).

1951: *National Census of De Facto Population.*

Eparkhia of the Ermionidha (population in parentheses):

Koinotis of Kranidhi (4,385): Kranidhi (4,280), Kambos (105).

Koinotis of Ermioni (3,322): Ermioni (2,239), convent of Ayioi Anaryiroi (30), Kineta (122), Thermisi (519), Pigadhia (148), Metokhi (264).

Koinotis of Dhidhima (1,569): Dhidhima (1,170), Loukaiti (224), Radho (99), Avgho (76).

Koinotis of Iliokastro (745): Iliokastro (631), Metalleia (P114).

Koinotis of Fournoi (432).

Koinotis of Koiladha (866).

Koinotis of Portokheli (584).

1961: *National Census of De Facto Population.*

Eparkhia of the Ermionidha (population in parentheses):

Koinotis of Kranidhi (4,028): Kranidhi (3,942), Kambos (86).

Koinotis of Ermioni (2,515): Ermioni (2,297), convent of Ayioi Anaryiroi (25), Kineta (193).

Koinotis of Thermisi (992): Thermisi (490), Pigadhia (264), Metokhi (238).

Koinotis of Dhidhima (1,683): Dhidhima (1,198), Loukaiti (284), Radho (98), Avgho (Pelei) (103).

Koinotis of Iliokastro (744): Iliokastro (665), Metalleia (P79).

Koinotis of Fournoi (422).

Koinotis of Koiladha (884).

Koinotis of Portokheli (690).

1971: *National Census of De Facto Population,* also given in Antonakatou and Mavros (1973: 139–52).

Eparkhia of the Ermionidha (population in parentheses):

Koinotis of Kranidhi (3,724): Kranidhi (3,657), Kambos (67).

Koinotis of Ermioni (2,479): Ermioni (2,186), convent of Ayioi Anaryiroi (60), Kineta (78), Akhladhitsa (Dardhiza) (155).

Koinotis of Thermisi (862): Thermisi (412), Pigadhia (112), Plepi (55), Solinari (127), Ayia Aikaterini (32), Akti Hydra (21), Metokhi (103).

Koinotis of Dhidhima (1,688): Dhidhima (1,252), Loukaiti (278), Radho

(127), Pelei (31).

Koinotis of Iliokastro (710): town of Iliokastro (706), Metalleia (4).

Koinotis of Fournoi (372).

Koinotis of Koiladha (995): Koiladha (983), Koronis (12).

Koinotis of Portokheli (964): Portokheli (885), Kosta (79).

1981: *National Census of De Facto Population.*

Eparkhia of the Ermionidha (population in parentheses):

Koinotis of Kranidhi (3,949): Kranidhi (3794), Kambos (98), Petrothalassa (45), Ayios Nikolaos (12).

Koinotis of Ermioni (2,458): Ermioni (2,104), convent of Ayioi Anaryiroi (14), Kineta (140), Akhladhitsa (52), Kouverta (97), Petrothalassa (51).

Koinotis of Thermisi (1,193): Thermisi (437), Pigadhia (121), Plepi (78), Solinari (91), Ayia Aikaterini (22), Akti Hydra (299), Metokhi (145).

Koinotis of Dhidhima (1,621): Dhidhima (1,217), Loukaiti (241), Radho (136), Pelei (17), Salandi (10).

Koinotis of Iliokastro (633).

Koinotis of Fournoi (371).

Koinotis of Koiladha (1,093): Koiladha (1,062), Kambos (27), Koronis (3), Dhouroufi (1).

Koinotis of Portokheli (904): Portokheli (754), Kosta (61), Ververonda (20), Hinitsa (69).

1991: *National Census of De Facto Population.*

Eparkhia of the Ermionidha (population in parentheses):

Koinotis of Kranidhi (4,403): Kranidhi (3,962), Kambos (54), Petrothalassa (94), Flamboura (116), Ayios Nikolaos (42), Vlachopouleika (32), Dhouroufi (2), Thinni (39), Lakkes (6), Tzemi (56).

Koinotis of Ermioni (2,939): Ermioni (2,395), convent of Ayioi Anaryiroi (95), Kineta (55), Akhladhitsa (68), Kouverta (54), Kambos (140), Kapari (41), Petrothalassa (46), Podhari (45).

Koinotis of Thermisi (900): Thermisi (467), Pigadhia (118), Plepi (75), Solinari (98), Ayia Aikaterini (21), Akti Hydra (53), Metokhi (68).

Koinotis of Dhidhima (1,541): Dhidhima (1,189), Loukaiti (252), Radho (82), Pelei (82), Salandi (4).

Koinotis of Iliokastro (611).

Koinotis of Fournoi (367).

Koinotis of Koiladha (1,091): Koiladha (1,044), Kambos (33), Dhouroufi (3), Koronis (11).

Koinotis of Portokheli (1,552): Portokheli (1,233), Kosta (72), Ververonda (42), Ayios Aimilianos (103), Oikismos DEH (25), Panorama (42), Hinitsa (35).

Reference Matter

Notes

CHAPTER ONE

1. See Jameson, Runnels, and van Andel (1994: 5–10) for a more detailed discussion of the history of archaeological research in this region.

2. The excavations at Halieis were directed by John Young in 1962, later by Jameson and Jacobsen, and still later by Wolf Rudolph. Work at the Franchthi Cave was directed by Jacobsen.

3. Jameson and Jacobsen worked out a plan for study of the whole area around 1970. Encouraged by these discussions, anthropological graduate students began ethnographic research in several communities in the region in 1970–71. In 1972, a permit was received for archaeological surveys of the Koiladha and Fournoi areas. Further archaeological fieldwork waited until 1979. At that time, Jameson, Runnels, and van Andel organized what constituted the second phase of the AEP, officially known as the Stanford University Archaeological and Environmental Survey of the Southern Argolid, a project that conducted survey fieldwork in many areas of the southern Argolid from 1979–1983. The present volume is part of the publication series of this second phase of the AEP, although it draws on some work done in the first phase and, indeed, some work done independently of the AEP altogether.

4. In rendering Greek toponyms, proper names, and vocabulary in this volume, we have generally used the system of transliteration employed by the *Journal of Modern Greek Studies*. This system provides English equivalencies for most Greek phonemes, but also suggests that when there is a long-standing and widely used English spelling of a Greek word or name this common form be used instead (e.g., the Argolid for Argolidha, Greece for Elladha). We have also honored the various transliterations that Greek authors have used for their own personal names.

5. For additional discussion of the area's environmental variation and the economic possibilities this has engendered, especially in the past, see Jameson, Runnels, and van Andel (1994: 322–324).

6. Spetses lies 2 km from the mainland, Hydra 6 km, Poros under 1 km, and Aegina 7 km.

7. For a more detailed account of the area's history, see Jameson, Runnels, and van Andel (1994: 57–148).

8. Ottoman conquest of the lands that constitute the present Greek nation followed their taking of the city of Constantinople in 1453. The gradual spread of Turkish control into the southern Argolid is described in more detail in Topping's contribution to this volume.

9. See Said (1978) and Fabian (1983) for two of the most influential discussions of the issues of "othering" and "orientalizing" in ethnographic and similar forms of representation.

10. For good discussions of the deployment of survivalism in Greece, see Angelomatis-Tsougarakis (1990), Constantine (1984), Eisner (1991), Fotiadis (1995), Herzfeld (1981), Kyriakidou-Nestoros (1971), Leontis (1992), Lowenthal (1985: 74–87), Morris (1994), Stewart (1991), Tsigakou (1981).

11. See Rogers (1988) for a parallel discussion for rural France.

12. See Nash (1981), Kearney (1986), and Gledhill (1985) for critiques of modernization theory on a general basis.

13. This shift reflected a mix of theoretical, political, and practical considerations that ranged from the fact that small-scale societies were disappearing as subject matter (although with as yet little recognition that they might not have been as isolated as often portrayed) to an ethical concern to make anthropology more inclusive.

14. See Herzfeld (1987) and Nadel-Klein (1991) for excellent discussions of how this operated in European community studies.

15. Their largely synchronic studies and standard use of the ethnographic present as a writing convention also added to this sense of timelessness. See Clifford and Marcus (1986) and Sanjek (1991) for entry into the now voluminous writing on this issue.

16. See Fotiadis (1995), Jameson (1994), and Morris (1994) for recent assessments of early survey work in Greek archaeology.

17. Indeed, within Greece, most archaeological efforts to find present equivalents for past behaviors have been made in conjunction with survey research, with ethnoarchaeological research on techniques of pottery manufacture a close second (Jacobsen 1985). Humphrey's (1983) use of anthropological theory to understand ancient social relations constitutes another important conjunction between anthropology and classical studies, but one more philologically oriented.

18. There are two earlier compilations of this work: Volume 19 of *Expedition* (Forbes 1976b, Gavrielides 1976a, 1976b; H. Koster 1976, J. Koster 1976, Clarke 1976b); and, *Regional Variation in Modern Greece and Cyprus*, edited by Dimen and Friedl (Clarke 1976a; Forbes 1976a, Forbes and Koster 1976; Jameson 1976; Koster and Koster 1976; Topping 1976).

19. Indeed, it was most likely his strong support of modern Greek statehood that led Finlay to render a description of the residents of the southern Argolid that was quite unusual for the nineteenth century. Finlay's account of the region included the statement that "the most influential . . . portion of the Albanian population in Greece consisted of the shipowners and sailors of Hydra and Spetzas, and of the boatmen of Poros, Kastri (Ermioni), and Kranidhi. A considerable portion of the coasting trade in the Archipelago was in the hands of the Albanians of Poros, Kastri, and Kranidhi, who possessed many decked boats" (1877, 6: 30–33). This was not, however, a very common or long-lived image, as evidenced by the many travelers such as Horton, who remarked at the end of his stay in the Argolid coastal community of Galatas, "I have had everything I wanted here. The mountains have closed around me in a loving circle, and my metropolis has been a little town of simple folk" (1902: 226).

20. This concept also coincides with Alexiou's (1978: 221) idea that those themes in contemporary Greek folklore that are also found in antiquity now carry different meaning because they operate in different circumstances.

21. See David (1992), Fotiadis (1994), Gould (1980, 1990), Hodder (1986), Kent (1987), Kramer (1979), Little (1994), Peebles (1992), Spencer (1992), Stahl (1993), and Wylie (1994) for general discussions of this shift in how to draw ethnoarchaeological analogies, plus Gallant (1991) and Fotiadis (1995) for Greece.

22. Not all environmental features, of course, remain constant, thus making diachronic environmental analysis a necessary feature of all long-term surveys. See van Andel's analysis of long-term environmental change in the southern Argolid (Jameson, Runnels, and van Andel 1994; van Andel and Runnels 1987; van Andel and Sutton 1987).

23. In any case, the realization that different populations have entered or left the southern Argolid over time, so that the same pattern of behavior can carry different meanings in different periods, renders all analogies at least somewhat comparative, even within the same geographical area.

24. Such conceptual reassessments are, of course, at the heart of much recent discussion within both ethnography and archaeology. For a start on archaeological deliberations, see Fotiadis (1992, 1994, 1995), Gardin and Peebles (1992), Hodder (1989), Little (1994), Morris (1994), Snodgrass (1987), and Wylie (1994). For the ethnographic ones, see Clifford and Marcus (1986) and Sanjek (1991).

25. Chang (1992) has recently given a general commentary on the site concept, while I (Sutton 1988, 1994) have discussed parallel issues connected to ethnographic use of the village concept.

26. Morris (1994: 38) notes that when the Council of Europe declined their support for returning the Elgin Marbles to Greece, one basis of their argument was that there had been little direct continuity between ancient and modern Greece.

27. This is an issue that deserves fuller treatment elsewhere. Both ethnographers and archaeologists have been wrestling with issues of responsibility and ethics in a postcolonial world. Ethnographers have focused on a more dialogical construction of knowledge, the impact of representation, and the effects, both intended and otherwise, of fieldwork on local communities. Archaeologists have expended much effort in preserving sites and artifacts and in working within Greek laws, both on collaborative projects with Greek scholars and against the illegal antiquities trade.

CHAPTER TWO

1. St. Peter died ca. 922.

2. The manuscript readings of the numerals leave no doubt. Although the rounding-out of the figures appears pronounced, they were, presumably, well-informed estimates of village elders. We should expect to find figures, even if modest, for Fournoi, Ilia, and Thermisi in the *catastico ordinario*. Unexpected is the absence of any figures for Kastri and Ayioi Anaryiroi in the *particolare*.

Most striking, perhaps, in these figures is the reversal of the ratio of sheep to goats—a little more than 2 to 1 in favor of sheep in the *ordinario*, but 2.5 to 1 in favor of goats in the *particolare*. We assume as a general rule for Greece that sheep normally outnumber goats (cf. the statistic for all Greece ca. 1930 cited in the *Enkyklopaidikon Lexikon Eleutheroudaki*: 6,500,000 sheep and 3,500,000 goats).

Obviously, there is much we can only guess at. Did the flocks of transhumant shepherds from outside Ermionidha somehow figure in the counting of animals in 1700 or 1705? Why do the Dhidhima figures drop so considerably for both species between 1700 and 1705? Did certain new families moving as settlers into Ermionidha from central Greece through the Isthmus, after 1700, bring large flocks of goats with them? But how do we account then for the drop in the combined total of both sheep and goats in 1705 compared with that of 1700? Do we perhaps have a rare instance in the *catastico particolare* of a clerical blunder whereby sheep were recorded as goats, and goats as sheep?

It is of interest to note the overall totals of sheep and goats in the district of Romania. In the *ordinario* (fol. 3r) they are recorded as 26,510 sheep and 10,860 goats. Actually, when we add up the numbers of animals given under the separate settlements throughout the district, we obtain slightly larger totals: 27,230 sheep and 11,060 goats. Thus for the entire district the ratio is 2.5 to 1 in favor of sheep. The *particolare*, as it happens, does not record comprehensive totals for the district. However, when we add up the figures under all the settlements, we get these totals: 18,672 sheep and 18,145 goats. (Exceptionally, for the settlements of Aria and Merse at Nafplio the figure is 620 sheep and goats together [Archival sources a: fol. 2R]. We have counted 310 for each species in obtaining the preceding totals.) Now the ratio is very close to 1:1.

The grand total, then, for both sheep and goats in Romania in 1700 was 37,370 (26,510 sheep and 10,860 goats); or 38,290 (27,230 sheep and 11,060 goats) on the basis of our own detailed addition. And in 1705, it was 36,817 (18,672 sheep and 18,145 goats).

CHAPTER THREE

1. While I was in the field I was much indebted to Curtis Runnels, Jerry van Andel, and Michael Jameson for help on a wide variety of matters. Especial thanks go to Susan Sutton for all her help, encouragement, and forbearance as a fieldwork collaborator and later as editor of this volume. This work also reflects many conversations with Harold and Joan Koster (not to mention their writings), through whom I was first introduced to the ethnographic situation in the Ermionidha during several stays in Dhidhima. My main debt, however, is to Peter Topping, whose transcripts of cadastral material, as well as published work on various aspects of the Venetian presence in Greece, have made the present contribution possible. Any shortcomings in this article, however, are purely my responsibility.

2. This contribution was originally conceived and largely written in 1986. It was revised in 1996, when publication seemed assured. However, there is an element in the revisions of new wine in old wineskins. It is inevitable that one's views change over a period of ten years, due not least to taking into account new publications. This has certainly been the case with this contribution: had I started it from scratch in 1996, it would probably have been significantly differently structured, and possibly differently angled, from the present one. However, since it is not possible to "unthink" and "unwrite" a piece, it is presented here as a revised version of the original. A number of the revisions are the result of insightful comments by Susan Sutton, to whom go my grateful thanks.

3. Names of the last three communities being written Coracha, Megalo Vugni, and Vorvoronda respectively.

4. The lowest age-group for both sexes is "1 sin 16." It is not immediately clear whether these numbers indicate a group aged from the year *following* the first birthday to the year *following* the sixteenth birthday (i.e., 1 to 16 years in modern terms) or whether it means from the *first year* of life to the *sixteenth year* of life (i.e., 0–15 years in our terms). It is therefore not obvious whether children under one year are included in the census. The only possible internal indicator of whether infants are included is the use of the term *anime* (souls). This could

be taken to indicate that unbaptized (and, in Greek Orthodox tradition, unnamed) children are not included in the census and that the one year figure is a kind of shorthand indicating baptized children. However, according to Cecil Clough (personal communication), the Venetians normally included children from birth in their censuses.

5. This suspicion is in line with one of the conclusions drawn in Appendix A on Venetian period land measurements: that the surveying was probably done by Greek, rather than Venetian surveyors.

6. Some glaring inaccuracies are revealed with close analysis of the Methana returns for the detailed agricultural census undertaken in 1971 by the Greek government: even the best efforts of the modern nation state cannot ensure complete accuracy.

7. The name Koiladhia is the original Albanian name, still occasionally heard in areas adjoining the *eparkhia*. The present name of Koilas/Koiladha is a twentieth-century introduction, part of a long-standing campaign in Greece to expunge non-Greek place-names wherever possible. Bory de Saint Vincent lists a monastery on the bay of Koiladha as Monastère du port Kiladia (Monastery of port Kiladia).

8. The mention of a settlement called Chieli in the *giurisdizione* of Porto Porro does not refer to Portokheli in the Ermionidha (Panayiotopoulos 1985: 247, 249).

9. This observation could be taken as a possible indication of a low level of population during the Second Venetian Occupation, although other interpretations are also possible. Other possible evidence of decline in the population—and perhaps the economy—comes from the numbers of ruined houses and churches noted in the cadastres, as well as the reference to "uncultivated cultivable" land in the *catastico particolare*. Numbers of ruined houses, however, are not an indisputable indicator of economic decline, if ethnographic studies in modern Greek villages are any indicator. On Methana, for instance, some houses were abandoned many years ago, when population numbers and economy were buoyant (cf. Clarke 1995: 519–523). A particularly common reason for abandonment was an inability among heirs to agree about who should inherit the family house, which would therefore stand empty and unmaintained until it decayed. Houses may also change their function from living accommodation to storage structures as inhabitants change or upgrade their living accommodation. Again, the following generation(s) may fail to agree who should inherit or use such storage structures, which

then decay through lack of upkeep. Houses should therefore be thought of as artifacts with finite, though variable, use-lives and potentially extended decay periods. Hence some ruined houses in any settlement of this period may be expectable.

10. Kranidhi's land area, while definitely larger than the others, is not disproportionately large.

11. These observations suggest that not everyone responsible for giving the answers required by the census-takers understood the questions in the same way. It would seem that some gave the area actually cultivated, while others gave the area potentially cultivable. Perhaps the later *catastico particolare* had a separate category of "uncultivated but cultivable" to resolve this confusion. This supposition suggests that the census-takers carried out relatively little actual land measurement and largely relied on verbal statements given by senior members of each community.

12. In 1851, 88.3 percent of the region's population was based in the two towns—76 percent in Kranidhi alone (Sutton, this volume).

13. The description here of farmers exploiting land at considerable distances from their villages is in keeping with studies made elsewhere in Greece. These other studies also indicate the use of temporarily occupied structures (*kalivia* or *spitakia*) by farmers for staying overnight during agricultural operations on distant fields (e.g., Methana—Forbes 1982: chapter 6; Melos—Wagstaff and Augustson 1982: 110).

14. An observation supported by fieldwork on Methana.

15. For discussion of labor allocation to specific crops and distribution of labor inputs throughout the year, with reference to Melos, see Wagstaff and Augustson (1982: 113–120). For discussion of distribution of labor inputs throughout the year on Methana, see Forbes (1982: 230–289). For labor inputs associated with different crops in Greece generally in the mid-twentieth century, see Pepelasis and Yotopoulos (1962).

16. I am most grateful to Tricia King (University College, London) for providing me with these references.

17. Conversely, it is conceivable that censuses, especially when not undertaken with the statistical rigor of the present day, could count households or individuals more than once.

18. This latter settlement is variously called in the Venetian documents Peligi, Pollezzi, Pellei, Pleis, Peleis, and Pellici. Plainly the Venetians had some problem with

this name. Panayiotopoulos (1985: 294) equates the Peligi of the 1700 census with modern Plepi: this is incorrect. Curiously, the settlement is not even mentioned by Jameson, Runnels, and van Andel in their discussion of "farming hamlets" of this period (1994: 131, 133–134).

19. The term *paglia* (straw) may refer quite literally to cereal straw, but more likely it refers to the giant cane-like reed, *Arundo donax*, called in modern Greek *kalami*. The same word in the plural (*kalamia*) is used in Greek for straw. Temporary shelters are still commonly built with *Arundo donax* in the region today. Another writer of this period describes houses at Thermisi in 1686 as "made of rushes . . . that grow where the Thermisi river reaches the coast" (Jameson, Runnels, and van Andel 1994: 134, quoting Locatelli 1691: 261). It is the kind of location where one would expect to find *Arundo donax* growing. Thus, temporary structures were quite possibly built of this material. This hypothesis suggests that the census-takers were relying heavily on verbal statements given in Greek and were translating them—not entirely correctly—into Italian. This language problem also occurred with the surveying of land areas (see Appendix A).

20. Milindra/Melindra is identified as site B5. Sakofoli is tentatively identified with B14, though B39 is an alternative candidate: the two sites are only some 100 m apart (Jameson, Runnels, and van Andel 1994: 131, 438, 441, 449–450).

21. Using the 4.3 hearth-multiplier noted above.

22. The Argolid Exploration Project survey did not determine the area of site B5, which is identified as Melindra/Milindra, but merely described it as large (Jameson, Runnels, and van Andel 1994, 438). Thirteen sherds out of a total of 209 (i.e., 6 percent) are listed as "modern" (a term that covers the period from the mid-sixteenth century to the present day) on this multi-period site. But the bulk of the sherds (number not stated) date to the mediaeval period—the twelfth to the fourteenth centuries (Jameson, Runnels, and van Andel 1994: 440). Although negative evidence is never conclusive, the archaeological evidence does not support the idea of a substantial permanent settlement during the early modern period at this site. A seasonally occupied site, however, might be expected to leave far fewer traces of its existence.

23. Loukaiti: 22; Iliokastro: 37; Pelei: 21 (Panayiotopoulos 1985: 248).

24. A directly comparable situation occurred on Methana in the nineteenth century, when cattle were still the main traction animals. In this rugged terrain, peasant farmers frequently maintained one or more *kalivia* in addition to their main house in their own village. Some kalivia were at distances of only 20–30 minutes' walk (for humans) from the settlement, but the time required for cattle to travel over the steep rocky paths caused farmers to build stone houses in which to stay temporarily when working their fields. Some of these temporary residences were grouped into small hamlets, but on Methana in the nineteenth century such hamlets were not associated with large estates. With the widespread introduction of equids (mules and donkeys) as the primary traction animals at the end of the nineteenth century, the need for these temporary shelters largely disappeared, and they were abandoned (Forbes, Mee and Foxhall 1995: 75; cf. Clarke Forbes 1976a: 254).

25. The list in the *catastico particolare* includes a range of statuses: *abate e religiosi da messa* (4); *diacono* (1); *laici o calogeri o sia monachi* (20); *secolari* (6); *serventi del monasterio* (35). By contrast, the *catastico ordinario* lists only three statuses: *calogeri sacerdotti* (2); *calogeri* (14); *serventi* (16). Some of the differences between the two documents probably indicate a genuine increase in the complement of the monastery in the few years between the surveys. However, given the different categories used in the two documents, it is conceivable that the smaller numbers in the earlier document are in part the result of its compilers failing to ask the right questions of their informants.

26. Walpole notes that in the late eighteenth and early nineteenth centuries the convent of Pendeli in Attica owned some 6,000 goats and sheep, guarded by forty dogs. On the basis of his evidence, it would seem that this convent employed some thirty shepherds. An additional twenty dogs guarded an unspecified number of horses and cattle.

27. In Methana it is said that in the old days, keeping plow cattle adequately nourished over the summer period, when grazing was scarcest, was so difficult that cattle sometimes dropped dead from hunger at autumn plowing time.

28. Another possibility is that the monastery had a business in running pack trains inside and/or outside the region, though the numbers of animals involved seem rather excessive for this. A combination of horse breeding and pack trains cannot be ruled out, however. Perhaps the monastery's seven mules listed in the *catastico ordinario* indicate a specialist pack train.

29. This observation even extends to beekeeping: the number of hives per head of the agricultural population at the monastery is far in excess of the figure for any other community.

30. It should be noted, however, that olive oil was one of the Peloponnesos's top exports in this period, but it was not classified as a food product because it was used exclusively for industrial purposes. Nevertheless, it seems unlikely that major quantities of olive oil were exported from the Ermionidha at this time: Nafplio was not one of the major olive oil exporting centers of the Peloponnesos in the earlier eighteenth century (Kremmydhas 1972: 144, 152). In any case, as will be demonstrated below, numbers of olive trees were generally rather restricted in the region at this time.

31. The thoroughly anomalous figure of about 120 ha per household for Iliokastro has been noted already.

32. According to statistics provided by the local agricultural officer.

33. It has crossed my mind that some sheep might have been reclassified by the monastery as "goats" for some reason, but there is no evidence to this effect.

34. I am using comparative data from the 1860s because, quite apart from mere availability, (a) the basic technology of mid-nineteenth-century agriculture in Greece can be expected to be very similar to that of the late seventeenth and early eighteenth centuries, and (b) any immediate effects of the Greek War of Independence should have worn off by the 1860s.

35. Of course, there is a possibility that the category *vacche* hides potential or actual traction cattle.

36. This figure of 0.15 ha is suspiciously close to the area measurement of the Turkish period's *stremma*—0.127 ha—which hints that the *stremma* was originally a notional figure for how much land could be plowed up and sown in one day.

37. My reference to these sources does not mean that I accept the idea that ancient Greek hoplites were the ancient equivalent of modern Greek peasants.

38. In fact, the actual average yield per tree in a fruiting year was probably significantly lower than this figure: for the problem of relating farmers' expectations to actual productivity, see Forbes 1992, especially p. 98.

39. For a wider discussion of the olive in the recent history of the Ermionidha, including the connection between increasing numbers of trees and increasing sophistication of press technology, see Forbes (1993).

CHAPTER FOUR

1. The social consequences of the flow of goods and persons from small communities to urban centers is stressed by Davis (1977: 69–70).

2. These oral accounts were collected during fieldwork in Kranidhi and neighboring areas (Hydra, Koiladha, Spetses) in 1981. The project was funded by the V. Papantoniou Foundation of Peloponnesian Folklore.

3. This approach has been analyzed by Thanopoulou and Petronoti (1987: 35).

4. For a detailed discussion of the factors that brought about the development of a Greek merchant navy, see Andreadis (1913: 14 ff.), Kremmydhas (1976–77: 16), Yiannakopoulou (1977: 115 ff.).

5. For an analysis of the influence that the expansion of European markets exerted on national economy, see Vergopoulos (1978: 12 ff.).

6. The role that the Greek merchant navy played in sea trade and transportation is discussed by Leontaritis (1981). Kremmydhas also provides relevant information (1973: 28).

7. Economic relations between Kranidhi and the island of Hydra are described in several documents published by Lignos (1961–1962). Relevant information can also be found in the *Yenika Arkhaia tou Kratous* (K47, file 9 a.o.). The population exchanges that took place in the Ermionidha and neighboring islands during the Turkish occupation are also documented in works by Vayiakakou (1968–1969: 59) and Evangelidhou (1934: 33). Finally, the arrival of Albanian populations in former centuries is discussed by Biris (1960) and Lambrinidou (1907).

8. See Hatzianaryirou (1925: 27), Vacalopoulos (1939: 60), and Gouda (1871, 4: 314). It is also worth noting the movement of farmers from Pigadhi Kinourias to Kranidhi, where they worked in vineyards for wages (*Kinouria* 1953: 4).

9. It is well known that shipowners in Kranidhi played a crucial role in the revolution (Hatzianargirou 1925: 249).

10. See Paraskevopoulos (1932: 14); and Konstantinidis (1954: 117), who mentions the existence of a shipyard in Kranidhi.

11. The Merchant Shipping Register in Hydra gives evidence of three shipbuilding operations in Koronidha (Koiladha), where all relevant documents have been destroyed.

12. The data presented in Figure 4.1 do not, of course,

reveal the total number of ships belonging to Kranidhiotes during the period with which I am concerned. A comprehensive estimation lies beyond the realm of this discussion and would require examination of a great variety of other sources (sale contracts, transfer documents, dividend warrants) for which access is very difficult, if not impossible.

13. According to the Merchant Shipping Registers in Hydra and Spetses, one-third of the ships had more than one owner. Likewise, the diary of a wealthy shipowner from Tsakonia reveals that a number of people from the Argolid owned shares in his ships (Kremmydhas 1973: 146). It is possible that some of them were from Kranidhi, since the town dominated the economic life of the Ermionidha (Leake 1830, 3: 463).

14. Barth has made an excellent analysis of the concept of entrepreneurship suggesting that this activity may be seen as the result of constrained choices (1963: 7–8).

15. Kranidhiotes' maritime power at the end of the nineteenth century is well documented. Karanikolas writes that Kranidhiotes owned 38 large and 80 smaller ships (1980: 20). Miliarakis reports that in 1886 Kranidhiotes owned 16 large ships, 60 small fishing boats, and 150–200 sponge-fishing boats (1886: 241). Strong (1842: 158–59) listed Kranidhi as having 217 ships of under 30 tons each, and 18 that weighed more than this. Finally, Urquhart reports that Kranidhi was a significant maritime center (1833: 54).

16. Kranidhiotes not only traded olive oil produced in the Ermionidha, but also collected significant quantities from Tsakonia, which has higher rates of production than Argolis. For example, 18,385 tons of olive oil were produced in Argolis and 70,762 in Tsakonia in 1963–64 (*Khorotaxiki Meleti Peloponnisou* 1973: Table 16).

17. The great number of windmills in Kranidhi (Bory de Saint Vincent 1837–38, 2: 461) indicates the existence of large quantities of wheat, which were probably imported, since the land of the region was arid and climatic conditions unfavorable.

18. Wealthy sea traders were the first to build large, two-storied houses in Kranidhi (Vatikioti 1976–77: 36–37).

19. Church construction constituted a symbolic sign of wealth in the years to come, too. Many landowners and migrants offered money for such constructions in Kranidhi (Gelti 1968).

20. Only two manufacturing operations were set up: Kondovrakis' weaving mill (1912), where women from Kranidhi and neighboring villages made clothes, fabrics, and dowry items; and a family enterprise for weaving rugs (*tserghes*). This enterprise stopped functioning during World War II because raw materials (goat hair) were not easily available.

21. For instance, they transported pears from Trikeri to the Aegean islands (Lignos 1961–62, 6: 214), as well as coal and lime from Kranidhi (Forbes and Koster 1976: 123).

22. Lending money with high interest was a rather common way of using private capital (Vergopoulos 1978: 19). According to a captain's diary, many capital owners made small loans in Kranidhi. As he writes, in 1909, he received interest of 320.50 drachmas. Unfortunately he does not specify the amount of money he had lent, but he says that one oka (1.28 kg) of olive oil cost 1.60 or 1.80 drachmas.

23. Adjudication abstracts (dated since 1807) show that houses, land, and plots were eventually appropriated by lenders. However, we do not know what the loss of such wealth meant to debtors. It must also be noted that such usury continued until the establishment of the Agricultural Bank in Kranidhi in the middle of the century.

24. *Karavokiridhes* were captains of small boats in contrast to *kapetanaioi* who were in charge of large ships.

25. Local population register books (dated since 1955) manifest that although the average family in Kranidhi had 3–4 children, this number was smaller among the families of merchants and civil servants but larger among those of farmers and wage laborers.

26. For the articulation of family social status with size and structure see Nimkoff (1960: 215) and Pasternack et al. (1976).

27. As Gavrielides reports (1976: 272), women in Fournoi comprise "significant wealth" and marital arrangements contribute to the improvement of the family's social status.

28. Daily wages in the Ermionida were about 3 drachmas in 1912. For a detailed discussion about fluctuations in wages between 1832–1912 see Asdrakhas (1983: 175–198).

29. Kranidhi had 4,813 inhabitants in 1830; 5,778 in 1848; 6,639 in 1861; 6,937 in 1896; 6,033 in 1907; 3,942 in 1961; and 3,962 in 1991 (Sutton, this volume). It must be stressed that in 1833, Kranidhi was part of the *demos* of Masitos, which included other settlements but became a distinct *koinotis* in 1912.

30. Thermisi had 263 inhabitants in 1896 and 467

in 1991, while Fournoi had 269 inhabitants in 1896, and 367 in 1991. As Baxevanis notes for the Peloponnesos in general, there has been a steady population increase in areas with large urban centers and irrigation projects (1972).

31. In 1973, there were more than 1,000 seamen in Kranidhi; and there were many more migrants, whose remittances could total as much as $150,000 per month (Gigizas 1973: 37).

32. Though many ethnographies stress the interaction between the local and the national, they do not analyze the villagers' entrepreneurial spirit and its impact on community organization.

CHAPTER FIVE

1. An *eparkhia* is one of several units of organization of the Greek state. A *sinoikismos* is a settlement that is part of a *koinotis* or *demos*, the basic municipal units of the Greek state. *Koinotis* or *demos* boundaries generally encompass several settlements and the open land between. They are grouped into *eparkhies* (singular = *eparkhia*), roughly equivalent to American counties, which, in turn, are grouped into *nomoi* (singular = *nomos*), roughly equivalent to states or provinces.

2. I gathered much of this information on the Ermionidha as a member of the Stanford University Archaeological and Environmental Survey phase of the Argolid Exploration Project (AEP) during the summers of 1982 and 1983. The second of these two field seasons was also supported by a National Endowment for the Humanities Summer Stipend directed toward my particular research. Additional information has been collected from various sources since that time, including the National Statistical Service and Gennadius Library in Athens. I am much indebted to other members of the AEP, especially Michael Jameson, Curtis Runnels, Tjeerd van Andel, Hamish Forbes, Nick Kardulias, Daniel Pullen, and my husband, Robert F. Sutton, Jr., as well as to the local officials who made their time and records available, to the many unofficial local historians and spokespersons who shared their knowledge with me, and to Susan Langdon and Bitten Skartvedt, who provided research assistance in analyzing this information.

3. In using the phrase "demographic transitions," I am playing off a body of demographic theory concerning a process sometimes known as the Demographic Transition (for a brief introduction, see Newell 1988:

10). The Demographic Transition refers to the initial growth followed by a subsequent decline in the rate of natural increase, which has occurred for various nations over the last few centuries. While such changes have occurred in Greece, they have not always been connected to the forces invoked for other nations. More important, by using the phrase in lower-case spelling and in the plural, I invoke the many other demographic changes occurring in the Ermionidha in the last three hundred years.

4. This paper builds on my contribution to van Andel and Sutton (1987), giving a more detailed look at the regional demographic trends of the entire Ermionidha.

5. Figures for the *eparkhia* as a whole, no matter what time period, have been adjusted to include all settlements within its present boundaries, including Radho but excluding Fourkaria. The figures for 1700 for Hydra and Spetses are estimates based on Kriezis (1860: 15), Orlandos (1877: 8), and Thomas (1977); those for the Ermionidha come from the Venetian census undertaken by Grimani (Panayiotopoulos 1985: 247–48). The 1829 figures for Hydra and Spetses, which range from 13,000 to 25,000 for Spetses, and 18,000 to 40,000 for Hydra, are averages of the estimates given by de Jassaud (1809: 33–59), Houliarakis (1973–6: 40), Kriezis (1860: 15–17), Pouqueville (1826: 304), Michaelides (1967: 13), and Finlay (1877: 30). The rest of the 1829 figures are from Bory de Saint Vincent (1834–36: 62–77). The 1851 figures are from Rangavis (1853: 285–86). The rest are from the national census reports listed under Greece, National Statistical Service in the References Cited.

6. For discussion of the nature and limitations of these censuses, see Drakakis and Koundhouros (1939: 12–14), Houliarakis (1973–76), and Kolodny (1974, 2: 765–6).

7. The population figures for the Expédition were collected in several ways, depending on the district of the Peloponnesos under consideration (Bory de Saint-Vincent 1834–36, 2: 59). For nine districts, local authorities gave estimates of total population size. For fifteen, only the numbers of families were recorded. The Expédition then multiplied these by 4.34 to calculate total population. For two, they had no figures but used an average settlement size of 165. In one other case, they reduced the figure to account for certain factors. Further discussion of the nature of these statistics may be found in Houliarakis (1973–76, 1: 40) and Frangakis and Wagstaff (1992).

8. The primary travelers and topographers referenced in this account are Pouqueville (1826), Gell (1810), Bursian (1868–72), Philippson (1892), Curtius (1852), and the Greek geographers Paraskevopoulos (1896), Miliarakis (1886), Noukhakis (1901), and Antonakatou and Mavros (1973).

9. Gender ratios from all nineteenth-century censuses for the Ermionidha show more men than women, indicating such under-enumeration operated there as well. See Topping (this volume) for discussions of this issue in early censuses.

10. Bory de Saint-Vincent (1834–36, 2: 61) states that some figures given to the French Expédition were raised or lowered to influence taxes.

11. This was most likely the case for the small settlements near Portokheli, which appear in reports for 1896, 1907, 1920, and 1928, then are missing for 1940, 1951, and 1961, only to reappear for 1971, 1981, and 1991.

12. Documents can also be ambiguous as to the nature of component parts of administrative divisions. Travelers' accounts are generally vague about their use of such terms as hamlet, place, village, and so forth. It is also unclear whether some of the places/components (*theseis/apartizonta*) listed in nineteenth-century accounts are settlements or simply placemarkers (e.g., Klados 1837: 202; Ragkavis 1853: 286). It seems likely, for example, that Hinitsa and Ayios Aimilianos, which are listed in nineteenth-century documents, only recently became places of habitation.

13. I have also made a few adjustments, such as estimating the distribution of total population between Portokheli and nearby small settlements for 1940, 1951, and 1961, based on the percentage of population in each in 1928 and 1971.

14. Net migration was calculated using residual methods (Newell 1988; Shryock and Siegel 1975: 777). For any period, population increase (or decrease) due to migration is equal to the total population growth (or decline) minus that due to natural increase (the excess of births over deaths). The following formula was first used to calculate the projected population size that should have been attained through natural increase alone from one census year to the next:

projected population = starting population $\times$
$e^{\text{rate of natural increase} \times \text{number of years between censuses}}$

This formula assumes exponential growth—that is, the growth rate was applied continuously during the time period and not just once a year. The projected population thus calculated was then subtracted from actual population recorded by the census to obtain the net migration.

Historical Greek rates of natural increase were taken from Valaoras (1960), Greece (1973), and United Nations (1992). Figures showing the national increase in birth rates throughout the nineteenth century (from .0100 annually around 1830, to .0157 in 1889) and subsequent decline during the twentieth century (to .0102 in 1920, .0093 in 1961, and .0050 in 1991) are supported in the Ermionidha by figures for the average number of children per family, calculated from the *dhimotoloyia* (local population registers) of Koiladha, Portokheli, and Kranidhi, which fall from an average of 5.28 in the late nineteenth century to 2.05 after World War II.

15. Agricultural intensification on family farms is thus seen as more the result of semi-peripheral economic conditions (Hadjimichalis 1987; Vergopoulos 1975), than of increasing population on limited land (Boserup 1965). See Netting (1993) for a discussion of the pros and cons of Boserup's thesis.

16. Parker and Jones (1975) discuss the increasing market involvement of European peasants in general at this time, something they see sparking a corresponding increase in population in the eighteenth and nineteenth centuries.

17. Before their rise, Hydra and Spetses were very sparsely inhabited (Forbes, this volume). They were populated during the fifteenth and sixteenth centuries by the same waves of Albanians as settled the southern Argolid (Jameson, Runnels, and van Andel 1994; Kolodny 1974, 1: 177; Kriezis 1860: 9–17; Thomas 1977: 3). Another wave of settlers in the seventeenth century was drawn almost entirely from Ermioni and Kranidhi (Orlandos 1877: 13). By the late eighteenth century, there were at least six hundred Kranidhiotes on Hydra (Kriezis 1860: 17).

18. A provisional government for the Greek forces under the direction of Hydriote leaders was temporarily established at Kranidhi (Petropulos 1968: 84), and Ermioni was the seat of the Third National Congress in 1827 (Antonakatou and Mavros 1973: 149).

19. These figures reflect occupations listed for adult male residents. The next largest grouping were laborers (*ergatai*), 11 percent of the total. Other smaller categories included manufacturers, merchants, professionals, public employees, and household servants (the latter a surprising 9 percent, almost all in Kranidhi). Very similar figures are given by Strong (1842: 186–87).

20. In addition to those economic activities already mentioned, chalcopyrite mines operated at Metalleia near Iliokastro for much of the twentieth century, and a thread factory, which employed local women, was built near Ermioni in the 1970s.

21. As Forbes (this volume) indicates, estimating the population of Hydra and Spetses in 1700 is particularly problematic, because the islands were omitted from the Venetian census. Orlandos (1877: 8) reports the local tradition that Spetses was not inhabited until after 1700. Other sources indicate, however, that there was probably a modest number of people on these islands at this time, a number which was to increase dramatically in the next century. In any case, the figures given in Table 5.1 for the islands for 1700 are to be taken with caution.

22. Anoyatis-Pele (1987: 30) disagrees with this view, feeling that the Peloponnesian population dropped at the end of the Tourkokratia. Whether or not this is generally true is a matter of debate, but it certainly does not apply to the Ermionidha.

23. Antoniadis-Bibicou gives an even longer chronological perspective on peasant mobility in Greece, as does Moch (1992) for Europe in general.

24. The one Peloponnesian area to lose population during the nineteenth century was Arcadia (Mansolas 1867: 9).

25. This is a pattern common throughout the Peloponnesos and Greece in general, as discussed by Baxevanis (1972: 33), Beuermann (1954), Bialor (1976), Burgel (1965: 11), Cvijic (1918), Sivignon (1981: 34), and Wagstaff (1982).

26. Law No. 2539 was passed in December 1997 and implemented in 1998. It eliminated most of the *koinotites* throughout Greece in favor of a revived *demos* system.

27. See 5. for elaboration of these calculations.

28. These indications of outward migration are also supported by the age/gender pyramids that can be constructed from the figures given with several censuses. That for Kranidhi in 1879, for example, shows significant loss of males, age 15–35 (Greece 1880).

29. Some of these can be presumed to have been temporarily living outside the *eparkhia* for work, study, or other reasons, while others probably had not yet switched their official residence, due either to uncertainty or oversight.

30. The *dhimotoloyio* for Iliokastro in the mid-1950s, for example, shows only 75 percent born there, while 12 percent were born in Dhidhima, 4 percent in the rest of the *eparkhia*, 2 percent in Arcadia, and the rest in a wide scatter of places throughout Greece. In Thermisi, only 39 percent had been born there, while 27 percent had been born in the Arcadian village of Valtetsi, 13 percent in the rest of the *eparkhia*, 6 percent on the Saronic Islands, and the rest again were scattered. In Portokheli, 59 percent had been born there, while 20 percent came from Kranidhi, and 11 percent from outside the *eparkhia*. In Koiladha, 73 percent had been born there, while 13 percent had come from Kranidhi, and 4 percent from outside the *eparkhia*.

31. Adding the net migration for the town of Kranidhi, from 1851 through 1991, yields a sum of −12,279. The corresponding figure for the rest of the *eparkhia* is −1,252.

32. See Sutton (1988) for a summary of my demographic work for Amorgos, Kea, and Nemea.

33. MacFarlane (1977) and Rosenberg (1988) have documented the historic role of migration in European villages in general.

34. This issue is complicated when Greek citizens, urban and otherwise, impute a backward or unchanging nature to the countryside. Such statements reflect views of what constitutes modernity, claims of longevity in an area, and other such issues (Sutton 1988; D. Sutton 1994). Comments, such as that of a government official sent to work in the Ermionidha, that the area's inhabitants were resistant to change, however, should not be taken as congruent with actual levels of change.

CHAPTER SIX

1. This paper is dedicated to Robert McC. Netting, who encouraged me to develop this and many other ideas and directed me to the work of Carol Kramer. An earlier version of this chapter, prepared in 1987, benefitted from critical review and comments from Stanley Aschenbrenner, Robert Bridges, Robert McC. Netting, Susan Sutton, and Malcolm Wagstaff. Ilianna Antonakopoulou and Maria Vellioti offered insights from their own research. My thinking on this topic also benefitted from two seasons of work (1987, 1988) with the Grevena regional survey, directed by Nancy Wilkie, particularly from my close collaboration with Stanley Aschenbrenner on the ethnoarchaeology of houses there. Discussion following my presentation of another version of this paper for the Anthropology Department at the University of Arizona in 1988 was also helpful.

During visits to Methana in 1992, 1995, and 1996, I updated the settlement and household history.

2. See, for example, Chang and Koster (1986), David (1991), Horne (1994), Kent (1987, 1990), Kramer (1982).

3. Wilk has proposed that ethnoarchaeology should approach households as units of consumption, that is, as products of consumer decisions. He argues that the analytical tools of consumer research can be used to focus on the way human actors balance various options within households (Wilk 1990). For the case of Methana, it is useful to think in terms of a transition from units driven by production decisions to units shaped by consumption decisions. Early houses were simple shelters for people, goods, and animals, so that the focus was on expansion of production.

4. I use the term smallholder as conceptualized by Netting (1989, 1993). I discuss this approach in more detail in my chapter on the changing household economy on Methana in this volume.

5. Consistent with this approach, Shutes has proposed to inform archaeology through production-oriented ethnography. This entails working with individual farmers to document changes in agricultural production strategies and to collect social histories (1994). Wilk, as noted earlier, has similarly stressed a focus on intrahousehold consumer decisions that shape houses (Wilk 1990).

6. See Clarke (1995) for a more detailed discussion of Methana settlement history and changing domestic architecture. Forbes and Mee (1997) present the results of an interdisciplinary archaeological survey, adding significant time depth to the settlement history of Methana.

7. One exception was the archaeologist Dawkins (1902), who described contemporary architectural details on the island of Karpathos based on an interest in folklore. Other early archaeologists such as Wace and Thompson made observations on local customs and structures (Philippides 1983). See McDonald and Aschenbrenner (1980) for a summary and discussion of archaeological evidence for ancient domestic architecture.

8. Herzfeld (1982) provides an excellent critical discussion of the political and ideological history of folklore in Greece. See Philippides (1983: 43), Meraklis (1984: 26–31, 129), and Kyriakidou-Nestoros (1978: 32) for discussions of the nationalism embedded in the folklore of house and settlement form in Greece.

Some other examples of the early folklore of traditional houses are Hadzimichalis (1949) and Loukopoulos (1925). See Pavlides and Sutton (1995) for a more detailed discussion.

9. For example, architect Michaelides' work (1967, 1995) relates the economic history of Hydra to the unplanned growth and form of the town, and functional areas within the town, and analyzes subsequent changes in the 1990s. Tzakou has described the central settlements of Sifnos in the context of history, geography, and social organization (1979). See also Saitas (1983) on Mani and Pavlides (1985, 1986, 1995) and on Lesvos; see as well Doumanis and Oliver (1974), a collection of architectural studies of Greek vernacular architecture. Essays by Phillipides (1983) and Bouras (1983) introduce an extensive collection of regional monographs on traditional architecture in Greece, edited by Phillipides. The Doxiades Institute of Ekistical Studies in Athens has also produced a number of studies on this topic. See Pavlides and Sutton (1995) for more detailed discussion.

10. Folklorist Alexakis's work on traditional Maniat society describes the social organization underlying the arrangement of houses in settlements and neighborhoods within them and the changing form, contents, and space utilization of houses (1980: 28–33, 183–192).

11. For example, Friedl provided a detailed description of the layout of the village of Vasilika in Boetia in the later 1950s, as it related to the landscape, the use of different areas within the settlement, and movement through the settlement (1962: 10–15). She also described the external and internal features of houses (1962: 39–42) and inheritance patterns associated with houses (1962: 60–68). T. Smith compared the social use of space in village Santorini (Cyclades) with that of a Santorinian migrant neighborhood in Amfiali, a suburb of Piraeus (1973). French-trained Greek rural sociologist Papiaoanou examined the relationship between natural conditions and social conditions in construction of houses and use of space within them on Ikaria in the Eastern Sporades (1978). Hirschon showed how the tradition of providing a house as dowry persists within the restricted space of an urban housing project for refugees from Asia Minor in a suburb of Athens (1983, 1989). To provide domestic structures for daughters' dowries, parents dug below the earth to create additional living space. Hirschon also worked with architects at the Doxiades Institute (Hirschon and Thakurdesi 1970).

12. For example, du Boulay characterized the house in Ambeli, Euboea, as a reflection of the family who maintains it—and its members' moral values (1974: 15–40). Hoffman's structural analysis of Santorini described a "cultural grammar" that orders the arrangement and meaning of objects and ranks people in houses and within the settlement (1976). Hirschon discussed the symbolic basis for the division and arrangement of interior and exterior space in the urban housing noted earlier, as well as the sacred connotations and symbolic attributes of house furnishings (1985). Similarly, Dubisch described the symbolic and functional association of women and houses in the Cyclades (1986b).

13. See Wagstaff (1969) for a detailed review of geographical studies of settlements. Wagstaff's own early work examined the relationship between house types, settlement form, and social organization in Mani (1965b, c, 1966). He also discussed the evolution of the coastal town of Gythion (Mani) in demographic, economic, and geographical terms. Wagstaff and Renfrew have more recently turned to applied locational analysis within the broader framework of general systems theory in an analysis of settlement pattern changes on the island of Melos over the last 10,000 years (Renfrew and Wagstaff 1982; Wagstaff and Cherry 1982).

14. See, for example, Aschenbrenner (1972, 1976a, 1976b), Clarke (1976a, 1976b, 1977, 1995), Chang (1981, 1984, 1989), Forbes (1976a, 1982, 1992, 1993), Gavrielides (1976a), H. Koster (1977), Koster and Koster (1976), Sutton (1988, 1991, van Andel, and Sutton 1987, Wright, Cherry, Davis, Mantzourani, and Sutton 1990), Whitelaw (1991).

15. See also Clarke (1988, 1995), Sutton (1988, 1991, 1994, 1995), Wagstaff and Cherry (1982), Whitelaw (1991).

16. Liakotera is a pseudonym based on a local place name. The village's house and settlement history is fairly representative of the other settlements on the Methana Peninsula. See Clarke (1988, 1995) for a more in-depth discussion of the types of settlements on the peninsula and of the history of Liakotera; see also my other chapter in this volume for discussion of local values and concepts regarding family, house, and household.

17. The methods used to construct this house history included analysis of local records, national census data, oral history, genealogy, landholding maps, focused interviews on inheritance practices, and observation and measurement of domestic structures, both occupied and abandoned. The case is fairly representative of the trans-

formation of house and household size in Liakotera and elsewhere on the peninsula, although in the postwar decades the case household was less engaged in wage labor and business than many of the other households.

18. All of the names used in this example are pseudonyms.

19. See Clarke (1995) for more detail on the construction of specific features of this form and the other house forms described here.

20. See my other chapter in this volume for photos of typical cisterns, threshing floor, and terrace walls.

21. The relationship of house, family, and family responsibilities is discussed in more detail in my other chapter in this volume. Clarke (1998) focuses on dowry, inheritance, and continuity of the family estate.

22. See Sutton (this volume, 1988, 1991) for discussion of the development of new rural settlements in the eighteenth through twentieth centuries in Greece.

CHAPTER SEVEN

1. The fieldwork conducted in Dhidhima was funded by a National Science Foundation Dissertation Improvement Grant in 1978–79, and a Wenner-Gren Foundation Grant in 1979. I am grateful for the long conversations about pastoralism I have had over the years with Harold and Joan Koster. In many ways, our work has been collaborative in the fullest sense of the word. I was a participant of the Grevena Archaeological Project under the direction of Nancy C. Wilkie from 1987–1993, an experience that expanded my research agenda, thus placing the Argolid research in a larger comparative context.

2. Netting (1993: 3) defined smallholders as those who practiced intensive agriculture. Nomadic pastoralists were excluded from this category, but many Dhidhima herders who also cultivated olives, cereal fields, and vegetable gardens seem to be qualified as intensive agriculturalists as well as herders.

3. The term landscape signature is taken from Marquardt and Crumley's (1987: 7) definition, which states that any material remains on the earth's surface that were caused by human groups is a signature.

4. Studies of this nature have also been conducted by Koster (1987) in the Grevena Province. There we have documented changes in land use reflected in the spatial distribution of modern herding sites (Chang 1992; Chang and Tourtellotte 1993; Chang 1993; 1994).

5. Gallant (1991: 125–26) describes the slaughtering

of livestock as one method peasant farmers in ancient Greece may have used to cope with declining agricultural harvests. It is surprising that he does not cite Koster (1977), who discussed at great length how cereal farming and sheep and goat husbandry articulated so as to provide a risk management system (e.g., when crops failed or market prices were low, a smallholder might invest more in a flock and vice-versa). Slaughtering members of one's flock in Dhidhima and elsewhere in Greece is a last recourse, since it means one destroys the potential reproductive capacity of the herd.

6. A lengthy discussion of the relative merits of land fragmentation over land consolidation in ancient and modern Greece is reviewed by Gallant (1991: 42–46). In the case of Dhidhima, land holdings were frequently fragmented for sound ecological reasons so as to minimize risks and maximize the use of microenvironments (Koster 1977). Herders often said they wished to keep some landholdings close to animal folds because it minimized travel to their fields and pastures and gave them a chance to use their holdings for cultivating green fodder and grazing their animals on the stubble and fallow areas. When I discuss the herder's desires to "consolidate resources" I do not mean to imply they did not practice land fragmentation.

CHAPTER EIGHT

1. The Stanford University Archaeological and Environmental Survey of the Southern Argolid was directed by Michael Jameson, Curtis Runnels, and Tjeerd van Andel under the auspices of the American School of Classical Studies in Athens and the Greek Department of Antiquities for the Argolid and Corinthia. An earlier version of this paper was published in the *Journal of Field Archaeology* (Murray and Kardulias 1986, 13: 21–41). It has been updated and revised for the present volume.

2. We were able to check briefly some of our 1982 field data and to gather new data on one additional site (MS#21) during the 1983 season.

3. Religious items are here defined as objects specifically manufactured for religious activity, such as icons, votives, oil lamps, and church furniture.

4. Agricultural artifacts are here defined as tools and other materials for use in the fields, as well as in the processing of agricultural products.

5. Animal-related artifacts include such things as feed troughs, harnessing, shepherd's staffs, etc., as well as tools for processing animal products.

6. Domestic articles include the following: appliances (tools for food processing, washing, etc.), furniture, cooking and serving aids, storage containers, personal sanitation items, cloth and clothing, cleaners and cleaning aids, leisure items, and decorative objects. Domestic objects are items usually found in habitational contexts, though they may also be found in other contexts. Manufacturing artifacts are most often stacks of useful materials, such as bricks or cement blocks, machine parts, pieces of wood or metal, and so forth, that are stored for use in building or repair. They can also be tools for making or repairing things.

CHAPTER NINE

1. This chapter is based on a manuscript originally drafted in 1987 from field research I had just completed. I examined intrahousehold and interhousehold relationships in one village of forty-seven households and their networks, which extended throughout the peninsula, the region, and the Greater Athens area. I also drew on earlier research that I had conducted in collaboration with Hamish A. Forbes between 1972 and 1974. The original draft of this chapter benefited from comments by Tom Gallant, William McGrew, Robert McC. Netting, Akis Papataxiarkis, Susan Sutton, and Malcolm Wagstaff. The discussion of regional and national lineages is based on a paper prepared for a graduate seminar on regional analysis conducted by Carol Smith at Duke University in 1978. The 1985–1986 research was funded by grants from the University of North Carolina at Chapel Hill and the Duke-UNC Women's Studies Research Center. Craig Mouzy did the copying and restoration of the text's photographs, which several Methanites kindly loaned me. I updated the household demography and economics data during field visits in 1992, 1995, and 1996. The basic approach and argument remain those developed in 1987, but have been enhanced by insights from more recent work.

2. I have discussed Folbre (1984) and the other literature associated with this critique in more detail in Clarke (1984). Also see Wilk (1989) and Sutton (1986).

3. The term stem household has been the subject of lengthy debates by social historians (Laslett and Wall 1972; Berkner 1972, 1975; Hammel and Laslett 1974; Wall, Robin, and Laslett 1983). See Kertzer (1984) for an excellent discussion of the debate and its methodological implications regarding the comparative study of households. Despite the controversy, I used the stem

household type in my analysis because it accurately describes a household form on Methana.

4. See "Wild Herbs in the Marketplace" (Clarke, 1977) and also Clarke (1996b) for more detailed discussions of the local ecology. Also see Forbes (1976a, this volume).

5. Because the term household has many meanings in both our everyday and our academic vocabularies, there is a tendency to confound those meanings in research. Many scholars who have described and compared households within and between cultures have confused family structure with household composition—erroneously equating the residential unit, the kinship unit, and domestic functions—in part because they treated the household as a "black box" and ignored its inner workings. For further discussion see Bender (1967), Clarke (1984), Guyer (1981), Netting, Wilk, and Arnould (1984), Wilk and Netting (1984), Wilk (1989), and Yanagisako (1979).

6. Albanians settled in many parts of Greece, starting roughly in the fourteenth century. During the late sixteenth century, the Turks resettled Albanians in Greece. The Greek Census of 1907 recorded 53,000 Albanians in the total population of two and a half million (Great Britain 1944, 1: 362–363). It is likely that the settlement of Albanians on Methana occurred during the late sixteenth or seventeenth century, or even later. Like many Aegean islands, Aegina was devastated by Barbarossa in 1537; Aegina was repopulated in 1579 by a partly Albanian population (Hasluck 1910–11: 162). It is possible that nearby Methana had a similar fate. For further discussion of Albanian settlement in the Aegean, see Hasluck (1908–1909).

7. See Clarke (1995, and Chapter 6 in this volume) for a detailed discussion of the changing form of houses in relation to changing family structure and economic change.

8. Scholars have discussed the nature of "honor" extensively in Mediterranean studies. The importance placed on this notion in Greek studies is reflected in the title of Campbell's classic ethnography of the Sarakatsani of Epiros, *Honour, Family and Patronage* (1964). See Herzfeld (1980a) for discussion of the problems and issues related to this concept in Greek ethnography.

9. See Sutton and Petronoti (this volume) for detailed discussions of the economic history and importance of seafaring in the Argolid. Leon (1972) offers a more general discussion of the history of the Greek merchant marine.

10. According to many Methanites, there were only a few local cargo boat owners, *kapitanoi*, and most of them come from Kounipitsa, the administrative center of Methana in the 1880s. The village controlled the tiny port of Saint George just below it. This is substantiated by the geographer Miliarakis who wrote that in 1880 there were fifteen trade boats that traveled from Saint George to Poros, Aegina, and Piraeus. The owners all came from Kounipitsa (1886: 204). Methanites' limited involvement in seagoing activities at this time can probably be explained by lack of capital for purchasing boats and the small size and limited number of harbors, as well as the richness and water-retentive volcanic soil and availability of land on the plain of Troizinia.

11. The lands of the plain were at least nominally controlled by the Turks prior to independence, although Dodwell notes that Turks neither resided in nor visited Troizinia in the early 1800s (Dodwell 1819). According to elder Methanites, large tracts of this land were awarded to ship captains from Hydra, Spetses, and Psara who made claims for their financial losses during the war. They sold the land to Methanites, transhumant shepherds, and others. See McGrew (1985) for discussion of land grants to veterans after the war. The villagers of Troizin protested against the granting of lands around their community. They used the courts and physical violence to resist the alienation of what they considered to be their own land (McGrew 1985: 186).

12. The village of Metamorphosis is an exception to this pattern of rapid population growth on the plain. The village had ninety-nine inhabitants in 1851 and ninety-four in 1940 (Rangavis 1853: 282; Greece, National Statistical Service 1950: 78). Elder Methanites say that this village had a serious problem with malaria. This was probably due to its proximity to a swampy coastal area that was not drained until after World War II. Even in 1940, malaria was a major cause of death in Greece (Great Britain 1944, 1: 270).

13. Until around 1935, when people began to space children using *coitus interruptus*, the only limit to family size was poor health conditions. Families often included up to six or eight children in the early part of the twentieth century. By World War II, most parents had only three or four children. This is consistent with trends in family size elsewhere in Greece (Symeonidou-Alatopoulou 1979: 91–92, Valaoras 1960). In 1931, the national crude birth rate (the ratio of the year's registered births to the total mid-year population) was 30.8 per thousand people as compared with 25.5 in 1940.

Earlier figures probably underestimate births due to ineffective registration. For example, on Methana the local register of births, deaths, marriage, and migration by household (*dhimotoloyio*) was only established in 1956. Earlier recording of such vital events was the responsibility of village priests, but not all priests kept these records. Since the late 1800s, the state has kept a register of male births (*Metroo Arenon*) for military conscription.

14. See Clarke (1997) for a discussion of the history of the street market on Methana.

15. See Forbes (1982) for a discussion of traditional agricultural technology on Methana. See Forbes (1992, 1993), Forbes and Foxhall (1978), and Gavrilides (1976b) for discussions of hand-driven and animal-driven olive press technology in Greece. See Belesioti (1978) for a general photographic essay on traditional agricultural techniques in Greece.

16. The major causes of death in Greece in 1936 in order of importance were pneumonia, diarrhea, tuberculosis, and malaria. Of 9,825 persons who died from diarrhea, 7,625 were children under two years of age (Great Britain 1944). These are the diseases that today plague the "developing" nations, where sanitation is poor and health systems are inadequate for serving the population.

17. Officially, from 1833–1928, the Greek government required four years of education for all children. In 1928, compulsory education was extended to six years. In actual practice many children did not attend school, particularly girls. In 1928, there were four times as many boys as girls in Greek primary schools. By 1938, the situation had improved so that girls constituted 45 percent of the primary school pupils. The 1928 census showed that 23 percent of the males and 56 percent of the females over eight years of age in Greece were illiterate (Great Britain 1944, 1: 295).

18. In actual practice, sibling shares of the family estate were never absolutely equal because sisters took their shares earlier as dowry. Some sisters received larger dowries than others, and some received more as dowry than their brothers did in inheritance, or the reverse. In some cases daughters who received a dowry also made claims for the inheritance. See Clarke (1998) for a detailed discussion of strategies used in transmission and perpetuation of the family estate on Methana. See Herzfeld (1980b, 1980c), Du Boulay (1974), Adams (this volume), Forbes (this volume), Kenna (1976), Friedl (1962), and Dubisch (1986b) for further discussion of issues related to dowry and inheritance in Greece.

19. See Clarke (1983) for more discussion of Methanites' notions regarding appropriate work for males and females.

20. Studies elsewhere in Greece also show the importance of women in economic decision making in the household. See, for example, Dubisch (1973), Friedl (1967), Galani-Moutafi (1993), Koster (1977), Sanders (1962), Stott (1985), Salamone and Stanton (1986), Seremetakis (1992), and Sutton (1986). See Dubisch (1986b) for a discussion of issues regarding woman's power in rural Greece.

21. See Koster and Forbes (this volume) for further discussion of the social and ecological aspects of charcoal and lime preparation in the Argolid.

22. In the 1960s, the political officials on Methana had an opportunity to rejoin the nomos of the Argolid with Nafplio as their capital. Not a single official voted in favor of this option because of the greater advantages offered by political links with the nation's capital, the Methanites' many social and economic ties there, and the ease of travel to Piraeus as compared with Nafplio.

23. To avoid distorting the rate of population increase of Loutrapolis, I combined the 1951 population of Vromo Limni and Loutrapolis because they were aggregated in 1981.

24. Much Greek migration until 1950 was transoceanic (to the United States, Australia, and Canada). After 1950, many more Greek emigrants went to European countries, especially West Germany. 1960–72 was a period of intense migration. While in 1950 there were 4,635 emigrants, in 1963 there were 100,072. This declined again by 1968, when there were only 18,882 emigrants. In 1976, 32,067 emigrants returned to Greece (Greece, National Statistical Service 1980: 96). In Greece as a whole the crude birth rate decreased from 20.3 per thousand inhabitants in 1951 to 13.47 in 1983 (Greece, National Statistical Service 1985: 35; Symeonidou-Alatopoulou 1979).

25. In Greece as a whole in 1964, only 19.7 percent of the rural households had electricity. By 1974, 95.8 percent had electricity (Karapostolis 1983: 443).

26. In Greece as a whole, health conditions and the health system improved dramatically after World War II. By 1983, the major causes of death were those of "developed" countries such as cancer, heart, cerebrovascular, and respiratory diseases, as well as accidents (Karapostolis 1983: 44).

27. The coffee shop (*kafeteria*) started in Loutrapolis in the late 1970s; it followed the style in Athens. In

contrast to the traditional coffeehouse (*kafeneio*), the kafeteria is a fancier place where younger people go in groups to drink coffee and soft drinks. It is also a place where younger men take their wives in the evening. The kafeneio continues to be a man's place for drinking coffee and cognac and playing cards. See Cowan (1990, 1991) for an analysis of the social and cultural construction of gender through socializing in the kafeteria in central Macedenia.

28. The names used in this and the following case are pseudonyms.

29. See Clarke (1989) for further discussion of conflict within the household reflected in physical symptoms of *nevra*. See Clarke (1998) for a discussion of household conflicts related to dowry and inheritance.

CHAPTER TEN

1. As late as the late 1970s, the benefits of plot fragmentation were not widely recognized; for example, they were ignored by Colson (1979) in her wide-ranging review of food strategies to combat hungry years.

2. This contribution is based on ethnographic field research conducted on Methana over a two-year period from 1972 to 1974. Much of the data presented here can be found in my Ph.D. dissertation, chapters 5 and 11 (Forbes 1982). When originally written for this volume in the mid 1980s, this article described a system that could be considered still current. By the time of publication, however, a whole generation has grown up—and many will have received family property—since the fieldwork on which this contribution is based. It must now therefore be considered to represent a historical situation. For this reason, both the property-transfer system and the agricultural system to which it was inextricably linked are described in the past tense. Nevertheless, many aspects of the system as it operated more than twenty years ago still function.

3. In addition to these small villages located away from the coast, there is a spa town, also called Methana, or colloquially Ta Loutra (The Baths), located on the coast. This was founded in the later nineteenth century, after the village settlements (see Clarke, this volume).

4. The system being described existed before the Greek government's 1984 legislation on dowries.

5. The amount of energy expended in cultivating trees, particularly olive and almond trees, was relatively small, and very few visits were needed for them over the year. Thus, to be at a considerable distance from crop trees was not as great a hardship as it was with agricultural land or especially vines.

6. Methanites used to say repeatedly: *i elia eine athanati*—the olive is immortal.

7. In this context, and all others unless otherwise stated, "plot" means an agricultural terrace or a group of contiguous terraces. Terraces are usually small, so one plot generally contains several such, unless the terrace is unusually large or fragmentation is particularly extreme.

8. Land is not generally measured in stremmata by Methanites, but in "days" (i.e., days of plowing) because the landscape is so rugged and terraces are frequently so irregular that accurate areal measurement is very difficult. Conversion of days to stremmata by Methanites generally seems to be based on a rule of thumb of 2 to 2.5 stremmata per day.

9. Several actual examples of how households acted to minimize the further fragmentation of their agricultural resources—and even to consolidate divided property—are given in Forbes 1982: 150–53.

10. Chisholm (1968: chap. 7) discusses a number of aspects of this link, but from the point of view of attempts to change settlement patterns in order to increase consolidation—and thus the "efficiency" of farming.

11. See Sutton (1988, 1995) for further discussion of kinship and legal forces favoring the formation of consolidated settlements in nineteenth-century Greece.

12. It is clear from historical research that the distribution of the present villages on the peninsula resulted from the choice of locations that had pre-existing churches, and that religious considerations were comparable in importance to those of safety and access to cultivable land in settlement foundation decisions (Forbes and Mee 1996: 82).

13. Harold Koster's observations (this volume) on the importance of maintaining bonds of mutual obligation in Dhidhima would argue that such destructive behavior would probably be minimized for the sake of good social relations. This is all the more likely since the fragmentation of holdings via dowry/inheritance means that the parties involved are likely to be related.

14. These expectable fluctuations have been termed "crises" (Galt 1979: 98), but this seems an inappropriate use of the term merely for climatic conditions that result in poorer than average productivity. The term also has rather specific connotations in other academic disciplines (e.g., demography). It is therefore probably better, if using the term "crisis," to restrict it to those occa-

sions for which the normal cultural coping mechanisms are inadequate.

15. In fact, certain "plots" documented here are not single plots, but groups of two or more plots situated close to each other. These figures were recorded, according to the household head, purely out of interest, as a record of the production of individual plots over the years, and as a record of total production of threshed wheat. Five plots have been eliminated from Table 10.2 because they only appear once in the farmer's records. Hence the columns for the years 1962 and 1970 do not add up to the figure in the *Total harvest* line.

16. The coefficient of variation is simply the standard deviation expressed as a percentage of the mean.

17. A very similar observation has been made in discussion of a community in Valais, Switzerland (Wiegandt 1977) where partible inheritance is also the rule. Here the Gini coefficient for the village was low, indicating a relatively equal distribution of wealth among all villagers.

18. McCloskey (1976) also notes that the dispersed plots of medieval English farms gave some protection against major losses due to localized hail storms.

19. It will be noted that a number of the toponyms in the list are distinctively non-Greek. As noted elsewhere (Forbes and Mee 1996: 78; Clarke, this volume) Methana's population has traditionally been Albanian speaking; virtually all toponyms seem to be derived from Albanian words.

20. The range of values 1.0–7.9 was chosen arbitrarily as a result of studying the range of conditions. The actual numbers assigned to each vine area as relative measures of moisture were not scientifically derived, but were assigned by me as a result of direct observation. The fieldwork methodology involved a heavy dependence on participating in agricultural work whenever and wherever possible. In this instance I participated in a considerable number of grape harvesting groups and some vine digging groups, as well as visiting all vine areas during times of high levels of activity in cultivating and harvesting. This gave me direct knowledge, inter alia, of the amount of shelter a location received and, as an amateur gardener, I found it relatively straightforward to evaluate the soil's structure at a basic level while actually engaged in working it.

21. This mean figure should not be considered as an exact balance of the factors of soil moisture retentiveness as against exposure to sun and wind, since both of the phenomena are in reality multifactorial, and the balance of their effects on crop production was dependent on different weather conditions.

22. The leaving of both the poorest and wealthiest classes corresponds to the general situation described for early migrants to Athens from many rural Greek areas by Sutton (1983).

23. The necessity of not taking an environmental determinist point of view is highlighted by Douglass's (1984: 111–13) argument that the Basques' tradition of impartible inheritance and their strong moral pressures *not* to fragment family holdings are directly related to the mountainous topography of their homeland.

CHAPTER ELEVEN

EPIGRAPH: Models of peasant life are indeed old! Here Hesiod presents a classic dilemma. On the one hand, in an intensive agricultural system, a large family provides the means to extract more production from the land. On the other hand, if the landholdings cannot be increased, then a large number of siblings may also mean the division of the resource base, the land.

1. This case study was originally completed as an M.A. thesis in the Department of Geography, University of North Carolina—Chapel Hill, in 1981 and was revised in 1986. Although I was reluctant to revisit old ground, a review of the relevant literature since 1986 convinced me that a longitudinal study of this type was still useful. Readers are referred to Bentley's review article (1987b) for a more global perspective on land fragmentation. I cannot claim to give voice to the people of Dhidhima, but by removing them from the constraints of an ahistorical perspective, I hope to give due respect to what they have actually done.

2. As late as 1990, Keeler and Skuras, in a paper on consolidation policy in Greece, note that consolidation has been hampered by "the attitudes of the farmer to change, social customs, and physical constraints" (1990: 76). In this way they continue the characterization of farmers as resistant to change and constrained by custom. These are McNall's villagers, inhibited from adjusting to a changing world (1974: 11). Fotiadis has criticized the perspective created by the Minnesota-Messenia Expedition's ethnoarchaeological approach as placing "the Messenians of the 1960's in the margins of modernity" (1995: 59). See also Sutton's critique of the ahistorical or timeless Greek villager (1994: 315; and this volume). Shutes characterizes two weaknesses of what he calls the "Peasant Approach": (1) portraying the

smallholder as passive and bound up in a rigid complex of traditional community values and (2) "rarely empirically examin[ing] the crucial economic variables that are clearly at work in such communities" (1994: 339).

3. I prefer the term smallholder to peasant as less constrained. Smallholder is also more descriptive of the farmers that are of concern in this study. I use the term following Netting (1993: 2–4). This case study deals with family holdings in an intensive though changing, complex agro-pastoral setting.

4. See Herzfeld (1985) and Chang (1993) for discussions of the ways in which shepherds negotiate identity vis-à-vis other herders, villagers, and townspeople. Also see Herzfeld (1991) for a discussion local versus national ideology.

5. Many thanks are due to the readers of my M.A. thesis, John Florin, Stephen Birdsall, and David Basile. Harold Koster gathered the original data for the study and provided ideas and criticism for the thesis. He also provided updated information for this revision. Mari Clarke afforded much support and information for the thesis based on her own fieldwork. Deborah L. Durham provided support and substantial criticism during the revisions for this volume. Though the value of this support and criticism is inestimable, all errors remain my own.

6. A number of the ethnographies that have been carried out in Greece have dealt extensively with agro-pastoral relationships. See especially the contributions of Harold Koster, Joan Koster, and Chang (this volume, as well as H. Koster 1977; H. Koster and Bouza 1976; Chang 1981, 1984) for descriptions of the situation in Dhidhima.

7. The perspective of risk reduction strategies such as polycropping (Forbes 1976a) and dispersed plots (Forbes, this volume) has been an important component of research in the Argolid for several decades. Risk reduction strategies such as dispersed holdings are not old-fashioned or limited to smallholders; modern large scale farmers routinely plant crops across diverse micro-ecologies or in widely dispersed fields to cover for yearly climatic variations and calamitous events such as hail or wind damage. See also Bentley's summary of the wider literature on risk reduction and land fragmentation (1987b: 50–52).

8. Although Dhidhima has grown substantially (especially in terms of architecture) since this study was carried out, the overall population density for the area still remains relatively low.

9. *Wakf* (from the Arabic "to stand"). A good discussion of the Koranic legal concept of *Wakf* (and *evlat wakf*) and its extension to Orthodox Christian foundations can be found in McGrew (1985: 25–27).

10. The "problem" of *minifundia* is sometimes discussed together with very large landholdings, *latifundia*. Latifundia are often associated with tenant farming, class distinctions, and contrasts of wealth and poverty. Where the two are found together, minifundia are to some extent a result of the disproportionate ratio of population to land brought about by latifundia.

11. Other terms used such as "pulverization" (Clout 1972: 106) are obvious in their negative depiction of fragmentation.

12. For a discussion of the pros and cons of fragmentation see Bentley (1987b: 42–58). Gallant (1991: 42–46) discusses the merits of fragmentation vis-à-vis consolidation. Bentley (1987b: 58–61) lays out the benefits and costs of consolidation.

13. Several sources are cited by Bentley that argue for the causal relationship between partible inheritance and fragmentation (Bentley 1987b: 35). In all of these cases, inheritance should only be seen as an agent, while population pressure and a dearth of economic alternatives would seem to better explain fragmentation. This is especially true for Silva's study (1983) of a parish on the northwest coast of Portugal. Silva's study involves differences in social class, fertility, and (one supposes) economic opportunity between the two study populations (see note 11 above). "Anthropologists conclude that inheritance divides fields relatively infrequently and that inheritance plays a functional role in peasant communities" (Bentley 1987: 37). Discussions of land inheritance practices in Greece can be found in Levy (1956) and Herzfeld (1980c). Forbes (this volume) discusses the relationship between dowry, inheritance, fragmentation, and risk reduction in a Greek village.

CHAPTER TWELVE

1. The dyadic nature of Foster's model has, over the years, received justified criticism, particularly with respect to the difficulty of separating the individual relationships of two persons from the matrices of their respective households (Silverman 1965: 177–78). Nevertheless, as has been argued by Galt, "the basic properties of the model—bi-polarity and exchange—lend it continuing utility. One can think of the two individuals as

the foci of two clusters of people who would not otherwise be related" (1974: 200–201).

2. Reina's work in Guatemala (1959) was a model for much of this. Brandes (1973) took a major step forward with his analysis of friendship ties in the Spanish village of Navagonal. It is probably more than coincidence that the basic economy and ecology of Navagonal and the Greek village of Dhidhima (the locus of this study) are similar and that they compare with respect to patterns of exchange and friendship.

3. The fieldwork on which this chapter is based was conducted in Dhidhima during 1971–1972, 1973, and 1975 with support from predoctoral fellowships from the National Institute of Mental Health and the University of Pennsylvania. During most of this period, I was assisted by Joan Bouza Koster, who contributed mightily to this work. I also must acknowledge the invaluable support and assistance of Mari Clarke, Hamish Forbes, Nicolas Gavrielides, Michael Jameson, Robert McC. Netting, Panos and Maria Spanos, and Brian Spooner, and the helpful editing of Susan Sutton.

4. It is also likely that both parties gained some advantage in avoiding taxation through the failure to record the transaction or to use cash.

5. The case for Dhidhimiote *tirovoli* is in marked contrast to the small-scale marketing of feta by Valtetsiotes and Roumeliotes in Arcadia and Corinthia. Herders in eastern Crete and in the northern Pindos successfully market home cheese production to their advantage (Koster 1997).

6. It should be stressed that speaking of a local marketplace does not imply that any physical market, other than stores or traveling merchants, exists in Dhidhima. There are no special market areas or places in the village such as exist, for example, on Methana (Clarke 1976c: 15).

7. This work group is very similar to a mutual aid group digging potatoes near Thebes described by Sanders (1955, 1966). In many respects the pressures leading to the formation of both groups appear to be similar in nature.

8. See Just (1991) for parallel discussion of fictions and economic strategies within the idiom of kinship.

CHAPTER THIRTEEN

1. We would like to thank Lin Foxhall and Joan Bouza Koster for their insights in discussing this topic. Robert McC. Netting and Brian Spooner made helpful comments on an earlier draft. An earlier version of this paper was presented at the symposium on "Deforestation, Erosion, and Ecology in the Ancient Mediterranean and Near East," sponsored by the Smithsonian Institution, held in Washington, D.C., April 1978 and organized by Robert Evans and Theodore Wertime. We dedicate this paper to the memory of Ted Wertime.

2. For discussion and restatement of traditional views of the causes of deforestation and erosion in Greece and the Mediterranean, see OECD (1983: 85–96) and Thirgood (1981). For a critical review by one of the present authors, see Forbes (1983). Excellent examples of detailed analyses of the historical evolution of plant communities in Greece are those of Rackham (1983) for Boeotia and Hansen (1991) for the Franchthi Cave.

3. For a recent consideration of these issues, see Kardulias and Shutes's 1997 volume, which includes articles by both of the present authors, as well as by others.

4. Not surprisingly, the period of the Civil War saw some of the lowest numbers of animals grazing on Dhidhimiote pastures. This pattern was replicated in many regions of Greece. The sudden increase in flock numbers using Dhidhima in the period 1951–1954 is primarily the result of a more than fourfold growth in the migratory and nonresident neighbor flocks. As elsewhere in Greece, herders responded to what they perceived as local increases in pasture productivity due to declines in grazing pressure by reduced flocks during the war years. It should also be observed that, although sheep/goats using Dhidhima pastures reached 20,000 in 1953, the more than 6,000 nonresident stock only used these pastures seasonally.

5. These data were collected by Forbes. The director of the office of the Greek Forest Service in Kranidhi was extremely helpful in making available his knowledge and his office's records. Of particular interest was a journal in which annual statistics concerning the exploitation of noncultivated land surface in the region were noted for different years discontinuously from 1931 to 1981. The most complete section was dated between 1931 and 1942. Besides giving actual statistics, there were occasional comments in the journal explaining why production had risen or fallen significantly in a given year.

6. The population of the Ermionidha for 1928 was 9,893 (Sutton, this volume). We base our calculation on a generous average consumption rate of 150 kg/ person/year (Foxhall and Forbes 1982: 65–68).

7. In these instances, however, costs and difficulties

involved in moving animals over distances continued to make cheese a more readily marketable item.

CHAPTER FOURTEEN

1. My deepest thanks go to Priscilla Murray, who conceived of the Modern-site Survey and allowed me to be an integral part of this project. She is also responsible for all the illustrations. During the course of the fieldwork and preparation of this report, Curtis Runnels provided his usual array of stimulating conversations and helpful criticisms. Susan Sutton has offered thoughtful comments and suggestions during the entire writing process.

2. Plastic containers possess certain attributes that contribute to a lower cost to consumers. Although purchase prices are not that disparate, the durability of plastic makes it cheaper to own than ceramic wares. Foster's (1977: 354–355) study of utilitarian pottery in Mexico indicates a life expectancy of one year for many vessels. More portable, thin-walled vessels, such as mugs, jars, and dishes, tend to have the shortest life span due to more frequent use (DeBoer and Lathrap 1979: 129). The ability of plastic to survive numerous mishaps reduces the need for regular replacement, and in this sense makes it a cheaper commodity.

3. In 1983, the exchange rate was 83.466 drachmas per U.S.$1.00.

CHAPTER FIFTEEN

1. Five main periods of field research (1970–1971, 1973, 1975, 1978, 1988) have been updated with research done in 1990 in Dhidhima and neighboring villages, as well as among the Sarakatsani and Valtetsiot groups, both in the Argolid and their home regions. Additional data for more recent periods have been obtained through correspondence with informants in the Argolid.

2. In writing this paper I am especially grateful for the assistance offered by my colleagues. Mari Clarke generously provided critical comment and comparative data from her fieldwork in Methana as well as numerous source materials. Discussions with Mary Martin, Jana Hesser, Lefteris Pavlides, and Linda Welters helped clarify many points. The encouragement and assistance of my husband, Harold Koster, has been vital to the development of this paper in its final form. Michael Jameson's gift of the writings of Loukopoulos and Hadzimichalis

has been invaluable, as has his encouragement through the years. Finally, I will always be indebted to my "teachers," the women of Dhidhima and Ghoura who taught me to spin and to weave textiles that would "last a lifetime" and who shared with me their love of the loom.

3. Much of the history and technology of Greek weaving has been recorded by noted Greek folklorists Angeliki Hatzimihalis (1929; 1957), Aliki Kyriakidou-Nestoros (1983), Demetrios Loukopoulos (1927, 1930), and Ioanna Papandoniou (1976), among others. Specific textile practices found in Greece have been described in my own previously published work (J. Koster 1976; 1978; 1979a; 1979b; 1981; 1985; 1996).

4. Small flocks of sheep and goats were routinely kept in these regions primarily for meat. Informants remember their grandmothers spinning, carding, and weaving. Some surviving spinning wheels and associated tools can be found. Comparative ethnographic data were collected in 1986 by the author in northern Appalachian communities in New York State and in the Maritime Provinces of Canada. A similar pattern of subsistence textile production is described by Ennew for the Hebrides (1982: 178–179).

5. In 1986, one woman—a widow and a "Vlach" or Valtetsiotissa—was weaving rag rugs in Fournoi for sale to other villagers. In the 1990s, a store in Kranidhi attempted, unsuccessfully, to market to tourists traditional woolen saddlebags woven by another settled Vlach in the Ermioni area.

6. A handwoven woolen *fustanela* (traditional shepherd's kilt), owned by a retired goatherd in Dhidhima, utilized three and a half yards of cloth in the pleated skirt alone.

7. Such weaving in the summer pastures by Sarakatsani has also been noted by Campbell (1964: 33) and Hadzimihalis (1955).

8. This distortion is created by the effect of synchronous sampling. One should not expect to see all households that weave actually engaging in the practice simultaneously, because of the effect of household cycles on the need for weavings. This is reminiscent of the "snapshot effect" of village censuses, which might, for example, underestimate the percentage of households that move through a stem family form in their developmental cycle (Berkner 1972).

9. Based on time and motion studies conducted in 1973, I found that the mean spinning rate was 161 cm per minute. This rate done on a simple spindle and distaff is comparable to that of contemporary profes-

sional North American hand spinners using simple spinning wheels.

10. In Dhidhima, on the day of the wedding, the *roukha* is carefully displayed so that each piece is clearly visible, and then female neighbors and kin slowly file in and pin on favors of net wrapped sugar-coated almonds, then throw rice, almonds, and coins on the piled linens or *stoiva*.

11. This shift in practice has also been reported for Amouliani in northern Greece (Salamone and Stanton 1986: 112–113), where it is explained as a way in which married women can continue to reaffirm their competence as *noikokires* (housewives) and as a means of providing increased wealth for the wedding couple. A third aspect of this shift may be found in its role in securing advantage for the groom's family in marriage negotiations. The *roukha*, whether handwoven or purchased, still holds considerable value, as in the past. With the rapid inflation that has occurred in village dowry values it is to be expected that the bride's family will attempt to increase the percentage of the total dowry value constituted by the *roukha*. This is even more likely if they have ready access to cheap sources of fiber and adequate labor. If the groom also brings a *proika* that duplicates articles in the bride's *roukha*, this will tend to depress the leverage that her trousseau will command in negotiations. The groom's family will want to see a higher percentage of the dowry's value in cash, or other assets that can be more readily liquidated. The trousseau has ultimate cash value, as all are aware, but to be compelled to sell it is a measure of desperation, and one that is within the memory of those who lived through years of economic depression, war, and civil war. As Schneider (1980: 343) has observed, the trousseau represents a line of last defense for the household economy, a reserve that can be drawn upon only under dire conditions. The sense of *anangi* (economic necessity) may mute some of the feelings of loss of family honor in having to sell trousseau, but only partially. For such reasons this is a form of property that is best insulated from a scheming husband's designs to appropriate from the wife's *proika*. It has the added advantage of often having less impact on the bride's family of origin than for example the transfer of land, cash, trees, or other fixed assets.

12. Washing wool removes dirt, sweat, and lanolin, which comprise about half the total weight of the raw fleece.

13. As can be seen in Table 15.3, knitting occupied far more time than did any of the other fiber arts. Knitted handspun wool sweaters, socks, petticoats, and *fanelles* (long johns) were essential garments for agriculturalists and herders who worked outdoors in all weather, and these garments required annual replacement. Woolen underwear made up the bulk of this knitting. While it appears odd to many non-Greeks that local inhabitants would wear rough wool underwear year-round in a relatively warm climate, this reflects the local belief that perspiration evaporating too rapidly from the body causes chills that lead to colds and grippe. People who have worn this underwear all their lives fear that removing it will cause such illnesses.

14. Weaving can serve many decorative purposes not found in the southern Argolid, such as table scarves, nonfunctional pillow covers, and wall hangings.

15. Papandoniou's excellent volumes (1974; 1976) on traditional Greek folk costumes provide numerous examples of the fine needlework employed.

16. This monetary difference has been compounded by the changing nature of Greek tourism as well. Rather than being drawn by the historical attractions of ancient Greece, northern Europeans have been flocking to the sunny beaches of the Mediterranean for summer holidays. Hot woven woolens prove of little interest to beachgoers, who find more use for T-shirts and beach wear. Woven items of all kinds have dropped in value and in some cases have even become unmarketable.

References Cited

ARCHIVAL SOURCES

Athens

1705. *Catastico particolare d'ogni villa e luocco del territorio di Romania*. Medieval Archive, Academy of Athens.

Nani, Antonio, proveditor general of Morea. 1703–1705. *Relazione* read to the Venetian Senate, 1706. Nani Family Archive, vol. 1, fols. 239r–244v. Mss. Division, National Library of Greece.

Venice, Archivio di Stato

Ca. 1700. *Catastico ordinario che segue il disegno dil territorio di Napoli di Romania*. Sindici Inquisitori in Levante, vol. 81.

Pisani, Marco, proveditor in district of Romania, 1695–97. Report in vol. 411 of Deliberationi del Senato 1697. Marzo fin tutt' agosto. Rettori. Also labeled as Senato I (Secreta) filza 130.

SECONDARY SOURCES

Acheson, James M. 1972. "The Territories of the Lobstermen." *Natural History* 81: 60–69.

———. 1975. "The Lobster Fiefs: Economic and Ecological Effects of Territoriality in the Maine Lobster Industry." *Human Ecology* 3: 183–208.

Adams, Keith. 1981. "The Effects of Land Value on Farm Plot Subdivision and Consolidation: Didyma, Greece, 1936–78." Master's thesis, Department of Geography, University of North Carolina.

Akritas, Takis. 1957. *Methana the Historic Peninsula*. Athens: Kayiafas.

Albaugh, L. G. 1953. *Crete: A Case Study of an Underdeveloped Area*. Princeton: Princeton University Press.

Alcock, Susan E., John F. Cherry, and Jack L. Davis. 1994. "Intensive Survey, Agricultural Practice, and the Classical Landscape of Greece." In Morris (1994), pp. 137–70.

Alexakis, Eleftherios. 1980. *Clan and Family in Traditional Maniat Society*. Athens.

———. 1984. *Bride Price: A Contribution to the Study of Marriage Institutions in Modern Greece*. Athens.

Alexander, J. C. 1974. *Toward a History of Post-Byzantine Greece: The Ottoman Kannunnames for the Greek Lands, circa 1500–circa 1600*. Ph.D. dissertation, Department of History, Columbia University.

Alexiou, Margaret. 1978. "Modern Greek Folklore and Its Relation to the Past: The Evolution of Charos in Greek Tradition." In S. Vryonis, ed., *The "Past" in Medieval and Modern Greek Culture*, pp. 221–36. Malibu, Calif.: Undena Press.

Allen, Peter. 1973. *Social and Economic Change in a De-populated Community in Southern Greece*. Ph.D. dissertation, Department of Anthropology, Brown University.

———. 1976. "Aspida: A Depopulated Maniat Community." In Dimen and Friedl (1976), pp. 168–98.

———. 1981. "Close Up of a Maniat Village." *The Athenian* (October): 21–24.

Ammerman, Albert J. 1981. "Surveys and Archaeological Research." *Annual Review of Anthropology* 10: 63–88.

Anderson-Gerfaud, P. 1992. "Experimental Cultivation, Harvest and Threshing of Wild Cereals and Their Relevance for Interpreting the Use of Epipaleolithic and Neolithic Artefacts." In P. Anderson-Gerfaud (1992), pp. 159–209.

———, ed. 1992. *Prehistoire de l'agriculture: nouvelles approaches experimentales et ethnographiques*. Paris: Monographie du CRA 6.

Andreadis, A. 1913. "La marine marchande Grecque." *Journal des Economistes.*

Andromedas, John. 1963. "The Enduring Ties of a Modern Greek Subculture." In John Peristiany, ed., *Contributions to Mediterranean Sociology*, pp. 269–73. Paris: Mouton.

Angelomatis-Tsougarakis, Helen. 1990. *The Eve of the Greek Revival: British Travellers' Perceptions of Early Nineteenth-Century Greece.* London: Routledge.

Anoyatis-Pele, Dimitris. 1987. *Connaissance de la population et des productions de la Morée a travers un manuscrit anonyme de la fin du XVIIIe siècle.* Athens: Manourtios.

Antonakatou, Diana and Takis Mavros. 1973. *Argolidhos Periiyisis.* Nafplio: Nomarkhias Argolidhos.

Antoniadis-Bibicou, H. 1965. "Villages desertes en Grèce: un bilan provisoire." In *Villages desertes et histoire economique, XIe–XVIIIe siècles*, pp. 343–417. Paris: École Pratique des Hautes Études.

Arnaoutoglou, Argiris. 1985. "Hydra." In Dimitri Philippides, ed., *Greek Traditional Architecture*, vol. 1, pp. 279–312. Athens: Melissa Press.

Aschenbrenner, Stanley. 1972. "A Contemporary Community." In McDonald and Rapp (1972), pp.47–63.

———. 1976a. "Archaeology and Ethnography in Messenia." In Dimen and Friedl (1976), pp. 158–67.

———. 1976b. "Karpofora: Reluctant Farmers on a Fertile Land." In Dimen and Friedl (1976), pp. 207–21.

———. 1986. *Life in a Changing Greek Village.* University of Minnesota, Publications in Ancient Studies No. 2.

Asdrakhas, S. 1879. I Oikonomiki domi ton Valanikon khoron (15-19 Aionas). Athens: Melissa Press.

———. 1983. *Zitimata Istorias.* Athens: Themelio.

Ataman, K. 1992. "Threshing Sledges and Archaeology." In Anderson-Gerfaud, ed. (1992), pp. 305–19.

Augustinos, Olga. 1994. *French Odysseys: Greece in French Travel Literature from the Renaissance to the Romantic Era.* Baltimore: Johns Hopkins University Press.

Bailey, F. G., ed. 1971. *Gifts and Poison: the Politics of Reputation.* New York: Schocken Books.

Bailey, H. P. 1979. "Semi-Arid Climates: Their Definition and Distribution." In Hall, Cannell, and Lawton (1979), pp. 73–97.

Baity, Elizabeth S. 1942. *Man is a Weaver.* New York: Viking Press.

Baldwin, Kennet. 1972. "Land Tenure in Crete, The Case of the Messara Plain." *Land Reform* 1: 73–89.

Banfield, Edward C. 1958. *The Moral Basis of a Backward Society.* New York: The Free Press.

Barkan, O. L. 1957. "Essai sur les données statistiques des registres de recensement dans l'empire Ottoman aux XVe et XVIe siècles." *Journal of the Economic and Social History of the Orient* 1: 9–36.

Barth, Fredrik. 1959. *Political Leadership Among Swat Pathans.* London: Athlone Press.

———. 1961. *Nomads of South Persia.* Boston: Little, Brown.

———. 1963. Introduction to *The Role of the Entrepreneur in Social Change in Northern Norway*, F. Barth, ed. Bergen: Norwegian Universities Press.

Bartlett, Peggy F. 1980. "Adaptive Strategies in Peasant Agricultural Production." *Annual Review of Anthropology* 9: 545–73.

Baxevanis, John J. 1965. "Population, Internal Migration and Urbanization in Greece." *Balkan Studies* 6: 83–98.

———. 1972. *Economy and Population Movements in the Peloponnesos of Greece.* Athens: National Centre of Social Research.

Beazley, John D. 1942. *Attic Red-Figure Vase-Painters.* Oxford: Clarendon Press.

———. 1956. *Attic Black-Figure Vase-Painters.* Oxford: Clarendon Press.

Beldiceanu, N., and Beldiceanu-Steinherr, Irène. 1980. "Recherches sur la Morée (1461–1512)." *Südost-Forschungen* 39: 17–74.

Belesioti, Niki. 1978. *Traditional Methods of Cultivation in Greece.* Athens: Benaki Museum.

Bender, D. 1967. "A Refinement of the Concept of the Household: Family, Coresidence and Domestic Functions." *American Anthropologist* 69: 293.

Benito, C. A. 1976. "Peasant's Response to Modernization Projects in Minifundia Economies." *American Journal of Agricultural Economics* 58: 143–51.

Bennett, Diane. 1988. "The Poor Have Much More Money: Changing Socio-economic Relations in a Greek Village." *Journal of Modern Greek Studies* 6: 217–44.

Bentley, J. W. 1987a. "A Parish Study in the Minho (Portugal)." In S. R. Pearson, ed., *Portuguese Agriculture in Transition.* Ithaca: Cornell University Press.

———. 1987b. "Economic and Ecological Approaches to Land Fragmentation: In Defense of a Much Maligned Phenomenon." *Annual Reviews In Anthropology* 16: 31–67.

———. 1990. "Wouldn't You Like to Have All of Your

Land in One Place? Land Fragmentation in Northwest Portugal." *Human Ecology* 18: 51–79.

Beopoulou, Ioanna. 1981. "Trikeri: mobilité et rapports d'appartenance." In Damaniakis (1981), pp. 191–99.

Berkner, Lutz. 1972. "The Stem Family and the Developmental Cycle of the Peasant Household: An Eighteenth Century Austrian Example." *American Historical Review* 77: 398–418.

———. 1975. "The Use and Misuse of Census Data for Historical Analysis of Family Structure." *Journal of Interdisciplinary Studies* 5: 721–38.

Berkowitz, Susan G. 1984. "Familism, Kinship and Sex Roles in Southern Italy: Contradictory Ideals and Real Contradictions." *Journal of Family History* 7: 289–98.

Bernard, Randolf. 1689. *The Present State of the Morea, Called Anciently Peloponnesus*. London: Will Notts.

Beuermann, Arnold. 1954. "Kalyviendörfer im Peloponnes." In *Ergebnisse und Probleme Moderner Geographischer Forschung*, pp. 229–38. Bremen: Walter Dorn.

Bialor, Perry A. 1973. "A Century and a Half of Change: Transformations of a Greek Farming Community in the Northwestern Peloponnesos, Greece." Ph.D. dissertation, Department of Anthropology, University of Chicago.

———. 1976. "The Northwestern Corner of the Peloponnesos: Mavrikion and its Region." In Dimen and Friedl (1976), pp. 222–35.

Binford, Lewis. 1978. "Dimensional Analysis of Behavior and Site Structure: Learning from an Eskimo Hunting Stand." *American Antiquity* 43: 330–61.

Binns, Bernard O. 1950. *The Consolidation of Fragmented Agricultural Holdings*. Washington, D.C.: UNFAO Agricultural Studies, 11.

Bintliff, J. L. 1977. "Natural Environment and Human Settlement in Prehistoric Greece." British Archaeological Reports, Supplementary Series, 28.

———. 1982. "Settlement Patterns, Land Tenure and Social Structure: A Diachronic Model." In C. Renfrew and S. Shennan, eds., *Ranking, Resource and Exchange: Aspects of the Archaeology of Early European Society*, pp. 106–11. Cambridge: Cambridge University Press.

Bintliff, J. L., and A. M. Snodgrass. 1985. "The Cambridge/Bradford Boeotian Expedition: the first four years." *Journal of Field Archaeology* 12: 123–61.

Biris, Kostas. 1960. *Arvanites, oi Dhorieis tou Neoterou Ellinismou*. Athens: G. Bizoumi.

Blaxter, Lorraine. 1971. "Rendre Service and Jalousie." In Bailey, F. G. (1971), pp. 119–38.

Blitzer, Harriet. 1982. "The Nineteenth and Early Twentieth Centuries." *Hesperia*, Supplement 18: 30–35.

———. 1990. "Koroneika Storage-Jar Production and Trade in the Traditional Aegean." *Hesperia* 59: 675–711.

Bloch, Marc. 1966. "The Rise of Dependent Cultivation and Seignorial Institutions." In M. M. Postan, ed., *The Cambridge Economic History of Europe*, vol. 1, pp. 235–89. 2d ed. Cambridge: Cambridge University Press.

Blok, Anton. 1969. "Variations in Patronage." *Sociologische Gids* 16: 365–78.

Boerio, Giuseppe. 1829. *Dizionario del Dialetto Veneziano*. Venice: Andrea Santini.

Boissevain, Jeremy. 1966. "Patronage in Sicily." *Man* 1: 18–23.

———. 1969. "Patrons as Brokers." *Sociologische Gids* 16: 379–86.

Bon, A. 1969. *La Morée franque: Recherches historiques, topographiques et archéologiques sur la principauté d'Achaïe (1205–1430)*. Paris: Bibliothèeque des Ecoles Françaises d'Athènes et de Rome, fasc. 213.

Bory de Saint Vincent, J. B. G. M. 1834–36. *Expédition scientifique de Morée: Travaux de la Section des Sciences Physiques*. Paris: F.G. Levrault.

Boserup, Ester. 1965. *The Conditions of Agricultural Growth*. Chicago: Aldine.

Bottomley, Gillian. 1992. *From Another Place: Migration and the Politics of Culture*. Cambridge: Cambridge University Press.

Bouras, Kharalambos. 1983. "The Approach to Vernacular Architecture, General Introduction." In Philippides (1983), vol. 1, pp. 21–32.

Bowden, L. 1979. "Development of Present Dryland Farming Systems." In Hall, Cannell, and Lawton (1979), pp. 45–72.

Bowles, Francis P. 1972. "The Fisherman as a Predator: The Role of the Lobster Fisherman in a Marine Ecosystem." Paper presented at the 71st Annual Meeting of the American Anthropological Association, Toronto.

Boyd, T. D., and W. W. Rudolph. 1978. "Excavations at Porto Cheli and vicinity, preliminary report IV: The Lower Town of Halieis, 1970–1977." *Hesperia* 47: 333–55.

Brandes, Stanley. 1973. "Social Structure and Interpersonal Relations in Navagonal (Spain)." *American Anthropologist* 75: 750–64.

———. 1975. *Migration, Kinship and Community: Tradition and Transition in a Spanish Village*. New York: Academic Press.

Brewster, John M. 1967. "Traditional Social Structures as Barriers to Change." In Herman M. Southworth and Bruce F. Johnson, eds., *Agricultural Development and Economic Growth*, Ithaca: Cornell University Press.

British School of Archaeology. 1985. "Methana." *Archaeological Reports* 31: 21–22.

———. 1986. "Methana." *Archaeological Reports* 32: 28.

Britton, D. K. 1977. "Some Explorations in the Analysis of Long-Term Changes in the Structure of Agriculture." *Journal of Agricultural Economics* 28: 197–209.

Brokensha, David W., Michael M. Horowitz, and Thayer Scudder. 1977. *The Anthropology of Rural Development in the Sahel: Proposals for Research*. Binghamton, N.Y.: Institute for Development Anthropology.

Bunzel, Ruth. 1929. *The Pueblo Potter: a Study of Creative Imagination in Primitive Art*. New York: Columbia University Press.

Burford, Alison. 1993. *Land and Labour in the Greek World*. Baltimore: Johns Hopkins University Press.

Burgel, Guy. 1965. *Pobia*. Athens: National Centre of Social Research.

———. 1972. *Recherches sur la Grèce rurale*. Memoires et documents, n.s. 13.

———. 1981. "La Grèce rurale revisitée." In Damianakis (1981), pp. 11–17.

Burrison, John A. 1983. *Brothers in Clay: The Story of Georgia Folk Pottery*. Athens: University of Georgia Press.

Bursian, Conrad. 1868–72. *Geographie von Griechenland*. Leipzig: B.G. Teubner.

Burton, S., and R. King. 1982. "Land Fragmentation and Consolidation in Cyprus." *Agricultural Administration* 11: 183–200.

Busch, Ruth C., Charles D. Busch, and Naki Uner. 1979. "Field Fragmentation on an Irrigated Plain in Turkey." *Human Organization* 18: 37–43.

Calligas, Haris. 1979. "The Evolution of Settlements in Mani." In Doumanis and Oliver (1979), pp. 115–37.

Cameron, Catherine M., and Steve A. Tomka, eds. 1992. *Abandonment of Settlements and Regions: Ethnoarchaeological and Archaeological Approaches*. Cambridge: Cambridge University Press.

Campbell, John K. 1964. *Honour, Family, and Patronage: A Study of Institutions and Moral Values in a Greek Mountain Village*. Oxford: Clarendon Press.

———. 1980. "Traditional Values and Continuities in Greek Society." In Richard Clogg, ed., *Greece in the 1980's*, pp. 184–297. London: Macmillan.

Campbell, John K., and Phillip Sherrard. 1968. *Modern Greece*. New York: Praeger.

Carlyle, W. J. 1983. "Fragmentation and Consolidation in Manitoba." *Canadian Geographer* 27: 17–34.

Carter, T. R., and N. T. Konijn. 1988. "The Choice of First-Order Impact Models for Semi-Arid Regions." In M. L. Parry, T. R. Carter, and N. T. Konijn, eds., *The Impact of Climatic Variations on Agriculture*, vol. 2, pp. 61–84. Dordrecht: Kluwer Academic.

Casagrande, Joseph. 1977. "Looms of Otavalo." *Natural History* 84, No. 8: 48–59.

Caskey, J. L. 1960. *The Early Helladic Period in the Argolid*. Hesperia 29: 285–303.

Cavounidis, Jennifer. 1983. "Capitalist Development and Women's Work in Greece." *Journal of Modern Greek Studies* 1: 321–38.

Champion, Timothy C. 1989. Introduction. In T. C. Champion, ed., *Centre and Periphery: Comparative Studies in Archaeology*, pp. 1–21. London: Unwin Hyman.

Chandler, Richard. 1776. *Travels in Greece*. Dublin: Price and Whitestone.

Chang, Claudia. 1981. "The Archaeology of Contemporary Herding Sites in Didyma, Greece." Ph.D. dissertation, Department of Anthropology, State University of New York, Binghamton.

———. 1984. "The Ethnoarchaeology of Herding Sites in Greece." *MASCA Journal* 3, No. 2: 44–48.

———. 1992. "Archaeological Landscapes: The Ethnoarchaeology of Pastoral Land Use in the Grevena Province of Greece." In Rossignol and Wandsnider (1992), pp. 65–89.

———. 1993. "Pastoral Transhumance in the Southern Balkans as a Social Ideology: Ethnoarchaeological Research in Northern Greece." *American Anthropologist* 95: 687–703.

———. 1994. "Sheep for the Ancestors: Ethnoarchaeology and the Study of Ancient Pastoralism." In Kardulias (1994), pp. 353–71.

Chang, C., and H. A. Koster. 1986. "Beyond Bones: Toward an Archaeology of Pastoralism." *Advances in Archaeological Method and Theory* 9: 97–148.

Chang, C., and H. A. Koster, eds. 1995. *Pastoralists at the*

Periphery: Herders in a Capitalist World. Tucson: University of Arizona Press.

Chang, C., and P. A. Tourtellotte. 1993. "The Ethnoarchaeological Survey of Pastoral Transhumant Sites in the Grevena Prefecture of Greece." *Journal of Field Archaeology* 20: 249–64.

Charlton, Thomas H. 1981. "Archaeology, Ethnohistory, and Ethnology: Interpretive Interfaces." *Advances in Archaeological Method and Theory* 4: 129–76.

Chase-Dunn, Christopher K., and Thomas D. Hall. 1991. *Core/Periphery Relations in Precapitalist Worlds.* Boulder: Westview Press.

Chayanov, A. V. 1986. *The Theory of Peasant Economy.* D. Thorner, B. Kerblay, and R. E. F. Smith, eds. Madison: University of Wisconsin.

Cheetham, N. 1981. *Mediaeval Greece.* Yale University Press, New Haven.

Cherry, John F. 1983. "Frogs Round the Pond: Perspectives on Current Archaeological Survey Projects in the Mediterranean Region." In Keller and Rupp (1983), pp. 375–416.

———. 1988. "Pastoralism and the Role of Animals in the Pre- and Protohistoric Economies of the Aegean." In C. R. Whittaker, ed., *Pastoral Economies in Classical Antiquity*, pp. 6–34. Cambridge Philogical Society, Supplementary Volume No. 14.

———. 1994. "Regional Survey in the Aegean: The 'New Wave' (and After)." In Kardulias (1994), pp. 91–112.

Cherry, John, Jack L. Davis, and Eleni Mantzourani, eds. 1991. *Landscape Archeology as Long-Term History: Northern Keos in the Cycladic Islands.* Monumenta Archaeologica, vol. 16, Institute of Archaeology, University of California at Los Angeles.

Chiotis, George. 1972. "Regional Development Policy in Greece." *Tijds. Econ. Soc. Geo.* (Rotterdam) 63 (2): 94–104.

Chisholm, Michael. 1968. *Rural Settlement and Land Use: An Essay in Location.* London: Hutchinson University Library.

Choras, G. A. 1975. *I Ayia Moni Areias en ti ekklisiastiki kai politiki istoria Nafpliou kai Argous.* Athens.

Christaller, W. 1933. *Die centralen Orte in Suddeutschland.* Jena.

Christodolou, Demetrios. 1959. *The Evolution of the Rural Land Use Patterns in Cyprus.* Regional Monograph No 8, Geographical Publications, Bude, Cornwall.

Clark, Colin. 1973. "The Economics of Overexploitation." *Science* 181: 631–634.

Clark, G. and L. Wagner. 1974. *Potters of Southern Africa.* Capetown: C. Struik.

Clarke, Mari H. 1976a. "Farming and Foraging in Prehistoric Greece." In Dimen and Friedl (1976), pp. 127–42.

———. 1976b. "Gathering in the Argolid: A Subsistence Subsystem in a Greek Agricultural Community." In Dimen and Friedl (1976), pp. 251–64.

———. 1976c. "In Pursuit of Wild Edibles, Present and Past." *Expedition* 19: 12–18.

———. 1977. "Farming and Foraging in Prehistoric Greece: the Nutritional Ecology of Wild Resource Use." In Thomas Fitzgerald, ed., *Nutrition and Anthropology in Action*, pp. 46–60. Amsterdam: Vangorcum.

———. 1983. "Variations on Themes of Male and Female: Reflections on Gender Bias in Fieldwork in Rural Greece." *Women's Studies* 10: 117–34.

———. 1984. "Woman Headed Households and Poverty: Insights from Kenya." *Signs* 10: 338–54.

———. 1985. *Household Economic Strategies and Support Networks of the Poor in Kenya: A Literature Review.* Washington, D.C.: World Bank.

———. 1988. "The Transformation of Households on Methana 1972–1987." In E. Papataxiarchis, ed., *Proceedings of the Symposium on Horizons of Anthropological Research in Greece*, Athens: University of the Aegean.

———. 1989. "'Nevra' in a Greek Village: Metaphor for Social Conflict." In Dona Davis, ed., *Gender and Illness*, pp. 195–217. New York: Hemisphere.

———. 1995. "From Shelters to Villas: Changing House and Settlement Form on Methana, 1880–1987." In Pavlides and Sutton (1995), pp. 511–36.

———. 1997. "Wild Herbs in the Marketplace: Gathering in Response to Market Demand." In Kardulias and Shutes (1997), pp. 214–35.

———. 1998. "Kali Sira: Perpetuating the Family Estate on Methana, Greece." *Ethnografika.*

Clarke, Mari H., and John P. Mason, eds. 1991. *New Directions in U. S. Foreign Assistance and New Roles for Anthropologists.* Williamsburg, Va.: Department of Anthropology, College of William and Mary.

Clifford, James. 1988. *The Predicament of Culture: Twentieth-Century Ethnography, Literature, and Art.* Cambridge: Harvard University Press.

Clifford, James, and George E. Marcus, eds. 1986. *Writ-*

ing Culture: the Poetics and Politics of Ethnography. Berkeley: University of California Press.

Clout, Hugh D. 1972. *Rural Geography.* New York: Pergamon.

———. 1984. *A Rural Policy for the EEC.* London. Methuen.

Clutton, A. E. 1978. "Review of Land Ownership in Cyprus (with Special Reference to Greek and Turkish Ownership)." *Geography.*

Cole, J. W., and E. R. Wolf. 1974. *The Hidden Frontier: Ecology and Ethnicity in an Alpine Valley.* New York: Academic Press.

Collard, Anna. 1981. "The Inequalities of Change in a Greek Mountain Village (Sterea Hellas: Evritania)." In Damianakis (1981), pp. 208–20.

Colson, Elizabeth. 1979. "In Good Years and in Bad: Food Strategies of Self-Reliant Societies." *Journal of Anthropological Research* 35: 8–29.

Common, R., and A. Prentice. 1956. "Some Observations on the Lowland Macedonian Village." *Tijds. Econ. Soc. Geo.* (Rotterdam) 47: 122–36.

Constantine, D. 1984. *Early Greek Travellers and the Hellenic Ideal.* Cambridge: Cambridge University Press.

Costa, Janeen Arnold. 1988. "The History of Migration and Political Economy in Rural Greece: A Case Study." *Journal of Modern Greek Studies* 6: 159–86.

Cotelazzo, Manlio, and Paolo Zolli. 1979. *Dizionario Etimologico della Lingua Italiana.* Bologna: Nicola Zanichelli.

Couroucli, Maria. 1981. "Changement et immobilité dans le montagne de Corfu." In Damianakis (1981), pp. 221–30.

———. 1985. *Les Oliviers du Lignage.* Paris: Maisonneuve et Larose.

———. 1989. "Review of D. Psychoyios, Proikes, foroi, stafida, kai psomi." *Journal of Modern Greek Studies* 7: 355–56.

Cowan, Jane. 1990. *Dance and the Body Politic in Northern Greece.* Princeton: Princeton University Press.

———. 1991. "Going Out for Coffee? Contesting the Grounds of Gendered Pleasures in Everyday Sociability." In Loizos and Papataxiarchis (1991), pp. 180–202.

Crist, Raymond E. 1964. "Review of Farm Fragmentation in Greece, by K. Thompson." *Geographical Review* 54: 449–50.

Crumley, Carole L., and William H. Marquardt, eds. 1987. *Regional Dynamics: Burgundian Landscapes in Historical Perspective.* New York: Academic Press.

Cullen, Tracey. 1984. "Social Implications of Ceramic Style in the Neolithic Peloponnese." In W. D. Kingery, ed., *Ancient Technology to Modern Science*, pp. 77–100. Columbus, Ohio: American Ceramic Society.

Curtius, Ernst. 1852. *Peloponnesos.* Gotha: Perthes.

Cvijic, Jovan. 1918. *La Peninsule Balkanique.* Paris: Armand Colin.

Damianakis, Stathis, ed. 1981. *Aspects du changement social dans la campagne grecque.* Athens: National Centre of Social Research.

Danforth, Loring M. 1989. *Firewalking and Religious Healing: The Anastenaria of Greece and the American Firewalking Movement.* Princeton: Princeton University Press.

———. 1995. *The Macedonian Conflict: Ethnic Nationalism in a Transnational World.* Princeton: Princeton University Press.

David, Nicholas. 1992. "Integrating Ethnoarchaeology: A Subtle Realist Perspective." *Journal of Anthropological Archaeology* 11: 330–59.

Davis, J. 1973. *Land and Family in Pesticci.* New York: Humanities Press.

———. 1977. *People of the Mediterranean.* London: Routledge.

Davis, Jack L. 1991. "Contributions to a Mediterranean Rural Archaeology: Historical Case Studies frm the Ottoman Cyclades." *Journal of Mediterranean Archaeology* 4: 131–215.

Dawkins, R. M. 1902. "Notes From Karpathos." *The Annual of the British School of Archaeology* 9: 177–201.

DeBoer, Warren B., and Donald Lathrap. 1979. "The Making and Breaking of Shipibo-Conibo Ceramics." In Carol Kramer, ed., *Ethno-archaeology: Implications of Ethnography for Archaeology*, pp. 102–38. New York: Columbia University Press.

Deetz, James. 1965. *The Dynamics of Stylistic Change in Arikara Ceramics.* Urbana: University of Illinois Press.

de Jassaud, Auguste. [1809] 1978. *Mémoire sur l'état physique et politique des isles d'Hydra, Spécié, Poro et Ipsera en l'année 1808.* Notes and introduction by Constantin Svolopoulos. Athens: Librairie N. Karavias.

Delano-Smith, Catherine, and Virginia Watson. 1964. "La geographie et l'histoire dans la region d'Argos (Grèce)." *Méditerranée* [GAP] 4: 329–40.

Dennell, R. 1983. *European Economic Prehistory: A New Approach.* London: Academic Press.

de Vooys, A. C. 1959. "Western Thessaly in Transition." *Tijks. K. Nederl. Gen.* 76 (1): 31–54.

deVooys, A. C., and J. J. C. Piket. 1959. "A Geographical Analysis of Two Villages in the Peloponnesos." *Tijds. Kon. Nederl. Aardr* 75 (1): 30–55; Geographisch Instituut der Rijks, Universiteit te Utrecht.

Dickenson, Robert E. 1954. "Land Reform in Southern Italy." *Economic Geography* 30: 157–76.

Dimen, Muriel. 1970. "Change and Continuity in a Greek Mountain Village." Ph.D. dissertation, Department of Anthropology, Columbia University.

———. 1986. "Servants and Sentries: Women, Power, and Social Reproduction in Kriovrisi." In Jill Dubisch (1986), pp. 53–67.

Dimen, Muriel, and Ernestine Friedl, eds. 1976. *Regional Variation in Modern Greece and Cyprus: Toward a Perspective on the Ethnography of Greece.* Annals of the New York Academy of Sciences. vol. 268.

Dodwell, Edward. 1819. *A Classical and Topographical Tour through Greece During 1801, 1805 and 1806.* 2 vols. London: Rodwell and Martin.

Dokos, Konstantinos. 1975. *I Sterea Ellas kata ton Enetotourkikon Polemon, 1684–1699, kai o Salonon Filotheos.* Athens: Etaireia Stereoelladikon Meleton.

———, ed. 1971–72. "I en Peloponneso ekklesiastiki periousia kata tin periodhon tis dhefteras venetokratias: Anekhdota engrafa ek ton arkheion Venetias." *Byzantinischneugriechische Jahrbücher* 21: 43–168.

———. 1971. *Sterea Hellas kata ton venetotourkikon polemon (1684–1699) kai o Salonon Filotheos.* Etaireia Stereoelladhikon Meleton, Text and Studies, No. 1. Athens.

Dolger, F. 1955. "Ein Chrysobull des Kaisers Andronikos II für Theodoros Nomikopoulos aus dem Jahre 1288." *Orientalia Christiana Periodica,* 21: 58–62.

Dorner, Peter. 1972. *Land Reform and Economic Development.* Baltimore: Penguin Books.

Douglas, Mary. 1972. "Symbolic Orders in the Use of Domestic Space." In Peter Ucko, Ruth Tringham, and G. W. Dimbleby, eds., *Man, Settlement and Urbanism,* pp. 515–22. London: Duckworth.

Douglass, W. A. 1969. *Death in Murelaga: Funerary Ritual in a Spanish Basque Village.* Seattle: University of Washington Press.

———. 1984. "Sheep Ranchers and Sugar Growers: Property Transmission in the Basque Immigrant Family of the American West and Australia." In Netting, Wilk, and Arnould (1984), pp. 109–29.

Doumanis, Orestis, and Paul Oliver, eds. 1979. *Shelter in Greece.* Athens: Architecture in Greece Press.

Dovring, Folke. 1962. "Flexibility and Security in Agrarian Reform Programs." In *Agrarian Reforms and Economic Growth in Developing Countries, Seminar on Research Perspectives and Problems,* pp. 30–40. Washington, D.C.: U.S. Dept. of Agriculture.

———. 1965. *Land and Labor in Europe in the Twentieth Century.* The Hague: Martinus Nijhoff.

Dow, Malcolm. 1985. "Agricultural Intensification and Craft Specialization: A Non-Recursive Model." *Ethnology* 24: 137–52.

Downing, Theodore E. 1973. "Zapotec Inheritance." Ph.D. dissertation, Department of Anthropology, Stanford University.

———. 1976. "Wealth Adjustment Mechanisms in Mesoamerican Communities." In Proceedings of the 41st International Congress of Americanists.

———. 1977. "Partible Inheritance and Land Fragmentation in a Oaxaca Village." *Human Organization* 36: 235–43.

Drakakis, A. T., and Stil. I. Koundhouros. 1939–40. *Arkheia peri tis sistaseos kai exelixeos ton dhimon kai koinotiton 1836–1939.* Athens: Ministry of the Interior.

Dubisch, Jill. 1972. "The Open Community: Migration from a Greek Island Village." Ph.D. dissertation, Department of Anthropology, University of Chicago.

———. 1973. "The Domestic Power of Women in a Greek Island Village." *Studies in European Society* 1: 23–33.

———. 1977. "The City as Resource: Migration from a Greek Island Village." *Urban Anthropology* 6: 65–82.

———. 1986a. Introduction. In Dubisch, ed. (1986), pp. 3–4.

———. 1986b. "Culture Enters Through the Kitchen: Women, Food and Social Boundaries in Rural Greece." In Dubisch, ed. (1986), pp. 195–214.

———. 1995a. *In a Different Place: Pilgrimage, Gender, and Politics at a Greek Island Shrine.* Princeton: Princeton University Press.

———. 1995b. "The Church of the Annunciation of Tinos and the Domestication of Institutional Space." In Pavlides and Sutton, pp. 389–418.

———, ed. 1986. *Gender and Power in Rural Greece.* Princeton: Princeton University Press.

Du Boulay, Juliet. 1974. *Portrait of a Greek Mountain Village.* Oxford: Clarendon Press.

———. 1983. "The Meaning of Dowry: Changing Values in Rural Greece." *Journal of Modern Greek Studies* 1: 243–70.

Dunnell, Robert C. 1992. "The Notion Site." In Rossignol and Wandsnider (1992), pp. 21–41.

Dyer, Louis. 1891. *Studies of the Gods in Greece at Certain Sanctuaries Recently Excavated*. London: Macmillan.

Edwards, C. J. W. 1978. "The Effects of Changing Farm Size Upon Levels of Farm Fragmentation: A Somerset Case Study." *Journal of Agricultural Economics* 29: 43–154.

Eisner, Robert. 1991. *Travelers to an Antique Land: The History and Literature of Travel to Greece*. Ann Arbor: University of Michigan Press.

Ekholm, Eric P. 1976. *The Dispossessed of the Earth: Land Reform and Sustainable Development*. Worldwatch Institute Paper No. 30. New York: Worldwatch.

Emo, A. 1709. "Relazione." Reprinted and edited by S. P. Lambros [1900]. *Dheltion tis historikes kai ethnoloyikes etairias tis Elladhos* 5: 644–706.

Enkyklopaidhikon Lexikon Eleftheroudhaki. 1930.

Ennew, Judith. 1982. "Harris Tweed: Construction, retention and representation of a cottage industry." In Goody (1982), pp. 166–99.

Erasmus, Charles. 1956. "Culture, Structure and Process: The Occurrence and Disappearance of Reciprocal Farm Labor." *Southwestern Journal of Anthropology* 12: 444–69.

Evangelidhou, T. 1934. *Istoria tou epikismou tis Idhras*. Athens: E. I. Khatziíoannou.

Evangelinides, Mary. 1979. "Core-Periphery Relations in the Greek Case." In D. Seers, B. Schaffer, and M. Kiljunen, eds., *Underdeveloped Europe: Studies in Core-Periphery Relations*, pp. 177–95. Atlantic Highlands, N.J.: Humanities Press.

Evelpidis, C., and S. Tsaousis. 1944. *The Rural House*. Athens.

Fabian, Johannes. 1983. *Time and the Other: How Anthropology Makes Its Object*. New York: Columbia University Press.

Faraklas, N. 1972. *Trizinia, Kalavria, Methana*. Athens: Center for Ekistics.

Farmer, B. H. 1960. "On Not Controlling Subdivision in Paddylands." *Transactions of Institute of British Geographers* 28: 225–35.

Fedalto, G. 1978. *La chiesa latina in oriente*, vol. III, Documenti veneziani, Verona.

Fenoaltea, S. 1976. "Risk, Transaction Costs and the Origin of Medieval Agriculture." *Explorations in Economic History* 13: 29–151.

Fife, Daniel. 1971. "Killing the Goose." *Environment* 13: 20–27.

Filipovic, Milenko S. 1970. "Reciprocity in Folk Life: the Serbian Case." *Ethnologia Europaea* 2: 123–126.

Finlay, George. 1877. *A History of Greece*. Oxford: Clarendon Press.

Fitzgerald, Denise A. 1951. "Land Tenure and Economic Development." *Land Economics* 27: 385–88.

Folbre, Nancy. 1984. "Household Production in the Philippines: A Non-Neoclassical Approach." *Economic Development and Cultural Change* 32: 303–30.

Forbes, D. K. 1984. *The Geography of Underdevelopment*. Baltimore: Johns Hopkins University Press.

Forbes, Hamish A. 1975. "From Bovine to Equine: Aspects of Agricultural Intensification in Modern Greece and Mediaeval Europe." Paper presented at the 74th Annual Meeting of the American Anthropological Association, San Francisco.

———. 1976a. "'We Have a Little of Everything': The Ecological Basis of Some Agricultural Practices in Methana, Trizinia." In Dimen and Friedl (1976), pp. 236–50.

———. 1976b. "The 'Thrice-Ploughed Field': Cultivation Techniques in Ancient and Modern Greece." *Expedition* 19: 5–11.

———. 1982. "Strategies and Soils: Technology, Production and the Environment in the Peninsula of Methana, Greece." Ph.D. dissertation, Department of Anthropology, University of Pennsylvania.

———. 1983. "The Struggle for Cash: The Integrated Exploitation of the Cultivated and Non-Cultivated Landscapes in the Southern Argolid, Peloponnesus, Greece." *Journal of Historical Geography* 9: 206–07.

———. 1987. Review of *The Poetics of Manhood*, by Michael Hertzfeld. *Liverpool Classical Monthly* 15, No. 1: 8–15.

———. 1989. "Of Grandfathers and Grand Theories: The Hierarchised Ordering of Responses to Hazard in a Greek Rural Community." In Paul Halstead and John O'Shea, eds., *Bad Year Economics: Cultural Responses to Risk and Uncertainty*, pp. 87–97. Cambridge: Cambridge University Press.

———. 1992. "The Ethnoarchaeological Approach to Ancient Greek Agriculture: Olive Cultivation as a Case Study." In B. Wells, ed., *Agriculture in Ancient Greece*, pp. 87–104. Stockholm: Proceedings of the Seventh International Symposium at the Swedish Institute at Athens, 4°, XLII.

———. 1993. "Ethnoarchaeology and the Place of the Olive in the Economy of the Southern Argolid,

Greece." *Bulletin de Correspondance Hellenique*, Supplement 26: 213–26.

Forbes, Hamish A., and Lynn Foxhall. 1978. "The Olive: Queen of All Trees: Some Preliminary Notes on the Archaeology of the Olive." *Expedition* 21: 37–47.

———. 1995. "Ethnoarchaeology and Storage in the Ancient Mediterranean: Beyond Risk and Survival." In J. Wilkins, D. Harvey, and M. Dobson, eds., *Food in Antiquity*, pp. 69–86. Exeter: University of Exeter Press.

Forbes, Hamish A., and Harold A. Koster. 1976. "Fire, Axe and Plow: Human Influence on Local Plant Communities in the Southern Argolid." In Dimen and Friedl (1976), pp. 109–26.

Forbes, Hamish A., Harold A. Koster, and Lin Foxhall. 1978. "Terrace Agriculture and Erosion: Environmental Effects of Population Instability in the Mediterranean." Paper presented at the Symposium on Deforestation, Erosion, and Ecology in the Ancient Mediterranean and Near East. Smithsonian Institution, Washington, D.C.

Forbes, Hamish A., and C. B. Mee. 1997. Introduction to *A Rough and Rocky Place: Settlement and Land Use on the Peninsula of Methana Greece*. Christopher Mee and Hamish Forbes, eds. Liverpool: University of Liverpool Press.

Forbes, Hamish A., C. B. Mee, and Lin Foxhall. 1996. "Six Hundred Years of Settlement History of the Methana Peninsula: An Interdisciplinary Approach." *Dialogos* 3: 72–94.

Foster, George M. 1961. "The Dyadic Contract: A Model for the Social Structure of a Mexican Peasant Village." *American Anthropologist* 63: 1173–1192.

———. 1965a. "The Sociology of Pottery: Questions and Hypotheses Arising from Contemporary Mexican Work." In Fredrick R. Matson, ed., *Ceramics and Man*, pp. 43–61. New York: Wenner-Gren.

———. 1965b. "Peasant Society and the Image of Limited Good." *American Anthropologist* 67: 293–315.

———. 1977. "Life Expectancy of Utilitarian Pottery in Tzintzuntzan, Michoacan, Mexico." In Daniel Ingersoll, John E. Yellen, and William McDonald, eds. *Experimental Archaeology*, pp. 352–58. New York: Columbia University Press.

Fotiadis, Michael. 1992. "Units of Data as Deployment of Disciplinary Codes." In Gardin and Peebles (1992), pp. 132–48.

———. 1994. "What is Archaeology's 'Mitigated Objectivism' Mitigated By? Comments on Wylie." *American Antiquity* 59: 545–55.

———. 1995. "Modernity and the Past-Still-Present: Politics of Time in the Birth of Regional Archaeological Projects in Greece." *American Journal of Archeology* 99: 59–78.

Fotos, Evan. 1957. "Land Tenure and Rural Organization in Turkey since 1923." Ph.D. dissertation, American University.

Fox, Richard G. 1985. *Lions of the Punjab: Culture in the Making*. Berkeley: University of California Press.

———. 1991. "Introduction: Working in the Present." In R. G. Fox, ed., *Recapturing Anthropology: Working in the Present*, pp. 1–16. School of American Research, Santa Fe.

Foxhall, Lin. 1986. "Greece Ancient and Modern: Subsistence and Survival." *History Today* 36 (July): 35–43.

———. 1987. "Ownership, Property and the Household in Classical Athens." *Classical Quarterly*.

Foxhall, Lin, and Hamish A. Forbes. 1982. "Sitometreia: The Role of Grain as a Staple Food in Classical Antiquity." *Chiron* 12: 41–90.

Frangakis, Elena, and J. Malcolm Wagstaff. 1987. "Settlement Pattern Change in the Morea (Peloponnisos), ca. A.D. 1700–1830." *Byzantine and Modern Greek Studies* 11: 163–92.

———. 1992. "The Height Zonation of Population in the Morea ca. 1830." *British School Annual* 87: 439–46.

Franke, Richard, and B. H. Chasin. 1980. *Seeds of Famine: Ecological Destruction and the Development Dilemma in the Western Sahel*. New Jersey: Allenheld, Osmun and Co.

Freeman, Susan Tax. 1970. *Neighbors: the Social Contract in a Castilian Hamlet*. Chicago: University of Chicago Press.

Friedl, Ernestine. 1959. "Dowry and Inheritance in Modern Greece." *Transactions of the New York Academy of Sciences* 22: 49–54.

———. 1962. *Vasilika: A Village in Modern Greece*. New York: Holt, Rinehart, Winston.

———. 1967. "The Position of Women: Appearance and Reality." *Anthropological Quarterly* 47: 97–108.

———. 1976. "Kinship, Class and Selective Migration." In John Peristiany, ed., *Mediterranean Family Structures*, pp. 363–88. Cambridge: Cambridge University Press.

———. 1995. "The Life of an Academic: A Personal Record of a Teacher, Administrator, and Anthropologist." *Annual Review of Anthropology* 24: 1–19.

Friedl, John. 1973. "Benefits of Fragmentation in a Traditional Society: A Case from the Swiss Alps." *Human Organization* 32: 29–36.

Friedmann, John. 1988. *Life Space and Economic Space: Essays in Third World Planning*. New Brunswick, N.J.: Transaction Books.

Frink, James C. 1973. "Greece Unveils Five-Year Plan to Revitalize Past Farm Goals." *Foreign Agriculture* 11(43): 6–8.

Fulin, R. et al., eds. 1879–1902. *I diarii di Marino Sanuto*. Venice, 58 vols.

Furse, G. A. 1895. *Military Transport*. London.

Galani-Moutafi, Vasiliki. 1993. "From Agriculture to Tourism: Property, Labor, Gender, and Kinship in a Greek Island Village." *Journal of Modern Greek Studies* 11: 113–31, 241–69.

Gallant, Thomas. 1991. *Risk and Survival in Ancient Greece: Reconstructing the Rural Domestic Economy*. Stanford: Stanford University Press.

Galt, Anthony H. 1974. "Rethinking Patron-Client Relationships: The Real System and the Official System in Southern Italy." *Anthropological Quarterly* 47: 182–202.

———. 1975. "Social Organization, Land Tenure and Ecological Adaptation on the Island of Pantellaria, Sicily." Paper presented at the Annual Meeting of the American Anthropological Association, San Francisco.

———. 1976. "Exploring the Cultural Ecology of Field Fragmentation and Scattering in South Italy." Unpublished manuscript.

———. 1977. "Greek Farm Policy Goals: More Output, Land Allocation." *Foreign Agriculture* 15 (11): 5–12.

———. 1979. "Exploring the Cultural Ecology of Field Fragmentation and Scattering on the Island of Pantellaria." *Journal of Anthropological Research* 35: 93–108.

Gamst, Frederick C. 1974. *Peasants in Complex Society*. New York: Holt, Rinehart and Winston.

Gardin, Jean-Claude, and Christopher S. Peebles, eds. 1992. *Representations in Archaeology*. Bloomington: Indiana University Press.

Gavrielides, Nicolas E. 1976a. "The Cultural Ecology of Olive Growing in the Fourni Valley." In Dimen and Friedl (1976), pp. 265–74.

———. 1976b. "The impact of olive growing on the landscape of the Fourni valley." In Dimen and Friedl (1976), pp. 143–57.

———. 1976c. "A Study of the Cultural Ecology of an Olive Growing Community in the Southern Argolid,

Greece." Ph.D. dissertation, Department of Anthropology, Indiana University.

Gell, William. 1810. *The Itinerary of Greece, Argolis*. London: T. Payne.

———. 1817. *The Itinerary of the Morea: Being a Description of the Routes of that Peninsula*. London: Rodwell and Martin.

———. 1823. *Narrative of a Journey in the Morea*. London: Longman, Hurst, Rees, Orme, and Brown.

Gelti, E. 1968. *Pernondas to Heimaro*. Athens: Ieras Monis Pandesiou Kranidhiou.

Georgas, Georgios E. 1937. *Meleti Peri Spongon, Spongalieias kai Spongemboriou*. Pireaus: Akadimias Athinon.

Georgios, Elias P. 1951. Istoria kai sinetairismos ton Amelakion. Ph.D. dissertation, University of Athens.

Gigizas, D. 1973. "To Kranidi." *Kranidiotika*, vol 2.

Gilmore, David. 1977. "Land Reform and Rural Revol. in Nineteenth Century Andalusia (Spain)." *Peasant Studies* 6: 142–46.

Gledhill, John. 1985. "The Peasantry in History: Some Notes on Latin American Research." *Critique of Anthropology* 5: 33–56.

Goody, Esther N., ed. 1982. *From Craft to Industry: The Ethnography of Proto-Industrial Cloth Production*. Cambridge: Cambridge University Press.

Gouda, A. 1871. *Vioi Parallili*. Athens.

Gould, P. R. 1963. "Man Against the Environment: A Game Theoretical Framework." *Annals of the Association of American Geographers* 53: 290–97.

Gould, Richard A. 1980. *Living Archaeology*. Cambridge: Cambridge University Press.

———. 1990. *Recovering the Past*. Albuquerque: University of New Mexico Press.

Gouldner, Alvin W. 1960. "The Norm of Reciprocity: A Preliminary Statement." *American Sociological Review* 25: 161–78.

Graburn, Nelson H., ed. 1976. *Ethnic and Tourist Arts: Cultural Expressions from the Fourth World*. Berkeley: University of California Press.

Great Britain, Admiralty. 1918. *The Mediterranean Pilot*. London: Taylor, Garnett and Evans. 5th ed. Vol. 4.

Great Britain, Naval Intelligence Division. 1918. *A Handbook of Greece*. London.

———. 1944–1945. *Greece*. Geographical Handbook Series B.R. 516. London.

Greece, National Centre of Social Research. 1972. *Greeks Abroad*. Athens: National Centre of Social Research.

Greece, National Statistical Service. 1872. *Statistiki tis Elladhos: Plithismos 1870*. Athens.

————. 1880. *Apografi tou Plithismou 1879*. Athens.

————. 1890. *Statistiki tis Elladhos: Plithismos 1889*. Athens.

————. 1909. *Apotelesmata tis yenikis apografis tou Plithismou 1907*. Athens.

————. 1913. *Agriculture and Livestock Census of 1911*. Athens.

————. 1921. *Plithismos tou Vasileiou tis Elladhos kata tin apografin tis 1920*. Athens.

————. 1929. *Population of Greece According to the Census of 15–16 May, 1928*. Athens.

————. 1933. *Statistika apotelesmata tis apografis tou Plithismou*. Athens.

————. 1946. *Plithismos tis Elladhos kata tin apografin tis 1940*. Athens.

————. 1948. *Atlas des municipalities et communes de la Grèce*. Athens.

————. 1955. *Plithismos tis Elladhos kata tin apografin tis 1951*. Athens.

————. 1962a. *Plithismos tis Elladhos kata tin apografin tis 1961*. Athens.

————. 1962b. *Katanomi tis ektasios tis khoras kata vasikas kategorias krisios aftes*. Pre-census data of the Agriculture-Livestock Census of March 1961. Athens.

————. 1971. *Agricultural Census of 14 March 1971*. Athens.

————. 1972. *Plithismos tis Elladhos kata tin apografin tis 1971*. Athens.

————. 1973. *Statistical Yearbook of Greece*. Athens.

————. 1975a. *Katanomi tis ektasios tes khoras kata vasikas kategorias krisios aftes*. Athens

————. 1975b. *Statistical Yearbook of Greece, 1973–1974*. Athens.

————. 1980. *The Population of Greece in the Second Half of the 20th Century*. Athens.

————. 1982. *Plithismos tis Elladhos kata tin apografin tis 1981*. Athens.

————. 1985. *National Statistical Yearbook of Greece, 1984*. Athens.

————. 1992. *Plithismos tis Elladhos kata tin apografin tis 1991* (computer file). Athens.

Grigg, David B. 1980. *Population Growth and Agrarian Change: A Historical Perspective*. Cambridge: Cambridge University Press.

Gusta, L. V., and T. H. H. Chen. 1988. "The Physiology of Temperature and Water Stress." In E. G. Heyne, ed., *Wheat and Wheat Improvement*, pp. 115–54. Madison, Wisc.: American Society of Agronomy, Crops Science Society of America, Soil Science Society of America.

Guyer, Jane I. 1981. "Household and Community in African Studies." *African Studies Review* 24: 87–137.

Hadjimichalis, Costis. 1987. *Uneven Development and Regionalism: State, Territory and Class in Southern Europe*. London: Croom Helm.

Hadjimihali, Angeliki. 1929. *Ipodemiata Ellinikis Diakosmitikis*. Athens: Pyrsou.

————. 1949. "La maison Greque." *L'Hellenisme Contemporain* 3: 167–90, 250–65.

————. 1957. *Sarakatsani*. Athens.

Halioris, Nikolaos. 1929. *To Monastiri*. Piraeus: Maraki and Daskalaki.

Hall, A. E., G. H. Cannell, and H. W. Lawton, eds., *Agriculture in Semi-Arid Environments*. Berlin: Springer-Verlag.

Hall, Thomas D. 1986. "Incorporation in the World-System: Toward A Critique." *American Sociological Review* 51: 390–402.

————. 1996 "Finding the Global in the Local." In R. Blanton, P. N. Peregrine, T. D. Hall, and D. Winslow, eds., *Economic Analysis: Beyond the Local System*, pp. 95–107. Lanham, Md.: University Press of America.

Halstead, Paul. 1981. "Counting Sheep in Neolithic and Bronze Age Greece." In I. Hodder, G. Isaac, and N. Hammond, eds., *Patterns of the Past: Studies in Honour of David Clarke*, pp. 307–39. Cambridge: Cambridge University Press.

————. 1987. "Traditional and Ancient Rural Economy in Mediterranean Europe: Plus ça Change?" *Journal of Hellenic Studies* 107: 77–87.

————. 1990. "Present to Past in the Pindhos: Diversification and Specialisation in Mountain Economies." *Revista di Studi Liguri, A.* 56: 61–80.

Halstead, Paul, and Glynis Jones. 1989. "Agrarian Ecology in the Greek Islands: Time, stress, scale and risk." *Journal of Hellenic Studies* 109: 41–55.

Hammel, E. A., and Peter Laslett. 1974. "Comparing Household Structure Over Time and Between Cultures." *Comparative Studies in Society and History* 16: 73–103.

Hansen, J. M. 1980. "The Palaeoethnobotany of Franchthi Cave, Greece." Ph.D. dissertation, University of Minnesota.

————. 1991. *The Palaeoethnobotany of the Franchthi Cave*. Bloomington: Indiana University Press.

Haraven, Tamara. 1982. Introduction. In Tamara Haraven, ed., *Family Time and Industrial Time.* Cambridge: Cambridge University Press.

Hardin, Garrett. 1968a. "The Tragedy of the Commons." *Science* 162: 1243–1248.

———. 1968b. "Ethical Implications of Carrying Capacity." In Garrett Hardin and John Baden, eds., *Managing the Commons*, pp. 112–25. San Francisco: W. H. Freeman.

———. 1977. *The Limits of Altruism: An Ecologist's View of Survival.* Bloomington: Indiana University Press.

Hart, Laurie Kain. 1992. *Time, Religion, and Social Experience in Rural Greece.* Lanham, Md.: Rowman and Littlefield.

Hasler, R. 1996. *Agriculture, Foraging, and Wildlife: Resources and Political Dynamics in the Zambezi Valley.* London: Kegan Paul.

Hasluck, F. M. 1908–1909. "Albanian Settlements in the Aegean Islands." *The Annual of the British School at Athens* 15: 223–28.

———. 1910–1911. "Depopulation in the Aegean Islands and the Turkish Conquest." *The Annual of the British School at Athens* 17: 151–81.

Hatzianaryirou, A. 1925. *Ta Spetsiotika.*

Hayden, Brian, and Aubrey Cannon. 1983. "Where the Garbage Goes: Refuse Disposal in the Maya Highlands." *Journal of Anthropological Archaeology* 2: 117–63.

Hector, J. 1973. "La plaine d'Argos: Repercussions socioeconomiques d'une specialisation agricole." *Mediterranée* 2: 1–17.

Hellenic Industrial Development Bank. 1970. *The Greek Wool Industry.* Athens: The Technical and Economic Studies Division.

Herzfeld, Michael. 1980a. "The Dowry in Greece: Terminological Usage and Historical Reconstruction." *Ethnohistory* 27: 225–41.

———. 1980b. "Honour and Shame: Problems in Comparative Analysis of Moral Systems." *Man, n.s.* 15: 339–51.

———. 1980c. "Social Tension and Inheritance by Lot in Three Greek Villages." *Anthropological Quarterly* 55: 91–100.

———. 1982. *Ours Once More: Folkore, Ideology and the Making of Modern Greece.* Austin: University of Texas Press.

———. 1985. *The Poetics of Manhood: Contest and Identity in a Cretan Mountain Village.* Princeton: Princeton University Press.

———. 1987. *Anthropology Through the Looking-Glass: Critical Ethnography in the Margins of Europe.* Cambridge: Cambridge University Press.

———. 1991. *A Place in History: Social and Monumental Time in a Cretan Town.* Princeton: Princeton University Press.

Hiday, Virginia Aldige. 1973. "Land Tenure and Population: A Study of the Effects of Land Tenure Structure on Population Growth and Distribution." Ph.D. dissertation, University of North Carolina.

Hirschon, Renée. 1981. "Essential Objects and the Sacred: Interior and Exterior Space in a Greek Urban Locality." In Shirley Ardener, ed., *Women and Space*, pp. 72–88. London: Croom Helm.

———. 1983. "Under One Roof: Marriage, Dowry and Family Relations in Piraeus." In Michael Kenny and David Kertzer, eds., *Urban Life in Mediterranean Europe*, pp. 288–333. Urbana: University of Illinois Press.

———. 1989. *Heirs of the Catastrophe: The Social Life of Asia Minor Refugees in Piraeus.* Oxford: Clarendon Press.

Hirschon, Renée, and S. Thakurdesi. 1970. "Society, Culture and Spatial Organization: An Athens Community." *Ekistics* 30: 187–96.

Hodder, Ian. 1983. *The Present Past.* New York: Pica Press.

———. 1986. *Reading the Past: Current Approaches to Interpretation in Archaeology.* Cambridge: Cambridge University Press.

———. 1989. "Post-Modernism, Post-Structuralism and Post-Processual Archaeology." In Hodder, ed. (1986), pp. 64–78.

———, ed. 1989. *The Meanings of Things: Material Culture and Symbolic Expression.* London: Unwin Hyman.

Hodder, I., and C. Orton. 1976. *Spatial Analysis in Archaeology.* Cambridge: Cambridge University Press.

Hodges, H. W. M. 1972. "Domestic Building Materials and Ancient Settlements." In Peter Ucko, Ruth Tringham, and G. W. Dimbleby, eds., *Man, Settlement and Urbanism*, pp. 523–30. London: Duckworth.

Hodkinson, Stephen. 1986. "Land Tenure and Inheritance in Classical Sparta." *Classical Quarterly* 36: 378–406.

———. 1988. "Animal Husbandry in the Greek Polis." In C. R. Whittaker, ed., *Pastoral Economies in Classical Antiquity*, pp. 35–74. Cambridge: Cambridge Philological Society, Supplementary vol. 14.

Hoffman, Susannah. 1976. "The Ethnography of the Islands: Thera." In Dimen and Friedl (1976), pp. 328–40.

Hole, Frank. 1978. "Pastoral Nomadism in Western Iran." In R. Gould, ed., *Explorations in Ethnoarchaeology*. pp. 127–79. Albuquerque: University of New Mexico Press.

———. 1979. "Rediscovering the Past in the Present: Ethnoarchaeology in Luristan, Iran." In C. Kramer, ed., *Ethnoarchaeology: Implications of Ethnography for Archaeology*, pp. 192–218. New York: Columbia University Press.

Holmes, Douglas. 1983. "A Peasant Worker Model in a North Italian Context." *American Ethnologist* 734–48.

Homans, George. 1941. *English Villagers of the Thirteenth Century*. Cambridge: Harvard University Press.

Horne, Lee. 1993. "Occupational and Locational Instability in Arid Land Settlement." In Cameron and Tomka (1993), pp. 43–53.

———. 1994. *Village Spaces: Settlement and Society in Northeastern Iran*. Washington, D.C.: Smithsonian Institution Press.

Horton, George. 1902. *In Argolis*. New York: McClure, Phillips.

Houliarakis, Michail. 1973–76. *Geografiki, Dhioikitiki kai Plithismiaki Exelixis tis Elladhos, 1821–1971*. Athens: National Center for Social Research.

Humphreys, S. C. 1983. *Anthropology and the Greeks*. Boston: Routledge and Kegan Paul.

Ingersoll, Daniel W., and Gordon Bronitsky, eds. 1987. *Mirror and Metaphor: Material and Social Constructions of Reality*. Lanham, Md.: University Press of America.

Instituto Centrale di Statistico. 1950. *Misure Locali per le Superficie Agrarie*. 2d ed. Rome.

International Bank for Reconstruction and Development. 1966. *The Development of Agriculture in Greece*. Washington D.C.

Ioakomidis, P. C. 1984. "Greece: From Military Dictatorship to Socialism." In Allen Williams, ed., *Southern Europe Transformed*. London: Harper and Row.

Isaac, Glynn. 1968. "Traces of Pleistocene Hunters: An East African Example." In R. Lee and I. DeVore, eds., *Man the Hunter*, pp. 268–273. Chicago: Aldine.

Ito, Masaru, Tatsuyoshi Sai Jo, and Masashi Une. 1994. *The Tragedy of the Commons Revisited: Identifying Behavioral Principles*. Osaka: Institute of Social and Economic Research, No. 338.

Jacobsen, Thomas W. 1976. "17,000 Years of Greek Prehistory." *Scientific American* 234: 76–87.

———. 1981. "Franchthi Cave and the Beginning of Settled Village Life in Greece." *Hesperia* 50: 303–19.

———. 1984. "Seasonal Pastoralism in Southern Greece: A Consideration of the Ecology of Neolithic Urfirnis Pottery." In P. M. Rice, ed., *Pots and Potters, Current Approaches in Ceramic Archaeology*, pp. 27–43. Los Angeles: University of California at Los Angeles, Institute of Archaeology, Monograph 24.

———. 1985. "Another Modest Proposal: Ethnoarchaeology in Greece." In Nancy Wilkie and William Coulson, eds., *Contributions to Aegean Archaeology*, pp. 91–107. Minneapolis: University of Minnesota, Center for Ancient Studies.

Jacoby, D. 1971. *La féodalité en Grèce médiévale: Les "Assises de Romanie" sources, application et diffusion*. P. Lemerle, ed. Paris and the Hague.

Jacoby, Erich H. 1953. *Interrelationship between Agrarian Reform and Agricultural Development*. Rome: UNFAO Agricultural Study No. 26.

Jameson, Michael H. 1954. "The System of Inheritance, in its Sociological and Historical Context, on the Island of Karpathos." *Yearbook of the American Philosophical Society* 210–12.

———. 1960. A Decree of Themistokles from Troizen. Princeton: Institute for Advanced Study.

———. 1962. "Palaeolithic in the Argolid." *American Journal of Archaeology* 66: 181–82.

———. 1969. "Excavations at Porto Cheli and Vicinity, Preliminary Report I: Halieis, 1962–1968." *Hesperia* 38: 311–42.

———. 1974. "The Excavation of a Drowned Greek Temple." *Scientific American* 231: 110–19.

———. 1976a. "The Southern Argolid: The Setting for Historical and Cultural Studies." In Dimen and Friedl, pp. 72–91.

———. 1976b. "A Greek Countryside: Reports from the Argolid Exploration Project." *Expedition* 19: 2–4.

———. 1977–1978. "Agriculture and Slavery in Classical Athens." *The Classical Journal* 73: 122–44.

———. 1990. "Private Space and the Greek City." In O. Murray and S. Price, eds., *The Greek City: From Homer to Alexander*, pp. 171–95. Oxford: Clarendon Press.

———. 1994a. "Class in the Ancient Greek Countryside." In P. N. Doukellis and L.G. Mendoni, eds.,

Structures rurales et sociétés antiques, pp. 55–63. Paris: Annales litteraires de l'Université de Besancon.

———. 1994b. "Response." In Morris (1994), pp. 193–96.

Jameson, Michael H., David R. Jordan, and Roy David Kotansky. 1993. *A 'Lex Sacra' from Selinous*. Durham, N.C.: Duke University.

Jameson, Michael H., Curtis N. Runnels, and Tjeerd H. van Andel. 1994. *A Greek Countryside: The Southern Argolid from Prehistory to the Present Day*. Stanford: Stanford University Press.

Jobes, Patrick C., William F. Stinner, and John M. Wardwell. 1992. "A Paradigm Shift in Migration Explanation." In P. C. Jobes, W. F. Stinner, and J. M. Wardwell, eds., *Community, Society and Migration: Noneconomic Migration in America*, pp. 1–31. Lanham, Md.: University Press of America.

Johnson, E. A. J. 1970. *The Organization of Space in Developing Countries*. Cambridge: Harvard University Press.

Jones, J. E., A. J. Graham, and L. H. Sackett. 1973. "The Attic Country House Below the Cave of Pan at Vari." *Annual of the British School at Athens* [BSA] 68: 355–443.

Just, Roger. 1985. "Les hommes plus riches, espouses plus jeunes: les cas de Meganisi." In Piault, ed. (1985), pp. 167–85.

———. 1988. "The Assessment of Dowry: Interpretation and Practice in Meganisiot Marriage Prestations." In J. G. Peristiany, ed., *Strategies et Prestations Matrimoniales en Mediterranée*. Marseilles.

———. 1991. "The Limits of Kinship." In Loizos and Papataxiarchis (1991), pp. 114–32.

Kahn, Joel S. 1980. *Minangkabau Social Formations: Indonesian Peasants and the World Economy*. Cambridge: Cambridge University Press.

Kalopissi-Verti, Sophia. 1975. *Die Kirche der Hagia Triada bei Kranidi in der Argolis (1244)*. University of Munich, Miscellanea Byzantina Monacensia, 20.

Karakasidou, Anastasia. 1993. "Politicizing Culture: Negating Ethnic Identity in Greek Macedonia." *Journal of Modern Greek Studies* 11: 1–28.

———. 1997. *Fields of Wheat, Hills of Blood: Passages to Nationhood in Greek Macedonia 1870–1990*. Chicago: University of Chicago Press.

Karanikolas, Pantelimonos K. 1980. *To Kranidhi*. Corinth: Holy Metropolitan of Corinth.

Kardulias, P. Nick. 1994. "Paradigms of the Past in Greek Archaeology." In Kardulias, ed. (1994), pp. 1–23.

———. 1996. "Microwear and Metric Analysis of Threshing Sledge Flints from Greece and Cyprus." *Journal of Archaeological Science*.

———. 1999. *World-Systems Theory in Practice: Leadership, Production, and Exchange*. Lanham, Md.: Rowan and Littlefield.

———, ed. 1994. *Beyond the Site: Regional Studies in the Aegean Area*. Lanham, Md.: University Press of America.

Kardulias, P. Nick, and Mark Shutes, eds. 1997. *Aegean Strategies: Studies of Culture and Environment on the European Fringe*. Lanham, Md.: Rowan and Littlefield.

Kardulias, P. Nick, and Richard W. Yerkes. 1996. "Microwear and Metric Analysis of Threshing Sledge Flints from Greece and Cyprus." *Journal of Archaeological Science* 23: 657–66.

Karopostolis, Vasilis. 1983. "Consumption Patterns in Rural Greek Communities: A Sociological Approach." *Ekistics* 50: 442–48.

Karouzis, George. 1977. *Land Ownership in Cyprus Past and Present (with Special Reference to Greek and Turkish Ownerships)*. Nicosia: Cosmos Press.

Kayser, Bernard. 1963. "Les migrations interieures en Grèce." In J. G. Peristiany, ed., *Contributions to Mediterranean Sociology*, pp. 192–200. The Hague: Mouton.

———. 1976. "Dynamics of Regional Integration in Modern Greece." In Dimen and Friedl (1976), pp. 10–15.

Kayser, Bernard, and Kenneth Thompson. 1964. *Economic and Social Atlas of Greece*. Athens: National Statistical Service of Greece.

Kayser, Bernard, Pierre-Yves Pechoux, and Michel Sivignon. 1971. *Exode rural et attraction urbaine en Grèce*. Athens: Social Science Research Center.

Kearney, Michael. 1986. "From the Invisible Hand to Visible Feet: Anthropological Studies of Migration and Development." *Annual Review of Anthropology* 15: 331–61.

Keeler, Murray E., and Dimitrios G. Skuras. 1990. "Land Fragmentation and Consolidation Policy in Greek Agriculture." *Geography* 76: 73–76.

Keller, Donald R., and David W. Rupp. 1983. "Introduction." In Keller and Rupp (1983), ed., pp. 1–6.

———, eds. 1983. *Archeological Survey in the Mediterranean Area*. BAR International Series No. 155.

Kelley, K. B. 1982. "Ethnoarchaeology of the Black Hat Navajos: Historical and Ethnohistorical Determinants of Site Features." *Journal of Anthropological Research* 38: 45–74.

Kenna, Margaret. 1976. "Houses, Fields and Graves: Property and Ritual Obligation on a Greek Island." *Ethnology* 15: 21–34.

———. 1983. "Institutional and Transformational Migration and the Politics of Community." *Archives Europeennes de Sociologie* 24: 263–87.

———. 1995. "Where the Streets Have No Name: Constructing and Reconstructing Tradition with Vaults and Cubes." In Pavlides and Sutton (1995), pp. 439–62.

Kennedy, Robinette. 1986. "Women's Friendships on Crete: A Psychological Perspective." In Dubisch (1986), pp. 121–38.

Kenny, Michael. 1960. "Patterns of Patronage in Spain." *Anthropological Quarterly* 33: 14–23.

Kenny, Michael, and David Kertzer. 1983. "Introduction." In Kenny and Kertzer (1983), pp. 3–21.

———, eds. 1983. *Urban Life in Mediterranean Europe: Anthropological Perspectives.* Champaign: University of Illinois Press.

Kent, Susan. 1987. "Understanding the Use of Space: An Ethnoarchaeological Approach." In S. Kent, ed., *Method and Theory for Activity Area Research: An Ethnoarchaeological Approach*, pp. 1–23. New York: Columbia University Press.

———. 1990. *Domestic Architecture and the Use of Space: an Interdisciplinary Cross-Cultural Study.* Cambridge: Cambridge University Press.

Keohane, Robert O., and Elinor Ostrom, eds. 1995. *Local Commons and Global Interdependence: Heterogeneity and Cooperation in Two Domains.* Thousand Oaks, Calif.: Sage.

Kertzer, David. 1984. *Family Life in Central Italy: 1880–1910.* New Brunswick: Rutgers University Press.

King, Russell L. 1973. *Land Reform: The Italian Experience.* London: Butterworth.

King, Russell L., and S. P. Burton. 1982. "Land Fragmentation: A Fundamental Rural Spatial Problem." *Problems in Human Geography* 6: 475–95.

———. 1983. "Structural Change in Agriculture: The Geography of Land Consolidation." *Problems in Human Geography* 7: 471–501.

Kish, George. 1956. "Land Reform in Italy: A Geographer's View." *Papers of the Michigan Academy of Science* (Ann Arbor) 41: 133–41.

Klados, A. I. 1837. *Efetiris tou Vasileiou tis Elladhos dhia to etos 1837.* Athens: Royal Printing Office.

Kohl, Philip L. 1987. "The Use and Abuse of World Systems Theory: The Case of the Pristine West Asian State." *Advances in Archaeological Method and Theory* 11: 1–35.

Kolodny, Emile Y. 1974. *La population des îles de la Grèce.* Aix-en-Provence: EDISUD.

Konstantinidhis, T. 1954. *Karavia, Kapetaneoi kai Sindhrofonaftai, 1800–1830.* Athens.

Konti, Voula. 1983. "Simvol. stin istoriki geografia tou nomou Argolidhos." *Symmeikta, Kentron Vizantinon Erevnon* (Ethnikon Idhrima Erevnon) 5: 169–203.

Kordhosis, M. S. 1986. *I kataktesi tis notias Elladhas apo tous Franghous.* Istorikogeographika 1: 53–194.

Koster, Harold A. 1976. "The Thousand Year Road." *Expedition* 19: 19–28.

———. 1977. "The Ecology of Pastoralism in Relation to Changing Patterns of Land Use in the Northeast Peloponnese." Ph.D. dissertation, Department of Anthropology, University of Pennsylvania.

———. 1987. Appendix IV: "The Ethnography of Herding in the Grevena Area." In Nancy C. Wilkie, ed., *The Grevena Report*, Manuscript on File at the Department of Anthropology, Carleton College.

———. 1997. "Yours, Mine and Ours: Private and Public Pasture in Greece." In Kardulias and Shutes (1997), pp. 141–85.

Koster, Harold A., and Claudia Chang. 1994. "Introduction." In Claudia Chang and Harold A. Koster, eds. *Pastoralists at the Periphery: Herders in a Capitalist World*, pp. 1–15. Tucson: University of Arizona Press.

Koster, Harold A., and Joan Bouza Koster. 1976. "Competition or Symbiosis?: Pastoral Adaptive Strategies in the Southern Argolid, Greece." In Dimen and Friedl (1976), pp. 275–85.

Koster, Joan Bouza. 1976. "From Spindle to Loom: Weaving in the Southern Argolid." *Expedition* 19: 29–39.

———. 1978. "Arachne's Children." *Shuttle, Spindle and Dyepot* 9 (3): 16–19.

———. 1979a. "The Carding Box." *Shuttle, Spindle and Dyepot* 10 (4): 24–25.

———. 1979b. *Handloom Construction: A Practical Guide for the Non-Expert.* Mt. Rainier, Md.: Volunteers in Technical Assistance.

———. 1981. "The Tagari: A Greek Saddlebag." *Weaver's Journal* 6 (2): 24–27.

———. 1985. "Contemporary Sarakatsani Weaving in the Northeast Peloponnese." Providence: Brown University, Haffenreffer Museum of Anthropology, Studies in Anthropology and Material Culture 1: 28–36.

———. 1996. "By the Waning of the Moon: Spinning, Weaving and Dyeing in Eastern Crete." *Shuttle, Spindle and Dyepot* 27 (2): 43–46.

———. 1997. *Growing Artists: Teaching Art to Young Children.* Albany, N.Y.: Delmar.

Koukkidi, K. 1948. *To Pnevma tou sinergatismou ton neoteron Ellinon kai t'Ambelakia.* Athens.

Kramer, Carol, ed. 1979. *Ethnoarchaeology: Implications of Ethnography for Archeology.* New York: Columbia University Press.

———. 1982. *Village Ethnoarchaeology: Rural Iran in Archaeological Perspective.* New York: Academic Press.

Kremmydhas, Vasilis. 1972. *To Emborio tis Peloponnisou sto 18o aiona (1715–1792).* Athens: Moskhonas.

———. 1973. *Arkhio Hatzipanayioti.* Athens: Konstantinidis and K. Mikhala.

———. 1976–77. "I Oikonomiki Krisi ston Elladhiko Khoro stis Arkhes tou 19ou aiona." *Mnimon,* No. 6.

———. 1980. *Singiria kai emborio stin proepanastatiki Peloponniso (1793–1821).* Athens: Istonki Ipiresia.

Kriezis, Georgios D. 1860. *Istoria tis nisou Idhras.* Patras: A.S. Agapitou.

Kroll, Ellen M., and T. Douglas Price, eds. 1991. *The Interpretation of Archaeological Spatial Patterning.* New York: Plenum Press.

Kyriakidou-Nestoros, A. 1971. "The Theory of Folklore in Greece: Laographia in its Contemporary Perspective." *East European Quarterly* 5: 487–504.

———. 1978. *The Theory of Greek Folklore.* Athens: Skholi Moraiti.

———. 1983. *Ta Ifanta tis Makedonias kai tis Thrakis.* Athens: Ellinikos Organismos Mikromesaion Metapoitikon Epikheriseon kai Kherotekhnias.

Lagopoulos, Alexandros Ph., and Karin Boklund-Lagopoulou. 1992. *Meaning and Geography: The Social Conception of the Region in Northern Greece.* New York: Mouton de Gruyter.

Laiou-Thomadakis, Angeliki E. 1977. *Peasant Society in the Late Byzantine Empire.* Princeton: Princeton University Press.

Lambiri-Dimaki, Ioanna. 1965. *Social Change in a Greek Country Town.* Athens: Centre of Planning and Economic Research.

———. 1972. "Dowry in Modern Greece: An Institution at the Crossroads between Persistence and Decline." In Constantina Safilios-Rothschild, ed., *Toward a Sociology of Women,* pp. 73–83. Lexington, Mass.: Xerox Publishing.

———. 1983. "Greece in the 1980's: Changing Evaluations of the Roles of Men and Women." In I. Lambiri-Dimaki, ed., *Social Stratification in Greece,* pp. 182–206. Athens: A. N. Sakkoulas.

Lambrinidou, M. 1907. *Istorikai Selides 1320–1821.* Athens.

Lambros, S. P. 1908. "Diathiki tou iz' aionos." *Neos Ellinomnemon* 5: 330–40.

Laslett, Peter, and Richard Wall. 1972. *Household and Family in Past Time.* Cambridge: Cambridge University Press.

Lattimore, Richmond. 1973. *Hesiod.* Ann Arbor: University of Michigan Press.

Lawrence, Denise L., and Setha M. Low. 1990. "The Built Environment and Spatial Form." *Annual Review of Anthropology* 19: 453–505.

Lawrence, Roderick. 1982. "Domestic Space and Society: A Cross-Cultural Study." *Comparative Studies in Society and History* 24: 104–30.

Lawson, John C. 1910. *Modern Greek Folklore and Ancient Greek Religion: A Study in Survivals.* Cambridge: Cambridge University Press.

Leake, W. M. 1830. *Travels in the Morea.* London: John Murray.

Leon, George B. 1972. "The Greek Merchant Marine (1435–1850)." In Stelios Papadopoulos, ed., *The Greek Merchant Marine,* pp. 13–44 and 469–83. Athens: National Bank of Greece.

Leonard, W. H., and J. H. Martin. 1963. *Cereal Crops.* New York: Macmillan.

Leone, Mark P. 1981. "Archaeology's Relationship to the Present and the Past." In Richard A. Gould and Michael B. Schiffer, eds., *Modern Material Culture: The Archaeology of Us,* pp. 5–14. New York: Academic Press.

Leontaritis, G. 1981. *Elliniki emboriki naftilia (1453–1850).* Athens: Mnimon.

Leontis, Artemis. 1991. "Cultural Politics and Populist Uses of the Ancients." *Journal of Modern Greek Studies* 9: 191–214.

———. 1992. *Topographies of Hellenism.* Princeton: Princeton University Press.

Levy, Harry L. 1956. "Property Distribution by Lot in Present Day Greece." *Transactions of the American Philological Society* 87: 42–46.

Lignos, A., ed. 1921–1932. *Arkheion tis koinotitos Idhras, 1778–1832.* Piraeus: Istorikon Arkheion Hydras.

———. 1961–62. *Arkheion tis koinotitos Idhras, 1778–1832.* Athens: Bauron.

Limp, W. F. 1983. "An Economic Model of Settlement

Aggregation and Dispersal." In G. Bronitsky, ed., *Ecological Models in Economic Prehistory*, pp. 18–45. Tempe: Arizona State University, Anthropological Research Papers, No. 29.

Little, Barbara. 1994. "Consider the Hermaphroditic Mind: Comment on 'The Interplay of Evidential Constraints and Political Interests: Recent Archaeological Research on Gender'." *American Antiquity* 59: 539–44.

Little, Michael A., and George E. B. Morren. 1976. *Ecology, Energetics and Human Variability*. Dubuque: William C. Brown.

Locatelli, Alessandro. 1691. *Racconto Storico Della Veneta Guerra in Levante*. Venice: G. Albrizzi.

Loizos, Peter. 1975. "Changes in Property Transfer Among Greek Peasants." *Man* 10: 503–24.

Loizos, Peter, and Evthymios Papataxiarchis, eds. 1991. *Contested Identities: Gender and Kinship in Modern Greece*. Princeton: Princeton University Press.

Long, N., J. D. Van der Ploeg, C. Curtin, and L. Box. 1986. *The Commoditization Debate*. The Netherlands: Agricultural University of Wageningen, Papers of the Department of Sociology, No. 17.

Longacre, William A. 1991. *Ceramic Ethnoarchaeology*. Tucson: University of Arizona Press.

Longacre, William A., and James M. Skibo, eds. 1994. *Kalinga Ethnoarchaeology: Expanding Archaeological Method and Theory*. Washington, D.C.: Smithsonian Institution Press.

Longnon, Jean, and Peter Topping. 1969. *Documents sur la regime des terres dans la principaute de Morée au 14e siècle*. Paris: Mouton.

Loukopoulos, Dimitrios. 1925. *Pos ifainoun kai dhinontai i Aitoloi*. Athens: I. Sideri.

Lowenthal, David. 1985. *The Past is a Foreign Country*. Cambridge: Cambridge University Press.

Luttrell, A. 1966. "The Latins of Argos and Nauplia 1311–1394." *Papers of the British School at Rome*. 34 (n.s. 21): 34–55.

MacFarlane, Alan. 1977. *Reconstructing Historical Communities*. Cambridge: Cambridge University Press.

Maclachlan, Morgan, ed. 1987. *Household Economies and Their Transformation*. Lanham, Md.: University Press of America.

Mansolas, A. 1867. *Politeiografikai pliroforiai peri Elladhos*. Athens: National Printing Office.

———. 1872. *Rapport sur l'état de la statistique en Grèce*. Athens: Perris.

Marcus, George E. 1989. "Imagining the Whole: Ethnography's Contemporary Efforts to Situate Itself." *Critique of Anthropology* 9: 7–30.

Mariolopoulos, E., G. Mistardis, and D. Catacousinos. 1963. "Three Articles on the Semi-Arid Regions of Greece." *B.S. Hellenique* 4: 180–98.

Marquardt, W. H. and C. L. Crumley. 1987. "Theoretical Issues in the Analysis of Spatial Patterning." In C. L. Crumley and W. H. Marquardt, eds., *Regional Dynamics: Burgundian Landscapes in Historical Perspective*, pp. 1–18. New York: Academic Press.

Martin, Mary. 1986. "The Socio-Cultural Context of Rural Textile Production: An Iranian Example." Unpublished manuscript.

Matson, Fredrick R. 1972. "Ceramic Studies." In McDonald and Rapp (1972), pp. 200–24.

Mauss, Marcel. [1925] 1967. *The Gift: Forms and Functions of Exchange in Archaic Societies*. Trans. I. Cunnison. New York: W.W. Norton.

McCloskey, Donald. 1975. "The Persistence of English Common Fields." In W. N. Parker and Eric L. Jones, eds., *European Peasants and Their Markets: Essays in Agrarian Economic History*, pp. 73–119. Princeton: Princeton University Press.

———. 1976. "English Open Fields as Behavior Towards Risk." In P. J. Uselding, ed., *Research in Economic History*, pp. 124–71. Greenwich, Conn: JAI Press.

McDonald, William A. 1972. "The Problems and the Program." In McDonald and Rapp (1972), pp. 3–17.

McDonald, William A., and Stanley Aschenbrenner. 1980. "Domestic Architecture and Village Layout in Mainland Greece, About 2200–800 B.C." *National Geographic Research Reports* 12: 463–71.

McDonald, William A., and G. R. Rapp. eds. 1972. *The Minnesota Messenia Expedition: Reconstructing a Bronze Age Regional Environment*. Minneapolis: University of Minnesota Press.

McGrew, William W. 1985. *Land and Revolution in Modern Greece, 1800–1881*. Kent, Ohio: Kent State University Press.

McLeod, W. E. 1962. "Kiveri and Thermisi." *Hesperia* 31: 378–92.

McNall, Scott G. 1974. *The Greek Peasant*. Washington, D.C.: American Sociological Association.

———. 1976. "Barriers to Development and Modernization in Greece." In Dimen and Friedl (1976), pp. 28–42.

Matson, Frederick R. 1972. "Ceramic Studies." In McDonald and Rapp (1972), pp. 200–224.

Megas, George. 1951. *The Greek House*. Athens: Ministry of Reconstruction.

———. 1958. *Greek Calendar Customs*. Athens: Press and Information Office, Prime Minister's Office.

Megaw, A., and R. Jones. 1983. "Byzantine and allied pottery: A contribution by chemical analysis to problems of origin and distribution." *Annual of the British School of Archaeology at Athens* 78: 235–63.

Meiggs, Russell, and David Lewis, eds. 1969. *Selection of Greek Historical Inscriptions to the End of the Fifth Century B.C.* Oxford: Clarendon Press.

Melas, E. M. 1989. "Etics, emics and emphathy in archaeological theory." In Hodder (1989), pp. 137–55.

Meraklis, Michaeli. 1984. *Greek Folklore*. Athens: Odysseas.

Meremiti, D. 1953. *Zitimata laografikis erevnis tis periokhis Ermionidhas*. Athens: Academy Manuscripts.

Meynaud, Jean. 1965. *Les forces politiques en Grèce*. Lausanne: Études de Science Politique No. 10.

Michaelides, Constantine E. 1967. *Hydra: A Greek Island Town*. Chicago: University of Chicago Press.

———. 1995. "Hydra: Tourist Economy and Traditional Architecture." In Pavlides and Sutton (1995), pp. 419–38.

Miliarakis, Antonios. 1886. *Geografia politiki nea kai arkhaia tou Nomou Argolidhos kai Korinthias*. Athens: Estias.

Moch, Leslie Page. 1992. *Moving Europeans: Migration in Western Europe Since 1650*. Bloomington: Indiana University Press.

Molinari, Vincenzo. 1873. *Metrologia Universale*. Naples: Sirena.

Moore, Roland S. 1995. "Constructing Tradition: Architecture in a Boeotian Tourist Town." In Pavlides and Sutton (1995), pp. 479–510.

Morris, Ian. 1994. "Archaeologies of Greece." In Morris (1994), ed., pp. 8–47.

———, ed. 1994. *Classical Greece: Ancient Histories and Modern Archaeologies*. Cambridge: Cambridge University Press.

Mouzelis, D. C., and Lawrence A. Witucki. 1971. *How Greece Developed Its Agriculture, 1947–67*. Washington, D.C.: U.S. Dept. of Agriculture, Economics Report No. 67.

Mouzelis, Nicos P. 1978. *Modern Greece: Facets of Underdevelopment*. New York: Holmes and Meier.

———. 1996. "The Concept of Modernization: Its Relevance for Greece." *Journal of Modern Greek Studies* 14: 215–27.

Munn, Mark H., and M. L. Z. Munn. Forthcoming. *Artifact and Assemblage*. vol. 2. Stanford: Stanford University Press.

Murray, Priscilla, and Claudia Chang. 1986. "An Ethnoarchaeological Study of a Contemporary Herder's Site." *Journal of Field Archaeology* 8: 372–81.

Murray, P., and P. N. Kardulias. 1985. "Modern-Site Survey in the Southern Argolid, Greece." *Journal of Field Archaeology* 12(3): 21–41.

Murray, Priscilla, and Curtis Runnels. 1984. "Ethnoarchaeology in Greece." Paper presented at the Archaeological Institute of America Annual Meeting, Toronto.

Nadel-Klein, Jane. 1991. "Reweaving the Fringe: Localism, Tradition, and Representation in British Ethnography." *American Ethnologist* 18: 500–517.

Nandris, J. G. 1985. "The Stina and the Katun: Foundations of a Research Design in European Highland Zone Ethnoarchaeology." *World Archaeology* 17: 256–68.

Nash, June. 1981. "Ethnographic Aspects of the World Capitalist System." *Annual Review of Anthropology* 10: 393–423.

Nelson, Ben A. 1985. *Decoding Prehistoric Ceramics*. Carbondale: Southern Illinois University Press.

Netting, Robert McC. 1968. *Hill Farmers of Nigeria: Cultural Ecology of the Kofyar of the Jos Plateau*. Seattle: University of Washington Press.

———. 1972. "Of Men and Meadows: Strategies of Alpine Land Use." *Anthropological Quarterly* 45: 132–44.

———. 1974. "Agrarian Ecology." *Annual Review of Anthropology* 3: 21–56.

———. 1977. *Cultural Ecology*. Prospect Heights Ill.: Waveland Press.

———. 1981. *Balancing on an Alp: Ecological Change and Continuity in a Swiss Mountain Community*. Cambridge: Cambridge University Press.

———. 1989. "Smallholders, Householders, Freeholders: Why the Family Farm Works Well Worldwide." In Richard Wilk, ed., *The Household Economy: Reconsidering the Domestic Mode of Production*, pp. 221–44. Boulder: Westview Press.

———. 1993. *Smallholders, Householders: Farm Families and the Ecology of Intensive, Sustainable Agriculture*. Stanford: Stanford University Press.

Netting, Robert McC., Richard Wilk, and Eric Arnould. 1984. *Households: Comparative and Historical Studies of the Domestic Group*. Berkeley: University of California Press.

Newell, Colin. 1988. *Methods and Models in Demography*. New York: Guilford Press.

Nimkoff, M., et al. 1960. "Types of Family and Types of Economy." *American Journal of Sociology* 66.

Noukhakis, Ioannis E. 1901. *Elliniki Khorografia*. Athens: S. Kousoulinos.

Nylon, John. 1959. "Land Consolidation in Spain." *Annals of the Association of American Geographers* 49: 361–73.

O'Brien, Jay, and William Roseberry, eds. 1991. *Golden Ages, Dark Ages: Imagining the Past in Anthropology and History*. Berkeley: University of California Press.

Ohnuki-Tierney, Emiko, ed. 1990. *Culture Through Time: Anthropological Approaches*. Stanford: Stanford University Press.

Oliver, Paul. 1979. "The Future of Studies in Greek Vernacular Architecture." In Doumanis and Oliver (1979), pp. 8–16.

Organization for Economic Co-operation and Development. 1983. *Environmental Policies in Greece*. Paris: Organization for Economic Co-operation and Development.

Orlandos, Anastasios K. 1877. *Peri tis nisou Petsas i Spetson*. Piraeus: Rousopoulou.

Orlove, Benjamin S. 1977. *Alpacas, Sheep, and Men: The Wool Export Economy and Regional Society in Southern Peru*. New York: Academic Press.

Osborne, Robin. 1987. *Classical Landscape with Figures: The Ancient Greek City and its Countryside*. London: George Philip.

Pacifico, Pier Antonio. 1704. *Breve Descrizzione Corografica del Peloponneso o' Morea*. Venice: Domenico Lovisa.

Panayiotopoulos, Vasilis. 1975. "Dhimographikes exelixeis istoria tou Ellenikou ethnous." In *O Ellenismos ipo xeni kiriarkhia, 1669–1821*, pp. 152–58. Athens.

———. 1979. "I Aporofisi ton oikonomikon poron kai tou plithismou apo tin anaptixi tis georgias ton 18o Aiona stin Peloponniso." In S. Asdrahas, ed., *I oikonomiki dhomi ton Valkanikon khoron 15os–19os Aionas*. Athens.

———. 1985. *Plithismos kai oikismoi tis Peloponnisou 13os – 18os Aionas*. Athens: Commercial Bank of Greece.

Panourgia, Neni. 1994. "A Native Narrative." *Anthropology and Humanism* 19: 40–51.

Papageorgiou, Euthemeous. 1963. "Fragmentation of Land Holdings and Measures for Consolidation in Greece." In Kenneth H. Persons, Raymond J. Penn, and Phillip M. Raup, eds., *Land Tenure*. Madison: University of Wisconsin Press.

Papaioanou, Vasilis. 1978. "Ethnology and Sociology of a Rural Village: Forms and Uses of the Built Space of Iakaria." *Texnika Khronika*, pp. 195–205.

Papandoniou, Ioanna. 1976. *Ellinikes Foresies*. Nafplion: Peloponnisiakon Laografikon Idhryma.

Papataxiarchis, Evthymios. 1991. "Friends of the Heart: Male Commensal Solidarity, Gender, and Kinship in Aegean Greece." In Loizos and Papataxiarchis (1991), pp. 156–179.

Paraskevopoulos, G. P. 1896. *Taxeidia me eikonas ana tin Elladha*. 2d ed. Athens: Korinnis.

———. 1932. *Aktines ke nefi*. Athens: Pyrsou.

Parker, William N., and Eric L. Jones, eds. 1975. *European Peasants and Their Markets*. Princeton: Princeton University Press.

Pasternack, B., et al. 1976. "On the Conditions Favoring Extended Family Households." *Journal of Anthropological Research* 32.

Patrakis, Joan. 1977. *The Needle Arts of Greece: Design and Techniques*. New York: Charles Scribner.

Pavlides, Eleftherios. 1985. "Vernacular Architecture in Social Context: A Case Sudy of Eressos Greece." Ph.D. dissertation, School of Architecture, University of Pennsylvania.

———. 1995. "The Expression of Institutional Meaning in Greek Domestic Architecture." In Pavlides and Sutton (1995), pp. 345–88.

Pavlides, Eleftherios, and Jana Hesser. 1986. "Women's Roles and House Form and Decoration in Eressos, Greece." In Dubisch (1986), pp. 68–96.

Pavlides, Eleftherios, and Susan Buck Sutton. 1995. "Introduction: Toward a Dialogue of Architecture and Anthropology in Greece." In Pavlides and Sutton (1995), ed., pp. 271–96.

———, eds. 1995. "Constructed Meaning: Form and Process in Greek Architecture." Special Issue of *The Modern Greek Studies Yearbook* 10/11: 271–543.

Payne, Sebastian. 1975. "Faunal Change at Franchthi Cave from 20,000 B.C.–3,000 B.C." In A. T. Clason, ed., *Archaeozoological Studies*, pp. 120–31. Amsterdam: Elsevier.

———. 1985. "Zoo-archaeology in Greece: A reader's guide." In N. C. Wilkie and W. D. Coulson, eds., *Contributions to Aegean Archaeology*, pp. 211–44. Dubuque: Kendall/Hunt.

Pechoux, Pierre-Yves. 1975. "La reforme agraire en Grèce." *Revue de geographie de Lyon* 50: 317–32.

Peebles, Christopher S. 1992. "Rooting Out Latent Behaviorism in Prehistory." In Gardin and Peebles (1992), pp. 357–84.

Pansiot, Fernand Paul, and Henri Rebour. 1961. *Improvement in Olive Cultivation*. Rome: Food and Agriculture Organization of the United Nations.

Pepelasis, Adamantos A. 1955. "Sociocultural Barriers to the Economic Development of Greece." Ph.D. dissertation, University of California at Berkeley.

———. 1976. "To Provlima tou mikrou klerou." *Agrotiki* 10: 2–4.

Pepelasis, Adamantos A., and Kenneth Thompson. 1960. "Agriculture in a Restrictive Environment: The Case of Greece." *Economic Geography* 36: 145–57.

———. 1976. "To Provlema tou mikrou klerou." *Agrotiki* 10: 2–4.

Pepelasis, Adamantos A., and P. A. Yotopoulos. 1962. *Surplus Labour in Greek Agriculture, 1953–1960*. Athens: Centre of Economic Research.

Peristiany, John G., ed. 1965. *Honour and Shame: The Values of Mediterranean Society*. London: Weidenfeld and Nicolson.

———. 1976. *Mediterranean Family Structures*. Cambridge: Cambridge University Press.

Perrin, Richard, and Don Winkleman. 1976. "Impediments to Technical Progress on Small versus Large Farms." *American Journal of Agricultural Economics* 59: 888–94.

Petronoti, Marina. 1985a. "*Skediasma yia ti meleti ton oikonomikon kai koinonikon skhimatismon sto Kranidhi (1821–1981)*." *Greek Review of Social Research* 57: 63–82.

———. 1985b. "The Organization of Production and Labour at Kranidi(1821–1900)." *Actes du IIe Colloque International D'Histoire, Economies Mediterraneennes: Equilibres et Intercommunications, XIIIe–XIXe siècles*. vol. 2, pp. 259–74.

———. 1985c. "I Dhiadhikasia esoterikis metanastefsis kai i koinoniki kinitikotita ton Kranidhioton." *Anthropologika* 7: 17–26.

———. 1998. *To Portraito mias diapolitismikis skhesis*. Athens: National Centre for Social Research.

Petropoulos, D. A. 1943–44. "Customs of Cooperation and Mutual Aid Among the Greek People." *Yearbook of the Greek Folklore Archives*, pp. 58–85.

Petropulos, John Anthony. 1968. *Politics and Statecraft in the Kingdom of Greece, 1833–1843*. Princeton: Princeton University Press.

Pezmazoglou, G. J. 1950. *Directives for Economic Policy [and] Greek Economy in 1949*. Athens: National Bank of Greece.

Philippides, Dimitris. 1983. "Historical Retrospect." In Dimitris Philippides, ed., *Greek Traditional Architecture*, vol. 1, pp. 33–49. Athens: Melissa Press.

Philippson, Alfred. 1892. *Der Peloponnes*. Berlin: R. Friedlander.

Piault, Colette. 1981. "L'absence vécue au village: l'ici entre l'ailleurs et autrefois." In Damianakis (1981), pp. 245–56.

———, ed. 1985. *Familles et biens en Grèce et a Chypre*. Paris: Editions Harmattan.

Pielou, E. C. 1960. "A Single Mechanism to Account for Regular, Random, and Aggregated Populations." *Journal of Ecology* 48: 575–84.

Pitt-Rivers, Julian A. 1954. *The People of the Sierra*. London: Weidenfeld and Nicolson.

Plog, Fred. 1980. *Generations in Clay: Pueblo Pottery of the American Southwest*. Flagstaff, Ariz.: Northland Press.

Polunin, Oleg, and Anthony Huxley. 1965. *Flowers of the Mediterranean*. London: Chatto and Windus.

Pope, Kevin O., and Tjeerd H. van Andel. 1984. "Late Quaternary alluviation and soil formation in the Southern Argolid: Its history, causes and archaeological implications." *Journal of Archaeological Science* 11: 281–306.

Pope, Kevin O., Curtis N. Runnels, and T. L. Ku. 1984. "Dating Middle Palaeolithic Red Beds in Southern Greece." *Nature* 312: 264–66.

Poretsanou, George. 1981. *The Loutrapolis of Methana*. Methana.

Poulopoulos, S. 1973. "Formation and Development of Cultivated Areas in Greece." *Sozialgeographische Probleme Südosteuropas: Aspekte raum-differenzierender Prozessabläufe* 7: 17–29.

Pouqueville, F. C. H. L. 1806. *Travels Through the Morea, Albania, and Several Other Parts of the Ottoman Empire to Constantinople. During the Years 1798, 1799, 1800, and 1801*. London: Richard Phillips.

———. 1826. *Voyage de la Grèce*. 2nd ed. Paris: Firman Didot.

Pred, Allan. 1990. *Making Histories and Constructing Human Geographies: The Local Transformation of Practice, Power Relations, and Consciousness*. Boulder: Westview Press.

Psikhoyios, Dimitris, et al. 1985. "Economic and Social Transformation of Rural Greek Communities." *Greek Review of Social Research* 58: 3–31.

Rackham, Oliver. 1983. "Observations on the Historical Ecology of Boetia." *Annals of the British School of Archaeology at Athens* 78: 291–351.

Radford, A., and G. Clark. 1979. "Cyclades, Studies of a Building Vernacular." In Doumanis and Oliver (1979), pp. 64–82.

Randolph, B. 1689. *The Present State of the Morea, Called Anciently Peloponnesus*. 3rd ed. London.

Rangavis, Iakovos. 1853. *Ta Ellinika: Perigrafi geografiki, istoriki, arkhaioloyiki, kai statistiki tis arkhaias kai neas Ellados*. Athens: K. Andoniadou.

Raup, Phillip M. 1972. "Societal Goals in Farm Size." In A. Gordon Ball and Earl O. Heady, eds., *Size, Structure and Future of Farms*, pp. 3–15. Ames: Iowa University Press.

RAVC (Royal Army Veterinary Corps). 1986. *Animal Transport Familiarisation Course*. Melton Mowbray, Eng.: Royal Army Veterinary Corps.

Raven, P. H. 1973. "Evolution of the Mediterranean Floras." In Di Castri and Mooney, pp. 213–24.

Redfield, Robert. 1956. *Peasant Society and Culture: An Anthropological Approach to Civilization*. Chicago: University of Chicago Press.

Reina, Ruben E. 1959. "Two Patterns of Friendship in a Guatemalan Community." *American Anthropologist* 61: 44–50.

Renfrew, Colin. 1972. "The Emergence of Civilisation." *In The Cyclades and the Aegean in the Third Millennium B.C.* London: Methuen.

———. 1982. "Polity and Power: Interaction, intensification and exploitation." In Renfrew and Wagstaff, pp. 264–90.

———. 1984. *Approaches to Social Archaeology*. Cambridge: Harvard University Press.

Renfrew, Colin, and Malcolm Wagstaff. 1982. "Introduction." In Renfrew and Wagstaff (1982) ed., pp. 1–8.

———, eds. 1982. *An Island Polity: The Archaeology of Exploitation in Melos*. Cambridge: Cambridge University Press.

Renfrew, J. M., and J. Hansen. 1978. "Palaeolithic-Neolithic Seed Remains at Franchthi Cave, Greece." *Nature* 271: 349–52.

Reynolds, Barbara, ed. 1962. *The Cambridge Italian Dictionary*. Cambridge: Cambridge University Press.

Rheubottom, D. H. n.d. "Strategy and Timing in Macedonian Domestic Groups." Unpublished paper.

Rhoades, Robert E., and Stephen I. Thompson. 1975. "Adaptive Strategies in Alpine Environments: Beyond Ecological Particularism." *American Ethnologist* 2: 535–52.

Rice, Prudence M. 1987. *Pottery Analysis: A Sourcebook*. Chicago: University of Chicago Press.

Rochefort, Renee. 1956. "Reflexions à propos du partage de terres en Sicile." *Annales geographiques de Lyon* 31: 99–106.

Rogers, Susan Carol. 1988. "Good to Think: The 'Peasant' in Contemporary France." *Anthropological Quarterly*, 56–63.

Rosenberg, Harriet G. 1988. *A Negotiated World: Three Centuries of Change in a French Alpine Community*. Toronto: University of Toronto Press.

Rossignol, Jacqueline, and LuAnn Wandsnider, eds. 1992. *Space, Time, and Archaeological Landscapes*. New York: Plenum Press.

Rudolph, W. 1979. "Excavations at Porto Cheli and Vicinity, Preliminary Report V: The Early Byzantine Remains." *Hesperia* 48: 294–324.

Runnels, Curtis N. 1981. *A Diachronic Study and Economic Analysis of Millstones from the Argolid, Greece*. Ph.D. dissertation, Department of Classical Archaeology, Indiana University.

———. 1983. "Trade and Communication in Prehistoric Greece." *Ekistics* 50: 417–20.

———. 1985. "Trade and the Demand for Millstones in Southern Greece in the Neolithic and the Early Bronze Age." In B. Knapp and T. Stech, eds., *Prehistoric Production and Exchange: The Aegean and Eastern Mediterranean*, pp. 30–43. Los Angeles: University of California at Los Angeles, Institute of Archaeology, Monograph 25.

Runnels, Curtis N., and Julie Hansen. 1986. "The Olive in the Prehistoric Aegean: The Evidence for Domestication in the Early Bronze Age." *Oxford Journal of Archaeology*.

Runnels, Curtis N., Daniel Pullen, and Susan Langdon. 1995. *Artifact and Assemblage*. vol. 1. Stanford: Stanford University Press.

Runnels, Curtis N., and Tjeerd H. van Andel. 1987. "The Evolution of Settlement in the Southern Argolid, Greece: An Economic Explanation." *Hesperia* 56: 303–34.

Rutter, Jeremy B. 1979. *Ceramic Change in the Aegean Early Bronze Age: A Theory Concerning the Origin of Early Helladic III Ceramics*. Occasional Paper 5, Institute of Archaeology, University of California at Los Angeles.

———. 1984. "The 'Early Cycladic III Gap': What It Is and How to Go About Filling It Without Making It Go Away." In J. A. MacGillivray and R. L. N. Barber, eds., *The Prehistoric Cyclades: Contributions to a Workshop on Cycladic Chronology*, pp. 95–107. Edinburgh.

Rye, Owen S. 1981. *Pottery Technology*. Washington: Taraxacum.

Rye, Owen S., and Clifford Evans. 1976. *Traditional Pottery Techniques of Pakistan*. Washington: Smithsonian Institution Press.

Said, Edward. 1978. *Orientalism*. New York: Pantheon.

Saitas, Iannis. 1983. "Mani: Settlement and Architectural Development in the Medieval and Modern Periods." In *Report of the Society of the Study of Modern Greek Culture and Basic Education*, pp. 79–100. Athens.

Sakellarios, M. [1939] 1978. *I Peloponnisos kata tin dhefteran Tourkokratian (1715–1821)*. Athens: Byzantinisch-Neugriechischen Jahrbücher.

Salamone, S. D., and Jill B. Stanton. 1986. "Introducing the Nikokyra: Ideality and Reality in Social Process." In Dubisch (1986), pp. 97–120.

Sanders, Irwin T. 1955. "Selection of Participants in a Mutual Aid Group in Rural Greece." *Sociometry* 18: 582–85.

———. 1962. *Rainbow in the Rock: The People of Rural Greece*. Boston: Harvard University Press.

Sanders, Irwin T., et al. 1976. *East European Peasantries: An Annotated Bibliography of Periodical Articles*. Boston: G.K. Hall.

Sandis, Eva E. 1973. *Refugees and Migrants in Greater Athens*. Athens: National Centre of Social Research.

Sanjek, Roger. 1991. "The Ethnographic Present." *Man* 26: 609–28.

Sant Cassia, Paul, with Constantina Bada. 1992. *The Making of the Modern Greek Family: Marriage and Exchange in Nineteenth-Century Athens*. Cambridge: Cambridge University Press.

Sarti, Roland. 1985. *Long Live the Strong: A History of Rural Society in the Apennine Mountains*. Amherst: University of Massachusetts Press.

Sathas, C. N., ed. 1880–1890. *Documents inédits relatifs à l'histoire de la Grèce au moyen âge*. Paris.

Sauerwein, Friedrich. 1971. "Die moderne Argolis: Probleme des Strukturwandels in einer griechischen Landschaft." *Frankfurter wirtschaft. u. sozialgeogr. Schr.* 9: 64.

Schiffer, Michael. 1972. "Archaeological Context and Systemic Context." *American Antiquity* 37: 156–65.

———. 1978. "Methodological Issues in Ethnoarchaeology." In R. Gould, ed., *Explorations in Ethnoarchaeology*, pp. 229–34. Albuquerque: University of New Mexico Press.

Schneider, Jane. 1980. "Trousseau as Treasure: Some Contradictions of Late Nineteenth Century Change in Sicily." In *Beyond the Myths of Culture: Essays in Cultural Materialism*, pp. 323–55. New York: Academic Press.

Scrofani, Saverio 1801. *Voyage en Grèce de Xavier Scrofani, Sicilien, fait en 1794 et 1795*. Paris and Strasbourg: Treuttel and Würtz.

Segalen, Martine. 1986. *Historical Anthropology of the Family*. Trans. J. C. Whitehouse and Sarah Matthews. Cambridge: Cambridge University Press.

Semple, Eleanor Church. 1932. *The Geography of the Mediterranean Region*. London: Constable.

Seremetakis, C. Nadia. 1991. *The Last Word: Women, Death, and Divination in Inner Mani*. Chicago: University of Chicago Press.

———. 1993. "Gender, Culture, and History: On the Anthropologies of Ancient and Modern Greece." In C. N. Seremetakis, ed., *Ritual, Power and the Body: Historical Perspectives on the Representation of Greek Women*, pp. 11–34. New York: Pella.

Sfikas, George. 1978. *Trees and Shrubs of Greece*. Athens: Efstathiadis.

———. 1984. *Medicinal Plants of Greece*. Athens: Efstathiadis.

Shanin, Teodor. 1988. "Expoliary Economies: A Political Economy of Margins." *Journal of Historical Sociology* 1: 107–15.

Shearer, Eric B. 1968. "Italian Land Reform Reappraised." *Land Economics* 49: 101–06.

Sherratt, A. G. 1981. "Plough and Pastoralism: Aspects of the Secondary Products Revolution." In Ian Hodder, Glyn Isaac, and N. Hammond, eds., *Patterns of the Past: Studies in Honour of David Clarke*, pp. 261–305. Cambridge: Cambridge University Press.

Shortman, Edward M., and Patricia A. Urban. 1987. "Modeling Interregional Interaction in Prehistory." *Advances in Archaeological Method and Theory* 11: 37–95.

Shryock, Henry, Jacob S. Siegel, and Associates. 1975. *The Methods and Materials of Demography*. Washington, D.C.: U.S. Department of Commerce.

Shutes, Mark T. 1994. "Production-Oriented Ethnography: The Cultural Anthropologist's Role in Understanding Long-Term Social Change." In Kardulias (1994), pp. 337–351.

———. 1996. "Tailored Research: On Getting the Right Fit Between Macro-Level Theory and Micro-Level Data." *Journal of World Systems Research* 2: 1–23.

Silva, R. F. M. 1983. "Contraste e mutcoes na paisagem agraria das planicies e colinas Minhotas." In *Comunidades Rurais, Estudos Interdisciplinares. Estud. Contemp.* 5: 9–16.

Silverman, Sydel. 1965. "Patronage and Community-Nation Relationships in Central Italy." *Ethnology* 4: 83–98.

———. 1968. "Agricultural Organization, Social Structure, and Values in Italy: Amoral Familism Reconsidered." *American Anthropologist* 70: 1–20.

Sivignon, Michel. 1977. "The Demographic and Economic Evolution of Thessaly (1881–1940)." In F. W. Carter, ed., *An Historical Geography of the Balkans*, pp. 379–407. New York: Academic Press.

———. 1981. "Evolution de la societé rurale dans l'ouest du Peloponnese-Metochi (Achaie)." In Damianakis (1981), pp. 32–41.

Skroubi, Byron G. 1978. *Rigani and its Cultivation.* Athens: Ministry of Agriculture Agricultural Research Service.

Smith, Carol A. 1976. "Regional Economic Systems: Linking Geographical Models and Socioeconomic Problems." In C. A. Smith, ed., *Regional Analysis*, vol. 1, pp. 3–63. New York: Academic Press.

———. 1984. "Does a Commodity Economy Enrich the Few While Ruining the Masses? Differentiation Among Petty Commodity Producers in Guatemala." *Journal of Peasant Studies* 11: 60–95.

———. 1985. "Theories and Measures of Urban Primacy: A Critique." In Carol A. Smith, ed., *Urbanization in the World-Economy*, pp. 87–117. New York: Academic Press.

Smith, E. G. 1975. "Fragmented Farms in the United States." *Annals of the Association of American Geographers* 65: 58–70.

Smith, Harvey. 1984. "Family and Class: The Household Economy of Languedoc Winegrowers 1830–1870." *Journal of Family History* 9: 64–87.

Smith, Joan, Immanuel Wallerstein, and Hans-Dieter Evers, eds. 1984. *Households and the World-Economy.* Beverly Hills: Sage.

Smith, Joyce. 1985. "Analysis of the Female Costume of the Sarakatsani." In *Female Costume of the Sarakatsani.* Providence, R.I.: Brown University, Haffenreffer Museum of Anthropology, Studies in Anthropology and Material Culture 1: 12–27.

Smith, Neil. 1984. *Uneven Development: Nature, Capital and the Production of Space.* Oxford: Basil Blackwell.

Smith, Timothy. 1973. "Social Space in a Greek Island Village and an Urban Migrant Community." Paper presented at the IX International Congress of Anthropological and Ethnological Sciences, Chicago.

Snodgrass, Anthony M. 1987. *An Archeology of Greece: The Present State and Future Scope of a Discipline.* Berkeley: University of California Press.

Soden, Dennis L. 1988. *The Tragedy of the Commons: Twenty Years of Policy Literature.* Monticello Ill.: Vance.

Sorocos, Eustache P. 1985. *La morphologie sociale du Pirée à travers son evolution.* Athens: National Social Science Research Center.

Sotiriou, G. A. 1935. I moniu tou Avghou para tous Dhidhimous tis Argolidhos imeroloyion tis megales Ellados, 457–64.

Spencer, Charles S. 1992. "Homology, Analogy, and Comparative Research in Archaeology." *Behavior Science Research* 26: 163–68.

Spencer, Terence. 1954. *Fair Greece, Sad Relic: Literary Philhellenism from Shakespeare to Byron.* London: Weidenfeld and Nicolson.

Sphyroeias, Vasilis, Anna Aniamea, and Spyros Asdrahas. 1985. *Maps and Mapmakers of the Aegean.* Athens: E. Louviou.

Spiridonakis, B. G. 1977. *Essays on the Historical Geography of the Greek World in the Balkans During the Tourkokratia.* Thessaloniki: Institute for Balkan Studies.

Spooner, Brian. 1972. *Population Growth, Anthropological Implications.* Cambridge: MIT Press.

———. 1986. "Weavers and Dealers: The Authenticity of an Oriental Carpet." In Arjun Appadurai, ed., *The Social Life of Things: Commodities in Cultural Perspective*, pp. 195–235. Cambridge: Cambridge University Press.

Stahl, Ann Brower. 1993. "Concepts of Time and Approaches to Analogical Reasoning in Historical Perspective." *American Antiquity* 58: 235–60.

Stamatiou, Ioannis. 1937. *Spaira and Poros with Troizinia: Historical Descriptions and Trips to Kalavria, Methana and Troizinia.* Athens: D.V. Dedilimntri.

Stanislawski, Michael B. 1974. "The Relationships of Ethnoarchaeology, Traditional and Systems Archaeology." In C. Donnan and C. Clewlow, eds., *Ethnoarchaeology.* Los Angeles: Institute of Archaeology, University of California, Los Angeles.

———. 1978. "If Pots Were Mortal." In Richard A. Gould, ed., *Explorations in Ethnoarchaeology,* pp. 201–27. Albuquerque: University of New Mexico Press.

Stavenhagen, Rodolfo. 1970. "Social Aspects of Agrarian Structure in Mexico." In Rodolfo Stavenhagen, ed., *Social Aspects of Agrarian Structure in Mexico.* Garden City, N.J.: Doubleday.

Stavrolakis, Niki. 1979. *Poros.* Athens: Lycabettus Press.

Stenning, D. J. 1959. "Household Viability among the Pastoral Fulani." In J. Goody, ed., *The Developmental Cycle in Domestic Groups,* pp. 92–119. Cambridge: Cambridge University Press.

Stevenson, Glenn G. 1991. *Common Property Economics: A General Theory and Land Use Applications.* Cambridge: Cambridge University Press.

Stewart, Charles. 1991. *Demons and the Devil: Moral Imagination in Modern Greek Culture.* Princeton: Princeton University Press.

Stott, Margaret. 1985. "Property, Labor and Household Economy: The Transition to Tourism in Myconos Greece." *Journal of Modern Greek Studies* 3: 182–206.

Strong, Frederick. 1842. *Greece as a Kingdom.* London: Longman, Brown, Green, and Longmans.

Sutton, David. 1994. "Tradition and Modernity: Kalymnian Constructions of Identity and Otherness." *Journal of Modern Greek Studies* 12: 239–60.

Sutton, Susan Buck. 1978. "Migrant Regional Associations: An Athenian Example and Its Implications." Ph.D. dissertation, Department of Anthropology, University of North Carolina.

———. 1983. "Rural-Urban Migration in Greece." In Kenny and Kertzer (1983), pp. 225–49.

———. 1985. "Women's Work in Nafplio, 1920–1940." *Ethnohistory* 32: 343–62.

———. 1986. "Family and Work: New Patterns for Village Women in Athens." *Journal of Modern Greek Studies* 4: 33–49.

———. 1988. "What is a Village in a Nation of Migrants?" *Journal of Modern Greek Studies* 6: 187–215.

———. 1991. "Settlement, Population and Economy in Post-Revolutionary Keos." In Cherry, Davis, and Mantzourani (1991), pp. 383–402.

———. 1994. "Settlement Patterns, Settlement Perceptions: Rethinking the Greek Village." In Kardulias (1994), pp. 313–35.

———. 1995. "Crumbling Walls and Bare Foundations: The Process of Housing in Greece." In Pavlides and Sutton (1995), pp. 319–44.

———. 1997. "Disconnected Landscapes: Ancient Sites, Travel Guides, and Local Identity in Modern Greece." *Anthropology of Eastern Europe Review* 15: 27–34.

Swallow, D. A. 1982. "Production and Control in the Indian Garment Export Industry." In Esther N. Goody, ed., *From Craft to Industry: The Ethnography of Proto-Industrial Cloth Production,* pp. 133–65.

Swanson, Timothy M., ed. 1996. *The Economics of Environmental Degradation: Tragedy for the Commons?* Brookfield, Vt.: Edward Elgar.

Sweet-Escott, Bickham. 1954. *Greece, A Political and Economic Survey, 1939–53.* London: Royal Institute of International Affairs.

Symeonidou-Alatopoulou, Haris. 1979. "An Account of Factors Affecting Fertility in Greece 1930–1975." *Greek Review of Social Research* 35.

Tank, Heide. 1977. "Wandel und Entwicklungstendenzen der Agrarstruktur Kretas seit 1948." *Erde* 108: 342–46.

Thanopoulou, M., and M. Petronoti. 1987. *Biografiki prosegisi: Mia alli protasi yia tin theorisi tis anthropinis embirias.* Epitheorisi Koinonikon Erevnon, vol. 64.

Thirgood, J. V. 1981. *Man and the Mediterranean Forest.* London: Academic Press.

Thiriet, F. 1961. *Réegestes des déeliberations du séenat de Venise concernant la Romanie.* vol. 3 (1413–1463). Paris and the Hague.

———. 1978. "Review of Greek Lands under Venetian Domination between the 2nd and 3rd Turko-Venetian War by G. S. Ploomides." *Rev. His.* 526: 528–30.

Thomas, Andrew. 1977. *Spetsai.* Athens: Lycabettus Press.

Thomlinson, Ralph. 1965. *Population Dynamics: Causes and Consequences of World Demographic Change.* New York: Random House.

Thompson, Kenneth. 1963. *Farm Fragmentation in Greece.* Athens: National Center of Planning and Economic Research.

Timberlake, Michael, ed. 1985. *Urbanization in the World Economy.* New York: Academic Press.

Timmons, John F. 1972. "Tenure and Size." In A. Gordon Ball and Earl O. Heady, eds., *Size, Structure and Future of Farms,* pp. 232–47. Ames: Iowa University Press.

Tomasevich, Jozo. 1955. *Peasants, Politics and Economic Change in Yugoslavia.* Stanford: Stanford University Press.

Topping, Peter. [1949] 1980. *Feudal Institutions, as Revealed in the Assizes of Romania: The Law Code of*

Frankish Greece. Philadelphia: University of Pennsylvania Press.

———. 1972. "The Post-Classical documents." In McDonald and Rapp (1972), pp. 64–80.

———. 1976a. "Premodern Peloponnesus: The Land and the People Under Venetian Rule (1685–1717)." In Dimen and Friedl (1976), pp. 92–108.

———. [1976b] 1977. *Studies in Latin Greece* A.D. *1205–1715*. London: Variorum Reprints.

———. 1976c. "The Population of the Morea 1685–1715." *Praktika protou dhiethnous synedriou peloponnisiakon spoudhon Sparti* 1: 119–28.

———. 1980a. Feudal Institutions as Revealed in the Assizes of Romania, the Law Code of Franish Greece: Translation of th Text of the Assizes with a Commentary on Feudal Instituions in Greece and in Medieval Europe. New York: AMS Press.

———. 1980b. "Albanian Settlements in Medieval Greece: Some Venetian Testimonies." In A. E. Laiou-Thomadakis, ed., *Essays in Honor of Peter Charanis*, pp. 261–71. New Brunswick: Rutgers University Press.

———. 1981. *I paragoge elaioladhou sti venetike Messenia*. Messeniaka Grammata 3: 33–40.

———. n.d. "Pre-modern Peloponessus: The Human and Economic Landscape as Seen Under Venetian Rule (1685–1715)." Unpublished paper.

Tringham, Ruth. 1972. "Introduction: Settlement Patterns and Urbanization." In Peter Ucko, Ruth Tringham, and G. W. Dimbleby, eds., *Man, Settlement and Urbanization*, pp. xiv–xxviii. London: Duckworth.

Tsaousis, D. G. 1976. "Future Research Strategies: Roundtable Discussion." In Dimen and Friedl (1976), pp. 455–56.

Tschopik, Harry. 1941. *Navaho Pottery Making: An Inquiry into the Affinities of Navaho Painted Pottery*. Cambridge: Peabody Museum of American Archaeology and Ethnology, Harvard University.

Tsigakou, Fani-Maria. 1981. *The Rediscovery of Greece: Travellers and Painters of the Romantic Era*. New Rochelle, N.Y.: Caratzas Bros.

Turner, B. L., and Stephen B. Brush, eds. 1987. *Comparative Farming Systems*. New York: Guilford Press.

Tzakou, Anastasia. 1976. *Central Settlements on the Island of Siphnos: Form and Evolution of a Traditional System*. Athens.

United Nations. 1954. *European Agriculture: A Statement of Problems*. Geneva: EEC/UNFAO.

———. 1992. *1991 Demographic Yearbook*. New York.

Urquhart, David. 1833. *Turkey and its Resources*. London: Henry Colburn.

Vacalopoulos, A. E. 1939. *Prosfiges kai to prosfiyiko zitima kata tin epanastasin tou 1821*. Thessaloniki: Marineli.

———. 1963. "La retraite des populations Grèques vers les regions éloignés et montagneuse pendant la domination Turque." *Balkan Studies* 4: 263–76.

Valaoras, Vasilios G. 1960. "A Reconstruction of the Demographic History of Modern Greece." *Milbank Memorial Fund Quarterly* 38: 115–39.

van Andel, Tjeerd H., and N. Lianos. 1983. "Prehistoric and Historic Shorelines of the Southern Argolid Peninsula: A Subbottom Profiler Study." *International Journal of Nautical Archaeology and Underwater Exploration* 12: 303–24.

van Andel, Tjeerd H., and Curtis Runnels. 1987. *Beyond the Acropolis: A Rural Greek Past*. Stanford: Stanford University Press.

van Andel, Tjeerd H., C. N. Runnels, and K. O. Pope. 1986. "Five Thousand Years of Land Use and Abuse in the Southern Argolid, Greece." *Hesperia* 55: 103–28.

van Andel, Tjeerd H., and J. C. Shackleton. 1982. "Late Paleolithic and Mesolithic Coastlines of Greece and the Aegean." *Journal of Field Archaeology* 9: 445–54.

van Andel, Tjeerd H., and Susan Buck Sutton. 1987. *Landscape and People of the Franchthi Region*. Bloomington: Indiana University Press.

Van der Meer, Paul. 1973. "Farm Plot Dispersal: Luliao Village, Taiwan." Ph.D. dissertation, University of Michigan.

———. 1975a. "Toward a Greater Precision in the Terminology and Analysis of Farm Fragmentation." *Peasant Studies Newsletter* 4(4): 14–16.

———. 1975b. "Land Consolidation through Land Fragmentation: Case Studies from Taiwan." *Land Economics* 51: 275–83.

Vanderpool, Eugene. 1930. "The Antiquities of the Peninsula of Methana." Paper submitted to the American School of Classical Studies of Athens.

van Wersch, Herman Joseph Mathias. 1969. "Land Tenure, Land Use, and Agricultural Development, a Comparative Analysis of Messenia (Greece) and Cape Bon (Tunesia)." Ph.D. dissertation, University of Minnesota.

———. 1972. "The agricultural economy." In McDonald and Rapp (1972), eds., pp. 177–87.

Varvaressos, A. 1950. "Land Ownership in Greece." *Foreign Agriculture* 14: 180–83.

Vasiliev, A. 1947. "The 'Life' of St. Peter of Argos and its Historical Significance." *Traditio* 5: 163–91.

Vatikioti, P. 1976–77. "Silloyi Laografikis Ilis Apo to Kranidhi." University of Athens, Center of Folklore Studies, manuscript No. 2972.

Vayiakakou, D. 1968–1969. *Engatastasis Pontion esi Lakonian*. Arkhion Pontou. No. 29.

Vellioti, Maria. 1987. "Le Parrainage, l'adoption et la fraternization dans un village Arvanite du Peloponese." *Études et documents Balkaniques et Mediterranéens* 13: 69–76.

Vergopoulos, Kostas. 1975. *To Agrotiko zitima stin Elladha: I koinoniki ensomatosi tis yeoryias*. Athens: Exandas.

———. 1977. *Le capitalisme difforme et la nouvelle question agraire: L'exemple de la Grèce moderne*. Paris: F. Maspero.

———. 1978. *Kratos kai oikonomiki politiki ston 19o aiona*. Athens: Exandas.

Vermeulen, Cornelis J. J. 1976. "Development and Migration in the Serres Basin." In Dimen and Friedl (1972), pp. 59–70.

Vernier, Bernard. 1984. "Putting Kin and Kinship to Good Use: The Circulation of Goods, Labor and Names on Karpathos, Greece." In H. Medick and D. W. Sabean, eds., *Interest and Emotion*, pp. 8–76. Cambridge: Cambridge University Press.

Vitelli, K. D. 1974. "The Greek Neolithic Patterned Urfirnis Ware from the Franchthi Cave and Lerna." Ph.D. dissertation, University of Pennsylvania.

———. 1984. "Greek Neolithic Pottery by Experiment." In Prudence Rice, ed., *Pots and Potters: Current Approaches in Ceramic Archaeology*, pp. 113–131. Institute of Archaeology Monograph XXIV. Los Angeles: University of California, Los Angeles.

von Brussel, A Ries. 1978. "Struktur der griechischen Agrarwirtschaft und die gemeinsame Agrarpolitik." *Ber. Landwirtschaft Bundesminster Ernahr Landwirtschaft Forsten*, n.s. 56: 240–53.

Voyatzoglou, M. 1979. "Traditional Ceramics in Modern Greece: An Example from Aghios Stefanos 1980 Mantamdo, Mytilini." *Ethnografika* 2: 37–46.

Wace, A. J. B. 1948. "Weaving or Embroidery?" *American Journal of Archaeology* 52: 51–55.

Wagstaff, J. Malcolm. 1965a. "An Outline of Agriculture in the Mani Region of Southern Greece." *Tijds. Kon. Nederl. Aard* 82: 270–80.

———. 1965b. "Traditional Houses in Modern Greece." *Geography* 50(9): 58–64.

———. 1965c. "House Types as an Index in Settlement Study: A Case Study from Greece." *Transactions and Papers of the Institute of British Geographers* 37: 6–75.

———. 1967. "A Small Coastal Town in Southern Greece: Its Evolution and Present Condition." *The Town Planning Review* 37: 255–70.

———. 1969. "The Study of Rural Greek Settlements: A Review of the Literature." *Erdkunde* 23: 306–17.

———. 1977. "War and Settlement Desertion in the Morea 1635–1830." *Transactions of the Institute of British Geographers*, n.s. 3: 295–308.

———. 1982. *The Development of Rural Settlements*. Avebury.

———. 1987. *Landscape and Culture: Geographical and Archaeological Perspectives*. Oxford: Blackwell.

———. 1996. "A review of Beyond the Site: Regional Studies in the Aegean Area, by Nick Kardulias." *American Journal of Archaeology* 78–79.

———. n.d. "Piracy and Settlements in the South Aegean: A Reconsideration of a Geographical Falacy." Unpublished manuscript.

Wagstaff, J. Malcolm, and J. F. Cherry. 1982. "Settlement and population change." In Renfrew and Wagstaff (1982), pp. 136–55.

Wagstaff, J. Malcolm, and Siv Augustson. 1982. "Traditional Land Use." In Renfrew and Wagstaff (1982), pp. 106–33.

Walker, D. S. 1964. *The Mediterranean Lands*. London: Methuen.

Wall, Richard, Jean Robin, and Peter Laslett, eds. 1983. *Family Forms in Historic Europe*. Cambridge: Cambridge University Press.

Wallerstein, Immanuel. 1974. *The Modern World-System*. San Diego: Academic Press.

Walpole, Robert, ed. 1818. *Memoirs Relating to European and Asiatic Turkey, and Other Countries of the East*. London: Longman, Hurst, Rees, Orme and Brown.

Ward, Benjamin. 1962. *Problems of Greek Regional Development*. Athens: Centre of Planning and Economic Research.

———. 1963. *Greek Regional Development*. Athens: Social Science Research Center.

Waterbury, R. 1989. "Embroidery for Tourists: A Contemporary Putting-Out System in Oaxaca, Mexico." In A. B. Weiner and J. Schneider, eds., *Cloth and the Human Experience*. Washington: Smithsonian Press.

Watrous, Vance. 1982. "Lasithi: A History of Settlement on a Highland Plain in Crete." *Hesperia* Supplement No. 23.

Watson, Patty Jo. 1979. *Archaeological Ethnography in Western Iran*. Tucson: University of Arizona Press.

Watson, Patty Jo, and Michael Fotiadis. 1990. "The Razor's Edge: Symbolic-Structuralist Archeology and the Expansion of Archeological Inference." *American Anthropologist* 92: 613–29.

Weber, A. [1929] 1958. *Theory of the Location of Industries*. Trans. Carl J. Friedrich. Chicago: University of Chicago Press.

Weinberd, D. 1972. "Cutting the Pie in the Swiss Alps." *Ethnohistory* 45: 125–31.

Weintraub, D., and Shapira, M. 1975. *Rural Reconstruction of Greece: Differential Social Prerequisites and Achievements During the Development Process*. London: Sage Publications.

Weissner, P. 1974. "A Functional Estimator of Population from the Floor Area." *American Antiquity* 39: 343–50.

Whipple, Clayton. 1943. "The Agriculture of Crete." *Foreign Agriculture* 7: 212–16.

———. 1944. "The Agriculture of Greece." *Foreign Agriculture* 8: 75–96.

White, Lynn Jr. 1962. *Medieval Technology and Social Change*. Oxford: Oxford University Press.

Whitelaw, Todd. 1991. "The Ethnoarcheology of Recent Rural Settlement and Land Use in Northwest Keos." In Cherry, Davis, and Mantzourani, pp. 403–54.

Wiegandt, Ellen. 1977. "Inheritance and Demography in the Swiss Alps." *Ethnohistory* 24: 133–48.

Wilk, Richard R. 1989. *The Household Economy: Reconsidering the Domestic Mode of Production*. Boulder: Westview Press.

———. 1990. "The Built Environment and Consumer Decisions." In S. Kent, ed., *Domestic Architecture and the Use of Space*, pp. 34–42. Cambridge: Cambridge University Press.

———. 1991. *Household Ecology: Economic Change and Domestic Life Among the Kekchi Maya in Belize*. Tucson: University of Arizona Press.

Wilk, Richard, and Robert McC. Netting. 1984. "Household Changing Form and Function." In Netting, Wilk, and Arnould (1984), pp. 1–28.

Willett, E. Henry, and Joey Brachner. 1983. *The Traditional Pottery of Alabama*. Montgomery: Montgomery Museum of Fine Arts.

Williams, Rory, and Juliet duBoulay. 1987. "Amoral Familism and the Image of the Limited Good: A Critique from a European Perspective." *Anthropological Quarterly* 60: 12–24.

Willigen, J. Dennis, and Katherine Lynch. 1982. *Sources and Methods of Historical Demography*. New York: Academic Press.

Wolf, Eric. 1956. "Types of Latin American Peasantry: A Preliminary Discussion." *American Anthropologist* 57: 452–71.

———. 1966. *Peasants*. Englewood Cliffs: Prentice Hall.

———. 1970. "The Inheritance of Land Among Bavarian and Tyrolese Peasants." *Anthropologica* 12: 99–114.

———. 1982. *Europe and the People Without History*. Berkeley: University of California Press.

Woodhouse, C. M. 1968. *A Short History of Modern Greece*. New York: Praeger.

Wolfart, U. 1966. "Die Reisen des Evliya Celebi durch die Morea." Ph.D. dissertation, University of Munich.

World Bank. 1975a. "Agricultural Credit." Sector Policy Paper. Washington, D.C.: World Bank.

———. 1975b. "Land Reform." Sector Policy Paper. Washington, D.C.: World Bank.

Wright, James C., John F. Cherry, Jack L. Davis, Eleni Mantzourani, and Susan Buck Sutton. 1990. "The Nemea Valley Archaeological Project: A Preliminary Report." *Hesperia* 59: 579–659.

Wylie, Alison. 1982. "An Analogy by Any Other Name Is Just as Analogical: A Commentary on the Gould-Watson Dialogue." *Journal of Anthropological Archaeology* 1: 382–401.

———. 1985. "The Reaction against Analogy." *Advances in Archaeological Method and Theory* 8: 63–111.

———. 1994. "On 'Capturing Facts Alive in the Past' (or Present): Response to Fotiadis and to Little." *American Antiquity* 59: 556–60.

Yanagisako, Sylvia Junko. 1979. "Family and Household: The Analysis of Domestic Groups." *Annual Review of Anthropology*: 161–205.

Yannopoulos, P. A. 1980. "La pénétration slave en Argolide." *Bulletin de correspondance hellénique*, Suppl. VI, pp. 323–71.

Yassoglou, N. J., D. Catacousinos, and A. Kouskalekas. 1972. "Land Use in the Semi-Arid Zone of Greece." In *Actes du colloque de geographie agraire: Les societés rurales mediteranées*, pp. 63–67. Madrid.

Yellen, John. 1977. *Archaeological Approaches to the Present.* New York: Academic Press.

Yiannakopoulou, Eleni. 1976. "To Emborio eis tin Peloponnison kata tin B' Pentaetian tou 19ou aionos." Peloponnisiaka 12: 103–51.

Yiannaropoulou, Ioanna. 1974. "Katalogoi Komopoleon kai khorion ton eparchion Nafplias kai Kato Nachayie (1830)." *Praktika tou Sindefriou Argolikon Spoudhon*, pp. 121–28.

Yotopoulos, Panagia A. 1967. *Allocative Efficiency in Economic Development.* Athens: National Center of Planning and Economic Research.

Young, J. H. 1956. "Studies in South Attica." *Hesperia* 25: 122–46.

Zakynthos, D. A. 1976. *The Making of Modern Greece: From Byzantium to Independence.* Trans. K. R. Johnstone. Totowa, N.J.: Rowman and Littlefield.

Zalvarlis, M. 1983. "Chiote Mastika." *Ta Agrotika* 20(May): 22–24.

Zorn, Elaine. 1979. "Textiles and Tourism: A Shift to Small Commodity Production in the Peruvian Highlands." *Andean Perspective Newsletter* 3: 11–13.

Contributors

Keith W. Adams is a geographer and public archaeologist who has conducted research on historical practices of land tenure and agriculture in Greece, Africa, and the United States. An independent scholar, Adams is currently involved in the reconstruction of land use, landscape, and economic change at Poplar Forest, the home retreat of Thomas Jefferson in Forest, Virginia.

Claudia Chang, Professor of Anthropology at Sweet Briar College, is a leading figure in the ethnoarchaeology of pastoralism. Together with Harold A. Koster, she has authored two highly regarded statements on this topic, their critical review article "Beyond Bones: Toward an Archaeology of Pastoralism" (1986) and their recent book *Pastoralists at the Periphery: Herders in a Capitalist World* (1995). Chang has conducted research in Greece, Alaska, and central Asia. She is the recipient of a recent National Science Foundation Grant for her field research on the evolution of pastoral nomadic steppe cultures in southeastern Kazakhstan.

Mari H. Clarke directs the Program Support Project for the Office of Private and Voluntary Cooperation at the U.S. Agency for International Development. Her wide-ranging career includes field research in ethnoarchaeology and cultural ecology in the southern Argolid and also applied work on the gender issues involved in various international development initiatives. Among Clarke's many publications are *Household Economic Strategies and Support Networks of the Poor in Kenya* (1985) and *New Directions in Foreign Assistance and New Roles for Anthropologists* (1991).

Hamish A. Forbes, Lecturer in Archaeology at the University of Nottingham, is a prominent scholar in the study of Mediterranean agriculture, both past and pres-

ent. Forbes has investigated the changing cultural ecology of Methana using a combination of ethnographic fieldwork and archaeological survey. His long-term program of field research in this region recently resulted in *A Rough and Rocky Place: The Landscape and Settlement History of the Methana Peninsula, Greece* (1997).

Michael H. Jameson is Crossett Professor of Humanistic Studies, Emeritus, at Stanford University. A distinguished classical scholar, Jameson has conducted epigraphical, historical, and archaeological research in the southern Argolid since the 1950s. He has been a guiding light for much of the research conducted by the other contributors to this volume. Jameson's numerous publications include *A Decree of Themistokles from Troizen* (1960), *A "lex sacra" from Selinous* (1993), and *A Greek Countryside: the Southern Argolid from Prehistory to the Present Day* (1994).

P. Nick Kardulias is Assistant Professor of Anthropology and Archaeology, and Chair of the Program in Archaeology, at the College of Wooster. He has combined an active field research program in survey archaeology with strong theoretical interests in cultural ecology and political economy. Kardulias has played a major role in bringing together a wide range of scholars interested in such issues through a series of influential edited volumes: *Beyond the Site: Regional Studies in the Aegean Area* (1994); *Aegean Strategies: Studies of Culture and Environment on the European Fringe* (1997); and *World-Systems Theory in Practice: Leadership, Production, and Exchange* (1999).

Harold A. Koster is Adjunct Assistant Professor of Anthropology at Binghamton University while also running an active sheep and goat farm. His ethno-

383

graphic research has been devoted to the material culture and economic strategies of Greek pastoralists. Koster has collaborated with Claudia Chang on two key statements on these issues: "Beyond Bones: Toward an Archaeology of Pastoralism" (1986) and *Pastoralists at the Periphery: Herders in a Capitalist World* (1995).

Joan Bouza Koster is a professional weaver who heads Smiling Shepherd Creations, while also serving as an instructor at Broome Community College in upstate New York. Koster has studied and worked with the women weavers of the southern Argolid for nearly three decades. She is the author of *Growing Artists: Teaching Art to Young Children* (1997).

Priscilla M. Murray is Membership Programs Administrator for the Archaeological Institute of America (AIA) in Boston. In this position, she oversees the Lecture Program of the AIA and serves as liaison between the national office and local AIA societies. Murray holds graduate degrees in anthropology and classical archaeology and has published on field methodology as well as the ethnoarchaeological study of discard practices. Since the Argolid Survey, she and husband Curtis Runnels, who is Professor of Archaeology at Boston University, have been concentrating on learning more about the Palaeolithic and Mesolithic periods in Greece.

Marina Petronoti holds the position of Senior Research Fellow at the National Centre for Social Research in Athens. As an anthropologist interested in history, politics, and migration, Petronoti has examined the social implication of Kranidhi's nineteenth century shipping boom as well as the conditions faced by contemporary Eritrean refugees in Athens. This latter work yielded her recent book *To Portraito mias diapolitismikis skhesis* (1998), the first major study of the refugee situation.

Susan Buck Sutton is Professor of Anthropology at Indiana University–Purdue University at Indianapolis. Her research interests have revolved around settlement, migration, the construction of communities, and the presentation of archaeological sites in Greece. Sutton's publications include *Landscape and People of the Franchthi Region* (1987) and *Constructed Meaning: Form and Process in Greek Architecture* (1995). She recently became Editor of the *Journal of Modern Greek Studies*.

Peter W. Topping is Senior Research Associate at the Dumbarton Oaks Institute in Washington, D.C. One of the foremost historians of late Byzantine and early modern Greece, Topping has devoted a long and distinguished career to examining the archival evidence on these little-known centuries of Greek history. His numerous articles and nearly a dozen books include the seminal studies *Feudal Institutions as Revealed in the Assizes of Romania* (1980) and *Studies on Latin Greece* A.D. *1205–1715* (1977).

Index

In this index an "f" after a number indicates a separate reference on the next page, and an "ff" indicates separate references on the next two pages. A continuous discussion over two or more pages is indicated by a span of page numbers, e.g., "57–59." *Passim* is used for a cluster of references in close but not consecutive sequence. References to tables and figures are given in italics.

Library of Congress Cataloging-in-Publication Data

Contingent countryside : settlement, economy, and land use in the
southern Argolid since 1700 / edited by Susan Buck Sutton;
contributors, Keith W. Adams . . . [et al.].
      p. cm.
    "A publication of the Argolid Exploration Project."
    Includes bibliographical references and index.
    ISBN 0-8047-3315-5 (cloth : alk. paper)
    1. Argolis Peninsula (Greece)—Economic conditions.
    2. Argolis Peninsula (Greece)—Social conditions.   3. Land use—
Greece—Argolis Peninsula.   4. Agriculture—Economic aspects—
Greece—Argolis Peninsula.   I. Sutton, Susan Buck.
II. Adams, Keith W.   III. Argolid Exploration Project.
HC297.A74C66   2000
330.9495′2—dc21   99-05596

⊗ This book is printed on acid-free, recycled paper.

Original printing 2000
Last figure below indicates year of this printing:
09 08 07 06 05 04 03 02 01 00

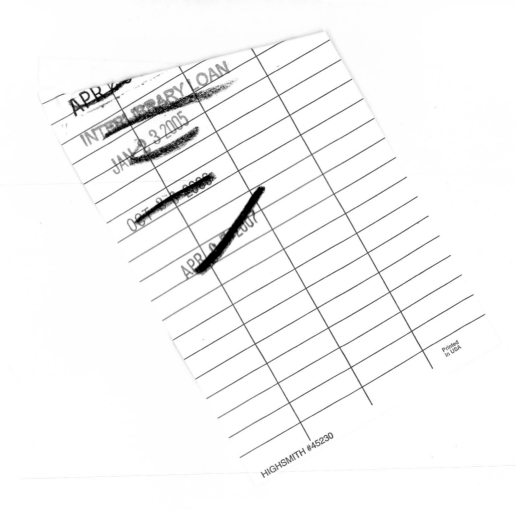